HIBERNATE WITH JAVA
—A PRACTICAL APPROACH

HIBERNATE WITH JAVA
—A PRACTICAL APPROACH

By

B. MOHAMED IBRAHIM

MCA., M.Phil., MBA.,

Software Technical Consultant

UNIVERSITY SCIENCE PRESS

(An Imprint of Laxmi Publications Pvt. Ltd.)

An ISO 9001:2008 Company

BENGALURU • CHENNAI • COCHIN • GUWAHATI • HYDERABAD
JALANDHAR • KOLKATA • LUCKNOW • MUMBAI • RANCHI • NEW DELHI
BOSTON (USA) • ACCRA (GHANA) • NAIROBI (KENYA)

HIBERNATE WITH JAVA–A PRACTICAL APPROACH

Printed and bound in India
Typeset at Kalyani Computer Services, Delhi
First Edition : 2016
ISBN 978-93-83828-34-0

Branches

Bengaluru	080-26 75 69 30	
Chennai	044-24 34 47 26,	24 35 95 07
Cochin	0484-237 70 04,	405 13 03
Guwahati	0361-254 36 69,	251 38 81
Hyderabad	040-27 55 53 83,	27 55 53 93
Jalandhar	0181-222 12 72	
Kolkata	033-22 27 43 84	
Lucknow	0522-220 99 16	
Mumbai	022-24 91 54 15,	24 92 78 69
Ranchi	0651-220 44 64	

PUBLISHED IN INDIA BY

UNIVERSITY SCIENCE PRESS
(An Imprint of Laxmi Publications Pvt. Ltd.)

An ISO 9001:2008 Company
113, GOLDEN HOUSE, DARYAGANJ,
NEW DELHI - 110002, INDIA
Telephone : 91-11-4353 2500, 4353 2501
Fax : 91-11-2325 2572, 4353 2528
www.laxmipublications.com info@laxmipublications.com

C—10062/015/03
Printed at : Repro Knowledgecast Limited, Thane

CONTENTS

PREFACE

The Object Relational Mapping (ORM) is a technique that maps the data represented in object type into relational model with a database schema. The Hibernate is an open source ORM tool for Java; it maps Java Objects into database objects such as tables. Hibernate also provides powerful querying tool that does the reverse process, converting database objects into Java objects. It simplifies the database interactions very much; otherwise the developers have to write complex JDBC statements. It is object oriented so that the developers can enjoy the features of Object Oriented Programming System (OOPS) features in handling data on any database.

Hibernate provides transparent persistence and Object-Oriented Query Language which is independent of any database. Hibernate supports native SQL queries as well.

The Chapter 1 (Getting Ready) make you get ready to work with Hibernate. It explains the installation procedure of Hibernate and other required supporting software tools such Java, Database, and Integrated Development Environment (IDE). This chapter introduces you the need of Hibernate and its architecture. It describes how to download and install supporting software components to work with Hibernate programs. The database MySQL is used for database interaction examples. However, the users may use other RDBMS databases, with minor changes in programs. The procedure for other databases is also given in this chapter. Like this, the user is not compelled to use only Tomcat as Application server and Eclipse as Java IDE.

The Chapter 2 (Persisting Student Data with Hibernate: Demo) demonstrates a complete working example with Hibernate. It explains how to insert one record of Student information into database table using Hibernate. Based on this example, this chapter explains briefly about the configuration details and required setups to work with Hibernate such as Creating database user, Creating Java Project in Eclipse, Setting up the required Hibernate and other library files with Eclipse, and Defining Hibernate configurations. The configurations are to be followed for examples shown in other chapters. The Hibernate API used this chapter are not explained in this chapter itself, but explained in the next chapters in detail.

The Chapter 3 (Hibernate Session) introduces working with Hibernate Sessions. All data definition and manipulation should be done in Hibernate through Session. Any object should be present in the Session before it is interacted with database. The Hibernate Session Factory acts a database connection pool and Hibernate Session acts a Connection, if it is compared with JDBC. The Hibernate Session Factory is used to provide Hibernate Session(s), which are used to do relational mappings of objects such as definition and manipulation of data with database. Hibernate

Session(s) are not thread-safe; data may be overwritten while a Session used in multi-threaded environment and the Session Factory provides remedy to the thread-safe issue as it is thread-safe among multi-threaded environment. This chapter explains how to create a Session Factory object and how to obtain Sessions from Session Factory. The important methods under Session are explained with sample programs. This chapter also explains the importance of using Transactions in applications.

The Chapter 4 (Defining POJOs using JPA/Hibernate Annotations) illustrates the uses of JPA/Hibernate annotations to define POJOs. A POJO (Plain Old Java Object) is a Java object that doesn't extend/implement any framework specific classes/interfaces. The POJOs look like a simple Java beans; they decouple your application code from any framework that you are using. We have to specify metadata information (such as name of the database table, column names, length of columns, data types, etc.) while using JPA/Hibernate persistence. Specifying metadata through XML is a common one; however, we can best use the annotation features of latest JPA/Hibernate API. While using Annotations, no need to depend on XML since the annotations (they are also Java classes) are compiled into Byte code and invoked during runtime using Java Reflection API. Some important JPA/Hibernate annotations for defining required POJOs (entities) are described in this chapter. The JPA can be also be used in EJB 3, keeping this flexibility in mind, many JPA annotations are used even though Hibernate equivalents are available. The Filters, Validator Framework, and Entity Manager concepts are explained with example code and output.

The Chapter 5 (HQL/JPAQL) discusses the techniques and Hibernate support to query data from database. HQL (Hibernate Query Language) is powerful object-oriented query feature supported by Hibernate. The syntaxes of HQL are similar to SQL, but not the same. HQL is independent of underlying database. Hibernate generates native SQL query for every HQL. The Java Persistent API Query Language (JPA QL, simply JPQL), based on EJB 3.0 standard, is an extension of EJBQL (Enterprise Java Bean Query Language) and has many features than EJBQL. It is also a database independent object-based query language and it is a subset of HQL so that all JPAQL queries are valid in HQL.

The Chapter 6 (Criteria Queries) introduces Criteria Queries, another easy way to create queries and retrieve data from database. Even though the HQL is based on object references, its query syntaxes are similar to SQL, so the programmer still needs to know SQL syntaxes and relational mappings to write HQL queries. The Hibernate provides *Criteria API*, which is purely based object-oriented approach; using this Criteria API, the programmer can use Java code for manipulating data with database, and no need to know SQL and relational mappings for building queries.

This book is well-suited for beginners and intermediates to Hibernate and Database Systems. All important concepts are chosen and explained with working examples. This book is written based on my working experience with Hibernate, and lot of efforts is taken to choose and organize the flow of concepts and suitable real-time examples given to each concepts.

First of all, I thank the Almighty; I can't be completed this book without His grace. All praise is due to him. I thank everyone for their direct and indirect support in all my success in my life.

—Author

CHAPTER

1

GETTING READY

1.0 INTRODUCTION

Hibernate is an Object Relational Mapping (ORM) tool, which is an Open Source. It maps objects (Java) with relational data (RDBMS) and vice versa, i.e., maps the Java classes to the database tables. So you can utilize the full features of Object Oriented Programming System (OOPS) in handling data on any database. Hibernate provides transparent persistence (storage) and Object-Oriented Query Language which is independent of any database. You can invoke native SQL queries (queries belonging to a particular database) as well.

1.1 HIBERNATE ARCHITECTURE

Hibernate sits in between the application (Java classes) and Database, as shown below.

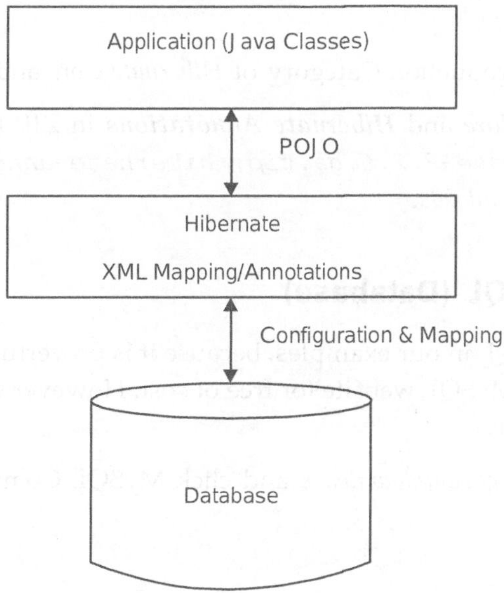

The POJOs are "Plain Old Java Objects" (like Java bean, class with fields and getter-setters), which are acting as persistence objects in Hibernate. They are data transmitter between your application and database. Each POJO is associated with a table in database and each field in the class maps the corresponding column in the database table, if configured. So your application needs to put the data on these POJOs, which are to be stored in database by Hibernate. When you instruct Hibernate to retrieve data from database, then Hibernate places the resultant data in the corresponding POJOs. That's how the POJOs are acting as value objects in Hibernate, but should be configured. These mapping configurations can be specified through an XML file, otherwise you can best use of Annotation features of latest JDK, which is supported by latest versions of Hibernate.

1.2 GET READY TO WORK WITH HIBERNATE

The following are main software components required to develop and test our hibernate programs.

- Hibernate Core API
- Hibernate Annotations API
- Any one RDBMS
- Additional Software & Tools (such as Application Server, IDE)

1.2.1 Download Hibernate

Download latest ***Hibernate Core*** and ***Hibernate Annotations*** from Hibernate web site (http://www.hibernate.org).

Choose to download Production Category of *Hibernate Core* and *Hibernate Annotations.*

Download ***Hibernate Core*** and ***Hibernate Annotations*** in ZIP format. And save them (the filenames looks like, *`hibernate-3.2.6.ga.zip`*, *`hibernate-annotations-3.3.1.GA.zip`*) on any directory, say *C:/Downloads*.

1.2.2 Download MySQL (Database)

I preferred to use MySQL in our examples, because it is powerful open source database. And it can be downloaded from MySQL website for free of cost. However you can use any RDBMS like Oracle, DB2, PostgreSQL, etc.

Browse to *http://dev.mysql.com/downloads* and click MySQL Community Server Download.

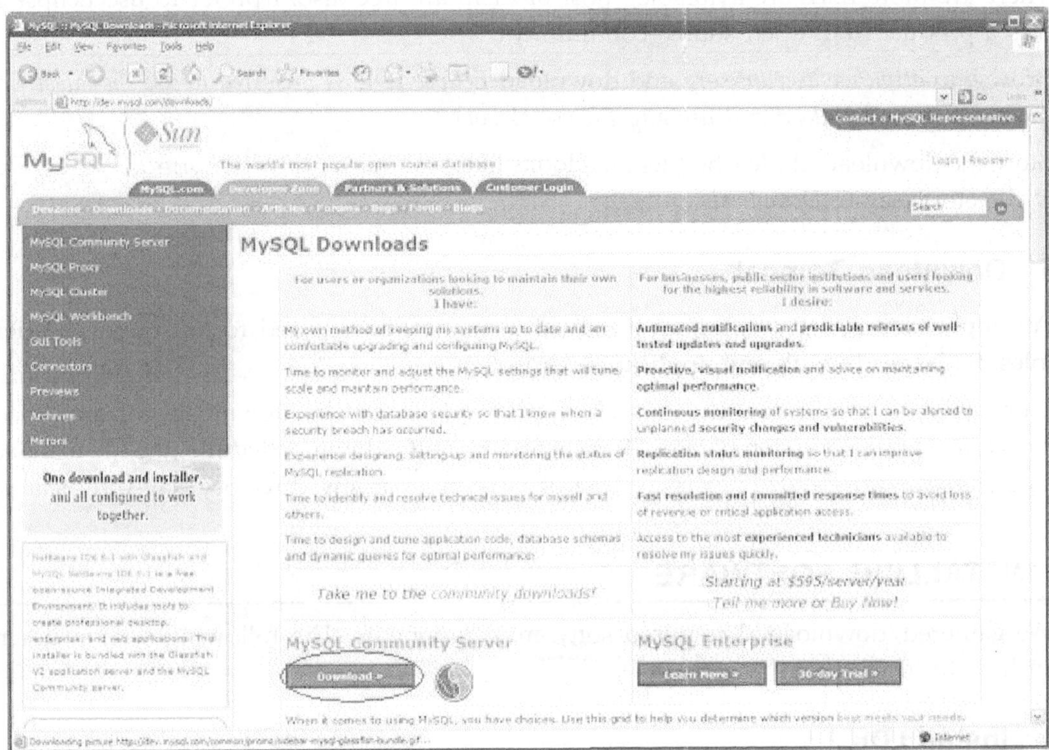

Then, Choose *Windows* (Operating System) download link → ***Windows Essentials (x86)*** download link. The downloaded file name looks like "`mysql-essential-5.0.51b-win32.msi`" (The filename may vary according to the version that you chosen).

1.2.3 Download MySQL Connector for Java

Browse to *http://dev.mysql.com/downloads* and download *MySQL Connector/J 5.1 - Generally Available (GA)* version in ZIP format and store it (the filename looks like, `mysql-connector-java-5.1.5.jar`) in any directory say, *C:/Downloads*. This is required to make MySQL database connection with Java.

1.2.4 Download Java Development Kit (JDK)

Browse to Java download page of *sun.com* (*http://java.sun.com/javase/downloads/*) and download latest JDK. Store the file (the filename looks like, `jdk-6u6-windows-i586-p.exe`, JDK 6) in any directory, say *C:/Downloads*.

1.2.5 Download Java IDE

It is always best to work with an IDE (Integrated Development Environment) for developing Java projects. It supports many features including auto-compilation, package organization, code assistance and environment to run and test your programs.

There are more IDEs are available, most of them are free also. I prefer to use Eclipse IDE, which is a product from open source community.

Browse to *http://www.eclipse.org* and download *Eclipse IDE. (I preferred to use the latest Eclipse Ganymede. You can download and use any Eclipse flavor).*

Store the downloaded file (the filename looks like, `eclipse-jee-ganymede-win32.zip`) in any directory, say *C:/Downloads*.

1.2.6 Download Tomcat

An application server (minimum a Servlet container) is required to test our web-oriented examples. So be ready with any application server.

I preferred to use open-source *Apache Tomcat*, which can be downloaded from Apache's website. Download ZIP version of latest Tomcat and Store the downloaded file (the file name looks like, `apache-tomcat-6.0.16.zip`, Tomcat version 6) in any directory, say *C:/Downloads*.

1.3 INSTALLING SOFTWARE

We gathered/downloaded required software components. The following section describes shortly how to install them.

1.3.1 Install J DK

Double click JDK executable file (*C:/Downloads/jdk-6u6-windows-i586-p.exe*) and install in your favorite directory (In our case, It is *C:/Development*. The Java Home directory is renamed to *jdk1.6*).

Follow the following procedure for setting `JAVA_HOME` Environment Variable to the Home directory of JDK installation.

Desktop → Right click on My Computer Icon → Properties → Advanced Tab → Click on Environment Variables button → click on *New* button → Set Variable name as `JAVA_HOME` and Variable value as the JDK installation directory → Click OK.

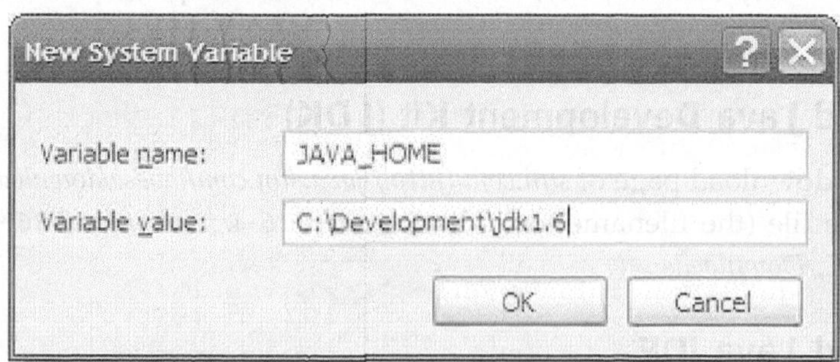

Once you set this environmental variable, it will be available throughout your session with the computer. And automatically set when the system is booted.

1.3.2 Install MySQL

Double click the downloaded MySQL Windows Installer File

(*mysql-essential-5.0.51b-win32.msi*). It will invoke MySQL installation.

For your Information: The file extension "*msi*" stands for **M**icrosoft **I**nstaller, now these *msi* files are called as Windows Installer Files.

Choose ***Next → Typical → Install***

Check "*Configure the MySQL Server now*" and click "*Finish*" button.

Press on "*Next*", Choose "*Standard Configuration*", and press "*Next*".

The check boxes for "*Install as Windows Service*" and "*Launch the MySQL Server automatically*" will be checked by default. Let them be checked. Check the checkbox for "*Include Bin directory in Windows PATH*".

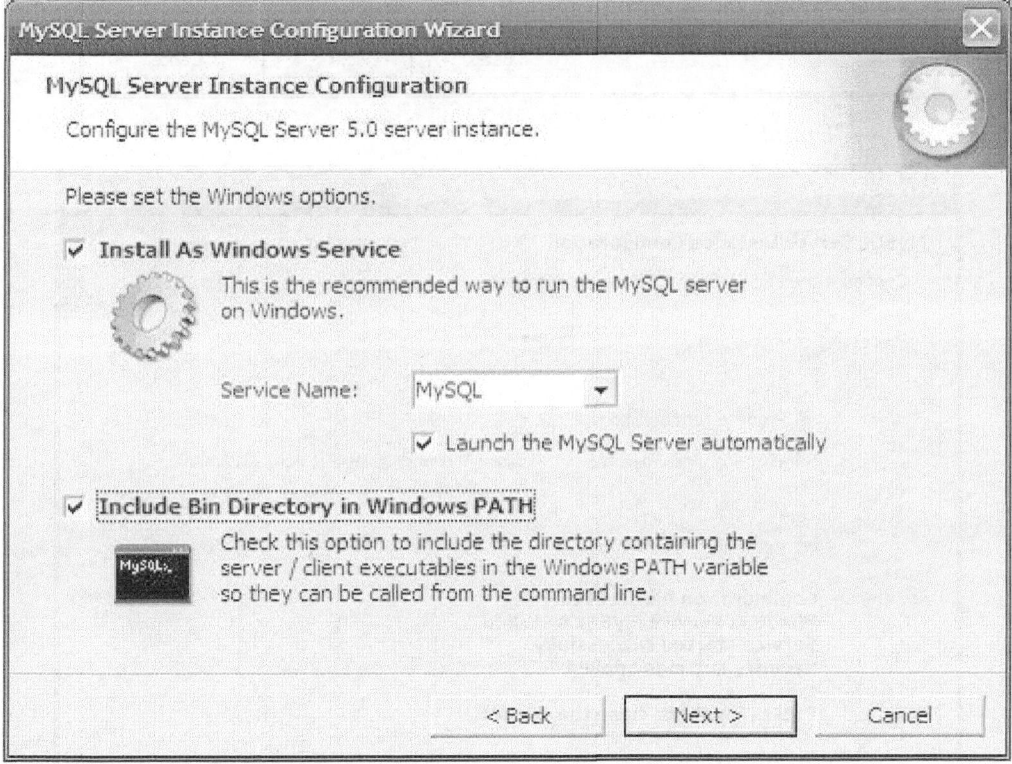

Press "*Next*". Enter the root (MySQL database system administrator) password and keep in mind, it is required for MySQL administration related activities such as creating users, allocating memory, etc. In our case, the root password is set as `'ibrahim'`. Choose "*Enable root access from remote machines*" feature.

Press "*Next*" → "*Execute*".

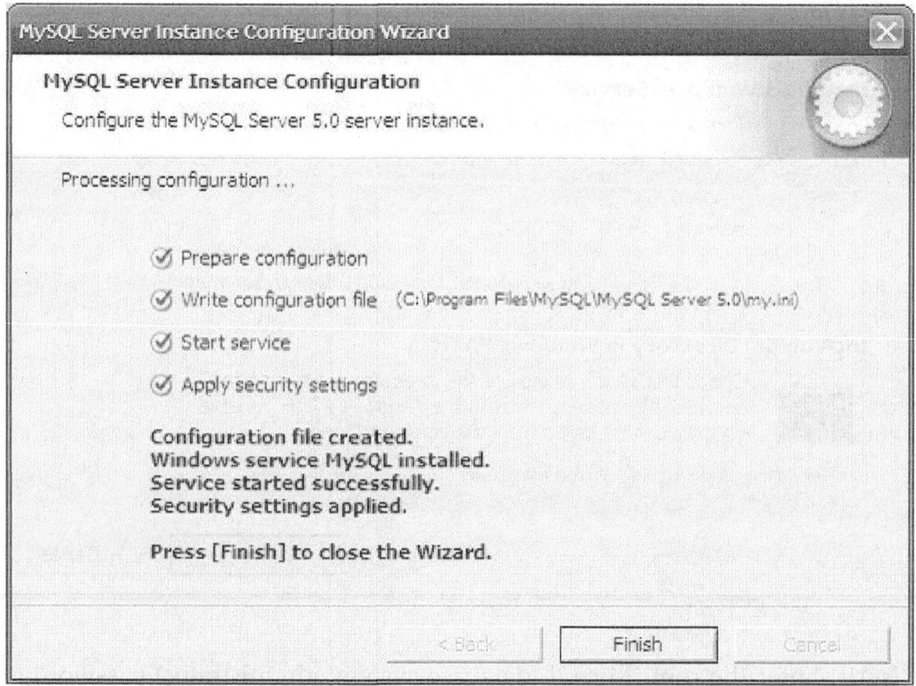

Click "*Finish*" to complete installation.

As per our settings, MySQLwill be automatically started when Windows is loaded. Any how, you can start/stop MySQL service. Choose Start → Control Panel → Administrative Tools → Services → MySQL start/restart/pause/stop.

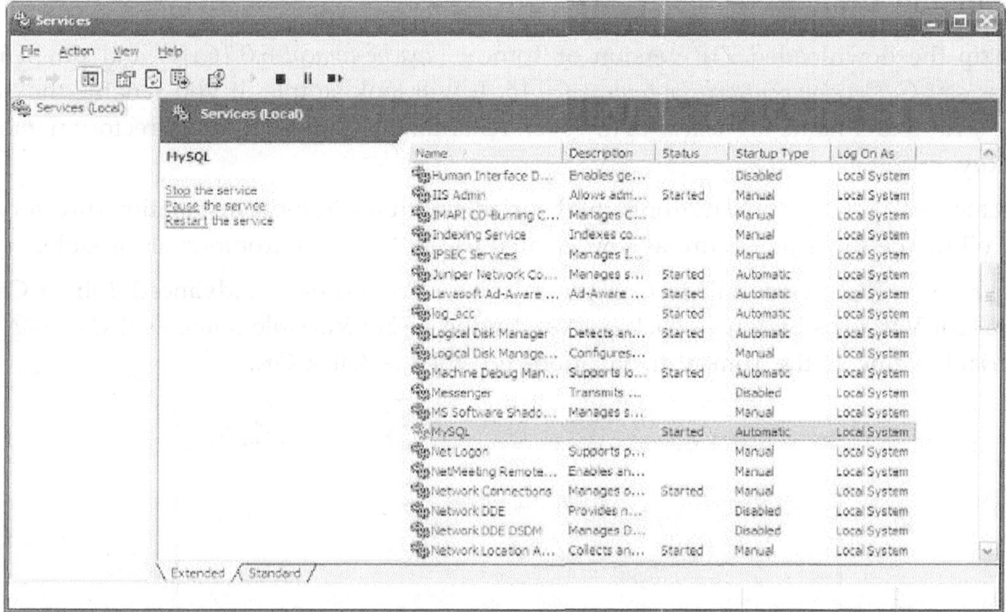

Working with MySQL:

You can use any third-party SQL manipulation software such as Oracle's SQL Developer, Aqua Data Studio, etc. Many of them are freeware / shareware. These software are basically Integrated Development Environments (IDEs) for easy access with databases.

We can also use DOS window for textual interaction with MySQL.

Open DOS window and give the following command to login to MySQL as root (administrator).

```
mysql  -u  root  -pibrahim
```

Here, *'ibrahim'* is the root password assigned while installing MySQL. Note that there is no space between `-p` and password.

```
C:\WINDOWS\system32\cmd.exe

C:\>mysql -u root -pibrahim
Welcome to the MySQL monitor.  Commands end with ; or \g.
Your MySQL connection id is 3
Server version: 5.0.51b-community-nt MySQL Community Edition (GPL)

Type 'help;' or '\h' for help. Type '\c' to clear the buffer.

mysql> select sysdate();
+---------------------+
| sysdate()           |
+---------------------+
| 2008-07-04 17:58:30 |
+---------------------+
1 row in set (0.00 sec)

mysql> exit
Bye

C:\>_
```

1.3.3 Install Tomcat

Unzip the downloaded ZIP version of Tomcat (*apache-tomcat-6.0.16.zip*) and put it in any directory, say *C:/Development/apache-tomcat-6.0.16*. It will look simple, if you rename the "*apache-tomcat-6.0.16*" folder name to "*tomcat*". However, renaming of Tomcat Home directory name is not mandatory.

Create `CATALINA_HOME` environmental variable with the Tomcat installation directory as its value. Follow the same procedure as you created `JAVA_HOME` environmental variable.

Desktop → Right click on My Computer Icon → Properties → Advanced Tab → Click on Environment Variables button → click on *New* button → Set Variable name as `CATALINA_HOME` and Variable value as the Tomcat installation directory → Click OK.

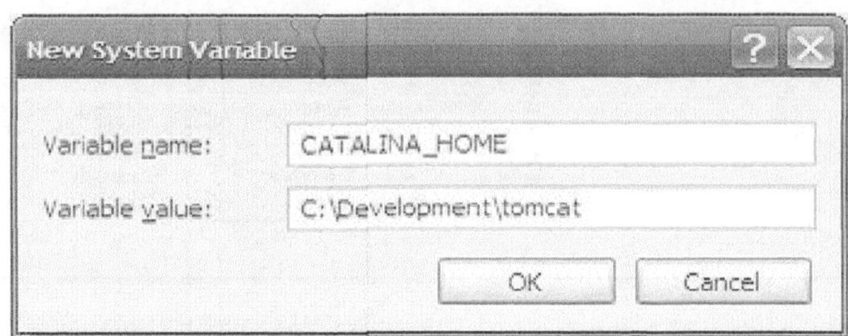

1.3.3.1 Testing Tomcat Installation

Do the following procedure to test Tomcat Installation.

Starting Tomcat: Go to "*bin*" folder of Tomcat (*C:/Development/tomcat/bin*) and invoke the "*startup.bat*" file (Double click on *startup.bat*, or type this command in command prompt; it is advised to make short-cut to *Desktop* for easy access).

```
Tomcat
Jul 7, 2008 11:52:12 AM org.apache.coyote.http11.Http11Protocol init
INFO: Initializing Coyote HTTP/1.1 on http-8080
Jul 7, 2008 11:52:12 AM org.apache.catalina.startup.Catalina load
INFO: Initialization processed in 1484 ms
Jul 7, 2008 11:52:12 AM org.apache.catalina.core.StandardService start
INFO: Starting service Catalina
Jul 7, 2008 11:52:12 AM org.apache.catalina.core.StandardEngine start
INFO: Starting Servlet Engine: Apache Tomcat/6.0.16
Jul 7, 2008 11:52:13 AM org.apache.catalina.core.StandardContext addApplicationL
istener
INFO: The listener "listeners.ContextListener" is already configured for this co
ntext. The duplicate definition has been ignored.
Jul 7, 2008 11:52:13 AM org.apache.catalina.core.StandardContext addApplicationL
istener
INFO: The listener "listeners.SessionListener" is already configured for this co
ntext. The duplicate definition has been ignored.
Jul 7, 2008 11:52:13 AM org.apache.coyote.http11.Http11Protocol start
INFO: Starting Coyote HTTP/1.1 on http-8080
Jul 7, 2008 11:52:14 AM org.apache.jk.common.ChannelSocket init
INFO: JK: ajp13 listening on /0.0.0.0:8009
Jul 7, 2008 11:52:14 AM org.apache.jk.server.JkMain start
INFO: Jk running ID=0 time=0/47  config=null
Jul 7, 2008 11:52:14 AM org.apache.catalina.startup.Catalina start
INFO: Server startup in 1637 ms
```

Once the Server is started up, invoke the browser (Internet Explorer, Firefox, etc.) with the address "*http://localhost:8080*". If you are working in networked environment, then you can access this page from any computer (including the local one) in the network by specifying the IP address / Domain name of the computer where the Tomcat server is installed, instead of "*localhost*". Note that "*localhost*" is look-back address that represents local (current) computer.

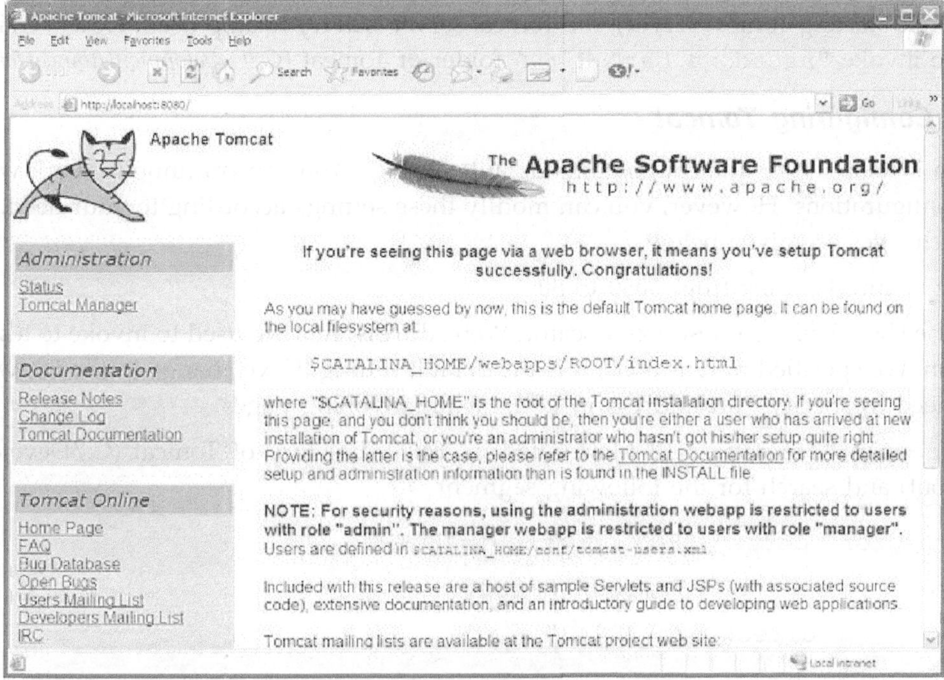

Invoking from the Local Computer (same computer where Tomcat server is running)

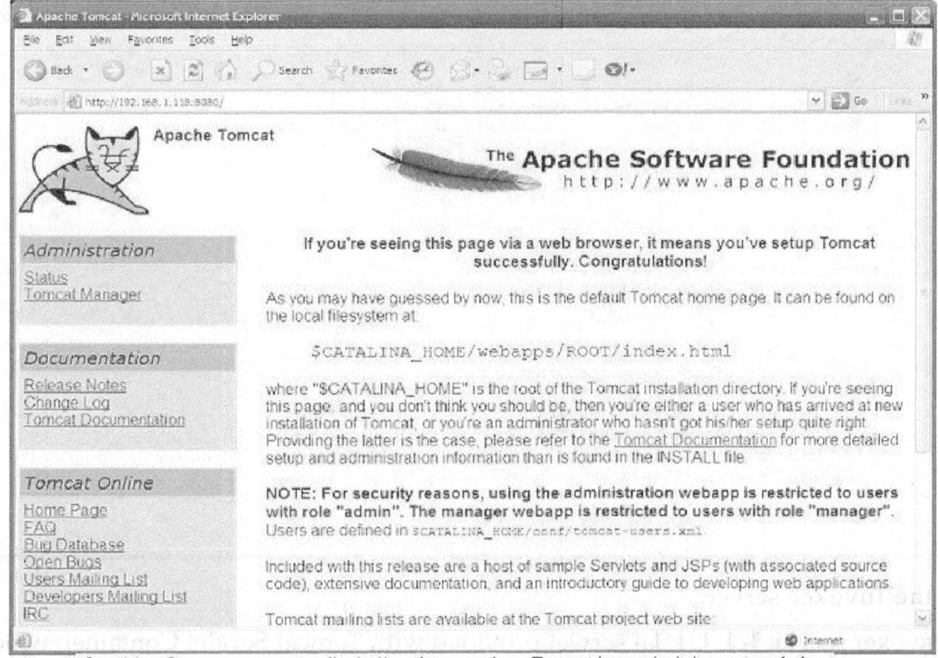

Invoking from any computer (including the one where Tomcat is running) in a network, by specifying the IP address of the computer where server Tomcat is running. Of course, the computer where Tomcat server is running must be with in the network

If you can see the web page like shown above, then it means that Tomcat installation is successful and Tomcat Server is running.

Shutting down Tomcat: If you try to close the Tomcat DOS window (the window that is opened while starting Tomcat server), the Tomcat server will try to stop itself. However, it is good practice to invoke "`shutdown.bat`" at "*bin*" folder of Tomcat (*C:/Development/tomcat/bin*).

1.3.3.2 Configuring Tomcat

Fresh installation of Tomcat contains default settings. You can continue to work with these default configurations. However, you can modify these settings according to your need. Some of common changes are given below.

Changing Connector Port from 8080 to 80:

See the URL (Uniform Resource Locator; Web address) that we used to invoke to test Tomcat installation. We specified port as 8080, it is the default setting. If we change it into 80 (web port), then no need to specify Port address in URLs while invoking pages.

To do, open "`server.xml`" file located in "*conf*" directory of Tomcat (C:/Development/tomcat/conf) and search for the following segment.

```
<Connector port="8080" protocol="HTTP/1.1"
        connectionTimeout="20000"
        redirectPort="8443" />
```

Then, change `port="8080"` to `port="80"`.

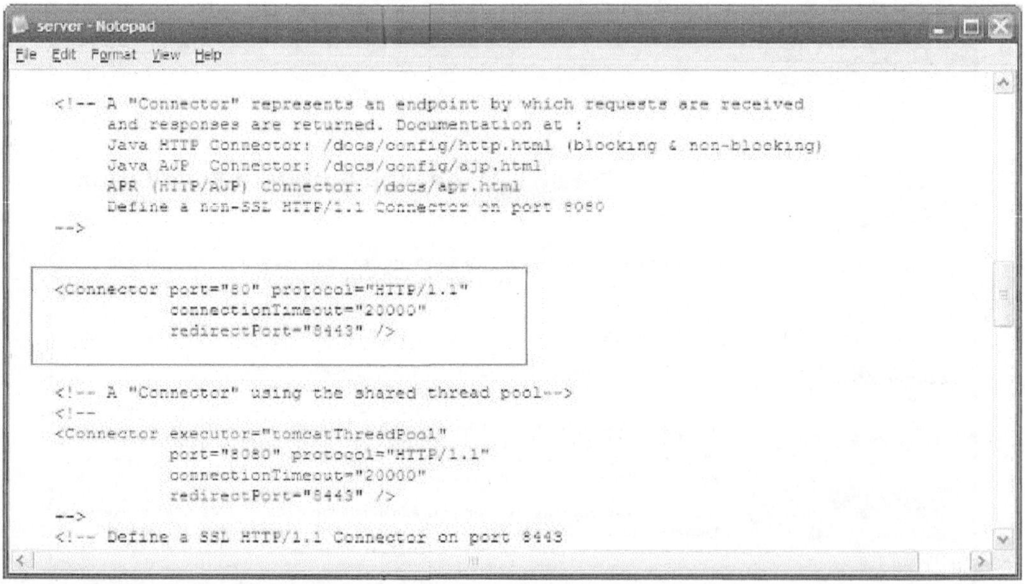

```
server - Notepad
File  Edit  Format  View  Help

    <!-- A "Connector" represents an endpoint by which requests are received
         and responses are returned. Documentation at :
         Java HTTP Connector: /docs/config/http.html (blocking & non-blocking)
         Java AJP  Connector: /docs/config/ajp.html
         APR (HTTP/AJP) Connector: /docs/apr.html
         Define a non-SSL HTTP/1.1 Connector on port 8080
    -->

    <Connector port="80" protocol="HTTP/1.1"
               connectionTimeout="20000"
               redirectPort="8443" />

    <!-- A "Connector" using the shared thread pool-->
    <!--
    <Connector executor="tomcatThreadPool"
               port="8080" protocol="HTTP/1.1"
               connectionTimeout="20000"
               redirectPort="8443" />
    -->
    <!-- Define a SSL HTTP/1.1 Connector on port 8443
```

Enabling the Invoker server:

The Invoker servlet is a special servlet provided with Tomcat Servlet Container, which allows servlets (servlet programs) to be called by simply using a */servlet* URL, without having to configure each servlet individually in web configuration XML (*web.xml*).

To enable this feature, follow the following procedure.

Open "*web.xml*" file under "*conf*" folder of Tomcat (C:/Development/tomcat/conf) and search for the following segment.

```
<!–
    <servlet>
        <servlet-name>invoker</servlet-name>
        <servlet-class>
          org.apache.catalina.servlets.InvokerServlet
        </servlet-class>
            <init-param>
                <param-name>debug</param-name>
                <param-value>0</param-value>
            </init-param>
            <load-on-startup>2</load-on-startup>
    </servlet>
–>
```

The `servlet` element contains the declarative data of a servlet.

Uncomment this segment (Remove <!– and –> lines).

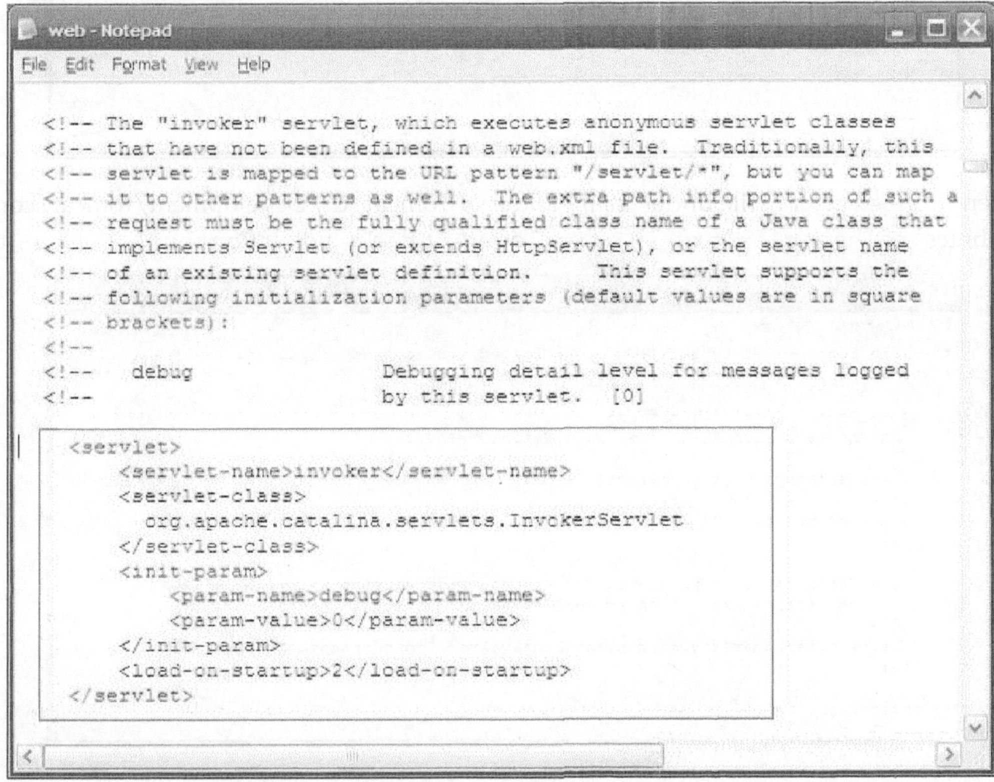


```
<!-- The "invoker" servlet, which executes anonymous servlet classes
<!-- that have not been defined in a web.xml file.  Traditionally, this
<!-- servlet is mapped to the URL pattern "/servlet/*", but you can map
<!-- it to other patterns as well.  The extra path info portion of such a
<!-- request must be the fully qualified class name of a Java class that
<!-- implements Servlet (or extends HttpServlet), or the servlet name
<!-- of an existing servlet definition.     This servlet supports the
<!-- following initialization parameters (default values are in square
<!-- brackets):
<!--
<!--   debug                Debugging detail level for messages logged
<!--                        by this servlet.  [0]

  <servlet>
      <servlet-name>invoker</servlet-name>
      <servlet-class>
        org.apache.catalina.servlets.InvokerServlet
      </servlet-class>
      <init-param>
          <param-name>debug</param-name>
          <param-value>0</param-value>
      </init-param>
      <load-on-startup>2</load-on-startup>
  </servlet>
```

And uncomment the following segment in the same file.

```
<!--
        <servlet-mapping>
                <servlet-name>invoker</servlet-name>
                <url-pattern>/servlet/*</url-pattern>
        </servlet-mapping>
-->
```

The servlet-mapping element defines a mapping between a servlet and a URL pattern.

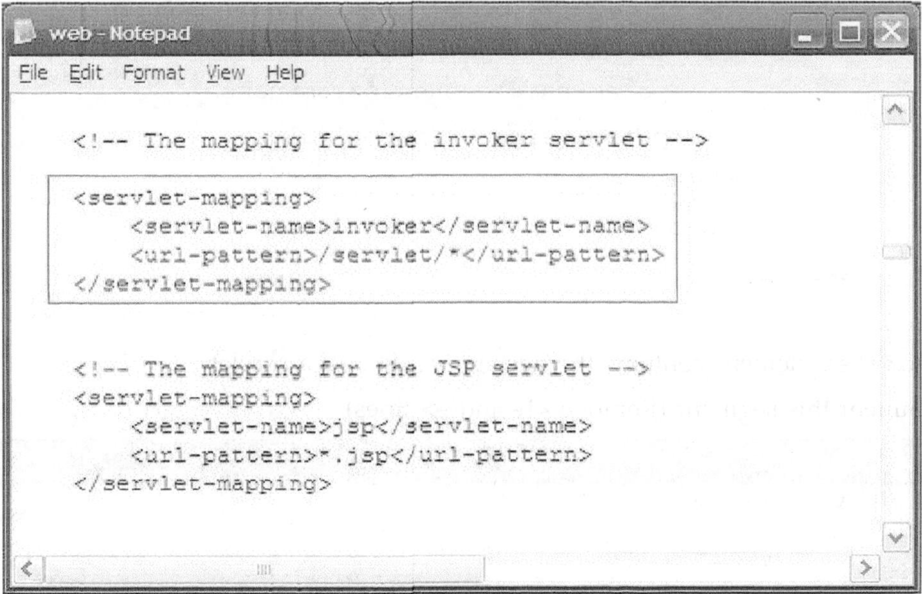

Open "*context.xml*" file under "*conf*" folder of Tomcat (C:/Development/tomcat/conf) and the attributes *reloadable="true" privileged="true"* to *<Context>* element.

```
context - Notepad
File Edit Format View Help
<!-- The contents of this file will be loaded for each web application -->
<Context reloadable="true" privileged="true">

    <!-- Default set of monitored resources -->
    <WatchedResource>WEB-INF/web.xml</WatchedResource>

    <!-- Uncomment this to disable session persistence across Tomcat restarts -->
    <!--
    <Manager pathname="" />
    -->

    <!-- Uncomment this to enable Comet connection tacking (provides events
         on session expiration as well as webapp lifecycle) -->
    <!--
    <Valve className="org.apache.catalina.valves.CometConnectionManagerValve" />
    -->

</Context>
```

The above setting makes Tomcat to reload the web-applications automatically, without restarting server after the web-application files are modified (deployed). This setting is good to use *InvokerServlet* facility.

1.3.4 Install Eclipse

Unzip the downloaded Eclipse zip file `(eclipse-jee-ganymede-win32.zip)` and put the resultant *'eclipse'* directory into your development directory (any directory of you choice), say *C:/Development*.

Go to *'eclipse'* folder and create a folder named *'workspace'*, which will contain all your projects. The structure of the *'eclipse'* directory looks like shown below.

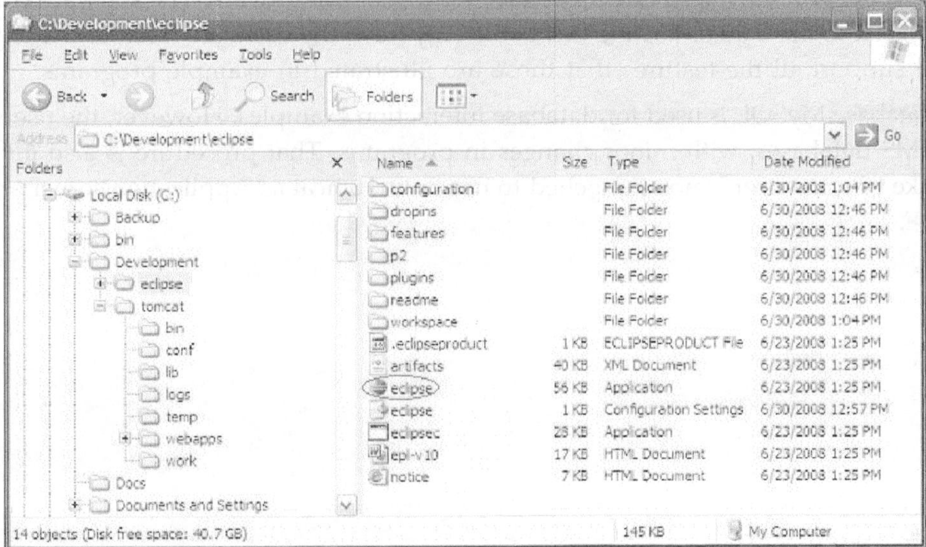

You can invoke (start) eclipse by clicking *'eclipse'* Application icon (Create short-cut in Desktop for easy access).

Invoke Eclipse. Then it will prompt for workspace.

Select the workspace directory (the directory in which your project code will reside, it may be any directory of your choice; in our case, select the directory just now we created).

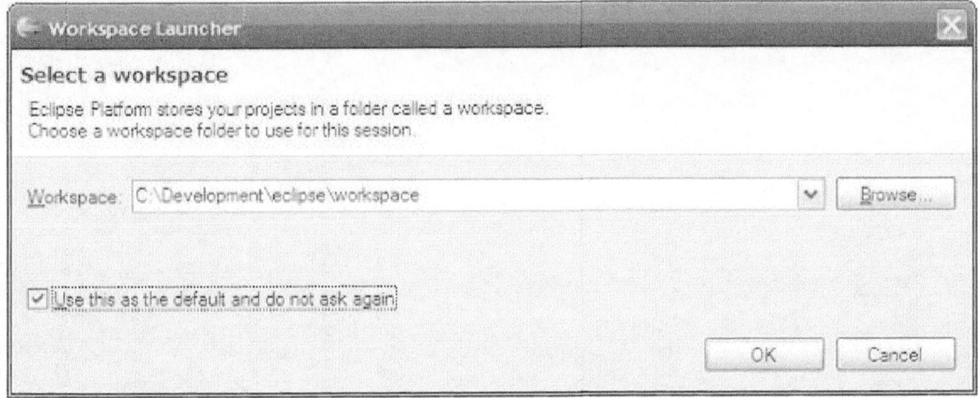

And check the "Use *this as the default and do not ask again*" checkbox to make this directory as default workspace.

Press "*OK*". Now you can start working with Eclipse IDE.

SUMMARY

This chapter introduces you the need of Hibernate and its architecture. It describes how to download and install supporting software components to work with Hibernate programs. If the user is already installed all or part of the above installation, there are not forced to install from the scratch. The installation directories are given for understanding purposes only. However, it is up to the users to follow the same procedure for installing software. The software components are almost latest to the date of writing this book. Any how, the users are freed to use any version, but should support all the features that those are illustrated in example programs.

The database MySQL is used for database interaction examples. However, the users may use other RDBMS databases, with minor changes in programs. That procedure is also given in this chapter. Like this, the user is not compelled to use only Tomcat as Application server and Eclipse as Java IDE.

CHAPTER

2

Persisting Student Data with Hibernate: Demo

2.0 INTRODUCTION

Some initial setups are required to work with Hibernate such as locating library files, configuring data sources, and defining persistence (storage) objects. This chapter demonstrates these initial configuration things with a simple program. These same Hibernate configurations are to be followed in other chapters.

Simple Program: Persisting Student Info

Now we will try to write and test a simple program using Hibernate. This program will insert one Student record (with fields, Roll number, Student name, Mark1, Mark2, Mark3, Total, Average, and Result) into the database table.

2.1 CREATING A DATABASE AND DATABASE USER

We already decided to use MySQL in our programs and we have already installed the same, now it is ready to use.

Note: *You may choose other databases also, if you do, you have to do little bit changes in code; that is more understandable.*

Open DOS window, and login to MySQL as root. Then, use the following command to create a database named "*hdemodb*".

```
create  database  hdemodb;
```

Note: *If you want to drop an existing database, use the command*

"drop database <database-name>"

The following commands create a user named "*huser*" with password "*hpword*" and set necessary rights for *huser* on the database *hdemodb*.

```
grant create, create view, create temporary tables on hdemodb.* to
'huser'@'localhost' identified by 'hpword';

grant delete, drop, update, select, alter, insert, index, show
view, lock tables on hdemodb.* to 'huser'@'localhost';
```

```
C:\Windows\system32\cmd.exe

C:\>mysql -u root -pibrahim
Welcome to the MySQL monitor.  Commands end with ; or \g.
Your MySQL connection id is 2
Server version: 5.0.51b-community-nt MySQL Community Edition (GPL)

Type 'help;' or '\h' for help. Type '\c' to clear the buffer.

mysql> create database hdemodb;
Query OK, 1 row affected (0.03 sec)

mysql> grant create, create view, create temporary tables on hdemodb.* to 'huser'@'localhost' identified by 'hpword';
Query OK, 0 rows affected (0.05 sec)

mysql> grant delete, drop, update, select, alter, insert, index, show view, lock tables on hdemodb.* to 'huser'@'localhost';
Query OK, 0 rows affected (0.00 sec)

mysql> exit
Bye

C:\>_
```

Now, try to login as *huser* for the database *hdemodb*.

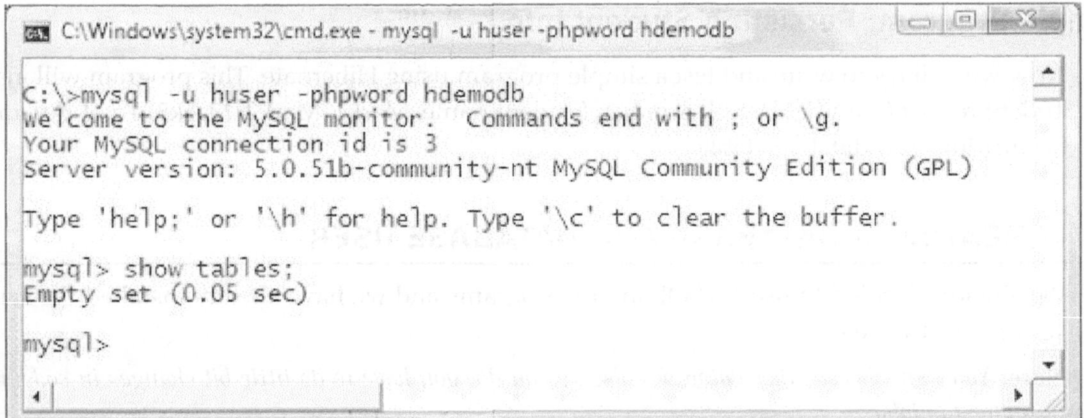

```
C:\Windows\system32\cmd.exe - mysql -u huser -phpword hdemodb

C:\>mysql -u huser -phpword hdemodb
Welcome to the MySQL monitor.  Commands end with ; or \g.
Your MySQL connection id is 3
Server version: 5.0.51b-community-nt MySQL Community Edition (GPL)

Type 'help;' or '\h' for help. Type '\c' to clear the buffer.

mysql> show tables;
Empty set (0.05 sec)

mysql>
```

If you get *mysql*> prompt with out any error, then the user creation is successful. This is the user that we going to use in our Hibernate programs to interact with *hdemodb* database in MySQL.

2.2 CREATING A JAVA PROJECT IN ECLIPSE

Invoke Eclipse IDE. Then, choose File → New → Other → Java Project

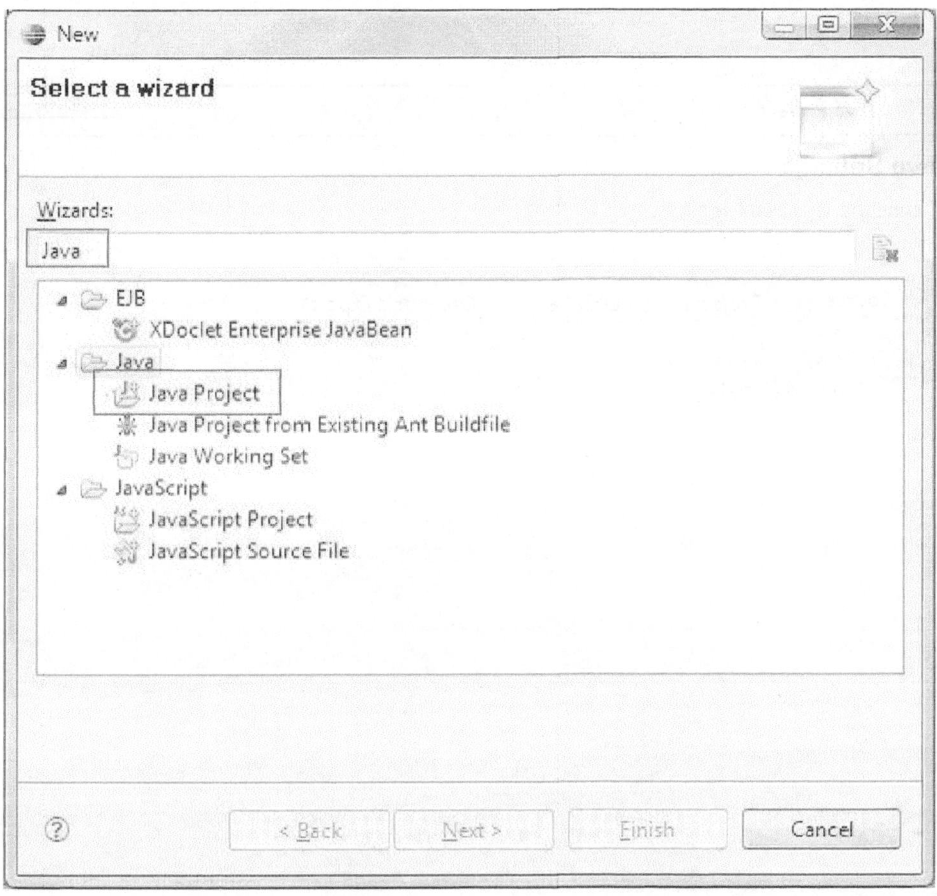

Click "*Next*". Type the string "*HibernateDemo*" in Project Name textbox and accept the defaults in the window.

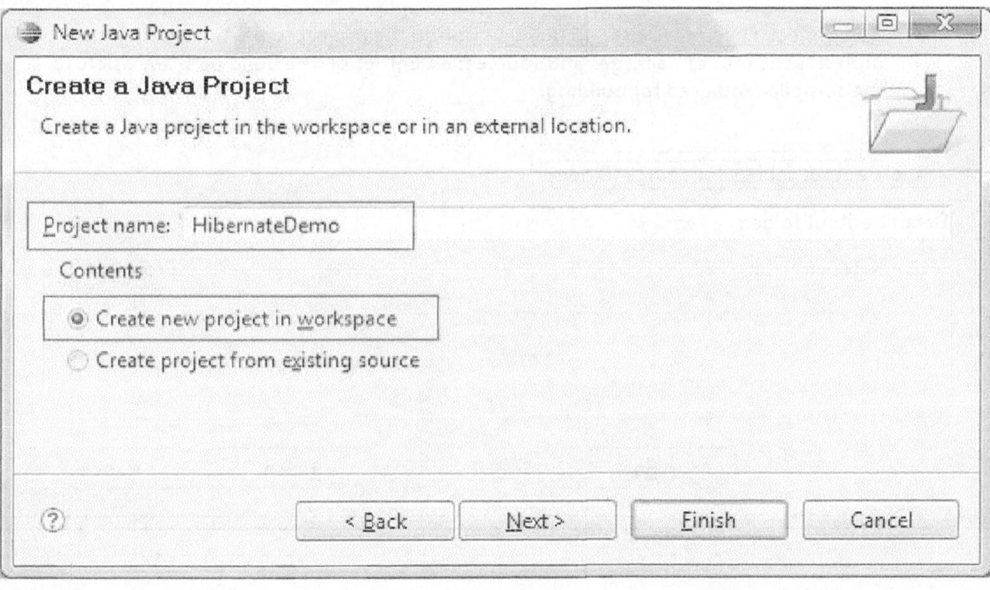

Click "*Next*".

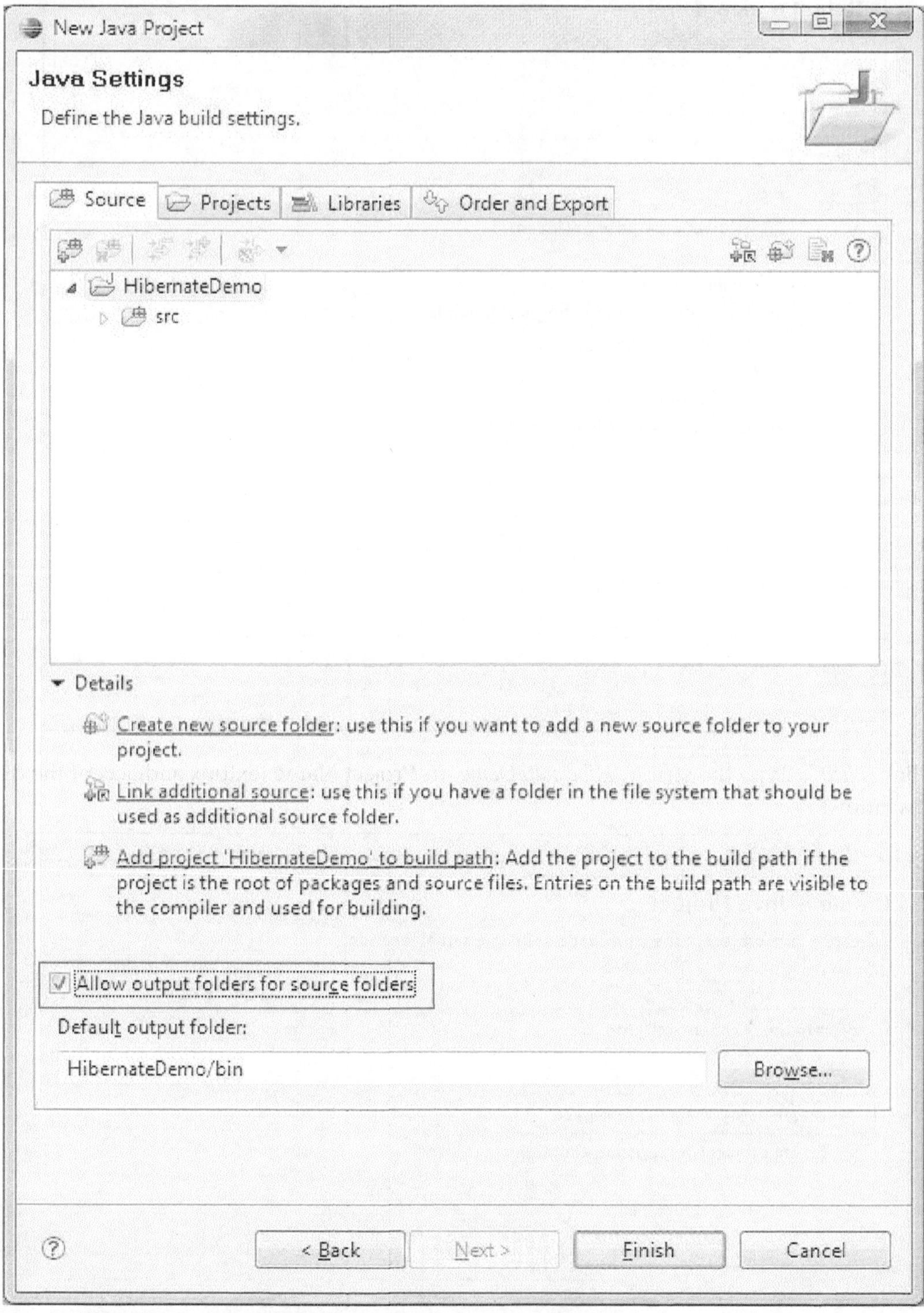
New Java Project
Java Settings
Define the Java build settings.
Source
Projects
Libraries
Order and Export
HibernateDemo
src
Details
Create new source folder: use this if you want to add a new source folder to your project.
Link additional source: use this if you have a folder in the file system that should be used as additional source folder.
Add project 'HibernateDemo' to build path: Add the project to the build path if the project is the root of packages and source files. Entries on the build path are visible to the compiler and used for building.
Allow output folders for source folders
Default output folder:
HibernateDemo/bin
Browse...
< Back
Next >
Finish
Cancel

Check the "*Allow output folders for source folders*" check box and then click "*Finish*".

Then, the Package Explorer window will look like below.

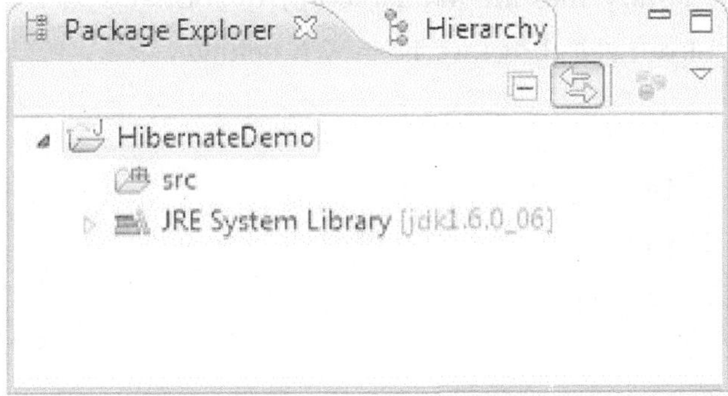

Select "*HibernateDemo*" project in Package Explorer and right click on it. From the popped-up menu, choose *New* → *Folder* and create a folder named "*lib*". Then, Package Explorer looks like below.

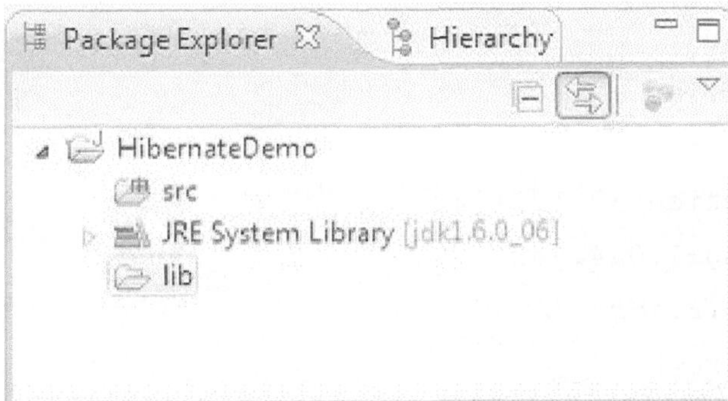

2.3 SETTING UP REQUIRED LIBRARY FILES FOR THE PROJECT

We have to find and collect what are the required library files needed for our program and set them on *classpath*. Instead of finding and collecting them one by one and deciding which one is needed for which functionality, simply copy all the library files from downloaded APIs (such as Hibernate API). Even though some of the libraries are not really needed now, simply copy because we may use them later. You are also most encouraged to study the actual purposes of these library files, if you are interested.

Unzip the MySQL Connector, Hibernate Core and Hibernate Annotations files (Already downloaded files: "*mysql-connector-java-5.1.6.zip*", "*hibernate-3.2.zip*", and "*hibernate-annotations-3.3.1.GA.zip*").

Copy

"/mysql-connector-java-5.1.6/mysql-connector-java-5.1.6-bin.jar",

"/hibernate-3.2/hibernate3.jar" and all jar files under "/hibernate-3.2/lib", and

"/hibernate-annotations-3.3.1.GA/hibernate-annotations.jar" and all jar files under

"/hibernate-annotations-3.3.1.GA/lib".

And paste them at "*/lib*" directory of our project (*/HibernateDemo/lib*).

Note: Generally the library files are available in *JAR* format.

A typical contents of our */lib* directory is shown below.

```
ant-1.6.5.jar
ant-antlr-1.6.5.jar
ant-junit-1.6.5.jar
ant-launcher-1.6.5.jar
ant-swing-1.6.5.jar
antlr-2.7.6.jar
asm-attrs.jar
asm.jar
c3p0-0.9.1.jar
cglib-2.1.3.jar
checkstyle-all.jar
cleanimports.jar
commons-collections-2.1.1.jar
commons-logging-1.0.4.jar
concurrent-1.3.2.jar
dom4j-1.6.1.jar
ehcache-1.2.3.jar
ejb3-persistence.jar
hibernate-annotations.jar
hibernate-commons-annotations.jar
hibernate3.jar
jaas.jar
jacc-1_0-fr.jar
javassist.jar
jaxen-1.1-beta-7.jar
jboss-cache.jar
jboss-common.jar
jboss-jmx.jar
jboss-system.jar
jgroups-2.2.8.jar
```

```
jta.jar
junit-3.8.1.jar
log4j-1.2.11.jar
mysql-connector-java-5.1.6-bin.jar
oscache-2.1.jar
proxool-0.8.3.jar
swarmcache-1.0rc2.jar
syndiag2.jar
versioncheck.jar
xerces-2.6.2.jar
xml-apis.jar
```

Select our project *HibernateDemo* in Package Explorer and right click, from the popped up menu, select *Properties*. Select *Java Build Path* item on left-hand side and select *Libraries* tab on the right-hand side. Click on "*Add JARs*" button which will open a *JAR Selection* window, select all the jar files under "*/lib*" directory of our project (*/HibernateDemo/lib*). Press "*OK*".

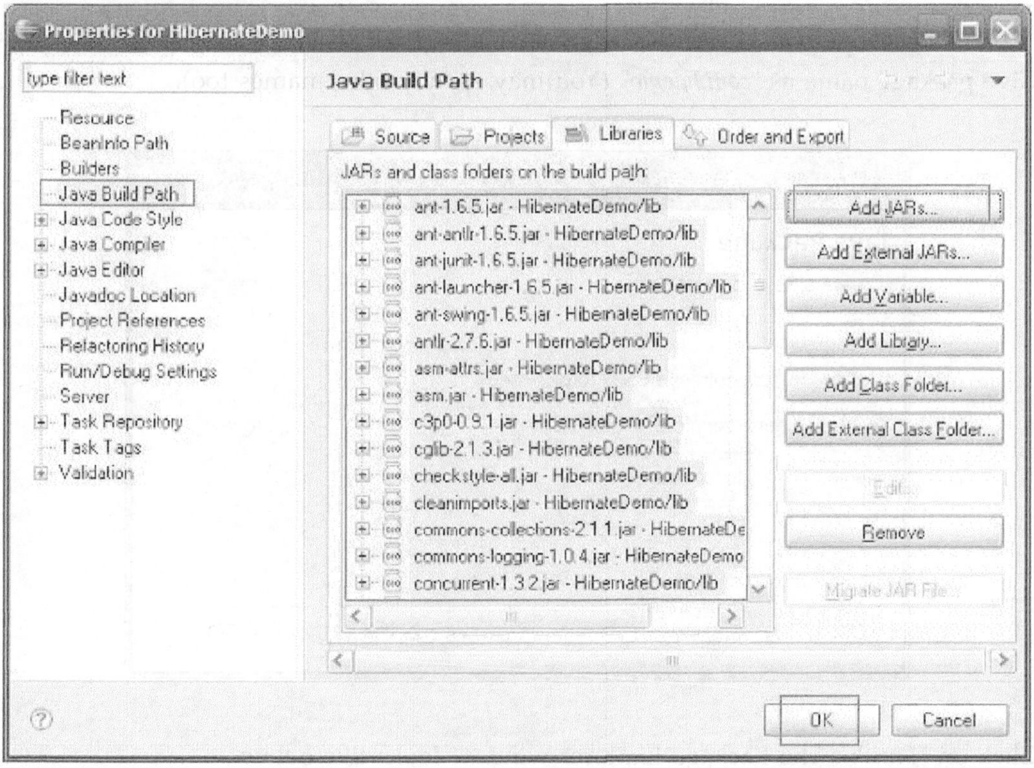

Press "*OK*", then the selected JARs will be available for our project.

2.4 SETTING UP LOG4J PROPERTIES

You may use Log4j (Log for Java; Logging –recording errors, warnings, output, etc. for auditing purpose) for logging purpose. Create a file named "*log4j.properties*" under "*src*" directory with the following contents.

```
log4j.rootCategory=INFO,  CONSOLE
log4j.logger.org.apache.axis.enterprise=WARN,  CONSOLE

log4j.appender.CONSOLE=org.apache.log4j.ConsoleAppender
log4j.appender.CONSOLE.Threshold=WARN
log4j.appender.CONSOLE.layout=org.apache.log4j.PatternLayout
log4j.appender.CONSOLE.layout.ConversionPattern=-  %m%n
```

2.5 CREATE A PACKAGE

For simple programs, you can start work with default package. However, it is good practice to create and work with packages in Java.

Right click on "*src*" of *SampleProgram* → From the popped-up menu select *New* → *Package*.

Give package name as "*com.hdemo*" (You may specify other names too).

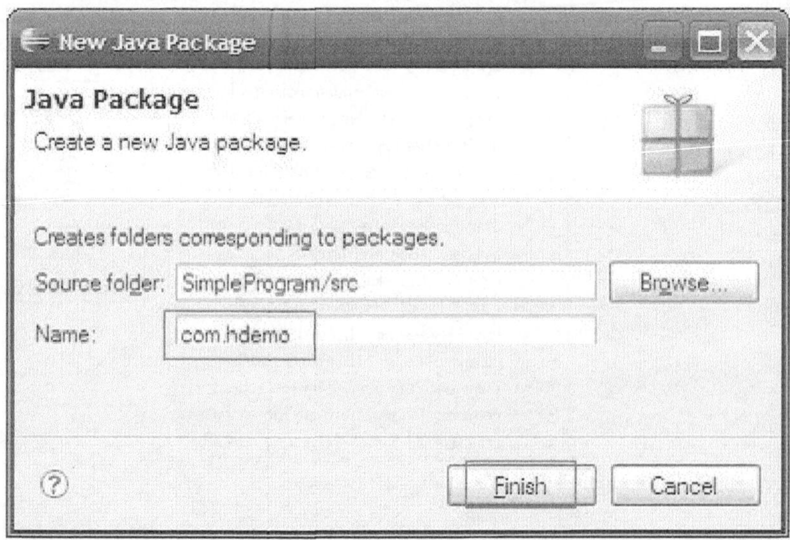

Click on "*Finish*". The Package Explorer window looks like below.

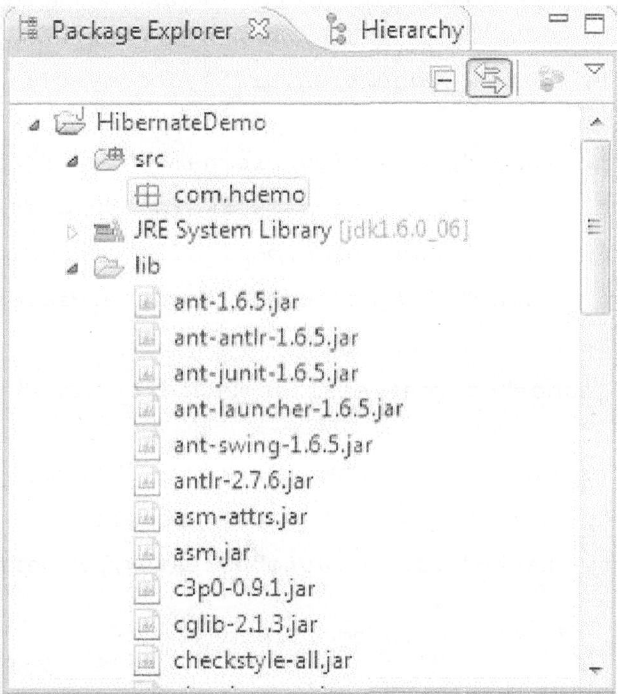

2.6 DEFINING HIBERNATE CONFIGURATIONS

Even though there are some alternate ways to define Hibernate configurations, defining them through XML is a good option.

Create a XML file named "*hibernate.cfg.xml*" under the *src* directory of our project. To do, Right click on *src* directory, then choose as follows in the popped-up menu.

Choose *New* → XML (Choose *Others* → Type XML as filter text, if you want to locate easily) → Type **hibernate.cfg.xml** as File name → Click on "*Finish*".

This XML file is used to configure Hibernate elements such as database connection, POJOs (Plain Old Java Objects). Save this file with the following content.

```
<?xml version='1.0' encoding='utf-8'?>
<!DOCTYPE hibernate-configuration PUBLIC
   "-//Hibernate/Hibernate Configuration DTD 3.0//EN"
   "http://hibernate.sourceforge.net/hibernate-configuration-3.0.dtd">
<hibernate-configuration>
  <session-factory>
```

```
    <property name="connection.driver_class">com.mysql.jdbc.Driver</
                                                                property>
     <property  name="connection.url">jdbc:mysql://localhost:3306/
                                                       hdemodb</property>
     <property  name="connection.username">huser</property>
     <property  name="connection.password">hpword</property>
     <property  name="connection.pool_size">1</property>
     <property  name="dialect">org.hibernate.dialect.MySQLDialect</
                                                                property>
    <property name="current_session_context_class">thread</property>
                                                              <property
name="cache.provider_class">org.hibernate.cache.NoCacheProvider</property>
     <property  name="show_sql">true</property>
     <property  name="hbm2ddl.auto">create</property>

     <mapping  class="com.hdemo.Student"  />

    </session-factory>
</hibernate-configuration>
```

The following properties (in the above configuration file) describe the database settings.

```
<property  name="connection.driver_class">com.mysql.jdbc.Driver</
                                                          property>
<property name="connection.url">jdbc:mysql://localhost:3306/hdemodb</
                                                          property>
<property  name="connection.username">huser</property>
<property  name="connection.password">hpword</property>
```

The "`connection.driver_class`" specifies the database driver.

The "`connection.url`" specifies JDBC URL, the "`connection.username`" and the "`connection.password`" specifies the username and password to connect to the database.

A typical setting for MySQL:

Driver Class	:	`com.mysql.jdbc.Driver`
Connection URL	:	`jdbc:mysql://<Database Host>:<Port>/<Database Name>` Here, `<Database Host>` is the IP-address / Domain-name of the computer in which database is running (database

		server). The <Port> is usually 3306, because it is the default setting while installing MySQL. The <Database Name> specifies the name of the database (usually created using command like *create database* by Database Administrator) that you are going to work with.
Driver Jar file	:	Can be downloaded from Internet. Try *http://dev.mysql.com/downloads* (Filename: mysql-connector-java-5.1.6-bin.jar)
Example	:	<property name="connection.driver_class"> com.mysql.jdbc.Driver </property> <property name="connection.url"> jdbc:mysql://localhost:3306/hdemodb </property>

A typical setting for Oracle:

Driver Class	:	oracle.jdbc.OracleDriver
Connection URL	:	jdbc:oracle:thin:@<Database Host>:<Port>:<Database Name>Here, <Database Host> is the IP-address / Domain-name of database server. The <Port> is usually 1521, because it is the default set while installing Oracle. The <Database Name> specifies the name of the database that you are going to work with.
Driver Jar file	:	Can be downloaded from Internet. Try *http://www.oracle.com* (Filename: ojdbc14.jar)
Example	:	<property name="*connection.driver_class*"> oracle.jdbc.OracleDriver </property> <property name="*connection.url*"> jdbc:oracle:thin:@localhost:1521:hdemodb </property>

The following property defines the maximum number of pooled (stack) database connections. It sets pool size as 1.

```
<property name="connection.pool_size">1</property>
```

It is advised to use third-party connection pooling in Hibernate for best performance and stability, instead of this Hibernate's internal connection pool.

Note: Connection pooling is a technique which is used to overcome the bottleneck of creating new database connections, particularly for applications which needs more database interaction. Generally, creation of database connection takes consider amount of time. Instead of creating and closing database connections every time, the connection pooling technique pools (stacks) the already opened connections. So that, when a database connection is needed, the application can get it from this connection pool. Of course, initially the required number of database connections should be created and pooled in connection pool.

However, Hibernate's default (internal) connection pooling algorithm is quite simple, not suitable for production environment. You should use a good third party connection pool (like C3P0 –An open source JDBC connection pool distributed along with Hibernate an you can find it in *lib* directory of Hibernate distribution) to achieve good performance. To do so, just replace the `hibernate.connection.pool_size` property with connection pool specific settings which will turn off Hibernate's default pool and direct to use specified pool. For example, you might like to use C3P0. The following *hibernate.c3p0* setting in *hibernate.properties* file makes Hibernate to use *C3P0ConnectionProvider* of C3P0 (C Three P Zero) for connection pooling.

```
<property  name="connection.pool_size">C3P0</property>
<property  name="hibernate.c3p0.min_size">5</property>
<property  name="hibernate.c3p0.max_size">20</property>
<property  name="hibernate.c3p0.timeout">1800</property>
<property  name="hibernate.c3p0.max_statements">50</property>
```

Another typical setting in *hibernate.cfg.xml* for C3P0 Connection pool.

```
<property  name="hibernate.connection.provider_class">
        org.hibernate.connection.C3P0ConnectionProvider
</property>

<property  name="hibernate.c3p0.min_size">2</property>
<property  name="hibernate.c3p0.max_size">10</property>
<property  name="hibernate.c3p0.acquire_increment">2</property>
<property  name="hibernate.c3p0.timeout">3600</property>
<property  name="hibernate.c3p0.idle_test_period">4000</property>
```

```
<property  name="hibernate.c3p0.max_statements">100</property>
```

The property "min_size" defines minimum number of connections will be maintained at any given time in the C3P0 Connection Pool, i.e., the minimum size of the C3P0 Connection Pool. Default is 3.

The property "max_size" defines maximum number of connections will be maintained at any given time in the C3P0 Connection Pool, i.e., the maximum size of the C3P0 Connection Pool. Default is 15.

The property "acquire_increment" defines how many connections will try to obtain (acquire) when the C3P0 Connection Pool is exhausted (no connection is available in the connection pool). Default is 3. You know that the applications get connections from Connection Pool, when they completed work with those connections, the connections will be collected (pooled) to the Connection Pool. To utilize the resources effectively, Hibernate will create "min_size" number of connections initially for Connection Pool, not the "max_size" number of connections. The acquireIncrement property determines how many "allowed connections" the C3P0 Connection Pool will attempt to acquire when the pool has run out of Connections (when the connection(s) are requested by the application). The "allowed connections" represents the meaning that the total number of connections in the Connection Pool must not exceed "max_size", that is the pool will never allow to exceed maximum number of connections regardless of this "acquire_increment". For example, if max_size is set as 10 and acquire_increment is set as 2, and application uses 9 connections, then only one connection will be created and added to the pool when application requires connection(s). If application uses 10 connections (the pool is empty) and the application requires some connections, then no connection will be created and added to the pool since maximum connections are already created, in this case the application should wait for connections, which are currently used and will be released by the application.

The property "timeout" defines timeout (maximum idle time) for C3P0 connections. Default is 0. This property defines how many seconds a connection in the C3P0 Connection Pool should be permitted to be idle (not required by the application), after that that connection will be expired. If a Connection pool created more number of connections (may be due to heavy load) and not all of them are used by applications at this time, then many of the connections will become "unused" and will be available in the connection pool for long time without requested by the application, and those "unused" connections will be unnecessarily maintained by the connection pool. In order to keep the connection poll always fresh, we can instruct the connection pool to delete those "unused" connections by setting the "timeout" property. The connection pool will wait for the number of seconds (specified in this "timeout" property) before deleting an "unused" connection from the connection pool. If a connection in the connection pool is not requested by the application for the specified number of seconds, then it will be deleted. The value 0 (zero) set to this property will never make to expire any connection, even if it is "unused". This *timeout* will not affect any other behaviors of the connection pool; it has the rights to create allowed number of connections again if necessary.

Note: For the connection pools used in large scale Enterprise Applications, do not set *timeout* (let it be defaulted to 0) or set to reasonable number of seconds (more than 30 minutes), otherwise *timeout* slows down the applications.

The property `"idle_test_period"` defines how long in seconds to wait before testing "*timeout*" connections (idle "unused" connection in connection pool, as explained above) to investigate. Default is 0. For every this number of seconds (set with this property), idle connections in connection pool are examined for deletion, however actual deletion process is depended on the value set in "timeout" property. A 0 (zero) value set to this property disables this feature, thus it will not set any specific time to invoke investigation process for idle connections.

The property `"max_statements"` defines the maximum number of already executed statements to cache for C3P0. Default is 0. It is a JDBC standard for controlling statement pooling in cache (a cache is a temporary storage in main memory where frequently accessed data can be stored for quick access). The `PreparedStatement` is a reference type in Java where a pre-compiled SQL statement will be stored to efficiently execute that statement multiple times. This `"max_statements"` property defines the total number of those `PreparedStatements`, generated by the present active connections and the connections in Connection Pool, to be kept in cache for the entire C3P0 connection pool. When the number of `PreparedStatements` in cache exceeded the value specified in this `"max_statements"`, then the least-recently-used (not accessed for the application for long time) `PreparedStatement` will be deleted from the cache to free one statement location in cache. Keep in mind that this cache is global for all connections. So it is important to set reasonable large number to this property, as each pooled connection requires its own, thus distinct group of cached statements.

The following property defines which database dialect (Dialect refers SQL, syntaxes, etc.). Provide proper dialect name according to the RDBMS database that you are going to use, so that Hibernate will generate SQL optimized for that database.

```
<property  name="dialect">Dialect  name</property>
```

Example:

The following statement set dialect for MySQL.

```
<property name="dialect">org.hibernate.dialect.MySQLDialect</property>
```

Some of the RDBMS databases and their corresponding dialect classes are given below.

RDBMS	Dialect
MySQL	`org.hibernate.dialect.MySQLDialect`
Oracle (any version)	`org.hibernate.dialect.OracleDialect`
Oracle 9i/10g	`org.hibernate.dialect.Oracle9Dialect`
Microsoft SQL Server	`org.hibernate.dialect.SQLServerDialect`

HypersonicSQL	org.hibernate.dialect.HSQLDialect
Sybase	org.hibernate.dialect.SybaseDialect
PostgreSQL	org.hibernate.dialect.PostgreSQLDialect
DB2	org.hibernate.dialect.DB2Dialect
HSQLDB	org.hibernate.dialect.HSQLDialect
MySQL	org.hibernate.dialect.MySQLDialect
PostgreSQL	org.hibernate.dialect.PostgreSQLDialect

If the following "show_sql" property is set to "true", then all the generated SQL (by Hibernate) will be displayed on the screen.

```
<property  name="show_sql">true</property>
```

The `"current_session_context_class"` property defines the scope of current session. The values for this property includes `jta, thread, and managed.`

```
<property  name="current_session_context_class">thread</property>
```

The following "hbm2ddl.auto" property is associated with DDL (Data Definition Language) to database. Some acceptable values for this property are *create, update, create-drop,* and *validate.*

```
<property  name="hbm2ddl.auto">create</property>
```

If it is set to `"create"`, then at the time of Hibernate Session Factory creation, the associated tables for all mapped POJOs (in our case, mapped using `<mapping class=" />`) are freshly created (dropped and re-created based on current mapped entities' properties) in database. If it is set to `"create-drop"`, it will re-create (freshly create) the associated tables and drop them at the end of Session Factory. If it is set to `"update"`, it will neither re-creates nor drops the existing tables; simply updates the incremental database (schema) changes, for example, creates the tables if those tables are not exists, alters (update the schema) the tables like adding new columns if the table already exists in the database. The setting `"validate"` enables *SchemaValidator* to run at the startup, which compares the associated Entities (POJOs, specified using `<mapping class="" />`) against the corresponding database tables (metadata) and raise an exception if there is a mismatch between them. These `hbm2ddl.auto` values investigate the mapped entities only; it will never touch other database tables present in the database, they will be available as they are.

Difference between `create` and `create-drop`:

Both of these values re-create the tables for mapped entities. However, a major difference is there: the `"create"` exports schema DDL to the database when the Session Factory is created, the `"create-drop"` exports schema DDL to the database when the Session Factory is created and destroys the schema when the Session Factory is destroyed.

Follow the below procedure to test the above said difference, but it uses some settings and programs. If you are very new to Hibernate, then skip this procedure now and complete this chapter, and then come back to this section to practice; otherwise you will be struck in executing programs.

Change `log4j rootLogger` property to `DEBUG` to get debug-level log messages.

Define Student entity. And map this entity in *hibernate.cfg.xml* file as below.

```
<mapping class="com.hdemo.Student" />
```

Set `hbm2ddl.auto` property to `create` in *hibernate.cfg.xml.*

```
<property name="hbm2ddl.auto">create</property>
```

Then execute the following program, which builds and closes the Session Factory.

```
package com.hdemo;

import org.hibernate.SessionFactory;
import org.hibernate.cfg.AnnotationConfiguration;

public class StudentInfo {

public static void main(String[] args) throws Exception {

SessionFactory sessionFactory = null;

try {
sessionFactory = new Annotation Configuration().configure().
buildSessionFactory();
}
catch (Exception e) {
System.out.println("Error in creating SessionFactory.");
                    e.printStackTrace();
                    return;
                }
                finally {
                    if (sessionFactory != null)
                        sessionFactory.close();
                }
```

```
        }
}
```

You can notice the following lines in the generated log.

```
DEBUG org.hibernate.tool.hbm2ddl.SchemaExport
- drop table if exists STUDENT

DEBUG org.hibernate.tool.hbm2ddl.SchemaExport
- create table STUDENT (
ROLL_NUMBER integer not null,
AVERAGE double precision, MARK1 integer,
MARK2 integer, MARK3 integer, RESULT varchar(8),
STUDENT_NAME varchar(64) not null,
TOTAL integer, primary key (ROLL_NUMBER))

INFO org.hibernate.tool.hbm2ddl.SchemaExport - schema export complete
```

In the case of "create", the following actions will be performed.

1. At the time of building SessionFactory, the associated tables (if exist) for the mapped entities will be dropped from the database.
2. At the time of building SessionFactory, the associated tables for the mapped entities (current entities) will be created (i.e., re-created). Of course, old data will not be available.
3. At the time of closing SessionFactory explicitly, no database schema based activities will be done. So that the created tables at database will exist even after the SessionFactory is closed.

```
mysql> desc student;
```

Field	Type	Null	Key	Default	Extra
ROLL_NUMBER	int(11)	NO	PRI	NULL	
AVERAGE	double	YES		NULL	
MARK1	int(11)	YES		NULL	
MARK2	int(11)	YES		NULL	
MARK3	int(11)	YES		NULL	
RESULT	varchar(8)	YES		NULL	
STUDENT_NAME	varchar(64)	NO		NULL	
TOTAL	int(11)	YES		NULL	

```
8 rows in set (0.00 sec)
```

Set `hbm2ddl.auto` property to `create-drop` in *hibernate.cfg.xml.*

```
<property  name="hbm2ddl.auto">create-drop</property>
```

Execute the given main program, and then you can notice the following lines in the generated log.

```
DEBUG  org.hibernate.tool.hbm2ddl.SchemaExport
- drop  table  if  exists  STUDENT

DEBUG  org.hibernate.tool.hbm2ddl.SchemaExport
- create  table  STUDENT  (
ROLL_NUMBER  integer  not  null,
AVERAGE  double  precision,  MARK1  integer,
MARK2  integer,  MARK3  integer,  RESULT  varchar(8),
STUDENT_NAME  varchar(64)  not  null,
TOTAL  integer,  primary  key  (ROLL_NUMBER))

INFO  org.hibernate.tool.hbm2ddl.SchemaExport - schema export complete

...

...

...

DEBUG  org.hibernate.tool.hbm2ddl.SchemaExport    -  drop  table  if
exists  STUDENT

INFO    org.hibernate.tool.hbm2ddl.SchemaExport    -  schema  export
complete
```

In the case of `"create-drop"`, the following actions will be performed.

1. At the time of building SessionFactory, the associated tables (if exist) for the mapped entities will be dropped from the database.
2. At the time of building SessionFactory, the associated tables for the mapped entities (current entities) will be created (i.e., re-created). Of course, old data will not be available.
3. At the time of closing SessionFactory explicitly, the associated tables for the mapped entities will be dropped from the database. So that the created tables at database will not exist after SessionFactory is closed.

```
mysql> desc student;
ERROR 1146 (42S02): Table 'hdemodb.student' doesn't exist
```

Difference between update and validate:

Both of these values will not re-create any database tables. Usually these *hbm2dll* values are set to append data to the database tables. However, major differences are there: the `"update"` alters/creates database table schema to the changes made on mapped entities. But, the `"validate"` immediately raise Hibernate Exception if there is schema mismatch between mapped entities and the corresponding database tables.

Set `hbm2ddl.auto` property to `update` in *hibernate.cfg.xml*.

```
<property name="hbm2ddl.auto">update</property>
```

Add one more filed named "grade" in the Student entity as below.

```
@Column(name = "GRADE", length = 16)
 private String grade;
```

Execute the given main program, and then you can notice the following lines in the generated log.

```
DEBUG org.hibernate.tool.hbm2ddl.SchemaUpdate
     - alter table STUDENT add column GRADE varchar(16)
INFO org.hibernate.tool.hbm2ddl.SchemaUpdate - schema update complete
```

In the case of `"update"`, the following actions will be performed.

1. At the time of building SessionFactory, no database table will be deleted.
   (i) If there is no corresponding table for a mapped entity exists in the database, then a new table for that entity will be created.
   (ii) If the corresponding table exists for a mapped entity and that entity is modified now, then the modified changes will be reflected on the database table by altering that existing table schema. Note that not all modified changes on the entity will be reflected on the database table. So, the words "*incremental changes*" are used in explaining `"update"` hbm2dll (hibernate mapping to data definition language) type.
      (a) If a new filed is added to the mapped entity, then the corresponding attribute for that filed will be added in the database table.
      (b) If a field is deleted from the mapped entity, then the corresponding attribute in the database table will not be removed.
      (c) If a field's attribute name is changed (in our examples, change at name attribute of `@Column`) in the mapped entity, then a new attribute with that

new name will be added to the database table. However, the old attribute (now it is not present in the mapped entity) in the database table will not be removed. Any other changes done at the `@Column` attribute of a field in the mapped entity will not be reflected into the database table. For example, if the `length` attribute in `@Column` annotation for a filed is incremented / decremented, then this change will not be done (reflected) with the database table.

2. At the time of closing SessionFactory explicitly, no database schema based activities will be done. So that the created tables at database will exist even after the SessionFactory is closed.

```
mysql> desc student;
```

Field	Type	Null	Key	Default	Extra
ROLL_NUMBER	int(11)	NO	PRI	NULL	
AVERAGE	double	YES		NULL	
MARK1	int(11)	YES		NULL	
MARK2	int(11)	YES		NULL	
MARK3	int(11)	YES		NULL	
RESULT	varchar(4)	YES		NULL	
STUDENT_NAME	varchar(32)	YES		NULL	
TOTAL	int(11)	YES		NULL	
GRADE	varchar(16)	YES		NULL	

```
9 rows in set (0.00 sec)
```

Set `hbm2ddl.auto` property to `validate` in *hibernate.cfg.xml.*

```
<property name="hbm2ddl.auto">validate</property>
```

Add one more filed named "grade" in the Student entity as below.

```
@Column(name = "REMARKS", length = 80)
private String remarks;
```

Execute the given main program, and then you can notice the following lines in the generated log.

```
Error in creating SessionFactory.
org.hibernate.HibernateException: Missing column: REMARKS in hdemodb.student
```

This `validate` hbm2dll will not add any modified changes on the mapped entity in to database table, or do any other schema alterations. It simply checks whether the schema specified in the mapped entities are matching with the corresponding database tables. If not, it throws an exception.

Note: Like "`update`" hbm2dll value, it will not check database column's properties such as length, nullable checks, etc.

The following property sets type of cache mechanism to be used.

```
<property  name="cache.provider_class">
org.hibernate.cache.NoCacheProvider
</property>
```

The value for this property is a custom cache provider class name, which includes the following.

```
org.hibernate.cache.NoCacheProvider
org.hibernate.cache.EhCacheProvider
org.hibernate.cache.ReadOnlyCache
```

All the POJOs that are representing as database entity should be defined in the *hibernate.cfg.xml* file using the *<mapping>* element. For example, the following element in Hibernate configuration file maps the *Student* POJO (which is located in *com.hdemo* package) with the specified database.

```
<mapping  class="com.hdemo.Student"  />
```

Use different *mapping* elements for each POJO entity class.

Miscellaneous Configuration Properties

The Hibernate configuration properties needed for our demonstration are explained in earlier. Here, some other important properties are given for interest. These properties can be specified in *hibernate.cfg.xml* file as usual.

`hibernate.connection.release_mode`

Generally, for JTA (Java Transaction API) based database source, database connections are released every JDBC call. And for non-JTA based data source, it is good to keep the database connection alive for every transaction.

This property is may be used to set database connection release mode for underlying data source. If you obtained database session using getCurrentSession() method, then this setting will have no effect since default global configuration for current session will take effect. This setting will have effect on all sessions obtained via openSession() method.

Allowed values for this property are,

`auto, on_close, after_transaction, after_statement`

The `value` auto, which is default, will set after_statement strategy for JTA based transactions and `after_transaction` for the JDBC based transactions. The `after_statement` setting aggressively releases connections after every JDBC call. The `after_transaction` setting releases connection at the end of each transaction. The `on_close` setting releases connection at the end of session.

Example

```
<property name="hibernate.connection.release_mode">
      after_transaction
</property>
```

hibernate.format_sql

If `show_sql` property is set to `true`, then Hibernate generated SQL queries will be displayed on screen (and/or stored in to log file, according to settings). This property neatly (by giving proper indentation and spaces) prints those SQL queries.

Acceptable values are,

`true` – Turns on this feature
`false` – Turns off this feature

Example

```
<property name="hibernate.format_sql">true</property>
```

hibernate.`use_sql_comments`

A true value set to this property makes Hibernate to generate comments inside the generated SQL for easier debugging. Its default value is false.

hibernate.query.substitutions -Defines Query Tokens

You may define new Hibernate query tokens using `hibernate.query.substitutions` property.

For example

The following setting cause the token "`true`" to be translated to integer value 1, and the token "`false`" to 0. This is very much used when you want to apply "group" operations, like summation, on boolean type filed of an entity.

```
hibernate.query.substitutions true=1, false=0
```

We can change the name of a function also as follows.

```
hibernate.query.substitutions toLowerCase=LOWER
```

The above setting renames the SQL function-name `LOWER` into `toLowerCase`.

2.7 CREATING POJO: *STUDENT*

This is the entity class whose fields are to be mapped in database table "STUDENT".

To create Student class: Right click on the package *com.hdemo* in Package explorer, and then choose New → Class → Type *Student* as Name → Finish. Make the following as the contents of this Student.java file.

```
// File Name: Student.java
// Student Entity class

package com.hdemo;

import java.io.Serializable;
import javax.persistence.Entity;
import javax.persistence.GeneratedValue;
import javax.persistence.Table;
import javax.persistence.Id;
import javax.persistence.Column;

import org.hibernate.annotations.GenericGenerator;

@Entity
@Table(name = "STUDENT")
public class Student implements Serializable {
private static final long serialVersionUID = 1L;

@Id
@Column(name = "ROLL_NUMBER", length = 8)
@GeneratedValue(generator = "idGen")
@GenericGenerator(name = "idGen", strategy = "assigned")
private Integer rollNumber;

@Column(name = "STUDENT_NAME", nullable = false, length = 64)
```

```
private String studentName;

@Column(name = "MARK1", length = 3)
private Integer mark1;

@Column(name = "MARK2", length = 3)
private Integer mark2;

@Column(name = "MARK3", length = 3)
private Integer mark3;

@Column(name = "TOTAL", length = 3)
private Integer total;

@Column(name = "AVERAGE")
private Double average;

@Column(name = "RESULT", length = 8)
private String result;

public Integer getRollNumber() {
  return rollNumber;
}

public void setRollNumber(Integer rollNumber) {
  this.rollNumber = rollNumber;
}

public String getStudentName() {
  return studentName;
}

public void setStudentName(String studentName) {
  this.studentName = studentName;
}
public Integer getMark1() {
  return mark1;
}

public void setMark1(Integer mark1) {
  this.mark1 = mark1;
}
```

```
public Integer getMark2() {
  return mark2;
}

public void setMark2(Integer mark2) {
  this.mark2 = mark2;
}

public Integer getMark3() {
  return mark3;
}

public void setMark3(Integer mark3) {
  this.mark3 = mark3;
}

public Integer getTotal() {
  return total;
}

public void setTotal(Integer total) {
  this.total = total;
}

public Double getAverage() {
  return average;
}
public void setAverage(Double average) {
  this.average = average;
}

public String getResult() {
  return result;
}

public void setResult(String result) {
  this.result = result;
}
}
```

Note: You can use IDE's features to generate Getters and Setters. In this program, several Annotations (starts with @ symbol) used. These annotations will be explained later.

2.8 CREATING MAIN PROGRAM

Create a class named "*StudentInfo*" with the following contents to insert one *Student* record into database.

```
// File Name: StudentInfo.java
// Main Program

package com.hdemo;

import org.hibernate.Session;
import org.hibernate.SessionFactory;
import org.hibernate.Transaction;
import org.hibernate.cfg.AnnotationConfiguration;

public class StudentInfo {

public static void main(String[] args) throws Exception {

        SessionFactory sessionFactory = null;

        try {
        sessionFactory = new Annotation Configuration().configure()
        .buildSessionFactory();
        }
        catch (Exception e) {
        System.out.println("Error in creating SessionFactory.");
        e.printStackTrace();
        return;
        }

        try {
        Session session = sessionFactory. openSession();
        Transaction txn = session.begin Transaction();

Student student = new Student();
student.setRollNumber(new Integer(1001));
```

```
    student.setStudentName("Mohamed  Ibrahim");

    student.setMark1(100);

    student.setMark2(80);

    student.setMark3(69);

    session.save(student);

    txn.commit();

    session.close();

    sessionFactory.close();

            System.out.println("Student record successfully inserted.");

      } catch (Exception e) {

            System.out.println("Error occured: " + e.getMessage());

                  e.printStackTrace();

            }

                  }

    }
```

The *Auto-boxing* feature of latest JDK will automatically converts *int* data type into *Integer* object. So it not compulsory to write as `student.setMark1(new Integer(100))`.

2.9 EXECUTING MAIN PROGRAM

Right click on the *StudentInfo.java* file in Package Explorer and Choose *Run As → Java Application*.

You can see the following result in the *Console* window. We set *show_sql* property to *true* in *hibernate.cfg.xml,* so that Hibernate displays the generated SQL statement.

```
    Hibernate: insert into student (AVERAGE, MARK1, MARK2, MARK3, RESULT, STUDENT_NAME, TOTAL, ROLL_NUMBER) values (?, ?, ?, ?, ?, ?, ?, ?)

    Student record successfully inserted.
```

2.10 VERIFYING DATA WITH DATABASE

Open DOS window and login to *hdemodb* database (As we specified in *hibernate.cfg.xml* file). And give the following SQL command.

```
select * from student;
```

There will be a record, which is inserted by Hibernate with the values present in the *student* object. That is, the *student* object is mapped into database table.

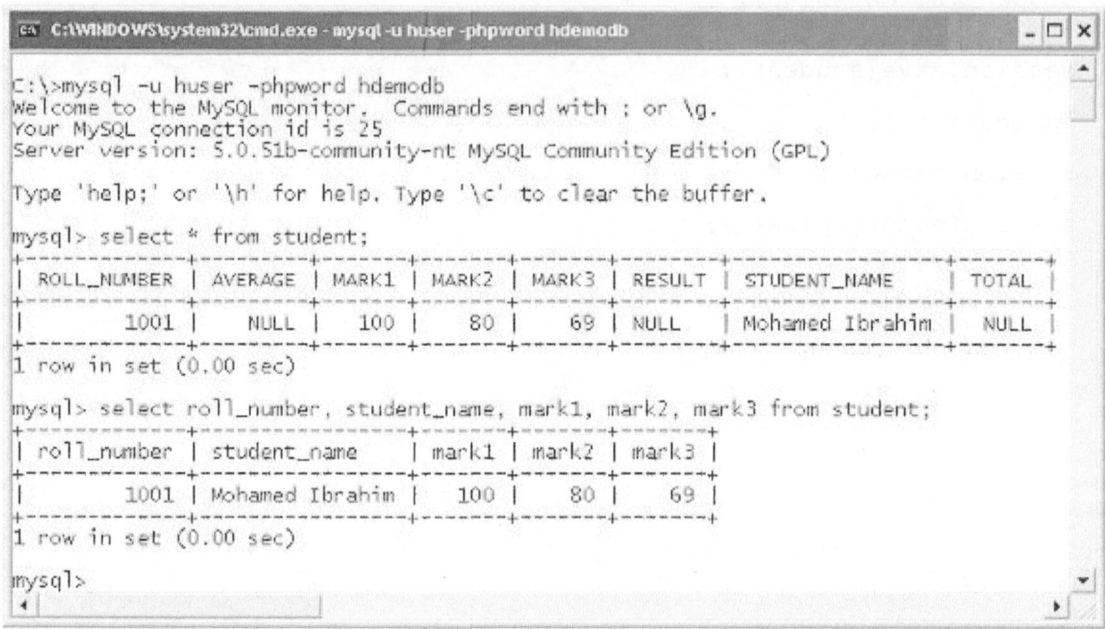

```
C:\WINDOWS\system32\cmd.exe - mysql -u huser -phpword hdemodb

C:\>mysql -u huser -phpword hdemodb
Welcome to the MySQL monitor.  Commands end with ; or \g.
Your MySQL connection id is 25
Server version: 5.0.51b-community-nt MySQL Community Edition (GPL)

Type 'help;' or '\h' for help. Type '\c' to clear the buffer.

mysql> select * from student;
+-------------+---------+-------+-------+-------+--------+-----------------+-------+
| ROLL_NUMBER | AVERAGE | MARK1 | MARK2 | MARK3 | RESULT | STUDENT_NAME    | TOTAL |
+-------------+---------+-------+-------+-------+--------+-----------------+-------+
|        1001 |    NULL |   100 |    80 |    69 | NULL   | Mohamed Ibrahim |  NULL |
+-------------+---------+-------+-------+-------+--------+-----------------+-------+
1 row in set (0.00 sec)

mysql> select roll_number, student_name, mark1, mark2, mark3 from student;
+-------------+-----------------+-------+-------+-------+
| roll_number | student_name    | mark1 | mark2 | mark3 |
+-------------+-----------------+-------+-------+-------+
|        1001 | Mohamed Ibrahim |   100 |    80 |    69 |
+-------------+-----------------+-------+-------+-------+
1 row in set (0.00 sec)

mysql>
```

Add code to set *Total, Average,* and *Result* in *Student* object in *StudentInfo.java* and run.

```
// File Name: StudentInfo.java
// Main Program

package com.hdemo;

import org.hibernate.Session;
import org.hibernate.SessionFactory;
import org.hibernate.Transaction;
import org.hibernate.cfg.AnnotationConfiguration;

public class StudentInfo {

public static void main(String[] args) throws Exception {

        SessionFactory sessionFactory = null;

        try {
        sessionFactory = new Annotation
```

```
                Configuration().configure().buildSessionFactory();
        } catch (Exception e) {
        System.out.println("Error in creating SessionFactory.");
e.printStackTrace();
 return;
 }

 try {
            Session session = sessionFactory.open Session();
            Transaction txn = session.begin Transaction();

 Student student = new Student();
 student.setRollNumber(new Integer(1001));
 student.setStudentName("Mohamed Ibrahim");
 student.setMark1(100);
 student.setMark2(80);
 student.setMark3(69);
 int total = student.getMark1() + student.getMark2() +
                                                    student.getMark3();
            double average = total / 3;
            String result = "PASS";

            if (student.getMark1() < 50 || student.getMark2() <
                                   50 || student.getMark3() < 50)
            result = "FAIL";

            student.setTotal(total);
            student.setAverage(average);
            student.setResult(result);

            session.save(student);
            txn.commit();
            session.close();
            sessionFactory.close();

            System.out.println("Student record successfully
                                                         inserted.");
```

```
            } catch (Exception e) {
                    System.out.println("Error occured: " + e.getMessage());
                                e.printStackTrace();
                            }

                    }

    }
```

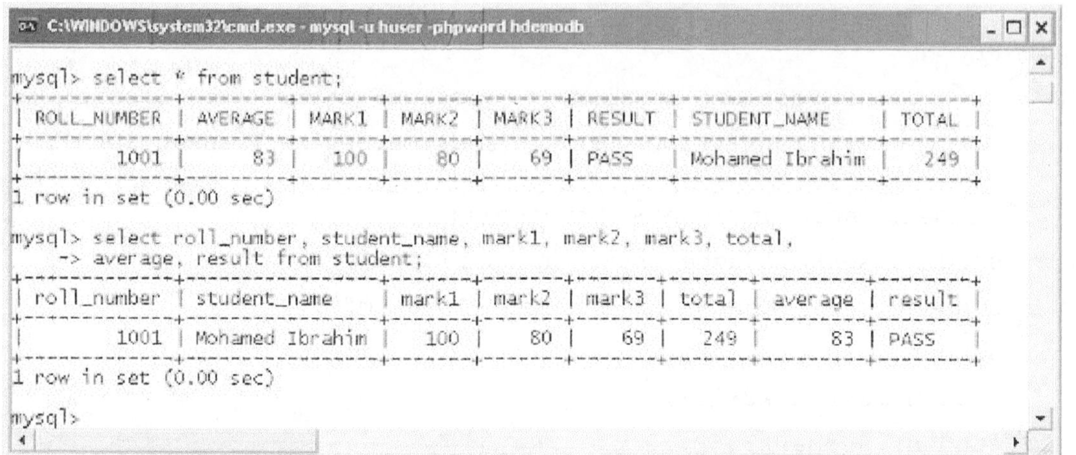

```
C:\WINDOWS\system32\cmd.exe - mysql -u huser -phpword hdemodb

mysql> select * from student;
+-------------+---------+-------+-------+-------+--------+-----------------+-------+
| ROLL_NUMBER | AVERAGE | MARK1 | MARK2 | MARK3 | RESULT | STUDENT_NAME    | TOTAL |
+-------------+---------+-------+-------+-------+--------+-----------------+-------+
|        1001 |      83 |   100 |    80 |    69 | PASS   | Mohamed Ibrahim |   249 |
+-------------+---------+-------+-------+-------+--------+-----------------+-------+
1 row in set (0.00 sec)

mysql> select roll_number, student_name, mark1, mark2, mark3, total,
    -> average, result from student;
+-------------+-----------------+-------+-------+-------+-------+---------+--------+
| roll_number | student_name    | mark1 | mark2 | mark3 | total | average | result |
+-------------+-----------------+-------+-------+-------+-------+---------+--------+
|        1001 | Mohamed Ibrahim |   100 |    80 |    69 |   249 |      83 | PASS   |
+-------------+-----------------+-------+-------+-------+-------+---------+--------+
1 row in set (0.00 sec)

mysql>
```

Change code as below to add multiple records.

```
// File Name: StudentInfo.java
// Main Program

package com.hdemo;

import java.util.Scanner;

import org.hibernate.Session;
import org.hibernate.SessionFactory;
import org.hibernate.Transaction;
import org.hibernate.cfg.AnnotationConfiguration;

public class StudentInfo {

public static void main(String[] args) throws Exception {

SessionFactory sessionFactory = null;
Scanner s = new Scanner(System.in);
```

```
    try {
    sessionFactory = new Annotation Configuration().configure().
buildSessionFactory();
        } catch (Exception e) {
            System.out.println("Error in creating SessionFactory.");
            e.printStackTrace();
            return;
        }

        try {
            Session session = sessionFactory.open Session();
            Transaction txn = session.begin Transaction();

            System.out.print("How many students? ");
            int num = s.nextInt();

    for (int i = 0; i < num; i++) {
                        System.out.println("\n\nEnter details of
Student [" + (i + 1) + "]\n");
    System.out.print("Enter Roll number:");
    int rollNumber = s.nextInt();
    System.out.println("Enter Student Name: ");
    s.nextLine(); // Clearing newline character
    String studentName = s.nextLine();
    System.out.println("Enter Mark1: ");
    int mark1 = s.nextInt();
    System.out.println("Enter Mark2: ");
    int mark2 = s.nextInt();
    System.out.println("Enter Mark3: ");
    int mark3 = s.nextInt();

    int total = mark1 + mark2 + mark3;
    double average = total / 3.0;
```

```
String result = "PASS";

if (mark1 < 50||mark2<50||mark3< 50)
result = "FAIL";

Student student = new Student();
student.setRollNumber(rollNumber);
student.setStudentName(studentName);
student.setMark1(mark1);
student.setMark2(mark2);
student.setMark3(mark3);
student.setTotal(total);
student.setAverage(average);
student.setResult(result);

session.save(student);
}

txn.commit();
session.close();
sessionFactory.close();

System.out.println("Student records are successfully inserted.");
        } catch (Exception e) {
System.out.println("Error occured: " + e.getMessage());
        e.printStackTrace();
        }
                }
}
```

Sample Run:

```
How many students? 3

Enter details of Student [1]

Enter Roll number: 1001
Enter Student Name:
```

```
Mohamed Ibrahim
Enter Mark1:
100
Enter Mark2:
90
Enter Mark3:
82

Enter details of Student [2]

Enter Roll number: 1002
Enter Student Name:
Karan Singh
Enter Mark1:
78
Enter Mark2:
98
Enter Mark3:
67
Enter details of Student [3]

Enter Roll number: 1003
Enter Student Name:
Kumar
Enter Mark1:
50
Enter Mark2:
49
Enter Mark3:
51
Hibernate: insert into STUDENT (AVERAGE, MARK1, MARK2, MARK3,
RESULT, STUDENT_NAME, TOTAL, ROLL_NUMBER) values (?, ?, ?, ?, ?, ?,
?, ?)
Hibernate: insert into STUDENT (AVERAGE, MARK1, MARK2, MARK3,
RESULT, STUDENT_NAME, TOTAL, ROLL_NUMBER) values (?, ?, ?, ?, ?, ?,
?, ?)
```

```
Hibernate: insert into STUDENT (AVERAGE, MARK1, MARK2, MARK3, RESULT, STUDENT_NAME, TOTAL, ROLL_NUMBER) values (?, ?, ?, ?, ?, ?, ?, ?)
Student records are successfully inserted.
```

```
C:\WINDOWS\system32\cmd.exe - mysql -u huser -phpword hdemodb

mysql> select roll_number, student_name, mark1, mark2, mark3, total, average, result from student;
+-------------+-----------------+-------+-------+-------+-------+------------------+--------+
| roll_number | student_name    | mark1 | mark2 | mark3 | total | average          | result |
+-------------+-----------------+-------+-------+-------+-------+------------------+--------+
|        1001 | Mohamed Ibrahim |   100 |    90 |    82 |   272 | 90.6666666666667 | PASS   |
|        1002 | Karan Singh     |    78 |    98 |    67 |   243 |               81 | PASS   |
|        1003 | Kumar           |    50 |    49 |    51 |   150 |               50 | FAIL   |
+-------------+-----------------+-------+-------+-------+-------+------------------+--------+
3 rows in set (0.00 sec)
```

SUMMARY

This chapter demonstrates how to insert one record of Student information into database table using Hibernate. Based on this example, this chapter explains briefly about the configuration details and required setups to work with Hibernate such as Creating database user, Creating Java Project in Eclipse, Setting up the required Hibernate and other library files with Eclipse, and Defining Hibernate configurations. The configurations are to be followed for examples shown in other chapters. The Hibernate API used in the example programs such as Annotations, SessionFactory, Session, and Transaction are not explained here and will be explained in the next chapters.

CHAPTER

3

HIBERNATE SESSION

3.0 INTRODUCTION

All data definition and manipulation should be done in Hibernate through Session. Any object should be present in the Session before it is interacted with database. The Hibernate SessionFactory acts a database connection pool and Hibernate Session acts a Connection, if you compare with JDBC. This chapter explains the uses of SessionFactory and the important methods in Session which are used for relational mappings of objects with database.

3.1 `SESSIONFACTORY` INTERFACE-CREATES AND MAINTAINS `SESSION(S)`

This is a global factory for entire application, responsible for a particular database. Hibernate allows your application to instantiate more than one `SessionFactory`, each for one (different) database software.

The Hibernate `Sessions` are created from this `SessionFactory`. The `SessionFactory` works similar to Connection Pool concept in JDBC, and the `Session` is similar to `Connection` in JDBC. Hibernate `Sessions` are not thread-safe, but `SessionFactory` is thread-safe. Thread safety ensures that the fields of an object/class always maintain valid state (original value, not changed by another thread) even when used by multiple threads concurrently.

A JNDI bound Hibernate `SessionFactory` can simplify the lookup of the factory and creation of new `Session`(s). Hibernate will automatically place the `SessionFactory` in JNDI after you call `buildSessionFactory()` method. And the associated current Session can be obtained through `getCurrentSession()` method, *i.e.*, when `getCurrentSession()` is called in the current thread, it creates a new Session for the first time and the created Session will be available as Current Session until the thread's transaction is ended (by commit/rollback) and the transaction's Session is closed. This `Session's` life cycle can be automatically bound to the scope of a JTA (Java Transaction API) transaction. The `"jta"` context is default to flush data before a transaction completes, to close Session after the transaction completes, and aggressively release JDBC connections after each statement in the transaction.

The method `openSession()`creates and returns a new `Session` while called with the object of `SessionFactory`. The method `close()` releases all the resources consumed by `SessionFactory` and closes the `SessionFactory`.

3.2 SESSION INTERFACE -HIBERNATE SESSION TO MANIPULATE DATA WITH DATABASE

The main functions of the `Session` are to offer *Create, Read, Update* and *Delete* (CRUD) operations for instances of mapped entity classes (POJOs). These instances can be in any one of the following three different states:

`Transient` → Never persistent with database, not associated with any *Session*

`Persistent` → Persistent, associated with a unique *Session*

`Detached` → Previously persistent, not associated with any *Session*

The *Transient* objects are not yet persisted in the database and not associated with any Hibernate Session. Hence, they are independent of any Hibernate operations. (If you will be getting confused, then do not compare these Hibernate Transient objects with Java "transient" variables; Hibernate Transient objects can be made associated with any Hibernate Session and then later can be persisted with database, but Java "transient" variables may not be serialized (persisted).

The *Persistent* objects are already persisted in the database and associated with one Hibernate session. Any changes on these objects will also be reflected on the corresponding database tables. Hibernate automatically generate and execute necessary query/queries to keep the states of persistent objects with the database.

The *Detached* objects are already persisted in the database and not associated with any Hibernate Session now. These objects are detached (separated) from any Hibernate Session in several occasions including that the object's associated Session may be closed, the object may be evicted (removed) from its associated Session by calling `evict()` method. A detached object can be associated with a new Hibernate Session (become as Persistent object for this session) by calling `load()`, `refresh()`, `merge()`, `update()`, or `save()` methods (any one) on the new session with a reference to the detached object.

Some methods under `Session` interface:

`Serializable save(Object object)`

Inserts (stores) the given object's data into corresponding database table. Do not call this method if the object already persisted in the database.

`void update(Object object)`

This `update()` method updates the persistent instance with the identifier of the given detached instance. Updates the given object's data to the corresponding database table. The persistent object should be in Session before updating values.

Note: Hibernate automatically persist the changes made on persistent objects into the database. The setReadOnly() method makes an persistent object as read_only, any changes made on this read only object will be reflected in to the database.

`void setReadOnly(Object entity, boolean readOnly)`

`void saveOrUpdate(Object object)`

Calls `save()` if object is not present in database table, otherwise it calls `update()`.

`void persist(Object object)`

Inserts (stores) the given object's data into corresponding database table. Do not call this method if the object already persisted in the database.

Difference between `save()` and `persist()`:

The `save()` generates and assigns the Id value to the persistent instance immediately and returns that Id value as `Serializable` object, but in the case of `persist()`, the assignment will not be done immediately which may happen at flush time of data and none will be returned (void).

`void refresh(Object object)`

Refreshes (takes original values) the persistent object from its database representation.

`Object get(Class class_name, Serializable id)`

Returns the persistent instance of the given entity class with the given identifier (object's primary key) if the instance presents in the database, else returns `null`. Cast the returned object to the class that you want.

`Object load(Class class_name, Serializable id)`

Returns the persistent instance of the given entity class with the given identifier (object's primary key), assuming that the instance exists. Cast the returned object to the class that you want. If the instance is not present in the database (object with the specified Id not found in database), then an Exception will be thrown.

`void delete(Object object)`

Deletes the specified object from the database. The object is not needed to be a persistent object (object associated with Session); Hibernate will take only Id value to perform deletion. Use "Cascade" features to delete all the associated objects of an object (to be deleted).

`Object merge(Object object)`

Copy the state (data members) of the object that is passed as argument onto the persistent object (and will be returned) with the same identifier `(@Id)` in the current Session. That is, copies the state of the given object onto the persistent object (associated with current Session) with the same identifier `(@Id)`.

If there is no persistent instance currently associated with the Session, then it loads the instance and returns that persistent instance. If the given instance is unsaved, then saves a copy of that instance and returns it as a newly persistent instance.

`void evict(Object object)`

Removes the specified object from the associated session, *i.e.*, it makes persistent object as detached object. (Note that the object should be present in the session before saving / updating to the database)

`void flush()`

Flushes data associated with the Session into database. It forces flush operation so that all pending changes into the database will be done (Dirty Session will be flushed).

Hibernate automatically persists the changes made on the persistent objects into the database, but not immediately; it queues up the changes and then commit with database. The Session becomes "dirty" when there are some changes on this queue. We can know the status of Session (dirty or all data are flushed out) by using the following method.

`boolean isDirty()`

The `setFlushMode()` method sets the flush mode to the invoking session and the `getFlushMode()` method gets the current flush mode set to the Session.

```
public void setFlushMode(FlushMode flushMode)
public FlushMode getFlushMode()
```

The possible flush modes are as follows.

`FlushMode.ALWAYS`

–The Session is flushed before a query is executed.

`FlushMode.AUTO`

–The Session will be flushed (if required) for ensuring that the data returned by a query is accurate to database (up-to-date). It is the default flush mode.

`FlushMode.COMMIT`

–The Session is flushed when a transaction associated with the Session is committed.

`FlushMode.MANUAL`

–The Session is flushed only when flush() method is called in application.

The following method clears the entire Session (clears all objects associated with the Session and simply cancels any queuing saves, updates, deletions ...).

`void clear()`

`boolean contains(Object object)`

Checks whether the specified instance is associated with this Session or not.

`Query createQuery(String queryString)`

Create an instance of `Query` for the specified HQL query.

`SQLQuery createSQLQuery(String queryString)`

Create an instance of `SQLQuery` for the specified SQL query.

`Criteria createCriteria(Class class_name)`

Create an instance of `Criteria` for the specified Entity class.

`Connection connection()`

Returns a JDBC `Connection` object of the underlying Session.

`Transaction beginTransaction()`

Begins a transaction with the associated session and returns the `Transaction` object.

`boolean isOpen()`

Checks whether the Session is still open or not.

`Connection close()`

Hibernate does clean-up operations and closes the Session.

In the previous chapter, we choose Student entity containing student information for demonstration. In this chapter, we will use Account entity which describes fields for account details as below.

```
// File Name: Account.java
// Account Entity class

package com.hdemo;

import javax.persistence.Column;
import javax.persistence.Entity;
import javax.persistence.GeneratedValue;
import javax.persistence.GenerationType;
import javax.persistence.Id;
import javax.persistence.Table;

import org.hibernate.validator.Min;

@Entity
@Table(name = "ACCOUNT")
public class Account {

                  @Id
@GeneratedValue(strategy = GenerationType.AUTO)
              int id;

@Column(name = "ACC_NUMBER", length = 64)
  String accountNumber;
@Column(name = "CUST_NAME", length = 64)
   String customerName;
       @Min(value = 0)
```

```
@Column(name = "AVAIL_BALANCE")
double availableBalance;

    public int getId() {
            return id;
    }

    public void setId(int id) {
            this.id = id;
    }

    public String getAccountNumber() {
            return accountNumber;
    }

    public void setAccountNumber(String accountNumber) {
            this.accountNumber = accountNumber;
    }

    public String getCustomerName() {
            return customerName;
    }

    public void setCustomerName(String customerName) {
            this.customerName = customerName;
    }

    public double getAvailableBalance() {
        return availableBalance;
    }

    public void setAvailableBalance(double availableBalance) {
        this.availableBalance = availableBalance;
    }
}
```

Since we are using annotations for checking minimum available balance (`@Min`), include Hibernate *validator.jar* (download it from Hibernate site) in `CLASSPATH` before executing this program. And do not forget to add the following *mapping* line in *hibernate.cfg.xml* file.

```
<mapping class="com.hdemo.Account" />
```

A typical content of *hibernate.cfg.xml* file is as below.

```
<?xml version='1.0' encoding='utf-8'?>
<!DOCTYPE hibernate-configuration PUBLIC
        "-//Hibernate/Hibernate Configuration DTD 3.0//EN"
        "http://hibernate.sourceforge.net/hibernate-configuration-
3.0.dtd">
<hibernate-configuration>
  <session-factory>
        <property name="connection.driver_class">
com.mysql.jdbc.Driver</property>
        <property name="connection.url">jdbc:mysql://localhost:3306/
hdemodb</property>
        <property name="connection.username">huser</property>
        <property name="connection.password">hpword</property>
        <property name="dialect">org.hibernate. dialect.MySQLDialect</
property>
        <property name="connection.pool_size">1</property>
        <property name="current_session_context_ class">thread</
property>
        <property name="cache.provider_class">
org.hibernate.cache.NoCacheProvider</property>
        <property name="show_sql">true</property>
        <property name="hbm2ddl.auto">create</property>
        <mapping class="com.hdemo.Account" />

  </session-factory>
</hibernate-configuration>
```

Instead of adding code for building SessionFactory in every main program, we will write a helper class named "HibernateUtil" as below. A static method named `getSessionFactory()` is written in this class to return the SessionFactory object.

```
package com.hdemo;

import org.hibernate.SessionFactory;
import org.hibernate.cfg.AnnotationConfiguration;
```

```
public class HibernateUtil {

   private static final SessionFactory sessionFactory;
   static {
         try {
         sessionFactory = new Annotation Configuration().configure().
         buildSessionFactory();
         }
         catch (Throwable e) {
         System.err.println("Error in crerating SessionFactory. " +
         e);
         throw new ExceptionInInitializerError(e);
         }
   }

   public static SessionFactory getSessionFactory() {
         return sessionFactory;
   }
}
```

Keep the above settings for all the demonstrations below, unless otherwise specified.

The following example illustrates the operation of `clear()` method of Session.

Program without `clear()`.

```
// File Name: AccountTransaction.java
// Main Program: Session without clear()

package com.hdemo;

import org.hibernate.Session;
import org.hibernate.SessionFactory;
import org.hibernate.Transaction;

public class AccountTransaction {

public static void main(String[] args) throws Exception {
         SessionFactory sessionFactory = Hibernate
                                          Util.getSessionFactory();
```

```
    Session session = sessionFactory.get CurrentSession();

    Transaction txn = session.beginTransaction();

    Account account1 = new Account();
    account1.setAccountNumber("SB5001");
    account1.setCustomerName("Mohamed Ibrahim");
    account1.setAvailableBalance(6000.00);

    Account account2 = new Account();
    account2.setAccountNumber("SB7501");
    account2.setCustomerName("Ajay");
    account2.setAvailableBalance(3000.00);

    session.save(account1);
    session.save(account2);

        // The following changes are also reflected into database
table automatically
        // since these two objects are persistent objects with
current Session
        account1.setAvailableBalance(2000.00);
        account2.setAvailableBalance(1000.00);

            txn.commit();
            sessionFactory.close();
            System.out.println("Data inserted successfully.");
        }
  }
```

```
  Hibernate: insert into ACCOUNT (ACC_NUMBER, AVAIL_BALANCE, CUST_NAME)
values (?, ?, ?)
  Hibernate: insert into ACCOUNT (ACC_NUMBER, AVAIL_BALANCE, CUST_NAME)
values (?, ?, ?)
  Hibernate: update ACCOUNT set ACC_NUMBER=?, AVAIL_BALANCE=?,
CUST_NAME=? where id=?
  Hibernate: update ACCOUNT set ACC_NUMBER=?, AVAIL_BALANCE=?,
CUST_NAME=? where id=?
```

```
Data inserted successfully.
```

```
C:\WINDOWS\system32\cmd.exe - mysql -u huser -phpword hdemodb

mysql> select * from account;
+----+------------+---------------+-----------------+
| id | ACC_NUMBER | AVAIL_BALANCE | CUST_NAME       |
+----+------------+---------------+-----------------+
|  1 | SB5001     |          2000 | Mohamed Ibrahim |
|  2 | SB7501     |          1000 | Ajay            |
+----+------------+---------------+-----------------+
2 rows in set (0.00 sec)

mysql>
```

Program with `clear()`.

```
// File Name: AccountTransaction.java
// Main Program: Session clear()

package com.hdemo;

import org.hibernate.Session;
import org.hibernate.SessionFactory;
import org.hibernate.Transaction;
public class AccountTransaction {

public static void main(String[] args) throws Exception {
SessionFactory sessionFactory = Hibernate Util.getSessionFactory();
Session session = sessionFactory.get CurrentSession();
Transaction txn = session.beginTransaction();

Account account1 = new Account();
account1.setAccountNumber("SB5001");
account1.setCustomerName("Mohamed Ibrahim");
account1.setAvailableBalance(6000.00);

Account account2 = new Account();
account2.setAccountNumber("SB7501");
account2.setCustomerName("Ajay");
```

```
    account2.setAvailableBalance(3000.00);

    session.save(account1);
    session.save(account2);

    session.clear();

                                 // The following changes will not be
reflected in to database table automatically
                                 // since these two objects are not persistent
objects with current Session.
                                 // The object became as detached. Use
update() method to update values with database.
    account1.setAvailableBalance(2000.00);
    account2.setAvailableBalance(1000.00);

              txn.commit();
              sessionFactory.close();
    System.out.println("Data inserted successfully.");
                        }
    }
    Hibernate: insert into ACCOUNT (ACC_NUMBER, AVAIL_BALANCE, CUST_NAME)
values (?, ?, ?)
    Hibernate: insert into ACCOUNT (ACC_NUMBER, AVAIL_BALANCE, CUST_NAME)
values (?, ?, ?)
    Data inserted successfully.
```

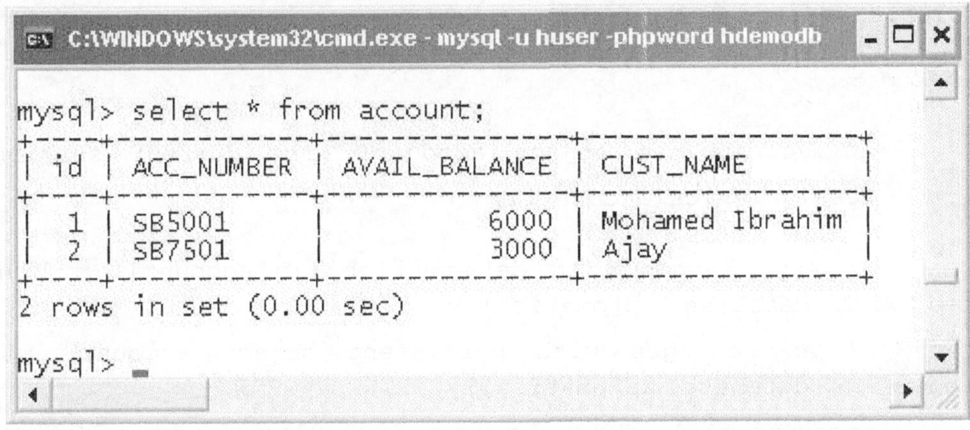

```
C:\WINDOWS\system32\cmd.exe - mysql -u huser -phpword hdemodb

mysql> select * from account;
+----+------------+---------------+-----------------+
| id | ACC_NUMBER | AVAIL_BALANCE | CUST_NAME       |
+----+------------+---------------+-----------------+
|  1 | SB5001     |          6000 | Mohamed Ibrahim |
|  2 | SB7501     |          3000 | Ajay            |
+----+------------+---------------+-----------------+
2 rows in set (0.00 sec)

mysql> _
```

The following example illustrates the operation of `evict()` method of `Session`.

```
// File Name: AccountTransaction.java
// Main Program: Session evict()

package com.hdemo;

import org.hibernate.Session;
import org.hibernate.SessionFactory;
import org.hibernate.Transaction;

public class AccountTransaction {

public static void main(String[] args) throws Exception {
SessionFactory sessionFactory = HibernateUtil.getSessionFactory();
Session session = sessionFactory.get CurrentSession();
Transaction txn = session.beginTransaction();

Account account1 = new Account();
account1.setAccountNumber("SB5001");
account1.setCustomerName("Mohamed Ibrahim");
account1.setAvailableBalance(6000.00);

Account account2 = new Account();
account2.setAccountNumber("SB7501");
account2.setCustomerName("Ajay");
account2.setAvailableBalance(3000.00);

session.save(account1);
session.save(account2);

        // Removes the object account1 from current session
        session.evict(account1);

        // Any changes with detached object account1 will not be
reflected with database automatically
        // Any changes with persistent object account2 will be
reflected with database automatically
        account1.setAvailableBalance(2000.00);
```

```
        account2.setAvailableBalance(1000.00);

        txn.commit();
        sessionFactory.close();
        System.out.println("Data inserted successfully.");
    }
}
```

```
Hibernate: insert into ACCOUNT (ACC_NUMBER, AVAIL_BALANCE, CUST_NAME) values (?, ?, ?)
Hibernate: insert into ACCOUNT (ACC_NUMBER, AVAIL_BALANCE, CUST_NAME) values (?, ?, ?)
Hibernate: update ACCOUNT set ACC_NUMBER=?, AVAIL_BALANCE=?, CUST_NAME=? where id=?
Data inserted successfully.
```

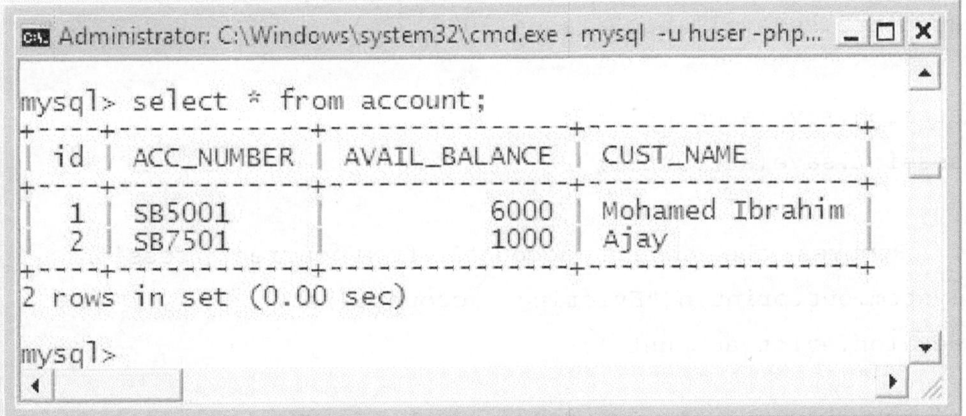

The following example illustrates the operation of `update()` method of `Session`.

```
// File Name: AccountTransaction.java
// Main Program: Session update()

package com.hdemo;

import org.hibernate.Session;
import org.hibernate.SessionFactory;
import org.hibernate.Transaction;

public class AccountTransaction {
```

```
public static void main(String[] args) throws Exception {
  SessionFactory sessionFactory = Hibernate Util.getSessionFactory();
  Session session = sessionFactory.get CurrentSession();

  Transaction txn = session.beginTransaction();

  Account account1 = new Account();
  account1.setAccountNumber("SB5001");
  account1.setCustomerName("Mohamed Ibrahim");
  account1.setAvailableBalance(6000.00);

  Account account2 = new Account();
  account2.setAccountNumber("SB7501");
  account2.setCustomerName("Ajay");
  account2.setAvailableBalance(3000.00);

  session.save(account1);
  session.save(account2);

  // Removes the object account1 from current session
  System.out.println("Evicting account1");
  session.evict(account1);

  // Any changes with detached object account1 will not be reflected
                                          with database automatically
  // Any changes with persistent object account2 will be reflected
                                          with database automatically
  System.out.println("Changing the value of Available Balance of
                                                          account1");
  account1.setAvailableBalance(2000.00);
  System.out.println("Changing the value of Available Balance of
                                                          account2");
  account2.setAvailableBalance(1000.00);
 // Makes the detached object account1 as persistent object and
                                  updates the changes with database
 System.out.println("Updating account1 with Session");
```

```
        session.update(account1);

        System.out.println("Committing the Transaction");
        txn.commit();
        sessionFactory.close();
        System.out.println("Data inserted successfully.");
    }
}
```

```
Hibernate: insert into ACCOUNT (ACC_NUMBER, AVAIL_BALANCE, CUST_NAME)
     values (?, ?, ?)
Hibernate: insert into ACCOUNT (ACC_NUMBER, AVAIL_BALANCE, CUST_NAME)
     values (?, ?, ?)
Evicting account1
Changing the value of Available Balance of account1
Changing the value of Available Balance of account2
Updating account1 with Session
Committing the Transaction
Hibernate: update ACCOUNT set ACC_NUMBER=?, AVAIL_BALANCE=?,
CUST_NAME=? where id=?
Hibernate: update ACCOUNT set ACC_NUMBER=?, AVAIL_BALANCE=?,
CUST_NAME=? where id=?
Data inserted successfully.
```

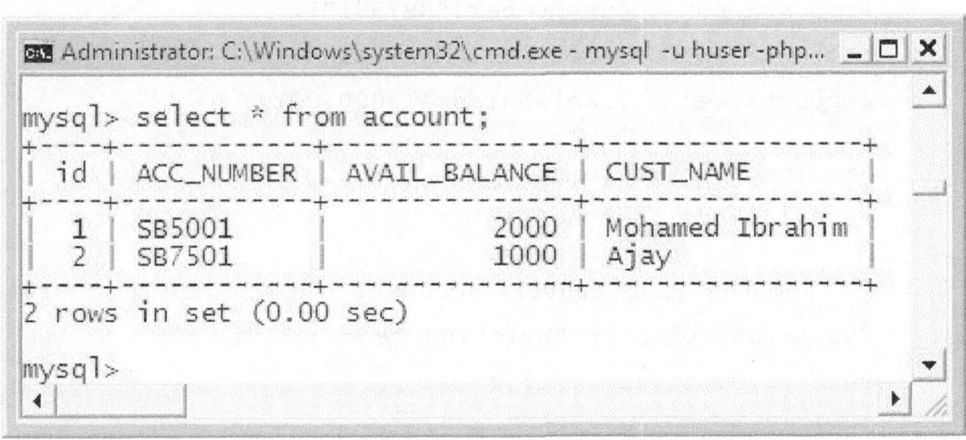

```
Administrator: C:\Windows\system32\cmd.exe - mysql -u huser -php...

mysql> select * from account;
+----+------------+---------------+-----------------+
| id | ACC_NUMBER | AVAIL_BALANCE | CUST_NAME       |
+----+------------+---------------+-----------------+
|  1 | SB5001     |          2000 | Mohamed Ibrahim |
|  2 | SB7501     |          1000 | Ajay            |
+----+------------+---------------+-----------------+
2 rows in set (0.00 sec)

mysql>
```

Observe from the above result that the update calls are made while committing the transaction. We can force to flush the data to database immediately after we invoked `update()` method using `flush()` method as follows.

```
// File Name: AccountTransaction.java
// Main Program: Session flush()
package com.hdemo;

import org.hibernate.Session;
import org.hibernate.SessionFactory;
import org.hibernate.Transaction;

public class AccountTransaction {

public static void main(String[] args) throws Exception {
        SessionFactory sessionFactory = Hibernate
                                        Util.getSessionFactory();
        Session session = sessionFactory.get CurrentSession();

        Transaction txn = session.beginTransaction();

        Account account1 = new Account();
        account1.setAccountNumber("SB5001");
        account1.setCustomerName("Mohamed Ibrahim");
        account1.setAvailableBalance(6000.00);

        Account account2 = new Account();
        account2.setAccountNumber("SB7501");
        account2.setCustomerName("Ajay");
        account2.setAvailableBalance(3000.00);

        session.save(account1);
        session.save(account2);

        // Removes the object account1 from current session
        System.out.println("Evicting account1");
        session.evict(account1);

        // Any changes with detached object account1 will not be
                             reflected with database automatically
        // Any changes with persistent object account2 will be
                             reflected with database automatically
```

```
        System.out.println("Changing the value of Available Balance
                                                  of account1");
        account1.setAvailableBalance(2000.00);
        System.out.println("Changing the value of Available Balance
                                                  of account2");
        account2.setAvailableBalance(1000.00);

        // Makes the detached object account1 as persistent object
                          and updates the changes with database
        System.out.println("Updating account1 with Session");
        session.update(account1);

        if (session.isDirty())
        System.out.println("Some data are to be updated with
                                                       database");
        else
        System.out.println("No data are to be updated with database");

        // Flushes the data in Session into database
        System.out.println("Flushing data");
        session.flush();

        if (session.isDirty())
        System.out.println("Some data are to be updated with
                                                       database");
        else
        System.out.println("No data are to be updated with database");

        System.out.println("Committing the Transaction");
        txn.commit();
        sessionFactory.close();
        System.out.println("Data inserted successfully.");
    }
}
```

```
Hibernate: insert into ACCOUNT (ACC_NUMBER, AVAIL_BALANCE, CUST_NAME)
                                                  values (?, ?, ?)
Hibernate: insert into ACCOUNT (ACC_NUMBER, AVAIL_BALANCE, CUST_NAME)
                                                  values (?, ?, ?)
Evicting account1
Changing the value of Available Balance of account1
Changing the value of Available Balance of account2
Updating account1 with Session
Some data are to be updated with database
Flushing data
Hibernate: update ACCOUNT set ACC_NUMBER=?, AVAIL_BALANCE=?,
                                        CUST_NAME=? where id=?
Hibernate: update ACCOUNT set ACC_NUMBER=?, AVAIL_BALANCE=?,
                                        CUST_NAME=? where id=?
No data are to be updated with database
Committing the Transaction
Data inserted successfully.
```

The following example illustrates the operation of refresh() method of Session.

```
// File Name: AccountTransaction.java
// Main Program: Session refresh()

package com.hdemo;

import org.hibernate.Session;
import org.hibernate.SessionFactory;
import org.hibernate.Transaction;

public class AccountTransaction {

public static void main(String[] args) throws Exception {
SessionFactory sessionFactory = Hibernate Util.getSessionFactory();
Session session = sessionFactory.get CurrentSession();

Transaction txn = session.beginTransaction();

Account account1 = new Account();
account1.setAccountNumber("SB5001");
```

```
account1.setCustomerName("Mohamed Ibrahim");
account1.setAvailableBalance(6000.00);

Account account2 = new Account();
account2.setAccountNumber("SB7501");
account2.setCustomerName("Ajay");
account2.setAvailableBalance(3000.00);

session.save(account1);
session.save(account2);

// Removes the object account1 from current session
System.out.println("Evicting account1");
session.evict(account1);

// Any changes with detached object account1 will not be
                reflected with database automatically
// Any changes with persistent object account2 will be
                reflected with database automatically
System.out.println("Changing the value of Available Balance
                                        of account1");
account1.setAvailableBalance(2000.00);
System.out.println("Changing the value of Available Balance
                                        of account2");
account2.setAvailableBalance(1000.00);

// Makes the detached object account1 as persistent object
               and updates the changes with database
System.out.println("Updating account1 with Session");
session.update(account1);

if (session.isDirty())
System.out.println("Some data are to be updated with database");
else
System.out.println("No data are to be updated with database");

// Session is dirty due to account1 and account2
// Flushes the data in Session into database
```

```
            System.out.println("Refreshing account1 from database. Any
changes done with account1 (dirty value, not committed with database
yet) will be overwritten.");
            session.refresh(account1);

            // Session is dirty due to account2
            // Flushes the data in Session into database
            System.out.println("Flushes session");
            session.flush();

            if (session.isDirty())
            System.out.println("Some data are to be updated with database");
            else
            System.out.println("No data are to be updated with database");

            System.out.println("Committing the Transaction");
            txn.commit();
            sessionFactory.close();
            System.out.println("Data inserted successfully.");
        }
    }
```

```
Hibernate: insert into ACCOUNT (ACC_NUMBER, AVAIL_BALANCE, CUST_NAME)
      values (?, ?, ?)
Hibernate: insert into ACCOUNT (ACC_NUMBER, AVAIL_BALANCE, CUST_NAME)
      values (?, ?, ?)
Evicting account1
Changing the value of Available Balance of account1
Changing the value of Available Balance of account2
Updating account1 with Session
Some data are to be updated with database
Refreshing account1 from database. Any changes done with account1
(dirty value, not committed with database yet) will be overwritten.
Hibernate: select account0_.id as id0_0_, account0_.ACC_NUMBER as
ACC2_0_0_, account0_.AVAIL_BALANCE as AVAIL3_0_0_, account0_.CUST_NAME
as CUST4_0_0_ from ACCOUNT account0_ where account0_.id=?
Flushes session
Hibernate: update ACCOUNT set ACC_NUMBER=?, AVAIL_BALANCE=?,
```

```
CUST_NAME=? where id=?
    No data are to be updated with database
    Committing the Transaction
    Data inserted successfully.
```

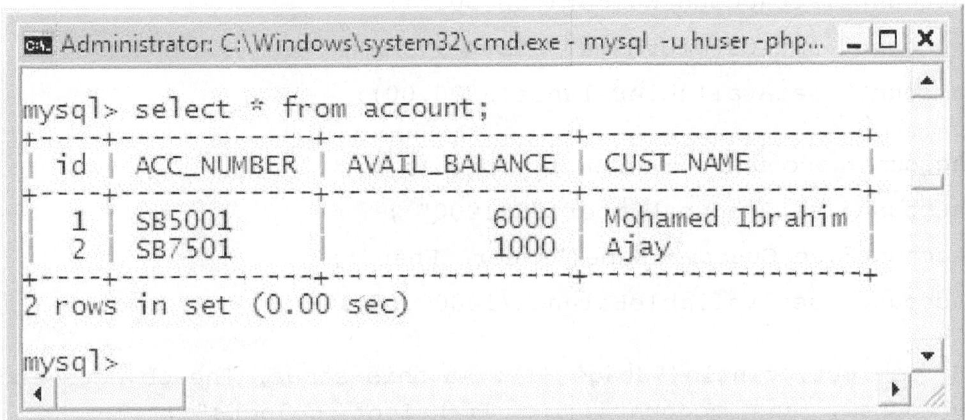

Administrator: C:\Windows\system32\cmd.exe - mysql -u huser -php...

mysql> select * from account;

id	ACC_NUMBER	AVAIL_BALANCE	CUST_NAME
1	SB5001	6000	Mohamed Ibrahim
2	SB7501	1000	Ajay

2 rows in set (0.00 sec)

mysql>

Observe from the above result that the changes we did on *account1* object is not updated into database, because we refreshes that object (synchronized data from database for that object) before the actual flush/updation to database is occurred.

The following example illustrates the operation of `merge()` method of `Session`.

```
// File Name: AccountTransaction.java
// Main Program: Session merge()

package com.hdemo;

import org.hibernate.Session;
import org.hibernate.SessionFactory;
import org.hibernate.Transaction;

public class AccountTransaction {

  public static void main(String[] args) throws Exception {
  SessionFactory sessionFactory = HibernateUtil.getSessionFactory();
  Session session = sessionFactory.getCurrentSession();

  Transaction txn = session.beginTransaction();

  Account account1 = new Account();
  account1.setAccountNumber("SB5001");
```

```
account1.setCustomerName("Mohamed Ibrahim");
account1.setAvailableBalance(6000.00);

Account account2 = new Account();
account2.setAccountNumber("SB7501");
account2.setCustomerName("Ajay");
account2.setAvailableBalance(3000.00);

Account account3 = new Account();
account3.setAccountNumber("SB1000");
account3.setCustomerName("Ameer Khan");
account3.setAvailableBalance(10000.00);

System.out.println("Stage (1): At this stage, The objects account1,
account2, and account3 are Transient objects");
session.save(account1);
session.save(account2);
session.merge(account3);
System.out.println("Stage (2): At this stage, The objects account1
and account2 are Persistent objects, and object3 is Transient
object");

// Changes on Persistent objects result in automatic database
updation, but not for Transient objects
account1.setAvailableBalance(8000.00);
account2.setAvailableBalance(7000.00);
account3.setAvailableBalance(9000.00);

System.out.println("Committing the Transaction");
txn.commit();
sessionFactory.close();
System.out.println("Data inserted successfully.");
                    }
}
```

```
Stage (1): At this stage, The objects account1, account2, and
                                   account3 are Transient objects
Hibernate: insert into ACCOUNT (ACC_NUMBER, AVAIL_BALANCE, CUST_NAME)
                                                values (?, ?, ?)
```

```
Hibernate: insert into ACCOUNT (ACC_NUMBER, AVAIL_BALANCE, CUST_NAME)
                                                  values (?, ?, ?)
Hibernate: insert into ACCOUNT (ACC_NUMBER, AVAIL_BALANCE, CUST_NAME)
                                                  values (?, ?, ?)
Stage (2): At this stage, The objects account1 and account2 are
           Persistent objects, and object3 is Transient object
Committing the Transaction
Hibernate: update ACCOUNT set ACC_NUMBER=?, AVAIL_BALANCE=?,
                                          CUST_NAME=? where id=?
Hibernate: update ACCOUNT set ACC_NUMBER=?, AVAIL_BALANCE=?,
                                          CUST_NAME=? where id=?
Data inserted successfully.
```

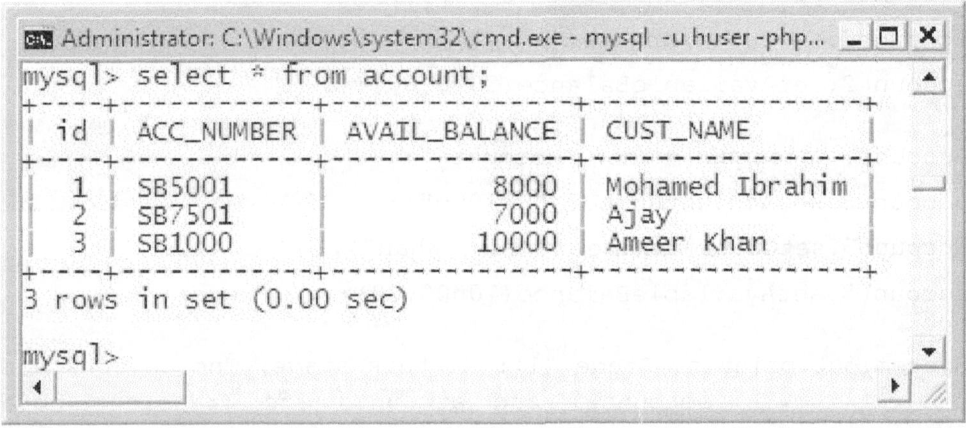

Observe from the above result that the `merge()` method adds one row to the database since it is not able to find any matching Id (Id value of *account3*) in existing records in the database. However, it will not become as a Persistent object. Actually, this `merge()` method returns the merged persistence object that we have to assign to a suitable reference variable as shown in the following example.

```
// File Name: AccountTransaction.java
// Main Program: Session merge()

package com.hdemo;

import org.hibernate.Session;
import org.hibernate.SessionFactory;
import org.hibernate.Transaction;

public class AccountTransaction {
```

```
public static void main(String[] args) throws Exception {
    SessionFactory sessionFactory = Hibernate Util.getSessionFactory();
    Session session = sessionFactory.get CurrentSession();

    Transaction txn = session.beginTransaction();
    Account account1 = new Account();
    account1.setAccountNumber("SB5001");
    account1.setCustomerName("Mohamed Ibrahim");
    account1.setAvailableBalance(6000.00);

    Account account2 = new Account();
    account2.setAccountNumber("SB7501");
    account2.setCustomerName("Ajay");
    account2.setAvailableBalance(3000.00);

    Account account3 = new Account();
    account3.setAccountNumber("SB1000");
    account3.setCustomerName("Ameer Khan");
    account3.setAvailableBalance(10000.00);

    System.out.println("Stage (1): At this stage, The objects account1,
                    account2, and account3 are Transient objects");
    session.save(account1);
    session.save(account2);
    // merge() returns merged Persistent object, we are assigning it
                                    to the reference variable object3.
    account3 = (Account) session.merge(account3);
    System.out.println("Stage (2): At this stage, The objects account1
            and account2 are Persistent objects due to save()," +
    "\n and object3 also become as Persistent object as merge()
                                                    returns it");

    // Changes on Persistent objects result in automatic database
                          updation, but not for Transient objects
    account1.setAvailableBalance(8000.00);
    account2.setAvailableBalance(7000.00);
    account3.setAvailableBalance(9000.00);
```

```
System.out.println("Committing  the  Transaction");
txn.commit();
sessionFactory.close();
System.out.println("Data  inserted  successfully.");
            }
}
```

```
Stage (1): At this stage, The objects account1, account2, and
account3 are Transient objects
Hibernate: insert into ACCOUNT (ACC_NUMBER, AVAIL_BALANCE, CUST_NAME)
values (?, ?, ?)
Hibernate: insert into ACCOUNT (ACC_NUMBER, AVAIL_BALANCE, CUST_NAME)
values (?, ?, ?)
Hibernate: insert into ACCOUNT (ACC_NUMBER, AVAIL_BALANCE, CUST_NAME)
values (?, ?, ?)
Stage (2): At this stage, The objects account1 and account2 are
Persistent objects due to save(),
and object3 also become as Persistent object as merge() returns it
Committing the Transaction
Hibernate: update ACCOUNT set ACC_NUMBER=?, AVAIL_BALANCE=?,
CUST_NAME=? where id=?
Hibernate: update ACCOUNT set ACC_NUMBER=?, AVAIL_BALANCE=?,
CUST_NAME=? where id=?
Hibernate: update ACCOUNT set ACC_NUMBER=?, AVAIL_BALANCE=?,
CUST_NAME=? where id=?
Data inserted successfully.
```

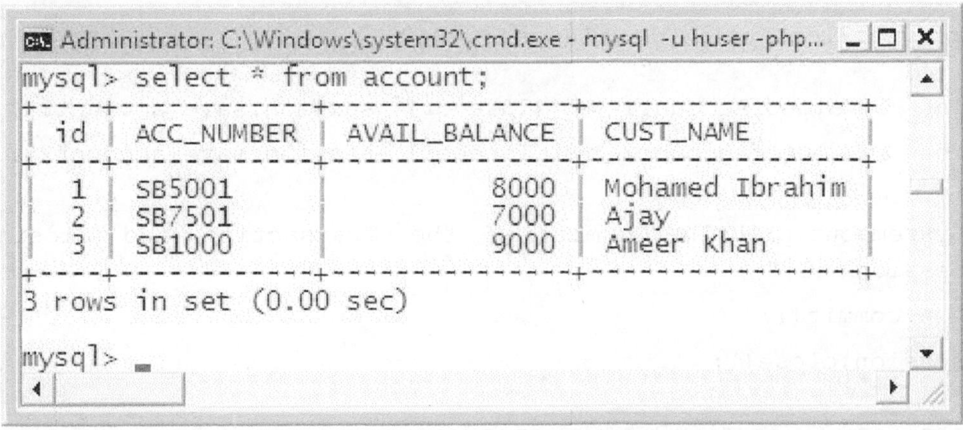

```
Administrator: C:\Windows\system32\cmd.exe - mysql -u huser -php...
mysql> select * from account;
+----+------------+---------------+------------------+
| id | ACC_NUMBER | AVAIL_BALANCE | CUST_NAME        |
+----+------------+---------------+------------------+
|  1 | SB5001     |          8000 | Mohamed Ibrahim  |
|  2 | SB7501     |          7000 | Ajay             |
|  3 | SB1000     |          9000 | Ameer Khan       |
+----+------------+---------------+------------------+
3 rows in set (0.00 sec)

mysql>
```

The following example illustrates how to merge an object in to existing persist object. Also, this example uses `get()` and `load()` method for retrieving object from database. In our example, we can either use `get()` or `load()`; however for demonstration purpose, both methods are used.

```
// File Name: AccountTransaction.java
// Main Program: Session merge()

package com.hdemo;

import org.hibernate.Session;
import org.hibernate.SessionFactory;
import org.hibernate.Transaction;

public class AccountTransaction {

public static void main(String[] args) throws Exception {
SessionFactory sessionFactory = Hibernate Util.getSessionFactory();
  Session session = sessionFactory.open Session();
  Transaction txn = session.beginTransaction();

  Account account1 = new Account();
  account1.setAccountNumber("SB5001");
  account1.setCustomerName("Mohamed Ibrahim");
  account1.setAvailableBalance(6000.00);

  Account account2 = new Account();
  account2.setAccountNumber("SB7501");
  account2.setCustomerName("Ajay");
  account2.setAvailableBalance(3000.00);

  int idValueOfAccount1 = (Integer) session.save(account1);
  int idValueOfAccount2 = (Integer) session.save(account2);

  System.out.println("Committing the Transaction and Closing the
  Session (1)");
  txn.commit();
  session.close();

  session = sessionFactory.openSession();
```

```
txn = session.beginTransaction();

//Retrieve the Persistent objects from the database by specifying
the Id values
Account retrievedAccount1 = (Account) session.get(Account.class,
idValueOfAccount1);
Account retrievedAccount2 = (Account) session.get(Account.class,
idValueOfAccount2);
System.out.println("retrievedAccount1 ==> " +
displayAccount(retrievedAccount1));
System.out.println("retrievedAccount2 ==> " +
displayAccount(retrievedAccount2));

Account account3 = new Account();
// Set Id value of account1 object to account3 object
// so that we can merge this object with account1
account3.setId(idValueOfAccount1);
account3.setAccountNumber("SB1000");
account3.setCustomerName("Ameer Khan");
account3.setAvailableBalance(10000.00);

// Find any object in database
// whose Id value matches the Id value of account3 (in our case
account1),
// If matches, then merge the values of account3 to that object,
// i.e., Copies the property values while property names matched
session.merge(account3);

System.out.println("Committing the Transaction and Closing the
Session (2)");
txn.commit();
session.close();

session = sessionFactory.openSession();
txn = session.beginTransaction();

Account rAccount1 = (Account) session.load(Account.class,
idValueOfAccount1);
```

```
Account rAccount2 = (Account) session.load(Account.class,
idValueOfAccount2);
System.out.println("retrievedAccount1 ==> " + displayAccount
(rAccount1));
System.out.println("retrievedAccount2 ==> " + displayAccount
(rAccount2));

txn.commit();
session.close();
sessionFactory.close();
}

static String displayAccount(Account account) {
return "id[" + account.getId() +
      "] accountNumber[" + account.getAccountNumber() +
      "] customerName[" + account.getCustomerName() +
      "] availableBalance[" + account.getAvailableBalance() + "]";
            }
}
```

```
Hibernate: insert into ACCOUNT (ACC_NUMBER, AVAIL_BALANCE, CUST_NAME)
    values (?, ?, ?)
Hibernate: insert into ACCOUNT (ACC_NUMBER, AVAIL_BALANCE, CUST_NAME)
    values (?, ?, ?)
Committing the Transaction and Closing the Session (1)
Hibernate: select account0_.id as id0_0_, account0_.ACC_NUMBER as
ACC2_0_0_, account0_.AVAIL_BALANCE as AVAIL3_0_0_, account0_.CUST_NAME
as CUST4_0_0_ from ACCOUNT account0_ where account0_.id=?
Hibernate: select account0_.id as id0_0_, account0_.ACC_NUMBER as
ACC2_0_0_, account0_.AVAIL_BALANCE as AVAIL3_0_0_, account0_.CUST_NAME
as CUST4_0_0_ from ACCOUNT account0_ where account0_.id=?
retrievedAccount1 ==> id[1] accountNumber[SB5001] customerName[Mohamed
Ibrahim] availableBalance[6000.0]
retrievedAccount2 ==> id[2] accountNumber[SB7501] customerName[Ajay]
availableBalance[3000.0]
Committing the Transaction and Closing the Session (2)
Hibernate: update ACCOUNT set ACC_NUMBER=?, AVAIL_BALANCE=?,
CUST_NAME=? where id=?
```

Hibernate: select account0_.id as id0_0_, account0_.ACC_NUMBER as ACC2_0_0_, account0_.AVAIL_BALANCE as AVAIL3_0_0_, account0_.CUST_NAME as CUST4_0_0_ from ACCOUNT account0_ where account0_.id=?

retrievedAccount1 ==> id[1] accountNumber[SB1000] customerName[Ameer Khan] availableBalance[10000.0]

Hibernate: select account0_.id as id0_0_, account0_.ACC_NUMBER as ACC2_0_0_, account0_.AVAIL_BALANCE as AVAIL3_0_0_, account0_.CUST_NAME as CUST4_0_0_ from ACCOUNT account0_ where account0_.id=?

retrievedAccount2 ==> id[2] accountNumber[SB7501] customerName[Ajay] availableBalance[3000.0]

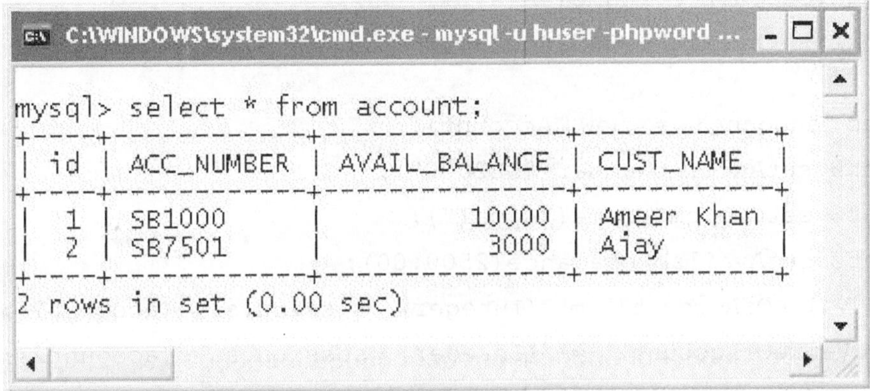

```
C:\WINDOWS\system32\cmd.exe - mysql -u huser -phpword ...

mysql> select * from account;
+----+------------+---------------+-------------+
| id | ACC_NUMBER | AVAIL_BALANCE | CUST_NAME   |
+----+------------+---------------+-------------+
|  1 | SB1000     |         10000 | Ameer Khan  |
|  2 | SB7501     |          3000 | Ajay        |
+----+------------+---------------+-------------+
2 rows in set (0.00 sec)
```

The following example illustrates the operation of `delete()` method of `Session`.

```
// File Name: AccountTransaction.java
// Main Program: Session delete()

package com.hdemo;

import java.util.List;

import org.hibernate.Session;
import org.hibernate.SessionFactory;
import org.hibernate.Transaction;

public class AccountTransaction {

@SuppressWarnings("unchecked")
public static void main(String[] args) throws Exception {
SessionFactory sessionFactory = Hibernate Util.getSessionFactory();
Session session = sessionFactory.open Session();
```

```
Transaction txn = session.beginTransaction();

Account account1 = new Account();
account1.setAccountNumber("SB5001");
account1.setCustomerName("Mohamed Ibrahim");
account1.setAvailableBalance(6000.00);

Account account2 = new Account();
account2.setAccountNumber("SB7501");
account2.setCustomerName("Ajay");
account2.setAvailableBalance(3000.00);

Account account3 = new Account();
account3.setAccountNumber("SB2000");
account3.setCustomerName("Ajmal");
account3.setAvailableBalance(2500.00);
int idValueOfAccount1 = (Integer) session.save(account1);
int idValueOfAccount2 = (Integer) session.save(account2);
session.persist(account3);

System.out.println("Committing the Transaction and Closing the Session
                                                                    (1)");
txn.commit();
session.close();

session = sessionFactory.openSession();
txn = session.beginTransaction();

// Retrieve the Persistent objects from the database
List<Account> list = session.createQuery ("from Account").list();
Account accountObj1 = null;
Account accountObj2 = null;
Account accountObj3 = null;

if (list.size() == 3) {
  accountObj1 = list.get(0);
  accountObj2 = list.get(1);
```

```
accountObj3 = list.get(2);
}
else {
System.out.println("Objects are not properly persisted.");
      return; //Exits the program
}

System.out.println("accountObj1 ==> " + displayAccount(accountObj1));
System.out.println("accountObj2 ==> " + displayAccount(accountObj2));
System.out.println("accountObj3 ==> " + displayAccount(accountObj3));

// Delete the account3 object from database
session.delete(accountObj3);

/* Deletion is based on Id, so that the argument to delete()
                                                   is not required
 * to be a persistent object. We will create a dummy Transient
                                                       object with
 * Id value of account1 (idValueOfAccount1), then we try to
                                                delete that object
 * (the object become Persistent, when passed as argument to
                                                   delete() method)
 * which makes deletion of actual account1 object in database.
                                                          However,
 * if you assign the Id value of account1 to another persistent
                                                           object,
 * then the account1 object should not be associated with
                                                    Session. That is,
 * no two persistent object have same Id in the same Session,
                                                         otherwise
 * NonUniqueObjectException with error message
 * "a different object with the same identifier value was
                         already associated with the session"
 * will be raised. To avoid this, we evicted accountObj1
                                              (account1, in our case)
 * object from the session before delete() is called.
```

```
*/

//Evict accountObj1 (account1)
session.evict(accountObj1);

//Create an Account object with id of account1
Account acc = new Account();
acc.setId(idValueOfAccount1);
//Delete the above created object
session.delete(acc);

System.out.println("Committing the Transaction and Closing the
                                                        Session (2)");
txn.commit();
session.close();

session = sessionFactory.openSession();
txn = session.beginTransaction();

// Retrieve the Persistent objects from the database
list = session.createQuery("from Account").list();

for (int i = 0; i < list.size(); i++) {
System.out.println("Object ==> " + displayAccount(list.get(i)));
}

txn.commit();
session.close();
sessionFactory.close();
}

static String displayAccount(Account account) {
return "id[" + account.getId() +
       "]accountNumber[" + account.getAccountNumber() +
       "]customerName[" + account.getCustomerName() +
```

```
        "] availableBalance[" + account.getAvailableBalance() + "]";
    }
  }
```

Hibernate: insert into ACCOUNT (ACC_NUMBER, AVAIL_BALANCE, CUST_NAME) values (?, ?, ?)

Hibernate: insert into ACCOUNT (ACC_NUMBER, AVAIL_BALANCE, CUST_NAME) values (?, ?, ?)

Hibernate: insert into ACCOUNT (ACC_NUMBER, AVAIL_BALANCE, CUST_NAME) values (?, ?, ?)

Committing the Transaction and Closing the Session (1)

Hibernate: select account0_.id as id0_, account0_.ACC_NUMBER as ACC2_0_, account0_.AVAIL_BALANCE as AVAIL3_0_, account0_.CUST_NAME as CUST4_0_ from ACCOUNT account0_

accountObj1 ==> id[1] accountNumber[SB5001] customerName[Mohamed Ibrahim] availableBalance[6000.0]

accountObj2 ==> id[2] accountNumber[SB7501] customerName[Ajay] availableBalance[3000.0]

accountObj3 ==> id[3] accountNumber[SB2000] customerName[Ajmal] availableBalance[2500.0]

Committing the Transaction and Closing the Session (2)

Hibernate: delete from ACCOUNT where id=?

Hibernate: delete from ACCOUNT where id=?

Hibernate: select account0_.id as id0_, account0_.ACC_NUMBER as ACC2_0_, account0_.AVAIL_BALANCE as AVAIL3_0_, account0_.CUST_NAME as CUST4_0_ from ACCOUNT account0_

Object ==> id[2] accountNumber[SB7501] customerName[Ajay] availableBalance[3000.0]

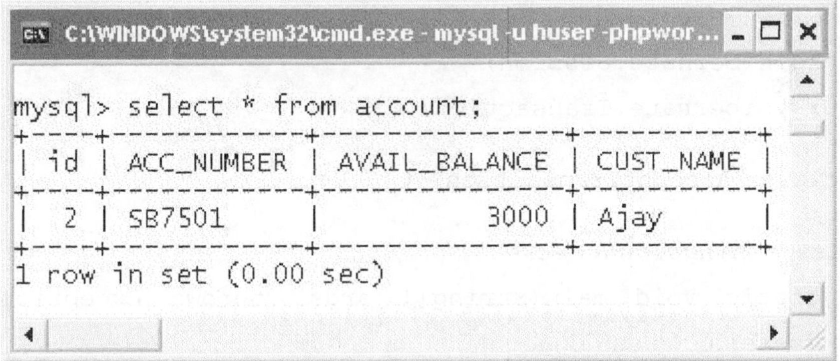

```
C:\WINDOWS\system32\cmd.exe - mysql -u huser -phpwor...
mysql> select * from account;
+----+------------+---------------+-----------+
| id | ACC_NUMBER | AVAIL_BALANCE | CUST_NAME |
+----+------------+---------------+-----------+
|  2 | SB7501     |          3000 | Ajay      |
+----+------------+---------------+-----------+
1 row in set (0.00 sec)
```

3.3 TRANSACTIONS

A group of database operations (statements, unit of work) is called as a *Transaction*. The aim is to execute all operations or none of them. We can make permanent those database operations (transaction), which is called as *commit* operation, or we can undo those database operations (transaction), which is called as *rollback*.

From `Session` object, we can create a new `Transaction` by calling `beginTransaction()` method.

```
Session  session  =  sessionFactory.openSession();
Transaction  txn  =  session.beginTransaction();
```

Some methods in `Transaction` interface:

`void begin()` : Begins a new transaction

`void commit()` : Make permanent the associated transaction

`void rollback()` : Undo (rollback) the associated transaction

A session is the conversation between a client and server during a time period. A single session can have "**n**" number of transactions.

Consider two banking transaction accounts, where the *balance* column will not accept negative values. Our aim is to detect (debit) specified amount from one account and deposit (credit) in another account, *i.e.*, both debit and credit should happen otherwise none should happen. The following example illustrates how to handle this kind of problems with the help of Hibernate *Transactions*.

The following program uses values in such a way that both debit and credit occur.

```
//  File Name:  AccountTransaction.java
//  Main Program:  Transactions

package com.hdemo;

import java.util.List;

import org.hibernate.Session;
import org.hibernate.Transaction;

public class  AccountTransaction  {

@SuppressWarnings("unchecked")
public  static  void  main(String[]  args)  throws  Exception  {
Session  session  =  null;
Transaction  txn  =  null;
```

```
try {
   session = HibernateUtil.getSession();
   txn = session.beginTransaction();
   Account account1 = new  Account();
   account1.setAccountNumber("SB5001");
   account1.setCustomerName("Mohamed  Ibrahim");
   account1.setAvailableBalance(6000.00);

   Account account2 = new Account();
   account2.setAccountNumber("SB7501");
   account2.setCustomerName("Ajay");
   account2.setAvailableBalance(3000.00);

   session.save(account1);
   session.save(account2);
   txn.commit();
   session.close();
   System.out.println("Data  inserted  successfully.");

   System.out.println("Before Transaction: Available Balance of Account
[" + account1.getAccountNumber() + "] is " + account1.getAvailableBalance
());

   System.out.println("Before Transaction: Available Balance of Account
[" + account2.getAccountNumber() + "] is " + account2.getAvailableBalance
());

   session  =  HibernateUtil.getSession();
   txn  =  session.beginTransaction();
   List accountList = session.createQuery("from  Account  a  where
a.accountNumber  =  :accountNumber").setString("accountNumber",
"SB5001").list();
   if (accountList == null || accountList.size() < 1)
   throw new Exception("The account [SB5001] is not found");
   else
   account1  =  (Account)  accountList.get(0);

   accountList = session.createQuery("from Account where accountNumber
=  :accountNumber").setString("accountNumber",  "SB7501").list();
```

```
    if (accountList == null || accountList.size() < 1)
    throw new Exception("The account [SB7501] is not found");
        else
    account2 = (Account) accountList.get(0);
    System.out.println("Debit 3000 from SB7501 and credit it in
                                                         SB5001");
    account1.setAvailableBalance(account1.getAvailableBalance() + 3000);
    account2.setAvailableBalance(account2.getAvailableBalance() - 3000);
    txn.commit();
    System.out.println("Account Transaction is successfully performed");
    System.out.println("After Transaction: Available Balance of Account
[" + account1.getAccountNumber() + "] is " +
account1.getAvailableBalance());
    System.out.println("After Transaction: Available Balance of Account
[" + account2.getAccountNumber() + "] is " +
account2.getAvailableBalance());
    } catch (Exception e) {
    if (txn != null && txn.isActive()) {
    System.out.println("Error occured. So, rolling back the
transaction");
            txn.rollback();
            }
            e.printStackTrace();
        }
    }
  }
```

```
  Hibernate: insert into ACCOUNT (ACC_NUMBER, AVAIL_BALANCE, CUST_NAME)
values (?, ?, ?)
  Hibernate: insert into ACCOUNT (ACC_NUMBER, AVAIL_BALANCE, CUST_NAME)
values (?, ?, ?)
  Data inserted successfully.
  Before Transaction: Available Balance of Account [SB5001] is 6000.0
  Before Transaction: Available Balance of Account [SB7501] is 3000.0
  Hibernate: select account0_.id as id1_, account0_.ACC_NUMBER as
ACC2_1_, account0_.AVAIL_BALANCE as AVAIL3_1_, account0_.CUST_NAME as
CUST4_1_ from ACCOUNT account0_ where account0_.ACC_NUMBER=?
```

```
Hibernate: select account0_.id as id1_, account0_.ACC_NUMBER as ACC2_1_, account0_.AVAIL_BALANCE as AVAIL3_1_, account0_.CUST_NAME as CUST4_1_ from ACCOUNT account0_ where account0_.ACC_NUMBER=?
Debit 3000 from SB7501 and credit it in SB5001
Hibernate: update ACCOUNT set ACC_NUMBER=?, AVAIL_BALANCE=?, CUST_NAME=? where id=?
Hibernate: update ACCOUNT set ACC_NUMBER=?, AVAIL_BALANCE=?, CUST_NAME=? where id=?
Account Transaction is successfully performed
After Transaction: Available Balance of Account [SB5001] is 9000.0
After Transaction: Available Balance of Account [SB7501] is 0.0
```

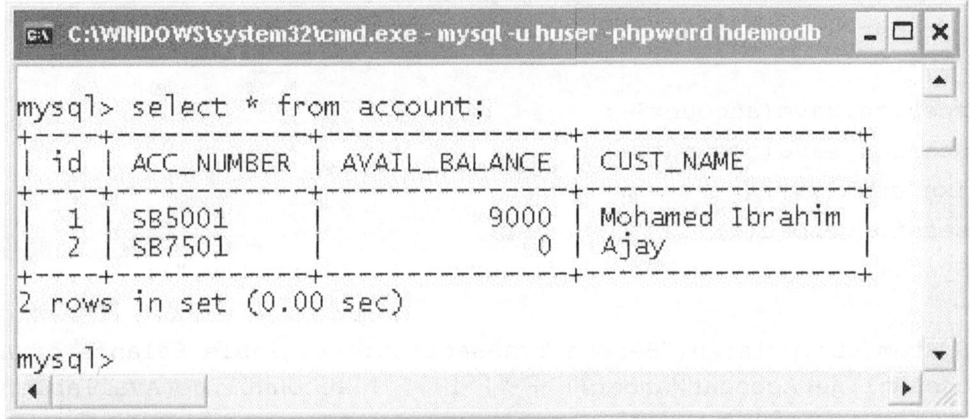

id	ACC_NUMBER	AVAIL_BALANCE	CUST_NAME
1	SB5001	9000	Mohamed Ibrahim
2	SB7501	0	Ajay

Now try to debit amount which is insufficient in available balance.

```
// File Name: AccountTransaction.java
// Main Program: Transactions

package com.hdemo;

import java.util.List;

import org.hibernate.Session;
import org.hibernate.Transaction;

public class AccountTransaction {

@SuppressWarnings("unchecked")
public static void main(String[] args) throws Exception {
                    Session session = null;
```

```
                    Transaction txn = null;
    try {
        session = HibernateUtil.getSession();
        txn = session.beginTransaction();
        Account account1 = new Account();
        account1.setAccountNumber("SB5001");
        account1.setCustomerName("Mohamed Ibrahim");
        account1.setAvailableBalance(6000.00);

        Account account2 = new Account();
        account2.setAccountNumber("SB7501");
        account2.setCustomerName("Ajay");
        account2.setAvailableBalance(3000.00);

        session.save(account1);
        session.save(account2);
        txn.commit();
        session.close();
        System.out.println("Data inserted successfully.");

        System.out.println("Before Transaction: Available Balance of Account
[" + account1.getAccountNumber() + "] is " + account1.getAvailableBalance
());
        System.out.println("Before Transaction: Available Balance of Account
[" + account2.getAccountNumber() + "] is " + account2.getAvailableBalance
());
        session = HibernateUtil.getSession();
        txn = session.beginTransaction();
        List accountList = session.createQuery("from Account a where
a.accountNumber = :accountNumber").setString("accountNumber",
"SB5001").list();
        if (accountList == null || accountList.size() < 1)
        throw new Exception("The account [SB5001] is not found");
            else
                account1 = (Account) accountList.get(0);

        accountList = session.createQuery("from Account where accountNumber
= :accountNumber").setString("accountNumber", "SB7501").list();
        if (accountList == null || accountList.size() < 1)
        throw new Exception("The account [SB7501] is not found");
```

```
      else
      account2 = (Account) accountList.get(0);

      System.out.println("Debit 4000 from SB7501 and credit it in
SB5001");

      account1.setAvailableBalance(account1.getAvailableBalance() + 4000);
      account2.setAvailableBalance(account2.getAvailableBalance() - 4000);
            txn.commit();
      System.out.println("Account Transaction is successfully performed");
      System.out.println("After Transaction: Available Balance of Account
[" + account1.getAccountNumber() + "] is " +
account1.getAvailableBalance());
      System.out.println("After Transaction: Available Balance of Account
[" + account2.getAccountNumber() + "] is " +
account2.getAvailableBalance());
      } catch (Exception e) {
            if (txn != null && txn.isActive()) {
      System.out.println("Error occured. So, rolling back the
transaction");
                  txn.rollback();
                  }
                  e.printStackTrace();
            }
      }
    }
```

```
   Hibernate: insert into ACCOUNT (ACC_NUMBER, AVAIL_BALANCE, CUST_NAME)
values (?, ?, ?)
   Hibernate: insert into ACCOUNT (ACC_NUMBER, AVAIL_BALANCE, CUST_NAME)
values (?, ?, ?)
   Data inserted successfully.
   Before Transaction: Available Balance of Account [SB5001] is 6000.0
   Before Transaction: Available Balance of Account [SB7501] is 3000.0
   Hibernate: select account0_.id as id1_, account0_.ACC_NUMBER as
ACC2_1_, account0_.AVAIL_BALANCE as AVAIL3_1_, account0_.CUST_NAME as
CUST4_1_ from ACCOUNT account0_ where account0_.ACC_NUMBER=?
   Hibernate: select account0_.id as id1_, account0_.ACC_NUMBER as
ACC2_1_, account0_.AVAIL_BALANCE as AVAIL3_1_, account0_.CUST_NAME as
CUST4_1_ from ACCOUNT account0_ where account0_.ACC_NUMBER=?
   Debit 4000 from SB7501 and credit it in SB5001
```

```
Hibernate: update ACCOUNT set ACC_NUMBER=?, AVAIL_BALANCE=?, CUST_NAME=? where id=?
Error occured. So, rolling back the transaction
org.hibernate.validator.InvalidStateException: validation failed for: com.hdemo.Account
at org.hibernate.validator.event.ValidateEventListener.validate(ValidateEventListener.java:148)
at org.hibernate.validator.event.ValidateEventListener.onPreUpdate(ValidateEventListener.java:177)
at org.hibernate.action.EntityUpdateAction.preUpdate(EntityUpdateAction.java:221)
at org.hibernate.action.EntityUpdateAction.execute(EntityUpdateAction.java:65)
at org.hibernate.engine.ActionQueue.execute(ActionQueue.java:279)
at org.hibernate.engine.ActionQueue.executeActions(ActionQueue.java:263)
at org.hibernate.engine.ActionQueue.executeActions(ActionQueue.java:168)
at org.hibernate.event.def.AbstractFlushingEventListener.performExecutions (AbstractFlushingEventListener.java:298)
at org.hibernate.event.def.DefaultFlushEventListener.onFlush(DefaultFlushEventListener.java:27)
at org.hibernate.impl.SessionImpl.flush(SessionImpl.java:1000)
at org.hibernate.impl.SessionImpl.managedFlush(SessionImpl.java:338)
at org.hibernate.transaction.JDBCTransaction.commit(JDBCTransaction.java:106)
at com.hdemo.AccountTransaction.main(AccountTransaction.java:54)
```

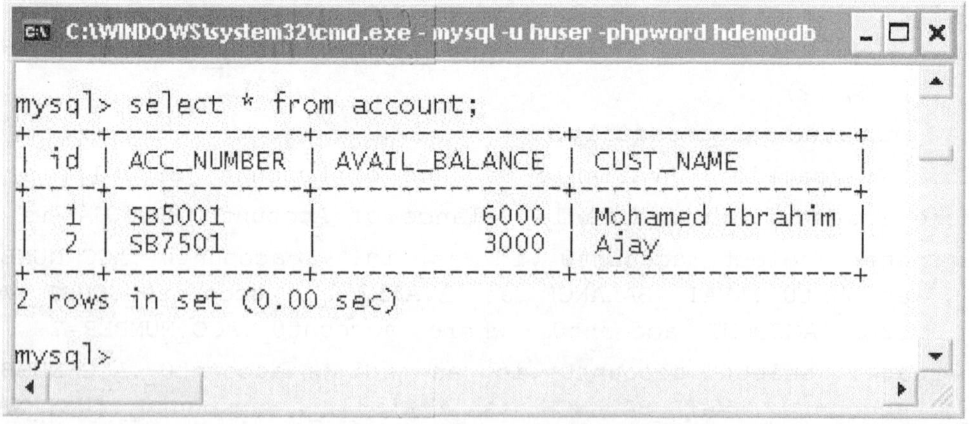

SUMMARY

The Hibernate SessionFactory interface is used to provide Hibernate Session(s) (interface), which are used to do relational mappings of objects such as definition and manipulation of data with database. Hibernate Session(s) are not thread-safe; data may be overwritten while a Session used in multi-threaded environment. And the SessionFactory provides remedy to the thread-safe issue as it is thread-safe among multi-threaded environment. This chapter explains how to create a SessionFactory object and how to obtain Sessions from SessionFactory. The important methods under Session are explained with sample programs. This chapter also explains the importance of using Transactions in applications.

CHAPTER

4

DEFINING POJOs USING JPA/ HIBERNATE ANNOTATIONS

4.0 INTRODUCTION

A POJO (Plain Old Java Object) is a Java object that doesn't extend/implement any framework specific classes/interfaces. The POJOs look like a simple Java beans; they decouple your application code from any framework that you are using.

JPA/Hibernate Annotations: We have to specify metadata information (such as name of the database table, column names, length of the columns, data types, etc.) while using JPA/Hibernate persistence. Specifying metadata through XML is a common one; however, we can best use the annotation features of latest JPA/Hibernate API. While using Annotations, no need to depend on XML since the annotations (they are also Java classes) are compiled into Byte code and invoked during runtime using Java Reflection API.

Some important JPA/Hibernate annotations for defining required POJOs (entities) are described below. The JPA can be also be used in EJB 3, keeping this flexibility in mind, many JPA annotations are used in the examples even though Hibernate equivalents are available.

4.1 `@Entity` - DEFINING AN ENTITY

This declares the POJO class as an entity bean (entity bean- persistent; stored with database).

General format

```
@Entity
```

Example

```
// File Name: Employee.java
// Illustrates @Entity

package com.hdemo;

import java.io.Serializable;
```

```
import javax.persistence.Entity;

@Entity
public class Employee implements Serializable {

}
```

The *serialVersionUID* can be generated using IDE.

4.2 @Table - DEFINING DATABASE SCHEMA

It defines the table associated with an Entity.

General format

```
        @Table (name="table_name")
```

Example

```
// File Name: Employee.java
// Illustrates @Table

package com.hdemo;

import java.io.Serializable;

import javax.persistence.Entity;
import javax.persistence.Table;

@Entity
@Table(name = "EMPLOYEE")
public class Employee implements Serializable {

  private static final long serialVersionUID = 1L;

}
```

4.3 @SecondaryTable/@SecondaryTables - MAPPING WITH MORE TABLES

It is possible to map a single entity bean (POJO) to multiple tables (some fields to one table, some others to another table, etc.). This is accomplished through `@SecondaryTable` and

@SecondaryTables annotations. Use @SecondaryTables annotation to specify multiple @SecondaryTable in an Entity.

General format

```
@SecondaryTable (name="Name_of_table")
```

Here name attribute is mandatory.

```
@SecondaryTables(Array of @SecondaryTable)
```

Here Array of @SecondaryTable is mandatory, this array should contain at least one @SecondaryTable.

We need to use @Column (explained later) annotation with *table* attribute, specifies which columns are belonging to which table.

Example

```
// File Name: Employee.java
// Illustrates @Entity

package com.hdemo;

import java.io.Serializable;

import javax.persistence.Column;
import javax.persistence.Entity;
import javax.persistence.Id;

import javax.persistence.SecondaryTable;
import javax.persistence.Table;

@Entity
@Table(name = "EMPLOYEE")
public class Employee implements Serializable {

  private static final long serialVersionUID = 1L;

  @Id
  @Column
  private int empNumber;

  @Column
```

```
 private String empName;

 @Column
 private double basicpay;

@Column
private double allowances;

@Column
private double deductions;

@Column
private double netpay;

@Column
private double da; // Dearness Allowance

@Column
private double hra; // House Rent Allowance

@Column
private double ma; // Medical Allowance

@Column
private double tax; // Income tax deduction

@Column
private double pf; // Provident fund deduction

@Column
private String addressDoorNumber;

@Column
private String addressBuildingName;

@Column
private String addressStreetName;

@Column
private String addressState;
```

```
    @Column
    private String addressCountry;

    @Column
    private int addressPostalCode;

    public int getEmpNumber() {
        return empNumber;
    }

    public void setEmpNumber(int empNumber) {
        this.empNumber = empNumber;
    }

    public String getEmpName() {
        return empName;
    }

    public void setEmpName(String empName) {
        this.empName = empName;
    }

    public double getBasicpay() {
        return basicpay;
    }

    public void setBasicpay(double basicpay) {
        this.basicpay = basicpay;
    }

    public double getAllowances() {
        return allowances;
    }

    public void setAllowances(double allowances) {
        this.allowances = allowances;
    }
```

```
 public double getDeductions() {
      return deductions;
 }

public void setDeductions(double deductions) {
    this.deductions = deductions;
}

public double getNetpay() {
    return netpay;
}

public void setNetpay(double netpay) {
    this.netpay = netpay;
}

public double getDa() {
    return da;
}

public void setDa(double da) {
    this.da = da;
}

public double getHra() {
    return hra;
}

public void setHra(double hra) {
    this.hra = hra;
}

public double getMa() {
    return ma;
}

public void setMa(double ma) {
    this.ma = ma;
```

```
    }

    public double getTax() {
            return tax;
    }

    public void setTax(double tax) {
        this.tax = tax;
    }

    public double getPf() {
        return pf;
    }

    public void setPf(double pf) {
        this.pf = pf;
    }

    public String getAddressDoorNumber() {
        return addressDoorNumber;
    }

    public void setAddressDoorNumber(String addressDoorNumber) {
        this.addressDoorNumber = addressDoorNumber;
    }

    public String getAddressBuildingName() {
        return addressBuildingName;
    }

    public void setAddressBuildingName(String addressBuildingName) {
        this.addressBuildingName = addressBuildingName;
    }

    public String getAddressStreetName() {
        return addressStreetName;
    }

    public void setAddressStreetName(String addressStreetName) {
```

```
        this.addressStreetName = addressStreetName;
    }

    public String getAddressState() {
        return addressState;
    }

    public void setAddressState(String addressState) {
        this.addressState = addressState;
    }

    public String getAddressCountry() {
        return addressCountry;
    }

    public void setAddressCountry(String addressCountry) {
        this.addressCountry = addressCountry;
    }

    public int getAddressPostalCode() {
        return addressPostalCode;
    }

    public void setAddressPostalCode(int addressPostalCode) {
        this.addressPostalCode = addressPostalCode;
    }

}
```

```
// File Name: EmployeeManipulation.java
// Main Program
package com.hdemo;

import org.hibernate.Session;
import org.hibernate.SessionFactory;

public class EmployeeManipulation {

public static void main(String[] args) throws Exception {
```

```
    SessionFactory sessionFactory = HibernateUtil.getSessionFactory();
          Session  session  =  sessionFactory.getCurrentSession();

       sessionFactory.close();
  }

}
```

Run the *EmployeeManipulation.java* application. Check created table structure in MySQL.

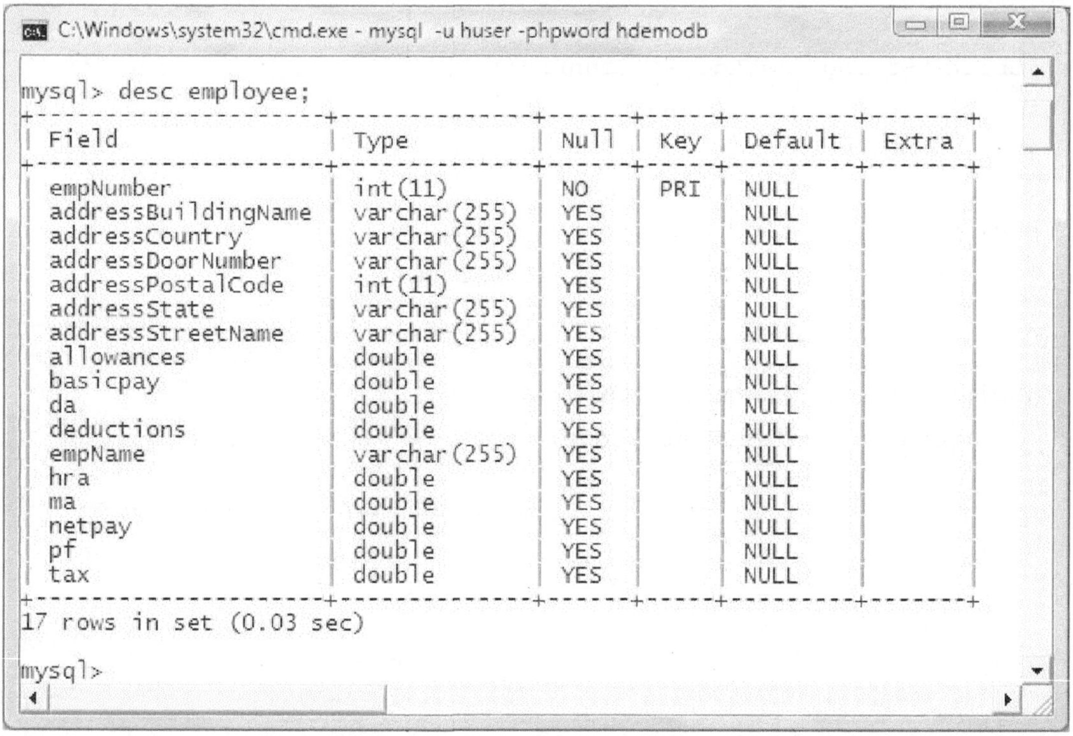

```
C:\Windows\system32\cmd.exe - mysql -u huser -phpword hdemodb

mysql> desc employee;
+---------------------+--------------+------+-----+---------+-------+
| Field               | Type         | Null | Key | Default | Extra |
+---------------------+--------------+------+-----+---------+-------+
| empNumber           | int(11)      | NO   | PRI | NULL    |       |
| addressBuildingName | varchar(255) | YES  |     | NULL    |       |
| addressCountry      | varchar(255) | YES  |     | NULL    |       |
| addressDoorNumber   | varchar(255) | YES  |     | NULL    |       |
| addressPostalCode   | int(11)      | YES  |     | NULL    |       |
| addressState        | varchar(255) | YES  |     | NULL    |       |
| addressStreetName   | varchar(255) | YES  |     | NULL    |       |
| allowances          | double       | YES  |     | NULL    |       |
| basicpay            | double       | YES  |     | NULL    |       |
| da                  | double       | YES  |     | NULL    |       |
| deductions          | double       | YES  |     | NULL    |       |
| empName             | varchar(255) | YES  |     | NULL    |       |
| hra                 | double       | YES  |     | NULL    |       |
| ma                  | double       | YES  |     | NULL    |       |
| netpay              | double       | YES  |     | NULL    |       |
| pf                  | double       | YES  |     | NULL    |       |
| tax                 | double       | YES  |     | NULL    |       |
+---------------------+--------------+------+-----+---------+-------+
17 rows in set (0.03 sec)

mysql>
```

Note: You can see that the table is not well defined according to the type and integrity of data (for example, salary field may accept *null* values). This example is given to illustrate `@Table`, `@SecondaryTable` and `@SecondaryTables` annotations. We will modify the same POJO according to our needs while explaining `@Column` annotation.

We can modify the above `Employee` class as below; to store address related fields to another table named "*employee_address*".

```
// File Name: Employee.java
// Illustrates @SecondaryTable
```

```
package com.hdemo;

import java.io.Serializable;

import javax.persistence.Column;
import javax.persistence.Entity;
import javax.persistence.Id;
import javax.persistence.SecondaryTable;
import javax.persistence.Table;

@Entity
@Table(name = "EMPLOYEE")
@SecondaryTable(name = "EMPLOYEE_ADDRESS")
public class Employee implements Serializable {

 private static final long serialVersionUID = 1L;

 @Id
 @Column
 private int empNumber;

 @Column
 private String empName;

 @Column
 private double basicpay;

 @Column
 private double allowances;

 @Column
 private double deductions;

 @Column
 private double netpay;

 @Column
 private double da; // Dearness Allowance
```

```
    @Column
    private double hra; // House Rent Allowance
    @Column
    private double ma; // Medical Allowance

    @Column
    private double tax; // Income tax deduction

    @Column
    private double pf; // Provident fund deduction

    @Column(table = "EMPLOYEE_ADDRESS")
    private String addressDoorNumber;

    @Column(table = "EMPLOYEE_ADDRESS")
    private String addressBuildingName;

    @Column(table = "EMPLOYEE_ADDRESS")
    private String addressStreetName;

    @Column(table = "EMPLOYEE_ADDRESS")
    private String addressState;

    @Column(table = "EMPLOYEE_ADDRESS")
    private String addressCountry;

    @Column(table = "EMPLOYEE_ADDRESS")
    private int addressPostalCode;

    public int getEmpNumber() {
        return empNumber;
    }

    public void setEmpNumber(int empNumber) {
        this.empNumber = empNumber;
    }

    public String getEmpName() {
```

```
        return empName;
    }

    public void setEmpName(String empName) {
        this.empName = empName;
    }

    public double getBasicpay() {
        return basicpay;
    }

    public void setBasicpay(double basicpay) {
        this.basicpay = basicpay;
    }

    public double getAllowances() {
        return allowances;
    }

    public void setAllowances(double allowances) {
        this.allowances = allowances;
    }

    public double getDeductions() {
        return deductions;
    }

    public void setDeductions(double deductions) {
        this.deductions = deductions;
    }

    public double getNetpay() {
        return netpay;
    }

    public void setNetpay(double netpay) {
        this.netpay = netpay;
    }
```

```
     public double getDa() {
          return da;
     }

    public void setDa(double da) {
        this.da = da;
    }

    public double getHra() {
        return hra;
    }

    public void setHra(double hra) {
        this.hra = hra;
    }

    public double getMa() {
        return ma;
    }

    public void setMa(double ma) {
        this.ma = ma;
    }

    public double getTax() {
        return tax;
    }

    public void setTax(double tax) {
        this.tax = tax;
    }

    public double getPf() {
        return pf;
    }

    public void setPf(double pf) {
        this.pf = pf;
```

```
    }

    public String getAddressDoorNumber() {
        return addressDoorNumber;
    }

    public void setAddressDoorNumber(String addressDoorNumber) {
        this.addressDoorNumber = addressDoorNumber;
    }

    public String getAddressBuildingName() {
        return addressBuildingName;
    }

    public void setAddressBuildingName(String addressBuildingName) {
        this.addressBuildingName = addressBuildingName;
    }

    public String getAddressStreetName() {
        return addressStreetName;
    }

    public void setAddressStreetName(String addressStreetName) {
        this.addressStreetName = addressStreetName;
    }

    public String getAddressState() {
        return addressState;
    }

    public void setAddressState(String addressState) {
        this.addressState = addressState;
    }

    public String getAddressCountry() {
        return addressCountry;
    }

    public void setAddressCountry(String addressCountry) {
```

```
        this.addressCountry = addressCountry;
    }

    public int getAddressPostalCode() {
        return addressPostalCode;
    }

    public void setAddressPostalCode(int addressPostalCode) {
        this.addressPostalCode = addressPostalCode;
    }

}
```

After a sample run, the database tables will be as shown below.

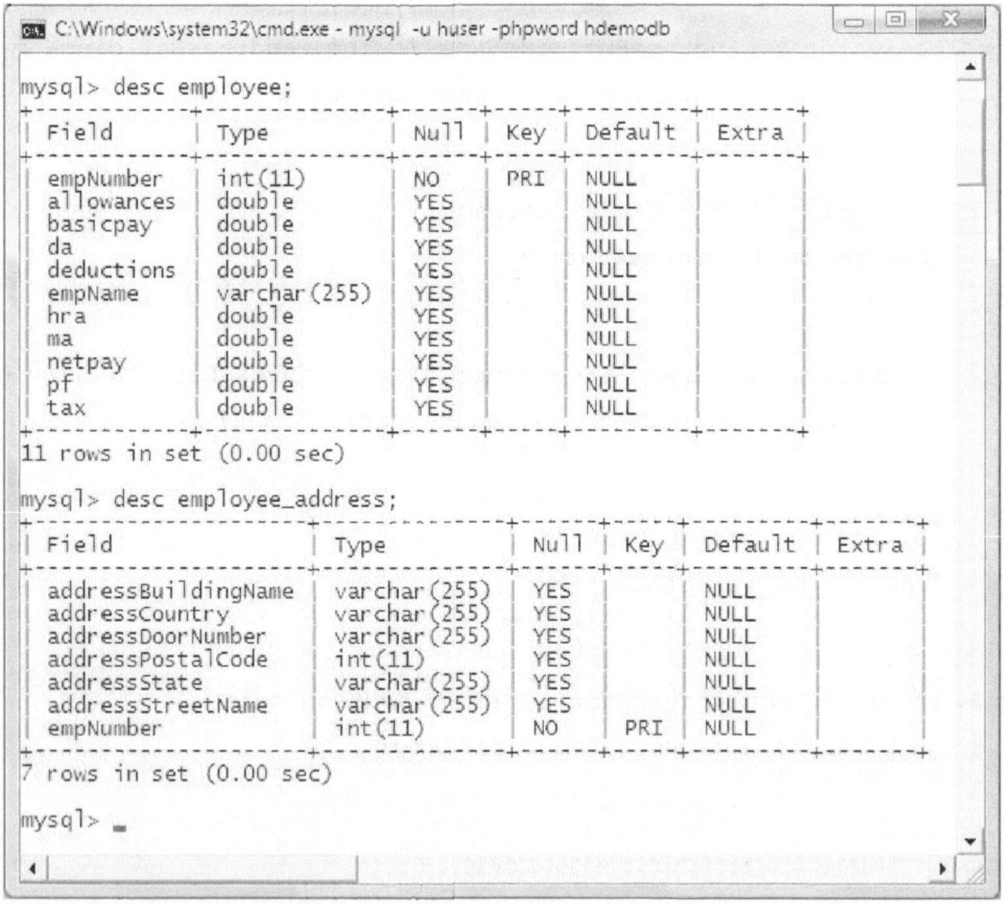

```
C:\Windows\system32\cmd.exe - mysql -u huser -phpword hdemodb

mysql> desc employee;
+-------------+--------------+------+-----+---------+-------+
| Field       | Type         | Null | Key | Default | Extra |
+-------------+--------------+------+-----+---------+-------+
| empNumber   | int(11)      | NO   | PRI | NULL    |       |
| allowances  | double       | YES  |     | NULL    |       |
| basicpay    | double       | YES  |     | NULL    |       |
| da          | double       | YES  |     | NULL    |       |
| deductions  | double       | YES  |     | NULL    |       |
| empName     | varchar(255) | YES  |     | NULL    |       |
| hra         | double       | YES  |     | NULL    |       |
| ma          | double       | YES  |     | NULL    |       |
| netpay      | double       | YES  |     | NULL    |       |
| pf          | double       | YES  |     | NULL    |       |
| tax         | double       | YES  |     | NULL    |       |
+-------------+--------------+------+-----+---------+-------+
11 rows in set (0.00 sec)

mysql> desc employee_address;
+---------------------+--------------+------+-----+---------+-------+
| Field               | Type         | Null | Key | Default | Extra |
+---------------------+--------------+------+-----+---------+-------+
| addressBuildingName | varchar(255) | YES  |     | NULL    |       |
| addressCountry      | varchar(255) | YES  |     | NULL    |       |
| addressDoorNumber   | varchar(255) | YES  |     | NULL    |       |
| addressPostalCode   | int(11)      | YES  |     | NULL    |       |
| addressState        | varchar(255) | YES  |     | NULL    |       |
| addressStreetName   | varchar(255) | YES  |     | NULL    |       |
| empNumber           | int(11)      | NO   | PRI | NULL    |       |
+---------------------+--------------+------+-----+---------+-------+
7 rows in set (0.00 sec)

mysql> _
```

Now, we will modify the Employee entity class in such as way that all address related fields will go to `EMPLOYEE_ADDRESS` table, all allowances related fields will go to `EMPLOYEE_ALLOWANCES` table, all deductions related fields will go to `EMPLOYEE_DEDUCTIONS` table, and all core fields will store in our EMPLOYEE table.

```
// File Name: Employee.java
// Illustrates @SecondaryTables

package com.hdemo;

import java.io.Serializable;

import javax.persistence.Column;
import javax.persistence.Entity;
import javax.persistence.Id;
import javax.persistence.SecondaryTable;
import javax.persistence.SecondaryTables;
import javax.persistence.Table;

@Entity
@Table(name = "EMPLOYEE")
@SecondaryTables( { @SecondaryTable(name = "EMPLOYEE_ADDRESS"),
@SecondaryTable(name = "EMPLOYEE_ALLOWANCES"),
@SecondaryTable(name = "EMPLOYEE_DEDUCTIONS") })
public class Employee implements Serializable {

 private static final long serialVersionUID = 1L;

 @Id
  @Column
  private int empNumber;

  @Column
  private String empName;

  @Column
  private double basicpay;

  @Column
  private double allowances;

  @Column
  private double deductions;
```

```
    @Column
    private double netpay;

    @Column(table = "EMPLOYEE_ALLOWANCES")
    private double da; // Dearness Allowance

    @Column(table = "EMPLOYEE_ALLOWANCES")
    private double hra; // House Rent Allowance

    @Column(table = "EMPLOYEE_ALLOWANCES")
    private double ma; // Medical Allowance

    @Column(table = "EMPLOYEE_DEDUCTIONS")
    private double tax; // Income tax deduction

    @Column(table = "EMPLOYEE_DEDUCTIONS")
    private double pf; // Provident fund deduction

    @Column(table = "EMPLOYEE_ADDRESS")
    private String addressDoorNumber;

    @Column(table = "EMPLOYEE_ADDRESS")
    private String addressBuildingName;

    @Column(table = "EMPLOYEE_ADDRESS")
    private String addressStreetName;

    @Column(table = "EMPLOYEE_ADDRESS")
    private String addressState;

    @Column(table = "EMPLOYEE_ADDRESS")
    private String addressCountry;

    @Column(table = "EMPLOYEE_ADDRESS")
    private int addressPostalCode;

    //Generate Getter and Setter methods using IDE

}
```

In the above program list, get and set methods for the fields are not included. Readers are advised to generate these getters/setters using any IDE such as Eclipse, or write them by own before executing the program.

A sample run results in the following database tables.

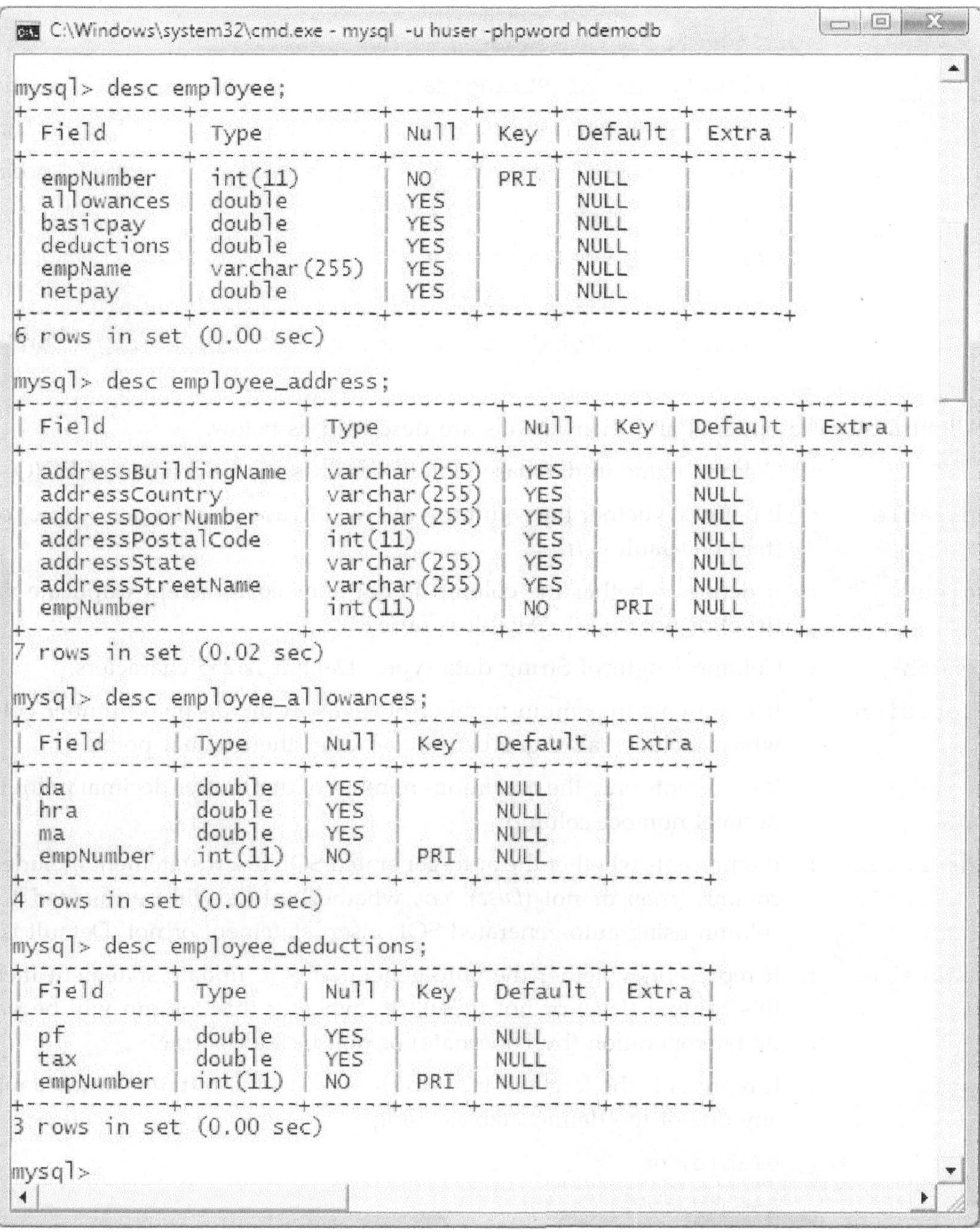

```
C:\Windows\system32\cmd.exe - mysql -u huser -phpword hdemodb

mysql> desc employee;
+-------------+--------------+------+-----+---------+-------+
| Field       | Type         | Null | Key | Default | Extra |
+-------------+--------------+------+-----+---------+-------+
| empNumber   | int(11)      | NO   | PRI | NULL    |       |
| allowances  | double       | YES  |     | NULL    |       |
| basicpay    | double       | YES  |     | NULL    |       |
| deductions  | double       | YES  |     | NULL    |       |
| empName     | varchar(255) | YES  |     | NULL    |       |
| netpay      | double       | YES  |     | NULL    |       |
+-------------+--------------+------+-----+---------+-------+
6 rows in set (0.00 sec)

mysql> desc employee_address;
+---------------------+--------------+------+-----+---------+-------+
| Field               | Type         | Null | Key | Default | Extra |
+---------------------+--------------+------+-----+---------+-------+
| addressBuildingName | varchar(255) | YES  |     | NULL    |       |
| addressCountry      | varchar(255) | YES  |     | NULL    |       |
| addressDoorNumber   | varchar(255) | YES  |     | NULL    |       |
| addressPostalCode   | int(11)      | YES  |     | NULL    |       |
| addressState        | varchar(255) | YES  |     | NULL    |       |
| addressStreetName   | varchar(255) | YES  |     | NULL    |       |
| empNumber           | int(11)      | NO   | PRI | NULL    |       |
+---------------------+--------------+------+-----+---------+-------+
7 rows in set (0.02 sec)

mysql> desc employee_allowances;
+-----------+---------+------+-----+---------+-------+
| Field     | Type    | Null | Key | Default | Extra |
+-----------+---------+------+-----+---------+-------+
| da        | double  | YES  |     | NULL    |       |
| hra       | double  | YES  |     | NULL    |       |
| ma        | double  | YES  |     | NULL    |       |
| empNumber | int(11) | NO   | PRI | NULL    |       |
+-----------+---------+------+-----+---------+-------+
4 rows in set (0.00 sec)

mysql> desc employee_deductions;
+-----------+---------+------+-----+---------+-------+
| Field     | Type    | Null | Key | Default | Extra |
+-----------+---------+------+-----+---------+-------+
| pf        | double  | YES  |     | NULL    |       |
| tax       | double  | YES  |     | NULL    |       |
| empNumber | int(11) | NO   | PRI | NULL    |       |
+-----------+---------+------+-----+---------+-------+
3 rows in set (0.00 sec)

mysql>
```

4.4 `@Column` - DEFINING DATABASE TABLE COLUMNS

This is used to map POJO field-name with database table's column-name.

General format

```
@Column (   name="Column name in database table",
          nullable="true | false",
          unique="true | false",
          length="width of String data-type columns such as varchar",
          precision="maximum number of decimal digits for Column",
          scale="maximum number of digits after decimal point",
          insertable="true | false",
          updatable="true | false",
          table="Secondary table name",
          columnDefinition="String- extra column definition"
       )
```

All attributes are optional and their actions are described as below.

`name` : Column name in database table. Default is the field name of POJO.

`nullable` : It defines whether the column is allowed to accept *null* values (true) or not (false). Default is *true.*

`unique` : It defines whether the column is not allowed to accept duplicate values (true) or not (false). Default is false.

`length` : Column length of String data types. Default is 255 characters.

`precision` : It represents maximum number of digits in the decimal number column, which includes all digits before and after the decimal point.

`scale` : It represents only the maximum number of digits after decimal point in the decimal number column.

`insertable` : It represents whether the auto-generated SQL insert statement includes this column (*true*) or not (*false*), *i.e.,* whether values will be inserted to this column using auto-generated SQL insert statement or not. Default is *true.*

`updatable` : It represents whether the auto-generated SQL update statement includes this column (*true*) or not (*false*), *i.e.,* whether this column will be part of update operation (by Hibernate) or not. Default is *true.*

`table` : It represents the targeted table to store this column (targeted table may be any one of the defined tables using

`@Table`, or

`@SeondaryTable`, or

`@SecondaryTables`.

Default is primary table, defined using `@Table` annotation).

`columnDefinition` : Specify any additional constraints / options here. All other attributes will create DDL Create statement; if you want to specify any additional ones, you can specify them here as String. You are also allowed to specify anything that the other optional attributes will do it for you.

Example

```
// File Name: Employee.java
// Illustrates @Column

package com.hdemo;

import java.io.Serializable;
import java.math.BigDecimal;

import javax.persistence.Column;
import javax.persistence.Entity;
import javax.persistence.Id;
import javax.persistence.Table;

@Entity
@Table(name = "EMPLOYEE")
public class Employee implements Serializable {

 private static final long serialVersionUID = 1L;

 @Id
  @Column(name = "EMP_NUMBER")
  private int empNumber;

  @Column(name = "EMP_NAME", nullable = false, length = 64)
  private String empName;

 @Column
 private double basicpay;

  @Column(name = "ALLOWANCES", nullable = false, precision = 10,
                                                      scale = 2)
  private BigDecimal allowances;
```

```
  @Column(name = "DEDUCTIONS", nullable = false, precision = 10,
                                                     scale = 2)
  private BigDecimal deductions;

  @Column(name = "NETPAY", nullable = false, precision = 10, scale
                                                           = 2)
  private BigDecimal netpay;

  private String address;

 public int getEmpNumber() {
     return empNumber;
 }

 public void setEmpNumber(int empNumber) {
     this.empNumber = empNumber;
 }

 public String getEmpName() {
     return empName;
 }

 public void setEmpName(String empName) {
     this.empName = empName;
 }

 public double getBasicpay() {
     return basicpay;
 }

 public void setBasicpay(double basicpay) {
     this.basicpay = basicpay;
 }

 public BigDecimal getAllowances() {
     return allowances;
  }
  public void setAllowances(BigDecimal allowances) {
```

```
        this.allowances = allowances;
    }

    public BigDecimal getDeductions() {
        return deductions;
    }

    public void setDeductions(BigDecimal deductions) {
        this.deductions = deductions;
    }

    public BigDecimal getNetpay() {
        return netpay;
    }

    public void setNetpay(BigDecimal netpay) {
        this.netpay = netpay;
    }

}
```

Note: I purposefully did not specify any `@Column` attribute for *"basicpay"* field and no annotation for *"address"* field. Do observe what defaults are applied to them from the following result.

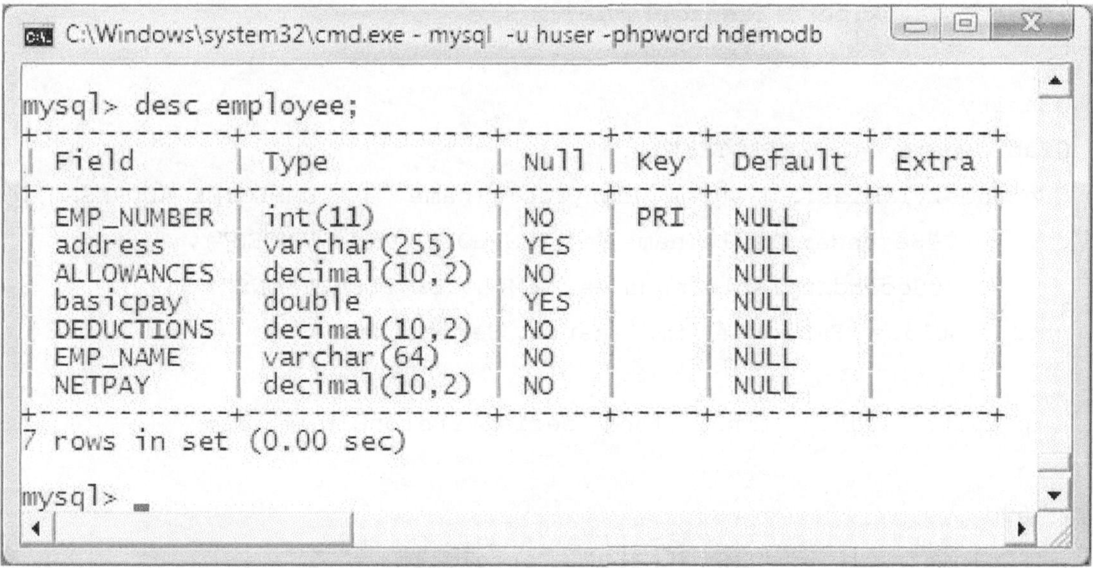

```
C:\Windows\system32\cmd.exe - mysql -u huser -phpword hdemodb

mysql> desc employee;
+------------+---------------+------+-----+---------+-------+
| Field      | Type          | Null | Key | Default | Extra |
+------------+---------------+------+-----+---------+-------+
| EMP_NUMBER | int(11)       | NO   | PRI | NULL    |       |
| address    | varchar(255)  | YES  |     | NULL    |       |
| ALLOWANCES | decimal(10,2) | NO   |     | NULL    |       |
| basicpay   | double        | YES  |     | NULL    |       |
| DEDUCTIONS | decimal(10,2) | NO   |     | NULL    |       |
| EMP_NAME   | varchar(64)   | NO   |     | NULL    |       |
| NETPAY     | decimal(10,2) | NO   |     | NULL    |       |
+------------+---------------+------+-----+---------+-------+
7 rows in set (0.00 sec)

mysql>
```

Observe that the field "*address*" also becomes persistent field by default, even if we did not specify `@Column` annotation and getter/setter methods. The Entity POJO will accept persistent field without getter/setter methods, but with out these methods mapping with database can be done automatically. We did not specify the *name* attribute in `@Column` annotation of *basicpay* field, so the field-name itself taken as persistent table-column name in database.

Now, we will take the same example that we used in explaining `@SecondaryTable` annotation for meaningfully and neatly defining database columns.

```
package com.hdemo;

import java.io.Serializable;
import java.math.BigDecimal;
import java.math.BigInteger;

// File Name: Employee.java
// Illustrates @SecondaryTables

import javax.persistence.Column;
import javax.persistence.Entity;
import javax.persistence.Id;
import javax.persistence.SecondaryTable;
import javax.persistence.SecondaryTables;
import javax.persistence.Table;

@Entity
@Table(name = "EMPLOYEE")
@SecondaryTables( { @SecondaryTable(name = "EMPLOYEE_ADDRESS"),
        @SecondaryTable(name = "EMPLOYEE_ALLOWANCES"),
        @SecondaryTable(name = "EMPLOYEE_DEDUCTIONS") })
public class Employee implements Serializable {

  private static final long serialVersionUID = 1L;

  @Id
  @Column(name = "EMP_NUMBER", precision = 5)
```

```
private BigInteger empNumber;

@Column(name = "EMP_NAME", nullable = false, length = 64)
private String empName;

@Column(name = "BASIC_PAY", nullable = false, precision = 9,
scale = 2)
private BigDecimal basicpay;

@Column(name = "ALLOWANCES", nullable = false, precision = 8,
scale = 2)
private BigDecimal allowances;

@Column(name = "DEDUCTIONS", nullable = false, precision = 8,
scale = 2)
private BigDecimal deductions;

@Column(name = "NET_PAY", nullable = false, precision = 9, scale
= 2)
private BigDecimal netpay;

@Column(name = "DA", precision = 8, scale = 2, table =
"EMPLOYEE_ALLOWANCES")
private BigDecimal da; // Dearness Allowance

@Column(name = "HRA", precision = 7, scale = 2, table =
"EMPLOYEE_ALLOWANCES")
private BigDecimal hra; // House Rent Allowance

@Column(name = "MA", precision = 7, scale = 2, table =
"EMPLOYEE_ALLOWANCES")
private BigDecimal ma; // Medical Allowance
```

```
    @Column(name = "TAX", precision = 7, scale = 2, table =
    "EMPLOYEE_DEDUCTIONS")
    private BigDecimal tax; // Income tax deduction

    @Column(name = "PF", precision = 7, scale = 2, table =
    "EMPLOYEE_DEDUCTIONS")
    private BigDecimal pf; // Provident fund deduction

    @Column(name = "ADDRESS_DOOR_NUMBER", length = 8, table =
    "EMPLOYEE_ADDRESS")
    private String addressDoorNumber;

    @Column(name = "ADDRESS_BUILDING_NAME", length = 64, table =
    "EMPLOYEE_ADDRESS")
    private String addressBuildingName;

    @Column(name = "ADDRESS_STREET_NAME", length = 64, table =
    "EMPLOYEE_ADDRESS")
    private String addressStreetName;

    @Column(name = "ADDRESS_STATE", length = 64, table =
    "EMPLOYEE_ADDRESS")
    private String addressState;

    @Column(name = "ADDRESS_COUNTRY", nullable = false, length = 64,
    table = "EMPLOYEE_ADDRESS")
    private String addressCountry;

    @Column(name = "ADDRESS_POSTAL_CODE", columnDefinition =
    "decimal(6,0) not null", table = "EMPLOYEE_ADDRESS")
    private int addressPostalCode;

    //Getter and setter methods

}
```

A sample run results as below.

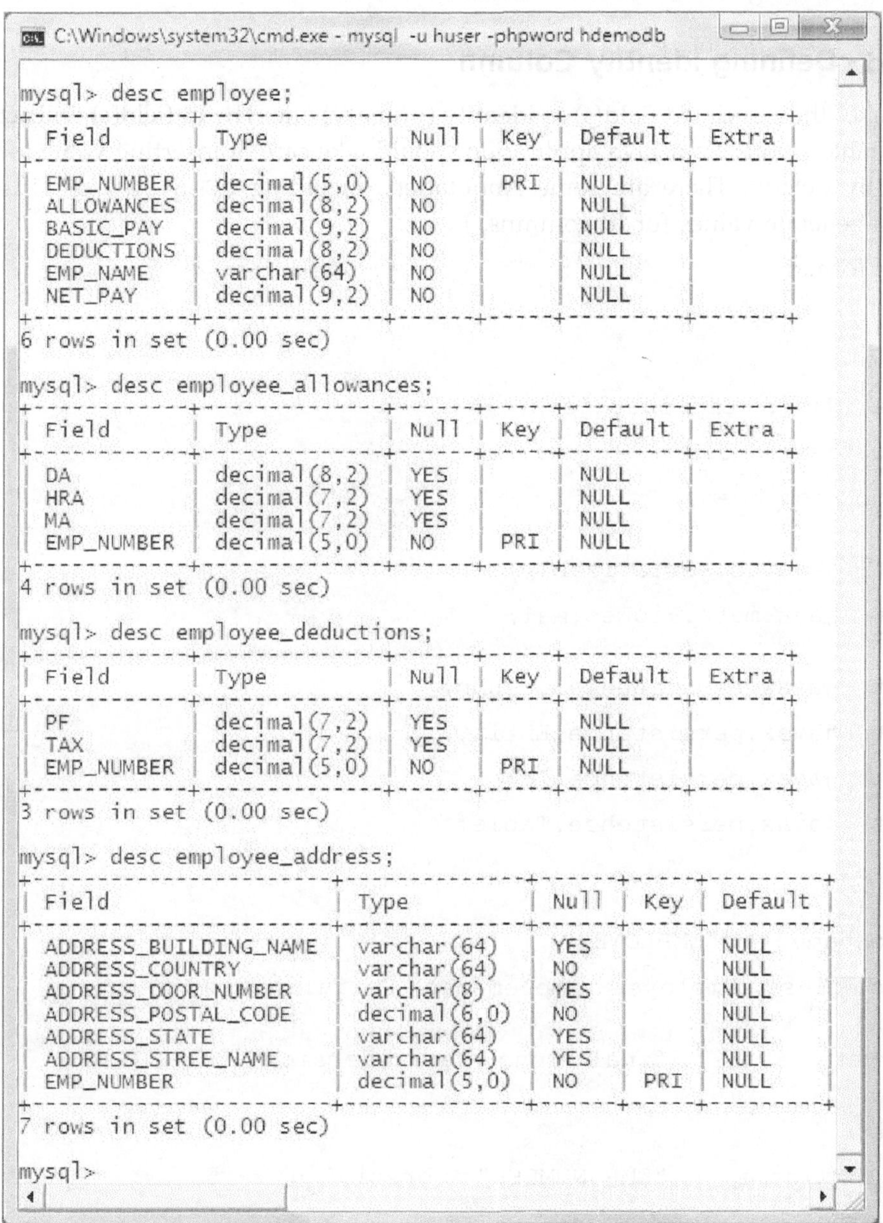

```
C:\Windows\system32\cmd.exe - mysql -u huser -phpword hdemodb

mysql> desc employee;
+-------------+--------------+------+-----+---------+-------+
| Field       | Type         | Null | Key | Default | Extra |
+-------------+--------------+------+-----+---------+-------+
| EMP_NUMBER  | decimal(5,0) | NO   | PRI | NULL    |       |
| ALLOWANCES  | decimal(8,2) | NO   |     | NULL    |       |
| BASIC_PAY   | decimal(9,2) | NO   |     | NULL    |       |
| DEDUCTIONS  | decimal(8,2) | NO   |     | NULL    |       |
| EMP_NAME    | varchar(64)  | NO   |     | NULL    |       |
| NET_PAY     | decimal(9,2) | NO   |     | NULL    |       |
+-------------+--------------+------+-----+---------+-------+
6 rows in set (0.00 sec)

mysql> desc employee_allowances;
+-------------+--------------+------+-----+---------+-------+
| Field       | Type         | Null | Key | Default | Extra |
+-------------+--------------+------+-----+---------+-------+
| DA          | decimal(8,2) | YES  |     | NULL    |       |
| HRA         | decimal(7,2) | YES  |     | NULL    |       |
| MA          | decimal(7,2) | YES  |     | NULL    |       |
| EMP_NUMBER  | decimal(5,0) | NO   | PRI | NULL    |       |
+-------------+--------------+------+-----+---------+-------+
4 rows in set (0.00 sec)

mysql> desc employee_deductions;
+-------------+--------------+------+-----+---------+-------+
| Field       | Type         | Null | Key | Default | Extra |
+-------------+--------------+------+-----+---------+-------+
| PF          | decimal(7,2) | YES  |     | NULL    |       |
| TAX         | decimal(7,2) | YES  |     | NULL    |       |
| EMP_NUMBER  | decimal(5,0) | NO   | PRI | NULL    |       |
+-------------+--------------+------+-----+---------+-------+
3 rows in set (0.00 sec)

mysql> desc employee_address;
+-----------------------+--------------+------+-----+---------+
| Field                 | Type         | Null | Key | Default |
+-----------------------+--------------+------+-----+---------+
| ADDRESS_BUILDING_NAME | varchar(64)  | YES  |     | NULL    |
| ADDRESS_COUNTRY       | varchar(64)  | NO   |     | NULL    |
| ADDRESS_DOOR_NUMBER   | varchar(8)   | YES  |     | NULL    |
| ADDRESS_POSTAL_CODE   | decimal(6,0) | NO   |     | NULL    |
| ADDRESS_STATE         | varchar(64)  | YES  |     | NULL    |
| ADDRESS_STREE_NAME    | varchar(64)  | YES  |     | NULL    |
| EMP_NUMBER            | decimal(5,0) | NO   | PRI | NULL    |
+-----------------------+--------------+------+-----+---------+
7 rows in set (0.00 sec)

mysql>
```

4.5 IDENTITY ANNOTATIONS

Each entity (POJO) must have at least one column that should serve as a primary key. A table may also have a composite key (a combination of columns in a table forms a primary key).

The following section explains some annotations that are dealing with this Identity definition.

Note: The Id column in a table should be a separate field, however in our following few examples we are using EMP_NUMBER column as Id column.

4.5.1 `@Id` - Defining Identity Column

This makes the associated field(s) as identity (primary) one. The Id field(s) will act as Primary key for that table. (Note: Your Java application should take care of inserting value to this Id field in database by default. There are some Annotations including `@GeneratedValue`, which is used to auto-generate values for Id columns.)

General format

```
        @Id
```

Example

```
//File Name: Employee.java
//Illustrates @ID
package com.hdemo;

import java.io.serializable;
import java.math.BigDecimal;

import javax.persistence.Column;
import javax.persistence.Entity;
import javax.persistence.Id;
import javax.persistence.Table;

@Entity
@Table(name = "EMPLOYEE")
public class Employee implements Serializable {

   Private static final long serialVersionUID = 1L;

   @Id
   @Column(name = "EMP_NUMBER", precision = 5)
   private int empNumber;

   @Column(name = "EMP_NAME", length = 64)
   private string empName;

   @Column(name = "SALARY", precision = 10, scale = 2)
   private BigDecimal Salary;
```

```
Public int getEmpNumber () {
      return empNumber;
}

public void setEmpNumber (int empNumber) {
      this.empNumber = empNumber;
}

public string getEmpName() {
      return empName;
}

public void setEmpName (String empName) {
      this.empName = empName;
{

public BigDecimal getSalary() {
      return salary;
}

public void setSalary (BigDecimal salary) {
      this.salary = salary;
}

}
```

A sample run of the main program results as below.

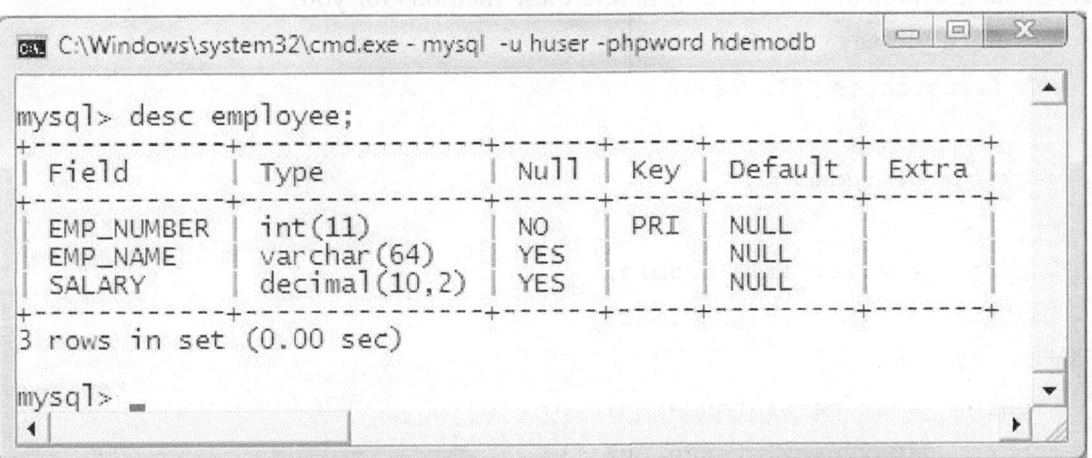

```
C:\Windows\system32\cmd.exe - mysql -u huser -phpword hdemodb

mysql> desc employee;
+------------+---------------+------+-----+---------+-------+
| Field      | Type          | Null | Key | Default | Extra |
+------------+---------------+------+-----+---------+-------+
| EMP_NUMBER | int(11)       | NO   | PRI | NULL    |       |
| EMP_NAME   | varchar(64)   | YES  |     | NULL    |       |
| SALARY     | decimal(10,2) | YES  |     | NULL    |       |
+------------+---------------+------+-----+---------+-------+
3 rows in set (0.00 sec)

mysql> _
```

4.5.2 `@IdClass` - Defining Composite Primary Key Class

A Composite Primary Key is made up of two or more fields (columns). This `@IdClass` annotation is used to specify a composite primary key class.

General format

```
@IdClass(PrimaryKeyClassName.class)
```

Use multiple `@Id` annotations in Entity class fields that you want to make them as composite key and they must be defined in the Primary Key Class which is defined through `@IdClass` annotation.

You should obey the following rules while defining Primary Key class.

- The Primary key class should be a POJO class, which implements *Serializable* interface.
- The fields (if we are using Annotations on field level, just above field declaration) or properties (if we are using Annotations on property –getter/setter level, just above *getter* method) of Primary Key class must correspond to the fields / properties of entity class (the entity POJO which refers this Primary key class through `@IdClass` annotation) that those fields / properties are declared as Identity columns using `@Id` annotation.
- The Primary key class must define `equals` and `hashCode` methods.

Every object has access to `equals` (`public boolean equals(Object obj)`and `hashCode public int hashCode()`) methods because they are inherited from *Object* class. All class (including user-defined ones) implicitly inherits *Object* class. These methods are used to check whether two objects are same or not. The `hashCode` method returns the hash code (number used in hash-based search techniques) value for the object on which this `hashCode` method is invoked. The `equals` method checks for equality of the object on which this method is invoked and the object that is passed as parameter to this `equals` method.

Instead of spending time and thinking logic in writing these *equals()* and *hashCode()* methods, you can just use IDE's features. In Eclipse, put cursor in any place with in the class, for that you want to write *equals()* and *hashCode()* method (assumed that the class contains required getters/ setters), then select *Source* menu-item from Main menu-bar, and select "*Generate hashCode() and equals()*" sub-menu-item, which will generate these methods for you.

```
// File Name: Employee.java
// Illustrates @IdClass

package com.hdemo;

import java.io.Serializable;
import java.math.BigDecimal;

import javax.persistence.Column;
import javax.persistence.Entity;
```

```
import javax.persistence.Id;
import javax.persistence.IdClass;
import javax.persistence.Table;

class EmployeePrimaryKey implements Serializable {

  @Column(name = "EMP_FIRST_NAME", length = 64)
  private String empFirstName;

  @Column(name = "EMP_LAST_NAME", length = 64)
  private String empLastName;

  public String getEmpFirstName() {
        return empFirstName;
  }

  public void setEmpFirstName(String empFirstName) {
        this.empFirstName = empFirstName;
  }

  public String getEmpLastName() {
        return empLastName;
  }

  public void setEmpLastName(String empLastName) {
        this.empLastName = empLastName;
  }

  @Override
  public int hashCode() {
        final int prime = 31;
        int result = 1;
        result = prime * result + ((empFirstName == null) ? 0 :
                                        empFirstName.hashCode());
        result = prime * result + ((empLastName == null) ? 0 :
```

```
                                                empLastName.hashCode());
        return result;
    }

    @Override
    public boolean equals(Object obj) {
        if (this == obj)
            return true;
        if (obj == null)
            return false;
        if (getClass() != obj.getClass())
            return false;
        EmployeePrimaryKey other = (EmployeePrimaryKey) obj;
        if (empFirstName == null) {
            if (other.empFirstName != null)
                return false;
        } else if (!empFirstName.equals(other.empFirstName))
            return false;
        if (empLastName == null) {
            if (other.empLastName != null)
                return false;
        } else if (!empLastName.equals(other.empLastName))
            return false;
        return true;
    }
}

@IdClass(EmployeePrimaryKey.class)
@Entity
@Table(name = "EMPLOYEE")
public class Employee implements Serializable {

    private static final long serialVersionUID = 1L;

    @Id
```

```
    private String empFirstName;

    @Id
    private String empLastName;

    @Column(name = "SALARY", precision = 10, scale = 2)
    private BigDecimal salary;

    public String getEmpFirstName() {
        return empFirstName;
    }

    public void setEmpFirstName(String empFirstName) {
        this.empFirstName = empFirstName;
    }

    public String getEmpLastName() {
        return empLastName;
    }

    public void setEmpLastName(String empLastName) {
        this.empLastName = empLastName;
    }

    public BigDecimal getSalary() {
        return salary;
    }

    public void setSalary(BigDecimal salary) {
        this.salary = salary;
    }
}
```

A sample run results as below.

```
C:\Windows\system32\cmd.exe - mysql -u huser -phpword hdemodb

mysql> desc employee;
+-----------------+---------------+------+-----+---------+-------+
| Field           | Type          | Null | Key | Default | Extra |
+-----------------+---------------+------+-----+---------+-------+
| EMP_FIRST_NAME  | varchar(64)   | NO   | PRI | NULL    |       |
| EMP_LAST_NAME   | varchar(64)   | NO   | PRI | NULL    |       |
| SALARY          | decimal(10,2) | YES  |     | NULL    |       |
+-----------------+---------------+------+-----+---------+-------+
3 rows in set (0.00 sec)

mysql> insert into employee (emp_first_name, emp_last_name, salary)
    -> values ('mohamed', 'ibrahim', 90000.00);
Query OK, 1 row affected (0.05 sec)

mysql> insert into employee (emp_first_name, emp_last_name, salary)
    -> values ('mohamed', 'rafi', 95000.00);
Query OK, 1 row affected (0.03 sec)

mysql> insert into employee (emp_first_name, emp_last_name, salary)
    -> values ('ahamed', 'ibrahim', 85000.00);
Query OK, 1 row affected (0.03 sec)

mysql> select * from employee;
+-----------------+---------------+----------+
| EMP_FIRST_NAME  | EMP_LAST_NAME | SALARY   |
+-----------------+---------------+----------+
| ahamed          | ibrahim       | 85000.00 |
| mohamed         | ibrahim       | 90000.00 |
| mohamed         | rafi          | 95000.00 |
+-----------------+---------------+----------+
3 rows in set (0.00 sec)

mysql> insert into employee (emp_first_name, emp_last_name, salary)
    -> values ('mohamed', 'ibrahim', 75000.00);
ERROR 1062 (23000): Duplicate entry 'mohamed-ibrahim' for key 1
mysql> insert into employee (emp_first_name, emp_last_name, salary)
    -> values ('ahamed', 'ibrahim', 85000.00);
ERROR 1062 (23000): Duplicate entry 'ahamed-ibrahim' for key 1
mysql>
mysql> insert into employee (emp_first_name, emp_last_name, salary)
    -> values ('mohamed', 'safi', 98000.00);
Query OK, 1 row affected (0.08 sec)

mysql> select * from employee;
+-----------------+---------------+----------+
| EMP_FIRST_NAME  | EMP_LAST_NAME | SALARY   |
+-----------------+---------------+----------+
| ahamed          | ibrahim       | 85000.00 |
| mohamed         | ibrahim       | 90000.00 |
| mohamed         | rafi          | 95000.00 |
| mohamed         | safi          | 98000.00 |
+-----------------+---------------+----------+
4 rows in set (0.00 sec)

mysql>
```

Note that when we try to insert the already existing *first name-lastname* pair, duplication error is raised. Check is made based on both *firstname* and *lastname* fields.

4.5.3 @EmbeddedId, @Embeddable - EMBEDDING @Embeddable PRIMARY KEY CLASS

The annotation `@EmbeddedId` is used to specify embeddable primary key class (which is defined as `@Embeddable`) to an Entity class.

General format

`@Embeddable`

It makes a Primary Key class as embeddable to entity/entities.

`@EmbeddedId`

Use this annotation at field level in Entity class for Primary Key class instance. This makes that Primary Key class embedded (fixed) with the entity.

The example used in explaining `@IdClass` can be written as follows using `@Embeddable` (Making a POJO as embeddable to some other POJO), and `@EmbeddedId` (Embedding an embeddable POJO).

```
// File Name: Employee.java
// Illustrates @Embeddable, @EmbeddedId

package com.hdemo;

import java.io.Serializable;
import java.math.BigDecimal;

import javax.persistence.Column;
import javax.persistence.Embeddable;
import javax.persistence.EmbeddedId;
import javax.persistence.Entity;
import javax.persistence.Id;
import javax.persistence.Table;

@Embeddable
class EmployeePrimaryKey implements Serializable {

  private static final long serialVersionUID = 1L;

  @Column(name = "EMP_FIRST_NAME", length = 64)
  private String empFirstName;
```

```
    @Column(name = "EMP_LAST_NAME", length = 64)
    private String empLastName;

    public String getEmpFirstName() {
        return empFirstName;
    }

    public void setEmpFirstName(String empFirstName) {
        this.empFirstName = empFirstName;
    }

    public String getEmpLastName() {
        return empLastName;
    }

    public void setEmpLastName(String empLastName) {
        this.empLastName = empLastName;
    }

    @Override
    public int hashCode() {
        final int prime = 31;
        int result = 1;
        result = prime * result + ((empFirstName == null) ? 0 :
        empFirstName.hashCode());
        result = prime * result + ((empLastName == null) ? 0 :
        empLastName.hashCode());
        return result;
    }

    @Override
    public boolean equals(Object obj) {
        if (this == obj)
            return true;
```

```
        if (obj == null)
            return false;
        if (getClass() != obj.getClass())
            return false;
        EmployeePrimaryKey other = (EmployeePrimaryKey) obj;
        if (empFirstName == null) {
            if (other.empFirstName != null)
                return false;
        } else if (!empFirstName.equals(other.empFirstName))
            return false;
        if (empLastName == null) {
            if (other.empLastName != null)
                return false;
        } else if (!empLastName.equals(other.empLastName))
            return false;
        return true;
    }
}

@Entity
@Table(name = "EMPLOYEE")
public class Employee implements Serializable {

  private static final long serialVersionUID = 1L;

  @EmbeddedId
  EmployeePrimaryKey employeePrimaryKey;

  @Id
  @Column(name = "EMP_FIRST_NAME", length = 64)
  private String empFirstName;

  @Id
  @Column(name = "EMP_LAST_NAME", length = 64)
  private String empLastName;

  @Column(name = "SALARY", precision = 10, scale = 2)
```

```
    private BigDecimal salary;

    public String getEmpFirstName() {
          return empFirstName;
    }

    public void setEmpFirstName(String empFirstName) {
          this.empFirstName = empFirstName;
    }

    public String getEmpLastName() {
          return empLastName;
    }

    public void setEmpLastName(String empLastName) {
          this.empLastName = empLastName;
    }

    public BigDecimal getSalary() {
          return salary;
    }

    public void setSalary(BigDecimal salary) {
          this.salary = salary;
    }

    public EmployeePrimaryKey getEmployeePrimaryKey() {
          return employeePrimaryKey;
    }
    public void setEmployeePrimaryKey(EmployeePrimaryKey employeePrimary
Key) {
          this.employeePrimaryKey = employeePrimaryKey;
    }

  }
```

A sample run results as below.

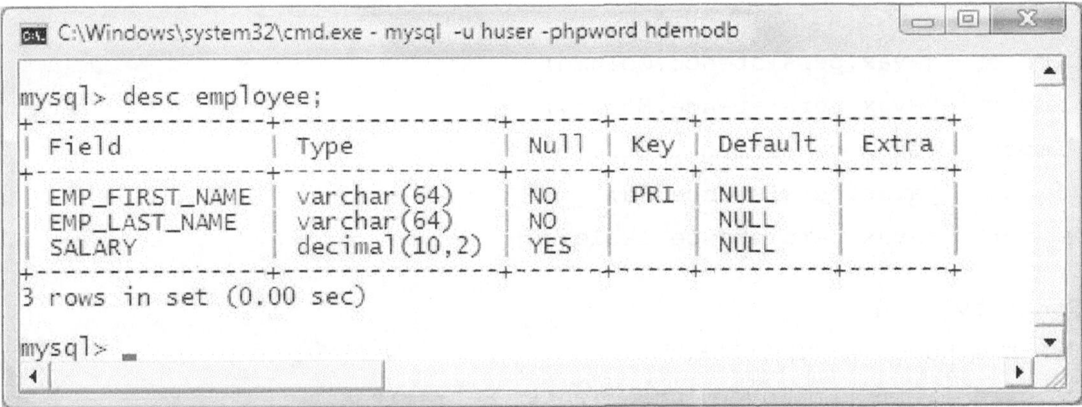
```
C:\Windows\system32\cmd.exe - mysql -u huser -phpword hdemodb

mysql> desc employee;
+----------------+---------------+------+-----+---------+-------+
| Field          | Type          | Null | Key | Default | Extra |
+----------------+---------------+------+-----+---------+-------+
| EMP_FIRST_NAME | varchar(64)   | NO   | PRI | NULL    |       |
| EMP_LAST_NAME  | varchar(64)   | NO   |     | NULL    |       |
| SALARY         | decimal(10,2) | YES  |     | NULL    |       |
+----------------+---------------+------+-----+---------+-------+
3 rows in set (0.00 sec)

mysql> _
```

4.6 @GeneratedValue - GENERATING VALUES FOR IDENTITY COLUMN

It is used to generate values for `@Id` columns in database tables.

General format

```
@GeneratedValue  (strategy  =  key_generator,
                   generator  =  name_of_generator_in_database)
```

The `strategy` attribute represents what type of generator class that you want to use for *id* generation. Some of the built-in generator types are:

`GenerationType.IDENTITY`	Uses database identity column (Identity key generation feature of database)
`GenerationType.SEQUENCE`	Uses the specified Sequence (database sequence) for key generation.
`GenerationType.TABLE`	Uses an existing database table holding the id value(s).
`GenerationType.AUTO`	Chooses a key generator (either `IDENTITY`, or `SEQUENCE`, or `TABLE`) that is more appropriate to the associated database.This is default, if no generator type is specified.

The `generator` attribute represents the name given to the key generator that is specified in `strategy`, which will be used to refer this with another annotation.

```
package  com.hdemo;
//  File  Name:  Employee.java
//  Illustrates  @GeneratedValue
```

```
import  java.io.Serializable;
import  java.math.BigDecimal;

import  javax.persistence.Column;
import  javax.persistence.Entity;
import  javax.persistence.GeneratedValue;
import  javax.persistence.Id;
import  javax.persistence.Table;

@Entity
@Table(name  =  "EMPLOYEE")
public  class  Employee  implements  Serializable  {

  private  static  final  long  serialVersionUID  =  1L;
  @Id
  @GeneratedValue
   @Column(name  =  "EMP_NUMBER")
   private  int  empNumber;

   @Column(name  =  "EMP_NAME",  nullable  =  false,  length  =  64)
   private  String  empName;

   @Column(name  =  "SALARY",  nullable = false, precision = 9,  scale  =  2)
   private  BigDecimal  salary;

  public  int  getEmpNumber()  {
      return  empNumber;
  }

  public  void  setEmpNumber(int  empNumber)  {
      this.empNumber  =  empNumber;
   }

   public  String  getEmpName()  {
       return  empName;
   }

   public  void  setEmpName(String  empName)  {
```

```
            this.empName = empName;
        }

      public BigDecimal getSalary() {
           return salary;
      }

      public void setSalary(BigDecimal salary) {
           this.salary = salary;
      }

    }
```

A sample run results as below. Observe how values *(ids)* are generated for `EMP_NUMBER` column.

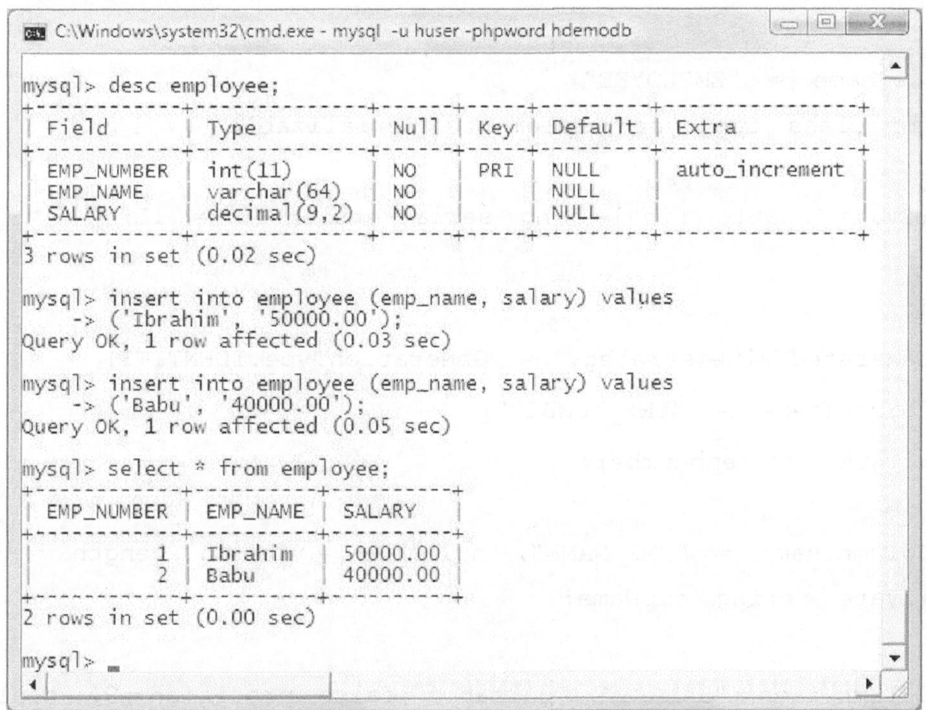

```
C:\Windows\system32\cmd.exe - mysql -u huser -phpword hdemodb

mysql> desc employee;
+------------+--------------+------+-----+---------+----------------+
| Field      | Type         | Null | Key | Default | Extra          |
+------------+--------------+------+-----+---------+----------------+
| EMP_NUMBER | int(11)      | NO   | PRI | NULL    | auto_increment |
| EMP_NAME   | varchar(64)  | NO   |     | NULL    |                |
| SALARY     | decimal(9,2) | NO   |     | NULL    |                |
+------------+--------------+------+-----+---------+----------------+
3 rows in set (0.02 sec)

mysql> insert into employee (emp_name, salary) values
    -> ('Ibrahim', '50000.00');
Query OK, 1 row affected (0.03 sec)

mysql> insert into employee (emp_name, salary) values
    -> ('Babu', '40000.00');
Query OK, 1 row affected (0.05 sec)

mysql> select * from employee;
+------------+----------+----------+
| EMP_NUMBER | EMP_NAME | SALARY   |
+------------+----------+----------+
|          1 | Ibrahim  | 50000.00 |
|          2 | Babu     | 40000.00 |
+------------+----------+----------+
2 rows in set (0.00 sec)

mysql> _
```

There will be no difference if you modify the above entity by specifying `GenerationType.`*`IDENTITY`* as value to *strategy* attribute of `@GeneratedValue`, which is chosen as default by `GenerationType.AUTO`

```
    // File Name: Employee.java
    // Illustrates @GeneratedValue(strategy = GenerationType.IDENTITY)
```

```
package com.hdemo;

import java.io.Serializable;
import java.math.BigDecimal;

import javax.persistence.Column;
import javax.persistence.Entity;
import javax.persistence.GeneratedValue;
import javax.persistence.GenerationType;
import javax.persistence.Id;
import javax.persistence.Table;

@Entity
@Table(name = "EMPLOYEE")
public class Employee implements Serializable {

  private static final long serialVersionUID = 1L;

  @Id
  @GeneratedValue(strategy = GenerationType.IDENTITY)
  @Column(name = "EMP_NUMBER")
  private int empNumber;

  @Column(name = "EMP_NAME", nullable = false, length = 64)
  private String empName;

  @Column(name="SALARY", nullable=false, precision=9, scale=2)
  private BigDecimal salary;

  //Getter and setter methods

}
```

You can find the same table structure.

```
C:\Windows\system32\cmd.exe - mysql -u huser -phpword hdemodb

mysql> desc employee;
+------------+--------------+------+-----+---------+----------------+
| Field      | Type         | Null | Key | Default | Extra          |
+------------+--------------+------+-----+---------+----------------+
| EMP_NUMBER | int(11)      | NO   | PRI | NULL    | auto_increment |
| EMP_NAME   | varchar(64)  | NO   |     | NULL    |                |
| SALARY     | decimal(9,2) | NO   |     | NULL    |                |
+------------+--------------+------+-----+---------+----------------+
3 rows in set (0.00 sec)
```

A bit about Sequences in MySQL: Sequences are often used to generate a unique series of numbers, which are used for identity columns across tables. They are also independent of any table. The sequences are supported by many available RDBMS software products. This direct sequence is not yet implemented in MySQL, however MySQL does this using *auto_increment*, but its limitation is that it depends on the corresponding table for which it had defined; you will get an error if you use `GenerationType.SEQUENCE` strategy with MySQL database dialect.

Sequence Id Generation Demo: Since MySQL does not support direct Sequence, we will use Oracle for the following Sequence Id generation example. Note that we are using MySQL for all other programs unless specified.

The content of *hibernate.cfg.xml* file will be,

```
<!– File Name: hibernate.cfg.xml –>

<?xml version='1.0' encoding='utf-8'?>
<!DOCTYPE hibernate-configuration PUBLIC
  "-//Hibernate/Hibernate Configuration DTD 3.0//EN"
  "http://hibernate.sourceforge.net/hibernate-configuration-3.0.dtd">
<hibernate-configuration>
  <session-factory>
        <property name="connection.driver_class">oracle.jdbc.driver.
                                              OracleDriver</property>
        <property name="connection.url">jdbc:oracle:thin:@localhost:
                                              1521:HDEMODB</property>
        <property name="connection.username">huser</property>
        <property name="connection.password">hpword</property>
        <property name="connection.pool_size">1</property>
        <property name="dialect">org.hibernate. dialect.OracleDialect
                                                          </property>
```

```
        <property name="current_session_context_ class">thread</
                                                    property>
        <property name="cache.provider_class">org. hibernate.cache.
                                         NoCacheProvider</property>
        <property name="show_sql">true</property>
        <property name="hbm2ddl.auto">create</property>
        <mapping class="com.hdemo.Employee" />
    </session-factory>
</hibernate-configuration>
```

Change the database setting such as `connection_url`, `database_username`, `database_password` according to your Oracle properties.

```
// File Name: Employee.java
// Illustrates @SequenceGenerator

package com.hdemo;

import java.io.Serializable;
import java.math.BigDecimal;

import javax.persistence.Column;
import javax.persistence.Entity;
import javax.persistence.GeneratedValue;
import javax.persistence.GenerationType;
import javax.persistence.Id;
import javax.persistence.SequenceGenerator;
import javax.persistence.Table;

@Entity
@Table(name = "EMPLOYEE")
public class Employee implements Serializable {

 private static final long serialVersionUID = 1L;

  @Id
   @SequenceGenerator(name = "ENO_SEQ", sequenceName =
"EMP_NUMBER_SEQ", initialValue = 1, allocationSize = 1)
   @GeneratedValue(strategy = GenerationType.SEQUENCE, generator =
"ENO_SEQ")
```

```
    @Column(name = "EMP_NUMBER")
    private int empNumber;

    @Column(name = "EMP_NAME", nullable = false, length = 64)
    private String empName;

    @Column(name = "SALARY", nullable = false, precision = 9, scale
    = 2)
    private BigDecimal salary;
    //Getter and Setter methods

}
```

```
// File Name: EmployeeManipulation.java
// Main Program

package com.hdemo;

import java.math.BigDecimal;

import org.hibernate.Session;
import org.hibernate.SessionFactory;
import org.hibernate.Transaction;

public class EmployeeManipulation {

    public static void main(String[] args) throws Exception {
    SessionFactory sessionFactory = HibernateUtil.getSessionFactory();
            Session session = sessionFactory.getCurrentSession();

        Transaction txn = session.beginTransaction();
        Employee employee1 = new Employee();
        Employee employee2 = new Employee();
        Employee employee3 = new Employee();

            employee1.setEmpName("Ibrahim");
            employee1.setSalary(new BigDecimal (92000.00));
            session.save(employee1);
```

```
            employee2.setEmpName("Karan");
            employee2.setSalary(new  BigDecimal  (96000.00));
            session.save(employee2);

            employee3.setEmpName("Ajay");
            employee3.setSalary(new  BigDecimal  (83000.00));
            session.save(employee3);

        txn.commit();

        sessionFactory.close();
    }

}
```

A sample run makes changes in database as below.

```
select  *  from  EMPLOYEE
     EMP_NUMBER                    EMP_NAME          SALARY
         1                         Ibrahim           92000
         2                         Karan             96000
         3                         Ajay              83000
  3  record(s)  selected  [Fetch  MetaData:  0/ms]  [Fetch  Data:  0/ms]
```

Observe that the sequence named "MP_NUMBER_SEQ" is created in underlying Oracle database.

4.7 @TableGenerator - GENERATING ID VALUES FROM A DATABASE TABLE

Set back to MySQL dialect, if you changed *hibernate.cfg.xml* file for the above sequence generation example.

This @TableGenerator uses one database table for generating Identity values. This annotation creates a table with key-value pair, from which the keys (identity values) are generated.

General format

```
@TableGenerator
        (name = "name of TableGenerator, used in @GeneratedValue",
         table = "name that is given to key generating table",
         pkColumnName = "key name; key column name",
```

```
        valueColumnName = "value name; value column name",
        pkColumnValue="primary key value; data of pkColumnName",
        allocationSize = "increment size for a new thread; next
        time"
    )
```

All attributes except name are optional.

```
// File Name: Employee.java
// Illustrates @TableGenerator

package com.hdemo;

import java.io.Serializable;
import java.math.BigDecimal;

import javax.persistence.Column;
import javax.persistence.Entity;
import javax.persistence.GeneratedValue;
import javax.persistence.GenerationType;
import javax.persistence.Id;
import javax.persistence.Table;
import javax.persistence.TableGenerator;

@Entity
@Table(name = "EMPLOYEE")
public class Employee implements Serializable {
  private static final long serialVersionUID = 1L;

  @Id
  @TableGenerator(name = "ENO_TABLE_GENERATOR",
                  table = "ENO_GENERATOR_TABLE",
                  pkColumnName = "NAME",
                  valueColumnName = "VALUE",
                  pkColumnValue = "EMP_TABLE_ID",
                  allocationSize = 1)
  @GeneratedValue(strategy = GenerationType.TABLE, generator =
"ENO_TABLE_GENERATOR")
  @Column(name = "EMP_NUMBER")
```

```
    private int empNumber;

    @Column(name = "EMP_NAME", nullable = false, length = 64)
    private String empName;

   @Column(name = "SALARY", nullable = false, precision = 9, scale = 2)
    private BigDecimal salary;
    //Getter and setter methods

}
```

```
// File Name: EmployeeManipulation.java
// Main Program

package com.hdemo;

import java.math.BigDecimal;

import org.hibernate.Session;
import org.hibernate.SessionFactory;
import org.hibernate.Transaction;

public class EmployeeManipulation {

public static void main(String[] args) throws Exception {
SessionFactory sessionFactory = HibernateUtil.getSessionFactory();
      Session session = sessionFactory.getCurrentSession();

      Transaction txn = session.beginTransaction();
      Employee employee1 = new Employee();
      Employee employee2 = new Employee();
      Employee employee3 = new Employee();

         employee1.setEmpName("Ibrahim");
         employee1.setSalary(new BigDecimal (92000.00));
         session.save(employee1);

         employee2.setEmpName("Karan");
         employee2.setSalary(new BigDecimal (96000.00));
         session.save(employee2);
```

```
            employee3.setEmpName("Ajay");
            employee3.setSalary(new  BigDecimal  (83000.00));
            session.save(employee3);

            txn.commit();

            sessionFactory.close();
      }
   }
```

Assumed that `hbm2ddl.auto` property in *hibernate.cfg.xml* is set to `create`, for this example. A sample run results as below.

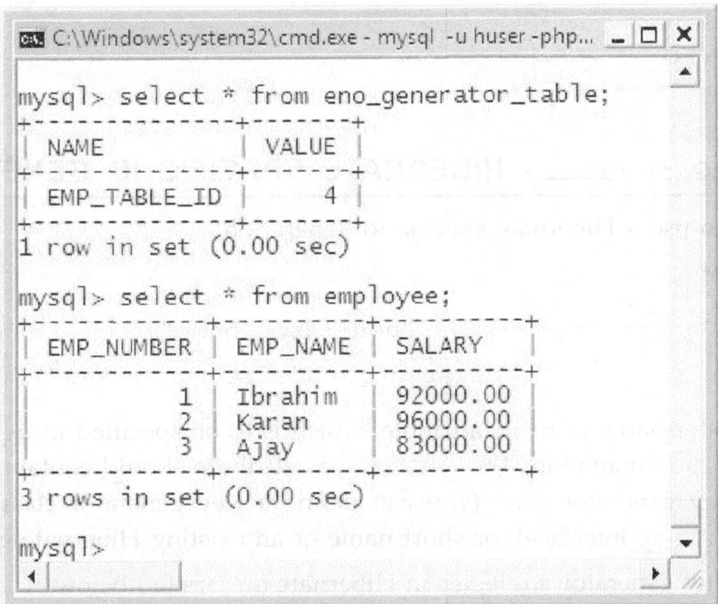

```
C:\Windows\system32\cmd.exe - mysql -u huser -php...
mysql> select * from eno_generator_table;
+--------------+-------+
| NAME         | VALUE |
+--------------+-------+
| EMP_TABLE_ID |     4 |
+--------------+-------+
1 row in set (0.00 sec)

mysql> select * from employee;
+------------+----------+----------+
| EMP_NUMBER | EMP_NAME | SALARY   |
+------------+----------+----------+
|          1 | Ibrahim  | 92000.00 |
|          2 | Karan    | 96000.00 |
|          3 | Ajay     | 83000.00 |
+------------+----------+----------+
3 rows in set (0.00 sec)

mysql>
```

Note that new table named `"ENO_GENERATOR_TABLE"` (`name="ENO_TABLE_ GENERATOR"` in `@TableGenerator`) is created with two fields namely `"NAME"` (`pkColumnName="NAME"`) and `"VALUE"` (`valueColumnName="VALUE"`) and one row with values `EMP_TABLE_ID` (`pkColumnValue="EMP_TABLE_ID"`) and `4` (This indicates the next value that is to be generated).

Just change *hbm2ddl.auto* property in *hibernate.cfg.xml* file into *update* (`<property name="hbm2ddl.auto">update</property>`) and save it. Now, run the same *EmployeeManipulation.java* and then check with database data. You can observe that how keys are generated for *emp_number* column of *employee* table.

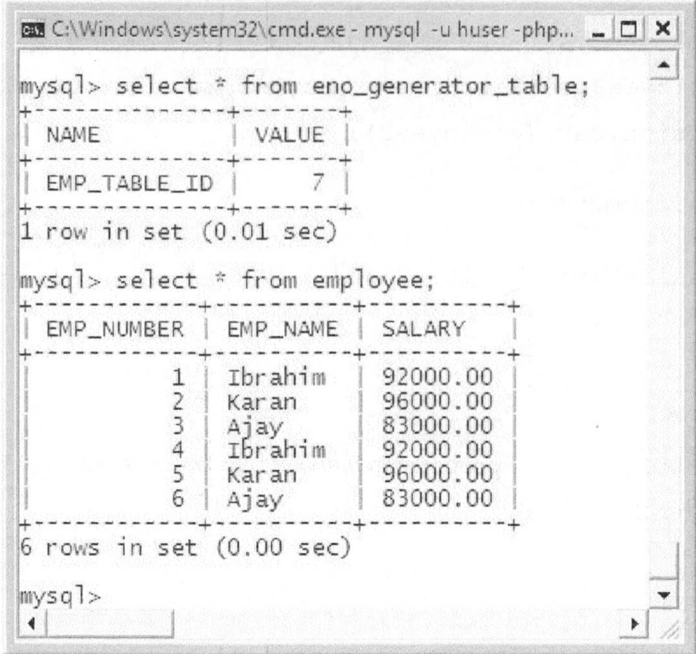
```
mysql> select * from eno_generator_table;
+--------------+-------+
| NAME         | VALUE |
+--------------+-------+
| EMP_TABLE_ID |     7 |
+--------------+-------+
1 row in set (0.01 sec)

mysql> select * from employee;
+------------+----------+----------+
| EMP_NUMBER | EMP_NAME | SALARY   |
+------------+----------+----------+
|          1 | Ibrahim  | 92000.00 |
|          2 | Karan    | 96000.00 |
|          3 | Ajay     | 83000.00 |
|          4 | Ibrahim  | 92000.00 |
|          5 | Karan    | 96000.00 |
|          6 | Ajay     | 83000.00 |
+------------+----------+----------+
6 rows in set (0.00 sec)

mysql>
```

4.8 @GenericGenerator - HIBERNATE SPECIFIC ID GENERATION

This is used to use a Hibernate specific Id generation.

General format

```
@GenericGenerator(name = "generator_name",
                  strategy = "strategy_class")
```

Specify generator-name in `name` attribute, which is to be specified in `generator` attribute of `@GeneratedValue` annotation. The `strategy` attribute should contain the fully qualified class name of a key generator class (you can define a Key generator class by implementing `IdentifierGenerator` interface), or short name of an existing Hibernate generator strategy.

Some of existing generator strategies in Hibernate are briefed below.

4.8.1 uuid - Universal Unique Identifier

A UUID (Universal Unique Identifier) is a 128-bit number used to uniquely identify an entity on the Internet. This *uuid* strategy uses this UUID technique to generate Ids and encode them in to 32 character length hexadecimal strings.

```
// File Name: Employee.java
// Illustrates 'uuid' Id generation


package com.hdemo;
```

```
import java.io.Serializable;
import java.math.BigDecimal;

import javax.persistence.Column;
import javax.persistence.Entity;
import javax.persistence.GeneratedValue;
import javax.persistence.Id;
import javax.persistence.Table;

import org.hibernate.annotations.GenericGenerator;

@Entity
@Table(name = "EMPLOYEE")
public class Employee implements Serializable {

  private static final long serialVersionUID = 1L;

  @Id
  @GeneratedValue(generator = "ENO_GEN_GENERATOR")
  @GenericGenerator(name = "ENO_GEN_GENERATOR", strategy = "uuid")
  @Column(name = "EMP_NUMBER")
  private String empNumber;

  @Column(name = "EMP_NAME", nullable = false, length = 64)
  private String empName;

 @Column(name = "SALARY", nullable = false, precision = 9, scale = 2)
  private BigDecimal salary;
  //Setter and Getter methods

}
```

A sample run of the main program results as below.

```
C:\Windows\system32\cmd.exe - mysql -u huser -phpword hdemodb

mysql> select * from employee;
+----------------------------------+----------+----------+
| EMP_NUMBER                       | EMP_NAME | SALARY   |
+----------------------------------+----------+----------+
| 402881f81b544a89011b544a8bd20001 | Ibrahim  | 92000.00 |
| 402881f81b544a89011b544a8bde0002 | Karan    | 96000.00 |
| 402881f81b544a89011b544a8bde0003 | Ajay     | 83000.00 |
+----------------------------------+----------+----------+
3 rows in set (0.00 sec)

mysql>
```

4.8.2 `guid` - Global Unique Identifier

This strategy can be used with GUID supported databases such as MySQL and MS SQL Server, which uses a database-generated GUID (**G**lobal **U**nique **ID**entifier) string for Id generation.

You can generate one UUID by using "`select uuid()`" command in MySQL.

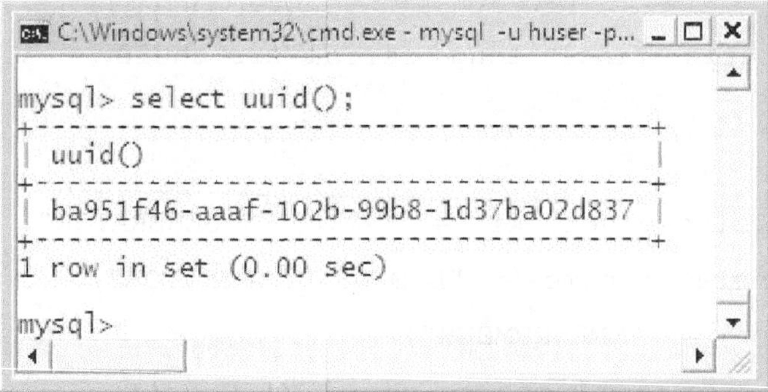


```
// File Name: Employee.java
// Illustrates 'guid' Id generation

package com.hdemo;

import java.io.Serializable;
import java.math.BigDecimal;

import javax.persistence.Column;
import javax.persistence.Entity;
import javax.persistence.GeneratedValue;
import javax.persistence.Id;
import javax.persistence.Table;
```

```
import org.hibernate.annotations.GenericGenerator;
@Entity
@Table(name = "EMPLOYEE")
public class Employee implements Serializable {

 private static final long serialVersionUID = 1L;

 @Id
  @GeneratedValue(generator = "ENO_GEN_GENERATOR")
  @GenericGenerator(name = "ENO_GEN_GENERATOR", strategy = "guid")
  @Column(name = "EMP_NUMBER")
  private String empNumber;

  @Column(name = "EMP_NAME", nullable = false, length = 64)
  private String empName;

 @Column(name="SALARY", nullable =false, precision = 9, scale = 2)
  private BigDecimal salary;
  //Setter and Getter methods

}
```

A sample run results as below.

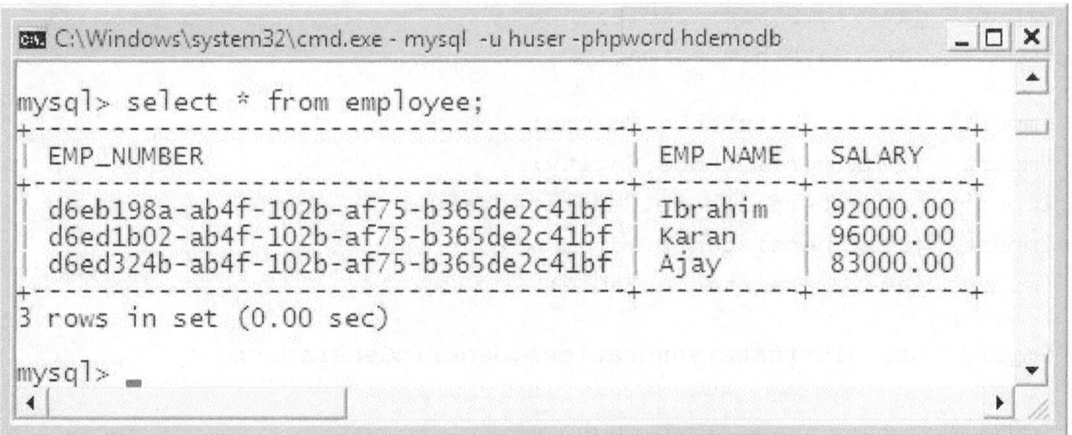

```
C:\Windows\system32\cmd.exe - mysql -u huser -phpword hdemodb

mysql> select * from employee;
+--------------------------------------+----------+----------+
| EMP_NUMBER                           | EMP_NAME | SALARY   |
+--------------------------------------+----------+----------+
| d6eb198a-ab4f-102b-af75-b365de2c41bf | Ibrahim  | 92000.00 |
| d6ed1b02-ab4f-102b-af75-b365de2c41bf | Karan    | 96000.00 |
| d6ed324b-ab4f-102b-af75-b365de2c41bf | Ajay     | 83000.00 |
+--------------------------------------+----------+----------+
3 rows in set (0.00 sec)

mysql> _
```

4.8.3 `hilo` - Using hi/lo Algorithm for Id generation

It uses *hi/lo* algorithm to generate integer type of unique identifiers, however the identifiers are unique only for a particular database. It requires a special database table to hold the next available "*hi*" value (like in `@TableGenerator`). The `seqhilo` strategy also uses *hi/lo* algorithm for generating ids, however it uses sequence (direct sequence like the one available in Oracle) instead of special database table, if sequence feature is supported by the underlying database.

Examples

Using *hilo* strategy:

```
@Id
   @GeneratedValue(generator = "ENO_GEN_GENERATOR")
   @GenericGenerator(name = "ENO_GEN_GENERATOR", strategy = "hilo")
   @Column(name = "EMP_NUMBER")
   private int empNumber;
```

Using *seqhilo* strategy:

```
@Id
   @GeneratedValue(generator = "ENO_GEN_GENERATOR")
   @GenericGenerator(name = "ENO_GEN_GENERATOR", strategy = "seqhilo")
   @Column(name = "EMP_NUMBER")
   private int empNumber;
```

Example:

```
// File Name: Employee.java
// Illustrates 'assigned' strategy

package com.hdemo;

import java.io.Serializable;
import java.math.BigDecimal;

import javax.persistence.Column;
import javax.persistence.Entity;
import javax.persistence.GeneratedValue;
import javax.persistence.Id;
import javax.persistence.Table;

import org.hibernate.annotations.GenericGenerator;

@Entity
@Table(name = "EMPLOYEE")
public class Employee implements Serializable {

  private static final long serialVersionUID = 1L;
```

```
    @Id
    @GeneratedValue(generator = "ENO_GEN_GENERATOR")
    @GenericGenerator(name = "ENO_GEN_GENERATOR", strategy = "assigned")
    @Column(name = "EMP_NUMBER")
    private int empNumber;

    @Column(name = "EMP_NAME", nullable = false, length = 64)
    private String empName;

    @Column(name = "SALARY", nullable = false, precision = 9, scale = 2)
    private BigDecimal salary;

    //Getter and Setter methods

}
```

```
// File Name: EmployeeManipulation.java
// Main Program

package com.hdemo;

import java.math.BigDecimal;

import org.hibernate.Session;
import org.hibernate.SessionFactory;
import org.hibernate.Transaction;

public class EmployeeManipulation {

    public static void main(String[] args) throws Exception {
    SessionFactory sessionFactory = HibernateUtil.getSessionFactory();
        Session session = sessionFactory.getCurrentSession();

      Transaction txn = session.beginTransaction();
      Employee employee1 = new Employee();
      Employee employee2 = new Employee();
        Employee employee3 = new Employee();

        employee1.setEmpNumber(5001);
```

```
        employee1.setEmpName("Ibrahim");
        employee1.setSalary(new  BigDecimal(92000.00));
        session.save(employee1);

      employee2.setEmpNumber(5002);
        employee2.setEmpName("Karan");
        employee2.setSalary(new  BigDecimal(96000.00));
        session.save(employee2);

      employee3.setEmpNumber(5003);
        employee3.setEmpName("Ajay");
        employee3.setSalary(new  BigDecimal(83000.00));
        session.save(employee3);
        txn.commit();

      sessionFactory.close();
  }

}
```

A sample run results as below.

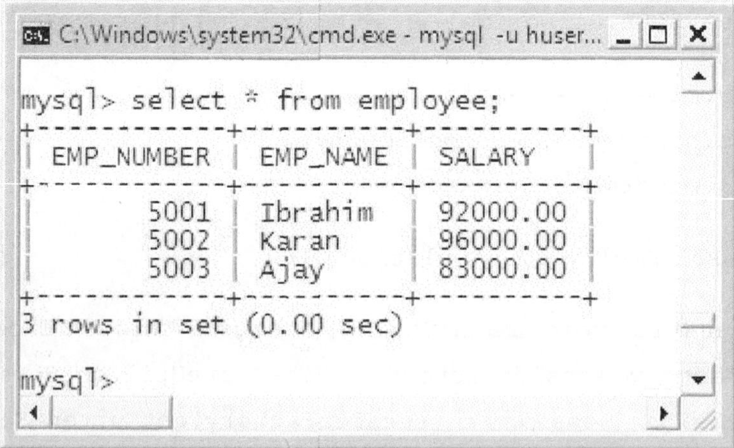

Note: It is not mandatory to give series of numbers for `@Id` field. You are also allowed to specify any number, but unique to table. However, it is good practice to use series of numbers.

Keeping the same `Employee` Entity, just change the `emp_number` field's values to 5000, 6000, and 7000 for the three employees' results as shown below.

```
// File Name: EmployeeManipulation.java
// Main program
```

```
package com.hdemo;

import java.math.BigDecimal;

import org.hibernate.Session;
import org.hibernate.SessionFactory;
import org.hibernate.Transaction;

public class EmployeeManipulation {

  public static void main(String[] args) throws Exception {
  SessionFactory sessionFactory = HibernateUtil.getSessionFactory();
      Session session = sessionFactory.getCurrentSession();
    Transaction txn = session.beginTransaction();
      Employee employee1 = new Employee();
      Employee employee2 = new Employee();
      Employee employee3 = new Employee();

      employee1.setEmpNumber(5000);
      employee1.setEmpName("Ibrahim");
      employee1.setSalary(new BigDecimal (92000.00));
      session.save(employee1);

    employee2.setEmpNumber(6000);
      employee2.setEmpName("Karan");
      employee2.setSalary(new BigDecimal(96000.00));
      session.save(employee2);

    employee3.setEmpNumber(7000);
      employee3.setEmpName("Ajay");
      employee3.setSalary(new BigDecimal(83000.00));
      session.save(employee3);
      txn.commit();
```

```
        sessionFactory.close();
    }

}
```

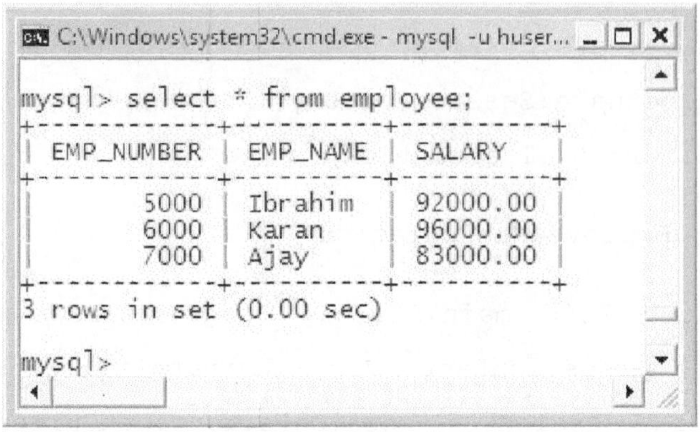

```
C:\Windows\system32\cmd.exe - mysql -u huser...

mysql> select * from employee;
+------------+----------+----------+
| EMP_NUMBER | EMP_NAME | SALARY   |
+------------+----------+----------+
|       5000 | Ibrahim  | 92000.00 |
|       6000 | Karan    | 96000.00 |
|       7000 | Ajay     | 83000.00 |
+------------+----------+----------+
3 rows in set (0.00 sec)

mysql>
```

The strategy "assigned" is the default one if no @GeneratedValue is used. A sample Entity looks below (the application should take care of assigning Id values for emp_number).

```
// File Name: Employee.java
// Illustrates assignment of values to @Id column

package com.hdemo;

import java.io.Serializable;
import java.math.BigDecimal;

import javax.persistence.Column;
import javax.persistence.Entity;
import javax.persistence.Id;
import javax.persistence.Table;

@Entity
@Table(name = "EMPLOYEE")
public class Employee implements Serializable {

 private static final long serialVersionUID = 1L;

 @Id
  @Column(name = "EMP_NUMBER")
  private int empNumber;

  @Column(name = "EMP_NAME", nullable = false, length = 64)
  private String empName;
```

```
    @Column(name = "SALARY", nullable = false, precision = 9, scale = 2)
    private BigDecimal salary;

    //Getter and Setter methods

}
```

4.8.4 Implementing Custom Key Generation Class

We can use custom (programmer-defined) key generation class for generating ids. We have to implement logic for unique id generation.

To use such custom key generation class, specify the fully qualified custom key generator class name as the value of `strategy` attribute of `@GenericGenerator` annotation. The custom Key generator class should implement `IdentifierGenerator` (as built-in key generator classes do), of course it should override the following only one method defined in that interface.

```
public Serializable generate(SessionImplementor arg0, Object arg1)
                                        throws HibernateException
{

}
```

This method should return a key, whose data-type is same as of Id filed in Entity. In the example program (KeyGenerator class), System's current time in milliseconds is fetched and returned as key (the *do..while* loop is used to get unique number; otherwise due to speed of your computer, the program may return the same number (same millisecond; if two or more statements are executed within a millisecond). However, this logic is given for only understanding how to generate custom ids, not for production system. There are many good methods which can be implemented in our custom key generating class. You can use also use a database table from which you get value and return as key.

```
// File Name: KeyGenerator.java
// Illustrates Custom Key generator classfor Id generation

package com.hdemo;

import java.io.Serializable;

import org.hibernate.HibernateException;
import org.hibernate.engine.SessionImplementor;
import org.hibernate.id.IdentifierGenerator;

public class KeyGenerator implements IdentifierGenerator {
```

```
    long key = 0, nextKey = 0;

    public KeyGenerator() {
    }

    public Serializable generate(SessionImplementor arg0, Object arg1)
throws HibernateException {
        try {
            do {
                nextKey = System.currentTimeMillis();
            } while (key == nextKey);

            key = nextKey;
        } catch (Exception e) {
            return -1;
        }
        return key;
    }
}
```

```
// File Name: EmployeeManipulation.java
// Main program

package com.hdemo;

import java.math.BigDecimal;

import org.hibernate.Session;
import org.hibernate.SessionFactory;
import org.hibernate.Transaction;

public class EmployeeManipulation {

    public static void main(String[] args) throws Exception {
    SessionFactory sessionFactory = HibernateUtil.getSessionFactory();
        Session session = sessionFactory.getCurrentSession();
```

```
        Transaction  txn  =  session.beginTransaction();
        Employee  employee1  =  new  Employee();

        Employee  employee2  =  new  Employee();

        Employee  employee3  =  new  Employee();


        employee1.setEmpName("Ibrahim");
        employee1.setSalary(new  BigDecimal  (92000.00));

        session.save(employee1);


        employee2.setEmpName("Karan");
        employee2.setSalary(new  BigDecimal  (96000.00));
        session.save(employee2);


        employee3.setEmpName("Ajay");
        employee3.setSalary(new  BigDecimal  (83000.00));

        session.save(employee3);
        txn.commit();


        sessionFactory.close();
    }
}
```

A sample run results as below.

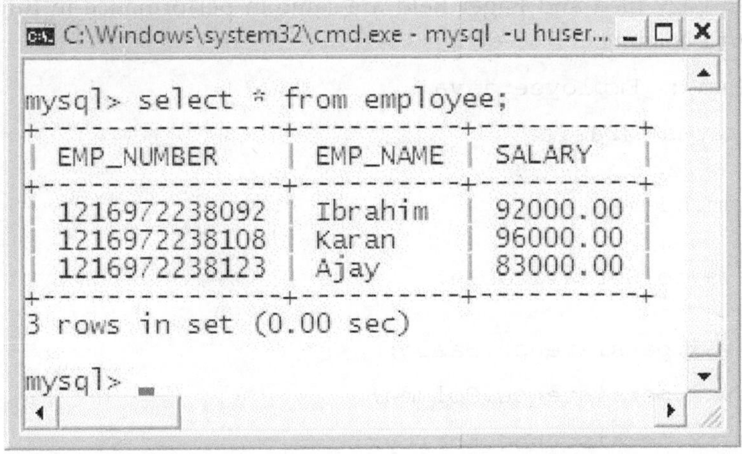

4.9 @Basic - DEFINING DATA FETCH MODE

This annotation is used to configure the fetch type of data for fields of an Entity.

General format

```
@Basic  (fetch=FetchType.EAGER  |  FetchType.LAZY)
```

By default, it is set to `FetchType.EAGER`. Use this annotation to a field/property of an Entity.

`FetchType.EAGER` -Fetches (data for) the field when the bean is loaded.

`FetchType.LAZY` -Fetches (data for) the field only when the field is used (It is also known as Dynamic Function Loading).

Eager Loading vs. Lazy Loading: By default, the System loader loads all dependents (including classes with data if present) into memory, when the main program is getting loaded. Lazy loading is design pattern, which allows the developer to specify some fields of an Entity that those should not be loaded into storage by default. The main advantage is that it very much increases the performance of program execution, if most of the Lazy fields are never referred (used) in your program. The main drawback occurs when many Lazy fields are referred as it consumes time for "on-the-fly" loading. Simply Lazy loading initializes the specified field to null, when it actually referred by somebody, then it will be originally loaded (with actual value); when the lazy fields are referred in second or further times, the effect is same as like eager fields since data is already fetched for that field.

Loading all the fields (dependents) into memory at the time loading is called Eager Loading. Think for a case, in an entity there is a field called "*comments*" which is very big length string. By default (EAGER loading), the Hibernate fetches data from database and puts on that field. This is wasted when we are not going to use this comments field. If this field is set as LAZY loaded, then Hibernate will not fetch as well as load that field in memory and actually it is set to *null*. Suppose you referred that field in a statement, then Hibernate will fetch the data and put on that field without knowing to the user (*on-the-fly*). Operationwise, in both of these techniques we are getting the data, but performance wise Lazy loading saving fetch time and memory if the corresponding lazy field is never used. Once Lazy fetch operation became successive and the lazy field got data, then Lazy filed and Eager field are same in performance in time and memory. It is based on *first time* loading.

```
// File Name: Employee.java
// Illustrates @Basic

package com.hdemo;

import java.io.Serializable;

import javax.persistence.Basic;
import javax.persistence.Column;
import javax.persistence.Entity;
```

```
import javax.persistence.FetchType;
import javax.persistence.Id;
import javax.persistence.Table;

@Entity
@Table(name = "EMPLOYEE")
public class Employee implements Serializable {

 private static final long serialVersionUID = 1L;

   @Id
   @Column(name = "EMP_NUMBER")
   private long empNumber;

   @Column(name = "EMP_NAME", nullable = false, length = 64)
   private String empName;

  @Basic(fetch = FetchType.LAZY)
   @Column(name = "BIO_DATA", length = 4000)
   private String bioData;

   //Getter and Setter methods

}
```

```
// File Name: EmployeeManipulation.java
// Main Program

package com.hdemo;

import org.hibernate.Session;
import org.hibernate.SessionFactory;
import org.hibernate.Transaction;

public class EmployeeManipulation {

   public static void main(String[] args) throws Exception {
   SessionFactory sessionFactory = HibernateUtil.getSessionFactory();
         Session session = sessionFactory.getCurrentSession();
```

```
            Transaction txn = session.beginTransaction();
            Employee employee1 = new Employee();
            Employee employee2 = new Employee();
            Employee employee3 = new Employee();

            employee1.setEmpNumber(1000);
            employee1.setEmpName("Ibrahim");
            employee1.setBioData("This is very long comment.");
            session.save(employee1);

        employee2.setEmpNumber(1001);
            employee2.setEmpName("Karan");
            session.save(employee2);

            employee3.setEmpNumber(1002);
            employee3.setEmpName("Ajay");
            session.save(employee3);
            txn.commit();

        sessionFactory.close();
    }
}
```

A sample run results as below.

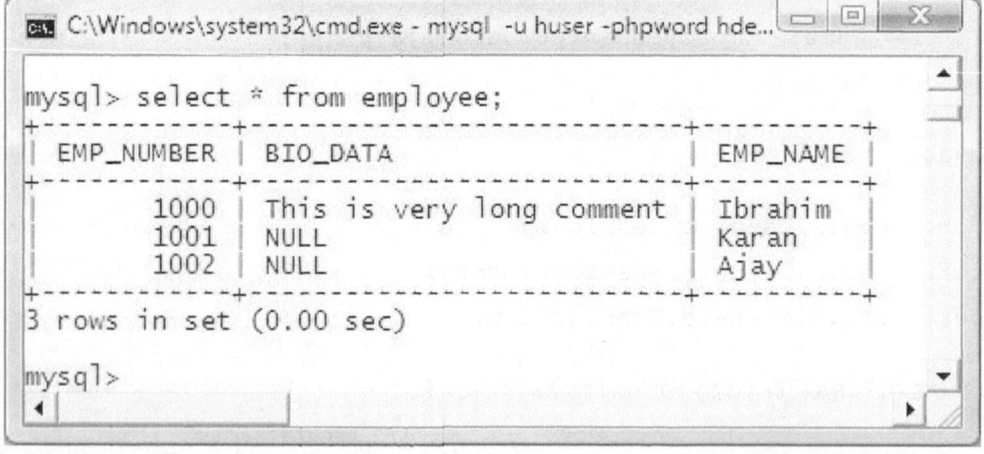

4.10 @Enumerated - DECLARING ENUMERATED DATA

It is used to declare an Enumerated field (the filed will accept only specified data in *enum* list).

General format

```
@Enumerated (value=EnumType.ORDINAL | EnumType.STRING)
```

If you specify `EnumType.ORDINAL` (It is default too), then the field will have index notation of Enumerated value. If you specify `EnumType.STRING`, the field will have String value of Enumerated value.

Note: If you do not use `@Enumerated` annotation in an Enumerated column, then the default is automatically `@Enumerated` and `value` attribute is set to `EnumType.ORDINAL`.

```
// File Name: EmployeeCategory.java
// Illustrates @Enumerated

package com.hdemo;

public enum EmployeeCategory {
  PERMANENT, CONTRACT, TEMPORARY
}
```

```
// File Name: Employee.java
// Illustrates @Enumerated

package com.hdemo;

import java.io.Serializable;

import javax.persistence.Column;
import javax.persistence.Entity;
import javax.persistence.Enumerated;
import javax.persistence.Id;
import javax.persistence.Table;

@Entity
@Table(name = "EMPLOYEE")
public class Employee implements Serializable {

 private static final long serialVersionUID = 1L;
```

```
    @Id
    @Column(name = "EMP_NUMBER")
    private long empNumber;

    @Column(name = "EMP_NAME", nullable = false, length = 64)
    private String empName;

    @Enumerated
    @Column(name = "EMP_CATEGORY", nullable = false)
    private EmployeeCategory empCategory;

    //Getter and Setter methods

}
```

```
// EmployeeManipulation.java
// Main Program

package com.hdemo;

import org.hibernate.Session;
import org.hibernate.SessionFactory;
import org.hibernate.Transaction;

public class EmployeeManipulation {

  public static void main(String[] args) throws Exception {
  SessionFactory sessionFactory = HibernateUtil.getSessionFactory();
        Session session = sessionFactory.getCurrentSession();

      Transaction txn = session.beginTransaction();
      Employee employee1 = new Employee();
      Employee employee2 = new Employee();
      Employee employee3 = new Employee();

        employee1.setEmpNumber(1000);
        employee1.setEmpName("Ibrahim");
        employee1.setEmpCategory(EmployeeCategory.PERMANENT);
        session.save(employee1);
```

```
        employee2.setEmpNumber(1001);
        employee2.setEmpName("Karan");
        employee2.setEmpCategory(EmployeeCategory.TEMPORARY);
        session.save(employee2);

        employee3.setEmpNumber(1002);
        employee3.setEmpName("Ajay");
        employee3.setEmpCategory(EmployeeCategory.CONTRACT);
        session.save(employee3);
        txn.commit();

        sessionFactory.close();
    }
}
```

A sample run results as below.

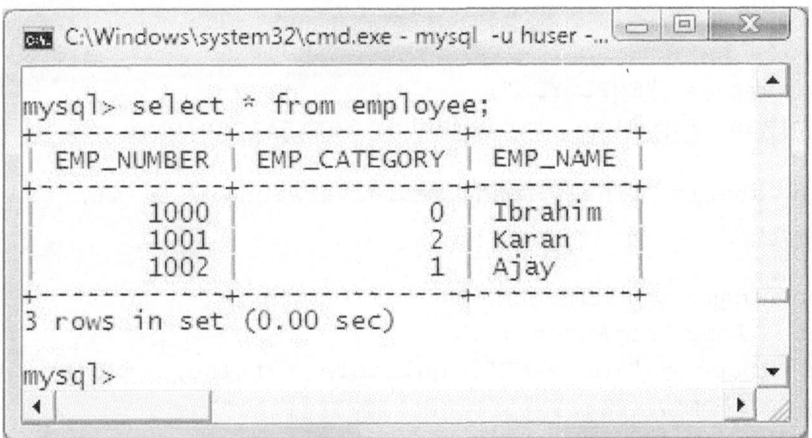

Change *value* to `EnumType.STRING` of `@Enumerated` and observe the result.

```
// File Name: Employee.java
// Illustrates @Enumerated

package com.hdemo;

import java.io.Serializable;

import javax.persistence.Column;
import javax.persistence.Entity;
import javax.persistence.EnumType;
import javax.persistence.Enumerated;
import javax.persistence.Id;
import javax.persistence.Table;

@Entity
```

```
@Table(name = "EMPLOYEE")
public class Employee implements Serializable {
```

Change value to `EnumType.STRING` of `@Enumerated` and observe the result.

```
// File Name: Employee.java
// Illustrates @Enumerated

Package com.hdemo;

import java.io.Serializable;

import javar. persistence.Column;
import javax.persistence.Entity;
import javax.persistence.EnumType;
import javax.persistence.Enumerated;
import javax.persistence.Id;
import javax.persistence.Table;

@Entity
@Table (name = "EMPLOYEE")
public class Employee implements Serializable {

 private static final long serialVersionUID = 1L;

 @Id
 @Column (name = "EMP_NUMBER")
 perivate long empNumber;
 @Column (name = "EMP_NAME", nullable = false, length = 64) private
 String empName;

 @Enumerated(value = EnumType.STRING)
 @Column(name = "EMP_CATEGORY", nullable = false)
 private EmployeeCategory empCategory;

}
```

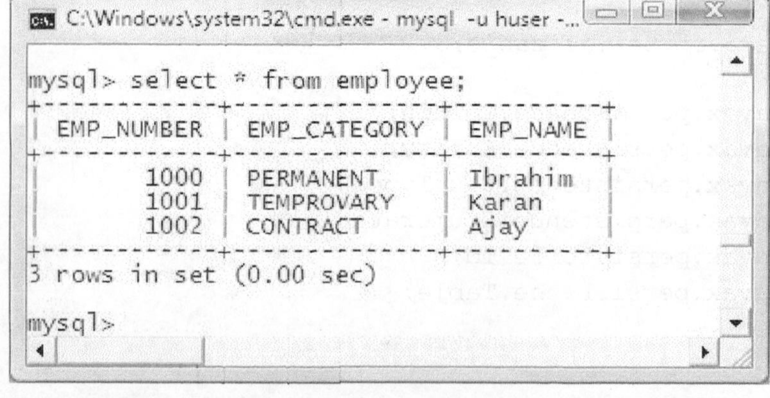

```
C:\Windows\system32\cmd.exe - mysql -u huser -...

mysql> select * from employee;
+------------+--------------+----------+
| EMP_NUMBER | EMP_CATEGORY | EMP_NAME |
+------------+--------------+----------+
|       1000 | PERMANENT    | Ibrahim  |
|       1001 | TEMPROVARY   | Karan    |
|       1002 | CONTRACT     | Ajay     |
+------------+--------------+----------+
3 rows in set (0.00 sec)

mysql>
```

4.11 `@Temporal` - DECLARING DATE/TIME VALUES

This annotation is used to define Date/Time fields (whose data type is `java.util.Date` / `java.util.Calendar`).

General format

```
@Temporal  (value=TemporalType.DATE  |
                  TemporalType.TIME  |
                  TemporalType.TIMESTAMP)
```

Here, `DATE` is equivalent to `java.sql.Date`, `TIME` is equivalent to `java.sql.Time` and `TIMESTAMP` is equivalent to `java.sql.Timestamp`.

If you do not use `@Temporal`, then the default is set to `TIMESTAMP` (both Date and Time will be persisted).

The following example illustrates how to store Date values `(DATE)`.

```
// File Name: Employee.java
// Illustrates @Temporal

package com.hdemo;

import java.io.Serializable;
import java.util.Calendar;

import javax.persistence.Column;
import javax.persistence.Entity;
import javax.persistence.Id;
import javax.persistence.Table;
import javax.persistence.Temporal;
import javax.persistence.TemporalType;

@Entity
@Table(name = "EMPLOYEE")
public class Employee implements Serializable {

  private static final long serialVersionUID = 1L;

  @Id
  @Column(name = "EMP_NUMBER")
  private long empNumber;

  @Column(name = "EMP_NAME", nullable = false, length = 64)
  private String empName;

 @Temporal(value = TemporalType.DATE)
 @Column(name = "DOJ", nullable = false)
```

```
  private Calendar dateOfJoining;
  //Getter and Setter methods

}
```

```
// File Name: EmployeeManipulation.java
// Main Program

package com.hdemo;

import java.util.Calendar;

import org.hibernate.Session;
import org.hibernate.SessionFactory;
import org.hibernate.Transaction;

public class EmployeeManipulation {

  public static void main(String[] args) throws Exception {
  SessionFactory sessionFactory = HibernateUtil.getSessionFactory();
        Session session = sessionFactory.getCurrentSession();

        Transaction txn = session.beginTransaction();
        Employee employee1 = new Employee();
        Employee employee2 = new Employee();
        Employee employee3 = new Employee();
        Calendar emp1DOJ = Calendar.getInstance();
        Calendar emp2DOJ = Calendar.getInstance();
        Calendar emp3DOJ = Calendar.getInstance();

        employee1.setEmpNumber(1000);
        employee1.setEmpName("Ibrahim");
        emp1DOJ.set(2001, 5, 1); // year, month, date; 1st June 2001
        employee1.setDateOfJoining(emp1DOJ);
        session.save(employee1);

        employee2.setEmpNumber(1001);
        employee2.setEmpName("Karan");
        emp2DOJ.set(2003, 0, 10); // 10th January 2003
        employee2.setDateOfJoining(emp2DOJ);
        session.save(employee2);
```

```
        employee3.setEmpNumber(1002);
        employee3.setEmpName("Ajay");
        emp3DOJ.set(1995, 10, 16); // 16th November 1995
        employee3.setDateOfJoining(emp3DOJ);
        session.save(employee3);
        txn.commit();

        sessionFactory.close();
    }

}
```

A sample run results as below.

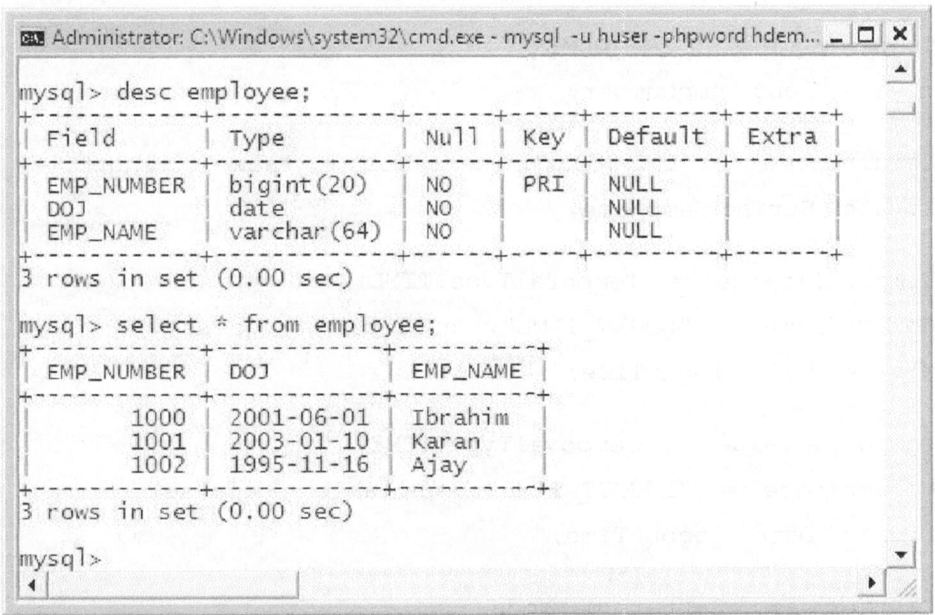

```
Administrator: C:\Windows\system32\cmd.exe - mysql -u huser -phpword hdem...

mysql> desc employee;
+------------+-------------+------+-----+---------+-------+
| Field      | Type        | Null | Key | Default | Extra |
+------------+-------------+------+-----+---------+-------+
| EMP_NUMBER | bigint(20)  | NO   | PRI | NULL    |       |
| DOJ        | date        | NO   |     | NULL    |       |
| EMP_NAME   | varchar(64) | NO   |     | NULL    |       |
+------------+-------------+------+-----+---------+-------+
3 rows in set (0.00 sec)

mysql> select * from employee;
+------------+------------+----------+
| EMP_NUMBER | DOJ        | EMP_NAME |
+------------+------------+----------+
|       1000 | 2001-06-01 | Ibrahim  |
|       1001 | 2003-01-10 | Karan    |
|       1002 | 1995-11-16 | Ajay     |
+------------+------------+----------+
3 rows in set (0.00 sec)

mysql>
```

The following example illustrates how to store Time (`TIME`). (**Note:** When you are persisting TIME only, prefer to use `java.util.Date` instead of `java.util.Calendar`)

```
// File Name: Employee.java
// Illustrates @Temporal

package com.hdemo;

import java.io.Serializable;
import java.util.Calendar;
import java.util.Date;

import javax.persistence.Column;
```

```
import javax.persistence.Entity;
import javax.persistence.Id;
import javax.persistence.Table;
import javax.persistence.Temporal;
import javax.persistence.TemporalType;

@Entity
@Table(name = "EMPLOYEE")
public class Employee implements Serializable {

  private static final long serialVersionUID = 1L;

  @Id
  @Column(name = "EMP_NUMBER")
  private long empNumber;

  @Column(name = "EMP_NAME", nullable = false, length = 64)
  private String empName;

  @Temporal(value = TemporalType.TIME)
  @Column(name = "LOGIN_TIME", nullable = false)
  private Date loginTime;

  @Temporal(value = TemporalType.TIME)
  @Column(name = "LOGOUT_TIME", nullable = false)
  private Date logoutTime;

  //Getter and Setter methods
}
```

```
// File Name: EmployeeManipulation.java
// Main Program

package com.hdemo;

import java.util.Calendar;

import org.hibernate.Session;
import org.hibernate.SessionFactory;
```

```
import  org.hibernate.Transaction;

public  class  EmployeeManipulation  {

   public  static  void  main(String[]  args)  throws  Exception  {
   SessionFactory sessionFactory = HibernateUtil.getSessionFactory();
         Session  session  =  sessionFactory.getCurrentSession();

         Transaction  txn  =  session.beginTransaction();
         Employee  employee1  =  new  Employee();
         Employee  employee2  =  new  Employee();
         Employee  employee3  =  new  Employee();

         Calendar  emp1LoginTime  =  Calendar.getInstance();
         Calendar  emp1LogoutTime  =  Calendar.getInstance();
         emp1LoginTime.set(Calendar.HOUR_OF_DAY,  10);
         emp1LoginTime.set(Calendar.MINUTE,  05);
         emp1LoginTime.set(Calendar.SECOND,  18);
         emp1LogoutTime.set(Calendar.HOUR_OF_DAY,  18);
         emp1LogoutTime.set(Calendar.MINUTE,  15);
         emp1LogoutTime.set(Calendar.SECOND,  45);

         Calendar  emp2LoginTime  =  Calendar.getInstance();
         Calendar  emp2LogoutTime  =  Calendar.getInstance();
         emp2LogoutTime.add(Calendar.HOUR,  8);

         Calendar  emp3LoginTime  =  Calendar.getInstance();
         Calendar  emp3LogoutTime  =  Calendar.getInstance();
         emp3LogoutTime.add(Calendar.MINUTE,  150);

         employee1.setEmpNumber(1000);
         employee1.setEmpName("Ibrahim");
         employee1.setLoginTime(emp1LoginTime.getTime());
         employee1.setLogoutTime(emp1LogoutTime.getTime());
         session.save(employee1);

         employee2.setEmpNumber(1001);
         employee2.setEmpName("Karan");
```

```
        employee2.setLoginTime(emp2LoginTime.getTime());
        employee2.setLogoutTime(emp2LogoutTime.getTime());
        session.save(employee2);

        employee3.setEmpNumber(1002);
        employee3.setEmpName("Ajay");
        employee3.setLoginTime(emp3LoginTime.getTime());
        employee3.setLogoutTime(emp3LogoutTime.getTime());
        session.save(employee3);
        txn.commit();

        sessionFactory.close();
    }

}
```

A sample run results as below.

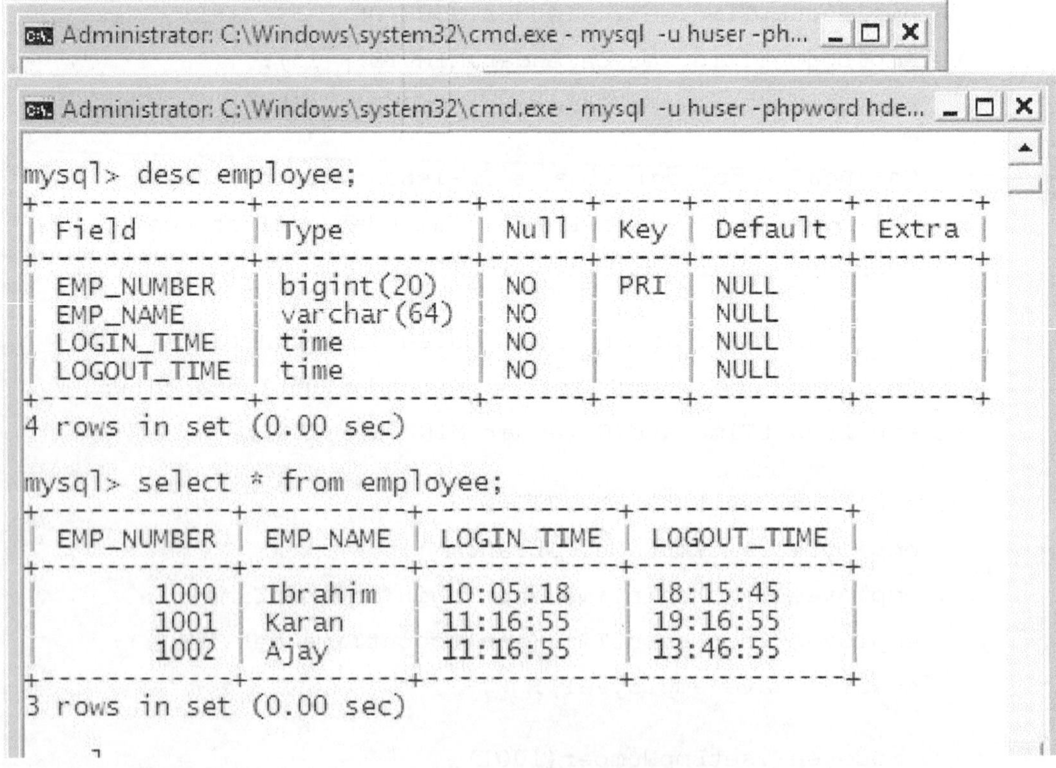

Administrator: C:\Windows\system32\cmd.exe - mysql -u huser -ph...

Administrator: C:\Windows\system32\cmd.exe - mysql -u huser -phpword hde...

```
mysql> desc employee;
+-------------+-------------+------+-----+---------+-------+
| Field       | Type        | Null | Key | Default | Extra |
+-------------+-------------+------+-----+---------+-------+
| EMP_NUMBER  | bigint(20)  | NO   | PRI | NULL    |       |
| EMP_NAME    | varchar(64) | NO   |     | NULL    |       |
| LOGIN_TIME  | time        | NO   |     | NULL    |       |
| LOGOUT_TIME | time        | NO   |     | NULL    |       |
+-------------+-------------+------+-----+---------+-------+
4 rows in set (0.00 sec)

mysql> select * from employee;
+------------+----------+------------+-------------+
| EMP_NUMBER | EMP_NAME | LOGIN_TIME | LOGOUT_TIME |
+------------+----------+------------+-------------+
|       1000 | Ibrahim  | 10:05:18   | 18:15:45    |
|       1001 | Karan    | 11:16:55   | 19:16:55    |
|       1002 | Ajay     | 11:16:55   | 13:46:55    |
+------------+----------+------------+-------------+
3 rows in set (0.00 sec)
```

The following example illustrates how to store Date and Time (TIMESTAMP).

```
// File Name: Employee.java
// Illustrates @Temporal

package com.hdemo;

import java.io.Serializable;
import java.util.Calendar;

import javax.persistence.Column;
import javax.persistence.Entity;
import javax.persistence.Id;
import javax.persistence.Table;
import javax.persistence.Temporal;
import javax.persistence.TemporalType;

@Entity
@Table(name = "EMPLOYEE")
public class Employee implements Serializable {

  private static final long serialVersionUID = 1L;

 @Id
  @Column(name = "EMP_NUMBER")
  private long empNumber;

  @Column(name = "EMP_NAME", nullable = false, length = 64)
  private String empName;

 @Temporal(value = TemporalType.TIMESTAMP)
  @Column(name = "LOGIN_TIME", nullable = false)
  private Calendar loginTime;

  @Temporal(value = TemporalType.TIMESTAMP)
  @Column(name = "LOGOUT_TIME", nullable = false)
  private Calendar logoutTime;

  //Getter and Setter methods

}
```

```
// File Name: EmployeeManipulation.java
// Main Program

package com.hdemo;

import java.util.Calendar;

import org.hibernate.Session;
import org.hibernate.SessionFactory;
import org.hibernate.Transaction;

public class EmployeeManipulation {

  public static void main(String[] args) throws Exception {
  SessionFactory sessionFactory = HibernateUtil.getSessionFactory();
       Session session = sessionFactory.getCurrentSession();

  Transaction txn = session.beginTransaction();
  Employee employee1 = new Employee();
  Employee employee2 = new Employee();
  Employee employee3 = new Employee();
  Calendar emp1LoginTime = Calendar.get Instance();
  Calendar emp1LogoutTime = Calendar.get Instance();
  emp1LoginTime.set(2001, 5, 1); // year, month, date; 1st June 2001
  emp1LoginTime.set(Calendar.HOUR_OF_DAY, 10);
  emp1LoginTime.set(Calendar.MINUTE, 05);
  emp1LoginTime.set(Calendar.SECOND, 18);
  emp1LogoutTime.set(2001, 5, 2); // year, month, date; 1st June 2001
  emp1LogoutTime.set(Calendar.HOUR_OF_DAY, 18);
  emp1LogoutTime.set(Calendar.MINUTE, 15);
  emp1LogoutTime.set(Calendar.SECOND, 45);

  Calendar emp2LoginTime = Calendar.get Instance();
  Calendar emp2LogoutTime = Calendar.get Instance();
  emp2LoginTime.set(2008, 0, 10); // 10th January 2008
  emp2LogoutTime.add(Calendar.HOUR, 8);

  Calendar emp3LoginTime = Calendar.get Instance();
       Calendar emp3LogoutTime = Calendar.get Instance();
       emp3LogoutTime.add(Calendar.MINUTE, 150);
```

```
        employee1.setEmpNumber(1000);
        employee1.setEmpName("Ibrahim");
        employee1.setLoginTime(emp1LoginTime);
        employee1.setLogoutTime(emp1LogoutTime);
        session.save(employee1);

      employee2.setEmpNumber(1001);
        employee2.setEmpName("Karan");
        employee2.setLoginTime(emp2LoginTime);
        employee2.setLogoutTime(emp2LogoutTime);
        session.save(employee2);

      employee3.setEmpNumber(1002);
        employee3.setEmpName("Ajay");
        employee3.setLoginTime(emp3LoginTime);
        employee3.setLogoutTime(emp3LogoutTime);
        session.save(employee3);
        txn.commit();

        sessionFactory.close();
  }
}
```

A sample run results as below.

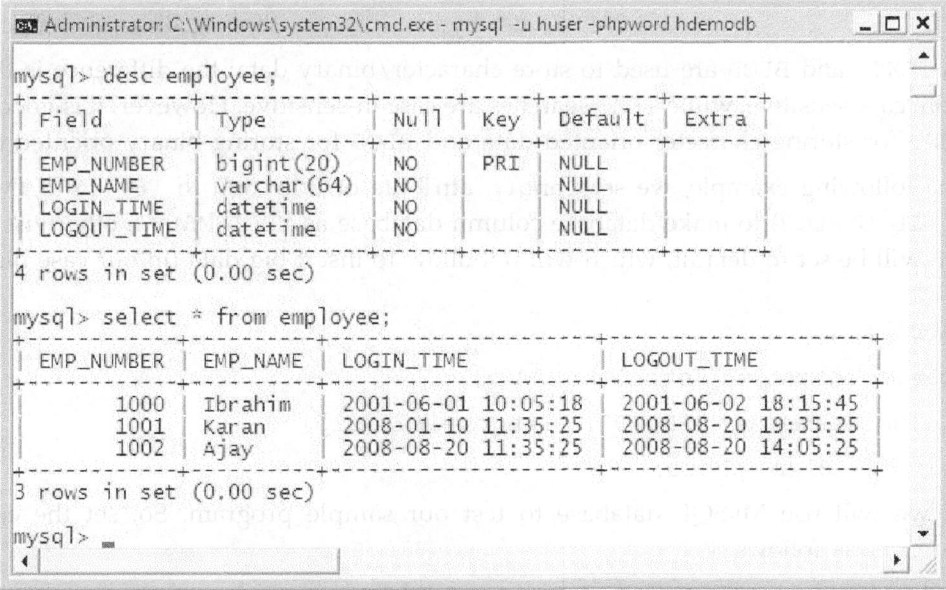

```
Administrator: C:\Windows\system32\cmd.exe - mysql -u huser -phpword hdemodb

mysql> desc employee;
+-------------+-------------+------+-----+---------+-------+
| Field       | Type        | Null | Key | Default | Extra |
+-------------+-------------+------+-----+---------+-------+
| EMP_NUMBER  | bigint(20)  | NO   | PRI | NULL    |       |
| EMP_NAME    | varchar(64) | NO   |     | NULL    |       |
| LOGIN_TIME  | datetime    | NO   |     | NULL    |       |
| LOGOUT_TIME | datetime    | NO   |     | NULL    |       |
+-------------+-------------+------+-----+---------+-------+
4 rows in set (0.00 sec)

mysql> select * from employee;
+------------+----------+---------------------+---------------------+
| EMP_NUMBER | EMP_NAME | LOGIN_TIME          | LOGOUT_TIME         |
+------------+----------+---------------------+---------------------+
|       1000 | Ibrahim  | 2001-06-01 10:05:18 | 2001-06-02 18:15:45 |
|       1001 | Karan    | 2008-01-10 11:35:25 | 2008-08-20 19:35:25 |
|       1002 | Ajay     | 2008-08-20 11:35:25 | 2008-08-20 14:05:25 |
+------------+----------+---------------------+---------------------+
3 rows in set (0.00 sec)

mysql> _
```

4.12 @Lob - DECLARING LONG OBJECTS (CHARACTER / BINARY)

This is used to define long objects (LOB) with database. Hibernate will decide to use whether the character based Clob or binary based Blob database data type depending on the field (class member) type. For example, java.lang.String, char array char[], Character class array Character[], or java.sql.Clob data are persisted in Clob type in database, if the corresponding field is annotated with @Lob. Similarly, the database data type Blob will be chosen for serialized objects, byte array byte[], Byte class array Byte[], and java.sql.Blob data type. (Note: Remember that you did not specify @Lob annotation on String field, and then the data type for that field will be varchar in database).

General format

```
@Lob
```

A Note on Storing Long Objects in MySQL: MySQL database defines the following data types for storing Long objects. There is no data type named Clob in MySQL database (as present in Oracle database), we can use TEXT as its alternative.

Data Type	Maximum Limit	Description
TINYTEXT	255 characters	Storing Binary/Character set
TEXT	65,535 characters	Storing Binary/Character set
MEDIUMTEXT	16,777,215 characters	Storing Binary/Character set
LONGTEXT	0–4,294,967,295 characters	Storing Binary/Character set
TINYBLOB	0–255 bytes	Storing Binary/Character set
BLOB	0–65,535 bytes	Storing Binary/Character set
MEDIUMBLOB	0–16,777,215 bytes	Storing Binary/Character set
LONGBLOB	0–4,294,967,295 bytes	Storing Binary/Character set

Both TEXT and BLOB are used to store character/binary data; the difference is that BLOB searches are case sensitive, while TEXT searches are case in-sensitive. However, it is good practice to use TEXT for storing character oriented data and BLOB for storing binary oriented data.

In the following example, we set length attribute of @Column to 16777215 (Maximum length of MEDIUMBLOB) to make database column database as MEDIUMBLOB, otherwise the data type BLOB will be set to default, which will not allow to insert big data (in our case big image).

```
@Lob
@Basic(fetch = FetchType.LAZY)
@Column(name = "PHOTO", length=16777215)
private Blob photo;
```

First we will use MySQL database to test our sample program. So, set the content of *hibernate.cfg.xml* as follows.

```
<?xml version='1.0' encoding='utf-8'?>
```

```
<!DOCTYPE hibernate-configuration PUBLIC
        "-//Hibernate/Hibernate Configuration DTD 3.0//EN"
        "http://hibernate.sourceforge.net/hibernate-configuration-
3.0.dtd">
<hibernate-configuration>
  <session-factory>
  <property name="connection.driver_class">com.mysql.jdbc.Driver</
property>
  <property name="connection.url">jdbc:mysql://localhost:3306/hdemodb</
property>
  <property name="connection.username">huser</property>
  <property name="connection.password">hpword</property>
  <property name="dialect">org.hibernate.dialect.MySQLDialect</property>

  <property name="hibernate.c3p0.minPoolSize">1</property>
  <property name="hibernate.c3p0.maxPoolSize">1</property>
  <property name="hibernate.c3p0.timeout">10</property>
  <property name="hibernate.c3p0.max_statement">50</property>
  <property name="hibernate.c3p0.testConnectionOnCheckout">false</
property>

  <property name="current_session_context_class">thread</property>
  <property name="cache.provider_class">org.hibernate.cache.NoCache
Provider</property>
  <property name="show_sql">true</property>
  <property name="hbm2ddl.auto">create</property>

  <mapping class="com.hdemo.Employee" />
  </session-factory>
</hibernate-configuration>
```

The program will fetch data from text file *ibrahim_biodata.txt* stored at `C:` drive to insert it into *bio_data* column of database table. Like wise, the program fetches data for *photo* field from the file *C:/ibrahim_photo.jpg*. You can change the file names and path locations as you want.

```
// File Name: Employee.java
// Illustrates @Lob

package com.hdemo;
```

```
import java.io.Serializable;
import java.sql.Blob;
import java.sql.Clob;

import javax.persistence.Basic;
import javax.persistence.Column;
import javax.persistence.Entity;
import javax.persistence.FetchType;
import javax.persistence.Id;
import javax.persistence.Lob;
import javax.persistence.Table;

@Entity
@Table(name = "EMPLOYEE")
public class Employee implements Serializable {

 private static final long serialVersionUID = 1L;

  @Id
  @Column(name = "EMP_NUMBER")
  private long empNumber;

  @Column(name = "EMP_NAME", nullable = false, length = 64)
  private String empName;

 @Lob
 @Basic(fetch = FetchType.LAZY)
  @Column(name = "PHOTO", length=16777215)
  private Blob photo;

 @Lob
  @Column(name = "BIO_DATA")
  private Clob bioData;

 @Lob
 @Column(name = "COMMENTS")
 private String comments;
```

```
    //Getter and Setter methods

  }
```

```
  // File Name: EmployeeManipulation.java
  // Main program

  package com.hdemo;

  import java.io.File;
  import java.io.FileInputStream;
  import java.io.FileReader;

  import org.hibernate.Hibernate;
  import org.hibernate.Session;
  import org.hibernate.SessionFactory;
  import org.hibernate.Transaction;

  public class EmployeeManipulation {

  public static void main(String[] args) throws Exception {
  SessionFactory sessionFactory = HibernateUtil.getSessionFactory();
    Session session = sessionFactory.openSession();

    Transaction txn = session.beginTransaction();
    Employee employee = new Employee();
    employee.setEmpNumber(1001);
    employee.setEmpName("Mohamed Ibrahim");

    File biodataFile = new File("C:/ibrahim_biodata.txt");
    FileReader reader = new FileReader(biodataFile);
    employee.setBioData(Hibernate.createClob(reader, (int) biodataFile.
    length()));

    FileInputStream stream = new FileInputStream("C:/ibrahim_photo.jpg");
```

```
    employee.setPhoto(Hibernate.createBlob(stream));

    employee.setComments("This record contains details about the Employee -Mohamed Ibrahim. ....");

            session.saveOrUpdate(employee);
            session.flush();
            txn.commit();

            session.close();
            sessionFactory.close();
    }
}
```

A sample run results as below.

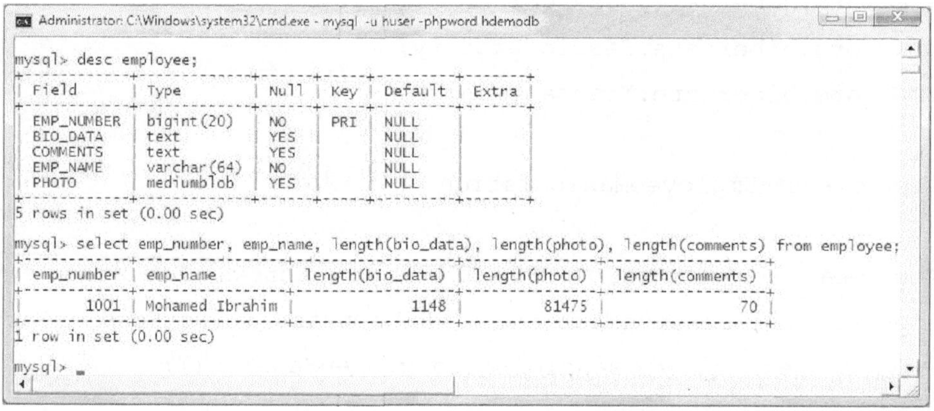

```
Administrator: C:\Windows\system32\cmd.exe - mysql -u huser -phpword hdemodb

mysql> desc employee;
+------------+-------------+------+-----+---------+-------+
| Field      | Type        | Null | Key | Default | Extra |
+------------+-------------+------+-----+---------+-------+
| EMP_NUMBER | bigint(20)  | NO   | PRI | NULL    |       |
| BIO_DATA   | text        | YES  |     | NULL    |       |
| COMMENTS   | text        | YES  |     | NULL    |       |
| EMP_NAME   | varchar(64) | NO   |     | NULL    |       |
| PHOTO      | mediumblob  | YES  |     | NULL    |       |
+------------+-------------+------+-----+---------+-------+
5 rows in set (0.00 sec)

mysql> select emp_number, emp_name, length(bio_data), length(photo), length(comments) from employee;
+------------+-----------------+------------------+---------------+------------------+
| emp_number | emp_name        | length(bio_data) | length(photo) | length(comments) |
+------------+-----------------+------------------+---------------+------------------+
|       1001 | Mohamed Ibrahim |             1148 |         81475 |               70 |
+------------+-----------------+------------------+---------------+------------------+
1 row in set (0.00 sec)

mysql> _
```

We will execute and observe the result of the same program with Oracle dialect.

Note: Use latest Oracle driver, I am using "`ojdbc14-10.2.0.3.0.jar`" driver file for testing this program; otherwise you may get "`java.sql.SQLException: Io exception: Connection reset`" exception.

Change the contents of *hibernate.cfg.xml* for Oracle settings as follows.

```
<?xml version='1.0' encoding='utf-8'?>
<!DOCTYPE hibernate-configuration PUBLIC
"-//Hibernate/Hibernate Configuration DTD 3.0//EN"
"http://hibernate.sourceforge.net/hibernate-configuration-3.0.dtd">
```

```
<hibernate-configuration>
<session-factory>
<property name="connection.driver_class"> oracle.jdbc.driver.
OracleDriver</property>
<property name="connection.url">jdbc: oracle:thin:@192.168.1.2:1521:
DEV</property>
<property name="connection.username"> hosetest</property>
<property name="connection.password"> hosetest</property>

<property name="hibernate.c3p0.minPoolSize"> 1</property>
        <property name="hibernate.c3p0.maxPoolSize"> 1</property>
            <property name="hibernate.c3p0.timeout">10</property>
    <property name="hibernate.c3p0. max_statement">50</property>
<property name="hibernate.c3p0. testConnectionOnCheckout">false</
property>
<property name="dialect">org.hibernate. dialect.OracleDialect</
property>
<property name="cache.provider_class">org. hibernate.cache.NoCache
Provider</property>
<property name="show_sql">true</property>
<property name="hibernate.jdbc.batch_size"> 0</property>
<property name="hbm2ddl.auto">create</property>

  <mapping class="com.hdemo.Employee" />
  </session-factory>
</hibernate-configuration>
```

Since Oracle database supports direct `Blob` data type, no need to set *length* field to required maximum byte as we did for MySQL.

```
@Lob
@Basic(fetch = FetchType.LAZY)
@Column(name = "PHOTO")
private Blob photo;
```

A sample run results as below.

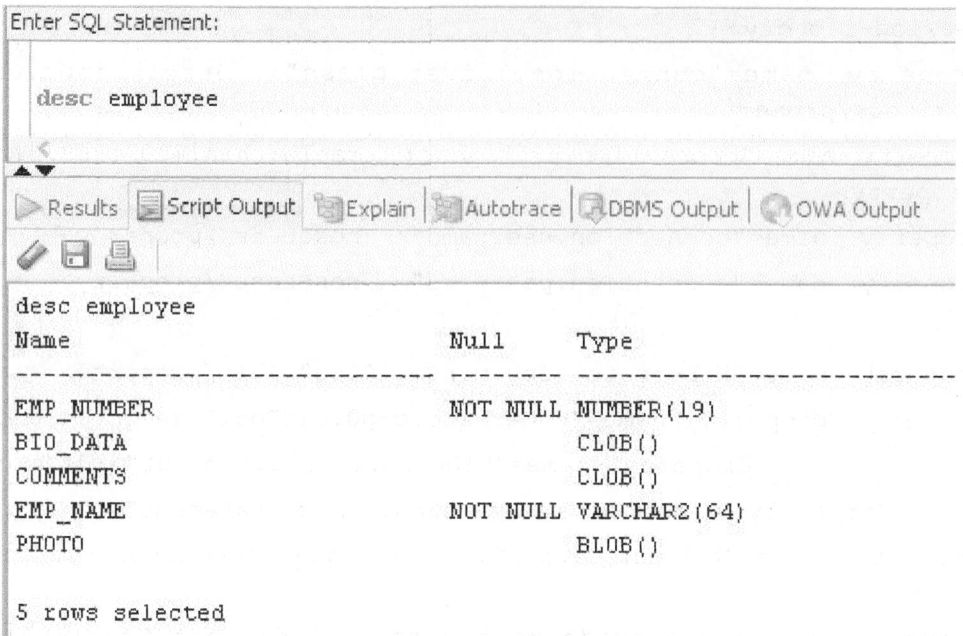

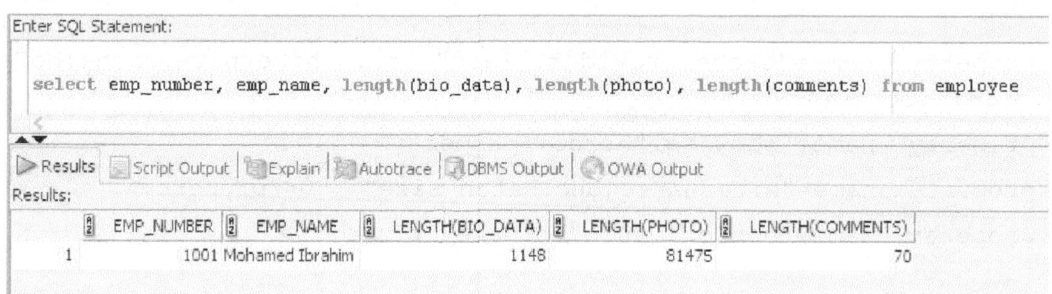

Now, we try to persist objects (The class should implement marker interface `Serializable`, then only we can persist the objects of that class in to secondary storage like database, file, or pass them as network stream.)

```
// File Name: Employee.java
// Illustrates @Lob

package com.hdemo;

import java.io.Serializable;

import javax.persistence.Column;
import javax.persistence.Entity;
import javax.persistence.Id;
import javax.persistence.Lob;
```

```
import javax.persistence.Table;

@Entity
@Table(name = "EMPLOYEE")
public class Employee implements Serializable {

 private static final long serialVersionUID = 1L;

 @Id
  @Column(name = "EMP_NUMBER")
  private long empNumber;

  @Column(name = "EMP_NAME", nullable = false, length = 64)
  private String empName;

 @Lob
 @Column(name = "SALARY_INFO")
 private SalaryInfo salaryInfo;
 //Getter and Setter methods

}
```

```
// File Name: EmployeeManipulation.java
// Main program

package com.hdemo;

import org.hibernate.Session;
import org.hibernate.SessionFactory;
import org.hibernate.Transaction;

public class EmployeeManipulation {

public static void main(String[] args) throws Exception {
SessionFactory sessionFactory = HibernateUtil.getSessionFactory();
  Session session = sessionFactory.getCurrentSession();

  Transaction txn = session.beginTransaction();
  SalaryInfo salaryInfo = new SalaryInfo();
        salaryInfo.setBasicPay(50000.0);
```

```
        salaryInfo.setDearnessAllowances(26000.0);
        salaryInfo.setMedicalAllowances(1000.0);
        salaryInfo.setHouseRentAllowances(3500.0);
        salaryInfo.setTransportAllowances(1500.0);
        salaryInfo.setProvidentFund(6000.0);
        salaryInfo.setIncomeTax(10900.0);
        salaryInfo.setLoanDeduction(0);

      Employee employee = new Employee();
      employee.setEmpNumber(3000);
        employee.setEmpName("Ibrahim");
        employee.setSalaryInfo(salaryInfo);
        session.save(employee);
        txn.commit();

        sessionFactory.close();
   }
}
```

A sample run results as below.

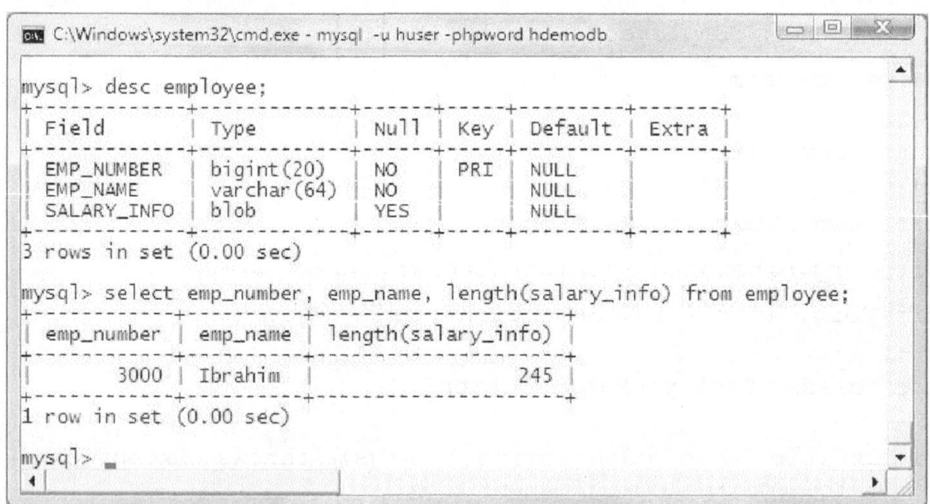

4.13 `@Transient` - DECLARING NON-PERSISTING FIELDS

This annotation is used to instruct not to persist a field. By default, all field in an Entity class (whether `@Column` is specified or not) will be persisted with database. To prevent such persistence, declare the required field as *transient* field using `@Transient` annotation.

The following program illustrates all fields in an Entity will be persisted irrespective of `@Column` fields.

```
// File Name: Employee.java
// Illustrates @Transient

package com.hdemo;

import java.io.Serializable;
import java.math.BigDecimal;

import javax.persistence.Column;
import javax.persistence.Entity;
import javax.persistence.Id;
import javax.persistence.Table;

@Entity
@Table(name = "EMPLOYEE")
public class Employee implements Serializable {

 private static final long serialVersionUID = 1L;

 @Id
  @Column(name = "EMP_NUMBER", precision = 5)
  private int empNumber;

  @Column(name = "EMP_NAME", nullable = false, length = 64)
  private String empName;

 @Column(name= "BASIC_PAY", nullable = false, precision = 9, scale=2)
  private BigDecimal basicPay;

 @Column(name="NET_PAY", nullable = false, precision = 9, scale=2)
  private BigDecimal netpay;

  private double allowances;
  private double deductions;
  private double da; // Dearness Allowance
  private double hra; // House Rent Allowance
  private double ma; // Medical Allowance
```

```
   private double tax; // Income tax deduction
   private double pf; // Provident fund deduction

   //Getter and Setter methods

}
```

```
// File Name: EmployeeManipulation.java
// Main program

package com.hdemo;

import java.math.BigDecimal;

import org.hibernate.Session;
import org.hibernate.SessionFactory;
import org.hibernate.Transaction;

public class EmployeeManipulation {

   public static void main(String[] args) throws Exception {
   SessionFactory sessionFactory = HibernateUtil.getSessionFactory();
         Session session = sessionFactory.getCurrentSession();
         Transaction txn = session.beginTransaction();

         Employee employee = new Employee();
         employee.setEmpNumber(3000);
         employee.setEmpName("Ibrahim");
         employee.setBasicPay(new BigDecimal(50000.0));
         employee.setDa(26000.0);
         employee.setMa(1000.0);
         employee.setHra(3500.0);
         employee.setPf(6000.0);
         employee.setTax(10900.0);
         employee.setAllowances( employee.getDa() + employee.getMa()
                                             + employee.getHra() );
         employee.setDeductions(employee.getPf()+employee.getTax() );
```

```
            employee.setNetpay(new  BigDecimal(  employee.getBasicPay().
doubleValue() + employee.getAllowances() - employee.getDeductions() ));

            session.save(employee);
            txn.commit();

            sessionFactory.close();
      }
   }
```

A sample run results as below.

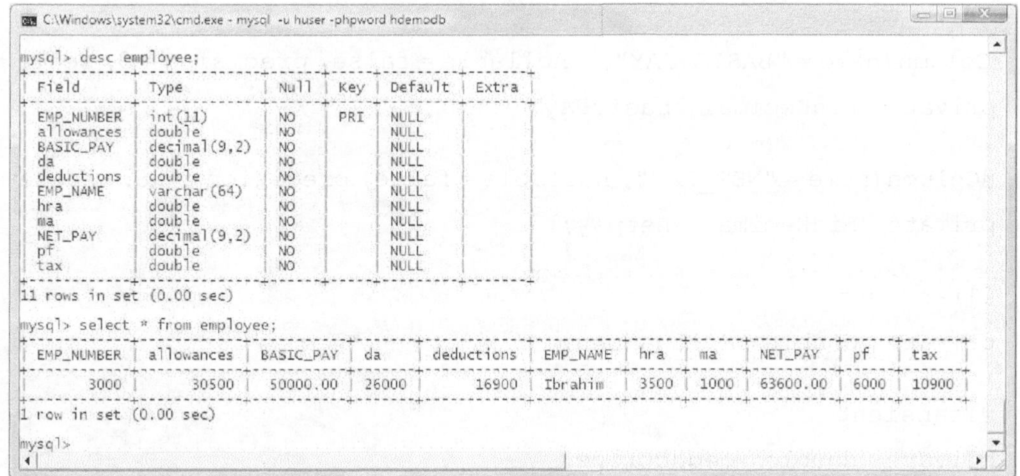

```
C:\Windows\system32\cmd.exe - mysql  -u huser -phpword hdemodb

mysql> desc employee;
+------------+--------------+------+-----+---------+-------+
| Field      | Type         | Null | Key | Default | Extra |
+------------+--------------+------+-----+---------+-------+
| EMP_NUMBER | int(11)      | NO   | PRI | NULL    |       |
| allowances | double       | NO   |     | NULL    |       |
| BASIC_PAY  | decimal(9,2) | NO   |     | NULL    |       |
| da         | double       | NO   |     | NULL    |       |
| deductions | double       | NO   |     | NULL    |       |
| EMP_NAME   | varchar(64)  | NO   |     | NULL    |       |
| hra        | double       | NO   |     | NULL    |       |
| ma         | double       | NO   |     | NULL    |       |
| NET_PAY    | decimal(9,2) | NO   |     | NULL    |       |
| pf         | double       | NO   |     | NULL    |       |
| tax        | double       | NO   |     | NULL    |       |
+------------+--------------+------+-----+---------+-------+
11 rows in set (0.00 sec)

mysql> select * from employee;
+------------+------------+-----------+-------+------------+----------+------+------+----------+------+-------+
| EMP_NUMBER | allowances | BASIC_PAY | da    | deductions | EMP_NAME | hra  | ma   | NET_PAY  | pf   | tax   |
+------------+------------+-----------+-------+------------+----------+------+------+----------+------+-------+
|       3000 |      30500 |  50000.00 | 26000 |      16900 | Ibrahim  | 3500 | 1000 | 63600.00 | 6000 | 10900 |
+------------+------------+-----------+-------+------------+----------+------+------+----------+------+-------+
1 row in set (0.00 sec)

mysql>
```

Now, we will modify the same entity with *transient* fields.

```
// File Name: Employee.java
// Illustrates @Transient

package com.hdemo;

import java.io.Serializable;
import java.math.BigDecimal;

import javax.persistence.Column;
import javax.persistence.Entity;
import javax.persistence.Id;
import javax.persistence.Table;
import javax.persistence.Transient;

@Entity
```

```
@Table(name = "EMPLOYEE")
public class Employee implements Serializable {

  private static final long serialVersionUID = 1L;

  @Id
  @Column(name = "EMP_NUMBER", precision = 5)
  private int empNumber;

  @Column(name = "EMP_NAME", nullable = false, length = 64)
  private String empName;

  @Column(name="BASIC_PAY", nullable=false, precision=9, scale= 2)
  private BigDecimal basicPay;

  @Column(name="NET_PAY", nullable=false, precision = 9, scale = 2)
  private BigDecimal netpay;

  @Transient
  private double allowances;

  @Transient
  private double deductions;

  @Transient
  private double da; // Dearness Allowance

  @Transient
  private double hra; // House Rent Allowance

  @Transient
  private double ma; // Medical Allowance

  @Transient
  private double tax; // Income tax deduction

  @Transient
  private double pf; // Provident fund deduction

  //Getter and Setter methods
```

}

A sample run results as below.

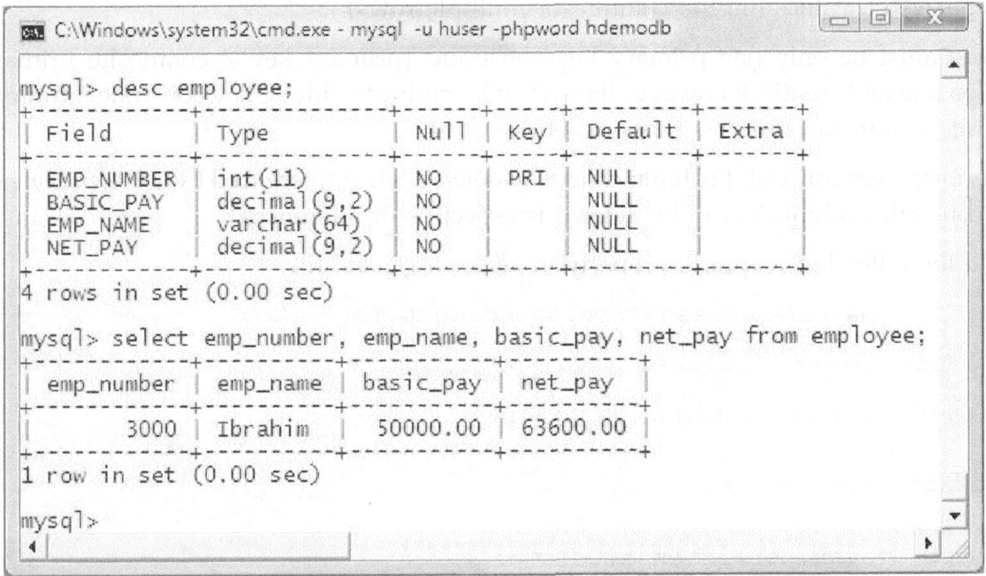

```
C:\Windows\system32\cmd.exe - mysql -u huser -phpword hdemodb

mysql> desc employee;
+------------+--------------+------+-----+---------+-------+
| Field      | Type         | Null | Key | Default | Extra |
+------------+--------------+------+-----+---------+-------+
| EMP_NUMBER | int(11)      | NO   | PRI | NULL    |       |
| BASIC_PAY  | decimal(9,2) | NO   |     | NULL    |       |
| EMP_NAME   | varchar(64)  | NO   |     | NULL    |       |
| NET_PAY    | decimal(9,2) | NO   |     | NULL    |       |
+------------+--------------+------+-----+---------+-------+
4 rows in set (0.00 sec)

mysql> select emp_number, emp_name, basic_pay, net_pay from employee;
+------------+----------+-----------+----------+
| emp_number | emp_name | basic_pay | net_pay  |
+------------+----------+-----------+----------+
|       3000 | Ibrahim  |  50000.00 | 63600.00 |
+------------+----------+-----------+----------+
1 row in set (0.00 sec)

mysql>
```

4.14 @UniqueConstraint - DEFINING UNIQUE COLUMNS AND COMPOSITE UNIQUE KEY

The *unique* attribute of `@Column` annotation defines unique (no duplicates) constraint for the corresponding column (column level) in an Entity. Similarly, the `@UniqueConstraint` annotation can be used in conjunction with `@Table` annotation (specify this `@UniqueConstraint` as value of `uniqueConstraint` attribute of `@Table` annotation) to define unique fields (columns) at Entity level. Even though both methods do the same function, `@UniqueConstraint` can also be used to define *Composite Unique Keys*, which can be generated using *unique* attribute of `@Column` annotation.

General formats

```
@UniqueConstraint(columnNames  =  {"Column-name-in-entity"})
```

You can use an array of `@UniqueConstraint` in `uniqueConstraints` attribute of `@Table` annotation to specify multiple unique keys (not composite unique keys) on that table.

```
@UniqueConstraint(columnNames=String-array-of-column-names-in-entity)
```

An array of column-names (multiple column names) specified in the `columnNames` attribute of `@UniqueConstraint` will result *Composite Unique Keys* on that table.

Unique key defined on a column will not accept duplicate (already stored value on that column) values. Composite unique key (like Composite primary key) defines a combination of unique columns, i.e., the data in this group of columns (as a bunch) should not be repeated.

A note on Primary key versus Unique key:

Primary key can not accept duplicate and *NULL* values. Unique key can not accept duplicates, but accepts *NULL* values (on the column for multiple rows).

There must be only one primary key constraint (primary key / composite primary key) defined on one table (entity); however there may be multiple unique key constraints (unique keys /composite unique keys) defined on one table (entity).

A primary key constraint column cannot be deleted when referenced by a *foreign key;* however unique constraint column(s) can be deleted irrespective of references.

Add the following mapping property in *hibernate.cfg.xml* file.

```
        <mapping class="com.hdemo.Customer" />
```

```
// File Name: Customer.java
// Illustrates @UniqueConstraint

package com.hdemo;

import javax.persistence.Column;
import javax.persistence.Entity;
import javax.persistence.GeneratedValue;
import javax.persistence.GenerationType;
import javax.persistence.Id;
import javax.persistence.Table;

@Entity
@Table(name = "CUSTOMER")
public class Customer {

   @Id
   @GeneratedValue(strategy = GenerationType.AUTO)
   @Column(name = "SEQ_NUMBER")
   private int seqNum;

   @Column(name = "CUST_NUMBER")
   private int customerNumber;

   @Column(name = "CUST_NAME")
   private String customerName;
```

```
  @Column(name = "SERVICE_NUMBER", unique = true)
  private String serviceNumber;

  @Column(name = "COMPLAINT_NUMBER")
  private String complaintNumber;

  @Column(name = "COMPLAINT_CATEGORY")
  private String complaintCategory;

  @Column(name = "REMARKS")
  private String remarks;

 //Getter and Setter methods

}
```

```
// File Name: CustomerService.java
// Main program

package com.hdemo;

import org.hibernate.Session;
import org.hibernate.SessionFactory;
import org.hibernate.Transaction;

public class CustomerService {

public static void main(String[] args) throws Exception {
SessionFactory sessionFactory = HibernateUtil.getSessionFactory();
  Session session = sessionFactory.getCurrentSession();
  Transaction txn = session.beginTransaction();

  Customer customer1 = new Customer();
  customer1.setCustomerNumber(2001);
  customer1.setCustomerName("Ajay");
  customer1.setServiceNumber("S3001");
  customer1.setComplaintNumber("C4001");
  customer1.setComplaintCategory("GENERAL_FAILURE");
```

```
    customer1.setRemarks("Please take necessary action.");

    Customer customer2 = new Customer();
    customer2.setCustomerNumber(2002);
    customer2.setCustomerName("Ibrahim");
    customer2.setServiceNumber("S3002");
    customer2.setComplaintNumber("C4002");
    customer2.setComplaintCategory("GENERAL_FAILURE");
    customer2.setRemarks("General failure.");

    Customer customer3 = new Customer();
    customer3.setCustomerNumber(2001);
    customer3.setCustomerName("Ajay");
    customer3.setComplaintNumber("C4001");
    customer3.setComplaintCategory("DAMAGE");
    customer3.setRemarks("Attention required.");

    Customer customer4 = new Customer();
    customer4.setCustomerNumber(2005);
    customer4.setCustomerName("Karan");
    customer4.setComplaintNumber("C4000");
    customer4.setComplaintCategory("GENERAL_FAILURE");
    customer4.setRemarks(null);

    session.save(customer1);
    session.save(customer2);
    session.save(customer3);
    session.save(customer4);

    txn.commit();
    sessionFactory.close();
    }
}
```

A sample run results as below.

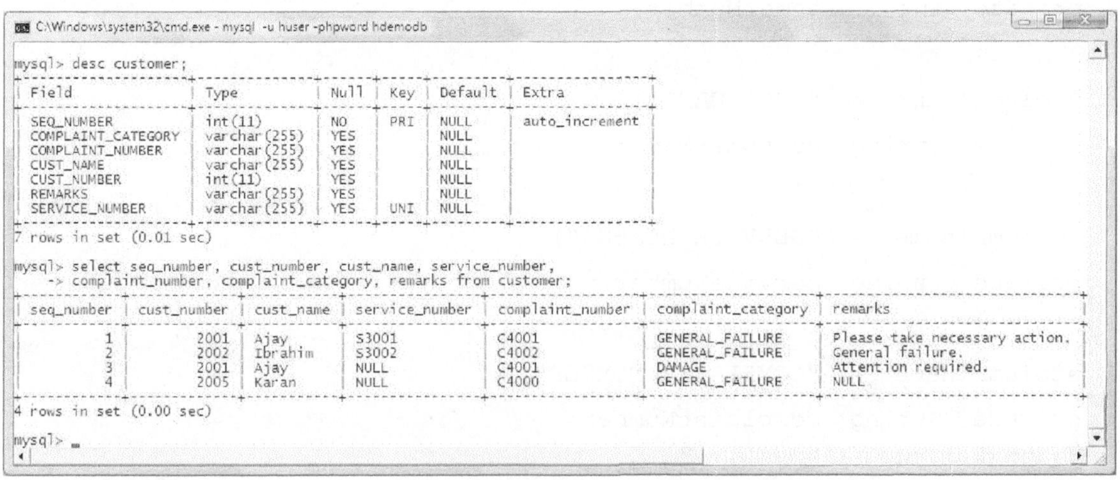

```
C:\Windows\system32\cmd.exe - mysql -u huser -phpword hdemodb

mysql> desc customer;
+--------------------+--------------+------+-----+---------+----------------+
| Field              | Type         | Null | Key | Default | Extra          |
+--------------------+--------------+------+-----+---------+----------------+
| SEQ_NUMBER         | int(11)      | NO   | PRI | NULL    | auto_increment |
| COMPLAINT_CATEGORY | varchar(255) | YES  |     | NULL    |                |
| COMPLAINT_NUMBER   | varchar(255) | YES  |     | NULL    |                |
| CUST_NAME          | varchar(255) | YES  |     | NULL    |                |
| CUST_NUMBER        | int(11)      | YES  |     | NULL    |                |
| REMARKS            | varchar(255) | YES  |     | NULL    |                |
| SERVICE_NUMBER     | varchar(255) | YES  | UNI | NULL    |                |
+--------------------+--------------+------+-----+---------+----------------+
7 rows in set (0.01 sec)

mysql> select seq_number, cust_number, cust_name, service_number,
    -> complaint_number, complaint_category, remarks from customer;
+------------+-------------+-----------+----------------+------------------+--------------------+-----------------------------+
| seq_number | cust_number | cust_name | service_number | complaint_number | complaint_category | remarks                     |
+------------+-------------+-----------+----------------+------------------+--------------------+-----------------------------+
|          1 |        2001 | Ajay      | S3001          | C4001            | GENERAL_FAILURE    | Please take necessary action. |
|          2 |        2002 | Ibrahim   | S3002          | C4002            | GENERAL_FAILURE    | General failure.            |
|          3 |        2001 | Ajay      | NULL           | C4001            | DAMAGE             | Attention required.         |
|          4 |        2005 | Karan     | NULL           | C4000            | GENERAL_FAILURE    | NULL                        |
+------------+-------------+-----------+----------------+------------------+--------------------+-----------------------------+
4 rows in set (0.00 sec)

mysql> _
```

We can rewrite the *Customer* entity as follows using `@UniqueConstraint` annotation.

```
// File Name: Customer.java
// Illustrates @UniqueConstraint

package com.hdemo;

import javax.persistence.Column;
import javax.persistence.Entity;
import javax.persistence.GeneratedValue;
import javax.persistence.GenerationType;
import javax.persistence.Id;
import javax.persistence.Table;
import javax.persistence.UniqueConstraint;

@Entity
@Table(name = "CUSTOMER", uniqueConstraints = { @UniqueConstraint
(columnNames = { "SERVICE_NUMBER" }) })
public class Customer {

@Id
@GeneratedValue(strategy = GenerationType.AUTO)
@Column(name = "SEQ_NUMBER")
private int seqNum;
```

```
@Column(name = "CUST_NUMBER")
private int customerNumber;

@Column(name = "CUST_NAME")
private String customerName;

@Column(name = "SERVICE_NUMBER")
private String serviceNumber;

@Column(name = "COMPLAINT_NUMBER")
private String complaintNumber;

@Column(name = "COMPLAINT_CATEGORY")
private String complaintCategory;

@Column(name = "REMARKS")
private String remarks;

//Getter and Setter methods

}
```

Now, we will add the following statement in the main program to try to insert duplicate value for *Service Number* column.

```
customer3.setServiceNumber("S3002");
```

A sample run results in the following error.

```
Hibernate: insert into CUSTOMER (COMPLAINT_CATEGORY, COMPLAINT_NUMBER, CUST_NAME, CUST_NUMBER, REMARKS, SERVICE_NUMBER) values (?, ?, ?, ?, ?, ?)
Hibernate: insert into CUSTOMER (COMPLAINT_CATEGORY, COMPLAINT_NUMBER, CUST_NAME, CUST_NUMBER, REMARKS, SERVICE_NUMBER) values (?, ?, ?, ?, ?, ?)
Hibernate: insert into CUSTOMER (COMPLAINT_CATEGORY, COMPLAINT_NUMBER, CUST_NAME, CUST_NUMBER, REMARKS, SERVICE_NUMBER) values (?, ?, ?, ?, ?, ?)
0 [main] ERROR org.hibernate.util.JDBCExceptionReporter - Duplicate entry 'S3002' for key 2
...
```

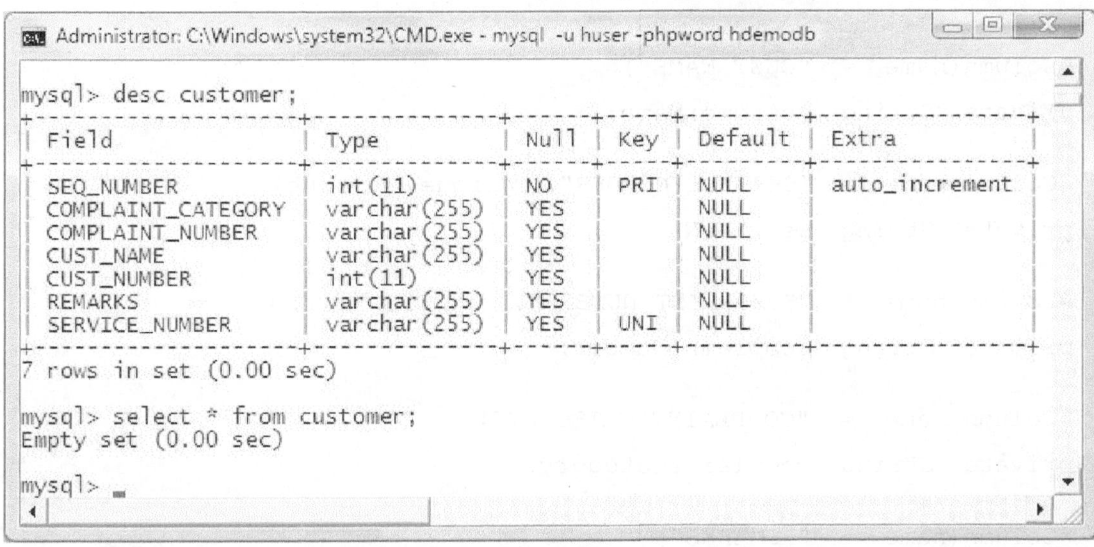

```
Administrator: C:\Windows\system32\CMD.exe - mysql  -u huser -phpword hdemodb

mysql> desc customer;
+--------------------+--------------+------+-----+---------+----------------+
| Field              | Type         | Null | Key | Default | Extra          |
+--------------------+--------------+------+-----+---------+----------------+
| SEQ_NUMBER         | int(11)      | NO   | PRI | NULL    | auto_increment |
| COMPLAINT_CATEGORY | varchar(255) | YES  |     | NULL    |                |
| COMPLAINT_NUMBER   | varchar(255) | YES  |     | NULL    |                |
| CUST_NAME          | varchar(255) | YES  |     | NULL    |                |
| CUST_NUMBER        | int(11)      | YES  |     | NULL    |                |
| REMARKS            | varchar(255) | YES  |     | NULL    |                |
| SERVICE_NUMBER     | varchar(255) | YES  | UNI | NULL    |                |
+--------------------+--------------+------+-----+---------+----------------+
7 rows in set (0.00 sec)

mysql> select * from customer;
Empty set (0.00 sec)

mysql> _
```

We will modify our entity to set *Service Number* and *Complaint Number* as unique (not composite unique key) using *unique* attribute of `@Column` annotation as follows.

```
// File Name: Customer.java
// Illustrates @UniqueConstraint

package com.hdemo;

import javax.persistence.Column;
import javax.persistence.Entity;
import javax.persistence.GeneratedValue;
import javax.persistence.GenerationType;
import javax.persistence.Id;
import javax.persistence.Table;

@Entity
@Table(name = "CUSTOMER")
public class Customer {

@Id
@GeneratedValue(strategy = GenerationType.AUTO)
@Column(name = "SEQ_NUMBER")
private int seqNum;

@Column(name = "CUST_NUMBER")
private int customerNumber;
```

```
@Column(name = "CUST_NAME")
private String customerName;

@Column(name = "SERVICE_NUMBER", unique = true)
private String serviceNumber;

@Column(name = "COMPLAINT_NUMBER", unique = true)
private String complaintNumber;

@Column(name = "COMPLAINT_CATEGORY")
private String complaintCategory;

@Column(name = "REMARKS")
private String remarks;

//Getter and Setter methods

}
```

```
// File Name: CustomerService.java
// Main program

package com.hdemo;

import org.hibernate.Session;
import org.hibernate.SessionFactory;
import org.hibernate.Transaction;

public class CustomerService {

  public static void main(String[] args) throws Exception {
  SessionFactory sessionFactory = HibernateUtil.getSessionFactory();
  Session session = sessionFactory.getCurrentSession();
  Transaction txn = session.beginTransaction();

  Customer customer1 = new Customer();
  customer1.setCustomerNumber(2001);
  customer1.setCustomerName("Ajay");
```

```
    customer1.setServiceNumber("S3001");
    customer1.setComplaintNumber("C5001");
    customer1.setComplaintCategory("GENERAL_FAILURE");
    customer1.setRemarks("Please take necessary action.");

    Customer customer2 = new Customer();
    customer2.setCustomerNumber(2002);
    customer2.setCustomerName("Ibrahim");
    customer2.setServiceNumber("S3002");
    customer2.setComplaintNumber("C5002");
    customer2.setComplaintCategory("GENERAL_FAILURE");
    customer2.setRemarks("General failure.");

    Customer customer3 = new Customer();
    customer3.setCustomerNumber(2001);
    customer3.setCustomerName("Ajay");
    customer3.setServiceNumber("S3003");
    customer3.setComplaintNumber("C5009");
    customer3.setComplaintCategory("DAMAGE");
    customer3.setRemarks("Attention required.");

    Customer customer4 = new Customer();
    customer4.setCustomerNumber(2005);
    customer4.setCustomerName("Karan");
    customer4.setComplaintCategory("GENERAL_FAILURE");
    customer4.setRemarks(null);

    session.save(customer1);
    session.save(customer2);
    session.save(customer3);
    session.save(customer4);

    txn.commit();
    sessionFactory.close();
    }

}
```

A sample run results as below.

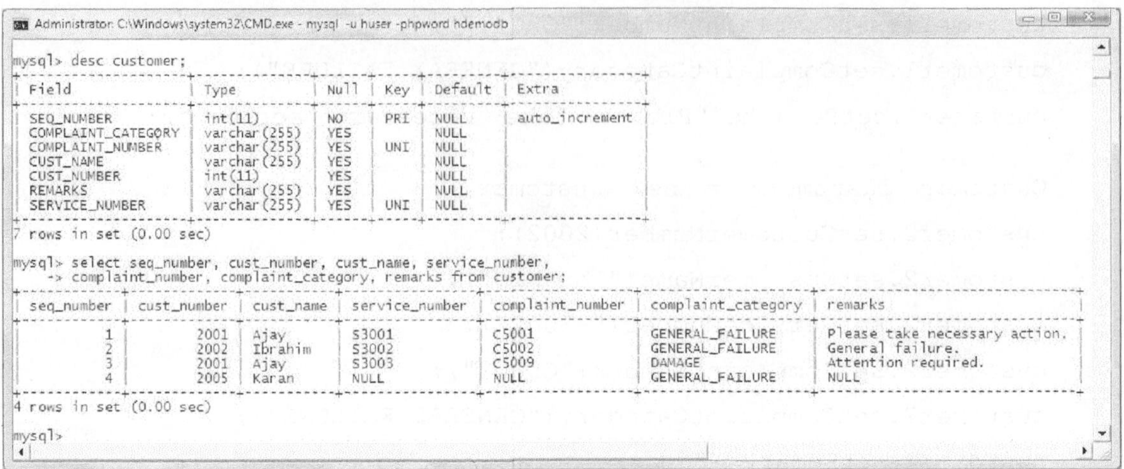

```
Administrator: C:\Windows\system32\CMD.exe - mysql -u huser -phpword hdemodb

mysql> desc customer;
+--------------------+--------------+------+-----+---------+----------------+
| Field              | Type         | Null | Key | Default | Extra          |
+--------------------+--------------+------+-----+---------+----------------+
| SEQ_NUMBER         | int(11)      | NO   | PRI | NULL    | auto_increment |
| COMPLAINT_CATEGORY | varchar(255) | YES  |     | NULL    |                |
| COMPLAINT_NUMBER   | varchar(255) | YES  | UNI | NULL    |                |
| CUST_NAME          | varchar(255) | YES  |     | NULL    |                |
| CUST_NUMBER        | int(11)      | YES  |     | NULL    |                |
| REMARKS            | varchar(255) | YES  |     | NULL    |                |
| SERVICE_NUMBER     | varchar(255) | YES  | UNI | NULL    |                |
+--------------------+--------------+------+-----+---------+----------------+
7 rows in set (0.00 sec)

mysql> select seq_number, cust_number, cust_name, service_number,
    -> complaint_number, complaint_category, remarks from customer;
+------------+-------------+-----------+----------------+------------------+--------------------+----------------------------+
| seq_number | cust_number | cust_name | service_number | complaint_number | complaint_category | remarks                    |
+------------+-------------+-----------+----------------+------------------+--------------------+----------------------------+
|          1 |        2001 | Ajay      | S3001          | C5001            | GENERAL_FAILURE    | Please take necessary action. |
|          2 |        2002 | Ibrahim   | S3002          | C5002            | GENERAL_FAILURE    | General failure.           |
|          3 |        2001 | Ajay      | S3003          | C5009            | DAMAGE             | Attention required.        |
|          4 |        2005 | Karan     | NULL           | NULL             | GENERAL_FAILURE    | NULL                       |
+------------+-------------+-----------+----------------+------------------+--------------------+----------------------------+
4 rows in set (0.00 sec)

mysql>
```

Now, we will modify our main program as below to try to insert duplicate value for *Service Number* column.

```
// File Name: CustomerService.java
// Main program

package com.hdemo;

import org.hibernate.Session;
import org.hibernate.SessionFactory;
import org.hibernate.Transaction;

public class CustomerService {

public static void main(String[] args) throws Exception {
   SessionFactory sessionFactory = HibernateUtil.getSessionFactory();
   Session session = sessionFactory.getCurrentSession();
   Transaction txn = session.beginTransaction();

   Customer customer1 = new Customer();
   customer1.setCustomerNumber(2001);
   customer1.setCustomerName("Ajay");
   customer1.setServiceNumber("S3001");
   customer1.setComplaintNumber("C4001");
   customer1.setComplaintCategory("GENERAL_FAILURE");
```

```
    customer1.setRemarks("Please  take  necessary  action.");

    Customer  customer2  =  new  Customer();
    customer2.setCustomerNumber(2002);
    customer2.setCustomerName("Ibrahim");
    customer2.setServiceNumber("S3002");
    customer2.setComplaintNumber("C4002");
    customer2.setComplaintCategory("GENERAL_FAILURE");
    customer2.setRemarks("General  failure.");

    Customer  customer3  =  new  Customer();
    customer3.setCustomerNumber(2001);
    customer3.setCustomerName("Ajay");
    customer3.setServiceNumber("S3002");
    customer3.setComplaintNumber("C4003");
    customer3.setComplaintCategory("DAMAGE");
    customer3.setRemarks("Attention  required.");

    Customer  customer4  =  new  Customer();
    customer4.setCustomerNumber(2005);
    customer4.setCustomerName("Karan");
    customer4.setComplaintNumber("C4000");
    customer4.setComplaintCategory("GENERAL_FAILURE");
    customer4.setRemarks(null);

    session.save(customer1);
    session.save(customer2);
    session.save(customer3);
    session.save(customer4);

    txn.commit();
    sessionFactory.close();
    }
}
```

A sample run results in the following error.

```
Hibernate: insert into CUSTOMER (COMPLAINT_CATEGORY, COMPLAINT_NUMBER, CUST_NAME, CUST_NUMBER, REMARKS, SERVICE_NUMBER) values (?, ?, ?, ?, ?, ?)

Exception in thread "main"

org.hibernate.exception.ConstraintViolation Exception: could not insert: [com.hdemo.Customer]

...
```

The following main program tries to insert duplicate value for *Complaint Number* column.

```
// File Name: CustomerService.java
// Main program

package com.hdemo;

import org.hibernate.Session;
import org.hibernate.SessionFactory;
import org.hibernate.Transaction;

public class CustomerService {

  public static void main(String[] args) throws Exception {
  SessionFactory sessionFactory = HibernateUtil.getSessionFactory();
  Session session = sessionFactory.getCurrentSession();
  Transaction txn = session.beginTransaction();

  Customer customer1 = new Customer();
  customer1.setCustomerNumber(2001);
  customer1.setCustomerName("Ajay");
  customer1.setServiceNumber("S3001");
  customer1.setComplaintNumber("C4001");
  customer1.setComplaintCategory("GENERAL_FAILURE");
  customer1.setRemarks("Please take necessary action.");

  Customer customer2 = new Customer();
  customer2.setCustomerNumber(2002);
  customer2.setCustomerName("Ibrahim");
  customer2.setServiceNumber("S3002");
```

```
    customer2.setComplaintNumber("C4002");
    customer2.setComplaintCategory("GENERAL_FAILURE");
    customer2.setRemarks("General failure.");

    Customer customer3 = new Customer();
    customer3.setCustomerNumber(2001);
    customer3.setCustomerName("Ajay");
    customer3.setServiceNumber("S3003");
    customer3.setComplaintNumber("C4002");
    customer3.setComplaintCategory("DAMAGE");
    customer3.setRemarks("Attention required.");

    Customer customer4 = new Customer();
    customer4.setCustomerNumber(2005);
    customer4.setCustomerName("Karan");
    customer4.setComplaintNumber("C4000");
    customer4.setComplaintCategory("GENERAL_FAILURE");
    customer4.setRemarks(null);

    session.save(customer1);
    session.save(customer2);
    session.save(customer3);
    session.save(customer4);

    txn.commit();
    sessionFactory.close();
    }
}
```

A sample run results in the following error.

```
Hibernate: insert into CUSTOMER (COMPLAINT_CATEGORY, COMPLAINT_NUMBER,
CUST_NAME, CUST_NUMBER, REMARKS, SERVICE_NUMBER) values (?, ?, ?,
?, ?, ?)
Hibernate: insert into CUSTOMER (COMPLAINT_CATEGORY, COMPLAINT_NUMBER,
CUST_NAME, CUST_NUMBER, REMARKS, SERVICE_NUMBER) values (?, ?, ?,
?, ?, ?)
Hibernate: insert into CUSTOMER (COMPLAINT_CATEGORY, COMPLAINT_NUMBER,
CUST_NAME, CUST_NUMBER, REMARKS, SERVICE_NUMBER) values (?, ?, ?,
?, ?, ?)
```

```
0 [main] ERROR org.hibernate.util.JDBCExceptionReporter  - Duplicate entry 'C4002' for key 2
Exception in thread "main" org.hibernate.exception.ConstraintViolationException: could not insert: [com.hdemo.Customer]
...
```

We can rewrite the *Customer* entity as follows using `@UniqueConstraint` annotation (to set *Service Number* and *Complaint Number).*

```
// File Name: Customer.java
// Illustrates @UniqueConstraint

package com.hdemo;

import javax.persistence.Column;
import javax.persistence.Entity;
import javax.persistence.GeneratedValue;
import javax.persistence.GenerationType;
import javax.persistence.Id;
import javax.persistence.Table;
import javax.persistence.UniqueConstraint;

@Entity
@Table(name = "CUSTOMER",
uniqueConstraints = { @UniqueConstraint (columnNames = { "SERVICE_NUMBER" }), @UniqueConstraint(columnNames = { "COMPLAINT_NUMBER" }) })
public class Customer {

  @Id
  @GeneratedValue(strategy = GenerationType.AUTO)
  @Column(name = "SEQ_NUMBER")
  private int seqNum;

  @Column(name = "CUST_NUMBER")
  private int customerNumber;

  @Column(name = "CUST_NAME")
  private String customerName;
```

```
@Column(name = "SERVICE_NUMBER")
private String serviceNumber;

@Column(name = "COMPLAINT_NUMBER")
private String complaintNumber;

@Column(name = "COMPLAINT_CATEGORY")
private String complaintCategory;

@Column(name = "REMARKS")
private String remarks;

//Getter and Setter methods

}
```

The following entity sets composite unique keys on *Service Number* and *Complaint Number* fields using @UniqueConstraint annotation.

```
// File Name: Customer.java
// Illustrates @UniqueConstraint

package com.hdemo;

import javax.persistence.Column;
import javax.persistence.Entity;
import javax.persistence.GeneratedValue;
import javax.persistence.GenerationType;
import javax.persistence.Id;
import javax.persistence.Table;
import javax.persistence.UniqueConstraint;

@Entity
@Table(name = "CUSTOMER",
uniqueConstraints = { @UniqueConstraint (columnNames = {
"SERVICE_NUMBER", "COMPLAINT_NUMBER" }) })
  public class Customer {

  @Id
  @GeneratedValue(strategy = GenerationType.AUTO)
  @Column(name = "SEQ_NUMBER")
```

```
    private int seqNum;

    @Column(name = "CUST_NUMBER")
    private int customerNumber;

    @Column(name = "CUST_NAME")
    private String customerName;

    @Column(name = "SERVICE_NUMBER")
    private String serviceNumber;

    @Column(name = "COMPLAINT_NUMBER")
    private String complaintNumber;

    @Column(name = "COMPLAINT_CATEGORY")
    private String complaintCategory;

    @Column(name = "REMARKS")
    private String remarks;

    //Getter and Setter methods

}
```

```
// File Name: CustomerService.java
// Main program

package com.hdemo;

import org.hibernate.Session;
import org.hibernate.SessionFactory;
import org.hibernate.Transaction;

public class CustomerService {

    public static void main(String[] args) throws Exception {
    SessionFactory sessionFactory = HibernateUtil.getSessionFactory();
    Session session = sessionFactory.getCurrentSession();
    Transaction txn = session.beginTransaction();
```

```
Customer customer1 = new Customer();
customer1.setCustomerNumber(2001);
customer1.setCustomerName("Ajay");
customer1.setServiceNumber("S3002");
customer1.setComplaintNumber("C5001");
customer1.setComplaintCategory("GENERAL_FAILURE");
customer1.setRemarks("Please take necessary action.");

Customer customer2 = new Customer();
customer2.setCustomerNumber(2002);
customer2.setCustomerName("Ibrahim");
customer2.setServiceNumber("S3002");
customer2.setComplaintNumber("C5002");
customer2.setComplaintCategory("GENERAL_FAILURE");
customer2.setRemarks("General failure.");

Customer customer3 = new Customer();
customer3.setCustomerNumber(2001);
customer3.setCustomerName("Ajay");
customer3.setServiceNumber("S3001");
customer3.setComplaintNumber("C4001");
customer3.setComplaintCategory("DAMAGE");
customer3.setRemarks("Attention required.");

Customer customer4 = new Customer();
customer4.setCustomerNumber(2005);
customer4.setCustomerName("Karan");
customer4.setServiceNumber("S3002");
customer4.setComplaintNumber("C4001");
customer4.setComplaintCategory("ERROR");
customer4.setRemarks(null);

session.save(customer1);
session.save(customer2);
session.save(customer3);
session.save(customer4);
```

```
            txn.commit();

            sessionFactory.close();

    }

}
```

A sample run results as below.

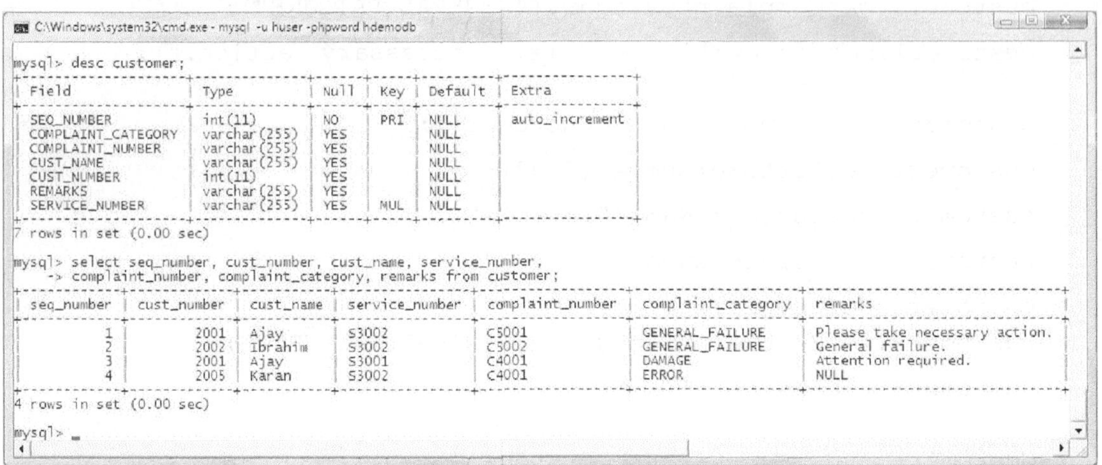

```
C:\Windows\system32\cmd.exe - mysql -u huser -phpword hdemodb

mysql> desc customer;
+--------------------+--------------+------+-----+---------+----------------+
| Field              | Type         | Null | Key | Default | Extra          |
+--------------------+--------------+------+-----+---------+----------------+
| SEQ_NUMBER         | int(11)      | NO   | PRI | NULL    | auto_increment |
| COMPLAINT_CATEGORY | varchar(255) | YES  |     | NULL    |                |
| COMPLAINT_NUMBER   | varchar(255) | YES  |     | NULL    |                |
| CUST_NAME          | varchar(255) | YES  |     | NULL    |                |
| CUST_NUMBER        | int(11)      | YES  |     | NULL    |                |
| REMARKS            | varchar(255) | YES  |     | NULL    |                |
| SERVICE_NUMBER     | varchar(255) | YES  | MUL | NULL    |                |
+--------------------+--------------+------+-----+---------+----------------+
7 rows in set (0.00 sec)

mysql> select seq_number, cust_number, cust_name, service_number,
    -> complaint_number, complaint_category, remarks from customer;
+------------+-------------+-----------+----------------+------------------+--------------------+-----------------------------+
| seq_number | cust_number | cust_name | service_number | complaint_number | complaint_category | remarks                     |
+------------+-------------+-----------+----------------+------------------+--------------------+-----------------------------+
|          1 |        2001 | Ajay      | S3002          | C5001            | GENERAL_FAILURE    | Please take necessary action. |
|          2 |        2002 | Ibrahim   | S3002          | C5002            | GENERAL_FAILURE    | General failure.            |
|          3 |        2001 | Ajay      | S3001          | C4001            | DAMAGE             | Attention required.         |
|          4 |        2005 | Karan     | S3002          | C4001            | ERROR              | NULL                        |
+------------+-------------+-----------+----------------+------------------+--------------------+-----------------------------+
4 rows in set (0.00 sec)

mysql> _
```

The combination of values (except NULL values) of Service Number and Complaint Number should not be repeated.

The following database insert will result in error, because already S3002-C5001 Service Number and Complaint Number pair exists in the table.

```
C:\Windows\system32\cmd.exe - mysql -u huser -phpword hdemodb

mysql> insert into customer (cust_number, cust_name, service_number, complaint_number, complaint_category, remarks)
    -> values (2006, 'Kumar', 'S3002', 'C5001', 'ERROR', 'Please check');
ERROR 1062 (23000): Duplicate entry 'S3002-C5001' for key 2
mysql>
```

The combination check is for data only, not for NULL values.

```
C:\Windows\system32\cmd.exe - mysql -u huser -phpword hdemodb
mysql> insert into customer (cust_number, cust_name, service_number, complaint_number, complaint_category, remarks)
    -> values (2006, 'Kumar', 'S3002', null, 'ERROR', null);
Query OK, 1 row affected (0.05 sec)

mysql> insert into customer (cust_number, cust_name, service_number, complaint_number, complaint_category, remarks)
    -> values (2006, 'Kumar', 'S3002', null, 'ERROR', null);
Query OK, 1 row affected (0.06 sec)

mysql> insert into customer (cust_number, cust_name, service_number, complaint_number, complaint_category, remarks)
    -> values (2006, 'Kumar', 'S3002', null, 'ERROR', null);
Query OK, 1 row affected (0.01 sec)

mysql> select seq_number, cust_number, cust_name, service_number,
    -> complaint_number, complaint_category, remarks from customer;
+------------+-------------+-----------+----------------+------------------+--------------------+-------------------------------+
| seq_number | cust_number | cust_name | service_number | complaint_number | complaint_category | remarks                       |
+------------+-------------+-----------+----------------+------------------+--------------------+-------------------------------+
|          1 |        2001 | Ajay      | S3002          | C5001            | GENERAL_FAILURE    | Please take necessary action. |
|          2 |        2002 | Ibrahim   | S3001          | NULL             | GENERAL_FAILURE    | General failure.              |
|          3 |        2001 | Ajay      | S3001          | NULL             | DAMAGE             | Attention required.           |
|          4 |        2005 | Karan     | S3002          | C4001            | ERROR              | NULL                          |
|          5 |        2006 | Kumar     | S3002          | NULL             | ERROR              | NULL                          |
|          6 |        2006 | Kumar     | S3002          | NULL             | ERROR              | NULL                          |
|          7 |        2006 | Kumar     | S3002          | NULL             | ERROR              | NULL                          |
+------------+-------------+-----------+----------------+------------------+--------------------+-------------------------------+
7 rows in set (0.00 sec)

mysql> _
```

Assume that the *customer* table had data as below.

```
Administrator: C:\Windows\system32\CMD.exe - mysql  -u huser -phpword hdemodb

mysql> desc customer;
+--------------------+--------------+------+-----+---------+----------------+
| Field              | Type         | Null | Key | Default | Extra          |
+--------------------+--------------+------+-----+---------+----------------+
| SEQ_NUMBER         | int(11)      | NO   | PRI | NULL    | auto_increment |
| COMPLAINT_CATEGORY | varchar(255) | YES  |     | NULL    |                |
| COMPLAINT_NUMBER   | varchar(255) | YES  |     | NULL    |                |
| CUST_NAME          | varchar(255) | YES  |     | NULL    |                |
| CUST_NUMBER        | int(11)      | YES  |     | NULL    |                |
| REMARKS            | varchar(255) | YES  |     | NULL    |                |
| SERVICE_NUMBER     | varchar(255) | YES  | MUL | NULL    |                |
+--------------------+--------------+------+-----+---------+----------------+
7 rows in set (0.00 sec)

mysql> select seq_number, cust_number, cust_name, service_number,
    -> complaint_number, complaint_category, remarks from customer;
+------------+-------------+-----------+----------------+------------------+--------------------+-------------------------------+
| seq_number | cust_number | cust_name | service_number | complaint_number | complaint_category | remarks                       |
+------------+-------------+-----------+----------------+------------------+--------------------+-------------------------------+
|          1 |        2001 | Ajay      | S3002          | C5001            | GENERAL_FAILURE    | Please take necessary action. |
|          2 |        2002 | Ibrahim   | S3002          | C5002            | GENERAL_FAILURE    | General failure.              |
|          3 |        2001 | Ajay      | S3001          | C4001            | DAMAGE             | Attention required.           |
|          4 |        2005 | Karan     | S3002          | C4001            | ERROR              | NULL                          |
+------------+-------------+-----------+----------------+------------------+--------------------+-------------------------------+
4 rows in set (0.00 sec)

mysql>
```

If we try to insert duplicate value pair `S3002-C5001` for *Service Number* and *Complaint Number* columns, then error is resulted. **Note:** Do not forget to set *hbm2ddl.auto property* in *hibernate.cfg.xml* file to *update* before executing the main program (as we want to keep existing data in database table; we don't want to re-create table).

```
// File Name: CustomerService.java
// Main program

package com.hdemo;

import org.hibernate.Session;
import org.hibernate.SessionFactory;
import org.hibernate.Transaction;

public class CustomerService {

    public static void main(String[] args) throws Exception {
    SessionFactory sessionFactory = HibernateUtil.getSessionFactory();
    Session session = sessionFactory.getCurrentSession();
    Transaction txn = session.beginTransaction();


    Customer customer1 = new Customer();
    customer1.setCustomerNumber(2006);
    customer1.setCustomerName("Kumar");
    customer1.setServiceNumber("S3002");
```

```
    customer1.setComplaintNumber("C5001");
    customer1.setComplaintCategory("ERROR");
    customer1.setRemarks("Please check.");

    session.save(customer1);

    txn.commit();
    sessionFactory.close();
    }
}
```

Result:

```
Hibernate: insert into CUSTOMER (COMPLAINT_CATEGORY, COMPLAINT_NUMBER,
CUST_NAME, CUST_NUMBER, REMARKS, SERVICE_NUMBER) values (?, ?, ?,
?, ?, ?)
0 [main] ERROR org.hibernate.util.JDBCExceptionReporter - Duplicate
entry 'S3002-C5001' for key 2
Exception in thread "main"
org.hibernate.exception. ConstraintViolationException: could not
insert: [com.hdemo.Customer]
...
```

4.15 @Embeddable - EMBEDDING ONE ENTITY INTO ANOTHER

A class which is declared as `@Embeddable` can be embedded (wholly inserted) with another class (entity) by using instance of `@Embeddable` class, of course the fields of the `@Embeddable` class will be mapped with the database table of the embedding entity. That's how a Primary Key class (declared as `@Embeddable`) is embedded with entity class in the earlier example.

Use `@Embeddable` at class level to define an Embeddable class. An embeddable object inherits the access type of its owning entity (which can be modified using `@AccessType` annotation).

An `@Embeddable` class can be embeddable in an entity by declaring an object of `@Embeddable` class. This object should be mapped (declared) as `@Embedded`, otherwise Hibernate will do for you, by default.

```
// File Name: Salary.java
// Illustrates @Embeddable

package com.hdemo;

import javax.persistence.Column;
import javax.persistence.Embeddable;
```

```
@Embeddable
public class Salary {

@Column(name = "BPAY")
private Double basicPay;

@Column(name = "ALLOWANCES")
private Double allowances;

@Column(name = "DEDUCTIONS")
private Double deductions;

@Column(name = "NETPAY")
private Double netPay;

//Getter and Setter methods

}
```

```
// File Name: Employee.java
// Illustrates @Embedded

package com.hdemo;

import java.io.Serializable;

import javax.persistence.Column;
import javax.persistence.Embedded;
import javax.persistence.Entity;
import javax.persistence.GeneratedValue;
import javax.persistence.Id;
import javax.persistence.Table;

import org.hibernate.annotations.GenericGenerator;

@Entity
@Table(name = "EMPLOYEE")
public class Employee implements Serializable {
```

```
    private static final long serialVersionUID = 1L;

    @Id
    @GeneratedValue(generator = "idGen")
    @GenericGenerator(name = "idGen", strategy = "uuid.hex")
    @Column(name = "ID", length = 32)
    private String id = "";

    @Column(name = "EMP_NUMBER", unique = true, nullable = false)
    private Integer empNumber;

    @Column(name = "EMP_NAME", length = 64, nullable = false)
    private String empName;

    @Embedded
    private Salary salary;

    //Getter and Setter methods

}
```

```
// File Name: EmployeeManipulation.java
// Main program

package com.hdemo;

import org.hibernate.Session;
import org.hibernate.SessionFactory;
import org.hibernate.Transaction;

public class EmployeeManipulation {

    public static void main(String[] args) throws Exception {
    SessionFactory sessionFactory = HibernateUtil.getSessionFactory();
    Session session = sessionFactory.getCurrentSession();
    Transaction txn = session.beginTransaction();

    Employee employee = new Employee();
    employee.setEmpNumber(2000);
    employee.setEmpName("Ibrahim");
```

```
    Salary salary = new Salary();
    salary.setBasicPay(10000.00);
    salary.setAllowances(3000.00);
    salary.setDeductions(2000.00);
    salary.setNetPay(salary.getBasicPay() + salary.getAllowances()
                                          - salary.getDeductions());
    employee.setSalary(salary);

    session.save(employee);
            txn.commit();
            sessionFactory.close();
    }
}
```

A sample run results as follows.

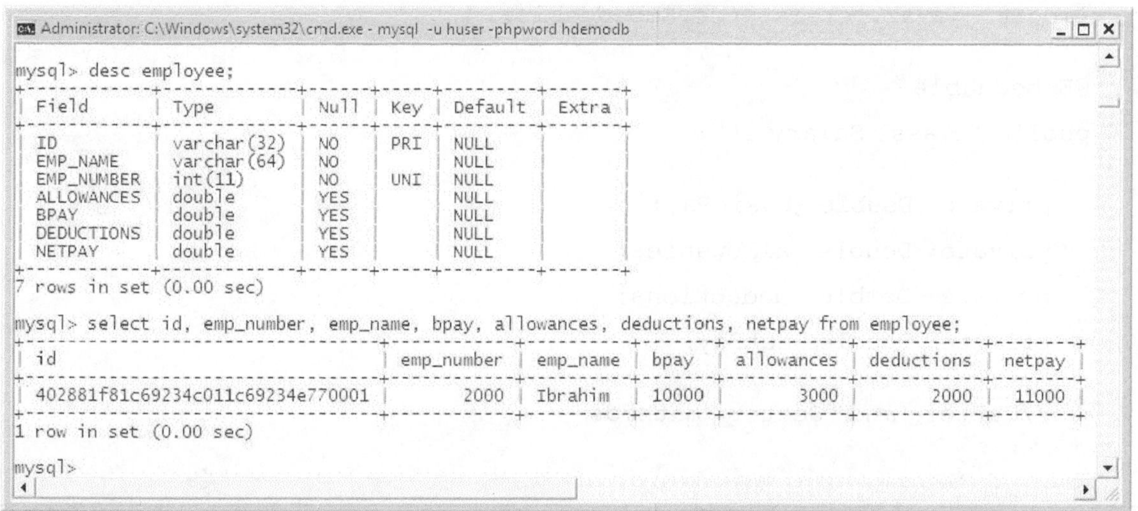

```
Administrator: C:\Windows\system32\cmd.exe - mysql -u huser -phpword hdemodb

mysql> desc employee;
+-------------+-------------+------+-----+---------+-------+
| Field       | Type        | Null | Key | Default | Extra |
+-------------+-------------+------+-----+---------+-------+
| ID          | varchar(32) | NO   | PRI | NULL    |       |
| EMP_NAME    | varchar(64) | NO   |     | NULL    |       |
| EMP_NUMBER  | int(11)     | NO   | UNI | NULL    |       |
| ALLOWANCES  | double      | YES  |     | NULL    |       |
| BPAY        | double      | YES  |     | NULL    |       |
| DEDUCTIONS  | double      | YES  |     | NULL    |       |
| NETPAY      | double      | YES  |     | NULL    |       |
+-------------+-------------+------+-----+---------+-------+
7 rows in set (0.00 sec)

mysql> select id, emp_number, emp_name, bpay, allowances, deductions, netpay from employee;
+----------------------------------+------------+----------+-------+------------+------------+--------+
| id                               | emp_number | emp_name | bpay  | allowances | deductions | netpay |
+----------------------------------+------------+----------+-------+------------+------------+--------+
| 402881f81c69234c011c69234e770001 |       2000 | Ibrahim  | 10000 |       3000 |       2000 |  11000 |
+----------------------------------+------------+----------+-------+------------+------------+--------+
1 row in set (0.00 sec)

mysql>
```

By default, column definitions of `@Embeddable` class applies to the table of the owning (embedding) entity, which (all attributes of `@Column`) can be modified by using `@AttributeOverride` (for single column) / `@AttributeOverrides` (for multiple columns) annotations in owning entity.

General format

To override one column,

```
@AttributeOverride(name="Overriding_Class_Field",
                   column=@Column(Column_Attributes))
```

The attribute *name* specifies the *field-name* of the base class (in our case, @Embeddable class). The *column* attribute defines new column definitions.

To override multiple columns (specify an array of `@AttributeOverride` as the argument in `@AttributeOverrides`),

```
@AttributeOverrides({
        @AttributeOverride,
        @AttributeOverride, ...
})
```

The `@AttributeOverride/@AttributeOverrides` can also be used to override fields of `@MappedSuperclass` class.

```
// File Name: Salary.java
// Illustrates @Embeddable

package com.hdemo;

import javax.persistence.Embeddable;

@Embeddable
public class Salary {

    private Double basicPay;
    private Double allowances;
    private Double deductions;
    private Double netPay;

    //Getter and Setter methods

}
```

```
// File Name: Employee.java
// Illustrates @Embedded

package com.hdemo;

import java.io.Serializable;

import javax.persistence.AttributeOverride;
import javax.persistence.AttributeOverrides;
```

```
import javax.persistence.Column;
import javax.persistence.Embedded;
import javax.persistence.Entity;
import javax.persistence.GeneratedValue;
import javax.persistence.Id;
import javax.persistence.Table;

import org.hibernate.annotations.GenericGenerator;

@Entity
@Table(name = "EMPLOYEE")
public class Employee implements Serializable {

  private static final long serialVersionUID = 1L;

  @Id
  @GeneratedValue(generator = "idGen")
  @GenericGenerator(name = "idGen", strategy = "uuid.hex")
  @Column(name = "ID", length = 32)
  private String id = "";

  @Column(name = "EMP_NUMBER", unique = true, nullable = false)
  private Integer empNumber;

  @Column(name = "EMP_NAME", length = 64, nullable = false)
  private String empName;

  @Embedded
  @AttributeOverrides({
  @AttributeOverride(name="basicPay",  column=@Column(name="BPAY")),
  @AttributeOverride(name="allowances", column=@Column(name="ALLOW")),
  @AttributeOverride(name="deductions", column=@Column(name="DEDUCT")),
  @AttributeOverride(name="netPay",  column=@Column(name="NETSAL"))
  })
  private Salary salary;

  //Getter and Setter methods
  }
```

Keep the same `EmployeeManipulation.java`

A sample run results as follows.

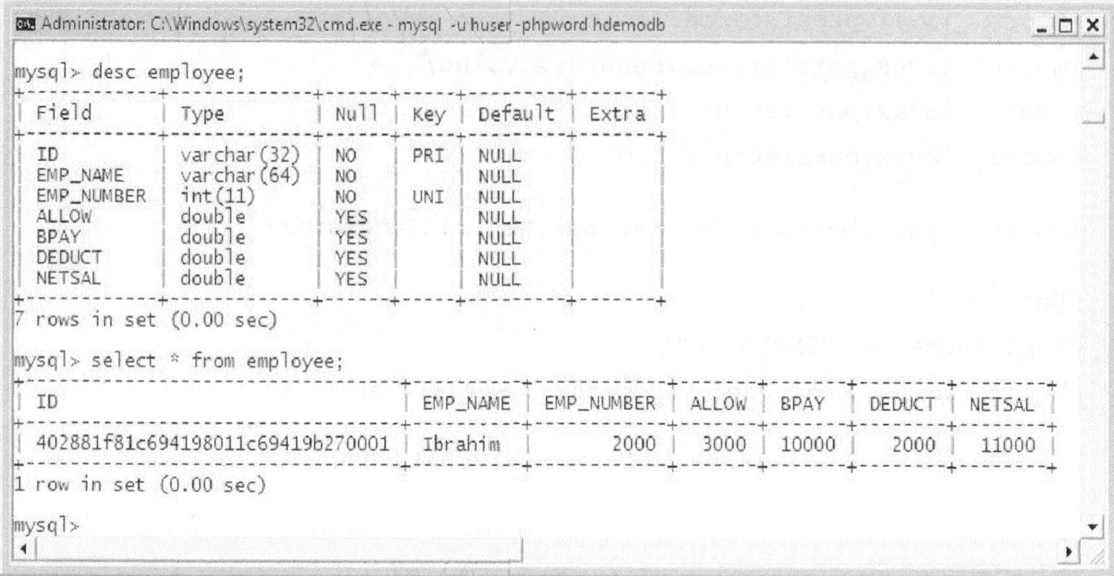

```
Administrator: C:\Windows\system32\cmd.exe - mysql -u huser -phpword hdemodb

mysql> desc employee;
+------------+-------------+------+-----+---------+-------+
| Field      | Type        | Null | Key | Default | Extra |
+------------+-------------+------+-----+---------+-------+
| ID         | varchar(32) | NO   | PRI | NULL    |       |
| EMP_NAME   | varchar(64) | NO   |     | NULL    |       |
| EMP_NUMBER | int(11)     | NO   | UNI | NULL    |       |
| ALLOW      | double      | YES  |     | NULL    |       |
| BPAY       | double      | YES  |     | NULL    |       |
| DEDUCT     | double      | YES  |     | NULL    |       |
| NETSAL     | double      | YES  |     | NULL    |       |
+------------+-------------+------+-----+---------+-------+
7 rows in set (0.00 sec)

mysql> select * from employee;
+----------------------------------+----------+------------+-------+-------+--------+--------+
| ID                               | EMP_NAME | EMP_NUMBER | ALLOW | BPAY  | DEDUCT | NETSAL |
+----------------------------------+----------+------------+-------+-------+--------+--------+
| 402881f81c694198011c69419b270001 | Ibrahim  |       2000 |  3000 | 10000 |   2000 |  11000 |
+----------------------------------+----------+------------+-------+-------+--------+--------+
1 row in set (0.00 sec)

mysql>
```

We try modifying some column attributes.

```
//  File  Name:  Salary.java
//  Illustrates  @Embeddable

package  com.hdemo;

import  javax.persistence.Column;
import  javax.persistence.Embeddable;

@Embeddable
public  class  Salary  {

   @Column(name  =  "BPAY")
   private  Double  basicPay;

   @Column(name  =  "ALLOWANCES")
   private  Double  allowances;

   @Column(name  =  "DEDUCTIONS")
   private  Double  deductions;

   @Column(name  =  "NETPAY")
```

```
  private Double netPay;

}
```

```
// File Name: Employee.java
// Illustrates @Embedded

package com.hdemo;

import java.io.Serializable;

import javax.persistence.AttributeOverride;
import javax.persistence.AttributeOverrides;
import javax.persistence.Column;
import javax.persistence.Embedded;
import javax.persistence.Entity;
import javax.persistence.GeneratedValue;
import javax.persistence.Id;
import javax.persistence.Table;

import org.hibernate.annotations.GenericGenerator;

@Entity
@Table(name = "EMPLOYEE")
public class Employee implements Serializable {

  private static final long serialVersionUID = 1L;

  @Id
  @GeneratedValue(generator = "idGen")
  @GenericGenerator(name = "idGen", strategy = "uuid.hex")
  @Column(name = "ID", length = 32)
  private String id = "";

  @Column(name = "EMP_NUMBER", unique = true, nullable = false)
  private Integer empNumber;

  @Column(name = "EMP_NAME", length = 64, nullable = false)
  private String empName;
```

```
@Embedded
@AttributeOverrides({
@AttributeOverride(name="basicPay", column=@Column(name=
"EMP_BASIC_PAY",  nullable=false)),
@AttributeOverride(name="allowances", column=@Column(name=
"EMP_SAL_ALLOWANCES")),
@AttributeOverride(name="deductions", column=@Column(name=
"EMP_SAL_DEDUCTIONS")),
@AttributeOverride(name="netPay", column=@Column(name=
"EMP_NET_SALARY",  nullable=false))
})
private Salary salary;

//Getter and Setter methods

}
```

Keep the same `EmployeeManipulation.java`

A sample run results as follows.

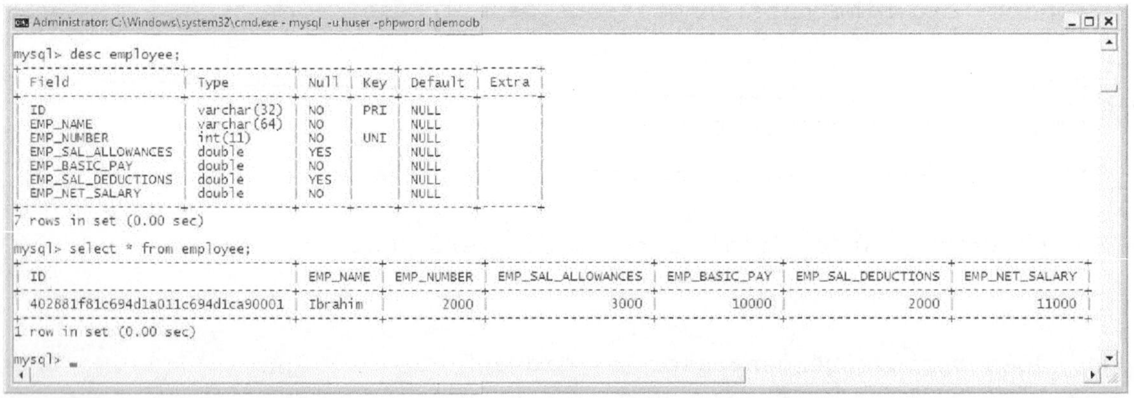


```
mysql> desc employee;
+--------------------+-------------+------+-----+---------+-------+
| Field              | Type        | Null | Key | Default | Extra |
+--------------------+-------------+------+-----+---------+-------+
| ID                 | varchar(32) | NO   | PRI | NULL    |       |
| EMP_NAME           | varchar(64) | NO   |     | NULL    |       |
| EMP_NUMBER         | int(11)     | NO   | UNI | NULL    |       |
| EMP_SAL_ALLOWANCES | double      | YES  |     | NULL    |       |
| EMP_BASIC_PAY      | double      | NO   |     | NULL    |       |
| EMP_SAL_DEDUCTIONS | double      | YES  |     | NULL    |       |
| EMP_NET_SALARY     | double      | NO   |     | NULL    |       |
+--------------------+-------------+------+-----+---------+-------+
7 rows in set (0.00 sec)

mysql> select * from employee;
+----------------------------------+----------+------------+--------------------+---------------+--------------------+----------------+
| ID                               | EMP_NAME | EMP_NUMBER | EMP_SAL_ALLOWANCES | EMP_BASIC_PAY | EMP_SAL_DEDUCTIONS | EMP_NET_SALARY |
+----------------------------------+----------+------------+--------------------+---------------+--------------------+----------------+
| 402881f81c694d1a011c694d1ca90001 | Ibrahim  |       2000 |               3000 |         10000 |               2000 |          11000 |
+----------------------------------+----------+------------+--------------------+---------------+--------------------+----------------+
1 row in set (0.00 sec)

mysql> _
```

4.16 `@Inheritance` - INHERITING PROPERTIES OF EXISTING ENTITIES

Inheritance is Object Oriented Programming System (OOPS) feature, which is used to create new classes (derived classes, sub classes) using already existing classes (base classes, super classes), so that the new classes will have properties (fields and methods) of existing classes. Thus Inheritance provides code reusability that the derived classes can use the properties (fields and methods) of base classes while adding their own functionalities.

4.16.1 Single Table Inheritance

The below example illustrates the default Hibernate settings (*Single Table Inheritance*), while using Inheritance.

We are defining three entity classes namely *Employee, EmployeeSalary,* and *EmployeeAddress.* The *Employee* acts as the super class, where the sub-classes *EmployeeSalary* and *EmployeeAddress* inherit it.

```
// File Name: Employee.java
// Illustrates @Inheritance

package com.hdemo;

import javax.persistence.Column;
import javax.persistence.Entity;
import javax.persistence.GeneratedValue;
import javax.persistence.Id;
import javax.persistence.Table;

import org.hibernate.annotations.GenericGenerator;

@Entity
@Table(name = "EMPLOYEE")
public class Employee {

   @Id
   @GeneratedValue(generator = "idGen")
   @GenericGenerator(name = "idGen", strategy = "uuid.hex")
   @Column(name = "ID", length = 32)
   private String id;

   @Column(name = "EMP_NUMBER", unique = true, nullable = false)
   private Integer empNumber;

   @Column(name = "EMP_NAME", length = 64, nullable = false)
   private String empName;

   //Getter and Setter methods
}
```

```
// File Name: EmployeeSalary.java
// Illustrates @Inheritance

package com.hdemo;

import javax.persistence.Column;
import javax.persistence.Entity;

@Entity
public class EmployeeSalary extends Employee {

  @Column(name = "BPAY")
  private Double basicPay;

  @Column(name = "ALLOWANCES")
  private Double allowances;

  @Column(name = "DEDUCTIONS")
  private Double deductions;

  @Column(name = "NETPAY")
  private Double netPay;

  //Getter and Setter methods

}
```

```
// File Name: EmployeeAddress.java
// Illustrates @Inheritance

package com.hdemo;

import javax.persistence.Column;
import javax.persistence.Entity;

@Entity
public class EmployeeAddress extends Employee {

  @Column(name = "HOUSE_NUMBER", length=8)
  private String houseNumber;
```

```
    @Column(name = "STREET_NAME", length=64)
    private String streetName;

    @Column(name = "CITY_NAME", length=64)
    private String cityName;

    @Column(name = "COUNTRY_NAME", length=64)
    private String countryName;

    @Column(name = "POSTAL_CODE", length=16)
    private String postalCode;

    //Getter and Setter methods

}
```

Don't forget to include the following mappings in *hibernate.cfg.xml* before running main class (`EmployeeManipulation.java`).

```
    <mapping class="com.hdemo.Employee" />
    <mapping class="com.hdemo.EmployeeSalary" />
    <mapping class="com.hdemo.EmployeeAddress" />
```

```
// File Name: EmployeeManipulation.java
// Main Program

package com.hdemo;

import org.hibernate.Session;
import org.hibernate.SessionFactory;
import org.hibernate.Transaction;

public class EmployeeManipulation {

    public static void main(String[] args) throws Exception {
    SessionFactory sessionFactory = HibernateUtil.getSessionFactory();
    Session session = sessionFactory.getCurrentSession();
    Transaction txn = session.beginTransaction();

    Employee employee = new Employee();
    employee.setEmpNumber(1000);
    employee.setEmpName("David");
    session.save(employee);
```

```
    EmployeeSalary  employeeSalary  =  new  EmployeeSalary();
    employeeSalary.setEmpNumber(2000);
    employeeSalary.setEmpName("Ibrahim");
    employeeSalary.setBasicPay(10000.00);
    employeeSalary.setAllowances(3000.00);
    employeeSalary.setDeductions(2000.00);
    employeeSalary.setNetPay(employeeSalary.getBasicPay()  +
    employeeSalary.getAllowances()  -  employeeSalary.getDeductions());
    session.save(employeeSalary);

    EmployeeAddress  employeeAddress  =  new  EmployeeAddress();
    employeeAddress.setEmpNumber(3000);
    employeeAddress.setEmpName("Ajay");
    employeeAddress.setHouseNumber("D-46-5");
    employeeAddress.setStreetName("Jalan  Bunus");
    employeeAddress.setCityName("Kuala  Lumpur");
    employeeAddress.setCountryName("Malaysia");
    employeeAddress.setPostalCode("50100");
    session.save(employeeAddress);

    txn.commit();
    sessionFactory.close();
    }
}
```

The successful execution of the above main class results in the following changes in the database.

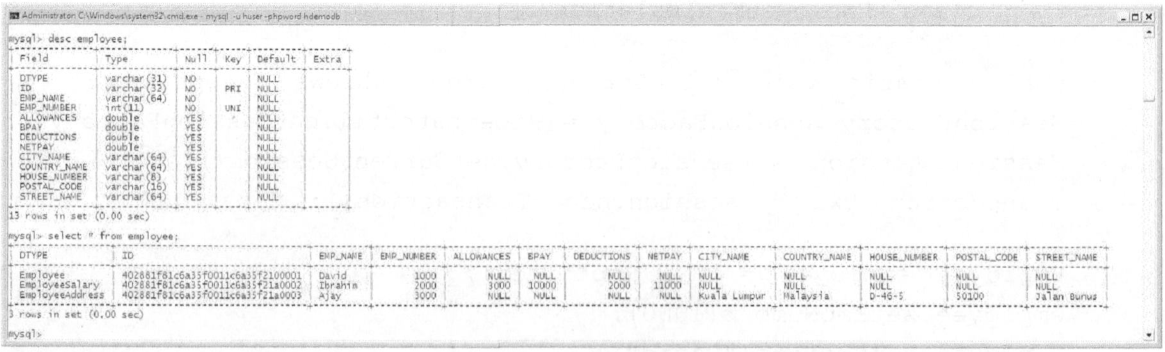

```
Administrator: C:\Windows\system32\cmd.exe - mysql -u huser -phpword hdemodb

mysql> desc employee;
+----------------+--------------+------+-----+---------+-------+
| Field          | Type         | Null | Key | Default | Extra |
+----------------+--------------+------+-----+---------+-------+
| DTYPE          | varchar(31)  | NO   |     | NULL    |       |
| ID             | varchar(32)  | NO   | PRI | NULL    |       |
| EMP_NAME       | varchar(64)  | NO   |     | NULL    |       |
| EMP_NUMBER     | int(11)      | NO   | UNI | NULL    |       |
| ALLOWANCES     | double       | YES  |     | NULL    |       |
| BPAY           | double       | YES  |     | NULL    |       |
| DEDUCTIONS     | double       | YES  |     | NULL    |       |
| NETPAY         | double       | YES  |     | NULL    |       |
| CITY_NAME      | varchar(64)  | YES  |     | NULL    |       |
| COUNTRY_NAME   | varchar(64)  | YES  |     | NULL    |       |
| HOUSE_NUMBER   | varchar(8)   | YES  |     | NULL    |       |
| POSTAL_CODE    | varchar(16)  | YES  |     | NULL    |       |
| STREET_NAME    | varchar(64)  | YES  |     | NULL    |       |
+----------------+--------------+------+-----+---------+-------+
13 rows in set (0.00 sec)

mysql> select * from employee;
+-----------------+----------------------------------+----------+------------+------------+-------+------------+--------+--------------+--------------+--------------+-------------+-------------+
| DTYPE           | ID                               | EMP_NAME | EMP_NUMBER | ALLOWANCES | BPAY  | DEDUCTIONS | NETPAY | CITY_NAME    | COUNTRY_NAME | HOUSE_NUMBER | POSTAL_CODE | STREET_NAME |
+-----------------+----------------------------------+----------+------------+------------+-------+------------+--------+--------------+--------------+--------------+-------------+-------------+
| Employee        | 402881f81c6a35f0011c6a35f2100001 | David    |       1000 |       NULL |  NULL |       NULL |   NULL | NULL         | NULL         | NULL         | NULL        | NULL        |
| EmployeeSalary  | 402881f81c6a35f0011c6a35f21a0002 | Ibrahim  |       2000 |       3000 | 10000 |       2000 |  11000 | NULL         | NULL         | NULL         | NULL        | NULL        |
| EmployeeAddress | 402881f81c6a35f0011c6a35f21a0003 | Ajay     |       3000 |       NULL |  NULL |       NULL |   NULL | Kuala Lumpur | Malaysia     | D-46-5       | 50100       | Jalan Bunus |
+-----------------+----------------------------------+----------+------------+------------+-------+------------+--------+--------------+--------------+--------------+-------------+-------------+
3 rows in set (0.00 sec)

mysql>
```

Observe that only one database table (for base class) is created with all the fields in base class and its all derived classes (of course, these classes should be mapped in *hibernate.cfg.xml* file) and with a special database-table column named "DTYPE", which is the *discriminator column* used to make a clear distinction that which set of field(s) are belong to which entity. When persisting one object, the non-present (not owned) field of those fields are set to *null*. For example, while persisting *Employee* object, the fields of *EmployeeSalary* and *EmployeeAddress* is set to *null*. Like wise while persisting *EmployeeSalary* object the fields, of *EmployeeAddress* fields are set to *null* automatically (of course, the *Employee* class fields cannot set to *null* automatically where they became part of *EmployeeSalary* as it inherits *Employee*). Note that only super class should have `@Id` fields, not at sub-classes.

Hibernate uses class-name of actual *object*, not the class-name of reference variable which refers the object, for discriminator column (DTYPE column). In the following main class, we used *base class* reference variable to refer *derived class* object and persisted that object through base class reference variable. However, Hibernate uses object content-type (derived class name) as DTYPE column value.

```
// File Name: EmployeeManipulation.java
// Main Program

package com.hdemo;

import org.hibernate.Session;
import org.hibernate.SessionFactory;
import org.hibernate.Transaction;

public class EmployeeManipulation {

  public static void main(String[] args) throws Exception {
  SessionFactory sessionFactory = HibernateUtil.getSessionFactory();
  Session session = sessionFactory.getCurrentSession();
  Transaction txn = session.beginTransaction();

  Employee employee = new Employee();
  employee.setEmpNumber(1000);
  employee.setEmpName("David");
  session.save(employee);

  Employee employeeSalary = new EmployeeSalary();
  employeeSalary.setEmpNumber(2000);
  employeeSalary.setEmpName("Ibrahim");
  session.save(employeeSalary);
```

```
        EmployeeAddress employeeAddress = new EmployeeAddress();
        employeeAddress.setEmpNumber(3000);
        employeeAddress.setEmpName("Ajay");
        session.save(employeeAddress);
        txn.commit();
        sessionFactory.close();
    }
}
```

The above main execution results in the following database changes.

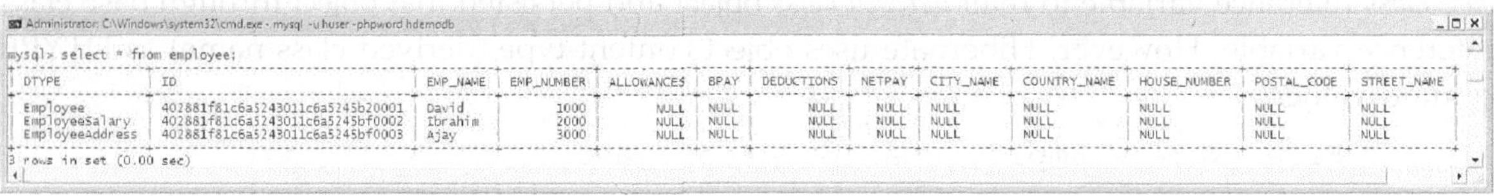

Administrator: C:\Windows\system32\cmd.exe - mysql -u huser -phpword hdemodb

mysql> select * from employee;

DTYPE	ID	EMP_NAME	EMP_NUMBER	ALLOWANCES	BPAY	DEDUCTIONS	NETPAY	CITY_NAME	COUNTRY_NAME	HOUSE_NUMBER	POSTAL_CODE	STREET_NAME
Employee	402881f81c6a5243011c6a5245b20001	David	1000	NULL	NULL	NULL	NULL	NULL	NULL	NULL	NULL	NULL
EmployeeSalary	402881f81c6a5243011c6a5245bf0002	Ibrahim	2000	NULL	NULL	NULL	NULL	NULL	NULL	NULL	NULL	NULL
EmployeeAddress	402881f81c6a5243011c6a5245bf0003	Ajay	3000	NULL	NULL	NULL	NULL	NULL	NULL	NULL	NULL	NULL

3 rows in set (0.00 sec)

The following entities do the same operation as defined above (by using default settings).

```
// File Name: Employee.java
// Illustrates @Inheritance

package com.hdemo;

import javax.persistence.Column;
import javax.persistence.DiscriminatorColumn;
import javax.persistence.DiscriminatorType;
import javax.persistence.DiscriminatorValue;
import javax.persistence.Entity;
import javax.persistence.GeneratedValue;
import javax.persistence.Id;
import javax.persistence.Inheritance;
import javax.persistence.InheritanceType;
import javax.persistence.Table;

import org.hibernate.annotations.GenericGenerator;

@Entity
@Table(name = "EMPLOYEE")
@Inheritance(strategy = InheritanceType.SINGLE_TABLE)
```

```
@DiscriminatorColumn(name = "DISCRIMINATOR_TYPE", discriminatorType
= DiscriminatorType.STRING, length = 20)
@DiscriminatorValue("EMP")
public class Employee {

 @Id
  @GeneratedValue(generator = "idGen")
  @GenericGenerator(name = "idGen", strategy = "uuid.hex")
  @Column(name = "ID", length = 32)
  private String id;

  @Column(name = "EMP_NUMBER", unique = true, nullable = false)
  private Integer empNumber;

  @Column(name = "EMP_NAME", length = 64, nullable = false)
  private String empName;

  //Getter and Setter methods

}
```

```
// File Name: EmployeeSalary.java
// Illustrates @Inheritance

package com.hdemo;

import javax.persistence.Column;
import javax.persistence.DiscriminatorValue;
import javax.persistence.Entity;

@Entity
@DiscriminatorValue("EMPSAL")
public class EmployeeSalary extends Employee {

  @Column(name = "BPAY")
  private Double basicPay;

  @Column(name = "ALLOWANCES")
  private Double allowances;
```

```
    @Column(name = "DEDUCTIONS")
    private Double deductions;

    @Column(name = "NETPAY")
    private Double netPay;

    //Getter and Setter methods

}
```

```
// File Name: EmployeeAddress.java
// Illustrates @Inheritance

package com.hdemo;

import javax.persistence.Column;
import javax.persistence.DiscriminatorValue;
import javax.persistence.Entity;

@Entity
@DiscriminatorValue("EMPADDR")
public class EmployeeAddress extends Employee {

    @Column(name = "HOUSE_NUMBER", length = 8)
    private String houseNumber;

    @Column(name = "STREET_NAME", length = 64)
    private String streetName;

    @Column(name = "CITY_NAME", length = 64)
    private String cityName;

    @Column(name = "COUNTRY_NAME", length = 64)
    private String countryName;

    @Column(name = "POSTAL_CODE", length = 16)
    private String postalCode;

    //Getter and Setter methods

}
```

The sample main program and its effect in database are shown below.

```
// File Name: EmployeeManipulation.java
// Main Program

package com.hdemo;

import org.hibernate.Session;
import org.hibernate.SessionFactory;
import org.hibernate.Transaction;

public class EmployeeManipulation {

  public static void main(String[] args) throws Exception {
  SessionFactory sessionFactory = HibernateUtil.getSessionFactory();
  Session session = sessionFactory.getCurrentSession();
  Transaction txn = session.beginTransaction();

  Employee employee = new Employee();
  employee.setEmpNumber(1000);
  employee.setEmpName("David");
  session.save(employee);

  EmployeeSalary employeeSalary = new EmployeeSalary();
  employeeSalary.setEmpNumber(2000);
  employeeSalary.setEmpName("Ibrahim");
  employeeSalary.setBasicPay(10000.00);
  employeeSalary.setAllowances(3000.00);
  employeeSalary.setDeductions(2000.00);
  employeeSalary.setNetPay(employeeSalary.getBasicPay() +
  employeeSalary.getAllowances() - employeeSalary.getDeductions());
  session.save(employeeSalary);

  EmployeeAddress employeeAddress = new EmployeeAddress();
  employeeAddress.setEmpNumber(3000);
  employeeAddress.setEmpName("Ajay");
  employeeAddress.setHouseNumber("D-46-5");
  employeeAddress.setStreetName("Jalan Bunus");
  employeeAddress.setCityName("Kuala Lumpur");
```

```
        employeeAddress.setCountryName("Malaysia");
        employeeAddress.setPostalCode("50100");
        session.save(employeeAddress);

        txn.commit();
        sessionFactory.close();
        }
    }
```

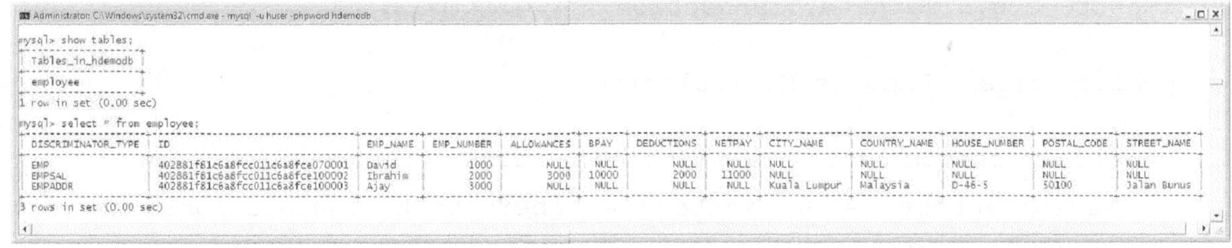

```
Administrator: C:\Windows\system32\cmd.exe - mysql -u huser -phpword hdemodb
mysql> show tables;
+-------------------+
| Tables_in_hdemodb |
+-------------------+
| employee          |
+-------------------+
1 row in set (0.00 sec)

mysql> select * from employee;
```

DISCRIMINATOR_TYPE	ID	EMP_NAME	EMP_NUMBER	ALLOWANCES	BPAY	DEDUCTIONS	NETPAY	CITY_NAME	COUNTRY_NAME	HOUSE_NUMBER	POSTAL_CODE	STREET_NAME
EMP	402881f81c6a8fcc011c6a8fce070001	David	1000	NULL	NULL	NULL	NULL	NULL	NULL	NULL	NULL	NULL
EMPSAL	402881f81c6a8fcc011c6a8fce100002	Ibrahim	2000	3000	10000	2000	11000	NULL	NULL	NULL	NULL	NULL
EMPADDR	402881f81c6a8fcc011c6a8fce100003	Ajay	3000	NULL	NULL	NULL	NULL	Kuala Lumpur	Malaysia	D-46-5	50100	Jalan Bunus

```
3 rows in set (0.00 sec)
```

The generated table has a discriminator column whose value represents the specific subclass to which the object that is represented by the row belongs to. By default, the discriminator column name is "DTYPE" and value for this column is the class-name of the object that is persisted with that row. The name of discriminator column can be modified through `@DiscriminatorColumn` annotation.

General format

```
@DiscriminatorColumn(name = "Column_Name_in_Table",
                     discriminatorType = DiscriminatorType.STRING,
                     length = column_length,
                     columnDefinition = "Extra_Column_Definitions")
```

The attribute *name* specifies the name of the discriminator column in the database table, the attribute *discriminatorType* specifies the type of data (*data type*) that the discriminator column will have to get (Hibernate provides pre-defined constants values for this column as follows, *DiscriminatorType.STRING, DiscriminatorType.CHAR, DiscriminatorType.INTEGER.* You can also use compactable custom class), the attribute *length* specifies maximum size of discriminator column for String type of values, and extra column constrains and definition can be specified through *columnDefinition* attribute.

The above cases, only one database table is created in the name of base class entity (of course if `@Table` is used, the table name is same as specified in `@Table` of base class `@Entity`) with all fields in base class and all derived classes. This approach is called ***SINGLE_TABLE Inheritance.***

4.16.2 Joined Table Inheritance

Every sub-class creates its own table (like base class creates a root table) with its own fields, not inherited fields. However, each sub-class shares data with the root table. Each sub-class table will be assigned a primary-key column (whose column-definitions are same as primary key column in base class table) and this column will contain the same value of primary key column of corresponding row in base table. And this column in sub-class table will acts as a foreign key to base table.

```
// File Name: Employee.java
// Illustrates @Inheritance

package com.hdemo;

import javax.persistence.Column;
import javax.persistence.Entity;
import javax.persistence.GeneratedValue;
import javax.persistence.Id;
import javax.persistence.Inheritance;
import javax.persistence.InheritanceType;
import javax.persistence.Table;

import org.hibernate.annotations.GenericGenerator;

@Entity
@Table(name = "EMPLOYEE")
@Inheritance(strategy = InheritanceType.JOINED)
public class Employee {

  @Id
  @GeneratedValue(generator = "idGen")
  @GenericGenerator(name = "idGen", strategy = "uuid.hex")
  @Column(name = "ID_PK", length = 32)
  private String id;

  @Column(name = "EMP_NUMBER", unique = true, nullable = false)
  private Integer empNumber;

  @Column(name = "EMP_NAME", length = 64, nullable = false)
  private String empName;
```

```
  //Getter and Setter methods
}
```

```
// File Name: EmployeeSalary.java
// Illustrates @Inheritance

package com.hdemo;

import javax.persistence.Column;
import javax.persistence.Entity;
import javax.persistence.Table;

@Entity
@Table(name = "EMPLOYEE_SAL")
public class EmployeeSalary extends Employee {

  @Column(name = "BPAY")
  private Double basicPay;

  @Column(name = "ALLOWANCES")
  private Double allowances;

  @Column(name = "DEDUCTIONS")
  private Double deductions;

  @Column(name = "NETPAY")
  private Double netPay;

  //Getter and Setter methods

}
```

```
// File Name: EmployeeAddress.java
// Illustrates @Inheritance

package com.hdemo;

import javax.persistence.Column;
```

```
import javax.persistence.Entity;
import javax.persistence.Table;

@Entity
@Table(name = "EMPLOYEE_ADDR")
public class EmployeeAddress extends Employee {

  @Column(name = "HOUSE_NUMBER", length = 8)
  private String houseNumber;

  @Column(name = "STREET_NAME", length = 64)
  private String streetName;

  @Column(name = "CITY_NAME", length = 64)
  private String cityName;

  @Column(name = "COUNTRY_NAME", length = 64)
  private String countryName;

  @Column(name = "POSTAL_CODE", length = 16)
  private String postalCode;

  //Getter and Setter methods

}
```

```
// File Name: EmployeeManipulation.java
// Main program

package com.hdemo;

import org.hibernate.Session;
import org.hibernate.SessionFactory;
import org.hibernate.Transaction;

public class EmployeeManipulation {

  public static void main(String[] args) throws Exception {
  SessionFactory sessionFactory = HibernateUtil.getSessionFactory();
```

```
    Session session = sessionFactory.getCurrentSession();
    Transaction txn = session.beginTransaction();

    Employee employee = new Employee();
    employee.setEmpNumber(1000);
    employee.setEmpName("David");
    session.save(employee);

    EmployeeSalary employeeSalary = new EmployeeSalary();
    employeeSalary.setEmpNumber(2000);
    employeeSalary.setEmpName("Ibrahim");
    employeeSalary.setBasicPay(10000.00);
    employeeSalary.setAllowances(3000.00);
    employeeSalary.setDeductions(2000.00);
    employeeSalary.setNetPay(employeeSalary.getBasicPay() +
      employeeSalary.getAllowances() - employeeSalary.getDeductions());
    session.save(employeeSalary);
    EmployeeAddress employeeAddress = new EmployeeAddress();
    employeeAddress.setEmpNumber(3000);
    employeeAddress.setEmpName("Ajay");
    employeeAddress.setHouseNumber("D-46-5");
    employeeAddress.setStreetName("Jalan Bunus");
    employeeAddress.setCityName("Kuala Lumpur");
    employeeAddress.setCountryName("Malaysia");
    employeeAddress.setPostalCode("50100");
    session.save(employeeAddress);

    txn.commit();
    sessionFactory.close();
    }
}
```

A sample run of the main program results in the following database changes.

```
Administrator: C:\Windows\system32\cmd.exe - mysql -u huser -phpword hde...

mysql> show tables;
+------------------+
| Tables_in_hdemodb |
+------------------+
| employee         |
| employee_addr    |
| employee_sal     |
+------------------+
3 rows in set (0.00 sec)

mysql> desc employee;
+------------+-------------+------+-----+---------+-------+
| Field      | Type        | Null | Key | Default | Extra |
+------------+-------------+------+-----+---------+-------+
| ID_PK      | varchar(32) | NO   | PRI | NULL    |       |
| EMP_NAME   | varchar(64) | NO   |     | NULL    |       |
| EMP_NUMBER | int(11)     | NO   | UNI | NULL    |       |
+------------+-------------+------+-----+---------+-------+
3 rows in set (0.00 sec)

mysql> desc employee_sal;
+------------+-------------+------+-----+---------+-------+
| Field      | Type        | Null | Key | Default | Extra |
+------------+-------------+------+-----+---------+-------+
| ALLOWANCES | double      | YES  |     | NULL    |       |
| BPAY       | double      | YES  |     | NULL    |       |
| DEDUCTIONS | double      | YES  |     | NULL    |       |
| NETPAY     | double      | YES  |     | NULL    |       |
| ID_PK      | varchar(32) | NO   | PRI | NULL    |       |
+------------+-------------+------+-----+---------+-------+
5 rows in set (0.00 sec)

mysql> desc employee_addr;
+--------------+-------------+------+-----+---------+-------+
| Field        | Type        | Null | Key | Default | Extra |
+--------------+-------------+------+-----+---------+-------+
| CITY_NAME    | varchar(64) | YES  |     | NULL    |       |
| COUNTRY_NAME | varchar(64) | YES  |     | NULL    |       |
| HOUSE_NUMBER | varchar(8)  | YES  |     | NULL    |       |
| POSTAL_CODE  | varchar(16) | YES  |     | NULL    |       |
| STREET_NAME  | varchar(64) | YES  |     | NULL    |       |
| ID_PK        | varchar(32) | NO   | PRI | NULL    |       |
+--------------+-------------+------+-----+---------+-------+
6 rows in set (0.00 sec)

mysql> _
```

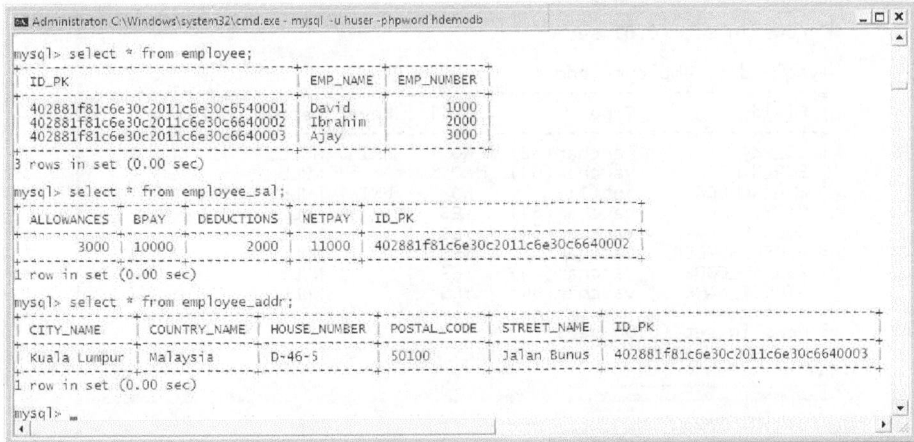

```
Administrator: C:\Windows\system32\cmd.exe - mysql -u huser -phpword hdemodb

mysql> select * from employee;
+----------------------------------+----------+------------+
| ID_PK                            | EMP_NAME | EMP_NUMBER |
+----------------------------------+----------+------------+
| 402881f81c6e30c2011c6e30c6540001 | David    |       1000 |
| 402881f81c6e30c2011c6e30c6640002 | Ibrahim  |       2000 |
| 402881f81c6e30c2011c6e30c6640003 | Ajay     |       3000 |
+----------------------------------+----------+------------+
3 rows in set (0.00 sec)

mysql> select * from employee_sal;
+------------+-------+------------+--------+----------------------------------+
| ALLOWANCES | BPAY  | DEDUCTIONS | NETPAY | ID_PK                            |
+------------+-------+------------+--------+----------------------------------+
|       3000 | 10000 |       2000 |  11000 | 402881f81c6e30c2011c6e30c6640002 |
+------------+-------+------------+--------+----------------------------------+
1 row in set (0.00 sec)

mysql> select * from employee_addr;
+--------------+--------------+--------------+-------------+-------------+----------------------------------+
| CITY_NAME    | COUNTRY_NAME | HOUSE_NUMBER | POSTAL_CODE | STREET_NAME | ID_PK                            |
+--------------+--------------+--------------+-------------+-------------+----------------------------------+
| Kuala Lumpur | Malaysia     | D-46-5       | 50100       | Jalan Bunus | 402881f81c6e30c2011c6e30c6640003 |
+--------------+--------------+--------------+-------------+-------------+----------------------------------+
1 row in set (0.00 sec)

mysql> _
```

4.16.3 Table per Class Inheritance

Each class (what ever it may be, base or derived one) creates its own table with all the fields, including the inherited fields from its super class. Since each table maps all of the fields in that entity's entire type hierarchy, there is no shared table and no columns are shared.

In the above example (Joint Table Inheritance), just change the value (parameter) of `@Inheritance` to `strategy=InheritanceType.TABLE_PER_CLASS` of *Employee* entity.

```
@Entity
@Table(name = "EMPLOYEE")
@Inheritance(strategy = InheritanceType.TABLE_PER_CLASS)
public class Employee {
{
    ...
}
```

A sample run of the main program results in the following database changes.

```
Administrator: C:\Windows\system32\cmd.exe - mysql -u huser -phpword hdem...

mysql> desc employee;
+------------+-------------+------+-----+---------+-------+
| Field      | Type        | Null | Key | Default | Extra |
+------------+-------------+------+-----+---------+-------+
| ID_PK      | varchar(32) | NO   | PRI | NULL    |       |
| EMP_NAME   | varchar(64) | NO   |     | NULL    |       |
| EMP_NUMBER | int(11)     | NO   | UNI | NULL    |       |
+------------+-------------+------+-----+---------+-------+
3 rows in set (0.00 sec)

mysql> desc employee_sal;
+------------+-------------+------+-----+---------+-------+
| Field      | Type        | Null | Key | Default | Extra |
+------------+-------------+------+-----+---------+-------+
| ID_PK      | varchar(32) | NO   | PRI | NULL    |       |
| EMP_NAME   | varchar(64) | NO   |     | NULL    |       |
| EMP_NUMBER | int(11)     | NO   | UNI | NULL    |       |
| ALLOWANCES | double      | YES  |     | NULL    |       |
| BPAY       | double      | YES  |     | NULL    |       |
| DEDUCTIONS | double      | YES  |     | NULL    |       |
| NETPAY     | double      | YES  |     | NULL    |       |
+------------+-------------+------+-----+---------+-------+
7 rows in set (0.01 sec)

mysql> desc employee_addr;
+--------------+-------------+------+-----+---------+-------+
| Field        | Type        | Null | Key | Default | Extra |
+--------------+-------------+------+-----+---------+-------+
| ID_PK        | varchar(32) | NO   | PRI | NULL    |       |
| EMP_NAME     | varchar(64) | NO   |     | NULL    |       |
| EMP_NUMBER   | int(11)     | NO   | UNI | NULL    |       |
| CITY_NAME    | varchar(64) | YES  |     | NULL    |       |
| COUNTRY_NAME | varchar(64) | YES  |     | NULL    |       |
| HOUSE_NUMBER | varchar(8)  | YES  |     | NULL    |       |
| POSTAL_CODE  | varchar(16) | YES  |     | NULL    |       |
| STREET_NAME  | varchar(64) | YES  |     | NULL    |       |
+--------------+-------------+------+-----+---------+-------+
8 rows in set (0.00 sec)
```

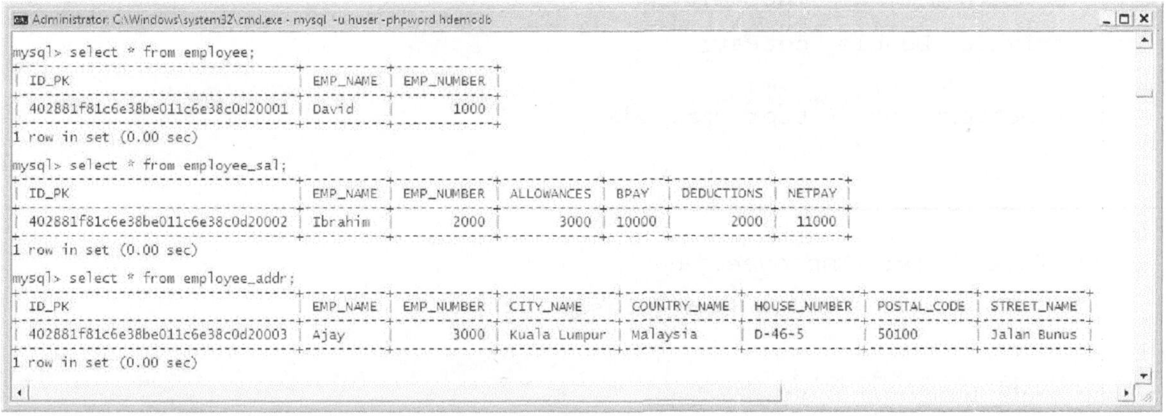

```
Administrator: C:\Windows\system32\cmd.exe - mysql -u huser -phpword hdemodb

mysql> select * from employee;
+----------------------------------+----------+------------+
| ID_PK                            | EMP_NAME | EMP_NUMBER |
+----------------------------------+----------+------------+
| 402881f81c6e38be011c6e38c0d20001 | David    |       1000 |
+----------------------------------+----------+------------+
1 row in set (0.00 sec)

mysql> select * from employee_sal;
+----------------------------------+----------+------------+------------+-------+------------+--------+
| ID_PK                            | EMP_NAME | EMP_NUMBER | ALLOWANCES | BPAY  | DEDUCTIONS | NETPAY |
+----------------------------------+----------+------------+------------+-------+------------+--------+
| 402881f81c6e38be011c6e38c0d20002 | Ibrahim  |       2000 |       3000 | 10000 |       2000 |  11000 |
+----------------------------------+----------+------------+------------+-------+------------+--------+
1 row in set (0.00 sec)

mysql> select * from employee_addr;
+----------------------------------+----------+------------+--------------+--------------+--------------+-------------+-------------+
| ID_PK                            | EMP_NAME | EMP_NUMBER | CITY_NAME    | COUNTRY_NAME | HOUSE_NUMBER | POSTAL_CODE | STREET_NAME |
+----------------------------------+----------+------------+--------------+--------------+--------------+-------------+-------------+
| 402881f81c6e38be011c6e38c0d20003 | Ajay     |       3000 | Kuala Lumpur | Malaysia     | D-46-5       | 50100       | Jalan Bunus |
+----------------------------------+----------+------------+--------------+--------------+--------------+-------------+-------------+
1 row in set (0.00 sec)
```

4.16.4 @MappedSuperclass

You may observe in the `@Inheritance` example that whatever the type of inheritance you use, the database table for base class will be created. This `@MappedSuperclass` is used create database table(s) for only sub-class/sub-classes, not for the base class. Simply declare the base class using `@MappedSuperclass`, then the database table columns will be created for all the fields in this base class along with the database table columns for sub-class while persisting `@Entity` sub-class object. That's how your entity sub-class inherits persistent fields from a `@MappedSuperclass` super class (which is common for other sub-classes).

```
// File Name: Salary.java
// Illustrates @MappedSuperclass

package com.hdemo;

import javax.persistence.Column;
import javax.persistence.MappedSuperclass;

@MappedSuperclass
public class Salary {

  @Column(name = "BPAY")
  private Double basicPay;

  @Column(name = "ALLOWANCES")
  private Double allowances;

  @Column(name = "DEDUCTIONS")
  private Double deductions;
```

```
    @Column(name = "NETPAY")
    private Double netPay;

    //Getter and Setter methods

}
```

```
// File Name: Employee.java
// Illustrates @MappedSuperclass

package com.hdemo;

import javax.persistence.Column;
import javax.persistence.Entity;
import javax.persistence.GeneratedValue;
import javax.persistence.Id;
import javax.persistence.Table;

import org.hibernate.annotations.GenericGenerator;
@Entity
@Table(name = "EMPLOYEE")
public class Employee extends Salary {

    private static final long serialVersionUID = 1L;

    @Id
    @GeneratedValue(generator = "idGen")
    @GenericGenerator(name = "idGen", strategy = "uuid.hex")
    @Column(name = "ID", length = 32)
    private String id = "";

    @Column(name = "EMP_NUMBER", unique = true, nullable = false)
    private Integer empNumber;

    @Column(name = "EMP_NAME", length = 64, nullable = false)
    private String empName;

    //Getter and Setter methods

}
```

```
// File Name: EmployeeManipulation.java
// Main program

package com.hdemo;

import org.hibernate.Session;
import org.hibernate.SessionFactory;
import org.hibernate.Transaction;

public class EmployeeManipulation {

  public static void main(String[] args) throws Exception {
  SessionFactory sessionFactory = HibernateUtil.getSessionFactory();
  Session session = sessionFactory.getCurrentSession();
  Transaction txn = session.beginTransaction();

  Employee employee = new Employee();
  employee.setEmpNumber(2000);
  employee.setEmpName("Ibrahim");
  employee.setBasicPay(10000.00);
  employee.setAllowances(3000.00);
  employee.setDeductions(2000.00);
  employee.setNetPay(employee.getBasicPay() + employee.getAllowances()
                                    - employee.getDeductions());

  session.save(employee);
  txn.commit();
  sessionFactory.close();
  }
}
```

Just add mapping entry for Employee class in *hibernate.cfg.xml,* no mapping for *Salary* class which is `@MappedSuperclass` not an `@Entity` class.

A sample run results as follows.

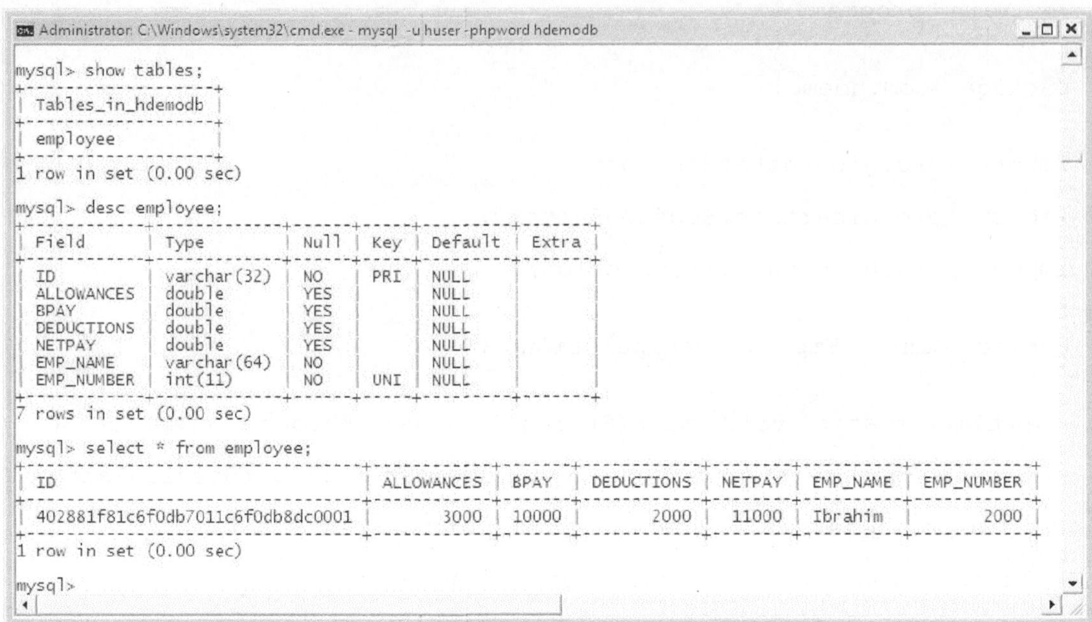

```
Administrator: C:\Windows\system32\cmd.exe - mysql -u huser -phpword hdemodb

mysql> show tables;
+-------------------+
| Tables_in_hdemodb |
+-------------------+
| employee          |
+-------------------+
1 row in set (0.00 sec)

mysql> desc employee;
+-------------+-------------+------+-----+---------+-------+
| Field       | Type        | Null | Key | Default | Extra |
+-------------+-------------+------+-----+---------+-------+
| ID          | varchar(32) | NO   | PRI | NULL    |       |
| ALLOWANCES  | double      | YES  |     | NULL    |       |
| BPAY        | double      | YES  |     | NULL    |       |
| DEDUCTIONS  | double      | YES  |     | NULL    |       |
| NETPAY      | double      | YES  |     | NULL    |       |
| EMP_NAME    | varchar(64) | NO   |     | NULL    |       |
| EMP_NUMBER  | int(11)     | NO   | UNI | NULL    |       |
+-------------+-------------+------+-----+---------+-------+
7 rows in set (0.00 sec)

mysql> select * from employee;
+----------------------------------+------------+-------+------------+--------+----------+------------+
| ID                               | ALLOWANCES | BPAY  | DEDUCTIONS | NETPAY | EMP_NAME | EMP_NUMBER |
+----------------------------------+------------+-------+------------+--------+----------+------------+
| 402881f81c6f0db7011c6f0db8dc0001 |       3000 | 10000 |       2000 |  11000 | Ibrahim  |       2000 |
+----------------------------------+------------+-------+------------+--------+----------+------------+
1 row in set (0.00 sec)

mysql>
```

This persistence operation is same as using `@Embeddable/@Embedded`. Here, we used the same example that is taken for illustrating `@Embeddable/@Embedded` annotations. Please go through these annotations once again to understand the similarity. Also, we can use `@AttributeOverride` (for single column)/`@AttributeOverrides` (for multiple columns) annotation to override base class field definitions (alter the field definitions of base class).

Change the *Employee* entity as follows and keep all other files intact.

```
// File Name: Employee.java
// Illustrates @MappedSuperclass

package com.hdemo;

import javax.persistence.AttributeOverride;
import javax.persistence.AttributeOverrides;
import javax.persistence.Column;
import javax.persistence.Entity;
import javax.persistence.GeneratedValue;
import javax.persistence.Id;
import javax.persistence.Table;

import org.hibernate.annotations.GenericGenerator;

@Entity
@Table(name = "EMPLOYEE")
```

```
@AttributeOverrides({
   @AttributeOverride(name="basicPay",  column=@Column(name="BPAY")),
   @AttributeOverride(name="allowances", column=@Column(name="ALLOW")),
   @AttributeOverride(name="deductions", column=@Column(name="DEDUCT")),
   @AttributeOverride(name="netPay",   column=@Column(name="NETSAL"))
   })
public class Employee extends Salary {

   private static final long serialVersionUID = 1L;

   @Id
   @GeneratedValue(generator = "idGen")
   @GenericGenerator(name = "idGen", strategy = "uuid.hex")
   @Column(name = "ID", length = 32)
   private String id = "";

   @Column(name = "EMP_NUMBER", unique = true, nullable = false)
   private Integer empNumber;

   @Column(name = "EMP_NAME", length = 64, nullable = false)
   private String empName;

   //Getter and Setter methods

}
```

A sample run results as follows.

```
Administrator: C:\Windows\system32\cmd.exe - mysql -u huser -phpword hdemodb
mysql> desc employee;
+------------+-------------+------+-----+---------+-------+
| Field      | Type        | Null | Key | Default | Extra |
+------------+-------------+------+-----+---------+-------+
| ID         | varchar(32) | NO   | PRI | NULL    |       |
| ALLOW      | double      | YES  |     | NULL    |       |
| BPAY       | double      | YES  |     | NULL    |       |
| DEDUCT     | double      | YES  |     | NULL    |       |
| NETSAL     | double      | YES  |     | NULL    |       |
| EMP_NAME   | varchar(64) | NO   |     | NULL    |       |
| EMP_NUMBER | int(11)     | NO   | UNI | NULL    |       |
+------------+-------------+------+-----+---------+-------+
7 rows in set (0.00 sec)

mysql> select * from employee;
+----------------------------------+-------+------+--------+--------+----------+------------+
| ID                               | ALLOW | BPAY | DEDUCT | NETSAL | EMP_NAME | EMP_NUMBER |
+----------------------------------+-------+------+--------+--------+----------+------------+
| 402881f81c6f17a7011c6f17a86a0001 |  NULL | NULL |   NULL |   NULL | Ibrahim  |       2000 |
+----------------------------------+-------+------+--------+--------+----------+------------+
1 row in set (0.00 sec)

mysql>
```

Note: If you are using inheritance, the base class should be either declared as `@Entity` or declared as `@MappedSuperclass`, then only its fields will become as persistent fields. Alternatively you can persist fields of `@Embeddable` class (it is not a base class, which is not also to be inherited) to another `@Entity` class using `@Embedded` object. Observe from the following example that the base class is neither `@Entity` nor `@MappedSuperclass`, so these fields are not became persisting fields of its sub-class.

```
// File Name: Salary.java
// Illustrates @MappedSuperclass

package com.hdemo;

import javax.persistence.Column;

public class Salary {

   @Column(name = "BPAY")
   private Double basicPay;

   @Column(name = "ALLOWANCES")
   private Double allowances;

   @Column(name = "DEDUCTIONS")
   private Double deductions;

   @Column(name = "NETPAY")
   private Double netPay;

   //Getter and Setter methods

}
```

```
// File Name: Employee.java
// Illustrates @MappedSuperclass

package com.hdemo;

import javax.persistence.Column;
import javax.persistence.Entity;
import javax.persistence.GeneratedValue;
import javax.persistence.Id;
import javax.persistence.Table;
```

```
import org.hibernate.annotations.GenericGenerator;

@Entity
@Table(name = "EMPLOYEE")
public class Employee extends Salary {

  private static final long serialVersionUID = 1L;

  @Id
  @GeneratedValue(generator = "idGen")
  @GenericGenerator(name = "idGen", strategy = "uuid.hex")
  @Column(name = "ID", length = 32)
  private String id = "";

  @Column(name = "EMP_NUMBER", unique = true, nullable = false)
  private Integer empNumber;

  @Column(name = "EMP_NAME", length = 64, nullable = false)
  private String empName;

  //Getter and setter methods

}
```

Keep the same main class and run this Java application.

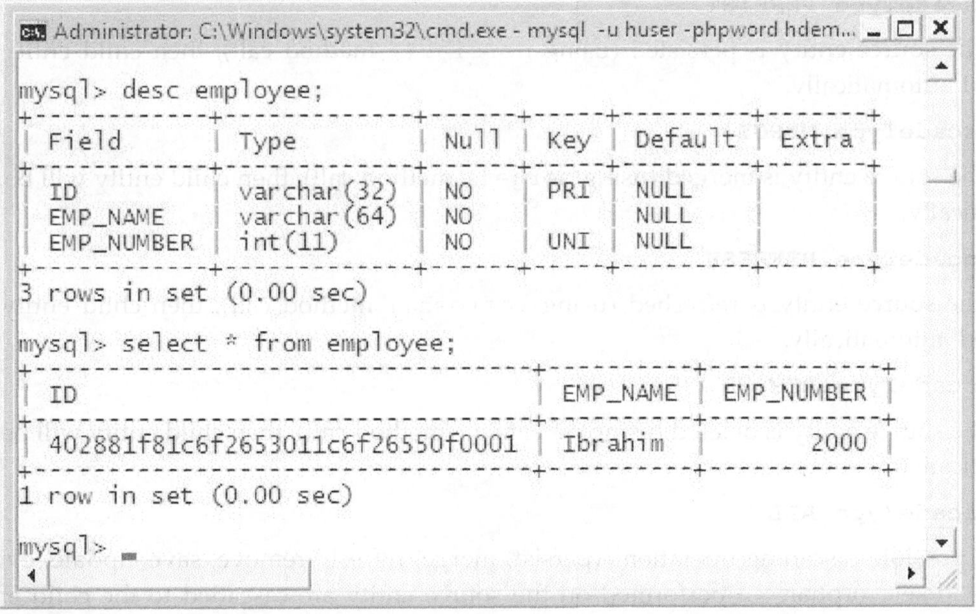

It is also acceptable to declare a class in the middle of inheritance hierarchy as `@MappedSuperclass`, of course any class in the said hierarchy which is not declared as `@Entity` or `@MappedSuperclass` will be ignored.

Cascading Types:

Assume that we are associating (declaring) one persistent filed as of type Entity (child entity /target entity of the association) in an Entity (parent entity/source entity).

```
class  Employee  {

String  empName;
...
Salary  salary;
...
}

class  Salary  {
...
}
```

Here Employee is the source entity and Salary is the child entity.

The Cascading operation determines what action should be taken on child entity when source entity is manipulated (persisted, merged, deleted ...).

The following are some of the supported Cascading types.

CascadeType.PERSIST

If the source entity is persisted (using `persist()` method call), then child entity will be persisted automatically.

CascadeType.MERGE

If the source entity is merged (using `merge()` method call), then child entity will be merged automatically.

CascadeType.REFRESH

If the source entity is refreshed (using `refresh()` method call), then child entity will be refreshed automatically.

CascadeType.REMOVE

If the source entity is deleted (using `delete()` method call), then child entity will be deleted automatically.

CascadeType.ALL

All possible cascading operations (persist, merge, refresh, remove, save_update, evict, lock, replicate, delete_orphan ...) performed on the source entity are cascaded to the child entity.

4.17 MAPPINGS

We can define Entities with the following relation (mapping).

- One-To-One
- One-To-Many
- Many-To-One
- Many-To-Many

4.17.1 One-To-One (@OneToOne)

Each row in parent table will have one and only one row in child table.

Example:

The *Employee* entity has a *Salary* field (entity), whose Entity-Relationship (ER) diagram is as follows.

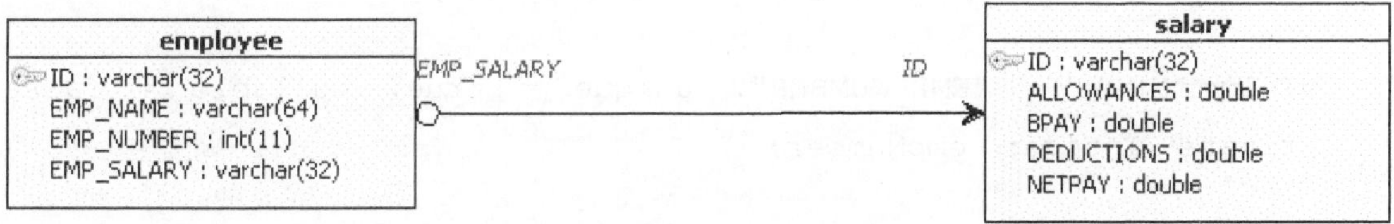

This One-To-One relationship can be achieved via three ways: through Shared Primary Keys, through Foreign-Key relationship, and through Join table.

One-To-One Mapping with Unidirectional Association using Foreign-key

One *Employee* will have only one *Salary*.

Employee → Salary

```
// File Name: Employee.java
// Illustrates @OneToOne

package com.hdemo;

import javax.persistence.CascadeType;
import javax.persistence.Column;
import javax.persistence.Entity;
import javax.persistence.GeneratedValue;
import javax.persistence.Id;
import javax.persistence.JoinColumn;
import javax.persistence.OneToOne;
import javax.persistence.Table;
```

```
import org.hibernate.annotations.GenericGenerator;

@Entity
@Table(name = "EMPLOYEE")
public class Employee {

   private static final long serialVersionUID = 1L;

   @Id
   @GeneratedValue(generator = "idGen")
   @GenericGenerator(name = "idGen", strategy = "uuid.hex")
   @Column(name = "ID", length = 32)
   private String id = "";

   @Column(name = "EMP_NUMBER", unique = true, nullable = false)
   private Integer empNumber;

   @Column(name = "EMP_NAME", length = 64, nullable = false)
   private String empName;
   @OneToOne(cascade = {CascadeType.PERSIST, CascadeType.REMOVE})
   @JoinColumn(name = "EMP_SALARY", unique=true)
   private Salary salary;

   //Getter and Setter methods

}
```

```
// File Name: Salary.java
// Illustrates @OneToOne

package com.hdemo;

import java.io.Serializable;

import javax.persistence.Column;
import javax.persistence.Entity;
import javax.persistence.GeneratedValue;
```

```
import javax.persistence.Id;
import javax.persistence.Table;
import org.hibernate.annotations.GenericGenerator;

@Entity
@Table(name = "SALARY")
public class Salary implements Serializable {

  private static final long serialVersionUID = 1L;

  @Id
  @GeneratedValue(generator = "idGen")
  @GenericGenerator(name = "idGen", strategy = "uuid.hex")
  @Column(name = "ID", length = 32)
  private String id = "";

  @Column(name = "BPAY")
  private Double basicPay;

  @Column(name = "ALLOWANCES")
  private Double allowances;

  @Column(name = "DEDUCTIONS")
  private Double deductions;

  @Column(name = "NETPAY")
  private Double netPay;

  //Getter and Setter methods

}
```

```
// File Name: EmployeeManipulation.java
// Main Program

package com.hdemo;

import org.hibernate.Session;
import org.hibernate.SessionFactory;
import org.hibernate.Transaction;
```

```
public class EmployeeManipulation {

  public static void main(String[] args) throws Exception {
  SessionFactory sessionFactory = HibernateUtil.getSessionFactory();
  Session session = sessionFactory.getCurrentSession();
  Transaction txn = session.beginTransaction();

  Employee employee1 = new Employee();
  employee1.setEmpNumber(5001);
  employee1.setEmpName("Ibrahim");
  Salary salary1 = new Salary();
  salary1.setBasicPay(10000.00);
  salary1.setAllowances(3000.00);
  salary1.setDeductions(2000.00);
  salary1.setNetPay(salary1.getBasicPay()
           + salary1.getAllowances() - salary1.getDeductions());
  employee1.setSalary(salary1);
  session.persist(employee1);

  Employee employee2 = new Employee();
  employee2.setEmpNumber(5002);
  employee2.setEmpName("Kumar");
  Salary salary2 = new Salary();
  salary2.setBasicPay(5000.00);
  salary2.setAllowances(1500.00);
  salary2.setDeductions(1000.00);
  salary2.setNetPay(salary2.getBasicPay()
           + salary2.getAllowances() - salary2.getDeductions());
  employee2.setSalary(salary2);
  session.persist(employee2);

  Employee employee3 = new Employee();
  employee3.setEmpNumber(5003);
  employee3.setEmpName("Ajay");
  Salary salary3 = new Salary();
```

```
    salary3.setBasicPay(15000.00);
    salary3.setAllowances(4000.00);
    salary3.setDeductions(2500.00);
    salary3.setNetPay(salary3.getBasicPay()
            + salary3.getAllowances() - salary3.getDeductions());
    employee3.setSalary(salary3);
    session.persist(employee3);

    txn.commit();
    sessionFactory.close();
    }
}
```

Do not forget to add <mapping> for these entities as below in *hibernate.cfg.xml file.*

```
        <mapping class="com.hdemo.Employee" />
        <mapping class="com.hdemo.Salary" />
```

A sample run results as below.

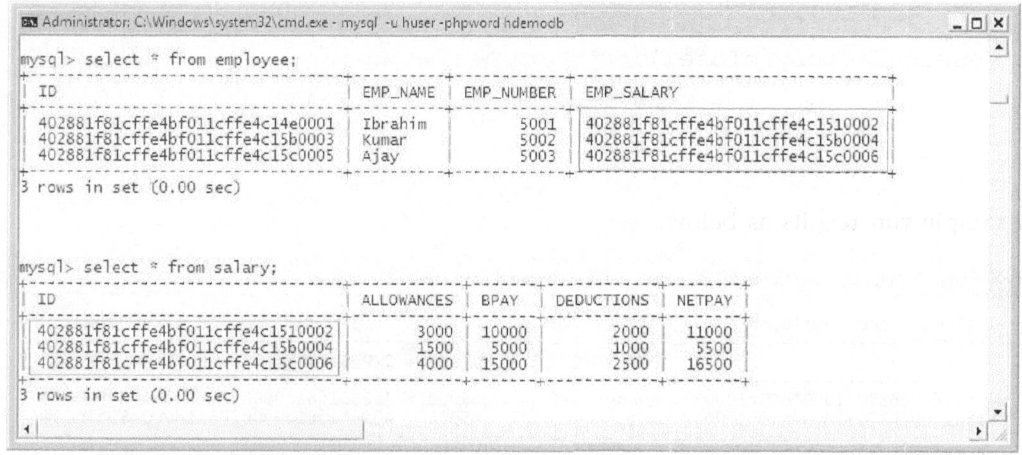

Administrator: C:\Windows\system32\cmd.exe - mysql -u huser -phpword hdemodb

mysql> select * from employee;

ID	EMP_NAME	EMP_NUMBER	EMP_SALARY
402881f81cffe4bf011cffe4c14e0001	Ibrahim	5001	402881f81cffe4bf011cffe4c1510002
402881f81cffe4bf011cffe4c15b0003	Kumar	5002	402881f81cffe4bf011cffe4c15b0004
402881f81cffe4bf011cffe4c15c0005	Ajay	5003	402881f81cffe4bf011cffe4c15c0006

3 rows in set (0.00 sec)

mysql> select * from salary;

ID	ALLOWANCES	BPAY	DEDUCTIONS	NETPAY
402881f81cffe4bf011cffe4c1510002	3000	10000	2000	11000
402881f81cffe4bf011cffe4c15b0004	1500	5000	1000	5500
402881f81cffe4bf011cffe4c15c0006	4000	15000	2500	16500

3 rows in set (0.00 sec)

Deleting parent record (Employee) will deletes the child record (Salary) also (as persisting parent record also inserts child record). This is due to *Cascade* type set in parent entity. All parent records (records using foreign-key of child record) should be deleted before deleting child record(s).

```
// File Name: EmployeeManipulation.java
// Main Program

package com.hdemo;

import java.util.List;
```

```
import  org.hibernate.Session;
import  org.hibernate.SessionFactory;
import  org.hibernate.Transaction;

public  class  EmployeeManipulation  {

  @SuppressWarnings("unchecked")
  public  static  void  main(String[]  args)  throws  Exception  {
  SessionFactory sessionFactory = HibernateUtil.getSessionFactory();
  Session  session  =  sessionFactory.getCurrentSession();
  Transaction  txn  =  session.beginTransaction();

  List<Employee>  listEmployee  =
  session.createQuery("from Employee where empNumber = 5001").list();
   if  (listEmployee.size()  >  0)  {
   session.delete(listEmployee.get(0));
  }

  txn.commit();
  sessionFactory.close();
 }
}
```

A sample run results as below.

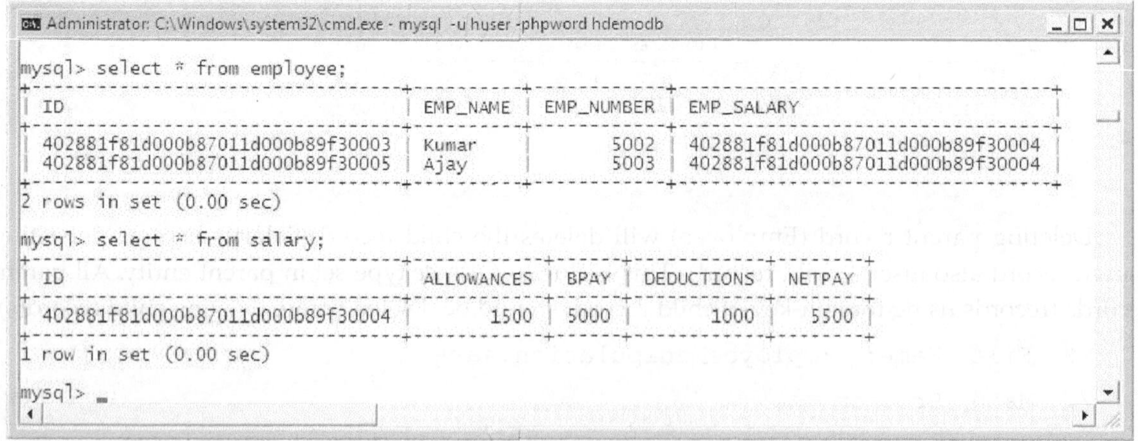

```
Administrator: C:\Windows\system32\cmd.exe - mysql -u huser -phpword hdemodb

mysql> select * from employee;
+----------------------------------+----------+------------+----------------------------------+
| ID                               | EMP_NAME | EMP_NUMBER | EMP_SALARY                       |
+----------------------------------+----------+------------+----------------------------------+
| 402881f81d000b87011d000b89f30003 | Kumar    |       5002 | 402881f81d000b87011d000b89f30004 |
| 402881f81d000b87011d000b89f30005 | Ajay     |       5003 | 402881f81d000b87011d000b89f30004 |
+----------------------------------+----------+------------+----------------------------------+
2 rows in set (0.00 sec)

mysql> select * from salary;
+----------------------------------+------------+------+------------+--------+
| ID                               | ALLOWANCES | BPAY | DEDUCTIONS | NETPAY |
+----------------------------------+------------+------+------------+--------+
| 402881f81d000b87011d000b89f30004 |       1500 | 5000 |       1000 |   5500 |
+----------------------------------+------------+------+------------+--------+
1 row in set (0.00 sec)

mysql> _
```

The above said delete operation should be performed through Hibernate `session.delete(employee_object)` code; however, deleting parent record through direct HSQL statement like below will not delete child records.

```
session.createQuery("delete  from  Employee").executeUpdate();
```

Of course, deleting parent records through SQL statements will not delete child records as shown below.

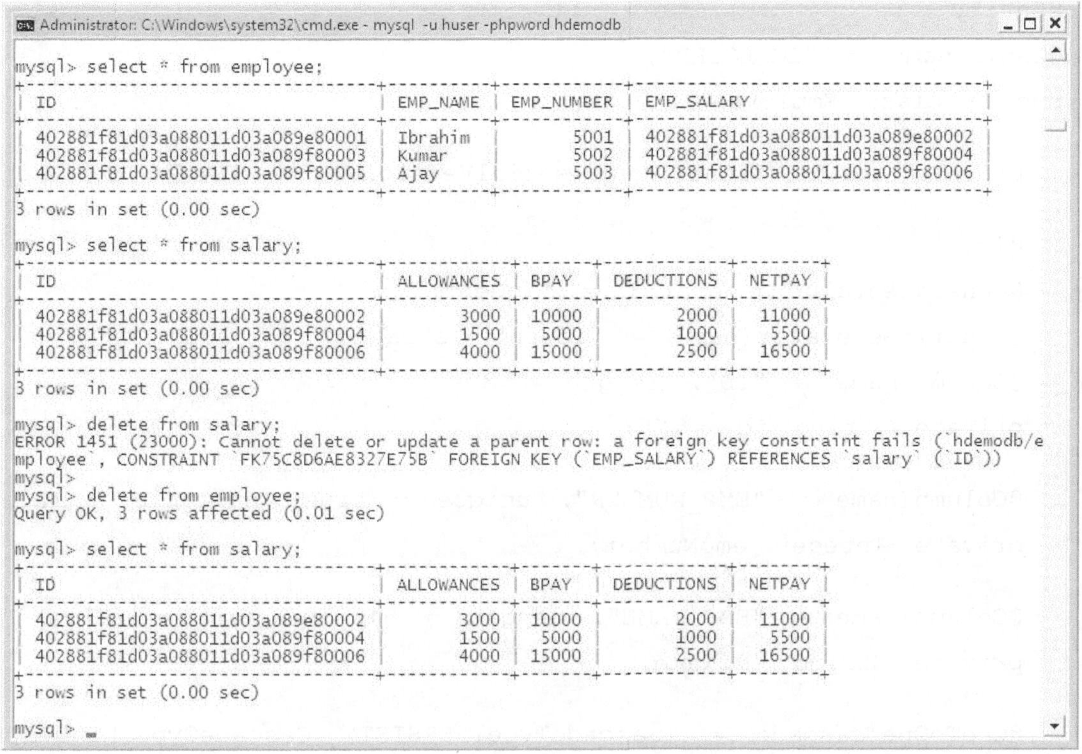

```
Administrator: C:\Windows\system32\cmd.exe - mysql -u huser -phpword hdemodb

mysql> select * from employee;
+----------------------------------+----------+------------+----------------------------------+
| ID                               | EMP_NAME | EMP_NUMBER | EMP_SALARY                       |
+----------------------------------+----------+------------+----------------------------------+
| 402881f81d03a088011d03a089e80001 | Ibrahim  |       5001 | 402881f81d03a088011d03a089e80002 |
| 402881f81d03a088011d03a089f80003 | Kumar    |       5002 | 402881f81d03a088011d03a089f80004 |
| 402881f81d03a088011d03a089f80005 | Ajay     |       5003 | 402881f81d03a088011d03a089f80006 |
+----------------------------------+----------+------------+----------------------------------+
3 rows in set (0.00 sec)

mysql> select * from salary;
+----------------------------------+------------+-------+------------+--------+
| ID                               | ALLOWANCES | BPAY  | DEDUCTIONS | NETPAY |
+----------------------------------+------------+-------+------------+--------+
| 402881f81d03a088011d03a089e80002 |       3000 | 10000 |       2000 |  11000 |
| 402881f81d03a088011d03a089f80004 |       1500 |  5000 |       1000 |   5500 |
| 402881f81d03a088011d03a089f80006 |       4000 | 15000 |       2500 |  16500 |
+----------------------------------+------------+-------+------------+--------+
3 rows in set (0.00 sec)

mysql> delete from salary;
ERROR 1451 (23000): Cannot delete or update a parent row: a foreign key constraint fails (`hdemodb/e
mployee`, CONSTRAINT `FK75C8D6AE8327E75B` FOREIGN KEY (`EMP_SALARY`) REFERENCES `salary` (`ID`))
mysql>
mysql> delete from employee;
Query OK, 3 rows affected (0.01 sec)

mysql> select * from salary;
+----------------------------------+------------+-------+------------+--------+
| ID                               | ALLOWANCES | BPAY  | DEDUCTIONS | NETPAY |
+----------------------------------+------------+-------+------------+--------+
| 402881f81d03a088011d03a089e80002 |       3000 | 10000 |       2000 |  11000 |
| 402881f81d03a088011d03a089f80004 |       1500 |  5000 |       1000 |   5500 |
| 402881f81d03a088011d03a089f80006 |       4000 | 15000 |       2500 |  16500 |
+----------------------------------+------------+-------+------------+--------+
3 rows in set (0.00 sec)

mysql> _
```

One-To-One Mapping with Bidirectional Association using Foreign-key

One *Employee* will have only one *Salary.*

Employee ⟷ Salary

```
//  File  Name:  Employee.java
//  Illustrates  @OneToOne

package  com.hdemo;

import  javax.persistence.CascadeType;
import  javax.persistence.Column;
import  javax.persistence.Entity;
import  javax.persistence.GeneratedValue;
import  javax.persistence.Id;
import  javax.persistence.JoinColumn;
import  javax.persistence.OneToOne;
```

```
import javax.persistence.Table;

import org.hibernate.annotations.GenericGenerator;

@Entity
@Table(name = "EMPLOYEE")
public class Employee {

  private static final long serialVersionUID = 1L;

  @Id
  @GeneratedValue(generator = "idGen")
  @GenericGenerator(name = "idGen", strategy = "uuid.hex")
  @Column(name = "ID", length = 32)
  private String id = "";

  @Column(name = "EMP_NUMBER", unique = true, nullable = false)
  private Integer empNumber;

  @Column(name = "EMP_NAME", length = 64, nullable = false)
  private String empName;

  @OneToOne(cascade = {CascadeType.PERSIST, CascadeType.REMOVE})
  @JoinColumn(name = "EMP_SALARY", nullable=false, unique=true)
  private Salary salary;

  //Getter and Setter methods

}
```

```
// File Name: Salary.java
// Illustrates @OneToOne

package com.hdemo;

import java.io.Serializable;

import javax.persistence.Column;
import javax.persistence.Entity;
import javax.persistence.GeneratedValue;
```

```
import javax.persistence.Id;
import javax.persistence.OneToOne;
import javax.persistence.Table;

import org.hibernate.annotations.GenericGenerator;

@Entity
@Table(name = "SALARY")
public class Salary implements Serializable {

  private static final long serialVersionUID = 1L;

  @Id
  @GeneratedValue(generator = "idGen")
  @GenericGenerator(name = "idGen", strategy = "uuid.hex")
  @Column(name = "ID", length = 32)
  private String id = "";

  @Column(name = "BPAY")
  private Double basicPay;

  @Column(name = "ALLOWANCES")
  private Double allowances;

  @Column(name = "DEDUCTIONS")
  private Double deductions;

  @Column(name = "NETPAY")
  private Double netPay;

  @OneToOne(mappedBy = "salary")
  private Employee employee;

  //Getter and Setter methods
}
```

```
// File Name: EmployeeManipulation.java
// Main Program
```

```
package com.hdemo;

import org.hibernate.Session;
import org.hibernate.SessionFactory;
import org.hibernate.Transaction;

public class EmployeeManipulation {

  public static void main(String[] args) throws Exception {
  SessionFactory sessionFactory = HibernateUtil.getSessionFactory();
  Session session = sessionFactory.getCurrentSession();
  Transaction txn = session.beginTransaction();

  Employee employee1 = new Employee();
  employee1.setEmpNumber(5001);
  employee1.setEmpName("Ibrahim");
  Salary salary1 = new Salary();
  salary1.setBasicPay(10000.00);
  salary1.setAllowances(3000.00);
  salary1.setDeductions(2000.00);
  salary1.setNetPay(salary1.getBasicPay() + salary1.getAllowances()
  - salary1.getDeductions());
  employee1.setSalary(salary1);
  session.persist(employee1);
  System.out.println("The object employee1 is persisted with
                                                    session");
  Employee employee2 = new Employee();
  employee2.setEmpNumber(5002);
  employee2.setEmpName("Kumar");
  Salary salary2 = new Salary();
  salary2.setBasicPay(5000.00);
  salary2.setAllowances(1500.00);
  salary2.setDeductions(1000.00);
  salary2.setNetPay(salary2.getBasicPay() + salary2.getAllowances()
  - salary2.getDeductions());
  employee2.setSalary(salary2);
```

```
        session.persist(employee2);
        System.out.println("The object employee2 is persisted with
        session");

        Employee employee3 = new Employee();
        employee3.setEmpNumber(5003);
        employee3.setEmpName("Ajay");
        Salary salary3 = new Salary();
        salary3.setBasicPay(15000.00);
        salary3.setAllowances(4000.00);
        salary3.setDeductions(2500.00);
        salary3.setNetPay(salary3.getBasicPay() + salary3.getAllowances()
        - salary3.getDeductions());
        employee3.setSalary(salary3);
        session.persist(employee3);
        System.out.println("The object employee3 is persisted with
        session");

        txn.commit();
        System.out.println("Transaction on this session is committed");
        sessionFactory.close();
        }
    }
```

A sample run results as below.

```
Administrator: C:\Windows\system32\cmd.exe - mysql -u huser -phpword hdemodb

mysql> select * from employee;
+----------------------------------+----------+------------+----------------------------------+
| ID                               | EMP_NAME | EMP_NUMBER | EMP_SALARY                       |
+----------------------------------+----------+------------+----------------------------------+
| 402881f81d03a9ea011d03a9ec410001 | Ibrahim  |       5001 | 402881f81d03a9ea011d03a9ec410002 |
| 402881f81d03a9ea011d03a9ec510003 | Kumar    |       5002 | 402881f81d03a9ea011d03a9ec510004 |
| 402881f81d03a9ea011d03a9ec510005 | Ajay     |       5003 | 402881f81d03a9ea011d03a9ec510006 |
+----------------------------------+----------+------------+----------------------------------+
3 rows in set (0.00 sec)

mysql> select * from salary;
+----------------------------------+------------+-------+------------+--------+
| ID                               | ALLOWANCES | BPAY  | DEDUCTIONS | NETPAY |
+----------------------------------+------------+-------+------------+--------+
| 402881f81d03a9ea011d03a9ec410002 |       3000 | 10000 |       2000 |  11000 |
| 402881f81d03a9ea011d03a9ec510004 |       1500 |  5000 |       1000 |   5500 |
| 402881f81d03a9ea011d03a9ec510006 |       4000 | 15000 |       2500 |  16500 |
+----------------------------------+------------+-------+------------+--------+
3 rows in set (0.00 sec)

mysql>
```

The following main program accesses *Salary* objects through *Employee* objects and vice-versa (bidirectional).

```
// File Name: EmployeeManipulation.java
// Main Program

package com.hdemo;

import java.util.List;

import org.hibernate.Session;
import org.hibernate.SessionFactory;
import org.hibernate.Transaction;

public class EmployeeManipulation {

  @SuppressWarnings("unchecked")
  public static void main(String[] args) throws Exception {
  SessionFactory sessionFactory = HibernateUtil.getSessionFactory();
  Session session = sessionFactory.getCurrentSession();
  Transaction txn = session.beginTransaction();

  System.out.println("Accessing Employee Objects\n\n");
  List<Employee> employeeList = session.createQuery("from
  Employee").list();
  for (int i = 0; i < employeeList.size(); i++) {
  Employee employee = employeeList.get(i);
  System.out.println("Employee Number: " + employee.getEmpNumber());
  System.out.println("Employee Name   : " + employee.getEmpName());
  System.out.println("NetPay : " + employee.getSalary().getNetPay());

  System.out.println("=======================================\n\n");
      }

  System.out.println("\n\nAccessing Salary Objects\n\n");
  List<Salary> salaryList = session.createQuery("from Salary").list();
  for (int i = 0; i < salaryList.size(); i++) {
  Salary salary = salaryList.get(i);
```

```
    System.out.println("Employee Number: " + salary.getEmployee().get
    EmpNumber());
    System.out.println("Employee Name   : " + salary.getEmployee().get
    EmpName());
    System.out.println("NetPay                : " + salary.getNetPay());

   System.out.println("========================================\n\n");
        }

    txn.commit();
    sessionFactory.close();
    }
}
```

A sample run results as below.

```
Accessing Employee Objects
```

Hibernate: select employee0_.ID as ID0_, employee0_.EMP_NAME as EMP2_0_, employee0_.EMP_NUMBER as EMP3_0_, employee0_.EMP_SALARY as EMP4_0_ from EMPLOYEE employee0_

Hibernate: select salary0_.ID as ID1_1_, salary0_.ALLOWANCES as ALLOWANCES1_1_, salary0_.BPAY as BPAY1_1_, salary0_.DEDUCTIONS as DEDUCTIONS1_1_, salary0_.NETPAY as NETPAY1_1_, employee1_.ID as ID0_0_, employee1_.EMP_NAME as EMP2_0_0_, employee1_.EMP_NUMBER as EMP3_0_0_, employee1_.EMP_SALARY as EMP4_0_0_ from SALARY salary0_ left outer join EMPLOYEE employee1_ on salary0_.ID=employee1_.EMP_SALARY where salary0_.ID=?

Hibernate: select employee0_.ID as ID0_1_, employee0_.EMP_NAME as EMP2_0_1_, employee0_.EMP_NUMBER as EMP3_0_1_, employee0_.EMP_SALARY as EMP4_0_1_, salary1_.ID as ID1_0_, salary1_.ALLOWANCES as ALLOWANCES1_0_, salary1_.BPAY as BPAY1_0_, salary1_.DEDUCTIONS as DEDUCTIONS1_0_, salary1_.NETPAY as NETPAY1_0_ from EMPLOYEE employee0_ inner join SALARY salary1_ on employee0_.EMP_SALARY=salary1_.ID where employee0_.EMP_SALARY=?

Hibernate: select salary0_.ID as ID1_1_, salary0_.ALLOWANCES as ALLOWANCES1_1_, salary0_.BPAY as BPAY1_1_, salary0_.DEDUCTIONS as DEDUCTIONS1_1_, salary0_.NETPAY as NETPAY1_1_, employee1_.ID as ID0_0_, employee1_.EMP_NAME as EMP2_0_0_, employee1_.EMP_NUMBER as EMP3_0_0_, employee1_.EMP_SALARY as EMP4_0_0_ from SALARY salary0_ left outer join EMPLOYEE employee1_ on salary0_.ID=employee1_.EMP_SALARY where salary0_.ID=?

```
Hibernate: select employee0_.ID as ID0_1_, employee0_.EMP_NAME as EMP2_0_1_, employee0_.EMP_NUMBER as EMP3_0_1_, employee0_.EMP_SALARY as EMP4_0_1_, salary1_.ID as ID1_0_, salary1_.ALLOWANCES as ALLOWANCES1_0_, salary1_.BPAY as BPAY1_0_, salary1_.DEDUCTIONS as DEDUCTIONS1_0_, salary1_.NETPAY as NETPAY1_0_ from EMPLOYEE employee0_ inner join SALARY salary1_ on employee0_.EMP_SALARY=salary1_.ID where employee0_.EMP_SALARY=?

Hibernate: select salary0_.ID as ID1_1_, salary0_.ALLOWANCES as ALLOWANCES1_1_, salary0_.BPAY as BPAY1_1_, salary0_.DEDUCTIONS as DEDUCTIONS1_1_, salary0_.NETPAY as NETPAY1_1_, employee1_.ID as ID0_0_, employee1_.EMP_NAME as EMP2_0_0_, employee1_.EMP_NUMBER as EMP3_0_0_, employee1_.EMP_SALARY as EMP4_0_0_ from SALARY salary0_ left outer join EMPLOYEE employee1_ on salary0_.ID=employee1_.EMP_SALARY where salary0_.ID=?

Hibernate: select employee0_.ID as ID0_1_, employee0_.EMP_NAME as EMP2_0_1_, employee0_.EMP_NUMBER as EMP3_0_1_, employee0_.EMP_SALARY as EMP4_0_1_, salary1_.ID as ID1_0_, salary1_.ALLOWANCES as ALLOWANCES1_0_, salary1_.BPAY as BPAY1_0_, salary1_.DEDUCTIONS as DEDUCTIONS1_0_, salary1_.NETPAY as NETPAY1_0_ from EMPLOYEE employee0_ inner join SALARY salary1_ on employee0_.EMP_SALARY=salary1_.ID where employee0_.EMP_SALARY=?

Employee Number  : 5001
Employee Name    : Ibrahim
NetPay           : 11000.0
========================================
Employee Number  : 5002
Employee Name    : Kumar
NetPay           : 5500.0
========================================
Employee Number  : 5003
Employee Name    : Ajay
NetPay           : 16500.0
========================================

Accessing Salary Objects

Hibernate: select salary0_.ID as ID1_, salary0_.ALLOWANCES as ALLOWANCES1_, salary0_.BPAY as BPAY1_, salary0_.DEDUCTIONS as
```

```
DEDUCTIONS1_, salary0_.NETPAY as NETPAY1_ from SALARY salary0_
    Employee Number   : 5001
    Employee Name     : Ibrahim
    NetPay            : 11000.0
    ========================================
    Employee Number   : 5002
    Employee Name     : Kumar
    NetPay            : 5500.0
    ========================================
    Employee Number   : 5003
    Employee Name     : Ajay
    NetPay            : 16500.0
    ========================================
```

One-To-One Mapping with Unidirectional Association using Association Table (Join table)

A parent table is linked to a child table through a association table (join table), which contains columns containing foreign-key values of each parent and child table to associate.

Employee → Salary

The Entity-Relationship (ER) diagram reflects the relationship.

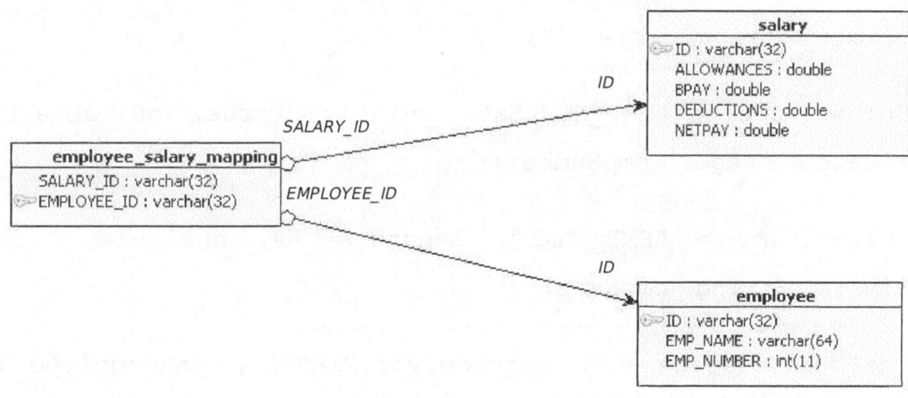


```
// File Name: Employee.java
// Illustrates @OneToOne

package com.hdemo;
```

```
import javax.persistence.CascadeType;
import javax.persistence.Column;
import javax.persistence.Entity;
import javax.persistence.GeneratedValue;
import javax.persistence.Id;
import javax.persistence.JoinColumn;
import javax.persistence.JoinTable;
import javax.persistence.OneToOne;
import javax.persistence.Table;

import org.hibernate.annotations.GenericGenerator;

@Entity
@Table(name = "EMPLOYEE")
public class Employee {

  private static final long serialVersionUID = 1L;
  @Id
  @GeneratedValue(generator = "idGen")
  @GenericGenerator(name = "idGen", strategy = "uuid.hex")
  @Column(name = "ID", length = 32)
  private String id = "";

  @Column(name = "EMP_NUMBER", unique = true, nullable = false)
  private Integer empNumber;

  @Column(name = "EMP_NAME", length = 64, nullable = false)
  private String empName;

  @OneToOne(cascade = { CascadeType.PERSIST, CascadeType.REMOVE })
  @JoinTable(name = "EMPLOYEE_SALARY_MAPPING",
  joinColumns = { @JoinColumn(name="EMPLOYEE_ID",unique = true) },
  inverseJoinColumns = { @JoinColumn(name = "SALARY_ID", unique =
  true) })
  private Salary salary;
```

```
    //Getter and Setter methods

}
```

```
// File Name: Salary.java
// Illustrates @OneToOne

package com.hdemo;

import java.io.Serializable;

import javax.persistence.Column;
import javax.persistence.Entity;
import javax.persistence.GeneratedValue;
import javax.persistence.Id;
import javax.persistence.Table;

import org.hibernate.annotations.GenericGenerator;

@Entity
@Table(name = "SALARY")
public class Salary implements Serializable {

    private static final long serialVersionUID = 1L;

    @Id
    @GeneratedValue(generator = "idGen")
    @GenericGenerator(name = "idGen", strategy = "uuid.hex")
    @Column(name = "ID", length = 32)
    private String id = "";

    @Column(name = "BPAY")
    private Double basicPay;

    @Column(name = "ALLOWANCES")
    private Double allowances;

    @Column(name = "DEDUCTIONS")
    private Double deductions;
```

```
    @Column(name = "NETPAY")
    private Double netPay;

    //Getter and Setter methods

}
```

```
// File Name: EmployeeManipulation.java
// Main Program

package com.hdemo;

import org.hibernate.Session;
import org.hibernate.SessionFactory;
import org.hibernate.Transaction;

public class EmployeeManipulation {

    public static void main(String[] args) throws Exception {
    SessionFactory sessionFactory = HibernateUtil.getSessionFactory();
    Session session = sessionFactory.getCurrentSession();
    Transaction txn = session.beginTransaction();

    Employee employee1 = new Employee();
    employee1.setEmpNumber(5001);
    employee1.setEmpName("Ibrahim");
    Salary salary1 = new Salary();
    salary1.setBasicPay(10000.00);
    salary1.setAllowances(3000.00);
    salary1.setDeductions(2000.00);
    salary1.setNetPay(salary1.getBasicPay() + salary1.getAllowances()
         - salary1.getDeductions());
    employee1.setSalary(salary1);
    session.persist(employee1);
    System.out.println("The object employee1 is persisted with session");
```

```
    Employee employee2 = new Employee();
    employee2.setEmpNumber(5002);
    employee2.setEmpName("Kumar");
    Salary salary2 = new Salary();
    salary2.setBasicPay(5000.00);
    salary2.setAllowances(1500.00);
    salary2.setDeductions(1000.00);
    salary2.setNetPay(salary2.getBasicPay() + salary2.getAllowances()
          - salary2.getDeductions());
    employee2.setSalary(salary2);
    session.persist(employee2);
    System.out.println("The object employee2 is persisted with
    session");

    Employee employee3 = new Employee();
    employee3.setEmpNumber(5003);
    employee3.setEmpName("Ajay");
    Salary salary3 = new Salary();
    salary3.setBasicPay(15000.00);
    salary3.setAllowances(4000.00);
    salary3.setDeductions(2500.00);
    salary3.setNetPay(salary3.getBasicPay() + salary3.getAllowances()
          - salary3.getDeductions());
    employee3.setSalary(salary3);
    session.persist(employee3);
    System.out.println("The object employee3 is persisted with
    session");

    txn.commit();
    System.out.println("Transaction on this session is committed");
    sessionFactory.close();
    }
}
```

A sample run results as below.

```
Administrator: C:\Windows\system32\cmd.exe - mysql -u huser -phpword hdemodb

mysql> desc employee;
+------------+-------------+------+-----+---------+-------+
| Field      | Type        | Null | Key | Default | Extra |
+------------+-------------+------+-----+---------+-------+
| ID         | varchar(32) | NO   | PRI | NULL    |       |
| EMP_NAME   | varchar(64) | NO   |     | NULL    |       |
| EMP_NUMBER | int(11)     | NO   | UNI | NULL    |       |
+------------+-------------+------+-----+---------+-------+
3 rows in set (0.02 sec)

mysql> desc salary;
+------------+-------------+------+-----+---------+-------+
| Field      | Type        | Null | Key | Default | Extra |
+------------+-------------+------+-----+---------+-------+
| ID         | varchar(32) | NO   | PRI | NULL    |       |
| ALLOWANCES | double      | YES  |     | NULL    |       |
| BPAY       | double      | YES  |     | NULL    |       |
| DEDUCTIONS | double      | YES  |     | NULL    |       |
| NETPAY     | double      | YES  |     | NULL    |       |
+------------+-------------+------+-----+---------+-------+
5 rows in set (0.00 sec)

mysql> desc employee_salary_mapping;
+-------------+-------------+------+-----+---------+-------+
| Field       | Type        | Null | Key | Default | Extra |
+-------------+-------------+------+-----+---------+-------+
| SALARY_ID   | varchar(32) | YES  | UNI | NULL    |       |
| EMPLOYEE_ID | varchar(32) | NO   | PRI | NULL    |       |
+-------------+-------------+------+-----+---------+-------+
2 rows in set (0.02 sec)

mysql> select * from employee;
+----------------------------------+----------+------------+
| ID                               | EMP_NAME | EMP_NUMBER |
+----------------------------------+----------+------------+
| 402881f81d040c1e011d040c233a0001 | Ibrahim  |       5001 |
| 402881f81d040c1e011d040c23490003 | Kumar    |       5002 |
| 402881f81d040c1e011d040c23490005 | Ajay     |       5003 |
+----------------------------------+----------+------------+
3 rows in set (0.00 sec)

mysql> select * from salary;
+----------------------------------+------------+-------+------------+--------+
| ID                               | ALLOWANCES | BPAY  | DEDUCTIONS | NETPAY |
+----------------------------------+------------+-------+------------+--------+
| 402881f81d040c1e011d040c233a0002 |       3000 | 10000 |       2000 |  11000 |
| 402881f81d040c1e011d040c23490004 |       1500 |  5000 |       1000 |   5500 |
| 402881f81d040c1e011d040c23490006 |       4000 | 15000 |       2500 |  16500 |
+----------------------------------+------------+-------+------------+--------+
3 rows in set (0.02 sec)

mysql> select * from employee_salary_mapping;
+----------------------------------+----------------------------------+
| SALARY_ID                        | EMPLOYEE_ID                      |
+----------------------------------+----------------------------------+
| 402881f81d040c1e011d040c233a0002 | 402881f81d040c1e011d040c233a0001 |
| 402881f81d040c1e011d040c23490004 | 402881f81d040c1e011d040c23490003 |
| 402881f81d040c1e011d040c23490006 | 402881f81d040c1e011d040c23490005 |
+----------------------------------+----------------------------------+
3 rows in set (0.00 sec)
```

One-To-One Mapping with Bidirectional Association using Association Table (Join table)

Employee ⟷ Salary

```
// File Name: Employee.java
// Illustrates @OneToOne

package com.hdemo;

import javax.persistence.Column;
import javax.persistence.Entity;
import javax.persistence.GeneratedValue;
import javax.persistence.Id;
import javax.persistence.JoinColumn;
import javax.persistence.JoinTable;
import javax.persistence.OneToOne;
import javax.persistence.Table;

import org.hibernate.annotations.GenericGenerator;

@Entity
@Table(name = "EMPLOYEE")
public class Employee {

  private static final long serialVersionUID = 1L;

  @Id
  @GeneratedValue(generator = "idGen")
  @GenericGenerator(name = "idGen", strategy = "uuid.hex")
  @Column(name = "ID", length = 32)
  private String id = "";

  @Column(name = "EMP_NUMBER", unique = true, nullable = false)
  private Integer empNumber;

  @Column(name = "EMP_NAME", length = 64, nullable = false)
  private String empName;

  @OneToOne
  @JoinTable(name = "EMPLOYEE_SALARY_MAPPING",
```

```
    joinColumns = { @JoinColumn(name = "EMPLOYEE_ID", unique = true) },
    inverseJoinColumns = { @JoinColumn(name = "SALARY_ID", unique =
         true) })
    private Salary salary;

    //Getter and Setter methods

  }
```

```
// File Name: Salary.java
// Illustrates @OneToOne

package com.hdemo;

import java.io.Serializable;

import javax.persistence.Column;
import javax.persistence.Entity;
import javax.persistence.GeneratedValue;
import javax.persistence.Id;
import javax.persistence.OneToOne;
import javax.persistence.Table;

import org.hibernate.annotations.GenericGenerator;

@Entity
@Table(name = "SALARY")
public class Salary implements Serializable {

 private static final long serialVersionUID = 1L;

  @Id
  @GeneratedValue(generator = "idGen")
  @GenericGenerator(name = "idGen", strategy = "uuid.hex")
  @Column(name = "ID", length = 32)
  private String id = "";

  @Column(name = "BPAY")
  private Double basicPay;
```

```
    @Column(name = "ALLOWANCES")
    private Double allowances;

    @Column(name = "DEDUCTIONS")
    private Double deductions;

    @Column(name = "NETPAY")
    private Double netPay;

    @OneToOne(mappedBy="salary")
    private Employee employee;

}
```

```
// File Name: EmployeeManipulation.java
// Main Program

package com.hdemo;

import org.hibernate.Session;
import org.hibernate.SessionFactory;
import org.hibernate.Transaction;

public class EmployeeManipulation {

    public static void main(String[] args) throws Exception {
    SessionFactory sessionFactory = HibernateUtil.getSessionFactory();
    Session session = sessionFactory.getCurrentSession();
    Transaction txn = session.beginTransaction();

    Employee employee1 = new Employee();
    employee1.setEmpNumber(5001);
    employee1.setEmpName("Ibrahim");
    Salary salary1 = new Salary();
    salary1.setBasicPay(10000.00);
    salary1.setAllowances(3000.00);
    salary1.setDeductions(2000.00);
    salary1.setNetPay(salary1.getBasicPay() + salary1.getAllowances()
        - salary1.getDeductions());
```

```
employee1.setSalary(salary1);
session.save(employee1);

System.out.println("The object employee1 is persisted with
session");

Employee employee2 = new Employee();
employee2.setEmpNumber(5002);
employee2.setEmpName("Kumar");
Salary salary2 = new Salary();
salary2.setBasicPay(5000.00);
salary2.setAllowances(1500.00);
salary2.setDeductions(1000.00);
salary2.setNetPay(salary2.getBasicPay() + salary2.getAllowances()
      - salary2.getDeductions());
employee2.setSalary(salary2);
session.save(employee2);
System.out.println("The object employee2 is persisted with
session");

Employee employee3 = new Employee();
employee3.setEmpNumber(5003);
employee3.setEmpName("Ajay");
Salary salary3 = new Salary();
salary3.setBasicPay(15000.00);
salary3.setAllowances(4000.00);
salary3.setDeductions(2500.00);
salary3.setNetPay(salary3.getBasicPay() + salary3.getAllowances()
      - salary3.getDeductions());
employee3.setSalary(salary3);
session.save(employee3);
System.out.println("The object employee3 is persisted with
session");
salary1.setEmployee(employee1);
salary2.setEmployee(employee2);
```

```
    salary3.setEmployee(employee3);
    session.save(salary1);
    session.save(salary2);
    session.save(salary3);

    txn.commit();
    System.out.println("Transaction on this session is committed");
    sessionFactory.close();
    }
}
```

Output:

```
The object employee1 is persisted with session
The object employee2 is persisted with session
The object employee3 is persisted with session
Hibernate: insert into EMPLOYEE (EMP_NAME, EMP_NUMBER, ID) values
(?, ?, ?)
Hibernate: insert into EMPLOYEE (EMP_NAME, EMP_NUMBER, ID) values
(?, ?, ?)
Hibernate: insert into EMPLOYEE (EMP_NAME, EMP_NUMBER, ID) values
(?, ?, ?)
Hibernate: insert into SALARY (ALLOWANCES, BPAY, DEDUCTIONS, NETPAY,
ID) values (?, ?, ?, ?, ?)
Hibernate: insert into SALARY (ALLOWANCES, BPAY, DEDUCTIONS, NETPAY,
ID) values (?, ?, ?, ?, ?)
Hibernate: insert into SALARY (ALLOWANCES, BPAY, DEDUCTIONS, NETPAY,
ID) values (?, ?, ?, ?, ?)
Hibernate: insert into EMPLOYEE_SALARY_MAPPING (SALARY_ID, EMPLOYEE_ID)
values (?, ?)
Hibernate: insert into EMPLOYEE_SALARY_MAPPING (SALARY_ID, EMPLOYEE_ID)
values (?, ?)
Hibernate: insert into EMPLOYEE_SALARY_MAPPING (SALARY_ID, EMPLOYEE_ID)
values (?, ?)
Transaction on this session is committed
```

A sample run results as below.

```
Administrator: C:\Windows\system32\cmd.exe - mysql -u huser -phpword hdemodb

mysql> desc employee;
+------------+-------------+------+-----+---------+-------+
| Field      | Type        | Null | Key | Default | Extra |
+------------+-------------+------+-----+---------+-------+
| ID         | varchar(32) | NO   | PRI | NULL    |       |
| EMP_NAME   | varchar(64) | NO   |     | NULL    |       |
| EMP_NUMBER | int(11)     | NO   | UNI | NULL    |       |
+------------+-------------+------+-----+---------+-------+
3 rows in set (0.00 sec)

mysql> desc salary;
+------------+-------------+------+-----+---------+-------+
| Field      | Type        | Null | Key | Default | Extra |
+------------+-------------+------+-----+---------+-------+
| ID         | varchar(32) | NO   | PRI | NULL    |       |
| ALLOWANCES | double      | YES  |     | NULL    |       |
| BPAY       | double      | YES  |     | NULL    |       |
| DEDUCTIONS | double      | YES  |     | NULL    |       |
| NETPAY     | double      | YES  |     | NULL    |       |
+------------+-------------+------+-----+---------+-------+
5 rows in set (0.00 sec)

mysql> desc employee_salary_mapping;
+-------------+-------------+------+-----+---------+-------+
| Field       | Type        | Null | Key | Default | Extra |
+-------------+-------------+------+-----+---------+-------+
| SALARY_ID   | varchar(32) | NO   | PRI |         |       |
| EMPLOYEE_ID | varchar(32) | NO   | MUL | NULL    |       |
+-------------+-------------+------+-----+---------+-------+
2 rows in set (0.00 sec)

mysql> select * from employee;
+----------------------------------+----------+------------+
| ID                               | EMP_NAME | EMP_NUMBER |
+----------------------------------+----------+------------+
| 402881f81d04f77a011d04f77d210001 | Ibrahim  |       5001 |
| 402881f81d04f77a011d04f77d2f0002 | Kumar    |       5002 |
| 402881f81d04f77a011d04f77d2f0003 | Ajay     |       5003 |
+----------------------------------+----------+------------+
3 rows in set (0.00 sec)

mysql> select * from salary;
+----------------------------------+------------+-------+------------+--------+
| ID                               | ALLOWANCES | BPAY  | DEDUCTIONS | NETPAY |
+----------------------------------+------------+-------+------------+--------+
| 402881f81d04f77a011d04f77d2f0004 |       3000 | 10000 |       2000 |  11000 |
| 402881f81d04f77a011d04f77d300005 |       1500 |  5000 |       1000 |   5500 |
| 402881f81d04f77a011d04f77d300006 |       4000 | 15000 |       2500 |  16500 |
+----------------------------------+------------+-------+------------+--------+
3 rows in set (0.00 sec)

mysql> select * from employee_salary_mapping;
+----------------------------------+----------------------------------+
| SALARY_ID                        | EMPLOYEE_ID                      |
+----------------------------------+----------------------------------+
| 402881f81d04f77a011d04f77d2f0004 | 402881f81d04f77a011d04f77d210001 |
| 402881f81d04f77a011d04f77d300005 | 402881f81d04f77a011d04f77d2f0002 |
| 402881f81d04f77a011d04f77d300006 | 402881f81d04f77a011d04f77d2f0003 |
+----------------------------------+----------------------------------+
3 rows in set (0.00 sec)
```

One-To-One Mapping with Unidirectional Association using Primary-key

Employee → Salary

The associated entities (Employee and Salary) share the same primary keys values, that is the Id value of Employee and the Id value of Salary are same (compositional relationship). The annotation `@PrimaryKeyJoinColumn` along with `@OneToOne` is used to achieve this relationship.

```
// File Name: Employee.java
// Illustrates @OneToOne

package com.hdemo;

import javax.persistence.CascadeType;
import javax.persistence.Column;
import javax.persistence.Entity;
import javax.persistence.GeneratedValue;
import javax.persistence.Id;
import javax.persistence.OneToOne;
import javax.persistence.PrimaryKeyJoinColumn;
import javax.persistence.Table;

import org.hibernate.annotations.GenericGenerator;
import org.hibernate.annotations.Parameter;

@Entity
@Table(name = "EMPLOYEE")
public class Employee {

  private static final long serialVersionUID = 1L;

  @Id
  @GeneratedValue(generator = "idGen")
  @GenericGenerator(name = "idGen",
                    strategy = "foreign",
  parameters = { @Parameter(name = "property", value = "salary") })
                    private String id = "";

  @Column(name = "EMP_NUMBER", unique = true, nullable = false)
  private Integer empNumber;
```

```
    @Column(name = "EMP_NAME", length = 64, nullable = false)
    private String empName;

    @OneToOne(cascade = { CascadeType.PERSIST, CascadeType.REMOVE })
    @PrimaryKeyJoinColumn
    private Salary salary;

    //Getter and Setter methods

}
```

```
// File Name: Salary.java
// Illustrates @OneToOne

package com.hdemo;

import java.io.Serializable;

import javax.persistence.Column;
import javax.persistence.Entity;
import javax.persistence.GeneratedValue;
import javax.persistence.Id;
import javax.persistence.Table;

import org.hibernate.annotations.GenericGenerator;

@Entity
@Table(name = "SALARY")
public class Salary implements Serializable {

    private static final long serialVersionUID = 1L;

    @Id
    @GeneratedValue(generator = "idGen")
    @GenericGenerator(name = "idGen", strategy = "uuid.hex")
    @Column(name = "ID", length = 32)
    private String id = "";

    @Column(name = "BPAY")
```

```
    private Double basicPay;

    @Column(name = "ALLOWANCES")
    private Double allowances;

    @Column(name = "DEDUCTIONS")
    private Double deductions;

    @Column(name = "NETPAY")
    private Double netPay;

    //Getter and Setter methods

}
```

```
// File Name: EmployeeManipulation.java
// Main Program

package com.hdemo;

import org.hibernate.Session;
import org.hibernate.SessionFactory;
import org.hibernate.Transaction;

public class EmployeeManipulation {

    public static void main(String[] args) throws Exception {
    SessionFactory sessionFactory = HibernateUtil.getSessionFactory();
    Session session = sessionFactory.getCurrentSession();
    Transaction txn = session.beginTransaction();

    Employee employee1 = new Employee();
    employee1.setEmpNumber(5001);
    employee1.setEmpName("Ibrahim");
    Salary salary1 = new Salary();
    salary1.setBasicPay(10000.00);
    salary1.setAllowances(3000.00);
    salary1.setDeductions(2000.00);
```

```
salary1.setNetPay(salary1.getBasicPay() + salary1.getAllowances()
     - salary1.getDeductions());
employee1.setSalary(salary1);
session.persist(employee1);

System.out.println("The object employee1 is persisted with
session");

Employee employee2 = new Employee();
employee2.setEmpNumber(5002);
employee2.setEmpName("Kumar");
Salary salary2 = new Salary();
salary2.setBasicPay(5000.00);
salary2.setAllowances(1500.00);
salary2.setDeductions(1000.00);
salary2.setNetPay(salary2.getBasicPay() + salary2.getAllowances()
     - salary2.getDeductions());
employee2.setSalary(salary2);
session.persist(employee2);
System.out.println("The object employee2 is persisted with
session");

Employee employee3 = new Employee();
employee3.setEmpNumber(5003);
employee3.setEmpName("Ajay");
Salary salary3 = new Salary();
salary3.setBasicPay(15000.00);
salary3.setAllowances(4000.00);
salary3.setDeductions(2500.00);
salary3.setNetPay(salary3.getBasicPay() + salary3.getAllowances()
     - salary3.getDeductions());
employee3.setSalary(salary3);
session.persist(employee3);
System.out.println("The object employee3 is persisted with
session");

txn.commit();
```

```
        System.out.println("Transaction on this session is committed");
        sessionFactory.close();
    }
}
```

A sample run results as below.

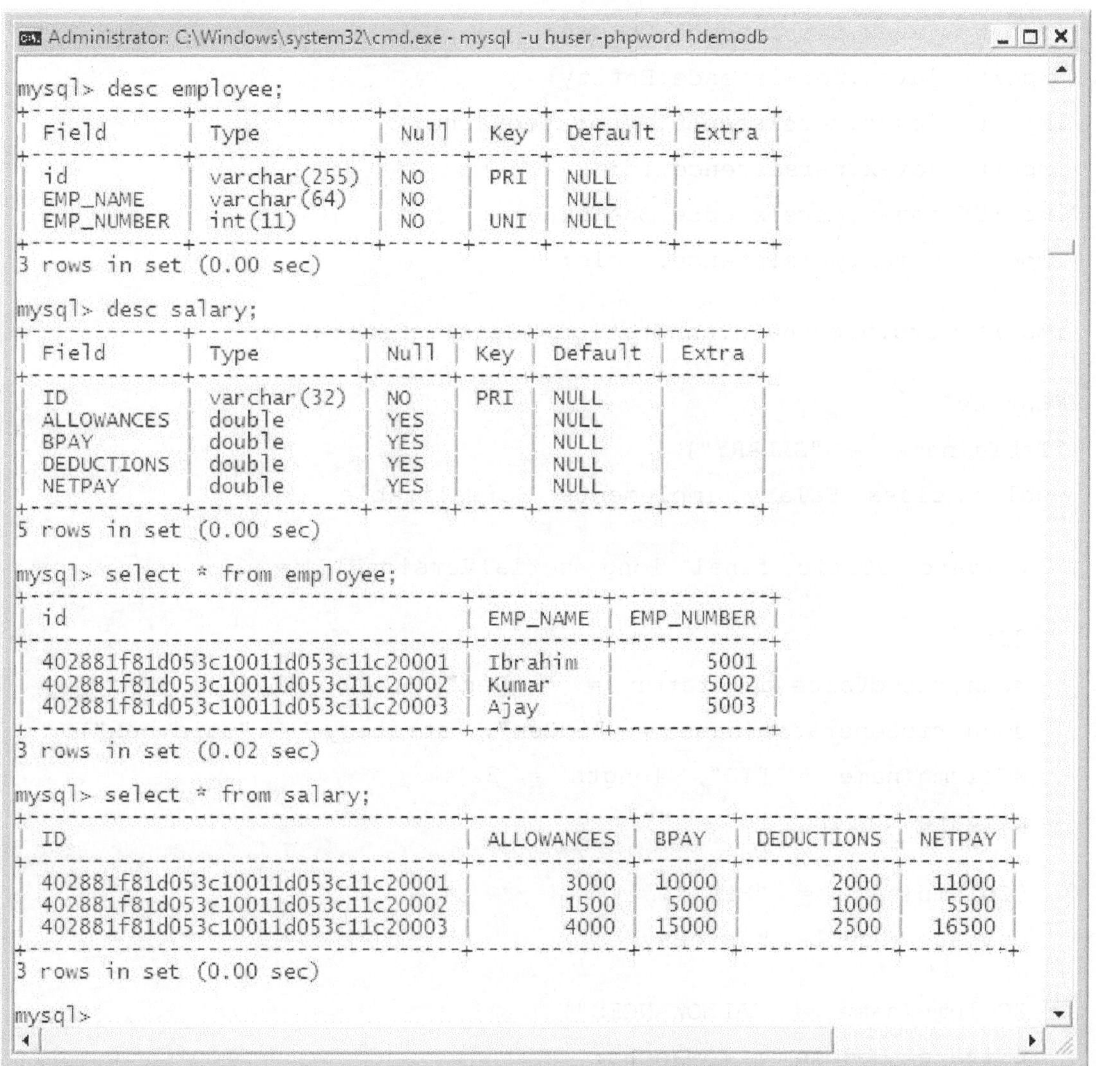

```
Administrator: C:\Windows\system32\cmd.exe - mysql -u huser -phpword hdemodb

mysql> desc employee;
+------------+--------------+------+-----+---------+-------+
| Field      | Type         | Null | Key | Default | Extra |
+------------+--------------+------+-----+---------+-------+
| id         | varchar(255) | NO   | PRI | NULL    |       |
| EMP_NAME   | varchar(64)  | NO   |     | NULL    |       |
| EMP_NUMBER | int(11)      | NO   | UNI | NULL    |       |
+------------+--------------+------+-----+---------+-------+
3 rows in set (0.00 sec)

mysql> desc salary;
+------------+-------------+------+-----+---------+-------+
| Field      | Type        | Null | Key | Default | Extra |
+------------+-------------+------+-----+---------+-------+
| ID         | varchar(32) | NO   | PRI | NULL    |       |
| ALLOWANCES | double      | YES  |     | NULL    |       |
| BPAY       | double      | YES  |     | NULL    |       |
| DEDUCTIONS | double      | YES  |     | NULL    |       |
| NETPAY     | double      | YES  |     | NULL    |       |
+------------+-------------+------+-----+---------+-------+
5 rows in set (0.00 sec)

mysql> select * from employee;
+----------------------------------+----------+------------+
| id                               | EMP_NAME | EMP_NUMBER |
+----------------------------------+----------+------------+
| 402881f81d053c10011d053c11c20001 | Ibrahim  |       5001 |
| 402881f81d053c10011d053c11c20002 | Kumar    |       5002 |
| 402881f81d053c10011d053c11c20003 | Ajay     |       5003 |
+----------------------------------+----------+------------+
3 rows in set (0.02 sec)

mysql> select * from salary;
+----------------------------------+------------+-------+------------+--------+
| ID                               | ALLOWANCES | BPAY  | DEDUCTIONS | NETPAY |
+----------------------------------+------------+-------+------------+--------+
| 402881f81d053c10011d053c11c20001 |       3000 | 10000 |       2000 |  11000 |
| 402881f81d053c10011d053c11c20002 |       1500 |  5000 |       1000 |   5500 |
| 402881f81d053c10011d053c11c20003 |       4000 | 15000 |       2500 |  16500 |
+----------------------------------+------------+-------+------------+--------+
3 rows in set (0.00 sec)

mysql>
```

One-To-One Mapping with Bidirectional Association using Primary-key

Employee ⟷ Salary

Take the same example shown in "One-To-One Mapping with Unidirectional Association using Primary-key" and change the *Salary* entity as follows.

```
// File Name: Salary.java
// Illustrates @OneToOne

package com.hdemo;

import java.io.Serializable;

import javax.persistence.Column;
import javax.persistence.Entity;
import javax.persistence.GeneratedValue;
import javax.persistence.Id;
import javax.persistence.OneToOne;
import javax.persistence.Table;

import org.hibernate.annotations.GenericGenerator;

@Entity
@Table(name = "SALARY")
public class Salary implements Serializable {

  private static final long serialVersionUID = 1L;

  @Id
  @GeneratedValue(generator = "idGen")
  @GenericGenerator(name = "idGen", strategy = "uuid.hex")
  @Column(name = "ID", length = 32)
  private String id = "";

  @Column(name = "BPAY")
  private Double basicPay;

  @Column(name = "ALLOWANCES")
  private Double allowances;

  @Column(name = "DEDUCTIONS")
  private Double deductions;

  @Column(name = "NETPAY")
  private Double netPay;
```

```
    @OneToOne(mappedBy = "salary")
    private Employee employee;

    //Getter and Setter methods

}
```

4.17.2 One-To-Many (@OneToMany) & Many-To-One (@ManyToOne)

One-To-Many mapping is used to represent the relationship between a single source object and a collection of target objects. Each row in parent table will have one or more rows in child table.

Example:

The *Employee* entity has many *Address* (entity) fields, whose Entity-Relationship (ER) diagram is as follows.

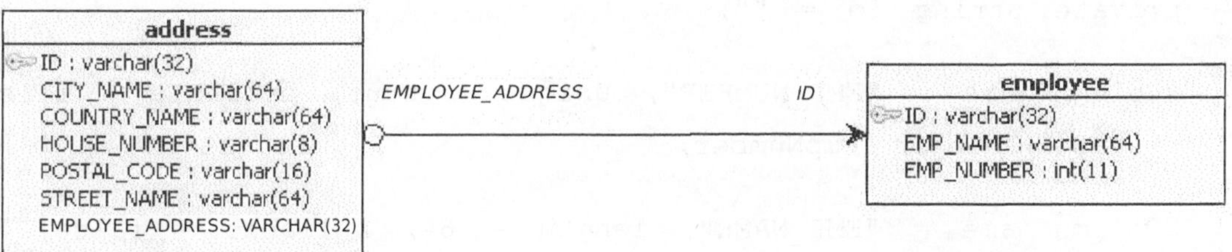

One-To-Many Mapping with Unidirectional Association using Foreign-Key

One *Employee* may have many addresses.

Employee (one) → Address (many)

```
// File Name: Employee.java
// Illustrates @OneToMany and @ManyToOne

package com.hdemo;

import java.util.List;

import javax.persistence.CascadeType;
import javax.persistence.Column;
import javax.persistence.Entity;
import javax.persistence.GeneratedValue;
import javax.persistence.Id;
import javax.persistence.JoinColumn;
```

```
import javax.persistence.OneToMany;
import javax.persistence.Table;

import org.hibernate.annotations.GenericGenerator;

@Entity
@Table(name = "EMPLOYEE")
public class Employee {

  private static final long serialVersionUID = 1L;

  @Id
  @GeneratedValue(generator = "idGen")
  @GenericGenerator(name = "idGen", strategy = "uuid.hex")
  @Column(name = "ID", length = 32)
  private String id = "";

  @Column(name = "EMP_NUMBER", unique = true, nullable = false)
  private Integer empNumber;

  @Column(name = "EMP_NAME", length = 64, nullable = false)
  private String empName;

  @OneToMany(cascade = CascadeType.ALL)
  @JoinColumn(name = "EMPLOYEE_ADDRESS")
  private List<Address> addresses;

  //Getter and Setter methods

}
```

```
// File Name: Address.java
// Illustrates @OneToMany and @ManyToOne

package com.hdemo;

import java.io.Serializable;

import javax.persistence.Column;
```

```
import javax.persistence.Entity;
import javax.persistence.GeneratedValue;
import javax.persistence.Id;
import javax.persistence.Table;

import org.hibernate.annotations.GenericGenerator;

@Entity
@Table(name = "ADDRESS")
public class Address implements Serializable {

  private static final long serialVersionUID = 1L;

  @Id
  @GeneratedValue(generator = "idGen")
  @GenericGenerator(name = "idGen", strategy = "uuid.hex")
  @Column(name = "ID", length = 32)
  private String id = "";

  @Column(name = "HOUSE_NUMBER", length = 8)
  private String houseNumber;

  @Column(name = "STREET_NAME", length = 64)
  private String streetName;

  @Column(name = "CITY_NAME", length = 64)
  private String cityName;

  @Column(name = "COUNTRY_NAME", length = 64)
  private String countryName;

  @Column(name = "POSTAL_CODE", length = 16)
  private String postalCode;

  //Getter and Setter methods

  public String toString() {
        return "[House Number:    " + houseNumber +
                  "\nStreet Name: " + streetName +
```

```
                "\nCity Name: " + cityName +
                "\nCountry Name: " + countryName +
                "\nPostal Code: " + postalCode +
                "]";
    }
}
```

```
// File Name: EmployeeManipulation.java
// Main Program

package com.hdemo;

import java.util.ArrayList;
import java.util.List;

import org.hibernate.Session;
import org.hibernate.SessionFactory;
import org.hibernate.Transaction;

public class EmployeeManipulation {

   @SuppressWarnings("unchecked")
   public static void main(String[] args) throws Exception {
   SessionFactory sessionFactory = HibernateUtil.getSessionFactory();
   Session session = sessionFactory.openSession();
   Transaction txn = session.beginTransaction();

   Employee employee1 = new Employee();
   employee1.setEmpNumber(5001);

   employee1.setEmpName("Ibrahim");
   Address employee1Address1 = new Address();
   employee1Address1.setHouseNumber("C-13-4");
   employee1Address1.setStreetName("Jalan Munsi Abdullah");
   employee1Address1.setCityName("Kuala Lumpur");
   employee1Address1.setCountryName("Malaysia");
   employee1Address1.setPostalCode("50100");
   Address employee1Address2 = new Address();
```

```
employee1Address2.setHouseNumber("3-121");
employee1Address2.setStreetName("Middle Street");
employee1Address2.setCityName("Tiruchirapalli");
employee1Address2.setCountryName("India");
employee1Address2.setPostalCode("621302");
List<Address> employee1Addresses = new ArrayList<Address>();
employee1Addresses.add(employee1Address1);
employee1Addresses.add(employee1Address2);
employee1.setAddresses(employee1Addresses);
session.save(employee1);
System.out.println("The object employee1 is persisted with
session");

Employee employee2 = new Employee();
employee2.setEmpNumber(5002);
employee2.setEmpName("Kumar");
Address employee2Address1 = new Address();
employee2Address1.setHouseNumber("T-4");
employee2Address1.setStreetName("Nehru Street");
employee2Address1.setCityName("Chennai");
employee2Address1.setCountryName("India");
employee2Address1.setPostalCode("600020");
List<Address> employee2Addresses = new ArrayList<Address>();
employee2Addresses.add(employee2Address1);
employee2.setAddresses(employee2Addresses);
session.save(employee2);
System.out.println("The object employee2 is persisted with
session");

Employee employee3 = new Employee();
employee3.setEmpNumber(5003);
employee3.setEmpName("Ajay");
employee3.setAddresses(null);
session.save(employee3);
System.out.println("The object employee3 is persisted with
session");
```

```
txn.commit();
System.out.println("Transaction on this session is committed");

txn = session.beginTransaction();
System.out.println("Accessing Employee Objects\n\n");
List<Employee> employeeList =
session.createQuery("from Employee").list();
      for (int i = 0; i < employeeList.size(); i++) {
Employee employee = employeeList.get(i);
System.out.println("Employee Number : " + employee.getEmpNumber());
System.out.println("Employee Name   : " + employee.getEmpName());
List<Address> addresses = employee.getAddresses();
for (int j=0; addresses != null && j < addresses.size(); j++) {
System.out.println("Employee Address (" + (j+1) + ") : " +
                                    addresses.get(j));
      }

System.out.println("=====================================\n\n");
      }
      txn.commit();
      sessionFactory.close();
   }
}
```

Output:

```
The object employee1 is persisted with session
The object employee2 is persisted with session
The object employee3 is persisted with session
Hibernate: insert into EMPLOYEE (EMP_NAME, EMP_NUMBER, ID) values
(?, ?, ?)
Hibernate: insert into ADDRESS (CITY_NAME, COUNTRY_NAME, HOUSE_NUMBER,
POSTAL_CODE, STREET_NAME, ID) values (?, ?, ?, ?, ?, ?)
Hibernate: insert into ADDRESS (CITY_NAME, COUNTRY_NAME, HOUSE_NUMBER,
POSTAL_CODE, STREET_NAME, ID) values (?, ?, ?, ?, ?, ?)
Hibernate: insert into EMPLOYEE (EMP_NAME, EMP_NUMBER, ID) values
(?, ?, ?)
Hibernate: insert into ADDRESS (CITY_NAME, COUNTRY_NAME, HOUSE_NUMBER,
POSTAL_CODE, STREET_NAME, ID) values (?, ?, ?, ?, ?, ?)
```

```
Hibernate: insert into EMPLOYEE (EMP_NAME, EMP_NUMBER, ID) values
(?, ?, ?)
Hibernate: update ADDRESS set EMPLOYEE_ADDRESS=? where ID=?
Hibernate: update ADDRESS set EMPLOYEE_ADDRESS=? where ID=?
Hibernate: update ADDRESS set EMPLOYEE_ADDRESS=? where ID=?
Transaction on this session is committed
Accessing Employee Objects

Hibernate: select employee0_.ID as ID0_, employee0_.EMP_NAME as
EMP2_0_, employee0_.EMP_NUMBER as EMP3_0_ from EMPLOYEE employee0_
Employee Number: 5001
Employee Name : Ibrahim
Employee Address (1) : [House Number: C-13-4
Street Name : Jalan Munsi Abdullah
City Name : Kuala Lumpur
Country Name: Malaysia
Postal Code : 50100]
Employee Address (2) : [House Number: 3-121
Street Name : Middle Street
City Name : Tiruchirapalli
Country Name: India
Postal Code : 621302]
============================================

Employee Number : 5002
Employee Name : Kumar
Employee Address (1) : [House Number: T-4
Street Name : Nehru Street
City Name : Chennai
Country Name : India
Postal Code : 600020]
============================================

Employee Number : 5003
Employee Name : Ajay
============================================
```

Do not forget to add <mapping> for these entities as below in *hibernate.cfg.xml file.*

```
<mapping class="com.hdemo.Employee" />
<mapping class="com.hdemo.Address" />
```

A sample run results as below.

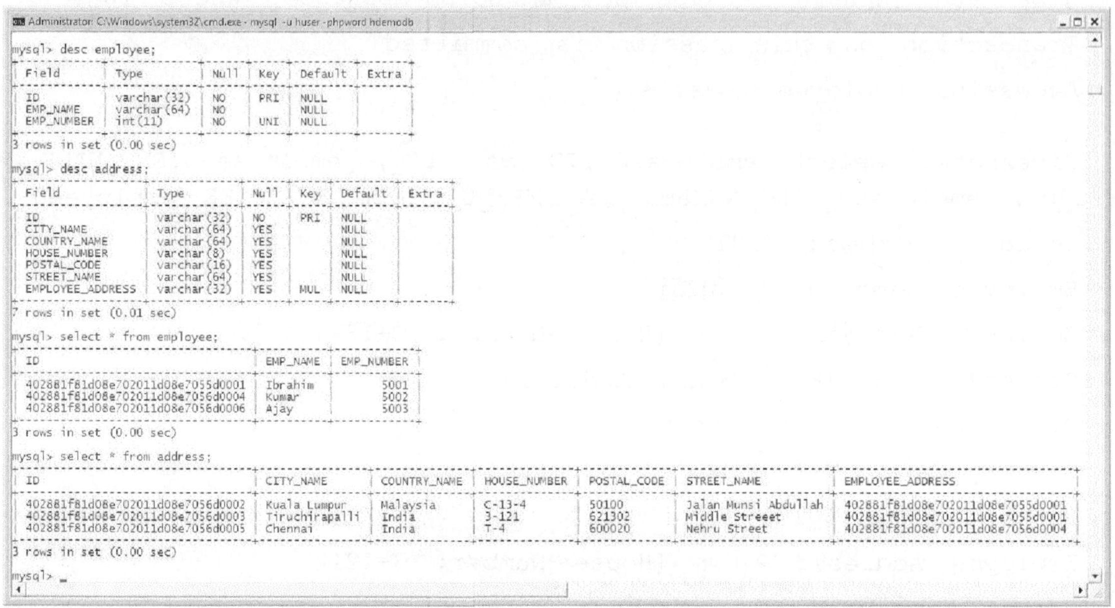

```
Administrator: C:\Windows\system32\cmd.exe - mysql -u huser -phpword hdemodb

mysql> desc employee;
+------------+-------------+------+-----+---------+-------+
| Field      | Type        | Null | Key | Default | Extra |
+------------+-------------+------+-----+---------+-------+
| ID         | varchar(32) | NO   | PRI | NULL    |       |
| EMP_NAME   | varchar(64) | NO   |     | NULL    |       |
| EMP_NUMBER | int(11)     | NO   | UNI | NULL    |       |
+------------+-------------+------+-----+---------+-------+
3 rows in set (0.00 sec)

mysql> desc address;
+------------------+-------------+------+-----+---------+-------+
| Field            | Type        | Null | Key | Default | Extra |
+------------------+-------------+------+-----+---------+-------+
| ID               | varchar(32) | NO   | PRI | NULL    |       |
| CITY_NAME        | varchar(64) | YES  |     | NULL    |       |
| COUNTRY_NAME     | varchar(64) | YES  |     | NULL    |       |
| HOUSE_NUMBER     | varchar(8)  | YES  |     | NULL    |       |
| POSTAL_CODE      | varchar(16) | YES  |     | NULL    |       |
| STREET_NAME      | varchar(64) | YES  |     | NULL    |       |
| EMPLOYEE_ADDRESS | varchar(32) | YES  | MUL | NULL    |       |
+------------------+-------------+------+-----+---------+-------+
7 rows in set (0.01 sec)

mysql> select * from employee;
+----------------------------------+----------+------------+
| ID                               | EMP_NAME | EMP_NUMBER |
+----------------------------------+----------+------------+
| 402881f81d08e702011d08e7055d0001 | Ibrahim  |       5001 |
| 402881f81d08e702011d08e7056d0004 | Kumar    |       5002 |
| 402881f81d08e702011d08e7056d0006 | Ajay     |       5003 |
+----------------------------------+----------+------------+
3 rows in set (0.00 sec)

mysql> select * from address;
+----------------------------------+-----------------+--------------+--------------+-------------+----------------------+----------------------------------+
| ID                               | CITY_NAME       | COUNTRY_NAME | HOUSE_NUMBER | POSTAL_CODE | STREET_NAME          | EMPLOYEE_ADDRESS                 |
+----------------------------------+-----------------+--------------+--------------+-------------+----------------------+----------------------------------+
| 402881f81d08e702011d08e7056d0002 | Kuala Lumpur    | Malaysia     | C-13-4       | 50100       | Jalan Munsi Abdullah | 402881f81d08e702011d08e7055d0001 |
| 402881f81d08e702011d08e7056d0003 | Tiruchirapalli  | India        | 3-121        | 621302      | Middle Streeet       | 402881f81d08e702011d08e7055d0001 |
| 402881f81d08e702011d08e7056d0005 | Chennai         | India        | T-4          | 600020      | Nehru Street         | 402881f81d08e702011d08e7056d0004 |
+----------------------------------+-----------------+--------------+--------------+-------------+----------------------+----------------------------------+
3 rows in set (0.00 sec)

mysql> _
```

One-To-Many Mapping with Unidirectional Association using Association Table (Join table)

Employee (one) → Address (many)

The Entity-Relationship (ER) diagram reflects the relationship.

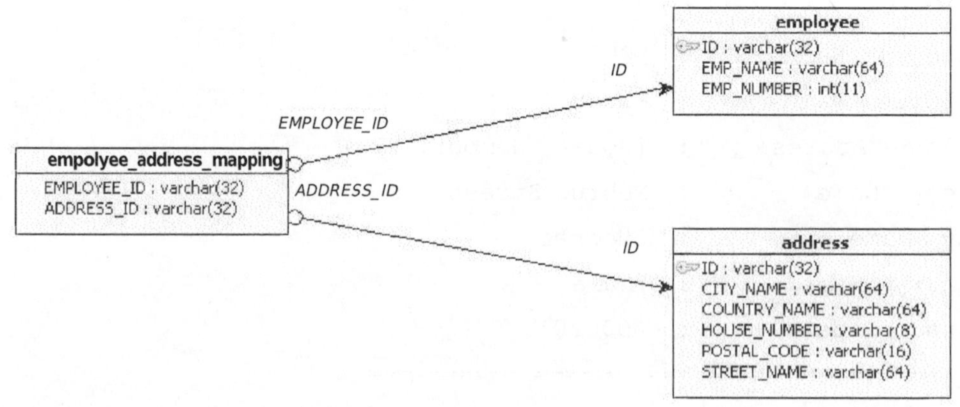


```
// File Name: Employee.java
// Illustrates @OneToMany and @ManyToOne
```

```
package com.hdemo;

import java.util.List;

import javax.persistence.CascadeType;
import javax.persistence.Column;
import javax.persistence.Entity;
import javax.persistence.GeneratedValue;
import javax.persistence.Id;
import javax.persistence.JoinColumn;
import javax.persistence.JoinTable;
import javax.persistence.OneToMany;
import javax.persistence.Table;

import org.hibernate.annotations.GenericGenerator;

@Entity
@Table(name = "EMPLOYEE")
public class Employee {

   private static final long serialVersionUID = 1L;

   @Id
   @GeneratedValue(generator = "idGen")
   @GenericGenerator(name = "idGen", strategy = "uuid.hex")
   @Column(name = "ID", length = 32)
   private String id = "";

   @Column(name = "EMP_NUMBER", unique = true, nullable = false)
   private Integer empNumber;

   @Column(name = "EMP_NAME", length = 64, nullable = false)
   private String empName;

   @OneToMany(cascade=CascadeType.ALL)
   @JoinTable(name = "EMPLOYEE_ADDRESS_MAPPING",
         joinColumns = { @JoinColumn(name = "EMPLOYEE_ID") },
         inverseJoinColumns ={ @JoinColumn(name = "ADDRESS_ID") })
```

```
    private List<Address> addresses;

    //Getter and Setter methods

  }
```

```
  // File Name: Address.java
  // Illustrates @OneToMany and @ManyToOne

  package com.hdemo;

  import java.io.Serializable;

  import javax.persistence.Column;
  import javax.persistence.Entity;
  import javax.persistence.GeneratedValue;
  import javax.persistence.Id;
  import javax.persistence.Table;

  import org.hibernate.annotations.GenericGenerator;

  @Entity
  @Table(name = "ADDRESS")
  public class Address implements Serializable {

    private static final long serialVersionUID = 1L;

    @Id
    @GeneratedValue(generator = "idGen")
    @GenericGenerator(name = "idGen", strategy = "uuid.hex")
    @Column(name = "ID", length = 32)
    private String id = "";

    @Column(name = "HOUSE_NUMBER", length = 8)
    private String houseNumber;

    @Column(name = "STREET_NAME", length = 64)
    private String streetName;

    @Column(name = "CITY_NAME", length = 64)
```

```
  private String cityName;

  @Column(name = "COUNTRY_NAME", length = 64)
  private String countryName;

  @Column(name = "POSTAL_CODE", length = 16)
  private String postalCode;

  //Getter and Setter methods

 public String toString() {
     return "[House Number: " + houseNumber +
           "\nStreet Name : " + streetName +
           "\nCity Name   : " + cityName +
           "\nCountry Name: " + countryName +
           "\nPostal Code : " + postalCode +
            "]";
  }
}
```

```
// File Name: EmployeeManipulation.java
// Main Program

package com.hdemo;

import java.util.ArrayList;
import java.util.List;

import org.hibernate.Session;
import org.hibernate.SessionFactory;
import org.hibernate.Transaction;

public class EmployeeManipulation {

  @SuppressWarnings("unchecked")
  public static void main(String[] args) throws Exception {
  SessionFactory sessionFactory = HibernateUtil.getSessionFactory();
  Session session = sessionFactory.openSession();
```

```
Transaction txn = session.beginTransaction();

Employee employee1 = new Employee();
employee1.setEmpNumber(5001);

employee1.setEmpName("Ibrahim");
Address employee1Address1 = new Address();
employee1Address1.setHouseNumber("C-13-4");
employee1Address1.setStreetName("Jalan Munsi Abdullah");
employee1Address1.setCityName("Kuala Lumpur");
employee1Address1.setCountryName("Malaysia");
employee1Address1.setPostalCode("50100");
Address employee1Address2 = new Address();
employee1Address2.setHouseNumber("3-121");
employee1Address2.setStreetName("Middle Street");
employee1Address2.setCityName("Tiruchirapalli");
employee1Address2.setCountryName("India");
employee1Address2.setPostalCode("621302");
List<Address> employee1Addresses = new ArrayList<Address>();
employee1Addresses.add(employee1Address1);
employee1Addresses.add(employee1Address2);
employee1.setAddresses(employee1Addresses);
session.save(employee1);
System.out.println("The object employee1 is persisted with
session");

Employee employee2 = new Employee();
employee2.setEmpNumber(5002);
employee2.setEmpName("Kumar");
Address employee2Address1 = new Address();
employee2Address1.setHouseNumber("T-4");
employee2Address1.setStreetName("Nehru Street");
employee2Address1.setCityName("Chennai");
employee2Address1.setCountryName("India");
employee2Address1.setPostalCode("600020");
List<Address> employee2Addresses = new ArrayList<Address>();
employee2Addresses.add(employee2Address1);
```

```
employee2.setAddresses(employee2Addresses);
session.save(employee2);
System.out.println("The object employee2 is persisted with session");

Employee employee3 = new Employee();
employee3.setEmpNumber(5003);
employee3.setEmpName("Ajay");
employee3.setAddresses(null);
session.save(employee3);
System.out.println("The object employee3 is persisted with session");

txn.commit();
System.out.println("Transaction on this session is committed");

txn = session.beginTransaction();
System.out.println("Accessing Employee Objects\n\n");
List<Employee> employeeList =
session.createQuery("from Employee").list();
for (int i = 0; i < employeeList.size(); i++) {
Employee employee = employeeList.get(i);
System.out.println("Employee Number : " + employee.getEmpNumber());
System.out.println("Employee Name   : " + employee.getEmpName());
List<Address> addresses = employee.getAddresses();
for (int j=0; addresses != null && j < addresses.size(); j++) {
System.out.println("Employee Address (" + (j+1) + ") : " +
addresses.get(j));
    }

System.out.println("========================================\n\n");
    }

txn.commit();
sessionFactory.close();
}
}
```

Output:

```
The object employee1 is persisted with session
The object employee2 is persisted with session
```

```
The object employee3 is persisted with session
Hibernate: insert into EMPLOYEE (EMP_NAME, EMP_NUMBER, ID) values
(?, ?, ?)
Hibernate: insert into ADDRESS (CITY_NAME, COUNTRY_NAME, HOUSE_NUMBER,
POSTAL_CODE, STREET_NAME, ID) values (?, ?, ?, ?, ?, ?)
Hibernate: insert into ADDRESS (CITY_NAME, COUNTRY_NAME, HOUSE_NUMBER,
POSTAL_CODE, STREET_NAME, ID) values (?, ?, ?, ?, ?, ?)
Hibernate: insert into EMPLOYEE (EMP_NAME, EMP_NUMBER, ID) values
(?, ?, ?)
Hibernate: insert into ADDRESS (CITY_NAME, COUNTRY_NAME, HOUSE_NUMBER,
POSTAL_CODE, STREET_NAME, ID) values (?, ?, ?, ?, ?, ?)
Hibernate: insert into EMPLOYEE (EMP_NAME, EMP_NUMBER, ID) values
(?, ?, ?)
Hibernate: insert into EMPLOYEE_ADDRESS_MAPPING (EMPLOYEE_ID,
ADDRESS_ID) values (?, ?)
Hibernate: insert into EMPLOYEE_ADDRESS_MAPPING (EMPLOYEE_ID,
ADDRESS_ID) values (?, ?)
Hibernate: insert into EMPLOYEE_ADDRESS_MAPPING (EMPLOYEE_ID,
ADDRESS_ID) values (?, ?)
Transaction on this session is committed
Accessing Employee Objects

Hibernate: select employee0_.ID as ID0_, employee0_.EMP_NAME as
EMP2_0_, employee0_.EMP_NUMBER as EMP3_0_ from EMPLOYEE employee0_
Employee Number : 5001
Employee Name   : Ibrahim
Employee Address (1) : [House Number: C-13-4
Street Name : Jalan Munsi Abdullah
City Name   : Kuala Lumpur
Country Name: Malaysia
Postal Code : 50100]
Employee Address (2) : [House Number: 3-121
Street Name : Middle Street
City Name   : Tiruchirapalli
Country Name: India
Postal Code : 621302]
=======================================

Employee Number : 5002
Employee Name   : Kumar
```

```
Employee Address (1) : [House Number: T-4
Street Name : Nehru Street
City Name   : Chennai
Country Name: India
Postal Code : 600020]
==========================================

Employee Number : 5003
Employee Name   : Ajay
==========================================
```

A sample run results as below.

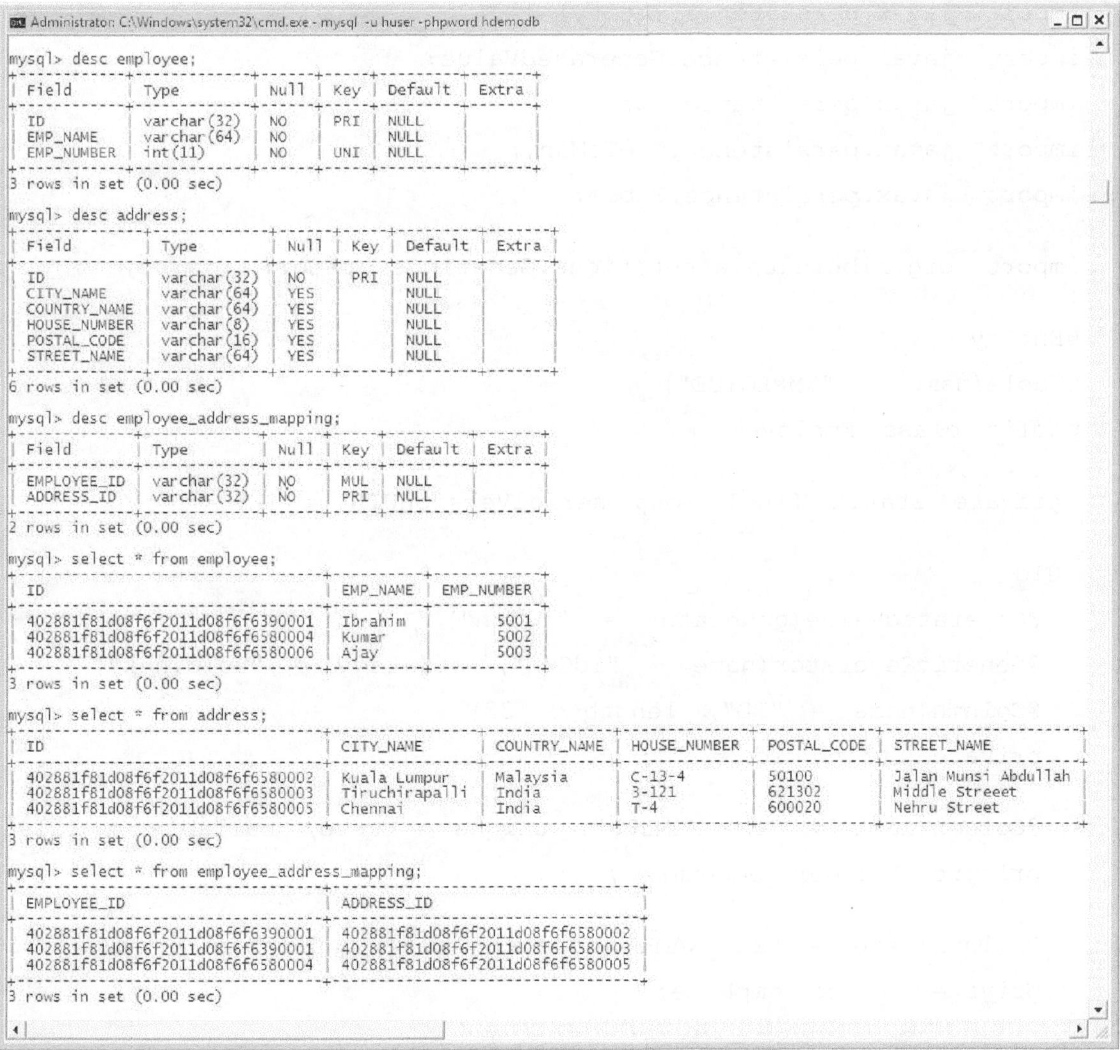

```
Administrator: C:\Windows\system32\cmd.exe - mysql -u huser -phpword hdemodb

mysql> desc employee;
+------------+-------------+------+-----+---------+-------+
| Field      | Type        | Null | Key | Default | Extra |
+------------+-------------+------+-----+---------+-------+
| ID         | varchar(32) | NO   | PRI | NULL    |       |
| EMP_NAME   | varchar(64) | NO   |     | NULL    |       |
| EMP_NUMBER | int(11)     | NO   | UNI | NULL    |       |
+------------+-------------+------+-----+---------+-------+
3 rows in set (0.00 sec)

mysql> desc address;
+--------------+-------------+------+-----+---------+-------+
| Field        | Type        | Null | Key | Default | Extra |
+--------------+-------------+------+-----+---------+-------+
| ID           | varchar(32) | NO   | PRI | NULL    |       |
| CITY_NAME    | varchar(64) | YES  |     | NULL    |       |
| COUNTRY_NAME | varchar(64) | YES  |     | NULL    |       |
| HOUSE_NUMBER | varchar(8)  | YES  |     | NULL    |       |
| POSTAL_CODE  | varchar(16) | YES  |     | NULL    |       |
| STREET_NAME  | varchar(64) | YES  |     | NULL    |       |
+--------------+-------------+------+-----+---------+-------+
6 rows in set (0.00 sec)

mysql> desc employee_address_mapping;
+-------------+-------------+------+-----+---------+-------+
| Field       | Type        | Null | Key | Default | Extra |
+-------------+-------------+------+-----+---------+-------+
| EMPLOYEE_ID | varchar(32) | NO   | MUL | NULL    |       |
| ADDRESS_ID  | varchar(32) | NO   | PRI | NULL    |       |
+-------------+-------------+------+-----+---------+-------+
2 rows in set (0.00 sec)

mysql> select * from employee;
+----------------------------------+----------+------------+
| ID                               | EMP_NAME | EMP_NUMBER |
+----------------------------------+----------+------------+
| 402881f81d08f6f2011d08f6f6390001 | Ibrahim  |       5001 |
| 402881f81d08f6f2011d08f6f6580004 | Kumar    |       5002 |
| 402881f81d08f6f2011d08f6f6580006 | Ajay     |       5003 |
+----------------------------------+----------+------------+
3 rows in set (0.00 sec)

mysql> select * from address;
+----------------------------------+-----------------+--------------+--------------+-------------+----------------------+
| ID                               | CITY_NAME       | COUNTRY_NAME | HOUSE_NUMBER | POSTAL_CODE | STREET_NAME          |
+----------------------------------+-----------------+--------------+--------------+-------------+----------------------+
| 402881f81d08f6f2011d08f6f6580002 | Kuala Lumpur    | Malaysia     | C-13-4       | 50100       | Jalan Munsi Abdullah |
| 402881f81d08f6f2011d08f6f6580003 | Tiruchirapalli  | India        | 3-121        | 621302      | Middle Streeet       |
| 402881f81d08f6f2011d08f6f6580005 | Chennai         | India        | T-4          | 600020      | Nehru Street         |
+----------------------------------+-----------------+--------------+--------------+-------------+----------------------+
3 rows in set (0.00 sec)

mysql> select * from employee_address_mapping;
+----------------------------------+----------------------------------+
| EMPLOYEE_ID                      | ADDRESS_ID                       |
+----------------------------------+----------------------------------+
| 402881f81d08f6f2011d08f6f6390001 | 402881f81d08f6f2011d08f6f6580002 |
| 402881f81d08f6f2011d08f6f6390001 | 402881f81d08f6f2011d08f6f6580003 |
| 402881f81d08f6f2011d08f6f6580004 | 402881f81d08f6f2011d08f6f6580005 |
+----------------------------------+----------------------------------+
3 rows in set (0.00 sec)
```

One-To-Many Mapping with Bidirectional Association using Foreign-Key

One *Employee* may have many addresses. Many addresses belong to one Employee.

Employee (one) ⟷ Address (many)

```
// File Name: Employee.java
// Illustrates @OneToMany and @ManyToOne

package com.hdemo;

import java.util.List;

import javax.persistence.CascadeType;
import javax.persistence.Column;
import javax.persistence.Entity;
import javax.persistence.GeneratedValue;
import javax.persistence.Id;
import javax.persistence.OneToMany;
import javax.persistence.Table;

import org.hibernate.annotations.GenericGenerator;

@Entity
@Table(name = "EMPLOYEE")
public class Employee {

 private static final long serialVersionUID = 1L;

 @Id
  @GeneratedValue(generator = "idGen")
  @GenericGenerator(name = "idGen", strategy = "uuid.hex")
  @Column(name = "ID", length = 32)
  private String id = "";

  @Column(name = "EMP_NUMBER", unique = true, nullable = false)
  private Integer empNumber;

  @Column(name = "EMP_NAME", length = 64, nullable = false)
  private String empName;

  @OneToMany(cascade=CascadeType.ALL, mappedBy="employee")
```

```
    private List<Address> addresses;

    //Getter and Setter methods

}
```

```
// File Name: Address.java
// Illustrates @OneToMany and @ManyToOnepackage
package com.hdemo;

import java.io.Serializable;

import javax.persistence.Column;
import javax.persistence.Entity;
import javax.persistence.GeneratedValue;
import javax.persistence.Id;
import javax.persistence.JoinColumn;
import javax.persistence.ManyToOne;
import javax.persistence.Table;

import org.hibernate.annotations.GenericGenerator;

@Entity
@Table(name = "ADDRESS")
public class Address implements Serializable {

    private static final long serialVersionUID = 1L;

    @Id
    @GeneratedValue(generator = "idGen")
    @GenericGenerator(name = "idGen", strategy = "uuid.hex")
    @Column(name = "ID", length = 32)
    private String id = "";

    @Column(name = "HOUSE_NUMBER", length = 8)
    private String houseNumber;

    @Column(name = "STREET_NAME", length = 64)
    private String streetName;
```

```
    @Column(name = "CITY_NAME", length = 64)
    private String cityName;

    @Column(name = "COUNTRY_NAME", length = 64)
    private String countryName;

    @Column(name = "POSTAL_CODE", length = 16)
    private String postalCode;

    @ManyToOne
    @JoinColumn(name="EMP_ID", nullable=false)
    private Employee employee;

    //Getter and Setter methods

    public String toString() {
          return "[House Number : " + houseNumber +
                "\nStreet Name  : " + streetName +
                "\nCity Name    : " + cityName +
                "\nCountry Name : " + countryName +
                "\nPostal Code  : " + postalCode +
                "]";
    }
}
```

```
// File Name: EmployeeManipulation.java
// Main Program

package com.hdemo;

import java.util.ArrayList;
import java.util.List;

import org.hibernate.Session;
import org.hibernate.SessionFactory;
import org.hibernate.Transaction;

public class EmployeeManipulation {
```

```
@SuppressWarnings("unchecked")
public static void main(String[] args) throws Exception {
SessionFactory sessionFactory = HibernateUtil.getSessionFactory();
Session session = sessionFactory.openSession();
Transaction txn = session.beginTransaction();

Employee employee1 = new Employee();
employee1.setEmpNumber(5001);

employee1.setEmpName("Ibrahim");
Address employee1Address1 = new Address();
employee1Address1.setHouseNumber("C-13-4");
employee1Address1.setStreetName("Jalan Munsi Abdullah");
employee1Address1.setCityName("Kuala Lumpur");
employee1Address1.setCountryName("Malaysia");
employee1Address1.setPostalCode("50100");
employee1Address1.setEmployee(employee1);
Address employee1Address2 = new Address();
employee1Address2.setHouseNumber("3-121");
employee1Address2.setStreetName("Middle Street");
employee1Address2.setCityName("Tiruchirapalli");
employee1Address2.setCountryName("India");
employee1Address2.setPostalCode("621302");
employee1Address2.setEmployee(employee1);
List<Address> employee1Addresses = new ArrayList<Address>();
employee1Addresses.add(employee1Address1);
employee1Addresses.add(employee1Address2);
employee1.setAddresses(employee1Addresses);

Employee employee2 = new Employee();
employee2.setEmpNumber(5002);
employee2.setEmpName("Kumar");
Address employee2Address1 = new Address();
employee2Address1.setHouseNumber("T-4");
employee2Address1.setStreetName("Nehru Street");
employee2Address1.setCityName("Chennai");
```

```
employee2Address1.setCountryName("India");
employee2Address1.setPostalCode("600020");
employee2Address1.setEmployee(employee2);
List<Address> employee2Addresses = new ArrayList<Address>();
employee2Addresses.add(employee2Address1);
employee2.setAddresses(employee2Addresses);

Employee employee3 = new Employee();
employee3.setEmpNumber(5003);
employee3.setEmpName("Ajay");
employee3.setAddresses(null);

session.save(employee1);
System.out.println("The object employee1 is persisted with session");
session.save(employee2);
System.out.println("The object employee2 is persisted with session");
session.save(employee3);
System.out.println("The object employee3 is persisted with session");

txn.commit();
System.out.println("Transaction on this session is committed");
session.close();

session = sessionFactory.openSession();
txn = session.beginTransaction();
System.out.println("Accessing Employee Objects through Employee
      ==> One To Many (One Employee has Many Addresses)\n\n");
List<Employee> employeeList = session.createQuery("from
      Employee").list();
for (int i = 0; i < employeeList.size(); i++) {
Employee employee = employeeList.get(i);
System.out.println("Employee Number : " + employee.getEmpNumber());
System.out.println("Employee Name   : " + employee.getEmpName());
List<Address> addresses = employee.getAddresses();
for (int j = 0; addresses != null && j < addresses.size(); j++) {
System.out.println("Employee Address (" + (j + 1)
      + ") : " + addresses.get(j));
```

```
        }

    System.out.println("========================================\n\n");
        }

    txn.commit();
    session.close();

    session = sessionFactory.openSession();
    txn = session.beginTransaction();
    System.out.println("Accessing Address Objects through Address ==>
    Many to One (Many Addresses belong to One Employee)\n\n");
    List<Address> addressList = session.createQuery("from
    Address").list();
    for (int i = 0; i < addressList.size(); i++) {
    Address address = addressList.get(i);
    System.out.println("Employee Number : " + address.getEmployee().
        getEmpNumber());
    System.out.println("Employee Name   : " + address.getEmployee().
        getEmpName());
    System.out.println("Address : " + address);

    System.out.println("========================================\n\n");
        }

      txn.commit();

      sessionFactory.close();
    }
}
```

Output:

```
The object employee1 is persisted with session
The object employee2 is persisted with session
The object employee3 is persisted with session
Hibernate: insert into EMPLOYEE (EMP_NAME, EMP_NUMBER, ID) values
(?, ?, ?)
Hibernate: insert into ADDRESS (CITY_NAME, COUNTRY_NAME, EMP_ID,
```

```
HOUSE_NUMBER, POSTAL_CODE, STREET_NAME, ID) values (?, ?, ?, ?, ?,
?, ?)
Hibernate: insert into ADDRESS (CITY_NAME, COUNTRY_NAME, EMP_ID,
HOUSE_NUMBER, POSTAL_CODE, STREET_NAME, ID) values (?, ?, ?, ?, ?,
?, ?)
Hibernate: insert into EMPLOYEE (EMP_NAME, EMP_NUMBER, ID) values
(?, ?, ?)
Hibernate: insert into ADDRESS (CITY_NAME, COUNTRY_NAME, EMP_ID,
HOUSE_NUMBER, POSTAL_CODE, STREET_NAME, ID) values (?, ?, ?, ?, ?, ?, ?)
Hibernate: insert into EMPLOYEE (EMP_NAME, EMP_NUMBER, ID) values
(?, ?, ?)
Transaction on this session is committed
Accessing Employee Objects through Employee ==> One To Many (One
Employee has Many Addresses)

Hibernate: select employee0_.ID as ID0_, employee0_.EMP_NAME as
EMP2_0_, employee0_.EMP_NUMBER as EMP3_0_ from EMPLOYEE employee0_
Employee Number : 5001
Employee Name    : Ibrahim
Hibernate: select addresses0_.EMP_ID as EMP7_1_, addresses0_.ID as
ID1_, addresses0_.ID as ID1_0_, addresses0_.CITY_NAME as CITY2_1_0_,
addresses0_.COUNTRY_NAME as COUNTRY3_1_0_, addresses0_.EMP_ID as
EMP7_1_0_, addresses0_.HOUSE_NUMBER as HOUSE4_1_0_,
addresses0_.POSTAL_CODE as POSTAL5_1_0_, addresses0_.STREET_NAME as
STREET6_1_0_ from ADDRESS addresses0_ where addresses0_.EMP_ID=?
Employee Address (1)   : [House Number: C-13-4
Street Name  : Jalan Munsi Abdullah
City Name    : Kuala Lumpur
Country Name : Malaysia
Postal Code  : 50100]
Employee Address (2)   : [House Number: 3-121
Street Name  : Middle Street
City Name    : Tiruchirapalli
Country Name : India
Postal Code  : 621302]
========================================

Employee Number: 5002
```

```
Employee Name : Kumar

Hibernate: select addresses0_.EMP_ID as EMP7_1_, addresses0_.ID as ID1_, addresses0_.ID as ID1_0_, addresses0_.CITY_NAME as CITY2_1_0_, addresses0_.COUNTRY_NAME as COUNTRY3_1_0_, addresses0_.EMP_ID as EMP7_1_0_, addresses0_.HOUSE_NUMBER as HOUSE4_1_0_, addresses0_.POSTAL_CODE as POSTAL5_1_0_, addresses0_.STREET_NAME as STREET6_1_0_ from ADDRESS addresses0_ where addresses0_.EMP_ID=?

Employee Address (1)   : [House Number: T-4

Street Name    : Nehru Street

City Name      : Chennai

Country Name : India

Postal Code    : 600020]

=========================================

Employee Number: 5003

Employee Name : Ajay

Hibernate: select addresses0_.EMP_ID as EMP7_1_, addresses0_.ID as ID1_, addresses0_.ID as ID1_0_, addresses0_.CITY_NAME as CITY2_1_0_, addresses0_.COUNTRY_NAME as COUNTRY3_1_0_, addresses0_.EMP_ID as EMP7_1_0_, addresses0_.HOUSE_NUMBER as HOUSE4_1_0_, addresses0_.POSTAL_CODE as POSTAL5_1_0_, addresses0_.STREET_NAME as STREET6_1_0_ from ADDRESS addresses0_ where addresses0_.EMP_ID=?

=========================================

Accessing Address Objects through Address ==> Many to One (Many Addresses belong to one Employee)

Hibernate: select address0_.ID as ID1_, address0_.CITY_NAME as CITY2_1_, address0_.COUNTRY_NAME as COUNTRY3_1_, address0_.EMP_ID as EMP7_1_, address0_.HOUSE_NUMBER as HOUSE4_1_, address0_.POSTAL_CODE as POSTAL5_1_, address0_.STREET_NAME as STREET6_1_ from ADDRESS address0_

Hibernate: select employee0_.ID as ID0_0_, employee0_.EMP_NAME as EMP2_0_0_, employee0_.EMP_NUMBER as EMP3_0_0_ from EMPLOYEE employee0_ where employee0_.ID=?

Hibernate: select employee0_.ID as ID0_0_, employee0_.EMP_NAME as EMP2_0_0_, employee0_.EMP_NUMBER as EMP3_0_0_ from EMPLOYEE employee0_ where employee0_.ID=?

Employee Number : 5001

Employee Name   : Ibrahim
```

```
Address        : [House Number: C-13-4
Street Name    : Jalan Munsi Abdullah
City Name      : Kuala Lumpur
Country Name   : Malaysia
Postal Code    : 50100]
===============================================

Employee Number: 5001
Employee Name  : Ibrahim
Address        : [House Number: 3-121
Street Name    : Middle Street
City Name      : Tiruchirapalli
Country Name   : India
Postal Code    : 621302]
===============================================

Employee Number: 5002
Employee Name  : Kumar
Address        : [House Number: T-4
Street Name    : Nehru Street
City Name      : Chennai
Country Name   : India
Postal Code    : 600020]
===============================================
```

A sample run results as below.

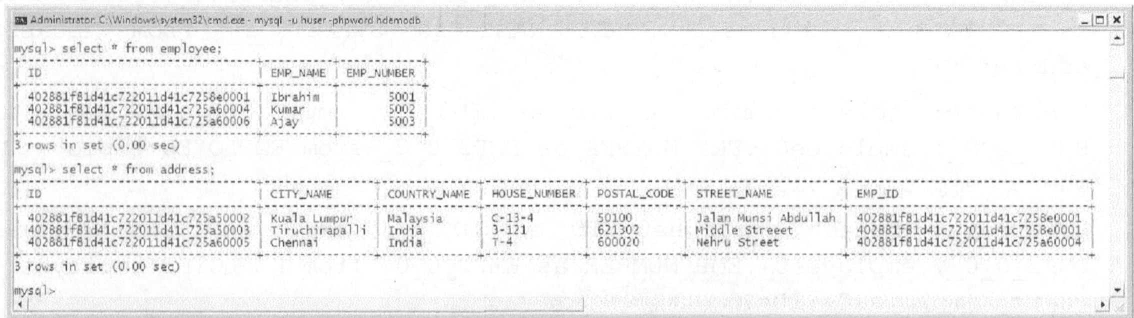

```
Administrator: C:\Windows\system32\cmd.exe - mysql -u huser -phpword hdemodb
mysql> select * from employee;
+----------------------------------+----------+------------+
| ID                               | EMP_NAME | EMP_NUMBER |
+----------------------------------+----------+------------+
| 402881f81d41c722011d41c7258e0001 | Ibrahim  |       5001 |
| 402881f81d41c722011d41c725a60004 | Kumar    |       5002 |
| 402881f81d41c722011d41c725a60006 | Ajay     |       5003 |
+----------------------------------+----------+------------+
3 rows in set (0.00 sec)

mysql> select * from address;
+----------------------------------+-----------------+--------------+--------------+-------------+----------------------+----------------------------------+
| ID                               | CITY_NAME       | COUNTRY_NAME | HOUSE_NUMBER | POSTAL_CODE | STREET_NAME          | EMP_ID                           |
+----------------------------------+-----------------+--------------+--------------+-------------+----------------------+----------------------------------+
| 402881f81d41c722011d41c725a50002 | Kuala Lumpur    | Malaysia     | C-13-4       | 50100       | Jalan Munsi Abdullah | 402881f81d41c722011d41c7258e0001 |
| 402881f81d41c722011d41c725a50003 | Tiruchirapalli  | India        | 3-121        | 621302      | Middle Streeet       | 402881f81d41c722011d41c7258e0001 |
| 402881f81d41c722011d41c725a60005 | Chennai         | India        | T-4          | 600020      | Nehru Street         | 402881f81d41c722011d41c725a60004 |
+----------------------------------+-----------------+--------------+--------------+-------------+----------------------+----------------------------------+
3 rows in set (0.00 sec)

mysql>
```

One-To-Many Mapping with Bidirectional Association using Association Table (Join table)

One *Employee* may have many addresses. Many addresses belong to One Employee.

Employee (one) ⟷ Address (many)

```
// File Name: Employee.java
// Illustrates @OneToMany and @ManyToOne

package com.hdemo;

import java.util.List;

import javax.persistence.CascadeType;
import javax.persistence.Column;
import javax.persistence.Entity;
import javax.persistence.GeneratedValue;
import javax.persistence.Id;
import javax.persistence.JoinColumn;
import javax.persistence.JoinTable;
import javax.persistence.OneToMany;
import javax.persistence.Table;

import org.hibernate.annotations.GenericGenerator;

@Entity
@Table(name = "EMPLOYEE")
public class Employee {

  private static final long serialVersionUID = 1L;

  @Id
  @GeneratedValue(generator = "idGen")
  @GenericGenerator(name = "idGen", strategy = "uuid.hex")
  @Column(name = "ID", length = 32)
  private String id = "";

  @Column(name = "EMP_NUMBER", unique = true, nullable = false)
  private Integer empNumber;

  @Column(name = "EMP_NAME", length = 64, nullable = false)
  private String empName;

  @OneToMany(cascade=CascadeType.ALL)
```

```
    @JoinTable(name = "EMPLOYEE_ADDRESS_MAPPING",
             joinColumns = { @JoinColumn(name = "EMPLOYEE_ID") },
              inverseJoinColumns = { @JoinColumn(name = "ADDRESS_ID") })
    private List<Address> addresses;

    //Getter and Setter methods

}
```

```
// File Name: Address.java
// Illustrates @OneToMany and @ManyToOne

package com.hdemo;

import java.io.Serializable;

import javax.persistence.Column;
import javax.persistence.Entity;
import javax.persistence.GeneratedValue;
import javax.persistence.Id;
import javax.persistence.JoinColumn;
import javax.persistence.JoinTable;
import javax.persistence.ManyToOne;
import javax.persistence.Table;

import org.hibernate.annotations.GenericGenerator;

@Entity
@Table(name = "ADDRESS")
public class Address implements Serializable {

    private static final long serialVersionUID = 1L;

    @Id
    @GeneratedValue(generator = "idGen")
    @GenericGenerator(name = "idGen", strategy = "uuid.hex")
    @Column(name = "ID", length = 32)
    private String id = "";
```

```
  @Column(name = "HOUSE_NUMBER", length = 8)
  private String houseNumber;

  @Column(name = "STREET_NAME", length = 64)
  private String streetName;

  @Column(name = "CITY_NAME", length = 64)
  private String cityName;

  @Column(name = "COUNTRY_NAME", length = 64)
  private String countryName;

  @Column(name = "POSTAL_CODE", length = 16)
  private String postalCode;

  @ManyToOne(optional = true)
  @JoinTable(name = "ADDRESS_EMPLOYEE_MAPPING",
  joinColumns = { @JoinColumn(name = "ADD_ID") },
  inverseJoinColumns = { @JoinColumn(name = "EMP_ID") })
  private Employee employee;

  //Getter and Setter methods

  public String toString() {
       return "[House Number: " + houseNumber +
            "\nStreet Name   : " + streetName +
            "\nCity Name     : " + cityName +
            "\nCountry Name  : " + countryName +
            "\nPostal Code   : " + postalCode +
            "]";
  }
}
```

```
// File Name: EmployeeManipulation.java
// Main Program

package com.hdemo;

import java.util.ArrayList;
```

```
import java.util.List;

import org.hibernate.Session;
import org.hibernate.SessionFactory;
import org.hibernate.Transaction;

public class EmployeeManipulation {

  @SuppressWarnings("unchecked")
  public static void main(String[] args) throws Exception {
  SessionFactory sessionFactory = HibernateUtil.getSessionFactory();
  Session session = sessionFactory.openSession();
  Transaction txn = session.beginTransaction();

  Employee employee1 = new Employee();
  employee1.setEmpNumber(5001);


  employee1.setEmpName("Ibrahim");
  Address employee1Address1 = new Address();
  employee1Address1.setHouseNumber("C-13-4");
  employee1Address1.setStreetName("Jalan Munsi Abdullah");
  employee1Address1.setCityName("Kuala Lumpur");
  employee1Address1.setCountryName("Malaysia");
  employee1Address1.setPostalCode("50100");
  employee1Address1.setEmployee(employee1);
  Address employee1Address2 = new Address();
  employee1Address2.setHouseNumber("3-121");
  employee1Address2.setStreetName("Middle Street");
  employee1Address2.setCityName("Tiruchirapalli");
  employee1Address2.setCountryName("India");
  employee1Address2.setPostalCode("621302");
  employee1Address2.setEmployee(employee1);
  List<Address> employee1Addresses = new ArrayList<Address>();
  employee1Addresses.add(employee1Address1);
  employee1Addresses.add(employee1Address2);
  employee1.setAddresses(employee1Addresses);

  Employee employee2 = new Employee();
```

```
employee2.setEmpNumber(5002);
employee2.setEmpName("Kumar");
Address employee2Address1 = new Address();
employee2Address1.setHouseNumber("T-4");
employee2Address1.setStreetName("Nehru Street");
employee2Address1.setCityName("Chennai");
employee2Address1.setCountryName("India");
employee2Address1.setPostalCode("600020");
employee2Address1.setEmployee(employee2);
List<Address> employee2Addresses = new ArrayList<Address>();
employee2Addresses.add(employee2Address1);
employee2.setAddresses(employee2Addresses);

Employee employee3 = new Employee();
employee3.setEmpNumber(5003);
employee3.setEmpName("Ajay");
employee3.setAddresses(null);

session.save(employee1);
System.out.println("The object employee1 is persisted with session");
session.save(employee2);
System.out.println("The object employee2 is persisted with session");
session.save(employee3);
System.out.println("The object employee3 is persisted with session");

txn.commit();
System.out.println("Transaction on this session is committed");
session.close();

session = sessionFactory.openSession();
txn = session.beginTransaction();
System.out.println("Accessing Employee Objects through Employee
==> One To Many (One Employee has Many Addresses)\n\n");
List<Employee> employeeList = session.createQuery("from
Employee").list();
for (int i = 0; i < employeeList.size(); i++) {
Employee employee = employeeList.get(i);
System.out.println("Employee Number : " + employee.getEmpNumber());
```

```
System.out.println("Employee Name    : " + employee.getEmpName());
List<Address> addresses = employee.getAddresses();
for (int j=0; addresses != null && j<addresses.size(); j++) {
System.out.println("Employee Address (" + (j + 1)
      + ") : " + addresses.get(j));
      }

System.out.println("============================================\n\n");
      }

txn.commit();
session.close();


session = sessionFactory.openSession();
txn = session.beginTransaction();
System.out.println("Accessing Address Objects through Address ==>
Many to One (Many Addresses belong to One Employee)\n\n");
List<Address> addressList =
session.createQuery("from Address").list();
for (int i = 0; i < addressList.size(); i++) {
Address address = addressList.get(i);
System.out.println("Employee Number : " +
address.getEmployee().get EmpNumber());
System.out.println("Employee Name   : " + address.getEmployee().get
EmpName());
System.out.println("Address : " + address);

System.out.println("============================================\n\n");
      }

txn.commit();

      sessionFactory.close();
  }
}
```

Output:

```
The object employee1 is persisted with session
The object employee2 is persisted with session
The object employee3 is persisted with session
```

```
Hibernate: insert into EMPLOYEE (EMP_NAME, EMP_NUMBER, ID) values
(?, ?, ?)
Hibernate: insert into ADDRESS (CITY_NAME, COUNTRY_NAME, HOUSE_NUMBER,
POSTAL_CODE, STREET_NAME, ID) values (?, ?, ?, ?, ?, ?)
Hibernate: insert into ADDRESS_EMPLOYEE_MAPPING (EMP_ID, ADD_ID)
values (?, ?)
Hibernate: insert into ADDRESS (CITY_NAME, COUNTRY_NAME, HOUSE_NUMBER,
POSTAL_CODE, STREET_NAME, ID) values (?, ?, ?, ?, ?, ?)
Hibernate: insert into ADDRESS_EMPLOYEE_MAPPING (EMP_ID, ADD_ID)
values (?, ?)
Hibernate: insert into EMPLOYEE (EMP_NAME, EMP_NUMBER, ID) values
(?, ?, ?)
Hibernate: insert into ADDRESS (CITY_NAME, COUNTRY_NAME, HOUSE_NUMBER,
POSTAL_CODE, STREET_NAME, ID) values (?, ?, ?, ?, ?, ?)
Hibernate: insert into ADDRESS_EMPLOYEE_MAPPING (EMP_ID, ADD_ID)
values (?, ?)
Hibernate: insert into EMPLOYEE (EMP_NAME, EMP_NUMBER, ID) values
(?, ?, ?)
Hibernate: insert into EMPLOYEE_ADDRESS_MAPPING (EMPLOYEE_ID,
ADDRESS_ID) values (?, ?)
Hibernate: insert into EMPLOYEE_ADDRESS_MAPPING (EMPLOYEE_ID,
ADDRESS_ID) values (?, ?)
Hibernate: insert into EMPLOYEE_ADDRESS_MAPPING (EMPLOYEE_ID,
ADDRESS_ID) values (?, ?)
Transaction on this session is committed
Accessing Employee Objects through Employee ==> One To Many (One
Employee has Many Addresses)

Hibernate: select employee0_.ID as ID0_, employee0_.EMP_NAME as
EMP2_0_, employee0_.EMP_NUMBER as EMP3_0_ from EMPLOYEE employee0_
Employee Number : 5001
Employee Name    : Ibrahim
Hibernate: select addresses0_.EMPLOYEE_ID as EMPLOYEE1_2_,
addresses0_.ADDRESS_ID as ADDRESS2_2_, address1_.ID as ID1_0_,
address1_.CITY_NAME as CITY2_1_0_, address1_.COUNTRY_NAME as
COUNTRY3_1_0_, address1_.HOUSE_NUMBER as HOUSE4_1_0_,
address1_.POSTAL_CODE as POSTAL5_1_0_, address1_.STREET_NAME as
STREET6_1_0_, address1_1_.EMP_ID as EMP1_2_0_, employee2_.ID as
ID0_1_, employee2_.EMP_NAME as EMP2_0_1_, employee2_.EMP_NUMBER as
EMP3_0_1_ from EMPLOYEE_ADDRESS_MAPPING addresses0_ left outer join
ADDRESS address1_ on addresses0_.ADDRESS_ID=address1_.ID left outer
```

```
join ADDRESS_EMPLOYEE_MAPPING address1_1_ on address1_.ID=
address1_1_.ADD_ID left outer join EMPLOYEE employee2_ on
address1_1_.EMP_ID=employee2_.ID where addresses0_.EMPLOYEE_ID=?
Employee Address (1) : [House Number: C-13-4
Street Name : Jalan Munsi Abdullah
City Name    : Kuala Lumpur
Country Name : Malaysia
Postal Code : 50100]
Employee Address (2) : [House Number: 3-121
Street Name : Middle Street
City Name    : Tiruchirapalli
Country Name : India
Postal Code : 621302]
========================================

Employee Number : 5002
Employee Name   : Kumar
Hibernate: select addresses0_.EMPLOYEE_ID as EMPLOYEE1_2_,
addresses0_.ADDRESS_ID as ADDRESS2_2_, address1_.ID as ID1_0_,
address1_.CITY_NAME as CITY2_1_0_, address1_.COUNTRY_NAME as
COUNTRY3_1_0_, address1_.HOUSE_NUMBER as HOUSE4_1_0_,
address1_.POSTAL_CODE as POSTAL5_1_0_, address1_.STREET_NAME as
STREET6_1_0_, address1_1_.EMP_ID as EMP1_2_0_, employee2_.ID as
ID0_1_, employee2_.EMP_NAME as EMP2_0_1_, employee2_.EMP_NUMBER as
EMP3_0_1_ from EMPLOYEE_ADDRESS_MAPPING addresses0_ left outer join
ADDRESS address1_ on addresses0_.ADDRESS_ID=address1_.ID left outer
join ADDRESS_EMPLOYEE_MAPPING address1_1_ on address1_.ID=
address1_1_.ADD_ID left outer join EMPLOYEE employee2_ on
address1_1_.EMP_ID=employee2_.ID where addresses0_.EMPLOYEE_ID=?
Employee Address (1) : [House Number: T-4
Street Name    : Nehru Street
City Name      : Chennai
Country Name   : India
Postal Code    : 600020]
========================================

Employee Number : 5003
Employee Name : Ajay
Hibernate: select addresses0_.EMPLOYEE_ID as EMPLOYEE1_2_,
addresses0_.ADDRESS_ID as ADDRESS2_2_, address1_.ID as ID1_0_,
```

```
address1_.CITY_NAME as CITY2_1_0_, address1_.COUNTRY_NAME as
COUNTRY3_1_0_, address1_.HOUSE_NUMBER as HOUSE4_1_0_,
address1_.POSTAL_CODE as POSTAL5_1_0_, address1_.STREET_NAME as
STREET6_1_0_, address1_1_.EMP_ID as EMP1_2_0_, employee2_.ID as
ID0_1_, employee2_.EMP_NAME as EMP2_0_1_, employee2_.EMP_NUMBER as
EMP3_0_1_ from EMPLOYEE_ADDRESS_MAPPING addresses0_ left outer join
ADDRESS address1_ on addresses0_.ADDRESS_ID=address1_.ID left outer
join ADDRESS_EMPLOYEE_MAPPING address1_1_ on address1_.ID=
address1_1_.ADD_ID left outer join EMPLOYEE employee2_ on
address1_1_.EMP_ID=employee2_.ID where addresses0_.EMPLOYEE_ID=?
========================================

Accessing Address Objects through Address ==> Many to One (Many
Addresses belong to One Employee)

Hibernate: select address0_.ID as ID1_, address0_.CITY_NAME as
CITY2_1_, address0_.COUNTRY_NAME as COUNTRY3_1_, address0_.HOUSE_NUMBER
as HOUSE4_1_, address0_.POSTAL_CODE as POSTAL5_1_,
address0_.STREET_NAME as STREET6_1_, address0_1_.EMP_ID as EMP1_2_
from ADDRESS address0_ left outer join ADDRESS_EMPLOYEE_MAPPING
address0_1_ on address0_.ID=address0_1_.ADD_ID
Hibernate: select employee0_.ID as ID0_0_, employee0_.EMP_NAME as
EMP2_0_0_, employee0_.EMP_NUMBER as EMP3_0_0_ from EMPLOYEE employee0_
where employee0_.ID=?
Hibernate: select employee0_.ID as ID0_0_, employee0_.EMP_NAME as
EMP2_0_0_, employee0_.EMP_NUMBER as EMP3_0_0_ from EMPLOYEE employee0_
where employee0_.ID=?
Employee Number : 5001
Employee Name   : Ibrahim
Address         : [House Number: C-13-4
Street Name     : Jalan Munsi Abdullah
City Name       : Kuala Lumpur
Country Name    : Malaysia
Postal Code     : 50100]
========================================

Employee Number : 5001
Employee Name   : Ibrahim
Address         : [House Number: 3-121
Street Name     : Middle Street
City Name       : Tiruchirapalli
```

```
Country Name     : India
Postal Code      : 621302]
========================================

Employee Number  : 5002
Employee Name    : Kumar
Address          : [House Number: T-4
Street Name      : Nehru Street
City Name        : Chennai
Country Name     : India
Postal Code      : 600020]
========================================
```

A sample run results as below.

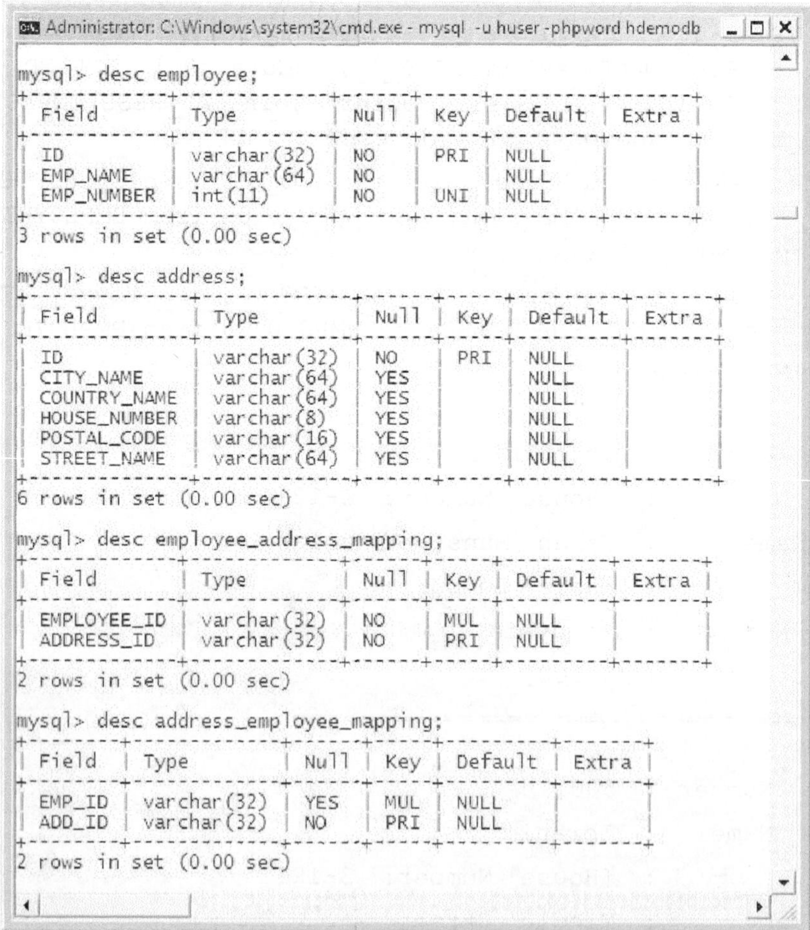

```
Administrator: C:\Windows\system32\cmd.exe - mysql -u huser -phpword hdemodb

mysql> desc employee;
+------------+-------------+------+-----+---------+-------+
| Field      | Type        | Null | Key | Default | Extra |
+------------+-------------+------+-----+---------+-------+
| ID         | varchar(32) | NO   | PRI | NULL    |       |
| EMP_NAME   | varchar(64) | NO   |     | NULL    |       |
| EMP_NUMBER | int(11)     | NO   | UNI | NULL    |       |
+------------+-------------+------+-----+---------+-------+
3 rows in set (0.00 sec)

mysql> desc address;
+--------------+-------------+------+-----+---------+-------+
| Field        | Type        | Null | Key | Default | Extra |
+--------------+-------------+------+-----+---------+-------+
| ID           | varchar(32) | NO   | PRI | NULL    |       |
| CITY_NAME    | varchar(64) | YES  |     | NULL    |       |
| COUNTRY_NAME | varchar(64) | YES  |     | NULL    |       |
| HOUSE_NUMBER | varchar(8)  | YES  |     | NULL    |       |
| POSTAL_CODE  | varchar(16) | YES  |     | NULL    |       |
| STREET_NAME  | varchar(64) | YES  |     | NULL    |       |
+--------------+-------------+------+-----+---------+-------+
6 rows in set (0.00 sec)

mysql> desc employee_address_mapping;
+-------------+-------------+------+-----+---------+-------+
| Field       | Type        | Null | Key | Default | Extra |
+-------------+-------------+------+-----+---------+-------+
| EMPLOYEE_ID | varchar(32) | NO   | MUL | NULL    |       |
| ADDRESS_ID  | varchar(32) | NO   | PRI | NULL    |       |
+-------------+-------------+------+-----+---------+-------+
2 rows in set (0.00 sec)

mysql> desc address_employee_mapping;
+--------+-------------+------+-----+---------+-------+
| Field  | Type        | Null | Key | Default | Extra |
+--------+-------------+------+-----+---------+-------+
| EMP_ID | varchar(32) | YES  | MUL | NULL    |       |
| ADD_ID | varchar(32) | NO   | PRI | NULL    |       |
+--------+-------------+------+-----+---------+-------+
2 rows in set (0.00 sec)
```

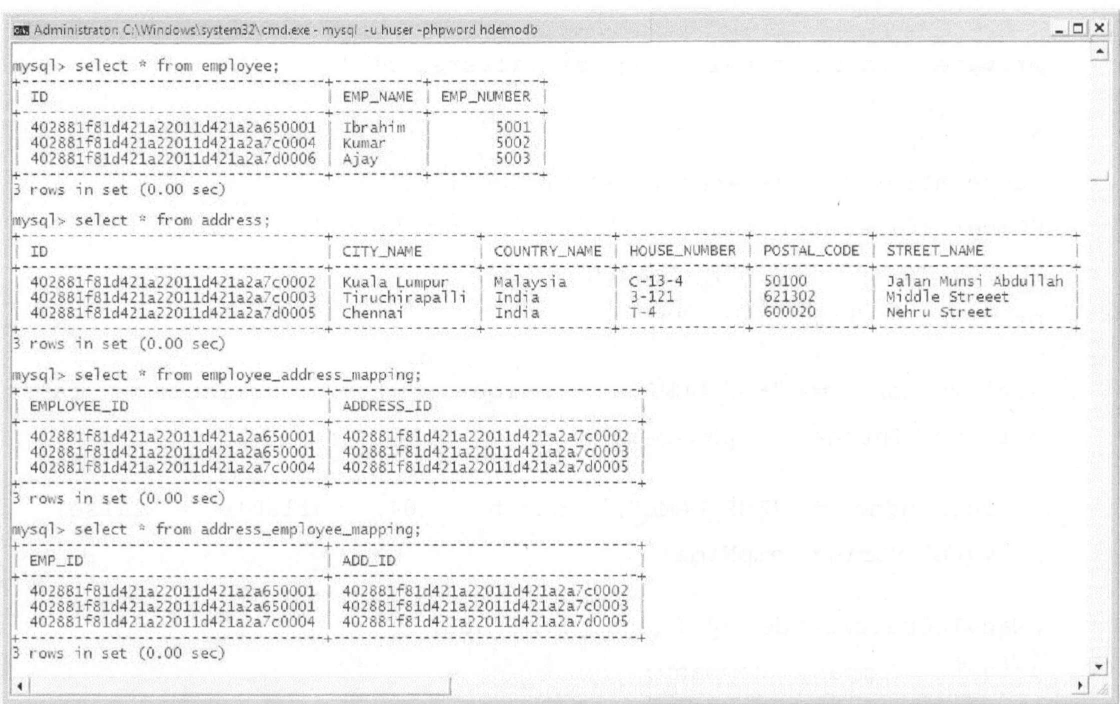

```
Administrator: C:\Windows\system32\cmd.exe - mysql -u huser -phpword hdemodb

mysql> select * from employee;
+----------------------------------+----------+------------+
| ID                               | EMP_NAME | EMP_NUMBER |
+----------------------------------+----------+------------+
| 402881f81d421a22011d421a2a650001 | Ibrahim  |       5001 |
| 402881f81d421a22011d421a2a7c0004 | Kumar    |       5002 |
| 402881f81d421a22011d421a2a7d0006 | Ajay     |       5003 |
+----------------------------------+----------+------------+
3 rows in set (0.00 sec)

mysql> select * from address;
+----------------------------------+-----------------+--------------+--------------+-------------+----------------------+
| ID                               | CITY_NAME       | COUNTRY_NAME | HOUSE_NUMBER | POSTAL_CODE | STREET_NAME          |
+----------------------------------+-----------------+--------------+--------------+-------------+----------------------+
| 402881f81d421a22011d421a2a7c0002 | Kuala Lumpur    | Malaysia     | C-13-4       | 50100       | Jalan Munsi Abdullah |
| 402881f81d421a22011d421a2a7c0003 | Tiruchirapalli  | India        | 3-121        | 621302      | Middle Streeet       |
| 402881f81d421a22011d421a2a7d0005 | Chennai         | India        | T-4          | 600020      | Nehru Street         |
+----------------------------------+-----------------+--------------+--------------+-------------+----------------------+
3 rows in set (0.00 sec)

mysql> select * from employee_address_mapping;
+----------------------------------+----------------------------------+
| EMPLOYEE_ID                      | ADDRESS_ID                       |
+----------------------------------+----------------------------------+
| 402881f81d421a22011d421a2a650001 | 402881f81d421a22011d421a2a7c0002 |
| 402881f81d421a22011d421a2a650001 | 402881f81d421a22011d421a2a7c0003 |
| 402881f81d421a22011d421a2a7c0004 | 402881f81d421a22011d421a2a7d0005 |
+----------------------------------+----------------------------------+
3 rows in set (0.00 sec)

mysql> select * from address_employee_mapping;
+----------------------------------+----------------------------------+
| EMP_ID                           | ADD_ID                           |
+----------------------------------+----------------------------------+
| 402881f81d421a22011d421a2a650001 | 402881f81d421a22011d421a2a7c0002 |
| 402881f81d421a22011d421a2a650001 | 402881f81d421a22011d421a2a7c0003 |
| 402881f81d421a22011d421a2a7c0004 | 402881f81d421a22011d421a2a7d0005 |
+----------------------------------+----------------------------------+
3 rows in set (0.00 sec)
```

Many-To-One Mapping with Unidirectional Association using Foreign Key

Employee (many) → Company (One)

Include mapping entry for Company entity in *hibernate.cfg.xml* file.

```
        <mapping class="com.hdemo.Company" />
```

```
// File Name: Employee.java
// Illustrates @ManyToOne

package com.hdemo;

import javax.persistence.CascadeType;
import javax.persistence.Column;
import javax.persistence.Entity;
import javax.persistence.GeneratedValue;
import javax.persistence.Id;
import javax.persistence.ManyToOne;
import javax.persistence.Table;

import org.hibernate.annotations.GenericGenerator;

@Entity
@Table(name = "EMPLOYEE")
public class Employee {
```

```
    private static final long serialVersionUID = 1L;

    @Id
    @GeneratedValue(generator = "idGen")
    @GenericGenerator(name = "idGen", strategy = "uuid.hex")
    @Column(name = "ID", length = 32)
    private String id = "";

    @Column(name = "EMP_NUMBER", unique = true, nullable = false)
    private Integer empNumber;

    @Column(name = "EMP_NAME", length = 64, nullable = false)
    private String empName;

    @ManyToOne(cascade = CascadeType.ALL)
    private Company company;

    //Getter and Setter methods

}
```

```
// File Name: Company.java
// Illustrates @ManyToOne

package com.hdemo;

import java.io.Serializable;

import javax.persistence.Column;
import javax.persistence.Entity;
import javax.persistence.GeneratedValue;
import javax.persistence.Id;
import javax.persistence.Table;

import org.hibernate.annotations.GenericGenerator;

@Entity
@Table(name = "COMPANY")
public class Company implements Serializable {
```

```
  private static final long serialVersionUID = 1L;

  @Id
  @GeneratedValue(generator = "idGen")
  @GenericGenerator(name = "idGen", strategy = "uuid.hex")
  @Column(name = "ID", length = 32)
  private String id = "";

  @Column(name = "COMPANY_NAME")
  private String companyName;

  @Column(name = "COUNTRY")
  private String country;

  //Getter and Setter methods

}
```

```
// File Name: EmployeeManipulation.java
// Main Program

package com.hdemo;

import java.util.List;

import org.hibernate.Session;
import org.hibernate.SessionFactory;
import org.hibernate.Transaction;

public class EmployeeManipulation {

  @SuppressWarnings("unchecked")
  public static void main(String[] args) throws Exception {
  SessionFactory sessionFactory = HibernateUtil.getSessionFactory();
  Session session = sessionFactory.openSession();
  Transaction txn = session.beginTransaction();

  Company company1 = new Company();
  company1.setCompanyName("ABC Pvt. Ltd.");
  company1.setCountry("India");
```

```
Company company2 = new Company();
company2.setCompanyName("XYZ Sdn. Bhd.");
company2.setCountry("Malaysia");

Employee employee1 = new Employee();
employee1.setEmpNumber(5001);
employee1.setEmpName("Ibrahim");
employee1.setCompany(company1);

Employee employee2 = new Employee();
employee2.setEmpNumber(5002);
employee2.setEmpName("Kumar");
employee2.setCompany(company1);

Employee employee3 = new Employee();
employee3.setEmpNumber(5003);
employee3.setEmpName("Ajay");
employee3.setCompany(company1);

Employee employee4 = new Employee();
employee4.setEmpNumber(5004);
employee4.setEmpName("Akhfa");
employee4.setCompany(company2);

session.save(employee1);
System.out.println("The object employee1 is persisted with session");
session.save(employee2);
System.out.println("The object employee2 is persisted with session");
session.save(employee3);
System.out.println("The object employee3 is persisted with session");
session.save(employee4);
System.out.println("The object employee4 is persisted with session");

txn.commit();
System.out.println("Transaction on this session is committed");
session.close();
```

```
session = sessionFactory.openSession();
txn = session.beginTransaction();
System.out.println("Accessing Employee Objects\n\n");
List<Employee> employeeList =
      session.createQuery("from Employee").list();
      for (int i = 0; i < employeeList.size(); i++) {
Employee employee = employeeList.get(i);
System.out.println("Employee Number : " + employee.getEmpNumber());
System.out.println("Employee Name : " + employee.getEmpName());
System.out.println("Company Name : " + employee.getCompany().get
CompanyName());

System.out.println("=====================================\n\n");
      }
txn.commit();
session.close();

sessionFactory.close();
}
}
```

Output:

```
The object employee1 is persisted with session
The object employee2 is persisted with session
The object employee3 is persisted with session
The object employee4 is persisted with session
Hibernate: insert into COMPANY (COMPANY_NAME, COUNTRY, ID) values
(?, ?, ?)
Hibernate: insert into EMPLOYEE (company_ID, EMP_NAME, EMP_NUMBER,
ID) values (?, ?, ?, ?)
Hibernate: insert into EMPLOYEE (company_ID, EMP_NAME, EMP_NUMBER,
ID) values (?, ?, ?, ?)
Hibernate: insert into EMPLOYEE (company_ID, EMP_NAME, EMP_NUMBER,
ID) values (?, ?, ?, ?)
```

```
Hibernate: insert into COMPANY (COMPANY_NAME, COUNTRY, ID) values
(?, ?, ?)
Hibernate: insert into EMPLOYEE (company_ID, EMP_NAME, EMP_NUMBER,
ID) values (?, ?, ?, ?)
Transaction on this session is committed
Accessing Employee Objects

Hibernate: select employee0_.ID as ID0_, employee0_.company_ID as
company4_0_, employee0_.EMP_NAME as EMP2_0_, employee0_.EMP_NUMBER
as EMP3_0_ from EMPLOYEE employee0_
Hibernate: select company0_.ID as ID1_0_, company0_.COMPANY_NAME as
COMPANY2_1_0_, company0_.COUNTRY as COUNTRY1_0_ from COMPANY company0_
where company0_.ID=?
Hibernate: select company0_.ID as ID1_0_, company0_.COMPANY_NAME as
COMPANY2_1_0_, company0_.COUNTRY as COUNTRY1_0_ from COMPANY company0_
where company0_.ID=?
Employee Number : 5001
Employee Name   : Ibrahim
Company Name    : ABC Pvt. Ltd.
========================================

Employee Number : 5002
Employee Name   : Kumar
Company Name    : ABC Pvt. Ltd.
========================================

Employee Number : 5003
Employee Name   : Ajay
Company Name    : ABC Pvt. Ltd.
========================================

Employee Number : 5004
Employee Name   : Akhfa
Company Name    : XYZ Sdn. Bhd.
========================================
```

A sample run results as below.

```
Administrator: C:\Windows\system32\cmd.exe - mysql -u huser -phpword hdemodb

mysql> select * from employee;
+----------------------------------+----------+------------+----------------------------------+
| ID                               | EMP_NAME | EMP_NUMBER | company_ID                       |
+----------------------------------+----------+------------+----------------------------------+
| 402881f81d4289cb011d4289cde10001 | Ibrahim  |       5001 | 402881f81d4289cb011d4289cde70002 |
| 402881f81d4289cb011d4289cdef0003 | Kumar    |       5002 | 402881f81d4289cb011d4289cde70002 |
| 402881f81d4289cb011d4289cdef0004 | Ajay     |       5003 | 402881f81d4289cb011d4289cde70002 |
| 402881f81d4289cb011d4289cdef0005 | Akhfa    |       5004 | 402881f81d4289cb011d4289cdef0006 |
+----------------------------------+----------+------------+----------------------------------+
4 rows in set (0.00 sec)

mysql> select * from company;
+----------------------------------+---------------+----------+
| ID                               | COMPANY_NAME  | COUNTRY  |
+----------------------------------+---------------+----------+
| 402881f81d4289cb011d4289cde70002 | ABC Pvt. Ltd. | India    |
| 402881f81d4289cb011d4289cdef0006 | XYZ Sdn. Bhd. | Malaysia |
+----------------------------------+---------------+----------+
2 rows in set (0.00 sec)

mysql>
```

Many-To-One Mapping with Unidirectional Association using Association Table (Join table)

Employee (many) → Company (One)

```
// File Name: Employee.java
// Illustrates @ManyToOne

package com.hdemo;

import javax.persistence.CascadeType;
import javax.persistence.Column;
import javax.persistence.Entity;
import javax.persistence.GeneratedValue;
import javax.persistence.Id;
import javax.persistence.JoinColumn;
import javax.persistence.JoinTable;
import javax.persistence.ManyToOne;
import javax.persistence.Table;

import org.hibernate.annotations.GenericGenerator;

@Entity
@Table(name = "EMPLOYEE")
public class Employee {

  private static final long serialVersionUID = 1L;
```

```
    @Id
    @GeneratedValue(generator = "idGen")
    @GenericGenerator(name = "idGen", strategy = "uuid.hex")
    @Column(name = "ID", length = 32)
    private String id = "";

    @Column(name = "EMP_NUMBER", unique = true, nullable = false)
    private Integer empNumber;

    @Column(name = "EMP_NAME", length = 64, nullable = false)
    private String empName;

    @ManyToOne(optional = true, cascade = CascadeType.ALL)
    @JoinTable(name = "EMPLOYEE_COMPANY_MAPPING",
    joinColumns={ @JoinColumn(name="EMPLOYEE_ID", unique = true) },
          inverseJoinColumns = { @JoinColumn(name = "COMPANY_ID") })
    private Company company;

    //Getter and Setter methods

}
```

```
// File Name: Company.java
// Illustrates @ManyToOne

package com.hdemo;

import java.io.Serializable;

import javax.persistence.Column;
import javax.persistence.Entity;
import javax.persistence.GeneratedValue;
import javax.persistence.Id;
import javax.persistence.Table;

import org.hibernate.annotations.GenericGenerator;

@Entity
```

```
@Table(name = "COMPANY")
public class Company implements Serializable {

  private static final long serialVersionUID = 1L;

  @Id
  @GeneratedValue(generator = "idGen")
  @GenericGenerator(name = "idGen", strategy = "uuid.hex")
  @Column(name = "ID", length = 32)
  private String id = "";

  @Column(name = "COMPANY_NAME")
  private String companyName;

  @Column(name = "COUNTRY")
  private String country;

  //Getter and Setter methods

}
```

```
// File Name: EmployeeManipulation.java
// Main Program

package com.hdemo;

import java.util.List;

import org.hibernate.Session;
import org.hibernate.SessionFactory;
import org.hibernate.Transaction;

public class EmployeeManipulation {

  @SuppressWarnings("unchecked")
  public static void main(String[] args) throws Exception {
  SessionFactory sessionFactory = HibernateUtil.getSessionFactory();
  Session session = sessionFactory.openSession();
  Transaction txn = session.beginTransaction();
```

```
Company company1 = new Company();
company1.setCompanyName("ABC Pvt. Ltd.");
company1.setCountry("India");

Company company2 = new Company();
company2.setCompanyName("XYZ Sdn. Bhd.");
company2.setCountry("Malaysia");

Employee employee1 = new Employee();
employee1.setEmpNumber(5001);
employee1.setEmpName("Ibrahim");
employee1.setCompany(company1);

Employee employee2 = new Employee();
employee2.setEmpNumber(5002);
employee2.setEmpName("Kumar");
employee2.setCompany(company1);

Employee employee3 = new Employee();
employee3.setEmpNumber(5003);
employee3.setEmpName("Ajay");
employee3.setCompany(company1);

Employee employee4 = new Employee();
employee4.setEmpNumber(5004);
employee4.setEmpName("Akhfa");
employee4.setCompany(company2);

session.save(employee1);
System.out.println("The object employee1 is persisted with session");
session.save(employee2);
System.out.println("The object employee2 is persisted with session");
session.save(employee3);
System.out.println("The object employee3 is persisted with session");
session.save(employee4);
System.out.println("The object employee4 is persisted with session");
```

```
    txn.commit();
    System.out.println("Transaction on this session is committed");
    session.close();

    session = sessionFactory.openSession();
    txn = session.beginTransaction();
    System.out.println("Accessing Employee Objects\n\n");
    List<Employee> employeeList =
                session.createQuery("from Employee").list();
                for (int i = 0; i < employeeList.size(); i++) {
                Employee employee = employeeList.get(i);
    System.out.println("Employee Number : " + employee.getEmpNumber());
    System.out.println("Employee Name   : " + employee.getEmpName());
    System.out.println("Company Name    : " +
                employee.getCompany().getCompanyName());

   System.out.println("====================================\n\n");
        }
    txn.commit();
    session.close();

    sessionFactory.close();
    }
}
```

Output:

```
The object employee1 is persisted with session
The object employee2 is persisted with session
The object employee3 is persisted with session
The object employee4 is persisted with session
Hibernate: insert into COMPANY (COMPANY_NAME, COUNTRY, ID) values
(?, ?, ?)
Hibernate: insert into EMPLOYEE (EMP_NAME, EMP_NUMBER, ID) values
(?, ?, ?)
Hibernate: insert into EMPLOYEE_COMPANY_MAPPING (COMPANY_ID,
EMPLOYEE_ID) values (?, ?)
Hibernate: insert into EMPLOYEE (EMP_NAME, EMP_NUMBER, ID) values
(?, ?, ?)
```

```
Hibernate: insert into EMPLOYEE_COMPANY_MAPPING (COMPANY_ID, EMPLOYEE_ID) values (?, ?)
Hibernate: insert into EMPLOYEE (EMP_NAME, EMP_NUMBER, ID) values (?, ?, ?)
Hibernate: insert into EMPLOYEE_COMPANY_MAPPING (COMPANY_ID, EMPLOYEE_ID) values (?, ?)
Hibernate: insert into COMPANY (COMPANY_NAME, COUNTRY, ID) values (?, ?, ?)
Hibernate: insert into EMPLOYEE (EMP_NAME, EMP_NUMBER, ID) values (?, ?, ?)
Hibernate: insert into EMPLOYEE_COMPANY_MAPPING (COMPANY_ID, EMPLOYEE_ID) values (?, ?)
Transaction on this session is committed
Accessing Employee Objects

Hibernate: select employee0_.ID as ID0_, employee0_.EMP_NAME as EMP2_0_, employee0_.EMP_NUMBER as EMP3_0_, employee0_1_.COMPANY_ID as COMPANY1_1_ from EMPLOYEE employee0_ left outer join EMPLOYEE_COMPANY_MAPPING employee0_1_ on employee0_.ID=employee0_1_.EMPLOYEE_ID
Hibernate: select company0_.ID as ID2_0_, company0_.COMPANY_NAME as COMPANY2_2_0_, company0_.COUNTRY as COUNTRY2_0_ from COMPANY company0_ where company0_.ID=?
Hibernate: select company0_.ID as ID2_0_, company0_.COMPANY_NAME as COMPANY2_2_0_, company0_.COUNTRY as COUNTRY2_0_ from COMPANY company0_ where company0_.ID=?
Employee Number : 5001
Employee Name   : Ibrahim
Company Name    : ABC Pvt. Ltd.
========================================

Employee Number : 5002
Employee Name   : Kumar
Company Name    : ABC Pvt. Ltd.
========================================

Employee Number : 5003
Employee Name   : Ajay
```

```
Company Name    : ABC Pvt. Ltd.
========================================

Employee Number : 5004
Employee Name   : Akhfa
Company Name    : XYZ Sdn. Bhd.
========================================
```

A sample run results as below.

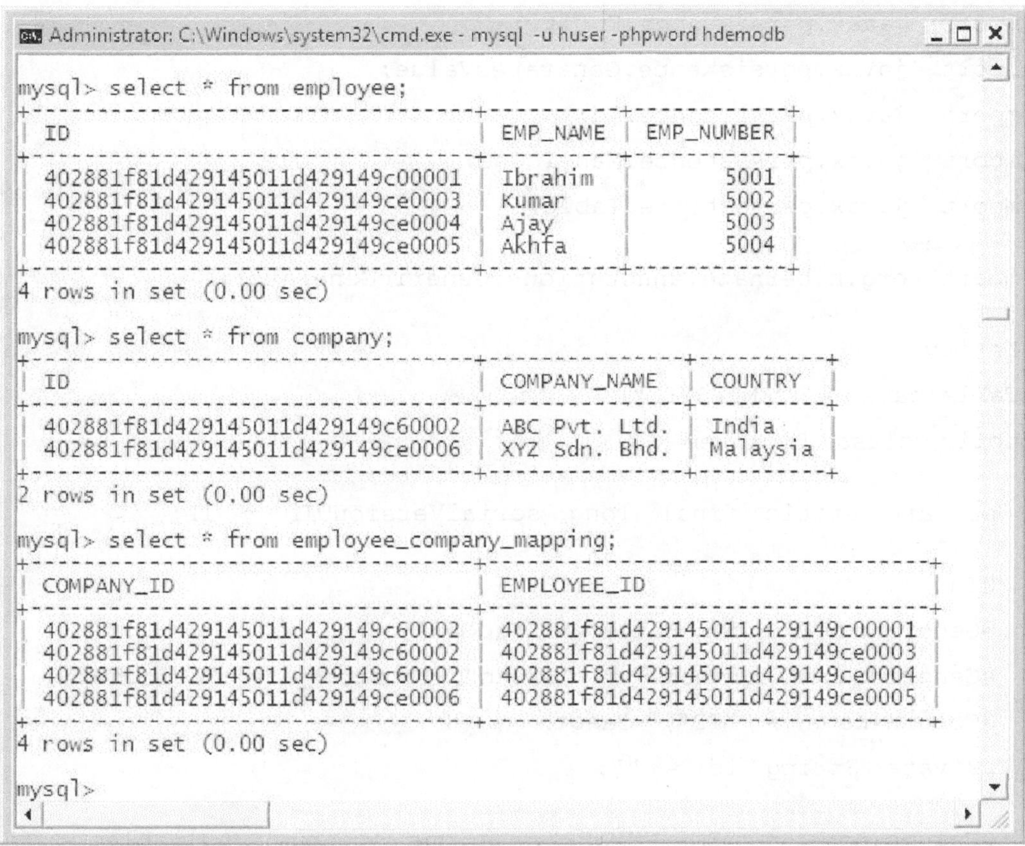

```
Administrator: C:\Windows\system32\cmd.exe - mysql -u huser -phpword hdemodb

mysql> select * from employee;
+----------------------------------+----------+------------+
| ID                               | EMP_NAME | EMP_NUMBER |
+----------------------------------+----------+------------+
| 402881f81d429145011d429149c00001 | Ibrahim  |       5001 |
| 402881f81d429145011d429149ce0003 | Kumar    |       5002 |
| 402881f81d429145011d429149ce0004 | Ajay     |       5003 |
| 402881f81d429145011d429149ce0005 | Akhfa    |       5004 |
+----------------------------------+----------+------------+
4 rows in set (0.00 sec)

mysql> select * from company;
+----------------------------------+---------------+----------+
| ID                               | COMPANY_NAME  | COUNTRY  |
+----------------------------------+---------------+----------+
| 402881f81d429145011d429149c60002 | ABC Pvt. Ltd. | India    |
| 402881f81d429145011d429149ce0006 | XYZ Sdn. Bhd. | Malaysia |
+----------------------------------+---------------+----------+
2 rows in set (0.00 sec)

mysql> select * from employee_company_mapping;
+----------------------------------+----------------------------------+
| COMPANY_ID                       | EMPLOYEE_ID                      |
+----------------------------------+----------------------------------+
| 402881f81d429145011d429149c60002 | 402881f81d429145011d429149c00001 |
| 402881f81d429145011d429149c60002 | 402881f81d429145011d429149ce0003 |
| 402881f81d429145011d429149c60002 | 402881f81d429145011d429149ce0004 |
| 402881f81d429145011d429149ce0006 | 402881f81d429145011d429149ce0005 |
+----------------------------------+----------------------------------+
4 rows in set (0.00 sec)

mysql>
```

Using Interface as Entity member and Mapping (Many-To-One Mapping with Unidirectional Association using Foreign Key)

Employee (many) → Company (One)

Where Company is not entity, it is an interface. Create an entity class (CompanyImpl) which implements this interface (Company).

The targetEntity attribute of the following mapping maps CompanyImpl entity to Employee entity.

```
@ManyToOne(cascade = CascadeType.ALL, targetEntity = CompanyImpl.class)
```

Include mapping entry for CompanyImpl entity in *hibernate.cfg.xml* file.

```
<mapping class="com.hdemo.CompanyImpl" />
```

```
// File Name: Employee.java
// Illustrates how to map Interfaces

package com.hdemo;

import javax.persistence.CascadeType;
import javax.persistence.Column;
import javax.persistence.Entity;
import javax.persistence.GeneratedValue;
import javax.persistence.Id;
import javax.persistence.ManyToOne;
import javax.persistence.Table;

import org.hibernate.annotations.GenericGenerator;

@Entity
@Table(name = "EMPLOYEE")
public class Employee {

  private static final long serialVersionUID = 1L;

  @Id
  @GeneratedValue(generator = "idGen")
  @GenericGenerator(name = "idGen", strategy = "uuid.hex")
  @Column(name = "ID", length = 32)
  private String id = "";

  @Column(name = "EMP_NUMBER", unique = true, nullable = false)
  private Integer empNumber;

  @Column(name = "EMP_NAME", length = 64, nullable = false)
  private String empName;

  @ManyToOne(cascade = CascadeType.ALL,
        targetEntity = CompanyImpl.class)
  private Company company;
```

```
    //Getter and Setter methods

    }
```

```
// File Name: Company.java
// Illustrates how to map Interfaces

package com.hdemo;

public interface Company {

    public String getCompanyName();
    public void setCompanyName(String companyName);
    public String getCountry();
    public void setCountry(String country);
}
```

```
// File Name: CompanyImpl.java
// Illustrates how to map Interfaces

package com.hdemo;

import javax.persistence.Column;
import javax.persistence.Entity;
import javax.persistence.GeneratedValue;
import javax.persistence.Id;
import javax.persistence.Table;

import org.hibernate.annotations.GenericGenerator;

@Entity
@Table(name = "COMPANY")
public class CompanyImpl implements Company {

    private static final long serialVersionUID = 1L;

    @Id
    @GeneratedValue(generator = "idGen")
    @GenericGenerator(name = "idGen", strategy = "uuid.hex")
```

```
    @Column(name = "ID", length = 32)
    private String id = "";

    @Column(name = "COMPANY_NAME")
    private String companyName;

    @Column(name = "COUNTRY")
    private String country;
    //Getter and Setter methods

  }
```

```
// File Name: EmployeeManipulation.java
// Main Program

package com.hdemo;

import java.util.List;

import org.hibernate.Session;
import org.hibernate.SessionFactory;
import org.hibernate.Transaction;

public class EmployeeManipulation {

  @SuppressWarnings("unchecked")
  public static void main(String[] args) throws Exception {
  SessionFactory sessionFactory = HibernateUtil.getSessionFactory();
  Session session = sessionFactory.openSession();
  Transaction txn = session.beginTransaction();

  CompanyImpl company1 = new CompanyImpl();
  company1.setCompanyName("ABC Pvt. Ltd.");
  company1.setCountry("India");

  CompanyImpl company2 = new CompanyImpl();
  company2.setCompanyName("XYZ Sdn. Bhd.");
  company2.setCountry("Malaysia");

  Employee employee1 = new Employee();
```

```
employee1.setEmpNumber(5001);
employee1.setEmpName("Ibrahim");
employee1.setCompany(company1);
Employee employee2 = new Employee();
employee2.setEmpNumber(5002);
employee2.setEmpName("Kumar");
employee2.setCompany(company1);

Employee employee3 = new Employee();
employee3.setEmpNumber(5003);
employee3.setEmpName("Ajay");
employee3.setCompany(company1);

Employee employee4 = new Employee();
employee4.setEmpNumber(5004);
employee4.setEmpName("Akhfa");
employee4.setCompany(company2);
      session.save(employee1);
System.out.println("The object employee1 is persisted with session");
session.save(employee2);
System.out.println("The object employee2 is persisted with session");
session.save(employee3);
System.out.println("The object employee3 is persisted with session");
session.save(employee4);
System.out.println("The object employee4 is persisted with session");
txn.commit();
System.out.println("Transaction on this session is committed");
session.close();

session = sessionFactory.openSession();
txn = session.beginTransaction();
System.out.println("Accessing Employee Objects\n\n");
List<Employee> employeeList =
      session.createQuery("from Employee").list();
      for (int i = 0; i < employeeList.size(); i++) {
```

```
    Employee employee = employeeList.get(i);
    System.out.println("Employee Number : " + employee.getEmpNumber());
    System.out.println("Employee Name   : " + employee.getEmpName());
    System.out.println("Company Name    : " + employee.getCompany().
          getC ompanyName());

   System.out.println("=====================================\n\n");
          }
    txn.commit();
    session.close();

    sessionFactory.close();
    }
}
```

```
The object employee1 is persisted with session
The object employee2 is persisted with session
The object employee3 is persisted with session
The object employee4 is persisted with session
Hibernate: insert into COMPANY (COMPANY_NAME, COUNTRY, ID) values
(?, ?, ?)
Hibernate: insert into EMPLOYEE (company_ID, EMP_NAME, EMP_NUMBER,
ID) values (?, ?, ?, ?)
Hibernate: insert into EMPLOYEE (company_ID, EMP_NAME, EMP_NUMBER,
ID) values (?, ?, ?, ?)
Hibernate: insert into EMPLOYEE (company_ID, EMP_NAME, EMP_NUMBER,
ID) values (?, ?, ?, ?)
Hibernate: insert into COMPANY (COMPANY_NAME, COUNTRY, ID) values
(?, ?, ?)
Hibernate: insert into EMPLOYEE (company_ID, EMP_NAME, EMP_NUMBER,
ID) values (?, ?, ?, ?)
Transaction on this session is committed
Accessing Employee Objects

Hibernate: select employee0_.ID as ID0_, employee0_.company_ID as
company4_0_, employee0_.EMP_NAME as EMP2_0_, employee0_.EMP_NUMBER
as EMP3_0_ from EMPLOYEE employee0_
```

```
Hibernate: select companyimp0_.ID as ID1_0_, companyimp0_.COMPANY_NAME
as COMPANY2_1_0_, companyimp0_.COUNTRY as COUNTRY1_0_ from COMPANY
companyimp0_ where companyimp0_.ID=?
Hibernate: select companyimp0_.ID as ID1_0_, companyimp0_.COMPANY_NAME
as COMPANY2_1_0_, companyimp0_.COUNTRY as COUNTRY1_0_ from COMPANY
companyimp0_ where companyimp0_.ID=?
Employee Number : 5001
Employee Name   : Ibrahim
Company Name    : ABC Pvt. Ltd.
========================================

Employee Number : 5002
Employee Name   : Kumar
Company Name    : ABC Pvt. Ltd.
========================================
Employee Number : 5003
Employee Name   : Ajay
Company Name    : ABC Pvt. Ltd.
========================================

Employee Number : 5004
Employee Name   : Akhfa
Company Name    : XYZ Sdn. Bhd.
========================================
```

A sample run results as below.

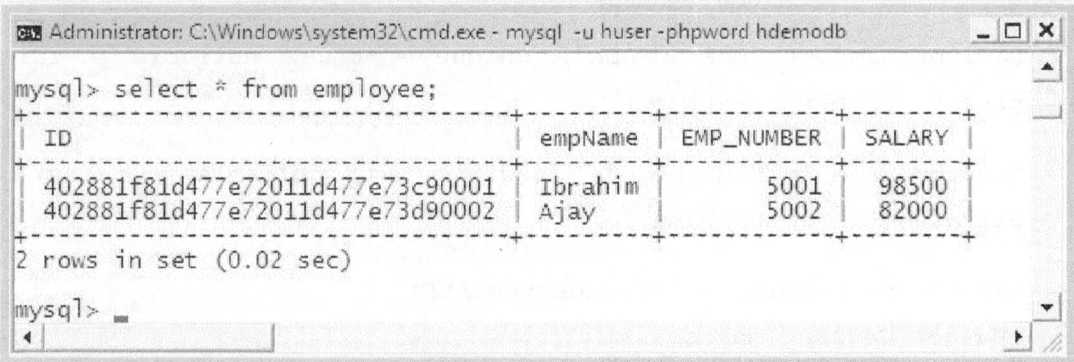

```
Administrator: C:\Windows\system32\cmd.exe - mysql -u huser -phpword hdemodb

mysql> select * from employee;
+----------------------------------+---------+------------+--------+
| ID                               | empName | EMP_NUMBER | SALARY |
+----------------------------------+---------+------------+--------+
| 402881f81d477e72011d477e73c90001 | Ibrahim |       5001 |  98500 |
| 402881f81d477e72011d477e73d90002 | Ajay    |       5002 |  82000 |
+----------------------------------+---------+------------+--------+
2 rows in set (0.02 sec)

mysql> _
```

The above Employee entity can be written as below, replacing `targetEntity` attribute with `@Target` annotation.

```
// File Name: Employee.java
// Illustrates how to map Interfaces with @Target

package com.hdemo;

import javax.persistence.CascadeType;
import javax.persistence.Column;
import javax.persistence.Entity;
import javax.persistence.GeneratedValue;
import javax.persistence.Id;
import javax.persistence.ManyToOne;
import javax.persistence.Table;

import org.hibernate.annotations.GenericGenerator;
import org.hibernate.annotations.Target;

@Entity
@Table(name = "EMPLOYEE")
public class Employee {

  private static final long serialVersionUID = 1L;

  @Id
  @GeneratedValue(generator = "idGen")
  @GenericGenerator(name = "idGen", strategy = "uuid.hex")
  @Column(name = "ID", length = 32)
  private String id = "";

  @Column(name = "EMP_NUMBER", unique = true, nullable = false)
  private Integer empNumber;

  @Column(name = "EMP_NAME", length = 64, nullable = false)
  private String empName;

  @ManyToOne(cascade = CascadeType.ALL)
  @Target(CompanyImpl.class)
  private Company company;
```

```
    //Getter and Setter methods

}
```

4.17.3 Many-To-Many (@ManyToMany)

Many-to-many mappings represent the relationships between a collection of source objects and a collection of target objects. An Association table (Join table) with Join conditions should be used to associate relation.

Example:

Many *Employee* entities have many *WorkOrder* (entity) fields and vice versa, whose Entity-Relationship (ER) diagram is as follows.

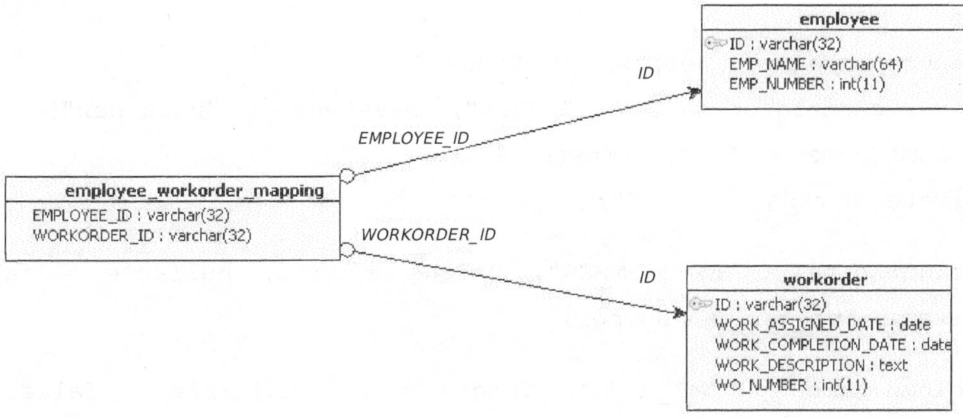

Many-To-Many Mapping with Unidirectional Association using Association Table (Join table)

Employee (many) → WorkOrder (many)

```
// File Name: Employee.java
// Illustrates @ManyToMany

package com.hdemo;

import java.util.List;

import javax.persistence.CascadeType;
import javax.persistence.Column;
import javax.persistence.Entity;
import javax.persistence.GeneratedValue;
import javax.persistence.Id;
import javax.persistence.JoinColumn;
```

```
import javax.persistence.JoinTable;
import javax.persistence.ManyToMany;
import javax.persistence.Table;

import org.hibernate.annotations.GenericGenerator;
@Entity
@Table(name = "EMPLOYEE")
public class Employee {
  private static final long serialVersionUID = 1L;

  @Id
  @GeneratedValue(generator = "idGen")
  @GenericGenerator(name = "idGen", strategy = "uuid.hex")
  @Column(name = "ID", length = 32)
  private String id = "";

  @Column(name = "EMP_NUMBER", unique = true, nullable = false)
  private Integer empNumber;

  @Column(name = "EMP_NAME", length = 64, nullable = false)
  private String empName;
  @ManyToMany(cascade=CascadeType.ALL)
  @JoinTable(name = "EMPLOYEE_WORKORDER_MAPPING",
        joinColumns = { @JoinColumn(name = "EMPLOYEE_ID") },
        inverseJoinColumns = { @JoinColumn(name = "WORKORDER_ID") })
  private List<WorkOrder> workOrders;

  //Getter and Setter methods

}
```

```
// File Name: WorkOrder.java
// Illustrates @ManyToMany

package com.hdemo;
```

```
import java.io.Serializable;
import java.text.SimpleDateFormat;
import java.util.Date;

import javax.persistence.Column;
import javax.persistence.Entity;
import javax.persistence.GeneratedValue;
import javax.persistence.Id;
import javax.persistence.Lob;
import javax.persistence.Table;
import javax.persistence.Temporal;
import javax.persistence.TemporalType;

import org.hibernate.annotations.GenericGenerator;

@Entity
@Table(name = "WORKORDER")
public class WorkOrder implements Serializable {

  private static final long serialVersionUID = 1L;

  @Id
  @GeneratedValue(generator = "idGen")
  @GenericGenerator(name = "idGen", strategy = "uuid.hex")
  @Column(name = "ID", length = 32)
  private String id = "";

  @Column(name = "WO_NUMBER")
  private int workOrderNumber;

  @Lob
  @Column(name = "WORK_DESCRIPTION")
  private java.sql.Clob workDescription;

  @Temporal(TemporalType.DATE)
  @Column(name = "WORK_ASSIGNED_DATE")
  private Date workAssignedDate;
```

```
    @Temporal(TemporalType.DATE)
    @Column(name = "WORK_COMPLETION_DATE")
    private Date workCompletionDate;

    //Getter and Setter methods

    public String toString() {
        String rStr = "[Work Order Number: " + workOrderNumber;
        try {
        rStr += "\nWork Description: " +
     workDescription.getSubString(1L, (int)workDescription.length());
        }
        catch(Exception e) {
            e.printStackTrace();
        }
        rStr += "\nWork Assigned Date: " + new SimpleDateFormat
        ("dd/MM/yyyy").format(workAssignedDate) +
        "\nWork Completion Date: " + new SimpleDateFormat
        ("dd/MM/yyyy").format(workCompletionDate) + "]";
        return rStr;
    }
}
```

```
// File Name: EmployeeManipulation.java
// Main Program

package com.hdemo;

import java.util.ArrayList;
import java.util.Calendar;
import java.util.List;

import org.hibernate.Hibernate;
import org.hibernate.Session;
import org.hibernate.SessionFactory;
import org.hibernate.Transaction;

public class EmployeeManipulation {
```

```
@SuppressWarnings("unchecked")
public static void main(String[] args) throws Exception {
SessionFactory sessionFactory = HibernateUtil.getSessionFactory();
Session session = sessionFactory.openSession();
Transaction txn = session.beginTransaction();

WorkOrder workOrder1 = new WorkOrder();
workOrder1.setWorkOrderNumber(2008111001);

workOrder1.setWorkDescription(
Hibernate.createClob("Complete Login screen"));
Calendar cal = Calendar.getInstance();
workOrder1.setWorkAssignedDate(cal.getTime());
cal.add(Calendar.DATE, 2);
workOrder1.setWorkCompletionDate(cal.getTime());

WorkOrder workOrder2 = new WorkOrder();
workOrder2.setWorkOrderNumber(2008111002);

workOrder2.setWorkDescription(
Hibernate.createClob("Complete Dashboard screen"));
cal = Calendar.getInstance();
workOrder2.setWorkAssignedDate(cal.getTime());
cal.add(Calendar.DATE, 7);
workOrder2.setWorkCompletionDate(cal.getTime());

WorkOrder workOrder3 = new WorkOrder();
workOrder3.setWorkOrderNumber(2008111003);
workOrder3.setWorkDescription(
Hibernate.createClob("Fix bug on Schedular"));
cal = Calendar.getInstance();
workOrder3.setWorkAssignedDate(cal.getTime());
cal.add(Calendar.DATE, 3);
workOrder3.setWorkCompletionDate(cal.getTime());

WorkOrder workOrder4 = new WorkOrder();
workOrder4.setWorkOrderNumber(2008111004);
```

```
workOrder4.setWorkDescription(
Hibernate.createClob("Perform unit testing"));
cal = Calendar.getInstance();
workOrder4.setWorkAssignedDate(cal.getTime());
cal.add(Calendar.DATE, 10);
workOrder4.setWorkCompletionDate(cal.getTime());

Employee employee1 = new Employee();
employee1.setEmpNumber(5001);
employee1.setEmpName("Ibrahim");
List<WorkOrder> employee1WorkOrders = new ArrayList<WorkOrder>();
employee1WorkOrders.add(workOrder1);
employee1WorkOrders.add(workOrder2);
employee1WorkOrders.add(workOrder4);
employee1.setWorkOrders(employee1WorkOrders);

Employee employee2 = new Employee();
employee2.setEmpNumber(5002);
employee2.setEmpName("Kumar");
List<WorkOrder> employee2WorkOrders = new ArrayList<WorkOrder>();
employee2WorkOrders.add(workOrder3);
employee2WorkOrders.add(workOrder4);
employee2.setWorkOrders(employee2WorkOrders);

Employee employee3 = new Employee();
employee3.setEmpNumber(5003);
employee3.setEmpName("Ajay");
List<WorkOrder> employee3WorkOrders = new ArrayList<WorkOrder>();
employee3WorkOrders.add(workOrder1);
employee3WorkOrders.add(workOrder2);
employee3WorkOrders.add(workOrder3);
employee3WorkOrders.add(workOrder4);
employee3.setWorkOrders(employee3WorkOrders);

session.save(employee1);
```

```
System.out.println("The object employee1 is persisted with session");
session.save(employee2);
System.out.println("The object employee2 is persisted with session");
session.save(employee3);
System.out.println("The object employee3 is persisted with session");

txn.commit();
System.out.println("Transaction on this session is committed");
session.close();

session = sessionFactory.openSession();
txn = session.beginTransaction();
System.out.println("Accessing Employee Objects through Employee
      (Many Employees have Many WorkOrders)\n\n");
List<Employee> employeeList =
      session.createQuery("from Employee").list();
      for (int i = 0; i < employeeList.size(); i++) {
Employee employee = employeeList.get(i);
System.out.println("Employee Number : " + employee.getEmpNumber());
System.out.println("Employee Name    : " + employee.getEmpName());
List<WorkOrder> workorders = employee.getWorkOrders();
for (int j = 0; workorders != null && j < workorders.size();
j++) {
System.out.println("\nWork Order (" + (j + 1) + ") : " +
workorders.get(j));
      }

System.out.println("======================================\n\n");
      }

txn.commit();
session.close();

sessionFactory.close();
}
}
```

A sample run results as below.

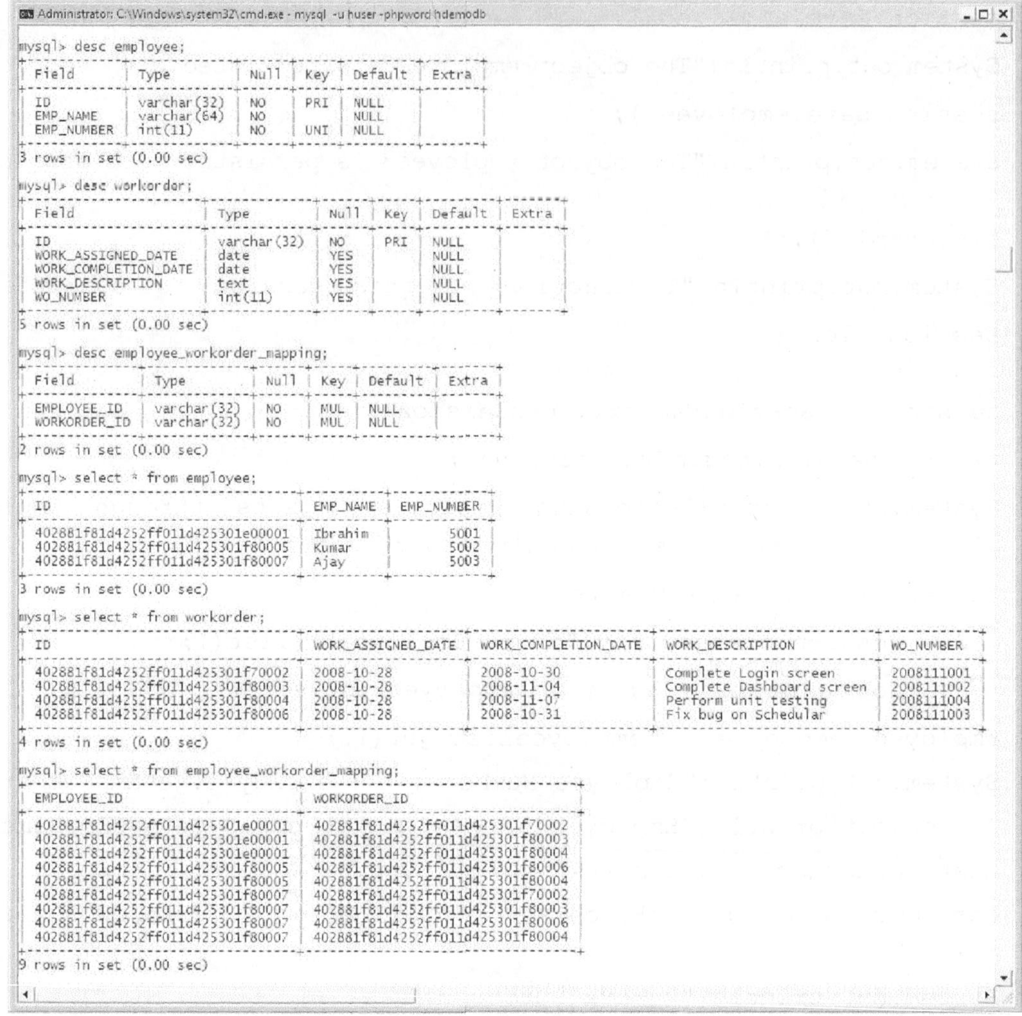

```
Administrator: C:\Windows\system32\cmd.exe - mysql -u huser -phpword hdemodb

mysql> desc employee;
+------------+-------------+------+-----+---------+-------+
| Field      | Type        | Null | Key | Default | Extra |
+------------+-------------+------+-----+---------+-------+
| ID         | varchar(32) | NO   | PRI | NULL    |       |
| EMP_NAME   | varchar(64) | NO   |     | NULL    |       |
| EMP_NUMBER | int(11)     | NO   | UNI | NULL    |       |
+------------+-------------+------+-----+---------+-------+
3 rows in set (0.00 sec)

mysql> desc workorder;
+----------------------+-------------+------+-----+---------+-------+
| Field                | Type        | Null | Key | Default | Extra |
+----------------------+-------------+------+-----+---------+-------+
| ID                   | varchar(32) | NO   | PRI | NULL    |       |
| WORK_ASSIGNED_DATE   | date        | YES  |     | NULL    |       |
| WORK_COMPLETION_DATE | date        | YES  |     | NULL    |       |
| WORK_DESCRIPTION     | text        | YES  |     | NULL    |       |
| WO_NUMBER            | int(11)     | YES  |     | NULL    |       |
+----------------------+-------------+------+-----+---------+-------+
5 rows in set (0.00 sec)

mysql> desc employee_workorder_mapping;
+-------------+-------------+------+-----+---------+-------+
| Field       | Type        | Null | Key | Default | Extra |
+-------------+-------------+------+-----+---------+-------+
| EMPLOYEE_ID | varchar(32) | NO   | MUL | NULL    |       |
| WORKORDER_ID| varchar(32) | NO   | MUL | NULL    |       |
+-------------+-------------+------+-----+---------+-------+
2 rows in set (0.00 sec)

mysql> select * from employee;
+----------------------------------+----------+------------+
| ID                               | EMP_NAME | EMP_NUMBER |
+----------------------------------+----------+------------+
| 402881f81d4252ff011d425301e00001 | Ibrahim  |       5001 |
| 402881f81d4252ff011d425301f80005 | Kumar    |       5002 |
| 402881f81d4252ff011d425301f80007 | Ajay     |       5003 |
+----------------------------------+----------+------------+
3 rows in set (0.00 sec)

mysql> select * from workorder;
+----------------------------------+--------------------+----------------------+--------------------------+------------+
| ID                               | WORK_ASSIGNED_DATE | WORK_COMPLETION_DATE | WORK_DESCRIPTION         | WO_NUMBER  |
+----------------------------------+--------------------+----------------------+--------------------------+------------+
| 402881f81d4252ff011d425301f70002 | 2008-10-28         | 2008-10-30           | Complete Login screen    | 2008111001 |
| 402881f81d4252ff011d425301f80003 | 2008-10-28         | 2008-11-04           | Complete Dashboard screen| 2008111002 |
| 402881f81d4252ff011d425301f80004 | 2008-10-28         | 2008-11-07           | Perform unit testing     | 2008111004 |
| 402881f81d4252ff011d425301f80006 | 2008-10-28         | 2008-10-31           | Fix bug on Schedular     | 2008111003 |
+----------------------------------+--------------------+----------------------+--------------------------+------------+
4 rows in set (0.00 sec)

mysql> select * from employee_workorder_mapping;
+----------------------------------+----------------------------------+
| EMPLOYEE_ID                      | WORKORDER_ID                     |
+----------------------------------+----------------------------------+
| 402881f81d4252ff011d425301e00001 | 402881f81d4252ff011d425301f70002 |
| 402881f81d4252ff011d425301e00001 | 402881f81d4252ff011d425301f80003 |
| 402881f81d4252ff011d425301e00001 | 402881f81d4252ff011d425301f80004 |
| 402881f81d4252ff011d425301f80005 | 402881f81d4252ff011d425301f80006 |
| 402881f81d4252ff011d425301f80005 | 402881f81d4252ff011d425301f80004 |
| 402881f81d4252ff011d425301f80007 | 402881f81d4252ff011d425301f70002 |
| 402881f81d4252ff011d425301f80007 | 402881f81d4252ff011d425301f80003 |
| 402881f81d4252ff011d425301f80007 | 402881f81d4252ff011d425301f80006 |
| 402881f81d4252ff011d425301f80007 | 402881f81d4252ff011d425301f80004 |
+----------------------------------+----------------------------------+
9 rows in set (0.00 sec)
```

Many-To-Many Mapping with Bidirectional Association using Association Table (Join table)

Employee (many) ⟷ WorkOrder (many)

Include mapping entry for WorkOrder entity in *hibernate.cfg.xml* file.

```
        <mapping  class="com.hdemo.WorkOrder"  />
```

```
//  File  Name:  Employee.java
//  Illustrates  @ManyToMany

package  com.hdemo;

import  java.util.List;
```

```
import javax.persistence.CascadeType;
import javax.persistence.Column;
import javax.persistence.Entity;
import javax.persistence.GeneratedValue;
import javax.persistence.Id;
import javax.persistence.JoinColumn;
import javax.persistence.JoinTable;
import javax.persistence.ManyToMany;
import javax.persistence.Table;

import org.hibernate.annotations.GenericGenerator;

@Entity
@Table(name = "EMPLOYEE")
public class Employee {

  private static final long serialVersionUID = 1L;

  @Id
  @GeneratedValue(generator = "idGen")
  @GenericGenerator(name = "idGen", strategy = "uuid.hex")
  @Column(name = "ID", length = 32)
  private String id = "";

  @Column(name = "EMP_NUMBER", unique = true, nullable = false)
  private Integer empNumber;

  @Column(name = "EMP_NAME", length = 64, nullable = false)
  private String empName;

  @ManyToMany(cascade=CascadeType.ALL)
  @JoinTable(name = "EMPLOYEE_WORKORDER_MAPPING",
        joinColumns = { @JoinColumn(name = "EMPLOYEE_ID") },
        inverseJoinColumns = { @JoinColumn(name = "WORKORDER_ID") })
  private List<WorkOrder> workOrders;

  //Getter and Setter methods

}
```

```
// File Name: WorkOrder.java
// Illustrates @ManyToMany

package com.hdemo;

import java.io.Serializable;
import java.text.SimpleDateFormat;
import java.util.Date;
import java.util.List;

import javax.persistence.Column;
import javax.persistence.Entity;
import javax.persistence.GeneratedValue;
import javax.persistence.Id;
import javax.persistence.Lob;
import javax.persistence.ManyToMany;
import javax.persistence.Table;
import javax.persistence.Temporal;
import javax.persistence.TemporalType;

import org.hibernate.annotations.GenericGenerator;

@Entity
@Table(name = "WORKORDER")
public class WorkOrder implements Serializable {

  private static final long serialVersionUID = 1L;

  @Id
  @GeneratedValue(generator = "idGen")
  @GenericGenerator(name = "idGen", strategy = "uuid.hex")
  @Column(name = "ID", length = 32)
  private String id = "";
  @Column(name = "WO_NUMBER")
  private int workOrderNumber;

  @Lob
```

```
    @Column(name = "WORK_DESCRIPTION")
    private java.sql.Clob workDescription;

    @Temporal(TemporalType.DATE)
    @Column(name = "WORK_ASSIGNED_DATE")
    private Date workAssignedDate;

    @Temporal(TemporalType.DATE)
    @Column(name = "WORK_COMPLETION_DATE")
    private Date workCompletionDate;

    @ManyToMany(mappedBy="workOrders")
    private List<Employee> employees;

    //Getter and Setter methods

    public String toString() {
          String rStr = "[Work Order Number: " + workOrderNumber;
          try {
          rStr += "\nWork Description: " + workDescription.get
                      SubString(1L, (int)workDescription.length());
          }
          catch(Exception e) {
          e.printStackTrace();
          }
          rStr += "\nWork Assigned Date: " + new SimpleDateFormat
                ("dd/MM/yyyy").format(workAssignedDate) +
          "\nWork Completion Date: " + new SimpleDateFormat
                      ("dd/MM/yyyy").format(workCompletionDate) + "]";
          return rStr;
    }
}
```

```
// File Name: EmployeeManipulation.java
// Main Program

package com.hdemo;
```

```
import java.util.ArrayList;
import java.util.Calendar;
import java.util.List;

import org.hibernate.Hibernate;
import org.hibernate.Session;
import org.hibernate.SessionFactory;
import org.hibernate.Transaction;

public class EmployeeManipulation {

  @SuppressWarnings("unchecked")
  public static void main(String[] args) throws Exception {
  SessionFactory sessionFactory = HibernateUtil.getSessionFactory();
  Session session = sessionFactory.openSession();
  Transaction txn = session.beginTransaction();

  WorkOrder workOrder1 = new WorkOrder();
  workOrder1.setWorkOrderNumber(2008111001);

  workOrder1.setWorkDescription(
  Hibernate.createClob("Complete Login screen"));
  Calendar cal = Calendar.getInstance();
  workOrder1.setWorkAssignedDate(cal.getTime());
  cal.add(Calendar.DATE, 2);
  workOrder1.setWorkCompletionDate(cal.getTime());

  WorkOrder workOrder2 = new WorkOrder();
  workOrder2.setWorkOrderNumber(2008111002);

  workOrder2.setWorkDescription(
  Hibernate.createClob("Complete Dashboard screen"));
  cal = Calendar.getInstance();
  workOrder2.setWorkAssignedDate(cal.getTime());
  cal.add(Calendar.DATE, 7);
  workOrder2.setWorkCompletionDate(cal.getTime());

  WorkOrder workOrder3 = new WorkOrder();
  workOrder3.setWorkOrderNumber(2008111003);
```

```
workOrder3.setWorkDescription(
Hibernate.createClob("Fix bug on Schedular"));
cal = Calendar.getInstance();
workOrder3.setWorkAssignedDate(cal.getTime());
cal.add(Calendar.DATE, 3);
workOrder3.setWorkCompletionDate(cal.getTime());

WorkOrder workOrder4 = new WorkOrder();
workOrder4.setWorkOrderNumber(2008111004);
workOrder4.setWorkDescription(
      Hibernate.createClob("Perform unit testing"));
cal = Calendar.getInstance();
workOrder4.setWorkAssignedDate(cal.getTime());
cal.add(Calendar.DATE, 10);
workOrder4.setWorkCompletionDate(cal.getTime());
Employee employee1 = new Employee();
employee1.setEmpNumber(5001);
employee1.setEmpName("Ibrahim");
List<WorkOrder> employee1WorkOrders = new ArrayList<WorkOrder>();
employee1WorkOrders.add(workOrder1);
employee1WorkOrders.add(workOrder2);
employee1WorkOrders.add(workOrder4);
employee1.setWorkOrders(employee1WorkOrders);

Employee employee2 = new Employee();
employee2.setEmpNumber(5002);
employee2.setEmpName("Kumar");
List<WorkOrder> employee2WorkOrders = new ArrayList<WorkOrder>();
employee2WorkOrders.add(workOrder3);
employee2WorkOrders.add(workOrder4);
employee2.setWorkOrders(employee2WorkOrders);

Employee employee3 = new Employee();
employee3.setEmpNumber(5003);
employee3.setEmpName("Ajay");
List<WorkOrder> employee3WorkOrders = new ArrayList<WorkOrder>();
employee3WorkOrders.add(workOrder1);
```

```
employee3WorkOrders.add(workOrder2);
employee3WorkOrders.add(workOrder3);
employee3WorkOrders.add(workOrder4);
employee3.setWorkOrders(employee3WorkOrders);

session.save(employee1);
System.out.println("The object employee1 is persisted with session");
session.save(employee2);
System.out.println("The object employee2 is persisted with session");
session.save(employee3);
System.out.println("The object employee3 is persisted with session");

txn.commit();
System.out.println("Transaction on this session is committed");
session.close();

session = sessionFactory.openSession();
txn = session.beginTransaction();
System.out.println("Accessing Employee Objects through Employee
            (Many Employees have Many WorkOrders)\n\n");
List<Employee> employeeList =
      session.createQuery("from Employee").list();
      for (int i = 0; i < employeeList.size(); i++) {
Employee employee = employeeList.get(i);
System.out.println("Employee Number : " + employee.getEmpNumber());
System.out.println("Employee Name   : " + employee.getEmpName());
List<WorkOrder> workorders = employee.getWorkOrders();
for (int j=0; workorders != null && j<workorders.size(); j++) {
System.out.println("\nWork Order (" + (j + 1) + ") : " +
      workorders.get(j));
            }

System.out.println("=====================================\n\n");
      }
txn.commit();
session.close();
```

```
  session = sessionFactory.openSession();
  txn = session.beginTransaction();
  System.out.println("Accessing Employee Objects through WorkOrder
  (Many WorkOrders belong to Many Employees)\n\n");
  List<WorkOrder> workOrderList =
  session.createQuery("from WorkOrder").list();
        for (int i = 0; i < workOrderList.size(); i++) {
        WorkOrder workOrder = workOrderList.get(i);
        System.out.println("Work Order : " + workOrder);
        List<Employee> employees = workOrder.getEmployees();
        for(int j=0; employees!=null && j<employees.size(); j++) {
        System.out.println("Employee (" + (j+1) + ")");
  System.out.println("Employee Number : " + employees.get(j).get
        EmpNumber());
  System.out.println("Employee Name    : " + employees.get(j).get
        EmpName());
        }

 System.out.println("=========================================\n\n");
        }
  txn.commit();
  session.close();

  sessionFactory.close();
  }
}
```

Output:

```
The object employee1 is persisted with session
The object employee2 is persisted with session
The object employee3 is persisted with session
Hibernate: insert into EMPLOYEE (EMP_NAME, EMP_NUMBER, ID) values
(?, ?, ?)
Hibernate: insert into WORKORDER (WORK_ASSIGNED_DATE,
WORK_COMPLETION_DATE, WORK_DESCRIPTION, WO_NUMBER, ID) values (?, ?,
?, ?, ?)
Hibernate: insert into WORKORDER (WORK_ASSIGNED_DATE,
WORK_COMPLETION_DATE, WORK_DESCRIPTION, WO_NUMBER, ID) values (?,
?, ?, ?, ?)
```

```
Hibernate: insert into WORKORDER (WORK_ASSIGNED_DATE, WORK_COMPLETION_DATE, WORK_DESCRIPTION, WO_NUMBER, ID) values (?, ?, ?, ?, ?)
Hibernate: insert into EMPLOYEE (EMP_NAME, EMP_NUMBER, ID) values (?, ?, ?)
Hibernate: insert into WORKORDER (WORK_ASSIGNED_DATE, WORK_COMPLETION_DATE, WORK_DESCRIPTION, WO_NUMBER, ID) values (?, ?, ?, ?, ?)
Hibernate: insert into EMPLOYEE (EMP_NAME, EMP_NUMBER, ID) values (?, ?, ?)
Hibernate: insert into EMPLOYEE_WORKORDER_MAPPING (EMPLOYEE_ID, WORKORDER_ID) values (?, ?)
Hibernate: insert into EMPLOYEE_WORKORDER_MAPPING (EMPLOYEE_ID, WORKORDER_ID) values (?, ?)
Hibernate: insert into EMPLOYEE_WORKORDER_MAPPING (EMPLOYEE_ID, WORKORDER_ID) values (?, ?)
Hibernate: insert into EMPLOYEE_WORKORDER_MAPPING (EMPLOYEE_ID, WORKORDER_ID) values (?, ?)
Hibernate: insert into EMPLOYEE_WORKORDER_MAPPING (EMPLOYEE_ID, WORKORDER_ID) values (?, ?)
Hibernate: insert into EMPLOYEE_WORKORDER_MAPPING (EMPLOYEE_ID, WORKORDER_ID) values (?, ?)
Hibernate: insert into EMPLOYEE_WORKORDER_MAPPING (EMPLOYEE_ID, WORKORDER_ID) values (?, ?)
Hibernate: insert into EMPLOYEE_WORKORDER_MAPPING (EMPLOYEE_ID, WORKORDER_ID) values (?, ?)
Hibernate: insert into EMPLOYEE_WORKORDER_MAPPING (EMPLOYEE_ID, WORKORDER_ID) values (?, ?)
Transaction on this session is committed
Accessing Employee Objects through Employee (Many Employees have Many WorkOrders)

Hibernate: select employee0_.ID as ID0_, employee0_.EMP_NAME as EMP2_0_, employee0_.EMP_NUMBER as EMP3_0_ from EMPLOYEE employee0_
Employee Number : 5001
Employee Name   : Ibrahim
Hibernate: select workorders0_.EMPLOYEE_ID as EMPLOYEE1_1_, workorders0_.WORKORDER_ID as WORKORDER2_1_, workorder1_.ID as ID1_0_, workorder1_.WORK_ASSIGNED_DATE as WORK2_1_0_,workorder1_.
```

```
WORK_COMPLETION_DATE as WORK3_1_0_, workorder1_.WORK_DESCRIPTION as
WORK4_1_0_, workorder1_.WO_NUMBER as WO5_1_0_ from EMPLOYEE_WORKORDER_
MAPPING workorders0_ left outer join WORKORDER workorder1_ on
workorders0_.WORKORDER_ID=workorder1_.ID where workorders0_.
EMPLOYEE_ID=?

Work Order (1)        : [Work Order Number: 2008111001
Work Description      : Complete Login screen
Work Assigned Date    : 28/10/2008
Work Completion Date  : 30/10/2008]

Work Order (2)        : [Work Order Number: 2008111002
Work Description      : Complete Dashboard screen
Work Assigned Date    : 28/10/2008
Work Completion Date  : 04/11/2008]

Work Order (3)        : [Work Order Number: 2008111004
Work Description      : Perform unit testing
Work Assigned Date    : 28/10/2008
Work Completion Date  : 07/11/2008]
=========================================

Employee Number       : 5002
Employee Name         : Kumar
Hibernate: select workorders0_.EMPLOYEE_ID as EMPLOYEE1_1_,
workorders0_.WORKORDER_ID as WORKORDER2_1_, workorder1_.ID as ID1_0_,
workorder1_.WORK_ASSIGNED_DATE as WORK2_1_0_, workorder1_.
WORK_COMPLETION_DATE as WORK3_1_0_, workorder1_.WORK_DESCRIPTION as
WORK4_1_0_, workorder1_.WO_NUMBER as WO5_1_0_ from EMPLOYEE_WORKORDER_
MAPPING workorders0_ left outer join WORKORDER workorder1_ on
workorders0_.WORKORDER_ID=workorder1_.ID where workorders0_.
EMPLOYEE_ID=?

Work Order (1)        : [Work Order Number: 2008111003
Work Description      : Fix bug on Schedular
Work Assigned Date    : 28/10/2008
Work Completion Date  : 31/10/2008]
Work Order (2)        : [Work Order Number: 2008111004
Work Description      : Perform unit testing
```

```
Work Assigned Date : 28/10/2008
Work Completion Date : 07/11/2008]
========================================

Employee Number : 5003
Employee Name : Ajay
Hibernate: select workorders0_.EMPLOYEE_ID as EMPLOYEE1_1_,
workorders0_.WORKORDER_ID as WORKORDER2_1_, workorder1_.ID as ID1_0_,
workorder1_.WORK_ASSIGNED_DATE as WORK2_1_0_, workorder1_.
WORK_COMPLETION_DATE as WORK3_1_0_, workorder1_.WORK_DESCRIPTION as
WORK4_1_0_, workorder1_.WO_NUMBER as WO5_1_0_ from EMPLOYEE_WORKORDER_
MAPPING workorders0_ left outer join WORKORDER workorder1_ on
workorders0_.WORKORDER_ID=workorder1_.ID where workorders0_.
EMPLOYEE_ID=?

Work Order (1)       : [Work Order Number: 2008111001
Work Description     : Complete Login screen
Work Assigned Date   : 28/10/2008
Work Completion Date : 30/10/2008]
Work Order (2)       : [Work Order Number: 2008111002
Work Description     : Complete Dashboard screen
Work Assigned Date   : 28/10/2008
Work Completion Date : 04/11/2008]

Work Order (3)       : [Work Order Number: 2008111003
Work Description     : Fix bug on Schedular
Work Assigned Date   : 28/10/2008
Work Completion Date : 31/10/2008]

Work Order (4)       : [Work Order Number: 2008111004
Work Description     : Perform unit testing
Work Assigned Date   : 28/10/2008
Work Completion Date : 07/11/2008]
========================================

Accessing Employee Objects through WorkOrder (Many WorkOrders belong
to Many Employees)

Hibernate: select workorder0_.ID as ID1_, workorder0_. WORK_ASSIGNED_
DATE as WORK2_1_, workorder0_.WORK_COMPLETION_DATE as WORK3_1_,
```

```
workorder0_.WORK_DESCRIPTION as WORK4_1_, workorder0_.WO_NUMBER as
WO5_1_ from WORKORDER workorder0_Work Order :
[Work Order Number: 2008111001
Work Description: Complete Login screen
Work Assigned Date: 28/10/2008
Work Completion Date: 30/10/2008]
Hibernate: select employees0_.WORKORDER_ID as WORKORDER2_1_,
employees0_.EMPLOYEE_ID as EMPLOYEE1_1_, employee1_.ID as ID0_0_,
employee1_.EMP_NAME as EMP2_0_0_, employee1_.EMP_NUMBER as EMP3_0_0_
from EMPLOYEE_WORKORDER_MAPPING employees0_ left outer join EMPLOYEE
employee1_ on employees0_.EMPLOYEE_ID=employee1_.ID where
employees0_.WORKORDER_ID=?
Employee (1)
Employee Number : 5001
Employee Name   : Ibrahim
Employee (2)
Employee Number : 5003
Employee Name   : Ajay
==============================================

Work Order : [Work Order Number: 2008111002
Work Description: Complete Dashboard screen
Work Assigned Date: 28/10/2008
Work Completion Date: 04/11/2008]
Hibernate: select employees0_.WORKORDER_ID as WORKORDER2_1_,
employees0_.EMPLOYEE_ID as EMPLOYEE1_1_, employee1_.ID as ID0_0_,
employee1_.EMP_NAME as EMP2_0_0_, employee1_.EMP_NUMBER as EMP3_0_0_
from EMPLOYEE_WORKORDER_MAPPING employees0_ left outer join EMPLOYEE
employee1_ on employees0_.EMPLOYEE_ID=employee1_.ID where
employees0_.WORKORDER_ID=?
Employee (1)
Employee Number : 5001
Employee Name   : Ibrahim
Employee (2)
Employee Number : 5003
Employee Name   : Ajay
==============================================
```

```
Work Order : [Work Order Number: 2008111004
Work Description: Perform unit testing
Work Assigned Date: 28/10/2008
Work Completion Date: 07/11/2008]
Hibernate: select employees0_.WORKORDER_ID as WORKORDER2_1_, employees0_.EMPLOYEE_ID as EMPLOYEE1_1_, employee1_.ID as ID0_0_, employee1_.EMP_NAME as EMP2_0_0_, employee1_.EMP_NUMBER as EMP3_0_0_ from EMPLOYEE_WORKORDER_MAPPING employees0_ left outer join EMPLOYEE employee1_ on employees0_.EMPLOYEE_ID=employee1_.ID where employees0_.WORKORDER_ID=?
Employee (1)
Employee Number : 5001
Employee Name   : Ibrahim
Employee (2)
Employee Number : 5002
Employee Name   : Kumar
Employee (3)
Employee Number : 5003
Employee Name   : Ajay
=======================================

Work Order : [Work Order Number: 2008111003
Work Description: Fix bug on Schedular
Work Assigned Date: 28/10/2008
Work Completion Date: 31/10/2008]
Hibernate: select employees0_.WORKORDER_ID as WORKORDER2_1_, employees0_.EMPLOYEE_ID as EMPLOYEE1_1_, employee1_.ID as ID0_0_, employee1_.EMP_NAME as EMP2_0_0_, employee1_.EMP_NUMBER as EMP3_0_0_ from EMPLOYEE_WORKORDER_MAPPING employees0_ left outer join EMPLOYEE employee1_ on employees0_.EMPLOYEE_ID=employee1_.ID where employees0_.WORKORDER_ID=?
Employee (1)
Employee Number : 5002
Employee Name   : Kumar
Employee (2)
Employee Number : 5003
Employee Name   : Ajay
=======================================
```

A sample run results as below.

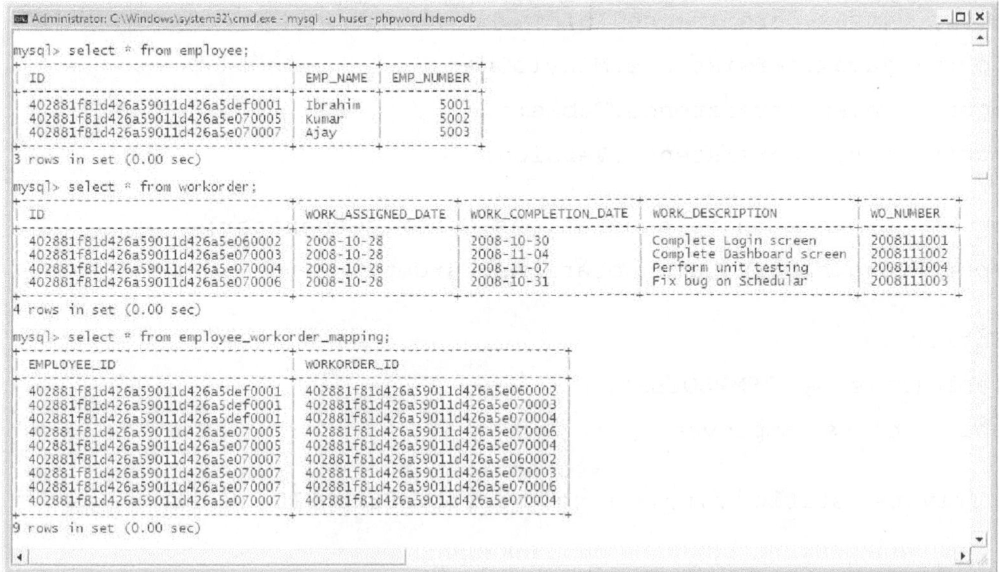

```
Administrator: C:\Windows\system32\cmd.exe - mysql -u huser -phpword hdemodb

mysql> select * from employee;
+-----------------------------------+----------+------------+
| ID                                | EMP_NAME | EMP_NUMBER |
+-----------------------------------+----------+------------+
| 402881f81d426a59011d426a5def0001  | Ibrahim  |       5001 |
| 402881f81d426a59011d426a5e070005  | Kumar    |       5002 |
| 402881f81d426a59011d426a5e070007  | Ajay     |       5003 |
+-----------------------------------+----------+------------+
3 rows in set (0.00 sec)

mysql> select * from workorder;
+-----------------------------------+--------------------+----------------------+-------------------------+------------+
| ID                                | WORK_ASSIGNED_DATE | WORK_COMPLETION_DATE | WORK_DESCRIPTION        | WO_NUMBER  |
+-----------------------------------+--------------------+----------------------+-------------------------+------------+
| 402881f81d426a59011d426a5e060002  | 2008-10-28         | 2008-10-30           | Complete Login screen   | 2008111001 |
| 402881f81d426a59011d426a5e070003  | 2008-10-28         | 2008-11-04           | Complete Dashboard screen | 2008111002 |
| 402881f81d426a59011d426a5e070004  | 2008-10-28         | 2008-11-07           | Perform unit testing    | 2008111004 |
| 402881f81d426a59011d426a5e070006  | 2008-10-28         | 2008-10-31           | Fix bug on Schedular    | 2008111003 |
+-----------------------------------+--------------------+----------------------+-------------------------+------------+
4 rows in set (0.00 sec)

mysql> select * from employee_workorder_mapping;
+-----------------------------------+-----------------------------------+
| EMPLOYEE_ID                       | WORKORDER_ID                      |
+-----------------------------------+-----------------------------------+
| 402881f81d426a59011d426a5def0001  | 402881f81d426a59011d426a5e060002  |
| 402881f81d426a59011d426a5def0001  | 402881f81d426a59011d426a5e070003  |
| 402881f81d426a59011d426a5def0001  | 402881f81d426a59011d426a5e070004  |
| 402881f81d426a59011d426a5e070005  | 402881f81d426a59011d426a5e070006  |
| 402881f81d426a59011d426a5e070005  | 402881f81d426a59011d426a5e070004  |
| 402881f81d426a59011d426a5e070007  | 402881f81d426a59011d426a5e060002  |
| 402881f81d426a59011d426a5e070007  | 402881f81d426a59011d426a5e070003  |
| 402881f81d426a59011d426a5e070007  | 402881f81d426a59011d426a5e070006  |
| 402881f81d426a59011d426a5e070007  | 402881f81d426a59011d426a5e070004  |
+-----------------------------------+-----------------------------------+
9 rows in set (0.00 sec)
```

4.18 IMPLEMENTING OPTIMISTIC LOCK

The Optimistic Lock is used while doing concurrency operations on RDBMS.

4.18.1 `@Version` - Adding Optimistic Locking Capability to an Entity

A transaction can set an optimistic lock for a row in a table (field in entity). The database system informs the transaction of the current version number of that table row. Each time a table row is changed, the database system increases the version number. By comparing the original and the current version number, database applications can determine whether the data read while setting the lock is still current or must be read again. For example, our application reads (selects) one row (each row also has a version number column) and assume that the version number is 1. If some other transaction updates the row, then the version number will became as 2 and so on. At present what we have selected is version 1, we should select latest updated row. How to know?, it is achieved by monitoring version number of that row. That is how this @version used to detect conflicting updates.

```
// File Name: Employee.java
// Illustrates @Version

package com.hdemo;

import javax.persistence.CascadeType;
import javax.persistence.Column;
import javax.persistence.Entity;
```

```
import javax.persistence.GeneratedValue;
import javax.persistence.Id;
import javax.persistence.ManyToOne;
import javax.persistence.Table;
import javax.persistence.Version;

import org.hibernate.annotations.GenericGenerator;
import org.hibernate.annotations.Target;

@Entity
@Table(name = "EMPLOYEE")
public class Employee {

  private static final long serialVersionUID = 1L;

  @Id
  @GeneratedValue(generator = "idGen")
  @GenericGenerator(name = "idGen", strategy = "uuid.hex")
  @Column(name = "ID", length = 32)
  private String id = "";
  @Version
  private int version;

  @Column(name = "EMP_NUMBER", unique = true, nullable = false)
  private Integer empNumber;

  @Column(name = "EMP_NAME", length = 64, nullable = false)
  private String empName;

  @ManyToOne(cascade = CascadeType.ALL)
  @Target(CompanyImpl.class)
  private Company company;

  //Getter and Setter methods

}
```

```
// File Name: EmployeeManipulation.java
// Main Program
```

```
package com.hdemo;

import org.hibernate.Session;
import org.hibernate.SessionFactory;
import org.hibernate.Transaction;

public class EmployeeManipulation {

  public static void main(String[] args) throws Exception {

  Employee employee = new Employee();

  SessionFactory sessionFactory = HibernateUtil.getSessionFactory();
  Session session = sessionFactory.openSession();
  Transaction txn = session.beginTransaction();

  Employee employee1 = new Employee();
  employee1.setEmpNumber(5001);
  employee1.setEmpName("Ibrahim");

  Employee employee2 = new Employee();
  employee2.setEmpNumber(5002);
  employee2.setEmpName("Kumar");

  Employee employee3 = new Employee();
  employee3.setEmpNumber(5003);
  employee3.setEmpName("Ajay");
  Employee employee4 = new Employee();
  employee4.setEmpNumber(5004);
  employee4.setEmpName("Akhfa");

  session.save(employee1);
  System.out.println("The object employee1 is persisted with session");
  session.save(employee2);
  System.out.println("The object employee2 is persisted with session");
  session.save(employee3);
  System.out.println("The object employee3 is persisted with session");
  session.save(employee4);
```

```
System.out.println("The object employee4 is persisted with session");

txn.commit();
System.out.println("Transaction on this session is committed");
session.close();

session = sessionFactory.openSession();
Transaction txn1 = session.beginTransaction();
Employee txn1obj1 = (Employee) session.createQuery("from Employee
where empNumber = :eno").setInteger("eno", 5001).list().get(0);
employee.setEmpNumber(txn1obj1.getEmpNumber());
employee.setEmpName(txn1obj1.getEmpName());
employee.setVersion(txn1obj1.getVersion());
System.out.println("Employee Number: " + employee.getEmpNumber()
+ "    Employee Name: " + employee.getEmpName() + "  Version:
" + employee.getVersion());

Employee txn1obj2 = (Employee) session
        .createQuery("from Employee where empNumber = :eno")
        .setInteger("eno", 5003)
        .list().get(0);
Employee txn1obj3 = (Employee) session.createQuery("from Employee
where empNumber = :eno").setInteger("eno", 5002).list().get(0);
txn1obj1.setEmpName("Ibrahim Sha");
session.update(txn1obj1);
txn1obj2.setEmpName("Ajay Naidu");
session.update(txn1obj2);
txn1obj3.setEmpName("Akshay Kumar");
session.update(txn1obj3);
txn1.commit();
session.close();

session = sessionFactory.openSession();
Transaction txn2 = session.beginTransaction();
Employee txn2obj1 = (Employee) session.createQuery("from Employee
where empNumber = :eno").setInteger("eno", 5001).list().get(0);
Employee txn2obj2 = (Employee) session.createQuery("from Employee
where empNumber = :eno").setInteger("eno", 5003).list().get(0);
```

```
    txn2obj1.setEmpName("Syed Ibrahim");
    session.update(txn2obj1);
    txn2obj2.setEmpName("Ajay Devgan");
    session.update(txn2obj2);
    txn2.commit();
    session.close();

    session = sessionFactory.openSession();
    Transaction txn3 = session.beginTransaction();
    Employee txn3obj1 = (Employee) session.createQuery("from Employee
    where empNumber = :eno").setInteger("eno", 5001).list().get(0);
    txn3obj1.setEmpName("Mohamed Ibrahim");
    session.update(txn3obj1);
    txn3.commit();
    System.out.println("Employee Number: " + employee.getEmpNumber()
    + "    Employee Name: " + employee.getEmpName() + "    Version:
    " + employee.getVersion());
    session.close();
    sessionFactory.close();
  }
}
```

Output:

```
The object employee1 is persisted with session
The object employee2 is persisted with session
The object employee3 is persisted with session
The object employee4 is persisted with session
Hibernate: insert into EMPLOYEE (company_ID, EMP_NAME, EMP_NUMBER,
version, ID) values (?, ?, ?, ?, ?)
Hibernate: insert into EMPLOYEE (company_ID, EMP_NAME, EMP_NUMBER,
version, ID) values (?, ?, ?, ?, ?)
Hibernate: insert into EMPLOYEE (company_ID, EMP_NAME, EMP_NUMBER,
version, ID) values (?, ?, ?, ?, ?)
Hibernate: insert into EMPLOYEE (company_ID, EMP_NAME, EMP_NUMBER,
version, ID) values (?, ?, ?, ?, ?)
Transaction on this session is committed
```

```
Hibernate: select employee0_.ID as ID0_, employee0_.company_ID as company5_0_, employee0_.EMP_NAME as EMP2_0_, employee0_.EMP_NUMBER as EMP3_0_, employee0_.version as version0_ from EMPLOYEE employee0_ where employee0_.EMP_NUMBER=?

Employee Number: 5001    Employee Name: Ibrahim    Version: 0

Hibernate: select employee0_.ID as ID0_, employee0_.company_ID as company5_0_, employee0_.EMP_NAME as EMP2_0_, employee0_.EMP_NUMBER as EMP3_0_, employee0_.version as version0_ from EMPLOYEE employee0_ where employee0_.EMP_NUMBER=?

Hibernate: select employee0_.ID as ID0_, employee0_.company_ID as company5_0_, employee0_.EMP_NAME as EMP2_0_, employee0_.EMP_NUMBER as EMP3_0_, employee0_.version as version0_ from EMPLOYEE employee0_ where employee0_.EMP_NUMBER=?

Hibernate: update EMPLOYEE set company_ID=?, EMP_NAME=?, EMP_NUMBER=?, version=? where ID=? and version=?

Hibernate: update EMPLOYEE set company_ID=?, EMP_NAME=?, EMP_NUMBER=?, version=? where ID=? and version=?

Hibernate: update EMPLOYEE set company_ID=?, EMP_NAME=?, EMP_NUMBER=?, version=? where ID=? and version=?

Hibernate: select employee0_.ID as ID0_, employee0_.company_ID as company5_0_, employee0_.EMP_NAME as EMP2_0_, employee0_.EMP_NUMBER as EMP3_0_, employee0_.version as version0_ from EMPLOYEE employee0_ where employee0_.EMP_NUMBER=?

Hibernate: select employee0_.ID as ID0_, employee0_.company_ID as company5_0_, employee0_.EMP_NAME as EMP2_0_, employee0_.EMP_NUMBER as EMP3_0_, employee0_.version as version0_ from EMPLOYEE employee0_ where employee0_.EMP_NUMBER=?

Hibernate: update EMPLOYEE set company_ID=?, EMP_NAME=?, EMP_NUMBER=?, version=? where ID=? and version=?

Hibernate: update EMPLOYEE set company_ID=?, EMP_NAME=?, EMP_NUMBER=?, version=? where ID=? and version=?

Hibernate: select employee0_.ID as ID0_, employee0_.company_ID as company5_0_, employee0_.EMP_NAME as EMP2_0_, employee0_.EMP_NUMBER as EMP3_0_, employee0_.version as version0_ from EMPLOYEE employee0_ where employee0_.EMP_NUMBER=?

Hibernate: update EMPLOYEE set company_ID=?, EMP_NAME=?, EMP_NUMBER=?, version=? where ID=? and version=?

Employee Number: 5001    Employee Name: Ibrahim    Version: 0
```

```
Administrator: C:\Windows\system32\cmd.exe - mysql -u huser -phpword hdemodb

mysql> select * from employee;
+----------------------------------+-----------------+------------+---------+
| ID                               | EMP_NAME        | EMP_NUMBER | OPTLOCK |
+----------------------------------+-----------------+------------+---------+
| 402881f81d4305d6011d4305d7d00001 | Mohamed Ibrahim |       5001 |       3 |
| 402881f81d4305d6011d4305d7e00002 | Akshay Kumar    |       5002 |       1 |
| 402881f81d4305d6011d4305d7e00003 | Ajay Devgan     |       5003 |       2 |
| 402881f81d4305d6011d4305d7e00004 | Akhfa           |       5004 |       0 |
+----------------------------------+-----------------+------------+---------+
4 rows in set (0.00 sec)

mysql> _
```

From the output of Java program, observe that we are having only old record, we don't know whether the record is updated or not. Now, we will compare versions to update the latest one.

```
// File Name: EmployeeManipulation.java
// Main Program

package com.hdemo;

import org.hibernate.Session;
import org.hibernate.SessionFactory;
import org.hibernate.Transaction;

public class EmployeeManipulation {

  public static void main(String[] args) throws Exception {

  Employee employee = new Employee();

  SessionFactory sessionFactory = HibernateUtil.getSessionFactory();
  Session session = sessionFactory.openSession();
  Transaction txn = session.beginTransaction();

  Employee employee1 = new Employee();
  employee1.setEmpNumber(5001);
  employee1.setEmpName("Ibrahim");

  Employee employee2 = new Employee();
  employee2.setEmpNumber(5002);
  employee2.setEmpName("Kumar");
```

```
Employee employee3 = new Employee();
employee3.setEmpNumber(5003);
employee3.setEmpName("Ajay");

Employee employee4 = new Employee();
employee4.setEmpNumber(5004);
employee4.setEmpName("Akhfa");

session.save(employee1);
System.out.println("The object employee1 is persisted with session");
session.save(employee2);
System.out.println("The object employee2 is persisted with session");
session.save(employee3);
System.out.println("The object employee3 is persisted with session");
session.save(employee4);
System.out.println("The object employee4 is persisted with session");

txn.commit();
System.out.println("Transaction on this session is committed");
session.close();

session = sessionFactory.openSession();
Transaction txn1 = session.beginTransaction();
Employee txn1obj1 = (Employee) session
.createQuery("from Employee where empNumber = :eno")
.setInteger("eno", 5001)
.list().get(0);
employee.setEmpNumber(txn1obj1.getEmpNumber());
employee.setEmpName(txn1obj1.getEmpName());
employee.setVersion(txn1obj1.getVersion());
System.out.println("Employee Number: " + employee.getEmpNumber()
+ "    Employee Name: " + employee.getEmpName() + "   Version:
" + employee.getVersion());

Employee txn1obj2 = (Employee) session.createQuery("from Employee
where empNumber = :eno").setInteger("eno", 5003).list().get(0);
Employee txn1obj3 = (Employee) session.createQuery("from Employee
where empNumber = :eno").setInteger("eno", 5002).list().get(0);
txn1obj1.setEmpName("Ibrahim Sha");
```

```
session.update(txn1obj1);
txn1obj2.setEmpName("Ajay  Naidu");
session.update(txn1obj2);
txn1obj3.setEmpName("Akshay  Kumar");
session.update(txn1obj3);
txn1.commit();
session.close();

session  =  sessionFactory.openSession();
Transaction  txn2  =  session.beginTransaction();
Employee  txn2obj1  =  (Employee)  session
.createQuery("from  Employee  where  empNumber  =  :eno")
.setInteger("eno",  5001)
.list().get(0);
Employee  txn2obj2  =  (Employee)  session.createQuery("from Employee
where  empNumber  =  :eno")
.setInteger("eno",  5003)
.list().get(0);
txn2obj1.setEmpName("Syed  Ibrahim");
session.update(txn2obj1);
txn2obj2.setEmpName("Ajay  Devgan");
session.update(txn2obj2);
txn2.commit();
session.close();

session  =  sessionFactory.openSession();
Transaction  txn3  =  session.beginTransaction();
Employee  txn3obj1  =  (Employee)  session.
createQuery("from  Employee  where  empNumber  =  :eno").
setInteger("eno",  5001).
list().get(0);  txn3obj1.setEmpName("Mohamed  Ibrahim");
session.update(txn3obj1);
txn3.commit();

Employee  currentEmployeeObj  =  (Employee)  session
.createQuery("from  Employee  where  empNumber  =  :eno")
.setInteger("eno",  5001)
.list().get(0);
if  (currentEmployeeObj.getVersion()  !=  employee.getVersion())  {

employee.setEmpNumber(currentEmployeeObj.getEmpNumber());
employee.setEmpName(currentEmployeeObj.getEmpName());
employee.setVersion(currentEmployeeObj.getVersion());
```

```
        }
    System.out.println("Employee Number: " + employee.getEmpNumber()
    + "    Employee Name: " + employee.getEmpName() + "   Version:
    " + employee.getVersion());
    session.close();
    sessionFactory.close();
    }
}
```

```
The object employee1 is persisted with session
The object employee2 is persisted with session
The object employee3 is persisted with session
The object employee4 is persisted with session
Hibernate: insert into EMPLOYEE (EMP_NAME, EMP_NUMBER, OPTLOCK, ID)
values (?, ?, ?, ?)
Hibernate: insert into EMPLOYEE (EMP_NAME, EMP_NUMBER, OPTLOCK, ID)
values (?, ?, ?, ?)
Hibernate: insert into EMPLOYEE (EMP_NAME, EMP_NUMBER, OPTLOCK, ID)
values (?, ?, ?, ?)
Hibernate: insert into EMPLOYEE (EMP_NAME, EMP_NUMBER, OPTLOCK, ID)
values (?, ?, ?, ?)
Transaction on this session is committed
Hibernate: select employee0_.ID as ID0_, employee0_.EMP_NAME as
EMP2_0_, employee0_.EMP_NUMBER as EMP3_0_, employee0_.OPTLOCK as
OPTLOCK0_ from EMPLOYEE employee0_ where employee0_.EMP_NUMBER=?
Employee Number: 5001   Employee Name: Ibrahim   Version: 0
Hibernate: select employee0_.ID as ID0_, employee0_.EMP_NAME as
EMP2_0_, employee0_.EMP_NUMBER as EMP3_0_, employee0_.OPTLOCK as
OPTLOCK0_ from EMPLOYEE employee0_ where employee0_.EMP_NUMBER=?
Hibernate: select employee0_.ID as ID0_, employee0_.EMP_NAME as
EMP2_0_, employee0_.EMP_NUMBER as EMP3_0_, employee0_.OPTLOCK as
OPTLOCK0_ from EMPLOYEE employee0_ where employee0_.EMP_NUMBER=?
Hibernate: update EMPLOYEE set EMP_NAME=?, EMP_NUMBER=?, OPTLOCK=?
where ID=? and OPTLOCK=?
Hibernate: update EMPLOYEE set EMP_NAME=?, EMP_NUMBER=?, OPTLOCK=?
where ID=? and OPTLOCK=?
Hibernate: update EMPLOYEE set EMP_NAME=?, EMP_NUMBER=?, OPTLOCK=?
where ID=? and OPTLOCK=?
```

```
Hibernate: select employee0_.ID as ID0_, employee0_.EMP_NAME as EMP2_0_, employee0_.EMP_NUMBER as EMP3_0_, employee0_.OPTLOCK as OPTLOCK0_ from EMPLOYEE employee0_ where employee0_.EMP_NUMBER=?

Hibernate: select employee0_.ID as ID0_, employee0_.EMP_NAME as EMP2_0_, employee0_.EMP_NUMBER as EMP3_0_, employee0_.OPTLOCK as OPTLOCK0_ from EMPLOYEE employee0_ where employee0_.EMP_NUMBER=?

Hibernate: update EMPLOYEE set EMP_NAME=?, EMP_NUMBER=?, OPTLOCK=? where ID=? and OPTLOCK=?

Hibernate: update EMPLOYEE set EMP_NAME=?, EMP_NUMBER=?, OPTLOCK=? where ID=? and OPTLOCK=?

Hibernate: select employee0_.ID as ID0_, employee0_.EMP_NAME as EMP2_0_, employee0_.EMP_NUMBER as EMP3_0_, employee0_.OPTLOCK as OPTLOCK0_ from EMPLOYEE employee0_ where employee0_.EMP_NUMBER=?

Hibernate: update EMPLOYEE set EMP_NAME=?, EMP_NUMBER=?, OPTLOCK=? where ID=? and OPTLOCK=?

Hibernate: select employee0_.ID as ID0_, employee0_.EMP_NAME as EMP2_0_, employee0_.EMP_NUMBER as EMP3_0_, employee0_.OPTLOCK as OPTLOCK0_ from EMPLOYEE employee0_ where employee0_.EMP_NUMBER=?

Employee Number: 5001 Employee Name: Mohamed Ibrahim  Version: 3
```

4.18.2 `@OptimisticLock` - Controlling Version Number Assigned for a Row

This annotation with excluded=true property settings stops increasing the version number of the row if the corresponding filed (only) is updated (by default it will increase the version number as shown above).

```
// File Name: Employee.java
// Illustrates @OptimisticLock

package com.hdemo;


import javax.persistence.Column;
import javax.persistence.Entity;
import javax.persistence.GeneratedValue;
import javax.persistence.Id;
import javax.persistence.Table;
import javax.persistence.Version;


import org.hibernate.annotations.GenericGenerator;
```

```
import org.hibernate.annotations.OptimisticLock;
@Entity
@Table(name = "EMPLOYEE")
public class Employee {
  private static final long serialVersionUID = 1L;

  @Id
  @GeneratedValue(generator = "idGen")
  @GenericGenerator(name = "idGen", strategy = "uuid.hex")
  @Column(name = "ID", length = 32)
  private String id = "";

  @Version
  private int version;

  @Column(name = "EMP_NUMBER", unique = true, nullable = false)
  private Integer empNumber;

  @OptimisticLock(excluded = true)
  @Column(name = "EMP_NAME", length = 64, nullable = false)
  private String empName;

  @Column(name = "COUNTRY", length = 64)
  private String country;

  //Getter and Setter methods

  pubic void setEmpNumber(Integer empNumber) {
       this.empNumer=empNumber;
  }

  public String getEmpName() {
       return empName;
```

```
    }

    Public void setEmpName(String empName) {
          this.empName=empName

    }

    Public String getCountry() {
          return country;
    }

    Public void setCountry(String country) {
          this.country = country;
    }

}
```

```
// File Name: EmployeeManipulation.java
// Main Program

package com.hdemo;

import org.hibernate.Session;
import org.hibernate.SessionFactory;
import org.hibernate.Transaction;

public class EmployeeManipulation {

  public static void main(String[] args) throws Exception {

  Employee employee = new Employee();

  SessionFactory sessionFactory = HibernateUtil.getSessionFactory();
  Session session = sessionFactory.openSession();
  Transaction txn = session.beginTransaction();

  Employee employee1 = new Employee();
  employee1.setEmpNumber(5001);
  employee1.setEmpName("Ibrahim");
```

```
employee1.setCountry("India");

Employee employee2 = new Employee();
employee2.setEmpNumber(5002);
employee2.setEmpName("Kumar");
employee2.setCountry("India");

Employee employee3 = new Employee();
employee3.setEmpNumber(5003);
employee3.setEmpName("Ajay");

Employee employee4 = new Employee();
employee4.setEmpNumber(5004);
employee4.setEmpName("Akhfa");

session.save(employee1);
System.out.println("The object employee1 is persisted with session");
session.save(employee2);
System.out.println("The object employee2 is persisted with session");
session.save(employee3);
System.out.println("The object employee3 is persisted with session");
session.save(employee4);
System.out.println("The object employee4 is persisted with session");

txn.commit();
System.out.println("Transaction on this session is committed");
session.close();

session = sessionFactory.openSession();
Transaction txn1 = session.beginTransaction();
Employee txn1obj1 = (Employee) session
.createQuery("from Employee where empNumber = :eno")
.setInteger("eno", 5001)
.list().get(0);
employee.setEmpNumber(txn1obj1.getEmpNumber());
employee.setEmpName(txn1obj1.getEmpName());
employee.setVersion(txn1obj1.getVersion());
System.out.println("Employee Number: " + employee.getEmpNumber()
+ "    Employee Name: " + employee.getEmpName() + "    Version:
" + employee.getVersion());
```

```
Employee txn1obj2 = (Employee) session
.createQuery("from Employee where empNumber = :eno")
.setInteger("eno", 5003)
.list().get(0); Employee txn1obj3 = (Employee) session
.createQuery("from Employee where empNumber = :eno")
.setInteger("eno", 5002)
.list().get(0);
txn1obj1.setEmpName("Ibrahim Sha");
session.update(txn1obj1);
txn1obj2.setEmpName("Ajay Naidu");
session.update(txn1obj2);
txn1obj3.setEmpName("Akshay Kumar");
session.update(txn1obj3);
txn1.commit();
session.close();

session = sessionFactory.openSession();
Transaction txn2 = session.beginTransaction();
Employee txn2obj1 = (Employee) session
.createQuery("from Employee where empNumber = :eno")
.setInteger("eno", 5001)
.list().get(0);
Employee txn2obj2 = (Employee) session.createQuery("from Employee
where empNumber = :eno")
.setInteger("eno", 5003)
.list().get(0); txn2obj1.setEmpName("Syed Ibrahim");
session.update(txn2obj1);
txn2obj2.setEmpName("Ajay Devgan");
txn2obj2.setCountry("Malaysia"); //This field update will change
the Version number
session.update(txn2obj2);
txn2.commit();
session.close();

session = sessionFactory.openSession();
Transaction txn3 = session.beginTransaction();
Employee txn3obj1 = (Employee) session.createQuery("from Employee
where empNumber = :eno").setInteger("eno", 5001).list().get(0);
txn3obj1.setEmpName("Mohamed Ibrahim");
session.update(txn3obj1);
txn3.commit();
```

```
Employee currentEmployeeObj = (Employee) session
.createQuery("from Employee where empNumber = :eno")
.setInteger("eno", 5001)
.list().get(0);
if (currentEmployeeObj.getVersion() != employee.getVersion()) {

employee.setEmpNumber(currentEmployeeObj.getEmpNumber());
      employee.setEmpName(currentEmployeeObj.getEmpName());
      employee.setVersion(currentEmployeeObj.getVersion());
      }
System.out.println("Employee Number: " + employee.getEmpNumber()
+ "    Employee Name: " + employee.getEmpName() + "    Version:
" + employee.getVersion());
session.close();
sessionFactory.close();
}
}
```

Output:

```
The object employee1 is persisted with session
The object employee2 is persisted with session
The object employee3 is persisted with session
The object employee4 is persisted with session
Hibernate: insert into EMPLOYEE (COUNTRY, EMP_NAME, EMP_NUMBER,
version, ID) values (?, ?, ?, ?, ?)
Hibernate: insert into EMPLOYEE (COUNTRY, EMP_NAME, EMP_NUMBER,
version, ID) values (?, ?, ?, ?, ?)
Hibernate: insert into EMPLOYEE (COUNTRY, EMP_NAME, EMP_NUMBER,
version, ID) values (?, ?, ?, ?, ?)
Hibernate: insert into EMPLOYEE (COUNTRY, EMP_NAME, EMP_NUMBER,
version, ID) values (?, ?, ?, ?, ?)
Transaction on this session is committed
Hibernate: select employee0_.ID as ID0_, employee0_.COUNTRY as
COUNTRY0_, employee0_.EMP_NAME as EMP3_0_, employee0_.EMP_NUMBER as
EMP4_0_, employee0_.version as version0_ from EMPLOYEE employee0_
where employee0_.EMP_NUMBER=?
Employee Number: 5001    Employee Name: Ibrahim    Version: 0
```

```
Hibernate: select employee0_.ID as ID0_, employee0_.COUNTRY as COUNTRY0_, employee0_.EMP_NAME as EMP3_0_, employee0_.EMP_NUMBER as EMP4_0_, employee0_.version as version0_ from EMPLOYEE employee0_ where employee0_.EMP_NUMBER=?

Hibernate: select employee0_.ID as ID0_, employee0_.COUNTRY as COUNTRY0_, employee0_.EMP_NAME as EMP3_0_, employee0_.EMP_NUMBER as EMP4_0_, employee0_.version as version0_ from EMPLOYEE employee0_ where employee0_.EMP_NUMBER=?

Hibernate: update EMPLOYEE set COUNTRY=?, EMP_NAME=?, EMP_NUMBER=?, version=? where ID=? and version=?

Hibernate: update EMPLOYEE set COUNTRY=?, EMP_NAME=?, EMP_NUMBER=?, version=? where ID=? and version=?

Hibernate: update EMPLOYEE set COUNTRY=?, EMP_NAME=?, EMP_NUMBER=?, version=? where ID=? and version=?

Hibernate: select employee0_.ID as ID0_, employee0_.COUNTRY as COUNTRY0_, employee0_.EMP_NAME as EMP3_0_, employee0_.EMP_NUMBER as EMP4_0_, employee0_.version as version0_ from EMPLOYEE employee0_ where employee0_.EMP_NUMBER=?

Hibernate: select employee0_.ID as ID0_, employee0_.COUNTRY as COUNTRY0_, employee0_.EMP_NAME as EMP3_0_, employee0_.EMP_NUMBER as EMP4_0_, employee0_.version as version0_ from EMPLOYEE employee0_ where employee0_.EMP_NUMBER=?

Hibernate: update EMPLOYEE set COUNTRY=?, EMP_NAME=?, EMP_NUMBER=?, version=? where ID=? and version=?

Hibernate: update EMPLOYEE set COUNTRY=?, EMP_NAME=?, EMP_NUMBER=?, version=? where ID=? and version=?

Hibernate: select employee0_.ID as ID0_, employee0_.COUNTRY as COUNTRY0_, employee0_.EMP_NAME as EMP3_0_, employee0_.EMP_NUMBER as EMP4_0_, employee0_.version as version0_ from EMPLOYEE employee0_ where employee0_.EMP_NUMBER=?

Hibernate: update EMPLOYEE set COUNTRY=?, EMP_NAME=?, EMP_NUMBER=?, version=? where ID=? and version=?

Hibernate: select employee0_.ID as ID0_, employee0_.COUNTRY as COUNTRY0_, employee0_.EMP_NAME as EMP3_0_, employee0_.EMP_NUMBER as EMP4_0_, employee0_.version as version0_ from EMPLOYEE employee0_ where employee0_.EMP_NUMBER=?

Employee Number: 5001    Employee Name: Ibrahim   Version: 0
```

```
Administrator: C:\Windows\system32\cmd.exe - mysql -u huser -phpword hdemodb

mysql> select * from employee;
+----------------------------------+-----------+------------------+------------+---------+
| ID                               | COUNTRY   | EMP_NAME         | EMP_NUMBER | version |
+----------------------------------+-----------+------------------+------------+---------+
| 402881f81d47ec68011d47ec6a670001 | India     | Mohamed Ibrahim  |       5001 |       0 |
| 402881f81d47ec68011d47ec6a740002 | India     | Akshay Kumar     |       5002 |       0 |
| 402881f81d47ec68011d47ec6a740003 | Malaysia  | Ajay Devgan      |       5003 |       1 |
| 402881f81d47ec68011d47ec6a740004 | NULL      | Akhfa            |       5004 |       0 |
+----------------------------------+-----------+------------------+------------+---------+
4 rows in set (0.00 sec)

mysql> _
```

4.19 `@OrderBy` - DEFINING SORT ORDER OF RECORDS TO RETRIEVE

By default, Hibernate retrieves the members of a `Collection` association in ascending order by primary key of the associated entity. We can change the sort key (order by column) and sort order (ascending/descending).

General format

```
@OrderBy ("field-name  ASC|DESC")
```

Use comma separated "`field-name  ASC|DESC`" specification for specifying multiple `orderBy` columns.

```
@OrderBy ("field-name  ASC|DESC,  field-name  ASC|DESC,  ...")
```

```
// File Name: Employee.java
// Illustrates @OrderBy

package com.hdemo;

import java.util.List;

import javax.persistence.CascadeType;
import javax.persistence.Column;
import javax.persistence.Entity;
import javax.persistence.GeneratedValue;
import javax.persistence.Id;
import javax.persistence.JoinColumn;
import javax.persistence.JoinTable;
import javax.persistence.ManyToMany;
import javax.persistence.OrderBy;
import javax.persistence.Table;
```

```
import org.hibernate.annotations.GenericGenerator;

@Entity
@Table(name = "EMPLOYEE")
public class Employee {

  private static final long serialVersionUID = 1L;

  @Id
  @GeneratedValue(generator = "idGen")
  @GenericGenerator(name = "idGen", strategy = "uuid.hex")
  @Column(name = "ID", length = 32)
  private String id = "";

  @Column(name = "EMP_NUMBER", unique = true, nullable = false)
  private Integer empNumber;

  @Column(name = "EMP_NAME", length = 64, nullable = false)
  private String empName;

  @OrderBy("workDescription DESC")
  @ManyToMany(cascade=CascadeType.ALL)
  @JoinTable(name = "EMPLOYEE_WORKORDER_MAPPING",
      joinColumns = { @JoinColumn(name = "EMPLOYEE_ID") },
      inverseJoinColumns = { @JoinColumn(name = "WORKORDER_ID") })
  private List<WorkOrder> workOrders;

  //Getter and Setter methods

}
```

```
// File Name: WorkOrder.java
// Illustrates @OrderBy

package com.hdemo;

import java.io.Serializable;
import java.text.SimpleDateFormat;
import java.util.Date;
```

```
import java.util.List;

import javax.persistence.Column;
import javax.persistence.Entity;
import javax.persistence.GeneratedValue;
import javax.persistence.Id;
import javax.persistence.Lob;
import javax.persistence.ManyToMany;
import javax.persistence.Table;
import javax.persistence.Temporal;
import javax.persistence.TemporalType;

import org.hibernate.annotations.GenericGenerator;

@Entity
@Table(name = "WORKORDER")
public class WorkOrder implements Serializable {

  private static final long serialVersionUID = 1L;

  @Id
  @GeneratedValue(generator = "idGen")
  @GenericGenerator(name = "idGen", strategy = "uuid.hex")
  @Column(name = "ID", length = 32)
  private String id = "";

  @Column(name = "WO_NUMBER")
  private int workOrderNumber;

  @Lob
  @Column(name = "WORK_DESCRIPTION")
  private java.sql.Clob workDescription;

  @Temporal(TemporalType.DATE)
  @Column(name = "WORK_ASSIGNED_DATE")
  private Date workAssignedDate;

  @Temporal(TemporalType.DATE)
```

```
  @Column(name = "WORK_COMPLETION_DATE")
  private Date workCompletionDate;

  @ManyToMany(mappedBy="workOrders")
  private List<Employee> employees;

  public String toString() {
        String rStr = "[Work Order Number: " + workOrderNumber;
        try {
        rStr += "\nWork Description: " + workDescription.
        getSubString(1L, (int)workDescription.length());
        }
  catch(Exception e) {
        e.printStackTrace();
        }
  rStr += "\nWork Assigned Date: " +
  new SimpleDateFormat("dd/MM/yyyy").format(workAssignedDate) +
  "\nWork Completion Date: " + new SimpleDateFormat
  ("dd/MM/yyyy").format(workCompletionDate) + "]";
   return rStr;
  }
}
```

```
// File Name: EmployeeManipulation.java
// Main Program

package com.hdemo;

import java.util.ArrayList;
import java.util.Calendar;
import java.util.List;

import org.hibernate.Hibernate;
import org.hibernate.Session;
import org.hibernate.SessionFactory;
import org.hibernate.Transaction;

public class EmployeeManipulation {
```

```
@SuppressWarnings("unchecked")
public static void main(String[] args) throws Exception {
SessionFactory sessionFactory = HibernateUtil.getSessionFactory();
Session session = sessionFactory.openSession();
Transaction txn = session.beginTransaction();

WorkOrder workOrder1 = new WorkOrder();
workOrder1.setWorkOrderNumber(2008111001);

workOrder1.setWorkDescription(
Hibernate.createClob("Complete Login screen"));
Calendar cal = Calendar.getInstance();
workOrder1.setWorkAssignedDate(cal.getTime());
cal.add(Calendar.DATE, 2);
workOrder1.setWorkCompletionDate(cal.getTime());

WorkOrder workOrder2 = new WorkOrder();
workOrder2.setWorkOrderNumber(2008111002);

workOrder2.setWorkDescription(
Hibernate.createClob("Complete Dashboard screen"));
cal = Calendar.getInstance();
workOrder2.setWorkAssignedDate(cal.getTime());
cal.add(Calendar.DATE, 7);
workOrder2.setWorkCompletionDate(cal.getTime());

WorkOrder workOrder3 = new WorkOrder();
workOrder3.setWorkOrderNumber(2008111003);
workOrder3.setWorkDescription(
Hibernate.createClob("Fix bug on Schedular"));
cal = Calendar.getInstance();
workOrder3.setWorkAssignedDate(cal.getTime());
cal.add(Calendar.DATE, 3);
workOrder3.setWorkCompletionDate(cal.getTime());

WorkOrder workOrder4 = new WorkOrder();
workOrder4.setWorkOrderNumber(2008111004);
```

```
workOrder4.setWorkDescription(
Hibernate.createClob("Perform unit testing"));
cal = Calendar.getInstance();
workOrder4.setWorkAssignedDate(cal.getTime());
cal.add(Calendar.DATE, 10);
workOrder4.setWorkCompletionDate(cal.getTime());

Employee employee1 = new Employee();
employee1.setEmpNumber(5001);
employee1.setEmpName("Ibrahim");
List<WorkOrder> employee1WorkOrders = new ArrayList<WorkOrder>();
employee1WorkOrders.add(workOrder1);
employee1WorkOrders.add(workOrder2);
employee1WorkOrders.add(workOrder4);
employee1.setWorkOrders(employee1WorkOrders);

Employee employee2 = new Employee();
employee2.setEmpNumber(5002);
employee2.setEmpName("Kumar");
List<WorkOrder> employee2WorkOrders = new ArrayList<WorkOrder>();
employee2WorkOrders.add(workOrder3);
employee2WorkOrders.add(workOrder4);
employee2.setWorkOrders(employee2WorkOrders);
Employee employee3 = new Employee();
employee3.setEmpNumber(5003);
employee3.setEmpName("Ajay");
List<WorkOrder> employee3WorkOrders = new ArrayList<WorkOrder>();
employee3WorkOrders.add(workOrder1);
employee3WorkOrders.add(workOrder2);
employee3WorkOrders.add(workOrder3);
employee3WorkOrders.add(workOrder4);
employee3.setWorkOrders(employee3WorkOrders);
      session.save(employee1);
System.out.println("The object employee1 is persisted with session");
session.save(employee2);
System.out.println("The object employee2 is persisted with session");
```

```
    session.save(employee3);
    System.out.println("The object employee3 is persisted with session");

    txn.commit();
    System.out.println("Transaction on this session is committed");
    session.close();

    session = sessionFactory.openSession();
    txn = session.beginTransaction();
    System.out.println("Accessing Employee Objects (Order by Work
    Order Description descending)\n\n");
    List<Employee> employeeList =
    session.createQuery("from Employee").list();
    for (int i = 0; i < employeeList.size(); i++) {
          Employee employee = employeeList.get(i);
    System.out.println("Employee Number : " + employee.getEmpNumber());
    System.out.println("Employee Name   : " + employee.getEmpName());
    List<WorkOrder> workorders = employee.getWorkOrders();
    for (int j = 0; workorders != null && j < workorders.size(); j++) {
    System.out.println("\nWork Order (" + (j + 1) + ") : " +
    workorders.get(j));
                }

   System.out.println("========================================\n\n");
          }
    txn.commit();
    session.close();
    sessionFactory.close();
    }
}
```

Output:

```
The object employee1 is persisted with session
The object employee2 is persisted with session
The object employee3 is persisted with session
Hibernate: insert into EMPLOYEE (EMP_NAME, EMP_NUMBER, ID) values
(?, ?, ?)
```

```
Hibernate: insert into WORKORDER (WORK_ASSIGNED_DATE, WORK_COMPLETION_DATE, WORK_DESCRIPTION, WO_NUMBER, ID) values (?, ?, ?, ?, ?)
Hibernate: insert into WORKORDER (WORK_ASSIGNED_DATE, WORK_COMPLETION_DATE, WORK_DESCRIPTION, WO_NUMBER, ID) values (?, ?, ?, ?, ?)
Hibernate: insert into WORKORDER (WORK_ASSIGNED_DATE, WORK_COMPLETION_DATE, WORK_DESCRIPTION, WO_NUMBER, ID) values (?, ?, ?, ?, ?)
Hibernate: insert into EMPLOYEE (EMP_NAME, EMP_NUMBER, ID) values (?, ?, ?)
Hibernate: insert into WORKORDER (WORK_ASSIGNED_DATE, WORK_COMPLETION_DATE, WORK_DESCRIPTION, WO_NUMBER, ID) values (?, ?, ?, ?, ?)
Hibernate: insert into EMPLOYEE (EMP_NAME, EMP_NUMBER, ID) values (?, ?, ?)
Hibernate: insert into EMPLOYEE_WORKORDER_MAPPING (EMPLOYEE_ID, WORKORDER_ID) values (?, ?)
Hibernate: insert into EMPLOYEE_WORKORDER_MAPPING (EMPLOYEE_ID, WORKORDER_ID) values (?, ?)
Hibernate: insert into EMPLOYEE_WORKORDER_MAPPING (EMPLOYEE_ID, WORKORDER_ID) values (?, ?)
Hibernate: insert into EMPLOYEE_WORKORDER_MAPPING (EMPLOYEE_ID, WORKORDER_ID) values (?, ?)
Hibernate: insert into EMPLOYEE_WORKORDER_MAPPING (EMPLOYEE_ID, WORKORDER_ID) values (?, ?)
Hibernate: insert into EMPLOYEE_WORKORDER_MAPPING (EMPLOYEE_ID, WORKORDER_ID) values (?, ?)
Hibernate: insert into EMPLOYEE_WORKORDER_MAPPING (EMPLOYEE_ID, WORKORDER_ID) values (?, ?)
Hibernate: insert into EMPLOYEE_WORKORDER_MAPPING (EMPLOYEE_ID, WORKORDER_ID) values (?, ?)
Hibernate: insert into EMPLOYEE_WORKORDER_MAPPING (EMPLOYEE_ID, WORKORDER_ID) values (?, ?)
Transaction on this session is committed
Accessing Employee Objects (Order by Work Order Description decending)

Hibernate: select employee0_.ID as ID0_, employee0_.EMP_NAME as EMP2_0_, employee0_.EMP_NUMBER as EMP3_0_ from EMPLOYEE employee0_
```

```
Employee Number : 5001
Employee Name    : Ibrahim
Hibernate: select workorders0_.EMPLOYEE_ID as EMPLOYEE1_1_, workorders0_.WORKORDER_ID as WORKORDER2_1_, workorder1_.ID as ID1_0_, workorder1_.WORK_ASSIGNED_DATE as WORK2_1_0_, workorder1_.WORK_COMPLETION_DATE as WORK3_1_0_, workorder1_.WORK_DESCRIPTION as WORK4_1_0_, workorder1_.WO_NUMBER as WO5_1_0_ from EMPLOYEE_WORKORDER_MAPPING workorders0_ left outer join WORKORDER workorder1_ on workorders0_.WORKORDER_ID=workorder1_.ID where workorders0_.EMPLOYEE_ID=? order by workorder1_.WORK_DESCRIPTION DESC

Work Order (1) : [Work Order Number: 2008111004
Work Description: Perform unit testing
Work Assigned Date: 29/10/2008
Work Completion Date: 08/11/2008]

Work Order (2) : [Work Order Number: 2008111001
Work Description: Complete Login screen
Work Assigned Date: 29/10/2008
Work Completion Date: 31/10/2008]

Work Order (3) : [Work Order Number: 2008111002
Work Description: Complete Dashboard screen
Work Assigned Date: 29/10/2008
Work Completion Date: 05/11/2008]
============================================

Employee Number : 5002
Employee Name    : Kumar
Hibernate: select workorders0_.EMPLOYEE_ID as EMPLOYEE1_1_, workorders0_.WORKORDER_ID as WORKORDER2_1_, workorder1_.ID as ID1_0_, workorder1_.WORK_ASSIGNED_DATE as WORK2_1_0_, workorder1_.WORK_COMPLETION_DATE as WORK3_1_0_, workorder1_.WORK_DESCRIPTION as WORK4_1_0_, workorder1_.WO_NUMBER as WO5_1_0_ from EMPLOYEE_WORKORDER_MAPPING workorders0_ left outer join WORKORDER workorder1_ on workorders0_.WORKORDER_ID=workorder1_.ID where workorders0_.EMPLOYEE_ID=? order by workorder1_.WORK_DESCRIPTION DESC

Work Order (1) : [Work Order Number: 2008111004
Work Description: Perform unit testing
```

```
Work Assigned Date: 29/10/2008
Work Completion Date: 08/11/2008]
Work Order (2) : [Work Order Number: 2008111003
Work Description: Fix bug on Schedular
Work Assigned Date: 29/10/2008
Work Completion Date: 01/11/2008]
=========================================

Employee Number : 5003
Employee Name    : Ajay
Hibernate: select workorders0_.EMPLOYEE_ID as EMPLOYEE1_1_,
workorders0_.WORKORDER_ID as WORKORDER2_1_, workorder1_.ID as ID1_0_,
workorder1_.WORK_ASSIGNED_DATE as WORK2_1_0_, workorder1_.
WORK_COMPLETION_DATE as WORK3_1_0_, workorder1_.WORK_DESCRIPTION as
WORK4_1_0_, workorder1_.WO_NUMBER as WO5_1_0_ from EMPLOYEE_WORKORDER_
MAPPING workorders0_ left outer join WORKORDER workorder1_ on
workorders0_.WORKORDER_ID=workorder1_.ID where workorders0_.
EMPLOYEE_ID=? order by workorder1_.WORK_DESCRIPTION DESC

Work Order (1)        : [Work Order Number: 2008111004
Work Description      : Perform unit testing
Work Assigned Date    : 29/10/2008
Work Completion Date  : 08/11/2008]

Work Order (2)        : [Work Order Number: 2008111003
Work Description      : Fix bug on Schedular
Work Assigned Date    : 29/10/2008
Work Completion Date  : 01/11/2008]

Work Order (3)        : [Work Order Number: 2008111001
Work Description      : Complete Login screen
Work Assigned Date    : 29/10/2008
Work Completion Date  : 31/10/2008]

Work Order (4)        : [Work Order Number: 2008111002
Work Description      : Complete Dashboard screen
Work Assigned Date    : 29/10/2008
Work Completion Date  : 05/11/2008]
=========================================
```

4.20 MAPPING `java.util.Map` TYPE FIELDS IN ENTITY (`@MapKey`)

While mapping java.util.Map field, Hibernate uses the primary key of the associated entity as the `Map` key for the field declared as `java.util.Map` type. If you want to use some other field as the `Map` key, set `name` property to the associated entity's field name.

```
// File Name: Employee.java
// Illustrates how to map Collections

package com.hdemo;

import java.util.Map;

import javax.persistence.CascadeType;
import javax.persistence.Column;
import javax.persistence.Entity;
import javax.persistence.GeneratedValue;
import javax.persistence.Id;
import javax.persistence.JoinColumn;
import javax.persistence.JoinTable;
import javax.persistence.ManyToMany;
import javax.persistence.MapKey;
import javax.persistence.OrderBy;
import javax.persistence.Table;

import org.hibernate.annotations.GenericGenerator;

@Entity
@Table(name = "EMPLOYEE")
public class Employee {

  private static final long serialVersionUID = 1L;

  @Id
  @GeneratedValue(generator = "idGen")
  @GenericGenerator(name = "idGen", strategy = "uuid.hex")
  @Column(name = "ID", length = 32)
  private String id = "";

  @Column(name = "EMP_NUMBER", unique = true, nullable = false)
  private Integer empNumber;
```

```
    @Column(name = "EMP_NAME", length = 64, nullable = false)
    private String emMaName;

    @ManyToMany(cascade=CascadeType.ALL)
    @JoinTable(name = "EMPLOYEE_WORKORDER_MAPPING",
          joinColumns = { @JoinColumn(name = "EMPLOYEE_ID") },
          inverseJoinColumns = { @JoinColumn(name = "WORKORDER_ID") })
    @MapKey(name="workOrderNumber")
    @OrderBy("workOrderNumber asc")
    private Map<Integer, WorkOrder> workOrders;

    //Getter and Setter methods
  }
```

```
// File Name: WorkOrder.java
// Illustrates how to map Collections

package com.hdemo;

import java.io.Serializable;
import java.text.SimpleDateFormat;
import java.util.Date;
import java.util.Set;

import javax.persistence.Column;
import javax.persistence.Entity;
import javax.persistence.GeneratedValue;
import javax.persistence.Id;
import javax.persistence.Lob;
import javax.persistence.ManyToMany;
import javax.persistence.OrderBy;
import javax.persistence.Table;
import javax.persistence.Temporal;
import javax.persistence.TemporalType;

import org.hibernate.annotations.GenericGenerator;
```

```
@Entity
@Table(name = "WORKORDER")
public class WorkOrder implements Serializable {

  private static final long serialVersionUID = 1L;

  @Id
  @GeneratedValue(generator = "idGen")
  @GenericGenerator(name = "idGen", strategy = "uuid.hex")
  @Column(name = "ID", length = 32)
  private String id = "";

  @Column(name = "WO_NUMBER", nullable = false, unique = true)
  private Integer workOrderNumber;

  @Lob
  @Column(name = "WORK_DESCRIPTION")
  private java.sql.Clob workDescription;

  @Temporal(TemporalType.DATE)
  @Column(name = "WORK_ASSIGNED_DATE")
  private Date workAssignedDate;

  @Temporal(TemporalType.DATE)
  @Column(name = "WORK_COMPLETION_DATE")
  private Date workCompletionDate;

  @ManyToMany(mappedBy = "workOrders")
  @OrderBy("empName ASC")
  private Set<Employee> employees;

  //Getter and Setter methods

  public String toString() {
        String rStr = "[Work Order Number: " + workOrderNumber;
        try {
        rStr += "\nWork Description: " + workDescription.get
        SubString(1L, (int) workDescription.length());
        }
```

```
        catch (Exception e) {
              e.printStackTrace();
        }
        rStr += "\nWork Assigned Date: " + new SimpleDateFormat
        ("dd/MM/yyyy").format(workAssignedDate) +
        "\nWork Completion Date: " + new SimpleDateFormat
        ("dd/MM/yyyy").format(workCompletionDate) + "]";
        return rStr;
  }
}
```

```
// File Name: EmployeeManipulation.java
// Main Program

package com.hdemo;

import java.util.Calendar;
import java.util.HashMap;
import java.util.Iterator;
import java.util.List;
import java.util.Map;
import java.util.Set;

import org.hibernate.Hibernate;
import org.hibernate.Session;
import org.hibernate.SessionFactory;
import org.hibernate.Transaction;

  public class EmployeeManipulation {

  @SuppressWarnings("unchecked")
  public static void main(String[] args) throws Exception {
  SessionFactory sessionFactory = HibernateUtil.getSessionFactory();
  Session session = sessionFactory.openSession();
  Transaction txn = session.beginTransaction();

  WorkOrder workOrder1 = new WorkOrder();
  workOrder1.setWorkOrderNumber(2008111001);
```

```
workOrder1.setWorkDescription(
Hibernate.createClob("Complete Login screen"));
Calendar cal = Calendar.getInstance();
workOrder1.setWorkAssignedDate(cal.getTime());
cal.add(Calendar.DATE, 2);
workOrder1.setWorkCompletionDate(cal.getTime());

WorkOrder workOrder2 = new WorkOrder();
workOrder2.setWorkOrderNumber(2008111002);

workOrder2.setWorkDescription(
Hibernate.createClob("Complete Dashboard screen"));
cal = Calendar.getInstance();
workOrder2.setWorkAssignedDate(cal.getTime());
cal.add(Calendar.DATE, 7);
workOrder2.setWorkCompletionDate(cal.getTime());

WorkOrder workOrder3 = new WorkOrder();
workOrder3.setWorkOrderNumber(2008111003);
workOrder3.setWorkDescription(
Hibernate.createClob("Fix bug on Schedular"));
cal = Calendar.getInstance();
workOrder3.setWorkAssignedDate(cal.getTime());
cal.add(Calendar.DATE, 3);
workOrder3.setWorkCompletionDate(cal.getTime());

WorkOrder workOrder4 = new WorkOrder();
workOrder4.setWorkOrderNumber(2008111004);
workOrder4.setWorkDescription(
Hibernate.createClob("Perform unit testing"));
cal = Calendar.getInstance();
workOrder4.setWorkAssignedDate(cal.getTime());
cal.add(Calendar.DATE, 10);
workOrder4.setWorkCompletionDate(cal.getTime());

Employee employee1 = new Employee();
employee1.setEmpNumber(5001);
```

```
employee1.setEmpName("Ibrahim");
Map<Integer, WorkOrder> employee1WorkOrders =
new HashMap<Integer, WorkOrder>();
employee1WorkOrders.put(
workOrder1.getWorkOrderNumber(), workOrder1);
employee1WorkOrders.put(
workOrder2.getWorkOrderNumber(), workOrder2);
employee1WorkOrders.put(
workOrder4.getWorkOrderNumber(), workOrder4);
employee1.setWorkOrders(
(Map<Integer, WorkOrder>) employee1WorkOrders);

Employee employee2 = new Employee();
employee2.setEmpNumber(5002);
employee2.setEmpName("Kumar");
Map<Integer, WorkOrder> employee2WorkOrders =
new HashMap<Integer,WorkOrder>();
employee2WorkOrders.put(
workOrder3.getWorkOrderNumber(), workOrder3);
employee2WorkOrders.put(
workOrder4.getWorkOrderNumber(), workOrder4);
employee2.setWorkOrders(
employee2WorkOrders);

Employee employee3 = new Employee();
employee3.setEmpNumber(5003);
employee3.setEmpName("Ajay");
Map<Integer, WorkOrder> employee3WorkOrders =
new HashMap<Integer, WorkOrder>();
employee3WorkOrders.put(
workOrder1.getWorkOrderNumber(), workOrder1);
employee3WorkOrders.put(
workOrder2.getWorkOrderNumber(), workOrder2);
employee3WorkOrders.put(
workOrder3.getWorkOrderNumber(), workOrder3);
employee3WorkOrders.put(
workOrder4.getWorkOrderNumber(), workOrder4);
employee3.setWorkOrders(employee3WorkOrders);
```

```
session.save(employee1);
System.out.println("The object employee1 is persisted with session");
session.save(employee2);
System.out.println("The object employee2 is persisted with session");
session.save(employee3);
System.out.println("The object employee3 is persisted with session");

txn.commit();
System.out.println("Transaction on this session is committed");
session.close();

session = sessionFactory.openSession();
txn = session.beginTransaction();
System.out.println("Accessing Employee Objects \n\n");
List<Employee> employeeList =
session.createQuery("from Employee").list();
      for (int i = 0; i < employeeList.size(); i++) {
      Employee employee = employeeList.get(i);
System.out.println("Employee Number : " + employee.getEmpNumber());
System.out.println("Employee Name   : " + employee.getEmpName());
Map<Integer, WorkOrder> workorders = employee.getWorkOrders();
for (Iterator iterator = workorders.entrySet().iterator();
iterator.hasNext();) {
      Map.Entry entry = (Map.Entry) iterator.next();
      Integer key = (Integer) entry.getKey();
      WorkOrder value = (WorkOrder) entry.getValue();
System.out.println("\nEmployee [Number: " + employee.getEmpNumber()
+ "] had the Work Order [Number: " + key + "] \n" +
value.toString());
            }

System.out.println("========================================\n\n");
      }

System.out.println("Accessing WorkOrder Objects \n\n");
List<WorkOrder> workOrderList =
session.createQuery("from WorkOrder").list();
```

```
for (int i = 0; i < workOrderList.size(); i++) {
      WorkOrder workOrder = workOrderList.get(i);
System.out.println("Work Order: \n" + workOrder.toString());
Set<Employee> employees = workOrder.getEmployees();
for(Iterator iterator=employees.iterator();iterator.hasNext();) {
      Employee employee = (Employee) iterator.next();
System.out.println("\nWork Order [Number: " + workOrder.get
          WorkOrderNumber() + "] belongs to Employee [Number:
          " + employee.getEmpNumber() + "] Name: [" +
          employee.getEmpName() + "]");
          }

System.out.println("========================================\n\n");
}
txn.commit();
session.close();
sessionFactory.close();
}
}
```

Output:

```
The object employee1 is persisted with session
The object employee2 is persisted with session
The object employee3 is persisted with session
Hibernate: insert into EMPLOYEE (EMP_NAME, EMP_NUMBER, ID) values
(?, ?, ?)
Hibernate: insert into WORKORDER (WORK_ASSIGNED_DATE,
WORK_COMPLETION_DATE, WORK_DESCRIPTION, WO_NUMBER, ID) values (?, ?, ?, ?, ?)
Hibernate: insert into WORKORDER (WORK_ASSIGNED_DATE,
WORK_COMPLETION_DATE, WORK_DESCRIPTION, WO_NUMBER, ID) values (?, ?, ?, ?, ?)
Hibernate: insert into WORKORDER (WORK_ASSIGNED_DATE,
WORK_COMPLETION_DATE, WORK_DESCRIPTION, WO_NUMBER, ID) values (?, ?, ?, ?, ?)
Hibernate: insert into EMPLOYEE (EMP_NAME, EMP_NUMBER, ID) values
(?, ?, ?)
Hibernate: insert into WORKORDER (WORK_ASSIGNED_DATE,
WORK_COMPLETION_DATE, WORK_DESCRIPTION, WO_NUMBER, ID) values (?, ?, ?, ?, ?)
Hibernate: insert into EMPLOYEE (EMP_NAME, EMP_NUMBER, ID) values
(?, ?, ?)
```

```
Hibernate: insert into EMPLOYEE_WORKORDER_MAPPING (EMPLOYEE_ID,
WORKORDER_ID) values (?, ?)
Hibernate: insert into EMPLOYEE_WORKORDER_MAPPING (EMPLOYEE_ID,
WORKORDER_ID) values (?, ?)
Hibernate: insert into EMPLOYEE_WORKORDER_MAPPING (EMPLOYEE_ID,
WORKORDER_ID) values (?, ?)
Hibernate: insert into EMPLOYEE_WORKORDER_MAPPING (EMPLOYEE_ID,
WORKORDER_ID) values (?, ?)
Hibernate: insert into EMPLOYEE_WORKORDER_MAPPING (EMPLOYEE_ID,
WORKORDER_ID) values (?, ?)
Hibernate: insert into EMPLOYEE_WORKORDER_MAPPING (EMPLOYEE_ID,
WORKORDER_ID) values (?, ?)
Hibernate: insert into EMPLOYEE_WORKORDER_MAPPING (EMPLOYEE_ID,
WORKORDER_ID) values (?, ?)
Hibernate: insert into EMPLOYEE_WORKORDER_MAPPING (EMPLOYEE_ID,
WORKORDER_ID) values (?, ?)
Hibernate: insert into EMPLOYEE_WORKORDER_MAPPING (EMPLOYEE_ID,
WORKORDER_ID) values (?, ?)
Transaction on this session is committed
Accessing Employee Objects

Hibernate: select employee0_.ID as ID0_, employee0_.EMP_NAME as
EMP2_0_, employee0_.EMP_NUMBER as EMP3_0_ from EMPLOYEE employee0_
Employee Number : 5001
Employee Name   : Ibrahim
Hibernate: select workorders0_.EMPLOYEE_ID as EMPLOYEE1_1_,
workorders0_.WORKORDER_ID as WORKORDER2_1_, (select a4.WO_NUMBER
from WORKORDER a4 where a4.ID=workorders0_.WORKORDER_ID) as
formula0_1_, workorder1_.ID as ID1_0_, workorder1_.WORK_ASSIGNED_DATE
as WORK2_1_0_, workorder1_.WORK_COMPLETION_DATE as WORK3_1_0_,
workorder1_.WORK_DESCRIPTION as WORK4_1_0_, workorder1_.WO_NUMBER
as WO5_1_0_ from EMPLOYEE_WORKORDER_MAPPING workorders0_ left outer
join WORKORDER workorder1_ on workorders0_.WORKORDER_ID=workorder1_.ID
where workorders0_.EMPLOYEE_ID=? order by workorder1_.WO_NUMBER asc

Employee [Number: 5001] had the Work Order [Number: 2008111001]
[Work Order Number: 2008111001
Work Description: Complete Login screen
Work Assigned Date: 29/10/2008
```

```
Work Completion Date: 31/10/2008]

Employee [Number: 5001] had the Work Order [Number: 2008111002]
[Work Order Number: 2008111002
Work Description: Complete Dashboard screen
Work Assigned Date: 29/10/2008
Work Completion Date: 05/11/2008]

Employee [Number: 5001] had the Work Order [Number: 2008111004]
[Work Order Number: 2008111004
Work Description: Perform unit testing
Work Assigned Date: 29/10/2008
Work Completion Date: 08/11/2008]
========================================

Employee Number : 5002
Employee Name   : Kumar
Hibernate: select workorders0_.EMPLOYEE_ID as EMPLOYEE1_1_,
workorders0_.WORKORDER_ID as WORKORDER2_1_, (select a4.WO_NUMBER
from WORKORDER a4 where a4.ID=workorders0_.WORKORDER_ID) as
formula0_1_, workorder1_.ID as ID1_0_, workorder1_.WORK_ASSIGNED_DATE
as WORK2_1_0_, workorder1_.WORK_COMPLETION_DATE as WORK3_1_0_,
workorder1_.WORK_DESCRIPTION as WORK4_1_0_, workorder1_.WO_NUMBER
as WO5_1_0_ from EMPLOYEE_WORKORDER_MAPPING workorders0_ left outer
join WORKORDER workorder1_ on workorders0_.WORKORDER_ID=workorder1_.ID
where workorders0_.EMPLOYEE_ID=? order by workorder1_.WO_NUMBER asc

Employee [Number: 5002] had the Work Order [Number: 2008111003]
[Work Order Number: 2008111003
Work Description: Fix bug on Schedular
Work Assigned Date: 29/10/2008
Work Completion Date: 01/11/2008]

Employee [Number: 5002] had the Work Order [Number: 2008111004]
[Work Order Number: 2008111004
Work Description: Perform unit testing
Work Assigned Date: 29/10/2008
Work Completion Date: 08/11/2008]
========================================
```

```
Employee Number : 5003
Employee Name   : Ajay
Hibernate: select workorders0_.EMPLOYEE_ID as EMPLOYEE1_1_, workorders0_.WORKORDER_ID as WORKORDER2_1_, (select a4.WO_NUMBER from WORKORDER a4 where a4.ID=workorders0_.WORKORDER_ID) as formula0_1_, workorder1_.ID as ID1_0_, workorder1_.WORK_ASSIGNED_DATE as WORK2_1_0_, workorder1_.WORK_COMPLETION_DATE as WORK3_1_0_, workorder1_.WORK_DESCRIPTION as WORK4_1_0_, workorder1_.WO_NUMBER as WO5_1_0_ from EMPLOYEE_WORKORDER_MAPPING workorders0_ left outer join WORKORDER workorder1_ on workorders0_.WORKORDER_ID=workorder1_.ID where workorders0_.EMPLOYEE_ID=? order by workorder1_.WO_NUMBER asc

Employee [Number: 5003] had the Work Order [Number: 2008111001]
[Work Order Number: 2008111001
Work Description: Complete Login screen
Work Assigned Date: 29/10/2008
Work Completion Date: 31/10/2008]

Employee [Number: 5003] had the Work Order [Number: 2008111002]
[Work Order Number: 2008111002
Work Description: Complete Dashboard screen
Work Assigned Date: 29/10/2008
Work Completion Date: 05/11/2008]

Employee [Number: 5003] had the Work Order [Number: 2008111003]
[Work Order Number: 2008111003
Work Description: Fix bug on Schedular
Work Assigned Date: 29/10/2008
Work Completion Date: 01/11/2008]

Employee [Number: 5003] had the Work Order [Number: 2008111004]
[Work Order Number: 2008111004
Work Description: Perform unit testing
Work Assigned Date: 29/10/2008
Work Completion Date: 08/11/2008]
=========================================

Accessing WorkOrder Objects
```

```
Hibernate: select workorder0_.ID as ID1_,workorder0_.WORK_ASSIGNED_DATE
as WORK2_1_, workorder0_.WORK_ COMPLETION_DATE as WORK3_1_,
workorder0_.WORK_DESCRIPTION as WORK4_1_, workorder0_.WO_NUMBER as
WO5_1_ from WORKORDER workorder0_
Work Order:
[Work Order Number: 2008111004
Work Description: Perform unit testing
Work Assigned Date: 29/10/2008
Work Completion Date: 08/11/2008]
Hibernate: select employees0_.WORKORDER_ID as WORKORDER2_1_,
employees0_.EMPLOYEE_ID as EMPLOYEE1_1_, employee1_.ID as ID0_0_,
employee1_.EMP_NAME as EMP2_0_0_, employee1_.EMP_NUMBER as EMP3_0_0_
from EMPLOYEE_WORKORDER_MAPPING employees0_ left outer join EMPLOYEE
employee1_ on employees0_.EMPLOYEE_ID=employee1_.ID where
employees0_.WORKORDER_ID=? order by employee1_.EMP_NAME ASC

Work Order [Number: 2008111004] belongs to Employee [Number: 5003]
Name: [Ajay]

Work Order [Number: 2008111004] belongs to Employee [Number: 5001]
Name: [Ibrahim]

Work Order [Number: 2008111004] belongs to Employee [Number: 5002]
Name: [Kumar]
========================================

Work Order:
[Work Order Number: 2008111002
Work Description: Complete Dashboard screen
Work Assigned Date: 29/10/2008
Work Completion Date: 05/11/2008]
Hibernate: select employees0_.WORKORDER_ID as WORKORDER2_1_,
employees0_.EMPLOYEE_ID as EMPLOYEE1_1_, employee1_.ID as ID0_0_,
employee1_.EMP_NAME as EMP2_0_0_, employee1_.EMP_NUMBER as EMP3_0_0_
from EMPLOYEE_WORKORDER_MAPPING employees0_ left outer join EMPLOYEE
employee1_ on employees0_.EMPLOYEE_ID=employee1_.ID where
employees0_.WORKORDER_ID=? order by employee1_.EMP_NAME ASC

Work Order [Number: 2008111002] belongs to Employee [Number: 5003]
Name: [Ajay]
```

```
Work Order [Number: 2008111002] belongs to Employee [Number: 5001]
Name: [Ibrahim]
==========================================

Work Order:
[Work Order Number: 2008111001
Work Description: Complete Login screen
Work Assigned Date: 29/10/2008
Work Completion Date: 31/10/2008]
Hibernate: select employees0_.WORKORDER_ID as WORKORDER2_1_,
employees0_.EMPLOYEE_ID as EMPLOYEE1_1_, employee1_.ID as ID0_0_,
employee1_.EMP_NAME as EMP2_0_0_, employee1_.EMP_NUMBER as EMP3_0_0_
from EMPLOYEE_WORKORDER_MAPPING employees0_ left outer join EMPLOYEE
employee1_ on employees0_.EMPLOYEE_ID=employee1_.ID where
employees0_.WORKORDER_ID=? order by employee1_.EMP_NAME ASC

Work Order [Number: 2008111001] belongs to Employee [Number: 5003]
Name: [Ajay]

Work Order [Number: 2008111001] belongs to Employee [Number: 5001]
Name: [Ibrahim]
==========================================

Work Order:
[Work Order Number: 2008111003
Work Description: Fix bug on Schedular
Work Assigned Date: 29/10/2008
Work Completion Date: 01/11/2008]
Hibernate: select employees0_.WORKORDER_ID as WORKORDER2_1_,
employees0_.EMPLOYEE_ID as EMPLOYEE1_1_, employee1_.ID as ID0_0_,
employee1_.EMP_NAME as EMP2_0_0_, employee1_.EMP_NUMBER as EMP3_0_0_
from EMPLOYEE_WORKORDER_MAPPING employees0_ left outer join EMPLOYEE
employee1_ on employees0_.EMPLOYEE_ID=employee1_.ID where
employees0_.WORKORDER_ID=? order by employee1_.EMP_NAME ASC

Work Order [Number: 2008111003] belongs to Employee [Number: 5003]
Name: [Ajay]

Work Order [Number: 2008111003] belongs to Employee [Number: 5002]
Name: [Kumar]
==========================================
```

4.21 @AccessType - DEFINING ANNOTATION ACCESS SPECIFICATIONS

We can specify annotations at field level (data member) or at property level (get member methods) of an entity. This @AccessType annotation is used to instruct which access type a filed should follow.

If the access type is marked as "*field*", the fields are scanned for annotations. If the access type is marked as "*property*", the getters are scanned for annotations. If no @AccessType is specified, then the elements marked with @Id or @EmbeddedId are scanned. This annotation can be used at Entity level or field/property level or both. Annotation at field/property level gets more precedence than annotation at entity level; this for only those annotated fields/properties only and other fields/properties will have Entity level settings.

```
// File Name: Employee.java
// Illustrates @AccessType

package com.hdemo;

import javax.persistence.Column;
import javax.persistence.Entity;
import javax.persistence.GeneratedValue;
import javax.persistence.Id;
import javax.persistence.Table;

import org.hibernate.annotations.AccessType;
import org.hibernate.annotations.GenericGenerator;

@Entity
@Table(name = "EMPLOYEE")
@AccessType("field")
public class Employee {

  private static final long serialVersionUID = 1L;

  @Id
  @GeneratedValue(generator = "idGen")
  @GenericGenerator(name = "idGen", strategy = "uuid.hex")
  @Column(name = "ID", length = 32)
  private String id = "";

  @Column(name = "EMP_NUMBER", unique = true, nullable = false)
  private Integer empNumber;
```

```
    private String empName;

    @Column(name = "SALARY")
    private double salary;

    public String getId() {
        return id;
    }

    public void setId(String id) {
        this.id = id;
    }

    public Integer getEmpNumber() {
        return empNumber;
    }

    public void setEmpNumber(Integer empNumber) {
        this.empNumber = empNumber;
    }

    @AccessType("property")
    @Column(name = "EMP_NAME", length = 64, nullable = false)
    public String getEmpName() {
        return "Mr. " + empName;
    }

    public void setEmpName(String empName) {
        this.empName = empName;
    }

    public double getSalary() {
        return salary;
    }

    public void setSalary(double salary) {
        this.salary = salary;
    }

}
```

```
// File Name: EmployeeManipulation.java
// Main Program

package com.hdemo;

import org.hibernate.Session;
import org.hibernate.SessionFactory;
import org.hibernate.Transaction;

public class EmployeeManipulation {

  public static void main(String[] args) throws Exception {
   SessionFactory sessionFactory = HibernateUtil.getSessionFactory();
   Session session = sessionFactory.openSession();
   Transaction txn = session.beginTransaction();

   Employee employee1 = new Employee();
   employee1.setEmpNumber(5001);
   employee1.setEmpName("Ibrahim");
   employee1.setSalary(98500.0);
   employee1.getEmpName();

   Employee employee2 = new Employee();
   employee2.setEmpNumber(5002);
   employee2.setEmpName("Ajay");
   employee2.setSalary(82000.0);

   session.persist(employee1);
   session.persist(employee2);
   System.out.println("The employee objects are persisted with session");

   txn.commit();
   System.out.println("Transaction on this session is committed");
   session.close();
   sessionFactory.close();
   }
}
```

```
Administrator: C:\Windows\system32\cmd.exe - mysql -u huser -phpword hdemodb

mysql> select * from employee;
+----------------------------------+---------+------------+--------+
| ID                               | empName | EMP_NUMBER | SALARY |
+----------------------------------+---------+------------+--------+
| 402881f81d477e72011d477e73c90001 | Ibrahim |       5001 |  98500 |
| 402881f81d477e72011d477e73d90002 | Ajay    |       5002 |  82000 |
+----------------------------------+---------+------------+--------+
2 rows in set (0.02 sec)

mysql> _
```

Now we will set Entity access type to "property". Observe the result. You will become to know the main difference of field and property access.

```
// File Name: Employee.java
// Illustrates @AccessType

package com.hdemo;

import javax.persistence.Column;
import javax.persistence.Entity;
import javax.persistence.GeneratedValue;
import javax.persistence.Id;
import javax.persistence.Table;

import org.hibernate.annotations.AccessType;
import org.hibernate.annotations.GenericGenerator;

@Entity
@Table(name = "EMPLOYEE")
@AccessType("property")
public class Employee {

   private static final long serialVersionUID = 1L;

   private String id = "";

   @AccessType("field")
   @Column(name = "EMP_NUMBER", unique = true, nullable = false)
   private Integer empNumber;
```

```
private String empName;

private double salary;

@Id
@GeneratedValue(generator = "idGen")
@GenericGenerator(name = "idGen", strategy = "uuid.hex")
@Column(name = "ID", length = 32)
public String getId() {
      return id;
}

public void setId(String id) {
      this.id = id;
}

public Integer getEmpNumber() {
      return empNumber;
}

public void setEmpNumber(Integer empNumber) {
      this.empNumber = empNumber;
}

@Column(name = "EMP_NAME", length = 64, nullable = false)
public String getEmpName() {
      return "Mr. " + empName;
}

public void setEmpName(String empName) {
      this.empName = empName;
}

@Column(name = "SALARY")
public double getSalary() {
      return salary;
}
```

```
    public void setSalary(double salary) {
        this.salary = salary;
    }

}
```

```
// File Name: EmployeeManipulation.java
// Main Program

package com.hdemo;

import org.hibernate.Session;
import org.hibernate.SessionFactory;
import org.hibernate.Transaction;

public class EmployeeManipulation {

  public static void main(String[] args) throws Exception {
   SessionFactory sessionFactory = HibernateUtil.getSessionFactory();
   Session session = sessionFactory.openSession();
   Transaction txn = session.beginTransaction();

   Employee employee1 = new Employee();
   employee1.setEmpNumber(5001);
   employee1.setEmpName("Ibrahim");
   employee1.setSalary(98500.0);
   employee1.getEmpName();

   Employee employee2 = new Employee();
   employee2.setEmpNumber(5002);
   employee2.setEmpName("Ajay");
   employee2.setSalary(82000.0);

   session.persist(employee1);
   session.persist(employee2);
   System.out.println("The employee objects are persisted with session");

   txn.commit();
```

```
   System.out.println("Transaction on this session is committed");
         session.close();
         sessionFactory.close();
   }
}
```

```
Administrator: C:\Windows\system32\cmd.exe - mysql -u huser -phpword hdemodb

mysql> select * from employee;
+----------------------------------+-------------+-----------+--------+
| ID                               | EMP_NAME    | empNumber | SALARY |
+----------------------------------+-------------+-----------+--------+
| 402881f81d4780e5011d4780e6d70001 | Mr. Ibrahim |      5001 |  98500 |
| 402881f81d4780e5011d4780e6e70002 | Mr. Ajay    |      5002 |  82000 |
+----------------------------------+-------------+-----------+--------+
2 rows in set (0.00 sec)

mysql> _
```

Yes, in property access the value returned by the get method will be persisted with the database.

As said earlier you can override the Entity level access type for individual fields/properties (data members), however the elements (fields/properties) to annotate will not be influenced as shown in the following example.

```
// File Name: Employee.java
// Illustrates @AccessType

package com.hdemo;

import javax.persistence.Column;
import javax.persistence.Entity;
import javax.persistence.GeneratedValue;
import javax.persistence.Id;
import javax.persistence.Table;

import org.hibernate.annotations.AccessType;
import org.hibernate.annotations.GenericGenerator;

@Entity
@Table(name = "EMPLOYEE")
@AccessType("property")
public class Employee {
```

```
    private static final long serialVersionUID = 1L;

    private String id = "";

    @AccessType("field")
    @Column(name = "EMP_NUMBER", unique = true, nullable = false)
    private Integer empNumber;

    @AccessType("field")
    @Column(name = "EMP_NAME", length = 64, nullable = false)
    private String empName;

   private double salary;

   @Id
    @GeneratedValue(generator = "idGen")
    @GenericGenerator(name = "idGen", strategy = "uuid.hex")
    @Column(name = "ID", length = 32)
    public String getId() {
          return id;
    }

   public void setId(String id) {
       this.id = id;
   }

    public Integer getEmpNumber() {
          return empNumber;
    }

   public void setEmpNumber(Integer empNumber) {
          this.empNumber = empNumber;
    }

    public String getEmpName() {
          return "Mr. " + empName;
    }
    public void setEmpName(String empName) {
```

```
        this.empName = empName;
    }

    @Column(name = "SALARY")
    public double getSalary() {
        return salary;
    }

   public void setSalary(double salary) {
        this.salary = salary;
    }

}
```

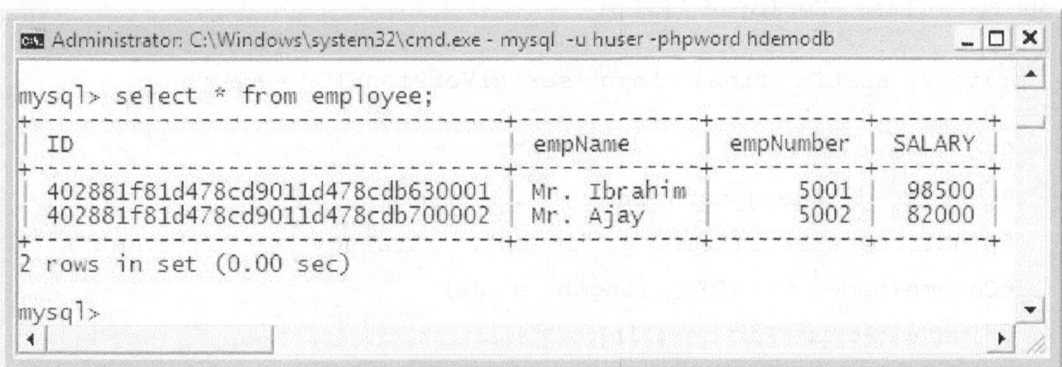


```
mysql> select * from employee;
+----------------------------------+-------------+-----------+--------+
| ID                               | empName     | empNumber | SALARY |
+----------------------------------+-------------+-----------+--------+
| 402881f81d478cd9011d478cdb630001 | Mr. Ibrahim |      5001 |  98500 |
| 402881f81d478cd9011d478cdb700002 | Mr. Ajay    |      5002 |  82000 |
+----------------------------------+-------------+-----------+--------+
2 rows in set (0.00 sec)

mysql>
```

Even though we did override entity level "`property`" access type to "`filed`" access type, the get method is called for data persistence (property access type). However, this provides extra convenience to the programmer as he can declare annotations wherever (field or get method) he want to specify.

4.22 `@Formula` - EVALUATING EXPRESSIONS

This field/property which is declared as `@Formula` will act as a virtual column in that entity table. No column for this filed/property is created in the table, of course no value will be persisted. However, the formula equation (should be compatible to underlying database, it is not Java expression/statement) specified as `@Formula` argument can use entity fields/properties for manipulation.

General format

```
        @Formula ("expression")
// File Name: Employee.java
// Illustrates @Formula
```

```
package com.hdemo;

import javax.persistence.Column;
import javax.persistence.Entity;
import javax.persistence.GeneratedValue;
import javax.persistence.Id;
import javax.persistence.Table;

import org.hibernate.annotations.Formula;
import org.hibernate.annotations.GenericGenerator;

@Entity
@Table(name = "EMPLOYEE")
public class Employee {

 private static final long serialVersionUID = 1L;

  @Id
  @GeneratedValue(generator = "idGen")
  @GenericGenerator(name = "idGen", strategy = "uuid.hex")
  @Column(name = "ID", length = 32)
  private String id = "";

  @Column(name = "EMP_NUMBER", unique = true, nullable = false)
  private Integer empNumber;

  @Column(name = "EMP_NAME", length = 64, nullable = false)
  private String empName;

  @Column(name = "SALARY")
  private double salary;

  @Formula("salary * 0.15")
  private double tax;

  //Getter and Setter methods

}
```

```
// File Name: EmployeeManipulation.java
// Main Program

package com.hdemo;

import java.util.List;

import org.hibernate.Session;
import org.hibernate.SessionFactory;
import org.hibernate.Transaction;

 public class EmployeeManipulation {

  @SuppressWarnings("unchecked")
  public static void main(String[] args) throws Exception {
  SessionFactory sessionFactory = HibernateUtil.getSessionFactory();
  Session session = sessionFactory.openSession();
  Transaction txn = session.beginTransaction();

  Employee employee1 = new Employee();
  employee1.setEmpNumber(5001);
  employee1.setEmpName("Ibrahim");
  employee1.setSalary(98500.0);
  employee1.getEmpName();

  Employee employee2 = new Employee();
  employee2.setEmpNumber(5002);
  employee2.setEmpName("Ajay");
  employee2.setSalary(82000.0);

  session.persist(employee1);
  session.persist(employee2);
  System.out.println("The employee objects are persisted with session");

  txn.commit();
  System.out.println("Transaction on this session is committed");
  session.close();
```

```
   session  =  sessionFactory.openSession();
   txn  =  session.beginTransaction();
   System.out.println("Accessing  Employee  Objects  \n\n");
   List<Employee>  employeeList  =
   session.createQuery("from  Employee").list();
   for  (int  i  =  0;  i  <  employeeList.size();  i++)  {
   Employee  employee  =  employeeList.get(i);
   System.out.println("Employee Number : " + employee.getEmpNumber());
   System.out.println("Employee Name   : " + employee.getEmpName());
   System.out.printf("Salary  :  %.2f  \n",  employee.getSalary());
   System.out.printf("Tax  :  %.2f   ",  employee.getTax());

  System.out.println("\n=========================================\n");
       }

   txn.commit();
   session.close();
   sessionFactory.close();
   }
}
```

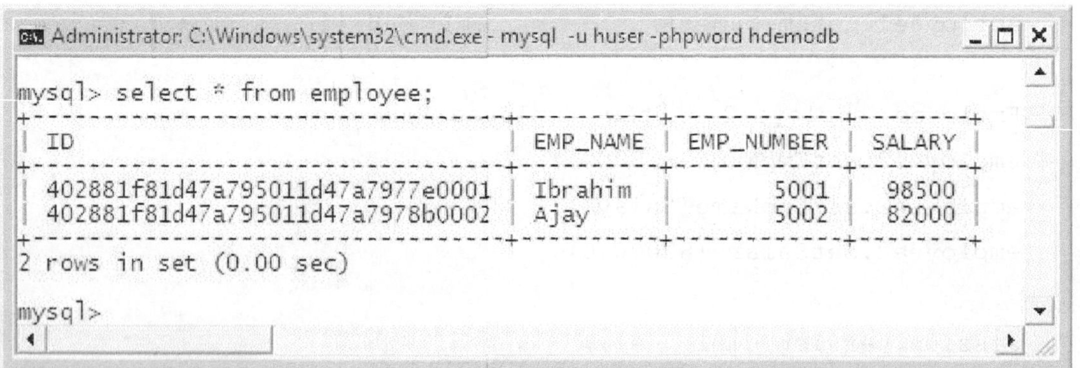

Administrator: C:\Windows\system32\cmd.exe - mysql -u huser -phpword hdemodb

```
mysql> select * from employee;
+----------------------------------+----------+------------+--------+
| ID                               | EMP_NAME | EMP_NUMBER | SALARY |
+----------------------------------+----------+------------+--------+
| 402881f81d47a795011d47a7977e0001 | Ibrahim  |       5001 |  98500 |
| 402881f81d47a795011d47a7978b0002 | Ajay     |       5002 |  82000 |
+----------------------------------+----------+------------+--------+
2 rows in set (0.00 sec)

mysql>
```

We will put conditions on expression.

```
// File Name: Employee.java
// Illustrates @Formula
package com.hdemo;
```

```
import  javax.persistence.Column;
import  javax.persistence.Entity;
import  javax.persistence.GeneratedValue;
import  javax.persistence.Id;
import  javax.persistence.Table;

import  org.hibernate.annotations.Formula;
import  org.hibernate.annotations.GenericGenerator;

@Entity
@Table(name  =  "EMPLOYEE")
public  class  Employee  {

  private  static  final  long  serialVersionUID  =  1L;

   @Id
   @GeneratedValue(generator  =  "idGen")
   @GenericGenerator(name  =  "idGen",  strategy  =  "uuid.hex")
   @Column(name  =  "ID",  length  =  32)
   private  String  id  =  "";

   @Column(name  =  "EMP_NUMBER",  unique  =  true,  nullable  =  false)
   private  Integer  empNumber;

   @Column(name  =  "EMP_NAME",  length  =  64,  nullable  =  false)
   private  String  empName;

   @Column(name  =  "SALARY")
   private  double  salary;

   @Formula("case when salary < 100000 then salary * 0.10 else case
   when salary < 200000 then 10000 + (salary - 100000) * 0.20 else
   salary  *  0.30  end  end")
   private  double  tax;

   //Getter  and  Setter  methods

}
```

```
// File Name: EmployeeManipulation.java
// Main Program

package com.hdemo;

import java.util.List;

import org.hibernate.Session;
import org.hibernate.SessionFactory;
import org.hibernate.Transaction;

public class EmployeeManipulation {

  @SuppressWarnings("unchecked")
  public static void main(String[] args) throws Exception {
  SessionFactory sessionFactory = HibernateUtil.getSessionFactory();
  Session session = sessionFactory.openSession();
  Transaction txn = session.beginTransaction();

  Employee employee1 = new Employee();
  employee1.setEmpNumber(5001);
  employee1.setEmpName("Ibrahim");
  employee1.setSalary(120000.0);
  employee1.getEmpName();

  Employee employee2 = new Employee();
  employee2.setEmpNumber(5002);
  employee2.setEmpName("Ajay");
  employee2.setSalary(82000.0);

  session.persist(employee1);
  session.persist(employee2);
  System.out.println("The employee objects are persisted with session");

  txn.commit();
  System.out.println("Transaction on this session is committed");
  session.close();

  session = sessionFactory.openSession();
```

```
txn = session.beginTransaction();
System.out.println("Accessing Employee Objects \n\n");
List<Employee> employeeList =
session.createQuery("from Employee").list();
for (int i = 0; i < employeeList.size(); i++) {
Employee employee = employeeList.get(i);
System.out.println("Employee Number : " + employee.getEmpNumber());
System.out.println("Employee Name   : " + employee.getEmpName());
System.out.printf("Salary   : %.2f \n", employee.getSalary());
System.out.printf("Tax : %.2f  ", employee.getTax());

System.out.println("\n========================================\n");
        }

txn.commit();
session.close();
sessionFactory.close();
}
}
```

Output:

```
The employee objects are persisted with session
Hibernate: insert into EMPLOYEE (EMP_NAME, EMP_NUMBER, SALARY, ID)
values (?, ?, ?, ?)
Hibernate: insert into EMPLOYEE (EMP_NAME, EMP_NUMBER, SALARY, ID)
values (?, ?, ?, ?)
Transaction on this session is committed
Accessing Employee Objects

Hibernate: select employee0_.ID as ID0_, employee0_.EMP_NAME as
EMP2_0_, employee0_.EMP_NUMBER as EMP3_0_, employee0_.SALARY as
SALARY0_, case when employee0_.salary < 100000 then employee0_.salary
* 0.10 else case when employee0_.salary < 200000 then 10000 +
(employee0_.salary - 100000) * 0.20 else employee0_.salary * 0.30
end end as formula0_ from EMPLOYEE employee0_
Employee Number : 5001
Employee Name   : Ibrahim
Salary          : 120000.00
```

```
Tax              : 14000.00
=========================================

Employee Number : 5002
Employee Name   : Ajay
Salary          : 82000.00
Tax             : 8200.00
=========================================
```

4.23 @Index - DEFINING INDEX ON A DATABASE COLUMN

It defines Index on a specified column.

Index speeds up reading a row (while doing search). However, index slows down the operations of inserting, updating and deleting records, so choose minimum number of index column(s) and which are not frequently updated.

General format

```
        @Index (name="Index Name")
// File Name: Employee.java
// Illustrates @Index

package com.hdemo;

import javax.persistence.Column;
import javax.persistence.Entity;
import javax.persistence.GeneratedValue;
import javax.persistence.Id;
import javax.persistence.Table;

import org.hibernate.annotations.GenericGenerator;
import org.hibernate.annotations.Index;

@Entity
@Table(name = "EMPLOYEE")
public class Employee {

  private static final long serialVersionUID = 1L;

   @Id
   @GeneratedValue(generator = "idGen")
```

```
  @GenericGenerator(name = "idGen", strategy = "uuid.hex")
  @Column(name = "ID", length = 32)
  private String id = "";

  @Index(name = "EmpNumberIndex")
  @Column(name = "EMP_NUMBER", unique = true, nullable = false)
  private Integer empNumber;

  @Column(name = "EMP_NAME", length = 64, nullable = false)
  private String empName;

  @Column(name = "SALARY")
  private double salary;

  //Getter and Setter methods

}
```

```
// File Name: EmployeeManipulation.java
// Main Program

package com.hdemo;

import java.util.List;

import org.hibernate.Session;
import org.hibernate.SessionFactory;
import org.hibernate.Transaction;

public class EmployeeManipulation {

  @SuppressWarnings("unchecked")
  public static void main(String[] args) throws Exception {
  SessionFactory sessionFactory = HibernateUtil.getSessionFactory();
  Session session = sessionFactory.openSession();
  Transaction txn = session.beginTransaction();

  Employee employee1 = new Employee();
  employee1.setEmpNumber(5001);
  employee1.setEmpName("Ibrahim");
```

```
employee1.setSalary(98500.0);
employee1.getEmpName();

Employee employee2 = new Employee();
employee2.setEmpNumber(5002);
employee2.setEmpName("Ajay");
employee2.setSalary(82000.0);

session.persist(employee1);
session.persist(employee2);
System.out.println("The employee objects are persisted with session");

txn.commit();
System.out.println("Transaction on this session is committed");
session.close();

session = sessionFactory.openSession();
txn = session.beginTransaction();
System.out.println("Accessing Employee Objects \n\n");
List<Employee> employeeList =
      session.createQuery("from Employee").list();
      for (int i = 0; i < employeeList.size(); i++) {
      Employee employee = employeeList.get(i);
System.out.println("Employee Number : " + employee.getEmpNumber());
System.out.println("Employee Name : " + employee.getEmpName());
System.out.printf("Salary : %.2f \n", employee.getSalary());

System.out.println("\n==================================\n");
      }

txn.commit();
session.close();
sessionFactory.close();
}
}
```

Administrator: C:\Windows\system32\cmd.exe - mysql -u huser -phpword hdemodb

mysql> show index from employee;

Table	Non_unique	Key_name	Seq_in_index	Column_name	Collation	Cardinality	Sub_part	Packed	Null	Index_type	Comment
employee	0	PRIMARY	1	ID	A	2	NULL	NULL		BTREE	
employee	0	EMP_NUMBER	1	EMP_NUMBER	A	2	NULL	NULL		BTREE	
employee	1	EmpNumber Index	1	EMP_NUMBER	A	2	NULL	NULL		BTREE	

3 rows in set (0.00 sec)

mysql>

4.24 `@NamedQueries` - PREDEFINE HQL/JPAQL QUERIES

This is used to specify more `@NamedQuery`(s) in an Entity.

General format

```
        @NamedQueries(Array_of_@NamedQuery)
```

```
// File Name: Employee.java
// Illustrates @NamedQueries

package com.hdemo;

import javax.persistence.Column;
import javax.persistence.Entity;
import javax.persistence.GeneratedValue;
import javax.persistence.Id;
import javax.persistence.NamedQueries;
import javax.persistence.NamedQuery;
import javax.persistence.Table;

import org.hibernate.annotations.GenericGenerator;

@Entity
@Table(name = "EMPLOYEE")

@NamedQueries({
@NamedQuery(name = "findEmployeeByEmpNumber",
  query = "SELECT e FROM Employee e WHERE e.empNumber = :empNumber"),
@NamedQuery(name = "findEmployeeBySalary",
  query = "SELECT e FROM Employee e WHERE e.salary > 100000")
})

public class Employee {
```

```
    private static final long serialVersionUID = 1L;

    @Id
    @GeneratedValue(generator = "idGen")
    @GenericGenerator(name = "idGen", strategy = "uuid.hex")
    @Column(name = "ID", length = 32)
    private String id = "";

    @Column(name = "EMP_NUMBER", unique = true, nullable = false)
    private Integer empNumber;

    @Column(name = "EMP_NAME", length = 64, nullable = false)
    private String empName;

    @Column(name = "SALARY")
    private double salary;

    //Getter and Setter methods

}
```

```
// File Name: EmployeeManipulation.java
// Main Program

package com.hdemo;

import java.util.List;

import org.hibernate.Session;
import org.hibernate.SessionFactory;
import org.hibernate.Transaction;

public class EmployeeManipulation {

    @SuppressWarnings("unchecked")
    public static void main(String[] args) throws Exception {
    SessionFactory sessionFactory = HibernateUtil.getSessionFactory();
    Session session = sessionFactory.openSession();
    Transaction txn = session.beginTransaction();
```

```
Employee employee1 = new Employee();
employee1.setEmpNumber(5001);
employee1.setEmpName("Ibrahim");
employee1.setSalary(120000.0);
employee1.getEmpName();

Employee employee2 = new Employee();
employee2.setEmpNumber(5002);
employee2.setEmpName("Ajay");
employee2.setSalary(82000.0);

session.persist(employee1);
session.persist(employee2);
System.out.println("The employee objects are persisted with session");
txn.commit();
System.out.println("Transaction on this session is committed");
session.close();

session = sessionFactory.openSession();
txn = session.beginTransaction();
System.out.println("Accessing Named Query findEmployee
ByEmpNumber\n");
List<Employee> employeeList = session.getNamedQuery("findEmployee
ByEmpNumber")
.setInteger("empNumber", 5002).list();
for (int i = 0; i < employeeList.size(); i++) {
      Employee employee = employeeList.get(i);
System.out.println("Employee Number : " + employee.getEmpNumber());
System.out.println("Employee Name   : " + employee.getEmpName());
System.out.printf("Salary : %.2f \n", employee.getSalary());

System.out.println("\n=======================================\n");
      }

System.out.println("Accessing Named Query findEmployeeBySalary\n");
employeeList = session.getNamedQuery("findEmployeeBySalary").list();
for (int i = 0; i < employeeList.size(); i++) {
```

```
        Employee employee = employeeList.get(i);
        System.out.println("Employee Number : " + employee.getEmpNumber());
        System.out.println("Employee Name   : " + employee.getEmpName());
        System.out.printf("Salary : %.2f \n", employee.getSalary());

       System.out.println("\n=======================================\n");
            }
        txn.commit();
        session.close();
        sessionFactory.close();
        }
    }
```

Output:

```
The employee objects are persisted with session
Hibernate: insert into EMPLOYEE (EMP_NAME, EMP_NUMBER, SALARY, ID)
values (?, ?, ?, ?)
Hibernate: insert into EMPLOYEE (EMP_NAME, EMP_NUMBER, SALARY, ID)
values (?, ?, ?, ?)
Transaction on this session is committed
Accessing Named Query findEmployeeByEmpNumber

Hibernate: select employee0_.ID as ID0_, employee0_.EMP_NAME as
EMP2_0_, employee0_.EMP_NUMBER as EMP3_0_, employee0_.SALARY as
SALARY0_ from EMPLOYEE employee0_ where employee0_.EMP_NUMBER=?
Employee Number : 5002
Employee Name   : Ajay
Salary          : 82000.00

========================================

Accessing Named Query findEmployeeBySalary

Hibernate: select employee0_.ID as ID0_, employee0_.EMP_NAME as
EMP2_0_, employee0_.EMP_NUMBER as EMP3_0_, employee0_.SALARY as
SALARY0_ from EMPLOYEE employee0_ where employee0_.SALARY>100000
Employee Number : 5001
Employee Name   : Ibrahim
Salary          : 120000.00

========================================
```

4.25 @NamedNativeQuery - PREDEFINE SQL QUERY

This is used to pre-define a query (native SQL query, depends on the database, like JDBC query) that can be executed by specifying its name at run time.

General format

`@NamedNativeQuery(name = "<query_name>" query = "<native_SQL_query>")`

We can also specify a class that will be mapped for query result in

`"resultClass = ClassName.class"` attribute.

```
// File Name: Employee.java
// Illustrates @NamedNativeQuery

package com.hdemo;

import javax.persistence.Column;
import javax.persistence.Entity;
import javax.persistence.GeneratedValue;
import javax.persistence.Id;
import javax.persistence.NamedNativeQuery;
import javax.persistence.Table;

import org.hibernate.annotations.GenericGenerator;

@Entity
@Table(name = "EMPLOYEE")
@NamedNativeQuery(name = "findEmployeeByEmpNumber",
query = "SELECT * FROM EMPLOYEE WHERE EMP_NUMBER = :empNumber",
resultClass = Employee.class)
public class Employee {

 private static final long serialVersionUID = 1L;

  @Id
  @GeneratedValue(generator = "idGen")
  @GenericGenerator(name = "idGen", strategy = "uuid.hex")
  @Column(name = "ID", length = 32)
  private String id = "";

  @Column(name = "EMP_NUMBER", unique = true, nullable = false)
```

```
    private Integer empNumber;
    @Column(name = "EMP_NAME", length = 64, nullable = false)
    private String empName;

    @Column(name = "SALARY")
    private double salary;

    //Getter and Setter methods

  }
```

```
// File Name: EmployeeManipulation.java
// Main Program

package com.hdemo;

import java.util.List;

import org.hibernate.Session;
import org.hibernate.SessionFactory;
import org.hibernate.Transaction;

public class EmployeeManipulation {

  @SuppressWarnings("unchecked")
  public static void main(String[] args) throws Exception {
  SessionFactory sessionFactory = HibernateUtil.getSessionFactory();
  Session session = sessionFactory.openSession();
  Transaction txn = session.beginTransaction();

  Employee employee1 = new Employee();
  employee1.setEmpNumber(5001);
  employee1.setEmpName("Ibrahim");
  employee1.setSalary(120000.0);
  employee1.getEmpName();

  Employee employee2 = new Employee();
  employee2.setEmpNumber(5002);
  employee2.setEmpName("Ajay");
```

```
    employee2.setSalary(82000.0);

    session.persist(employee1);
    session.persist(employee2);
    System.out.println("The employee objects are persisted with session");

    txn.commit();
    System.out.println("Transaction on this session is committed");
    session.close();

    session = sessionFactory.openSession();
    txn = session.beginTransaction();
    System.out.println("Accessing Named Query findAllEmployees\n");
    List<Employee> employeeList = session
    .getNamedQuery ("findEmployeeByEmpNumber")
    .setInteger("empNumber", 5002).list();
        for (int i = 0; i < employeeList.size(); i++) {
        Employee employee = employeeList.get(i);
    System.out.println("Employee Number : " + employee.getEmpNumber());
    System.out.println("Employee Name : " + employee.getEmpName());
    System.out.printf("Salary : %.2f \n", employee.getSalary());

   System.out.println("\n=====================================\n");
        }

    txn.commit();
    session.close();
    sessionFactory.close();
    }
}
```

Output:

```
The employee objects are persisted with session
Hibernate: insert into EMPLOYEE (EMP_NAME, EMP_NUMBER, SALARY, ID)
values (?, ?, ?, ?)
Hibernate: insert into EMPLOYEE (EMP_NAME, EMP_NUMBER, SALARY, ID)
values (?, ?, ?, ?)
Transaction on this session is committed
Accessing Named Query findAllEmployees
```

```
Hibernate: SELECT * FROM EMPLOYEE WHERE EMP_NUMBER = ?
Employee Number : 5002
Employee Name   : Ajay
Salary          : 82000.00
========================================
```

4.26 @NamedNativeQueries - PREDEFINE SQL QUERIES

This is used to specify more **@NamedNativeQuery**(s) in an Entity.

General format

```
@NamedNativeQueries(Array_of_@NamedNativeQuery)
```

```
// File Name: Employee.java
// Illustrates @NamedNativeQueries

package com.hdemo;

import javax.persistence.Column;
import javax.persistence.Entity;
import javax.persistence.GeneratedValue;
import javax.persistence.Id;
import javax.persistence.NamedNativeQueries;
import javax.persistence.NamedNativeQuery;
import javax.persistence.Table;

import org.hibernate.annotations.GenericGenerator;

@Entity
@Table(name = "EMPLOYEE")
@NamedNativeQueries( {
  @NamedNativeQuery(name = "findEmployeeByEmpNumber",
  query = "SELECT * FROM EMPLOYEE WHERE EMP_NUMBER = :empNumber",
  resultClass = Employee.class),
  @NamedNativeQuery(name = "findEmployeeBySalary", query = "SELECT
  * FROM EMPLOYEE WHERE SALARY > 100000", resultClass =
  Employee.class)
  } )
  public class Employee {
```

```
    private static final long serialVersionUID = 1L;

    @Id
    @GeneratedValue(generator = "idGen")
    @GenericGenerator(name = "idGen", strategy = "uuid.hex")
    @Column(name = "ID", length = 32)
    private String id = "";

    @Column(name = "EMP_NUMBER", unique = true, nullable = false)
    private Integer empNumber;

    @Column(name = "EMP_NAME", length = 64, nullable = false)
    private String empName;

    @Column(name = "SALARY")
    private double salary;

    //Getter and Setter Methods

}
```

```
// File Name: EmployeeManipulation.java
// Main Program

package com.hdemo;

import java.util.List;

import org.hibernate.Session;
import org.hibernate.SessionFactory;
import org.hibernate.Transaction;

public class EmployeeManipulation {

    @SuppressWarnings("unchecked")
    public static void main(String[] args) throws Exception {
    SessionFactory sessionFactory = HibernateUtil.getSessionFactory();
    Session session = sessionFactory.openSession();
    Transaction txn = session.beginTransaction();
```

```
Employee employee1 = new Employee();
employee1.setEmpNumber(5001);
employee1.setEmpName("Ibrahim");
employee1.setSalary(120000.0);
employee1.getEmpName();

Employee employee2 = new Employee();
employee2.setEmpNumber(5002);
employee2.setEmpName("Ajay");
employee2.setSalary(82000.0);

session.persist(employee1);
session.persist(employee2);
System.out.println("The employee objects are persisted with session");

txn.commit();
System.out.println("Transaction on this session is committed");
session.close();

session = sessionFactory.openSession();
txn = session.beginTransaction();
System.out.println("Accessing Named Query findAllEmployees\n");
List<Employee> employeeList = session
.getNamedQuery ("findEmployeeByEmpNumber")
.setInteger("empNumber", 5002).list();
      for (int i = 0; i < employeeList.size(); i++) {
      Employee employee = employeeList.get(i);
System.out.println("Employee Number : " + employee.getEmpNumber());
System.out.println("Employee Name   : " + employee.getEmpName());
System.out.printf("Salary : %.2f \n", employee.getSalary());

System.out.println("\n=======================================\n");
      }

System.out.println("Accessing Named Query findEmployeeBySalary\n");
employeeList = session.getNamedQuery("findEmployeeBySalary").list();
      for (int i = 0; i < employeeList.size(); i++) {
      Employee employee = employeeList.get(i);
System.out.println("Employee Number : " + employee.getEmpNumber());
```

```
    System.out.println("Employee Name   : " + employee.getEmpName());
    System.out.printf("Salary  :  %.2f  \n", employee.getSalary());

   System.out.println("\n======================================\n");
      }
    txn.commit();
    session.close();
    sessionFactory.close();
   }
 }
```

Output:

```
The employee objects are persisted with session
Hibernate: insert into EMPLOYEE (EMP_NAME, EMP_NUMBER, SALARY, ID)
values (?, ?, ?, ?)
Hibernate: insert into EMPLOYEE (EMP_NAME, EMP_NUMBER, SALARY, ID)
values (?, ?, ?, ?)
Transaction on this session is committed
Accessing Named Query findAllEmployees

Hibernate: SELECT * FROM EMPLOYEE WHERE EMP_NUMBER = ?
Employee Number  : 5002
Employee Name    : Ajay
Salary           : 82000.00

====================================

Accessing Named Query findEmployeeBySalary

Hibernate: SELECT * FROM EMPLOYEE WHERE SALARY > 100000
Employee Number  : 5001
Employee Name    : Ibrahim
Salary           : 120000.00

====================================
```

Named Native Queries with Join:

The above examples illustrate how to execute named native queries and their results are based on single entity. The following example demonstrates how to use Native Named Queries with Joining of tables (entities).

Declare one `@SqlResultSetMapping` and specify its name as value to the attribute **resultSetMapping** of `@NamedNativeQuery`.

In `@SqlResultSetMapping`, pass an array of `@EntityResult` as the value to *entities* attribute value. And each `@EntityResult` should have Entity Class name specified in `entityClass` attribute and an array of `@FieldResult` specified as value to *fields* attribute. Note that all the filed (data members of the entity) should be specified in fields attribute of `@EntityResult` and all the fields should be selected from native SQL query. In `@FieldResult` annotation, the name attribute refers field-name (data member) of the entity class and column attribute specifies the actual column-name in the database table (the column name that the native SQL will return if we say exactly). Of course, if you are using alias-name in native SQL query, that alias-name only should be specified as column attribute value, not the actual database table column name.

Other fields returned by native SQL query (not part of any entity) can be specified in *columns* attribute of `@SqlResultSetMapping` which contains an array of `@ColumnResult`. Each `@ColumnResult` should have an attribute named *name* with native SQL select column name as its value.

```
// File Name: Employee.java
// Illustrates @SqlResultSetMapping

package com.hdemo;

import javax.persistence.CascadeType;

@SqlResultSetMapping (
                        name = "EmployeeResultSetMapping",
                             entities = {
                   @EntityResult(

 entityClass = Employee.class,
                   fields = {

 @FieldResult(name="id", column="ID"),

 @FieldResult(name="empNumber", column="EMP_NUM"),

 @FieldResult(name="empName", column="EMP_NAME"),

 @FieldResult(name="salary", column="EMP_SALARY"),

 @FieldResult(name="address", column="EMP_ADDRESS"),

 }
```

```
            ),
            @EntityResult(

   entityClass = Address.class,

   fields = {

   @FieldResult(name="id", column="ADDRESS_ID"),

   @FieldResult(name="houseNumber", column="HOUSE_NUMBER"),

   @FieldResult(name="streetName", column="STREET_NAME"),

   @FieldResult(name="cityName", column="CITY_NAME"),

   @FieldResult(name="countryName", column="COUNTRY_NAME"),

   @FieldResult(name="postalCode", column="PIN"),

         }
                  }
                        },

            columns = {
            @ColumnResult(
                              name = "TODAY"
                        }

                  )
      }

@Entity
@Table(name = "EMPLOYEE")
@NamedNativeQuery(name = "findEmployeeByEmpNumber",
     query = "SELECT E.ID AS ID, E.EMP_NUMBER AS EMP_NUM, E.EMP_NAME,
E.SALARY AS EMP_SALARY, E.ADDRESS_ID AS EMP_ADDRESS, "+
     "A.ID AS ADDRESS_ID, A.HOUSE_NUMBER, A.STREET_NAME, A.CITY_NAME,
A.COUNTRY_NAME, A.POSTAL_CODE AS PIN, " +
     "DATE_FORMAT(SYSDATE(), '%d/%m/%Y') AS TODAY FROM EMPLOYEE E,
```

```
    ADDRESS A WHERE E.ADDRESS_ID = A.ID AND E.EMP_NUMBER = :EmpNumber",
    resultSetMapping="EmployeeResultSetMapping")
    public class Employee {

    private static final long serialVersionUID = 1L;

    @Id
    @GeneratedValue(generator = "idGen")
    @GenericGenerator(name = "idGen", strategy = "uuid.hex")
    @Column(name = "ID", length = 32)
    private String id = "";

    @Column(name = "EMP_NUMBER", unique = true, nullable = false)
    private Integer empNumber;

    @Column(name = "EMP_NAME", length = 64, nullable = false)
    private String empName;

    @Column(name = "SALARY")
    private double salary;

    @OneToOne(cascade = CascadeType.ALL)
    @JoinColumn(name = "ADDRESS_ID")
    Address address;

    //Getter and Setter methods

}
```

```
// File Name: Address.java
// Illustrates @SqlResultSetMapping

package com.hdemo;

import java.io.Serializable;

import javax.persistence.Column;
import javax.persistence.Entity;
import javax.persistence.GeneratedValue;
import javax.persistence.Id;
```

```
import javax.persistence.Table;

import org.hibernate.annotations.GenericGenerator;

@Entity
@Table(name = "ADDRESS")
public class Address implements Serializable {

  private static final long serialVersionUID = 1L;

  @Id
  @GeneratedValue(generator = "idGen")
  @GenericGenerator(name = "idGen", strategy = "uuid.hex")
  @Column(name = "ID", length = 32)
  private String id = "";

  @Column(name = "HOUSE_NUMBER", length = 8)
  private String houseNumber;

  @Column(name = "STREET_NAME", length = 64)
  private String streetName;

  @Column(name = "CITY_NAME", length = 64)
  private String cityName;

  @Column(name = "COUNTRY_NAME", length = 64)
  private String countryName;


  @Column(name = "POSTAL_CODE", length = 16)
  private String postalCode;

  //Getter and Setter methods

}
```

```
// File Name: EmployeeManipulation.java
// Main Program

package com.hdemo;
```

```
import java.util.List;

import org.hibernate.Session;
import org.hibernate.SessionFactory;
import org.hibernate.Transaction;

public class EmployeeManipulation {

  @SuppressWarnings("unchecked")
  public static void main(String[] args) throws Exception {
  SessionFactory sessionFactory = HibernateUtil.getSessionFactory();
  Session session = sessionFactory.openSession();
  Transaction txn = session.beginTransaction();

  Employee employee1 = new Employee();
  employee1.setEmpNumber(5001);
  employee1.setEmpName("Ibrahim");
  employee1.setSalary(120000.0);
  Address address1 = new Address();
  address1.setHouseNumber("C-48-2");
  address1.setStreetName("Jalan Munsi Abdullah");
  address1.setCityName("Kuala Lumpur");
  address1.setPostalCode("50100");
  address1.setCountryName("Malaysia");
  employee1.setAddress(address1);

  Employee employee2 = new Employee();
  employee2.setEmpNumber(5002);
  employee2.setEmpName("Ajay");
  employee2.setSalary(82000.0);
  Address address2 = new Address();
  address2.setHouseNumber("3/121");
  address2.setStreetName("Nehru Street");
  address2.setCityName("Trichy");
  address2.setPostalCode("621302");
  address2.setCountryName("India");
  employee2.setAddress(address2);
```

```
session.persist(employee1);
session.persist(employee2);
System.out.println("The employee objects are persisted with session");

txn.commit();
System.out.println("Transaction on this session is committed");
session.close();
session = sessionFactory.openSession();
txn = session.beginTransaction();
System.out.println("Accessing Named Query findEmployeeByEmp
      Number\n");
List employeeList = session
.getNamedQuery("findEmployeeByEmpNumber"). setInteger("EmpNumber",
      5002).list();
      for (int i = 0; i < employeeList.size(); i++) {

      Object[] row = (Object[]) employeeList.get(i);
      Employee employee = (Employee) row[0];
      Address address = (Address) row[1];
      String today = (String) row[2];
System.out.println("Employee: Id[" +
            employee.getId() + "] Emp Number[" +
            employee.getEmpNumber() +
            "] Emp Name[" + employee.getEmpName() + "]");
System.out.println("Address: Id[" +
            address.getId() + "] House Number[" +
            address.getHouseNumber() + "] Street Name[" +
            address.getStreetName() + "] City Name[" +
            address.getCityName() + "] Postal Code[" +
            address.getPostalCode() + "] Country[" + address.
            getCountryName() + "]");
System.out.println("Date [" + today + "]");

System.out.println("\n=====================================\n");
      }

      txn.commit();
```

```
            session.close();
            sessionFactory.close();
        }
    }
```

Suppose if we want to select only few columns from one entity and some few columns from another entity using join, the above `@SqlResultSetMapping` will not work. Because we specifies entities attribute will expect all the fields in the entity/entities should be defined and should be selected in native SQL.

However, the above query can be accomplished by only using columns attribute of `@SqlResultSetMapping` as follows. Keep the same Address entity.

```
// File Name: Employee.java
// Illustrates @SqlResultSetMapping

package com.hdemo;

import javax.persistence.CascadeType;

@SqlResultSetMapping (name = "EmployeeResultSetMapping",
                columns = {
                            @ColumnResult(name = "EMP_NUM"),
                            @ColumnResult(name = "EMP_NAME"),
                            @ColumnResult(name = "COUNTRY_NAME")
                                          }
                            )

@Entity
@Table(name = "EMPLOYEE")
@NamedNativeQuery(name = "findEmployeeByEmpNumber",
                query = "SELECT E.EMP_NUMBER AS EMP_NUM, E.EMP_NAME,
A.COUNTRY_NAME FROM EMPLOYEE E, ADDRESS A WHERE E.ADDRESS_ID = A.ID
AND E.EMP_NUMBER = :EmpNumber",
                  resultSetMapping="EmployeeResultSetMapping")
public class Employee {

  private static final long serialVersionUID = 1L;

  @Id
```

```
    @GeneratedValue(generator = "idGen")
    @GenericGenerator(name = "idGen", strategy = "uuid.hex")
    @Column(name = "ID", length = 32)
    private String id = "";

    @Column(name = "EMP_NUMBER", unique = true, nullable = false)
    private Integer empNumber;

    @Column(name = "EMP_NAME", length = 64, nullable = false)
    private String empName;

    @Column(name = "SALARY")
    private double salary;

    @OneToOne(cascade = CascadeType.ALL)
    @JoinColumn(name = "ADDRESS_ID")
    Address address;

    //Getter and Setter methods

}
```

```
// File Name: EmployeeManipulation.java
// Main Program

package com.hdemo;

import java.util.List;

import org.hibernate.Session;
import org.hibernate.SessionFactory;
import org.hibernate.Transaction;

public class EmployeeManipulation {

    @SuppressWarnings("unchecked")
    public static void main(String[] args) throws Exception {
    SessionFactory sessionFactory = HibernateUtil.getSessionFactory();
    Session session = sessionFactory.openSession();
    Transaction txn = session.beginTransaction();
```

```
Employee employee1 = new Employee();
employee1.setEmpNumber(5001);
employee1.setEmpName("Ibrahim");
employee1.setSalary(120000.0);
Address address1 = new Address();
address1.setHouseNumber("C-48-2");
address1.setStreetName("Jalan Munsi Abdullah");
address1.setCityName("Kuala Lumpur");
address1.setPostalCode("50100");
address1.setCountryName("Malaysia");
employee1.setAddress(address1);

Employee employee2 = new Employee();
employee2.setEmpNumber(5002);
employee2.setEmpName("Ajay");
employee2.setSalary(82000.0);
Address address2 = new Address();
address2.setHouseNumber("3/121");
address2.setStreetName("Nehru Street");
address2.setCityName("Trichy");
address2.setPostalCode("621302");
address2.setCountryName("India");
employee2.setAddress(address2);

session.persist(employee1);
session.persist(employee2);
System.out.println("The employee objects are persisted with session");

txn.commit();
System.out.println("Transaction on this session is committed");
session.close();

session = sessionFactory.openSession();
txn = session.beginTransaction();
System.out.println("Accessing Named Query findEmployeeByEmp
Number\n");
```

```
List employeeList = session
.getNamedQuery("findEmployeeByEmpNumber").setInteger("EmpNumber",
5002).list();
for (int i = 0; i < employeeList.size(); i++) {
Object[] row = (Object[]) employeeList.get(i);
System.out.println("Employee: Emp Number[" + row[0] + "] Emp
Name[" + row[1] + "] Country[" + row[2] + "]");

System.out.println("\n=========================================\n");
    }
txn.commit();
session.close();
sessionFactory.close();
}
}
```

Output:

```
The employee objects are persisted with session
Hibernate: insert into ADDRESS (CITY_NAME, COUNTRY_NAME, HOUSE_NUMBER,
POSTAL_CODE, STREET_NAME, ID) values (?, ?, ?, ?, ?, ?)
Hibernate: insert into EMPLOYEE (ADDRESS_ID, EMP_NAME, EMP_NUMBER,
SALARY, ID) values (?, ?, ?, ?, ?)
Hibernate: insert into ADDRESS (CITY_NAME, COUNTRY_NAME, HOUSE_NUMBER,
POSTAL_CODE, STREET_NAME, ID) values (?, ?, ?, ?, ?, ?)
Hibernate: insert into EMPLOYEE (ADDRESS_ID, EMP_NAME, EMP_NUMBER,
SALARY, ID) values (?, ?, ?, ?, ?)
Transaction on this session is committed
Accessing Named Query findEmployeeByEmpNumber

Hibernate: SELECT E.EMP_NUMBER AS EMP_NUM, E.EMP_NAME, A.COUNTRY_NAME
FROM EMPLOYEE E, ADDRESS A WHERE E.ADDRESS_ID = A.ID AND E.EMP_NUMBER
= ?

Employee: Emp Number[5002] Emp Name[Ajay] Country[India]

=========================================
```

An array of `@SqlResultSetMapping` can be specified using `@SqlResultSetMappings`.

4.27 HIBERNATE VALIDATOR

To use Hibernate Validator, download `hibernate-validator.jar` and make it available in the `CLASSPATH`. (Download Validator library file (in our case, hibernate-validator-3.0.0.GA.zip) from Hibernate site, and unzip to get the required jar file, add this hibernate-validator.jar file in Eclipse via Right Click on HibernateDemo Project → Properties → Java Build Path → Libraries Tab/ → Add JAR... (if the jar file present in the Project directory)/Add External JARs... (if jar file present in any directory) → Select the jar file → Press OK → Press OK from Properties window).

4.27.1 @Length

–Defines minimum and maximum length of String datum.

General format

```
@Length (min = <minimum_value>, max = <maximum_value>)
```

4.27.2 @Min

–Checks minimum value for Numeric datum.

General format

```
@Min (value = <minimum_value>)
```

4.27.3 @Max

–Checks maximum value for Numeric datum.

General format

```
@Max (value = <maximum_value>)
```

4.27.4 @Range

–Checks minimum and maximum value for Numeric datum.

General format

```
@Range(min = <value>, max = <value>)
```

4.27.5 @NotNull

–Checks the value is not null, and will not accept null value.

General format

```
@NotNull
```

4.27.6 @NotEmpty

–Checks the string is not null and not empty.

General format

```
@NotEmpty
```

4.27.7 @Past

–Applied on Date / Calendar field/property. Checks the date is past (earlier) than current one.

General format

```
@Past
```

4.27.8 @Future

–Applied on Date / Calendar field/property. Checks the date is future (later) than current one.

General format

```
@Future
```

4.27.9 @Size

–Applied on array/collection/map field/property. Define the size of the field/property.

General format

```
@Size(min = <value>, max = <value>)
```

4.27.10 @Email

–Checks whether the string datum is conformed to a valid e-mail id.

General format

```
@Email
```

The following example uses some of the data validation annotations to check Student data. Add the below mapping definition for `Student` entity in *hibernate.cfg.xml*.

```
<mapping class="com.hdemo.Student" />
```

```
// File Name: Student.java
// Entity class -Hibernate Validations

package com.hdemo;

import java.util.Date;

import javax.persistence.Column;
import javax.persistence.Entity;
import javax.persistence.GeneratedValue;
import javax.persistence.Id;
import javax.persistence.Table;
import javax.persistence.Temporal;
import javax.persistence.TemporalType;
```

```
import org.hibernate.annotations.GenericGenerator;
import org.hibernate.validator.Email;
import org.hibernate.validator.Length;
import org.hibernate.validator.Max;
import org.hibernate.validator.Min;
import org.hibernate.validator.NotEmpty;
import org.hibernate.validator.Past;
import org.hibernate.validator.Range;

import com.sun.istack.internal.NotNull;

@Entity
@Table(name = "STUDENT")
public class Student {

   @Id
   @GeneratedValue(generator = "idGen")
   @GenericGenerator(name = "idGen", strategy = "uuid.hex")
   @Column(name = "ID", length = 32)
   private String id = "";

   @Min(value = 0, message = "Roll Number should be a positive non-
   zero number")
   @Column(name = "ROLL_NUMBER", nullable = false)
   private int rollNumber;

   @Length(min = 5, max = 64)
   @Column(name = "STUD_NAME", nullable = false, length = 64)
   private String studName;

   @Email
   @Column(name = "EMAIL", nullable = false, length = 64)
   private String email;

   @Past(message = "Admission Date should be past date")
   @Temporal(TemporalType.DATE)
   @Column(name = "ADMISSION_DATE")
```

```
  private Date admissionDate;

  @Range(min = 0, max = 100,
  message = "Mark1 should be within the range 0-100")
  @Column(name = "MARK1", nullable = false)
  private int mark1;

  @Range(min = 0, max = 100,
  message = "Mark2 should be within the range 0-100")
  @Column(name = "MARK2", nullable = false)
  private int mark2;

  @Range(min = 0, max = 100,
  message = "Mark3 should be within the range 0-100")
  @Column(name = "MARK3", nullable = false)
  private int mark3;

  @Min(value = 0,
  message = "Total marks should not be less than 0")
  @Max(value = 300, message = "Total marks should not exceed 300")
  @NotNull
  @Column(name = "TOTAL")
  private int total;

  @NotEmpty(message = "Result should not be null or empty")
  @Column(name = "RESULT", length = 4)
  private String result;

  //Getter and Setter methods
}
```

```
// File Name: StudentManipulation.java
// Hibernate Validations

package com.hdemo;

import java.util.Date;

import org.hibernate.Session;
```

```
import  org.hibernate.SessionFactory;
import  org.hibernate.Transaction;

public  class  StudentManipulation  {

  public  static  void  main(String[]  args)  throws  Exception  {
   SessionFactory sessionFactory = HibernateUtil.getSessionFactory();
   Session  session  =  sessionFactory.openSession();
   Transaction  txn  =  session.beginTransaction();

   Student  student  =  new  Student();
   student.setRollNumber(0);
   student.setStudName("Amar");
   student.setEmail("amar#yahoo.com");
   student.setAdmissionDate(new  Date());
   student.setMark1(550);
   student.setMark2(12);
   student.setMark3(-80);
   student.setResult("");

   try  {
          session.save(student);
          txn.commit();
          System.out.println("Data confirms the Validation Rules. Record
          inserted  successfully.");
   }
   catch  (Exception  e)  {
          System.out.println("Validation  Failed.");
          e.printStackTrace();
          txn.rollback();
   }

   session.close();
   sessionFactory.close();
   }
}
```

Output:

The validation exception is thrown, when we execute the given mail program as it violates validation rules defined in the Entity.

```
Validation Failed.
org.hibernate.validator.InvalidStateException: validation failed for:
com.hdemo.Student
at org.hibernate.validator.event.ValidateEventListener.
validate(ValidateEventListener.java:148)
at org.hibernate.validator.event.ValidateEventListener.
onPreInsert(ValidateEventListener.java:172)
at org.hibernate.action.EntityInsertAction. preInsert(EntityInsert
Action.java:160)
at org.hibernate.action.EntityInsertAction.execute (EntityInsertAction.
java:53)
at org.hibernate.engine.ActionQueue.execute(ActionQueue.java:279)
at org.hibernate.engine.ActionQueue.executeActions (ActionQueue.
java:263)
at org.hibernate.engine.ActionQueue.executeActions (ActionQueue.
java:167)
at org.hibernate.event.def.AbstractFlushingEventListener.
performExecutions(AbstractFlushingEventListener.java:298)
at org.hibernate.event.def.DefaultFlushEventListener. onFlush(Default
FlushEventListener.java:27)
at org.hibernate.impl.SessionImpl.flush(SessionImpl.java:1000)
at org.hibernate.impl.SessionImpl.managedFlush(SessionImpl.java:338)
at org.hibernate.transaction.JDBCTransaction.commit (JDBCTransaction.
java:106)
at com.hdemo.StudentManipulation.main(StudentManipulation.java:31)
```

Change the main program as below, which try to insert only valid data for *Student* entity.

```
// File Name: StudentManipulation.java
// Hibernate Validations

package com.hdemo;

import java.util.Calendar;

import org.hibernate.Session;
import org.hibernate.SessionFactory;
```

```
import org.hibernate.Transaction;

public class StudentManipulation {

 public static void main(String[] args) throws Exception {
  SessionFactory sessionFactory = HibernateUtil.getSessionFactory();
  Session session = sessionFactory.openSession();
  Transaction txn = session.beginTransaction();

  Student student = new Student();
  student.setRollNumber(1001);
  student.setStudName("Amar Singh");
  student.setEmail("amar@yahoo.com");
  Calendar calendar = Calendar.getInstance();
  calendar.add(Calendar.DATE, -5);
  student.setAdmissionDate(calendar.getTime());
  student.setMark1(50);
  student.setMark2(62);
  student.setMark3(80);
  student.setTotal(192);
  student.setResult("PASS");

  try {
        session.save(student);
        txn.commit();
        System.out.println("Data confirms the Validation Rules. Record
        inserted successfully.");
  }
        catch (Exception e) {
        System.out.println("Validation Failed.");
        e.printStackTrace();
        txn.rollback();
        }

        session.close();
        sessionFactory.close();
  }
```

```
}
```

Output:

```
Hibernate: insert into STUDENT (ADMISSION_DATE, EMAIL, MARK1, MARK2, MARK3, RESULT, ROLL_NUMBER, STUD_NAME, TOTAL, ID) values (?, ?, ?, ?, ?, ?, ?, ?, ?, ?)
Data confirms the Validation Rules. Record inserted successfully.

mysql> select * from student;
```

ID	ADMISSION_DATE	EMAIL	MARK1	MARK2	MARK3	RESULT	ROLL_NUMBER	STUD_NAME	TOTAL
402 ...	2009-02-14	amar@ yahoo .com	50	62	80	PASS	1001	Amar Singh	192

```
1 row in set (0.00 sec)
```

4.28 `@FilterDef`, `@Filter` - FILTERING QUERY RESULT

Hibernate Filter, as it name specifies, filters the records retrieved from database table using Hibernate Session. It is a programmatic way to restrict the result of query through Hibernate. Its function is same like "where" conditions specified while retrieving data ("where condition" in HQL, `Restrictions` criterions in Criteria Query), however these filter conditions can be parameterized and we can pass values to parameters in conditions at runtime.

These pre-defined Filters can be attached at both a class (Entity) and a Collection (Set, List ...) level. Thus Filters act like "database views", but not at database level. Filters should be accessed with Hibernate Session. These Filters can be enabled and disabled (by default) during a Hibernate session. No Filter is enabled (active filters) for a Session, by default.

The following are some methods of `org.hibernate.Session` Interface to handle Filters in Hibernate Session.

```
Filter enableFilter(String filterName)
```

This method enables the named filter for the current session (the session where this method is invoked).

```
void disableFilter(String filterName)
```

This method disables the named filter for the current session.

```
Filter getEnabledFilter(String filterName)
```

This method retrieves the currently enabled (already activated filter with the current session) filter by name.

The following are some methods of `org.hibernate.Filter` Interface to set parameter values for a Filter.

```
Filter setParameter(String name, Object value)
```

Sets the specified value to the specified parameter-name of the Filter.

```
Filter setParameterList(String name, Collection|Object[] values)
```

Sets the specified Collection or Array values to the specified parameter (used for doing in comparison to filter data).

The annotation `@FilterDef` (Hibernate Annotation) defines a single filter and `@FilterDefs` define multiple filters, which are to be used by `@Filter` to implement filtration.

General formats

Defining a Filter Definition using `@FilterDef`:

```
@FilterDef(name = "filter_name",
           parameters = @ParamDef_Array,
           defaultCondition = "condition")
```

The attribute `name` specifies the name of the filter, which will be referred by `@Filters`. The parameter-names, which are used in the condition part of Filter (in `defaultCondition` attribute of `@FilterDef`, or in `condition` attribute of `@Filter`), are specified in `parameters` attribute as `@ParamDef` **`array`**.

Each parameter is defined by a `@ParamDef` which has a name and a type.

```
@ParamDef(name = "parameter_name",
     type = "Hibernate_data_type")
```

Some Hibernate data types for corresponding to Java data types are given below.

Java Data Type	Hibernate Data Type
short	short
Integer, int	integer
long	long
char	character
float	float
double	double
String	string (if it is a very long String, then use the data type text)
java.util.Date	date, time, timestamp (according to the datum; Date only, Time only, Data & Time)
java.util.Calendar	calendar, calendar_date
java.sql.Clob	clob
java.sql.Blob	blob
Any Java Object	serializable
byte Array	binary

Defining multiple Filter Definitions using `@FilterDefs`:

```
@FilterDefs(value = @FilterDef_Array)
```

Creating a Filter:

```
@Filter(name = "filter_name", condition = "condition")
```

Creating Multiple Filters:

```
@Filters(value = @Filter_Array)
```

The `@FilterDefs` can be defined at the class or package level. The `@Filter` should be placed either on the entity or the collection element (field).

The following example inserts some sample data initially, and queries those data on database and filtered them using filtering condition based on Employee Type. (Adjust configuration in *hibernate.cfg.xml* file).

```
// File Name: Employee.java
// Filtering Query result using @Filter

package com.hdemo;

import java.util.List;

import javax.persistence.CascadeType;
import javax.persistence.Column;
import javax.persistence.Entity;
import javax.persistence.GeneratedValue;
import javax.persistence.Id;
import javax.persistence.JoinColumn;
import javax.persistence.OneToMany;
import javax.persistence.Table;

import org.hibernate.annotations.Filter;
import org.hibernate.annotations.FilterDef;
import org.hibernate.annotations.GenericGenerator;
import org.hibernate.annotations.ParamDef;

@Entity
@Table(name = "EMPLOYEE")
@FilterDef(name = "EmployeeCategory",
parameters = @ParamDef(name = "empCategory", type = "string"))
```

```
@Filter(name = "EmployeeCategory",
condition = ":empCategory = EMP_TYPE")

public class Employee {

   @Id
   @GeneratedValue(generator = "idGen")
   @GenericGenerator(name = "idGen", strategy = "uuid.hex")
   @Column(name = "ID", length = 32)
   private String id = "";

   @Column(name = "EMP_NUMBER", unique = true, nullable = false)
   private Integer empNumber;

   @Column(name = "EMP_NAME", length = 64, nullable = false)
   private String empName;

   @Column(name = "EMP_TYPE", length = 64, nullable = false)
   private String empType;

   @OneToMany(cascade = CascadeType.ALL)
   @JoinColumn(name = "EMPLOYEE_ADDRESS")
   private List<Address> addresses;

   //Getter and Setter methods

}
```

```
// File Name: Address.java
// Filtering Query result using @Filter

package com.hdemo;

import java.io.Serializable;

import javax.persistence.Column;
import javax.persistence.Entity;
import javax.persistence.GeneratedValue;
```

```
import javax.persistence.Id;
import javax.persistence.Table;

import org.hibernate.annotations.GenericGenerator;

@Entity
@Table(name = "ADDRESS")
public class Address implements Serializable {

  private static final long serialVersionUID = 1L;

  @Id
  @GeneratedValue(generator = "idGen")
  @GenericGenerator(name = "idGen", strategy = "uuid.hex")
  @Column(name = "ID", length = 32)
  private String id = "";

  @Column(name = "HOUSE_NUMBER", length = 8)
  private String houseNumber;

  @Column(name = "STREET_NAME", length = 64)
  private String streetName;

  @Column(name = "CITY_NAME", length = 64)
  private String cityName;

  @Column(name = "COUNTRY_NAME", length = 64)
  private String countryName;

  @Column(name = "POSTAL_CODE", length = 16)
  private String postalCode;

  //Getter and Setter methods

  public String toString() {
        return "[House Number: " + houseNumber +
                  "\nStreet Name : " + streetName +
                  "\nCity Name    : " + cityName +
```

```
                    "\nCountry Name: " + countryName +
                    "\nPostal Code : " + postalCode +
                    "]";
    }
}
```

```
// File Name: EmployeeManipulation.java
// Filtering Query result using @Filter

package com.hdemo;

import java.util.ArrayList;
import java.util.List;

import org.hibernate.Filter;
import org.hibernate.Session;
import org.hibernate.SessionFactory;
import org.hibernate.Transaction;

public class EmployeeManipulation {

  @SuppressWarnings("unchecked")
  public static void main(String[] args) throws Exception {
  SessionFactory sessionFactory = HibernateUtil.getSessionFactory();
  Session session = sessionFactory.openSession();
  Transaction txn = session.beginTransaction();

  Employee employee1 = new Employee();
  employee1.setEmpNumber(5001);
  employee1.setEmpName("Ibrahim");
  employee1.setEmpType("PERMANENT");
  Address employee1Address1 = new Address();
  employee1Address1.setHouseNumber("C-13-4");
  employee1Address1.setStreetName("Jalan Munsi Abdullah");
  employee1Address1.setCityName("Kuala Lumpur");
  employee1Address1.setCountryName("Malaysia");
  employee1Address1.setPostalCode("50100");
  Address employee1Address2 = new Address();
```

```
employee1Address2.setHouseNumber("3-121");
employee1Address2.setStreetName("Middle  Street");
employee1Address2.setCityName("Tiruchirapalli");
employee1Address2.setCountryName("India");
employee1Address2.setPostalCode("621302");
List<Address>  employee1Addresses  =  new  ArrayList<Address>();
employee1Addresses.add(employee1Address1);
employee1Addresses.add(employee1Address2);
employee1.setAddresses(employee1Addresses);
session.save(employee1);
System.out.println("The object employee1 is persisted with session");

Employee  employee2  =  new  Employee();
employee2.setEmpNumber(5002);
employee2.setEmpName("Kumar");
employee2.setEmpType("PERMANENT");
Address  employee2Address1  =  new  Address();
employee2Address1.setHouseNumber("T-4");
employee2Address1.setStreetName("Nehru  Street");
employee2Address1.setCityName("Chennai");
employee2Address1.setCountryName("India");
employee2Address1.setPostalCode("600020");
List<Address>  employee2Addresses  =  new  ArrayList<Address>();
employee2Addresses.add(employee2Address1);
employee2.setAddresses(employee2Addresses);
session.save(employee2);
System.out.println("The object employee2 is persisted with session");

Employee  employee3  =  new  Employee();
employee3.setEmpNumber(5003);
employee3.setEmpName("Ajay");
employee3.setEmpType("CONTRACT");
employee3.setAddresses(null);
session.save(employee3);
System.out.println("The object employee3 is persisted with session");
```

```
txn.commit();
System.out.println("Transaction on this session is committed");

txn = session.beginTransaction();
System.out.println("##### Accessing Employee Objects #####\n\n");
List<Employee> employeeList =
session.createQuery("from Employee").list();
      for (int i = 0; i < employeeList.size(); i++) {
      Employee employee = employeeList.get(i);
System.out.println("Employee Number : " + employee.getEmpNumber());
System.out.println("Employee Name   : " + employee.getEmpName());
System.out.println("Employment Type : " + employee.getEmpType());
List<Address> addresses = employee.getAddresses();
for (int j=0; addresses != null && j < addresses.size(); j++) {
System.out.println("Employee Address (" + (j+1) + ") : " +
addresses.get(j));
            }

System.out.println("========================================\n\n");
      }
txn.commit();

txn = session.beginTransaction();
System.out.println("##### Accessing Employee Objects after Filtering
(Select PERMANENT Employees) #####\n\n");
Filter filter = session.enableFilter("EmployeeCategory");
filter.setParameter("empCategory", "PERMANENT");

employeeList = session.createQuery("from Employee").list();
for (int i = 0; i < employeeList.size(); i++) {
      Employee employee = employeeList.get(i);
System.out.println("Employee Number : " + employee.getEmpNumber());
System.out.println("Employee Name   : " + employee.getEmpName());
System.out.println("Employment Type : " + employee.getEmpType());
      List<Address> addresses = employee.getAddresses();
      for(int j=0; addresses!= null && j<addresses.size();j++){
```

```
System.out.println("Employee Address (" + (j+1) + ") : " +
addresses.get(j));
            }

System.out.println("=========================================\n\n");
        }
        txn.commit();

        txn = session.beginTransaction();
System.out.println("##### Accessing Employee Objects after Filtering
(Select CONTRACT Employees) #####\n\n");
        filter.setParameter("empCategory", "CONTRACT");

        employeeList = session.createQuery("from Employee").list();
        for (int i = 0; i < employeeList.size(); i++) {
        Employee employee = employeeList.get(i);
System.out.println("Employee Number : " + employee.getEmpNumber());
System.out.println("Employee Name   : " + employee.getEmpName());
System.out.println("Employment Type : " + employee.getEmpType());
        List<Address> addresses = employee.getAddresses();
        for (int j=0; addresses != null && j < addresses.size(); j++) {
System.out.println("Employee Address (" + (j+1) + ") : " +
addresses.get(j));
            }

System.out.println("=========================================\n\n");
        }
        txn.commit();

        sessionFactory.close();
    }
}
```

Output:

```
The object employee1 is persisted with session
The object employee2 is persisted with session
The object employee3 is persisted with session
```

```
Hibernate: insert into EMPLOYEE (EMP_NAME, EMP_NUMBER, EMP_TYPE,
ID) values (?, ?, ?, ?)
Hibernate: insert into ADDRESS (CITY_NAME, COUNTRY_NAME, HOUSE_NUMBER,
POSTAL_CODE, STREET_NAME, ID) values (?, ?, ?, ?, ?, ?)
Hibernate: insert into ADDRESS (CITY_NAME, COUNTRY_NAME, HOUSE_NUMBER,
POSTAL_CODE, STREET_NAME, ID) values (?, ?, ?, ?, ?, ?)
Hibernate: insert into EMPLOYEE (EMP_NAME, EMP_NUMBER, EMP_TYPE,
ID) values (?, ?, ?, ?)
Hibernate: insert into ADDRESS (CITY_NAME, COUNTRY_NAME, HOUSE_NUMBER,
POSTAL_CODE, STREET_NAME, ID) values (?, ?, ?, ?, ?, ?)
Hibernate: insert into EMPLOYEE (EMP_NAME, EMP_NUMBER, EMP_TYPE,
ID) values (?, ?, ?, ?)
Hibernate: update ADDRESS set EMPLOYEE_ADDRESS=? where ID=?
Hibernate: update ADDRESS set EMPLOYEE_ADDRESS=? where ID=?
Hibernate: update ADDRESS set EMPLOYEE_ADDRESS=? where ID=?
Transaction on this session is committed
##### Accessing Employee Objects #####

Hibernate: select employee0_.ID as ID0_, employee0_.EMP_NAME as
EMP2_0_, employee0_.EMP_NUMBER as EMP3_0_, employee0_.EMP_TYPE as
EMP4_0_ from EMPLOYEE employee0_
Employee Number      : 5001
Employee Name        : Ibrahim
Employment Type      : PERMANENT
Employee Address (1) : [House Number: C-13-4
Street Name          : Jalan Munsi Abdullah
City Name            : Kuala Lumpur
Country Name         : Malaysia
Postal Code          : 50100]
Employee Address (2) : [House Number: 3-121
Street Name          : Middle Street
City Name            : Tiruchirapalli
Country Name         : India
Postal Code          : 621302]
========================================

Employee Number      : 5002
```

```
Employee Name        : Kumar
Employment Type      : PERMANENT
Employee Address (1) : [House Number: T-4
Street Name          : Nehru Street
City Name            : Chennai
Country Name         : India
Postal Code          : 600020]
========================================
Employee Number      : 5003
Employee Name        : Ajay
Employment Type      : CONTRACT
========================================

##### Accessing Employee Objects after Filtering (Select PERMANENT
Employees) #####

Hibernate: select employee0_.ID as ID0_, employee0_.EMP_NAME as
EMP2_0_, employee0_.EMP_NUMBER as EMP3_0_, employee0_.EMP_TYPE as
EMP4_0_ from EMPLOYEE employee0_ where ? = employee0_.EMP_TYPE
Employee Number      : 5001
Employee Name        : Ibrahim
Employment Type      : PERMANENT
Employee Address (1) : [House Number: C-13-4
Street Name          : Jalan Munsi Abdullah
City Name            : Kuala Lumpur
Country Name         : Malaysia
Postal Code          : 50100]
Employee Address (2) : [House Number: 3-121
Street Name          : Middle Street
City Name            : Tiruchirapalli
Country Name         : India
Postal Code          : 621302]
========================================

Employee Number      : 5002
Employee Name        : Kumar
```

```
Employment Type     : PERMANENT
Employee Address (1) : [House Number: T-4
Street Name         : Nehru Street
City Name           : Chennai
Country Name        : India
Postal Code         : 600020]
=========================================

##### Accessing Employee Objects after Filtering (Select CONTRACT
Employees) #####

Hibernate: select employee0_.ID as ID0_, employee0_.EMP_NAME as
EMP2_0_, employee0_.EMP_NUMBER as EMP3_0_, employee0_.EMP_TYPE as
EMP4_0_ from EMPLOYEE employee0_ where ? = employee0_.EMP_TYPE
Employee Number    : 5003
Employee Name      : Ajay
Employment Type    : CONTRACT
=========================================
```

The above main program uses HQL to retrieve the records. This program can be written using Criteria Query as follows.

```
// File Name: EmployeeManipulation.java
// Filtering Query result using @Filter

package com.hdemo;

import java.util.ArrayList;
import java.util.List;

import org.hibernate.Filter;
import org.hibernate.Session;
import org.hibernate.SessionFactory;
import org.hibernate.Transaction;

public class EmployeeManipulation {

  @SuppressWarnings("unchecked")
  public static void main(String[] args) throws Exception {
```

```
SessionFactory sessionFactory = HibernateUtil.getSessionFactory();
Session session = sessionFactory.openSession();
Transaction txn = session.beginTransaction();

Employee employee1 = new Employee();
employee1.setEmpNumber(5001);
employee1.setEmpName("Ibrahim");
employee1.setEmpType("PERMANENT");
Address employee1Address1 = new Address();
employee1Address1.setHouseNumber("C-13-4");
employee1Address1.setStreetName("Jalan Munsi Abdullah");
employee1Address1.setCityName("Kuala Lumpur");
employee1Address1.setCountryName("Malaysia");
employee1Address1.setPostalCode("50100");
Address employee1Address2 = new Address();
employee1Address2.setHouseNumber("3-121");
employee1Address2.setStreetName("Middle Street");
employee1Address2.setCityName("Tiruchirapalli");
employee1Address2.setCountryName("India");
employee1Address2.setPostalCode("621302");
List<Address> employee1Addresses = new ArrayList<Address>();
employee1Addresses.add(employee1Address1);
employee1Addresses.add(employee1Address2);
employee1.setAddresses(employee1Addresses);
session.save(employee1);
System.out.println("The object employee1 is persisted with session");

Employee employee2 = new Employee();
employee2.setEmpNumber(5002);
employee2.setEmpName("Kumar");
employee2.setEmpType("PERMANENT");
Address employee2Address1 = new Address();
employee2Address1.setHouseNumber("T-4");
employee2Address1.setStreetName("Nehru Street");
employee2Address1.setCityName("Chennai");
employee2Address1.setCountryName("India");
```

```
employee2Address1.setPostalCode("600020");
List<Address> employee2Addresses = new ArrayList<Address>();
employee2Addresses.add(employee2Address1);
employee2.setAddresses(employee2Addresses);
session.save(employee2);
System.out.println("The object employee2 is persisted with session");

Employee employee3 = new Employee();
employee3.setEmpNumber(5003);
employee3.setEmpName("Ajay");
employee3.setEmpType("CONTRACT");
employee3.setAddresses(null);
session.save(employee3);
System.out.println("The object employee3 is persisted with session");

txn.commit();
System.out.println("Transaction on this session is committed");

txn = session.beginTransaction();
System.out.println("##### Accessing Employee Objects #####\n\n");
List<Employee> employeeList = session.createCriteria
(Employee.class).list();
      for (int i = 0; i < employeeList.size(); i++) {
      Employee employee = employeeList.get(i);
System.out.println("Employee Number : " + employee.getEmpNumber());
System.out.println("Employee Name   : " + employee.getEmpName());
System.out.println("Employment Type : " + employee.getEmpType());
      List<Address> addresses = employee.getAddresses();
      for (int j=0; addresses != null && j < addresses.size(); j++) {
System.out.println("Employee Address (" + (j+1) + ") : " +
addresses.get(j));
           }

System.out.println("=====================================\n\n");
      }
      txn.commit();
```

```
        txn = session.beginTransaction();
    System.out.println("##### Accessing Employee Objects after Filtering
    (Select PERMANENT Employees) #####\n\n");
        Filter filter = session.enableFilter("EmployeeCategory");
        filter.setParameter("empCategory", "PERMANENT");

        employeeList = session.createCriteria(Employee.class).list();
        for (int i = 0; i < employeeList.size(); i++) {
            Employee employee = employeeList.get(i);
    System.out.println("Employee Number : " + employee.getEmpNumber());
    System.out.println("Employee Name    : " + employee.getEmpName());
    System.out.println("Employment Type : " + employee.getEmpType());
        List<Address> addresses = employee.getAddresses();
        for(int j=0; addresses != null && j < addresses.size(); j++) {
    System.out.println("Employee Address (" + (j+1) + ") : " +
    addresses.get(j));
            }

    System.out.println("========================================\n\n");
        }
        txn.commit();

        txn = session.beginTransaction();
    System.out.println("##### Accessing Employee Objects after Filtering
    (Select CONTRACT Employees) #####\n\n");
        filter.setParameter("empCategory", "CONTRACT");

        employeeList = session.createCriteria(Employee.class).list();
        for (int i = 0; i < employeeList.size(); i++) {
    Employee employee = employeeList.get(i);
    System.out.println("Employee Number : " + employee.getEmpNumber());
    System.out.println("Employee Name    : " + employee.getEmpName());
    System.out.println("Employment Type : " + employee.getEmpType());
        List<Address> addresses = employee.getAddresses();
        for(int j=0; addresses != null && j < addresses.size(); j++) {
    System.out.println("Employee Address (" + (j+1) + ") : " +
    addresses.get(j));
```

```
                  }

      System.out.println("=========================================\n\n");
            }
            txn.commit();

            sessionFactory.close();
      }
  }
```

The following example defines and uses two filters to get employees where they are PERMANENT and their names contain the string 'rahim'. Keep the same code for Address class.

```
// File Name: Employee.java
// Filtering Query result using @Filters

package com.hdemo;

import java.util.List;

import javax.persistence.CascadeType;
import javax.persistence.Column;
import javax.persistence.Entity;
import javax.persistence.GeneratedValue;
import javax.persistence.Id;
import javax.persistence.JoinColumn;
import javax.persistence.OneToMany;
import javax.persistence.Table;

import org.hibernate.annotations.Filter;
import org.hibernate.annotations.FilterDef;
import org.hibernate.annotations.FilterDefs;
import org.hibernate.annotations.Filters;
import org.hibernate.annotations.GenericGenerator;
import org.hibernate.annotations.ParamDef;

@Entity
@Table(name = "EMPLOYEE")
```

```
@FilterDefs(value = {@FilterDef(name = "EmployeeCategoryFilter",
parameters = @ParamDef(name = "employeeCategory", type="string")) ,
@FilterDef(name = "EmployeeNameFilter",
parameters = @ParamDef(name = "employeeName", type = "string"))  })
@Filters(value = {@Filter(name = "EmployeeCategoryFilter",
condition = "EMP_TYPE = :employeeCategory") ,
@Filter(name = "EmployeeNameFilter",
condition = "EMP_NAME like :employeeName")     })

public class Employee {

  @Id
  @GeneratedValue(generator = "idGen")
  @GenericGenerator(name = "idGen", strategy = "uuid.hex")
  @Column(name = "ID", length = 32)
  private String id = "";

  @Column(name = "EMP_NUMBER", unique = true, nullable = false)
  private Integer empNumber;

  @Column(name = "EMP_NAME", length = 64, nullable = false)
  private String empName;

  @Column(name = "EMP_TYPE", length = 64, nullable = false)
  private String empType;

  @OneToMany(cascade = CascadeType.ALL)
  @JoinColumn(name = "EMPLOYEE_ADDRESS")
  private List<Address> addresses;

  //Getter and Setter methods

}
```

```
// File Name: EmployeeManipulation.java
// Filtering Query result using @Filter

package com.hdemo;
```

```
import  java.util.ArrayList;
import java.util.List;

import  org.hibernate.Filter;
import  org.hibernate.Session;
import  org.hibernate.SessionFactory;
import  org.hibernate.Transaction;

public  class  EmployeeManipulation  {

  @SuppressWarnings("unchecked")
  public  static  void  main(String[]  args)  throws  Exception  {
  SessionFactory sessionFactory = HibernateUtil.getSessionFactory();
  Session  session  =  sessionFactory.openSession();
  Transaction  txn  =  session.beginTransaction();

  Employee  employee1  =  new  Employee();
  employee1.setEmpNumber(5001);
  employee1.setEmpName("Ibrahim");
  employee1.setEmpType("PERMANENT");
  Address  employee1Address1  =  new  Address();
  employee1Address1.setHouseNumber("C-13-4");
  employee1Address1.setStreetName("Jalan  Munsi  Abdullah");
  employee1Address1.setCityName("Kuala  Lumpur");
  employee1Address1.setCountryName("Malaysia");
  employee1Address1.setPostalCode("50100");
  Address  employee1Address2  =  new  Address();
  employee1Address2.setHouseNumber("3-121");
  employee1Address2.setStreetName("Middle  Street");
  employee1Address2.setCityName("Tiruchirapalli");
  employee1Address2.setCountryName("India");
  employee1Address2.setPostalCode("621302");
  List<Address>  employee1Addresses  =  new  ArrayList<Address>();
  employee1Addresses.add(employee1Address1);
  employee1Addresses.add(employee1Address2);
  employee1.setAddresses(employee1Addresses);
```

```
session.save(employee1);
System.out.println("The object employee1 is persisted with session");

Employee employee2 = new Employee();
employee2.setEmpNumber(5002);
employee2.setEmpName("Kumar");
employee2.setEmpType("PERMANENT");
Address employee2Address1 = new Address();
employee2Address1.setHouseNumber("T-4");
employee2Address1.setStreetName("Nehru Street");
employee2Address1.setCityName("Chennai");
employee2Address1.setCountryName("India");
employee2Address1.setPostalCode("600020");
List<Address> employee2Addresses = new ArrayList<Address>();
employee2Addresses.add(employee2Address1);
employee2.setAddresses(employee2Addresses);
session.save(employee2);
System.out.println("The object employee2 is persisted with session");

Employee employee3 = new Employee();
employee3.setEmpNumber(5003);
employee3.setEmpName("Ajay");
employee3.setEmpType("CONTRACT");
employee3.setAddresses(null);
session.save(employee3);
System.out.println("The object employee3 is persisted with session");

txn.commit();
System.out.println("Transaction on this session is committed");

txn = session.beginTransaction();
System.out.println("##### Accessing Employee Objects #####\n\n");
List<Employee> employeeList = session.createQuery("from
Employee").list();
      for (int i = 0; i < employeeList.size(); i++) {
      Employee employee = employeeList.get(i);
```

```
System.out.println("Employee Number : " + employee.getEmpNumber());
System.out.println("Employee Name   : " + employee.getEmpName());
System.out.println("Employment Type : " + employee.getEmpType());
      List<Address> addresses = employee.getAddresses();
      for(int j=0; addresses != null && j < addresses.size(); j++) {
System.out.println("Employee Address (" + (j+1) + ") : " +
addresses.get(j));
      }

System.out.println("========================================\n\n");
      }
      txn.commit();

      txn = session.beginTransaction();
System.out.println("##### Accessing Employee Objects after Filtering
\n" + "(Select Employees where their Emp_Types are PERMANENT and
Emp_Names contain the string 'rahim' #####\n\n");
Filter filterEmpCategory = session.enableFilter("EmployeeCategory
Filter");filterEmpCategory.setParameter("employeeCategory",
"PERMANENT");

Filter filterEmpName = session.enableFilter("EmployeeNameFilter");
      filterEmpName.setParameter("employeeName", "%rahim%");

      employeeList = session.createQuery("from Employee").list();
      for (int i = 0; i < employeeList.size(); i++) {
      Employee employee = employeeList.get(i);
System.out.println("Employee Number : " + employee.getEmpNumber());
System.out.println("Employee Name   : " + employee.getEmpName());
System.out.println("Employment Type : " + employee.getEmpType());
      List<Address> addresses = employee.getAddresses();
      for(int j=0; addresses != null && j < addresses.size(); j++) {
System.out.println("Employee Address (" + (j+1) + ") : " +
addresses.get(j));
            }

System.out.println("========================================\n\n");
```

```
        }
        txn.commit();
        sessionFactory.close();
    }
}
```

Output:

```
The object employee1 is persisted with session
The object employee2 is persisted with session
The object employee3 is persisted with session
Hibernate: insert into EMPLOYEE (EMP_NAME, EMP_NUMBER, EMP_TYPE,
ID) values (?, ?, ?, ?)
Hibernate: insert into ADDRESS (CITY_NAME, COUNTRY_NAME, HOUSE_NUMBER,
POSTAL_CODE, STREET_NAME, ID) values (?, ?, ?, ?, ?, ?)
Hibernate: insert into ADDRESS (CITY_NAME, COUNTRY_NAME, HOUSE_NUMBER,
POSTAL_CODE, STREET_NAME, ID) values (?, ?, ?, ?, ?, ?)
Hibernate: insert into EMPLOYEE (EMP_NAME, EMP_NUMBER, EMP_TYPE,
ID) values (?, ?, ?, ?)
Hibernate: insert into ADDRESS (CITY_NAME, COUNTRY_NAME, HOUSE_NUMBER,
POSTAL_CODE, STREET_NAME, ID) values (?, ?, ?, ?, ?, ?)
Hibernate: insert into EMPLOYEE (EMP_NAME, EMP_NUMBER, EMP_TYPE,
ID) values (?, ?, ?, ?)
Hibernate: update ADDRESS set EMPLOYEE_ADDRESS=? where ID=?
Hibernate: update ADDRESS set EMPLOYEE_ADDRESS=? where ID=?
Hibernate: update ADDRESS set EMPLOYEE_ADDRESS=? where ID=?
Transaction on this session is committed
##### Accessing Employee Objects #####

Hibernate: select employee0_.ID as ID0_, employee0_.EMP_NAME as
EMP2_0_, employee0_.EMP_NUMBER as EMP3_0_, employee0_.EMP_TYPE as
EMP4_0_ from EMPLOYEE employee0_
Employee Number      : 5001
Employee Name        : Ibrahim
Employment Type      : PERMANENT
Employee Address(1)  : [House Number: C-13-4
Street Name          : Jalan Munsi Abdullah
City Name            : Kuala Lumpur
```

```
Country Name          : Malaysia
Postal Code           : 50100]
Employee Address(2)  : [House Number: 3-121
Street Name           : Middle Street
City Name             : Tiruchirapalli
Country Name          : India
Postal Code           : 621302]
========================================

Employee Number       : 5002
Employee Name         : Kumar
Employment Type       : PERMANENT
Employee Address(1)  : [House Number: T-4
Street Name           : Nehru Street
City Name             : Chennai
Country Name          : India
Postal Code           : 600020]
========================================

Employee Number       : 5003
Employee Name         : Ajay
Employment Type       : CONTRACT
========================================

##### Accessing Employee Objects after Filtering
(Select Employees where their Emp_Types are PERMANENT and Emp_Names
contain the string 'rahim' #####

Hibernate: select employee0_.ID as ID0_, employee0_.EMP_NAME as
EMP2_0_, employee0_.EMP_NUMBER as EMP3_0_, employee0_.EMP_TYPE as
EMP4_0_ from EMPLOYEE employee0_ where employee0_.EMP_TYPE = ? and
employee0_.EMP_NAME like ?
Employee Number       : 5001
Employee Name         : Ibrahim
Employment Type       : PERMANENT
Employee Address(1)  : [House Number: C-13-4
Street Name           : Jalan Munsi Abdullah
```

```
City Name           : Kuala Lumpur
Country Name        : Malaysia
Postal Code         : 50100]
Employee Address(2) : [House Number: 3-121
Street Name         : Middle Street
City Name           : Tiruchirapalli
Country Name        : India
Postal Code         : 621302]
=========================================
```

In the above entity, we are using two @FilterDefs and two @Filters to filter data. We can achieve the same using single @FilterDef with two parameters and single @Filter as follows.

```
// File Name: Employee.java
// Filtering Query result using @Filter

package com.hdemo;

import java.util.List;

import javax.persistence.CascadeType;
import javax.persistence.Column;
import javax.persistence.Entity;
import javax.persistence.GeneratedValue;
import javax.persistence.Id;
import javax.persistence.JoinColumn;
import javax.persistence.OneToMany;
import javax.persistence.Table;

import org.hibernate.annotations.Filter;
import org.hibernate.annotations.FilterDef;
import org.hibernate.annotations.GenericGenerator;
import org.hibernate.annotations.ParamDef;

@Entity
@Table(name = "EMPLOYEE")
@FilterDef(name = "EmployeeCategoryNameFilter",
```

```
        parameters = { @ParamDef(name = "employeeCategory",
        type = "string"),
        @ParamDef(name = "employeeName",
        type = "string")
                                    }
                  )
@Filter(name = "EmployeeCategoryNameFilter",
condition = "EMP_TYPE = :employeeCategory AND EMP_NAME like:
employeeName")

public class Employee {

   @Id
   @GeneratedValue(generator = "idGen")
   @GenericGenerator(name = "idGen", strategy = "uuid.hex")
   @Column(name = "ID", length = 32)
   private String id = "";

   @Column(name = "EMP_NUMBER", unique = true, nullable = false)
   private Integer empNumber;

   @Column(name = "EMP_NAME", length = 64, nullable = false)
   private String empName;

   @Column(name = "EMP_TYPE", length = 64, nullable = false)
   private String empType;

   @OneToMany(cascade = CascadeType.ALL)
   @JoinColumn(name = "EMPLOYEE_ADDRESS")
   private List<Address> addresses;

   //Getter and Setter methods

}
```

```
// File Name: EmployeeManipulation.java
// Filtering Query result using @Filter

package com.hdemo;
```

```
import java.util.ArrayList;
import java.util.List;

import org.hibernate.Filter;
import org.hibernate.Session;
import org.hibernate.SessionFactory;
import org.hibernate.Transaction;

public class EmployeeManipulation {

   @SuppressWarnings("unchecked")
   public static void main(String[] args) throws Exception {
   SessionFactory sessionFactory = HibernateUtil.getSessionFactory();
   Session session = sessionFactory.openSession();
   Transaction txn = session.beginTransaction();

   Employee employee1 = new Employee();
   employee1.setEmpNumber(5001);
   employee1.setEmpName("Ibrahim");
   employee1.setEmpType("PERMANENT");
   Address employee1Address1 = new Address();
   employee1Address1.setHouseNumber("C-13-4");
   employee1Address1.setStreetName("Jalan Munsi Abdullah");
   employee1Address1.setCityName("Kuala Lumpur");
   employee1Address1.setCountryName("Malaysia");
   employee1Address1.setPostalCode("50100");
   Address employee1Address2 = new Address();
   employee1Address2.setHouseNumber("3-121");
   employee1Address2.setStreetName("Middle Street");
   employee1Address2.setCityName("Tiruchirapalli");
   employee1Address2.setCountryName("India");
   employee1Address2.setPostalCode("621302");
   List<Address> employee1Addresses = new ArrayList<Address>();
   employee1Addresses.add(employee1Address1);
   employee1Addresses.add(employee1Address2);
   employee1.setAddresses(employee1Addresses);
```

```
session.save(employee1);
System.out.println("The object employee1 is persisted with session");

Employee employee2 = new Employee();
employee2.setEmpNumber(5002);
employee2.setEmpName("Kumar");
employee2.setEmpType("PERMANENT");
Address employee2Address1 = new Address();
employee2Address1.setHouseNumber("T-4");
employee2Address1.setStreetName("Nehru Street");
employee2Address1.setCityName("Chennai");
employee2Address1.setCountryName("India");
employee2Address1.setPostalCode("600020");
List<Address> employee2Addresses = new ArrayList<Address>();
employee2Addresses.add(employee2Address1);
employee2.setAddresses(employee2Addresses);
session.save(employee2);
System.out.println("The object employee2 is persisted with session");

Employee employee3 = new Employee();
employee3.setEmpNumber(5003);
employee3.setEmpName("Ajay");
employee3.setEmpType("CONTRACT");
employee3.setAddresses(null);
session.save(employee3);
System.out.println("The object employee3 is persisted with session");

txn.commit();
System.out.println("Transaction on this session is committed");

txn = session.beginTransaction();
System.out.println("##### Accessing Employee Objects #####\n\n");
List<Employee> employeeList = session.createQuery("from
Employee").list();
      for (int i = 0; i < employeeList.size(); i++) {
      Employee employee = employeeList.get(i);
```

```
System.out.println("Employee Number : " + employee.getEmpNumber());
System.out.println("Employee Name    : " + employee.getEmpName());
System.out.println("Employment Type : " + employee.getEmpType());
List<Address> addresses = employee.getAddresses();
for (int j=0; addresses != null && j < addresses.size(); j++) {
System.out.println("Employee Address (" + (j+1) +
") : " + addresses.get(j));
        }

System.out.println("========================================\n\n");
      }

      txn.commit();

      txn = session.beginTransaction();
System.out.println("##### Accessing Employee Objects after Filtering
\n" +
"(Select Employees where their Emp_Types are PERMANENT and Emp_Names
contain the string 'rahim' #####\n\n");
Filter filterEmpCategoryName = session.enableFilter("Employee
CategoryNameFilter");
filterEmpCategoryName.setParameter("employeeCategory", "PERMANENT");
filterEmpCategoryName.setParameter("employeeName", "%rahim%");

employeeList = session.createQuery("from Employee").list();
for (int i = 0; i < employeeList.size(); i++) {
      Employee employee = employeeList.get(i);
System.out.println("Employee Number : " + employee.getEmpNumber());
System.out.println("Employee Name    : " + employee.getEmpName());
System.out.println("Employment Type : " + employee.getEmpType());
List<Address> addresses = employee.getAddresses();
for (int j=0; addresses != null && j < addresses.size(); j++) {
System.out.println("Employee Address (" + (j+1) +
") : " + addresses.get(j));
      }

System.out.println("========================================\n\n");
      }
```

```
            txn.commit();

            sessionFactory.close();
      }
}
```

Output:

```
The object employee1 is persisted with session
The object employee2 is persisted with session
The object employee3 is persisted with session
Hibernate: insert into EMPLOYEE (EMP_NAME, EMP_NUMBER, EMP_TYPE,
ID) values (?, ?, ?, ?)
Hibernate: insert into ADDRESS (CITY_NAME, COUNTRY_NAME, HOUSE_NUMBER,
POSTAL_CODE, STREET_NAME, ID) values (?, ?, ?, ?, ?, ?)
Hibernate: insert into ADDRESS (CITY_NAME, COUNTRY_NAME, HOUSE_NUMBER,
POSTAL_CODE, STREET_NAME, ID) values (?, ?, ?, ?, ?, ?)
Hibernate: insert into EMPLOYEE (EMP_NAME, EMP_NUMBER, EMP_TYPE,
ID) values (?, ?, ?, ?)
Hibernate: insert into ADDRESS (CITY_NAME, COUNTRY_NAME, HOUSE_NUMBER,
POSTAL_CODE, STREET_NAME, ID) values (?, ?, ?, ?, ?, ?)
Hibernate: insert into EMPLOYEE (EMP_NAME, EMP_NUMBER, EMP_TYPE,
ID) values (?, ?, ?, ?)
Hibernate: update ADDRESS set EMPLOYEE_ADDRESS=? where ID=?
Hibernate: update ADDRESS set EMPLOYEE_ADDRESS=? where ID=?
Hibernate: update ADDRESS set EMPLOYEE_ADDRESS=? where ID=?
Transaction on this session is committed
##### Accessing Employee Objects #####

Hibernate: select employee0_.ID as ID0_, employee0_.EMP_NAME as
EMP2_0_, employee0_.EMP_NUMBER as EMP3_0_, employee0_.EMP_TYPE as
EMP4_0_ from EMPLOYEE employee0_
Employee Number     : 5001
Employee Name       : Ibrahim
Employment Type     : PERMANENT
Employee Address(1) : [House Number: C-13-4
Street Name         : Jalan Munsi Abdullah
City Name           : Kuala Lumpur
```

```
Country Name          : Malaysia
Postal Code           : 50100]
Employee Address(2)   : [House Number: 3-121
Street Name           : Middle Street
City Name             : Tiruchirapalli
Country Name          : India
Postal Code           : 621302]
=========================================

Employee Number       : 5002
Employee Name         : Kumar
Employment Type       : PERMANENT
Employee Address(1)   : [House Number: T-4
Street Name           : Nehru Street
City Name             : Chennai
Country Name          : India
Postal Code           : 600020]
=========================================

Employee Number       : 5003
Employee Name         : Ajay
Employment Type       : CONTRACT
=========================================

##### Accessing Employee Objects after Filtering
(Select Employees where their Emp_Types are PERMANENT and Emp_Names
contain the string 'rahim' #####

Hibernate: select employee0_.ID as ID0_, employee0_.EMP_NAME as
EMP2_0_, employee0_.EMP_NUMBER as EMP3_0_, employee0_.EMP_TYPE as
EMP4_0_ from EMPLOYEE employee0_ where employee0_.EMP_TYPE = ? AND
employee0_.EMP_NAME like ?
Employee Number       : 5001
Employee Name         : Ibrahim
Employment Type       : PERMANENT
Employee Address(1)   : [House Number: C-13-4
Street Name           : Jalan Munsi Abdullah
```

```
City Name               : Kuala Lumpur
Country Name            : Malaysia
Postal Code             : 50100]
Employee Address (2) : [House Number: 3-121
Street Name             : Middle Street
City Name               : Tiruchirapalli
Country Name            : India
Postal Code             : 621302]
========================================
```

The following example uses filter operation at Query level (not at Entities) to retrieve all Employees with their Addresses where Country Name is "India".

```
// File Name: Employee.java
// Filtering Query result

package com.hdemo;

import java.util.List;

import javax.persistence.CascadeType;
import javax.persistence.Column;
import javax.persistence.Entity;
import javax.persistence.GeneratedValue;
import javax.persistence.Id;
import javax.persistence.JoinColumn;
import javax.persistence.OneToMany;
import javax.persistence.Table;

import org.hibernate.annotations.GenericGenerator;

@Entity
@Table(name = "EMPLOYEE")
public class Employee {

   @Id
   @GeneratedValue(generator = "idGen")
   @GenericGenerator(name = "idGen", strategy = "uuid.hex")
   @Column(name = "ID", length = 32)
```

```
    private String id = "";

    @Column(name = "EMP_NUMBER", unique = true, nullable = false)
    private Integer empNumber;

    @Column(name = "EMP_NAME", length = 64, nullable = false)
    private String empName;

    @Column(name = "EMP_TYPE", length = 64, nullable = false)
    private String empType;

    @OneToMany(cascade = CascadeType.ALL)
    @JoinColumn(name = "EMPLOYEE_ADDRESS")
    private List<Address> addresses;

    //Getter and Setter methods

}
```

```
// File Name: Address.java
// Filtering Query result

package com.hdemo;

import javax.persistence.Column;
import javax.persistence.Entity;
import javax.persistence.GeneratedValue;
import javax.persistence.Id;
import javax.persistence.Table;

import org.hibernate.annotations.GenericGenerator;

@Entity
@Table(name = "ADDRESS")

public class Address {

    @Id
    @GeneratedValue(generator = "idGen")
    @GenericGenerator(name = "idGen", strategy = "uuid.hex")
```

```
    @Column(name = "ID", length = 32)
    private String id = "";

    @Column(name = "HOUSE_NUMBER", length = 8)
    private String houseNumber;

    @Column(name = "STREET_NAME", length = 64)
    private String streetName;

    @Column(name = "CITY_NAME", length = 64)
    private String cityName;

    @Column(name = "COUNTRY_NAME", length = 64)
    private String countryName;

    @Column(name = "POSTAL_CODE", length = 16)
    private String postalCode;

    //Getter and Setter methods

    public String toString() {
          return "[House Number       : " + houseNumber +
                       "\nStreet Name  : " + streetName +
                       "\nCity Name    : " + cityName +
                       "\nCountry Name : " + countryName +
                       "\nPostal Code  : " + postalCode +
                       "]";
    }
}
```

```
// File Name: EmployeeManipulation.java
// Filtering Query result

package com.hdemo;

import java.util.ArrayList;
import java.util.List;
```

```
import org.hibernate.Session;
import org.hibernate.SessionFactory;
import org.hibernate.Transaction;

public class EmployeeManipulation {

  @SuppressWarnings("unchecked")
  public static void main(String[] args) throws Exception {
  SessionFactory sessionFactory = HibernateUtil.getSessionFactory();
  Session session = sessionFactory.openSession();
  Transaction txn = session.beginTransaction();

  Employee employee1 = new Employee();
  employee1.setEmpNumber(5001);
  employee1.setEmpName("Ibrahim");
  employee1.setEmpType("PERMANENT");
  Address employee1Address1 = new Address();
  employee1Address1.setHouseNumber("C-13-4");
  employee1Address1.setStreetName("Jalan Munsi Abdullah");
  employee1Address1.setCityName("Kuala Lumpur");
  employee1Address1.setCountryName("Malaysia");
  employee1Address1.setPostalCode("50100");
  Address employee1Address2 = new Address();
  employee1Address2.setHouseNumber("3-121");
  employee1Address2.setStreetName("Middle Street");
  employee1Address2.setCityName("Tiruchirapalli");
  employee1Address2.setCountryName("India");
  employee1Address2.setPostalCode("621302");
  List<Address> employee1Addresses = new ArrayList<Address>();
  employee1Addresses.add(employee1Address1);
  employee1Addresses.add(employee1Address2);
  employee1.setAddresses(employee1Addresses);
  session.save(employee1);
  System.out.println("The object employee1 is persisted with session");

  Employee employee2 = new Employee();
       employee2.setEmpNumber(5002);
```

```
employee2.setEmpName("Kumar");
employee2.setEmpType("PERMANENT");
Address employee2Address1 = new Address();
employee2Address1.setHouseNumber("T-4");
employee2Address1.setStreetName("Nehru Street");
employee2Address1.setCityName("Chennai");
employee2Address1.setCountryName("India");
employee2Address1.setPostalCode("600020");
List<Address> employee2Addresses = new ArrayList<Address>();
employee2Addresses.add(employee2Address1);
employee2.setAddresses(employee2Addresses);
session.save(employee2);
System.out.println("The object employee2 is persisted with session");

Employee employee3 = new Employee();
employee3.setEmpNumber(5003);
employee3.setEmpName("Ajay");
employee3.setEmpType("CONTRACT");
employee3.setAddresses(null);
session.save(employee3);
System.out.println("The object employee3 is persisted with session");

      txn.commit();
System.out.println("Transaction on this session is committed");

      txn = session.beginTransaction();
System.out.println("##### Accessing Employee Objects #####\n\n");
List<Employee> employeeList =
session.createQuery("from Employee").list();
      for (int i = 0; i < employeeList.size(); i++) {
      Employee employee = employeeList.get(i);
System.out.println("Employee Number : " + employee.getEmpNumber());
System.out.println("Employee Name   : " + employee.getEmpName());
System.out.println("Employment Type : " + employee.getEmpType());
      List<Address> addresses = employee.getAddresses();
      for (int j = 0; addresses != null && j < addresses.size(); j++) {
```

```
System.out.println("Employee Address (" +
(j + 1) + ") : " + addresses.get(j));
        }

System.out.println("========================================\n\n");
    }
    txn.commit();

    txn = session.beginTransaction();
System.out.println("##### Accessing Employee Objects after Filtering
\n" + "(Select Employees where their Country is India) ####\n\n");

employeeList = session.createQuery("from Employee").list();
    for (int i = 0; i < employeeList.size(); i++) {
    Employee employee = employeeList.get(i);
System.out.println("Employee Number : " + employee.getEmpNumber());
System.out.println("Employee Name   : " + employee.getEmpName());
System.out.println("Employment Type : " + employee.getEmpType());
    List<Address> addresses = employee.getAddresses();
    if (addresses != null) {
List<Address> filteredAddresses = session.createFilter(addresses,
"where this.countryName is ?").setString(0, "India").list();
    for (int j = 0; filteredAddresses != null && j <
    filteredAddresses.size(); j++) {
System.out.println("Employee Address (" +
(j + 1) + ") : " + filteredAddresses.get(j));
            }
        }

System.out.println("========================================\n\n");
    }
    txn.commit();

    sessionFactory.close();
}

}
```

Output:

```
The object employee1 is persisted with session
The object employee2 is persisted with session
The object employee3 is persisted with session
Hibernate: insert into EMPLOYEE (EMP_NAME, EMP_NUMBER, EMP_TYPE,
ID) values (?, ?, ?, ?)
Hibernate: insert into ADDRESS (CITY_NAME, COUNTRY_NAME, HOUSE_NUMBER,
POSTAL_CODE, STREET_NAME, ID) values (?, ?, ?, ?, ?, ?)
Hibernate: insert into ADDRESS (CITY_NAME, COUNTRY_NAME, HOUSE_NUMBER,
POSTAL_CODE, STREET_NAME, ID) values (?, ?, ?, ?, ?, ?)
Hibernate: insert into EMPLOYEE (EMP_NAME, EMP_NUMBER, EMP_TYPE,
ID) values (?, ?, ?, ?)
Hibernate: insert into ADDRESS (CITY_NAME, COUNTRY_NAME, HOUSE_NUMBER,
POSTAL_CODE, STREET_NAME, ID) values (?, ?, ?, ?, ?, ?)
Hibernate: insert into EMPLOYEE (EMP_NAME, EMP_NUMBER, EMP_TYPE,
ID) values (?, ?, ?, ?)
Hibernate: update ADDRESS set EMPLOYEE_ADDRESS=? where ID=?
Hibernate: update ADDRESS set EMPLOYEE_ADDRESS=? where ID=?
Hibernate: update ADDRESS set EMPLOYEE_ADDRESS=? where ID=?
Transaction on this session is committed
##### Accessing Employee Objects #####

Hibernate: select employee0_.ID as ID0_, employee0_.EMP_NAME as
EMP2_0_, employee0_.EMP_NUMBER as EMP3_0_, employee0_.EMP_TYPE as
EMP4_0_ from EMPLOYEE employee0_
Employee Number      : 5001
Employee Name        : Ibrahim
Employment Type      : PERMANENT
Employee Address(1)  : [House Number: C-13-4
Street Name          : Jalan Munsi Abdullah
City Name            : Kuala Lumpur
Country Name         : Malaysia
Postal Code          : 50100]
Employee Address(2)  : [House Number: 3-121
Street Name          : Middle Street
City Name            : Tiruchirapalli
```

```
Country Name        : India
Postal Code         : 621302]
========================================

Employee Number     : 5002
Employee Name       : Kumar
Employment Type     : PERMANENT
Employee Address(1) : [House Number: T-4
Street Name         : Nehru Street
City Name           : Chennai
Country Name        : India
Postal Code         : 600020]
========================================

Employee Number     : 5003
Employee Name       : Ajay
Employment Type     : CONTRACT
========================================

##### Accessing Employee Objects after Filtering
(Select Employees where their Country is India) ####

Hibernate: select employee0_.ID as ID0_, employee0_.EMP_NAME as
EMP2_0_, employee0_.EMP_NUMBER as EMP3_0_, employee0_.EMP_TYPE as
EMP4_0_ from EMPLOYEE employee0_
Employee Number     : 5001
Employee Name       : Ibrahim
Employment Type     : PERMANENT
Hibernate: select address0_.ID as ID1_, address0_.CITY_NAME as
CITY2_1_, address0_.COUNTRY_NAME as COUNTRY3_1_, address0_.HOUSE_NUMBER
as HOUSE4_1_, address0_.POSTAL_CODE as POSTAL5_1_,
address0_.STREET_NAME as STREET6_1_ from ADDRESS address0_ where
address0_.EMPLOYEE_ADDRESS = ? and address0_.COUNTRY_NAME=?
Employee Address (1) : [House Number: 3-121
Street Name         : Middle Street
City Name           : Tiruchirapalli
Country Name        : India
Postal Code         : 621302]
========================================
```

```
Employee Number      : 5002
Employee Name        : Kumar
Employment Type      : PERMANENT
Hibernate: select address0_.ID as ID1_, address0_.CITY_NAME as CITY2_1_, address0_.COUNTRY_NAME as COUNTRY3_1_, address0_.HOUSE_NUMBER as HOUSE4_1_, address0_.POSTAL_CODE as POSTAL5_1_, address0_.STREET_NAME as STREET6_1_ from ADDRESS address0_ where address0_.EMPLOYEE_ADDRESS = ? and address0_.COUNTRY_NAME=?
Employee Address(1): [House Number: T-4
Street Name          : Nehru Street
City Name            : Chennai
Country Name         : India
Postal Code          : 600020]
========================================

Employee Number      : 5003
Employee Name        : Ajay
Employment Type      : CONTRACT
========================================
```

4.29 LIFECYCLE EVENT ANNOTATIONS AND `EntityManager`

In every state of Entity's lifecycle (before loading, after loading, before its object is removed, after its object is removed ...) we can make some methods to be invoked automatically (yes, you can compare EJB 2 *callback* methods). Some of Lifecycle event annotations are briefed below.

These annotations can be applied to any public no-argument no-return method and the method name should not start with *'ejb'*. We can directly annotate to an entity or we can also use Entity Listener classes and specifying them in Entity using `@EntityListeners`.

Note that in our examples, we are using `Session` object for CRUD (Create, Read, Update, and Delete) and other operations on entities with database. We can do these operations with some other methods also, for example `EntityManager` also supports these operations. But, we must take care of method call as the method names will vary accordingly. For example, to delete an entity object we use `delete()` method in Session, but we should use `remove()` method in `EntityManager` as `delete()` method is not present in `EntityManager`. However, these Entity lifecycle callback methods will be called based on events, not based on method names. So, we can use either `Session` **or** `EntityManager`, the required callback methods will be called.

4.29.1 `@PrePersist`

The corresponding callback method (the method we declared this annotation) will be invoked before the entity is going to be persisted with database. (While calling `save()`, `persist()` methods; the callback method will also be called when `merge()` is also called which creates newly managed instance of the entity.). This Pre-persist event will happen just before inserting the row in to database (usually during session is flushed / transaction on the session is committed).

4.29.2 `@PostPersist`

The corresponding callback method is called after the entity is persisted with the database. This Post-persist event will happen just after the row is inserted into the database. (Usually after session is flushed / transaction on the session is committed).

4.29.3 `@PreRemove`

The corresponding callback method will be invoked before the entity is going to be deleted from the database. (While calling `delete()` method, in case of Session). This Pre-persist event will happen just before deleting a row from the database.

4.29.4 `@PostRemove`

The corresponding callback method is called after the entity is deleted from the database. This Post-remove event will happen just after the row is deleted from the database. (Usually after session is flushed / transaction on the session is committed).

4.29.5 `@PreUpdate`

The corresponding callback method will be invoked before the entity is going to be updated with the database. (While calling `update()` method, in case of Session, while `merge()` results in updation). This Pre-update event will happen just before updating a row with the database.

4.29.6 `@PostUpdate`

The corresponding callback method is called after the entity is updated in the database. This Post-update event will happen just after the row is updated from the database. (Usually after session is flushed/transaction on the session is committed).

4.29.7 `@PreLoad`

The corresponding callback method is called after the entity has been loaded into the current persistence context from the database (after select the row from database), also after refreshing the entity (using `refresh()` method).

Working with EntityManager

The Hibernate EntityManager provides the programming interfaces and lifecycle rules as defined by the EJB3 persistence specification. Generally these persistence are used in an EJB3 containers (application server is required). However, this persistence is also available for standalone Java applications (JSE applications).

We have used `org.hibernate.Session` for persisting and manipulating entities in earlier sections. Those operations can also be done using EntityManager. The above said Life cycle callback methods will not be invoked if you are using Hibernate Session to persist and manipulate objects. You are needed to use EntityManager interface which will invoke those lifecycle callback methods automatically. In general, this EntityManager is used in EJB3 environment, requires EJB3 supported application server like JBoss. This application server EJB3 environment provides sophistication to instantiate EntityManager and persist entities. However, we can instantiate EntityManager in a standalone Java application, no need to have an application server. The following example is a standalone Java application which uses EntityManager for persistence, with additional settings. Note that we can also use both Hibernate Session and EntityManager in a same application.

Just to remind you, we are using the following versions of hibernate components

Hibernate Core: `hibernate-3.2.6.GA`

Hibernate Annotations: `hibernate-annotations-3.3.1.GA`

For working with EntityManager we require Hibernate Entity Manager. Download it from `hibernate.org`. I am downloading `hibernate-entitymanager-3.3.2.GA`. Be care about downloading compatibility versions of Hibernate components. For example, for `Hibernate Core 3.2.6 GA`, the `Hibernate Entity Manager 3.4.x` is not compactable; if you try to use, error will be the result.

Currently the following jars are set in the `CLASSPATH` (These jars are present in `HibernateDemo/lib` directory of our project and added in class path).

```
ant-1.6.5.jar                      ant-antlr-1.6.5.jar
ant-junit-1.6.5.jar                ant-launcher-1.6.5.jar
ant-swing-1.6.5.jar                antlr-2.7.6.jar
asm-attrs.jar                      asm.jar
c3p0-0.9.1.jar                     cglib-2.1.3.jar
checkstyle-all.jar                 cleanimports.jar
commons-collections-2.1.1.jar      commons-logging-1.0.4.jar
concurrent-1.3.2.jar               dom4j-1.6.1.jar
ehcache-1.2.3.jar                  ejb3-persistence.jar
hibernate-annotations.jar          hibernate-commons-annotations.jar
hibernate-entitymanager.jar        hibernate3.jar
jaas.jar                           jacc-1_0-fr.jar
javassist.jar                      jaxen-1.1-beta-7.jar
jboss-cache.jar                    jboss-common.jar
jboss-jmx.jar                      jboss-system.jar
jgroups-2.2.8.jar                  jta.jar
junit-3.8.1.jar                    lib2
log4j-1.2.11.jar                   mysql-connector-java-5.1.6-bin.jar
ojdbc14-10.2.0.3.0.jar             ojdbc14.jar
```

oscache-2.1.jar proxool-0.8.3.jar

swarmcache-1.0rc2.jar syndiag2.jar

versioncheck.jar xerces-2.6.2.jar

xml-apis.jar

Unzip downloaded `hibernate-entitymanager-3.3.2.GA.zip` file and find all `.jar` files. The jar filenames are as below.

hibernate-entitymanager.jar

ejb3-persistence.jar

hibernate-annotations.jar

hibernate-commons-annotations.jar

ivy-1.4.1.jar

Add these files to CLASSPATH.

Note: To add these jars in to class_path in our project, copy these jar files to `HibernateDemo/lib` directory. Then choose project_name in package_explorer window of our Eclipse → Right click → Properties → Libraries Tab → click Add JARs button → Select jar files (You need to select only `hibernate-entitymanager.jar` and `ivy-1.4.1.jar`, other three jar files (`ejb3-persistence.jar`, `hibernate-annotations.jar`, `hibernate-commons-annotations.jar`) are already included in class_path; if not, select them also) → Press OK

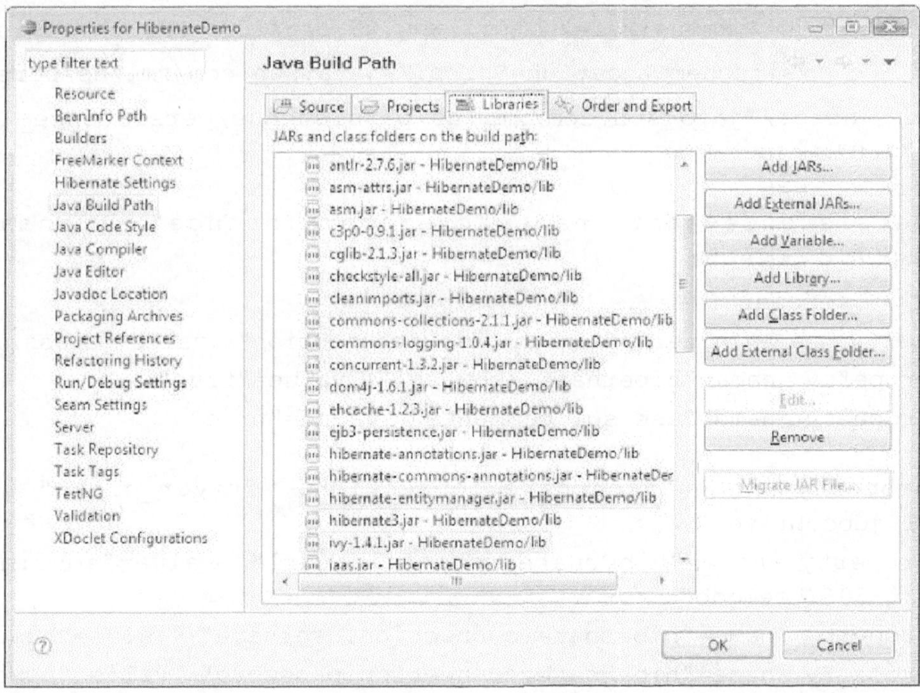

Like *hibernate.cfg.xml* file, in EntityManager we have to use *persistence.xml* file. It will define the required properties such as database, annotation auto-deduction, and SQL settings. The

EntityManager will look this file in WEB-INF directory (as EntityManager works on EJB3 container). Our application is a simple standalone Java application; we are not having EJB3 environment, so create a directory named WEB-INF under /src directory of our project. And place the *persistence.xml* file there. A typical directory structure appears below.

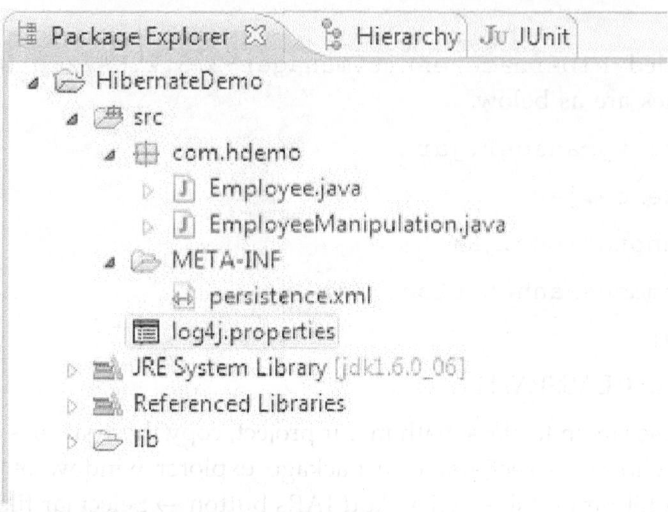

The content of *persistent.xml* file is as below.

```
<?xml version="1.0" encoding="UTF-8"?>
<persistence xmlns="http://java.sun.com/xml/ns/persistence"
             xmlns:xsi="http://www.w3.org/2001/XMLSchema-instance"
         xsi:schemaLocation="http://java.sun.com/xml/ns/persistence
       http://java.sun.com/xml/ns/persistence/persistence_1_0.xsd"
version="1.0">

   <persistence-unit name="hdemopersistence" transaction-
type="RESOURCE_LOCAL">
        <properties>
  <property name="hibernate.archive.autodetection" value="class, hbm"/>
   <property name="hibernate.show_sql" value="true" />
   <property name="use_sql_comments" value="true" />

   <property name="hibernate.connection. driver_class" value="
com.mysql.jdbc.Driver" />
   <property name="hibernate.connection.url" value="jdbc:mysql://
localhost:3306/hdemodb" />
   <property name="hibernate.connection.username" value="huser" />
   <property name="hibernate.connection.password" value="hpword" />
  <property name="hibernate.dialect" value="org.hibernate.dialect.
MySQLDialect" />
```

```
<property name="hibernate.c3p0.min_size" value="1" />
<property name="hibernate.c3p0.max_size" value="5" />
<property name="hibernate.c3p0.timeout" value="300" />
<property name="hibernate.c3p0.max_statements" value="50" />
<property name="hibernate.c3p0.idle_test_period" value="3000" />

<property name="hibernate.hbm2ddl.auto" value="create" />
    </properties>
</persistence-unit>

</persistence>
```

That's all configurations to work with EntityManager in a standalone Java application.

```
// File Name: Employee.java
// Illustrates Lifecycle event annotations

package com.hdemo;

import javax.persistence.Column;
import javax.persistence.Entity;
import javax.persistence.GeneratedValue;
import javax.persistence.Id;
import javax.persistence.PostLoad;
import javax.persistence.PostPersist;
import javax.persistence.PostRemove;
import javax.persistence.PostUpdate;
import javax.persistence.PrePersist;
import javax.persistence.PreRemove;
import javax.persistence.PreUpdate;
import javax.persistence.Table;

import org.hibernate.annotations.GenericGenerator;

@Entity
@Table(name = "EMPLOYEE")
public class Employee {

  private static final long serialVersionUID = 1L;

  @Id
  @GeneratedValue(generator = "idGen")
```

```
@GenericGenerator(name = "idGen", strategy = "uuid.hex")
@Column(name = "ID", length = 32)
private String id = "";

@Column(name = "EMP_NUMBER", unique = true, nullable = false)
private Integer empNumber;

@Column(name = "EMP_NAME", length = 64, nullable = false)
private String empName;

@Column(name = "SALARY")
private double salary;

//Getter and Setter methods

@PrePersist
public void beforePersist() throws Exception {
      System.out.println("\nbeforePersist() is called");
      empName = "Mr. " + empName;
      if (empNumber < 5000 || empNumber >= 6000)
      throw new Exception("Emp Number should be in the range 5000
      - 5999");
}

@PostPersist
public void afterPersist() {
System.out.println("\nafterPersist() is called");
System.out.println("Employee record is persisted into database");
}

@PreRemove
public void beforeDelete() {
      System.out.println("\nbeforeDelete() is called");
}

@PostRemove
public void afterDelete() {
System.out.println("\nafterDelete() is called");
System.out.println("Employee record is deleted from database");
```

```
  }

  @PreUpdate
  public void beforeUpdate() {
        System.out.println("\nbeforeUpdate() is called");
  }

  @PostUpdate
  public void afterUpdate() {
        System.out.println("\nafterUpdate() is called");
        System.out.println("Employee record is updated in database");
  }

 @PostLoad
 public void afterLoad() {
        System.out.println("\nafterLoad() is called");
  }

}
```

```
// File Name: EmployeeManipulation.java
// Main Program

package com.hdemo;

import javax.persistence.EntityManager;
import javax.persistence.EntityManagerFactory;
import javax.persistence.EntityTransaction;
import javax.persistence.Persistence;

public class EmployeeManipulation {

 public static void main(String[] args) throws Exception {

  EntityManagerFactory emf = Persistence.createEntityManagerFactory
  ("hdemopersistence");
        EntityManager em = emf.createEntityManager();

        EntityTransaction tx = em.getTransaction();
        tx.begin();
```

```
        Employee employee = new Employee();
        employee.setEmpNumber(5001);
        employee.setEmpName("Ibrahim");
        employee.setSalary(120000.0);
        em.persist(employee);
        tx.commit();
        System.out.println("Emp Name is " + employee.getEmpName());

        tx.begin();
        employee.setEmpName("Mohamed Ibrahim");
        em.merge(employee);
        tx.commit();
        System.out.println("Emp Name is " + employee.getEmpName());

        tx.begin();
        em.refresh(employee);
        tx.commit();

        tx.begin();
        em.remove(employee);
        tx.commit();

        em.close();
    }
}
```

Output:

```
beforePersist() is called
Hibernate: insert into EMPLOYEE (EMP_NAME, EMP_NUMBER, SALARY, ID)
values (?, ?, ?, ?)

afterPersist() is called
Employee record is persisted into database
Emp Name is Mr. Ibrahim

beforeUpdate() is called
Hibernate: update EMPLOYEE set EMP_NAME=?, EMP_NUMBER=?, SALARY=?
where ID=?
```

```
afterUpdate() is called
Employee record is updated in database
Emp Name is Mohamed Ibrahim
Hibernate: select employee0_.ID as ID0_0_, employee0_.EMP_NAME as EMP2_0_0_, employee0_.EMP_NUMBER as EMP3_0_0_, employee0_.SALARY as SALARY0_0_ from EMPLOYEE employee0_ where employee0_.ID=?

afterLoad() is called

beforeDelete() is called
Hibernate: delete from EMPLOYEE where ID=?

afterDelete() is called
Employee record is deleted from database
```

Pass persistence_unit_name (*hdemopersistence)* defined in *persistence.xml* file as argument of `createEntityManagerFactory()` factory method to get `EntityManagerFactory` **`object`**.

```
EntityManagerFactory emf = Persistence.createEntityManagerFactory
("hdemopersistence");
```

Invoke `createEntityManager()` method of `EntityManagerFactory` to create an `EntityManager`.

```
EntityManager em = emf.createEntityManager();
```

Once you get object of `EntityManager`, do persistence and query operations as you want.

SUMMARY

This chapter discussed the important JPA/Hibernate Annotations to define POJOs with syntaxes and example source code. Various types of ID generation techniques are given. Complex operations on POJO such as Inheritance, Mappings and locking are explained with illustrations. Some advanced concepts such as Hibernate validator, Filtering and Entity Manager are given with their features.

CHAPTER

5

HQL/JPAQL

5.0 INTRODUCTION

HQL (Hibernate Query Language) is powerful object-oriented query feature supported by Hibernate. The syntaxes of HQL are similar to SQL, but not the same. HQL is independent of underlying database. Hibernate generates native SQL query for every HQL.

The Java Persistent API Query Language (JPAQL, simply JPQL), based on EJB 3.0 standard, is an extension of EJB QL (Enterprise Java Bean Query Language) and has many features than EJB QL. It is also a database independent object-based query language. And it is a subset of HQL so that all JPAQL queries are valid in HQL.

5.1 GENERATING SAMPLE DATA FOR DEMONSTRATIONS

Before we begin to demonstrate the features of HQL, we will have a database table named "EMPLOYEE" with some initial data. The required files for generating these sample data are given below. Follow the already explained instructions to run these programs.

Configuration File (`hibernate.cfg.xml`):

```
<?xml version='1.0' encoding='utf-8'?>
<!DOCTYPE hibernate-configuration PUBLIC
        "-//Hibernate/Hibernate Configuration DTD 3.0//EN"
        "http://hibernate.sourceforge.net/hibernate-configuration-
        3.0.dtd">
<hibernate-configuration>
  <session-factory>
        <property name="connection.driver_class"> com.mysql.jdbc.
        Driver</property>
        <property name="connection.url">jdbc:mysql://localhost:3306/
        hdemodb</property>
```

```
   <property  name="connection.username">huser</property>
   <property  name="connection.password">hpword</property>
   <property  name="dialect">org.hibernate.  dialect.MySQLDialect</
   property>

   <property  name="hibernate.c3p0.minPoolSize">  1</property>
   <property  name="hibernate.c3p0.maxPoolSize">  1</property>
   <property  name="hibernate.c3p0.timeout">10</property>
   <property  name="hibernate.c3p0.max_statement">50</property>
   <property  name="hibernate.c3p0.testConnectionOnCheckout">  false</
   property>

   <property  name="current_session_  context_class">thread</property>
   <property name="cache.provider_class">org. hibernate.cache.NoCache
   Provider</property>
   <property  name="show_sql">true</property>
   <property  name="hbm2ddl.auto">create</property>

   <mapping  class="com.hdemo.Employee"/>

   </session-factory>
</hibernate-configuration>
```

Entity File:

```
//  File  Name:  Employee.java
//  Entity  class

package  com.hdemo;

import  java.io.Serializable;
import  java.math.BigDecimal;

import  javax.persistence.Column;
import  javax.persistence.Entity;
import  javax.persistence.GeneratedValue;
import  javax.persistence.Id;
```

```
import javax.persistence.Table;

import org.hibernate.annotations.GenericGenerator;

@Entity
@Table(name = "EMPLOYEE")
public class Employee implements Serializable {

  private static final long serialVersionUID = 1L;

  @Id
  @GeneratedValue(generator = "idGen")
  @GenericGenerator(name = "idGen", strategy = "uuid.hex")
  @Column(name = "ID", length = 32)
  private String id = "";

  @Column(name = "EMP_NUMBER", nullable = false)
  private int empNumber;

  @Column(name = "EMP_NAME", nullable = false, length = 64)
  private String empName;

  @Column(name = "DEPT", nullable = false, length = 64)
  private String department;

  @Column(name = "BASIC_PAY", nullable = false, precision = 10,
  scale = 2)
  private BigDecimal basicpay;

  @Column(name = "ALLOWANCES", precision = 10, scale = 2)
  private BigDecimal allowances;

  @Column(name = "DEDUCTIONS", precision = 10, scale = 2)
  private BigDecimal deductions;

  @Column(name = "NETPAY", precision = 10, scale = 2)
  private BigDecimal netpay;

  Employee() {
```

```
    }

    Employee(int empNumber, String empName, String department, BigDecimal
basicpay, BigDecimal allowances, BigDecimal deductions) {
            this.empNumber = empNumber;
            this.empName = empName;
            this.department = department;
            this.basicpay = basicpay;
            this.allowances = allowances;
            this.deductions = deductions;
            this.netpay = basicpay.add(allowances).subtract(deductions);
      }

      public String getId() {
            return id;
      }

      public void setId(String id) {
            this.id = id;
      }

      public int getEmpNumber() {
            return empNumber;
      }

      public void setEmpNumber(int empNumber) {
            this.empNumber = empNumber;
      }

      public String getEmpName() {
            return empName;
      }

      public void setEmpName(String empName) {
            this.empName = empName;
      }

      public String getDepartment() {
```

```
        return department;
    }

    public void setDepartment(String department) {
        this.department = department;
    }

    public BigDecimal getBasicpay() {
        return basicpay;
    }

    public void setBasicpay(BigDecimal basicpay) {
        this.basicpay = basicpay;
    }

    public BigDecimal getAllowances() {
        return allowances;
    }

    public void setAllowances(BigDecimal allowances) {
        this.allowances = allowances;
    }

    public BigDecimal getDeductions() {
        return deductions;
    }

    public void setDeductions(BigDecimal deductions) {
        this.deductions = deductions;
    }

    public BigDecimal getNetpay() {
        return netpay;
    }

    public void setNetpay(BigDecimal netpay) {
        this.netpay = netpay;
    }
```

```
}
```

SessionFactory Helper File:

```
// File Name: HibernateUtil.java
// Helper class to ger SessionFactory object

package com.hdemo;

import org.hibernate.SessionFactory;
import org.hibernate.cfg.AnnotationConfiguration;

public class HibernateUtil {

  private static final SessionFactory sessionFactory;
  static {
       try {
            sessionFactory = new
AnnotationConfiguration().configure().buildSessionFactory();
       }
       catch (Throwable e) {
            System.err.println("Error in crerating SessionFactory."
+ e);
            throw new ExceptionInInitializerError(e);
       }
  }
  public static SessionFactory getSessionFactory() {
       return sessionFactory;
  }
}
```

Main Program:

```
// File Name: EmployeeManipulation.java
// Main Program

package com.hdemo;

import java.math.BigDecimal;
```

```
import org.hibernate.Session;
import org.hibernate.SessionFactory;
import org.hibernate.Transaction;

public class EmployeeManipulation {

public static void main(String[] args) throws Exception {
    SessionFactory sessionFactory = HibernateUtil.getSessionFactory();
    Session session = sessionFactory.openSession();
    Transaction txn = session.beginTransaction();

    Employee employee1 = new Employee(5001, "Ibrahim", "IT", new
BigDecimal(98000.0), new BigDecimal(30000.0), new BigDecimal(15000.0));
    Employee employee2 = new Employee(5002, "Ananad Desai", "IT", new
BigDecimal(93000.0), new BigDecimal(29000.0), new BigDecimal(15000.0));
    Employee employee3 = new Employee(5003, "Karan Singh", "SALES",
new BigDecimal(88000.0), new BigDecimal(27000.0), new
BigDecimal(14500.0));
    Employee employee4 = new Employee(5004, "Sudhir", "SALES", new
BigDecimal(83000.0), new BigDecimal(25000.0), new BigDecimal(14100.0));
    Employee employee5 = new Employee(5005, "Ajay", "SALES", new
BigDecimal(78000.0), new BigDecimal(23000.0), new BigDecimal(14000.0));
    Employee employee6 = new Employee(5006, "Achfa", "SALES", new
BigDecimal(74000.0), new BigDecimal(22500.0), new BigDecimal(12500.0));
    Employee employee7 = new Employee(5007, "Indiran", "PERSONAL",
new BigDecimal(69000.0), new BigDecimal(16000.0), new BigDecimal(8000.0));
    Employee employee8 = new Employee(5008, "Nitin Otagiri", "PERSONAL",
new BigDecimal(67000.0), new BigDecimal(15800.0), new BigDecimal(7000.0));
    Employee employee9 = new Employee(5009, "Kumar", "STATIONARY",
new BigDecimal(65000.0), new BigDecimal(15700.0), new BigDecimal(7000.0));
    Employee employee10 = new Employee(5010, "Ravi Chandran",
"INVENTORY", new BigDecimal(55800.0), new BigDecimal(15100.0), new
BigDecimal(7000.0));
```

```
        session.persist(employee1);
        session.persist(employee2);
        session.persist(employee3);
        session.persist(employee4);
        session.persist(employee5);
        session.persist(employee6);
        session.persist(employee7);
        session.persist(employee8);
        session.persist(employee9);
        session.persist(employee10);
        System.out.println("The employee objects are persisted with
        session");

        txn.commit();
        System.out.println("Transaction on this session is committed");
        session.close();
        sessionFactory.close();
        }
    }
```

Program Result:

```
The employee objects are persisted with session
Hibernate: insert into EMPLOYEE (ALLOWANCES, BASIC_PAY, DEDUCTIONS, DEPT, EMP_NAME, EMP_NUMBER, NETPAY, ID) values (?, ?, ?, ?, ?, ?, ?, ?)
Hibernate: insert into EMPLOYEE (ALLOWANCES, BASIC_PAY, DEDUCTIONS, DEPT, EMP_NAME, EMP_NUMBER, NETPAY, ID) values (?, ?, ?, ?, ?, ?, ?, ?)
Hibernate: insert into EMPLOYEE (ALLOWANCES, BASIC_PAY, DEDUCTIONS, DEPT, EMP_NAME, EMP_NUMBER, NETPAY, ID) values (?, ?, ?, ?, ?, ?, ?, ?)
Hibernate: insert into EMPLOYEE (ALLOWANCES, BASIC_PAY, DEDUCTIONS, DEPT, EMP_NAME, EMP_NUMBER, NETPAY, ID) values (?, ?, ?, ?, ?, ?, ?, ?)
Hibernate: insert into EMPLOYEE (ALLOWANCES, BASIC_PAY, DEDUCTIONS, DEPT, EMP_NAME, EMP_NUMBER, NETPAY, ID) values (?, ?, ?, ?, ?, ?, ?, ?)
Hibernate: insert into EMPLOYEE (ALLOWANCES, BASIC_PAY, DEDUCTIONS, DEPT, EMP_NAME, EMP_NUMBER, NETPAY, ID) values (?, ?, ?, ?, ?, ?, ?, ?)
Hibernate: insert into EMPLOYEE (ALLOWANCES, BASIC_PAY, DEDUCTIONS, DEPT, EMP_NAME, EMP_NUMBER, NETPAY, ID) values (?, ?, ?, ?, ?, ?, ?, ?)
```

```
Hibernate: insert into EMPLOYEE (ALLOWANCES, BASIC_PAY, DEDUCTIONS, DEPT, EMP_NAME, EMP_NUMBER, NETPAY, ID) values (?, ?, ?, ?, ?, ?, ?, ?)
Hibernate: insert into EMPLOYEE (ALLOWANCES, BASIC_PAY, DEDUCTIONS, DEPT, EMP_NAME, EMP_NUMBER, NETPAY, ID) values (?, ?, ?, ?, ?, ?, ?, ?)
Hibernate: insert into EMPLOYEE (ALLOWANCES, BASIC_PAY, DEDUCTIONS, DEPT, EMP_NAME, EMP_NUMBER, NETPAY, ID) values (?, ?, ?, ?, ?, ?, ?, ?)
Transaction on this session is committed
```

Database Result:

Administrator: C:\Windows\system32\cmd.exe - mysql -u huser -phpword hdemodb

```
mysql> desc employee;
+-------------+---------------+------+-----+---------+-------+
| Field       | Type          | Null | Key | Default | Extra |
+-------------+---------------+------+-----+---------+-------+
| ID          | varchar(32)   | NO   | PRI | NULL    |       |
| ALLOWANCES  | decimal(10,2) | YES  |     | NULL    |       |
| BASIC_PAY   | decimal(10,2) | NO   |     | NULL    |       |
| DEDUCTIONS  | decimal(10,2) | YES  |     | NULL    |       |
| DEPT        | varchar(64)   | NO   |     | NULL    |       |
| EMP_NAME    | varchar(64)   | NO   |     | NULL    |       |
| EMP_NUMBER  | int(11)       | NO   |     | NULL    |       |
| NETPAY      | decimal(10,2) | YES  |     | NULL    |       |
+-------------+---------------+------+-----+---------+-------+
8 rows in set (0.00 sec)

mysql> select id, emp_number, emp_name, dept, basic_pay, allowances, deductions, netpay from employee;
+----------------------------------+------------+----------------+------------+-----------+------------+------------+-----------+
| id                               | emp_number | emp_name       | dept       | basic_pay | allowances | deductions | netpay    |
+----------------------------------+------------+----------------+------------+-----------+------------+------------+-----------+
| 402881f81eab16b6011eab16b7e40001 |       5001 | Ibrahim        | IT         |  98000.00 |   30000.00 |   15000.00 | 113000.00 |
| 402881f81eab16b6011eab16b7f00002 |       5002 | Ananad Desai   | IT         |  93000.00 |   29000.00 |   15000.00 | 107000.00 |
| 402881f81eab16b6011eab16b7f00003 |       5003 | Karan Singh    | SALES      |  88000.00 |   27000.00 |   14500.00 | 100500.00 |
| 402881f81eab16b6011eab16b7f00004 |       5004 | Sudhir         | SALES      |  83000.00 |   25000.00 |   14100.00 |  93900.00 |
| 402881f81eab16b6011eab16b7f00005 |       5005 | Ajay           | SALES      |  78000.00 |   23000.00 |   14000.00 |  87000.00 |
| 402881f81eab16b6011eab16b7f00006 |       5006 | Achfa          | SALES      |  74000.00 |   22500.00 |   12500.00 |  84000.00 |
| 402881f81eab16b6011eab16b7f10007 |       5007 | Indiran        | PERSONAL   |  69000.00 |   16000.00 |    8000.00 |  77000.00 |
| 402881f81eab16b6011eab16b7f10008 |       5008 | Nitin Otagiri  | PERSONAL   |  67000.00 |   15800.00 |    7000.00 |  75800.00 |
| 402881f81eab16b6011eab16b7f10009 |       5009 | Kumar          | STATIONARY |  65000.00 |   15700.00 |    7000.00 |  73700.00 |
| 402881f81eab16b6011eab16b7f1000a |       5010 | Ravi Chandran  | INVENTORY  |  55800.00 |   15100.00 |    7000.00 |  63900.00 |
+----------------------------------+------------+----------------+------------+-----------+------------+------------+-----------+
10 rows in set (0.00 sec)
```

5.2 SELECTING RECORDS FROM DATABASE TABLE

The 'from'clause is used to retrieve records from database tables. This is similar to select statement in SQL.

5.2.1 `from` Clause-Selecting Rows from Database Table

This from clause selects values from database table and assigns them on entity object(s).

General format

```
from entity_clsss_name [where condition]
from entity_clsss_name1, entity_clsss_name2, ... [where condition]
```

`[where condition]` part is optional.

We can use alias names also to refer those entities in the query.

```
from entity_clsss_name as alias_name [where condition]
```

```
from entity_clsss_name1    as alias_name,
     entity_clsss_name2 as alias_name, ... [where condition]
```

The word "as" is optional while specifying alias name(s).

Example

```
from Student
```

-Selects all rows from the database table where the entity `Student` relates.

```
from Student s, Employee e
```

-Selects all rows from the database tables where the entities `Student` and `Employee` relate.

```
// File Name: EmployeeManipulation.java
// Illustrates HQL: from clause

package com.hdemo;

import java.util.List;

import org.hibernate.Session;
import org.hibernate.SessionFactory;
import org.hibernate.Transaction;

public class EmployeeManipulation {
   @SuppressWarnings("unchecked")
   public static void main(String[] args) throws Exception {
   SessionFactory sessionFactory =
                              HibernateUtil.getSessionFactory();
   Session session = sessionFactory.openSession();
   Transaction txn = session.beginTransaction();

   List<Employee> employeeList = session.createQuery("from
                                           Employee").list();
   for (int i = 0; i < employeeList.size(); i++) {
        Employee employee = employeeList.get(i);
        System.out.println("Employee Number : " +
                                   employee.getEmpNumber());
        System.out.println("Employee Name   : " +
                                     employee.getEmpName());
        System.out.println("Department      : " +
```

```
                                          employee.getDepartment());
        System.out.println("Basic  Pay        : " +
                                            employee.getBasicpay());
        System.out.println("Allowances        : " +
                                          employee.getAllowances());
        System.out.println("Deductions        : " +
                                          employee.getDeductions());
        System.out.println("Netpay                    : " +
                                              employee.getNetpay());
   System.out.println("=================================\n\n");
        }

        txn.commit();
        session.close();
        sessionFactory.close();
    }
  }
```

```
Hibernate: select employee0_.ID as ID0_, employee0_.ALLOWANCES as ALLOWANCES0_, employee0_.BASIC_PAY as BASIC3_0_, employee0_.DEDUCTIONS as DEDUCTIONS0_, employee0_.DEPT as DEPT0_, employee0_.EMP_NAME as EMP6_0_, employee0_.EMP_NUMBER as EMP7_0_, employee0_.NETPAY as NETPAY0_ from EMPLOYEE employee0_

Employee  Number    :  5001
Employee  Name      :  Ibrahim
Department          :  IT
Basic  Pay          :  98000.00
Allowances          :  30000.00
Deductions          :  15000.00
Netpay              :  113000.00
=======================================

Employee  Number    :  5002
Employee  Name      :  Ananad  Desai
Department          :  IT
Basic  Pay          :  93000.00
```

```
Allowances          :  29000.00
Deductions          :  15000.00
Netpay              :  107000.00
=========================================

Employee  Number    :  5003
Employee  Name      :  Karan  Singh
Department          :  SALES
Basic  Pay          :  88000.00
Allowances          :  27000.00
Deductions          :  14500.00
Netpay              :  100500.00
=========================================

Employee  Number    :  5004
Employee  Name      :  Sudhir
Department          :  SALES
Basic  Pay          :  83000.00
Allowances          :  25000.00
Deductions          :  14100.00
Netpay              :  93900.00
=========================================

Employee  Number    :  5005
Employee  Name      :  Ajay
Department          :  SALES
Basic  Pay          :  78000.00
Allowances          :  23000.00
Deductions          :  14000.00
Netpay              :  87000.00
=========================================

Employee  Number    :  5006
Employee  Name      :  Achfa
Department          :  SALES
Basic  Pay          :  74000.00
```

```
Allowances          :  22500.00
Deductions          :  12500.00
Netpay              :  84000.00
========================================

Employee  Number    :  5007
Employee  Name      :  Indiran
Department          :  PERSONAL
Basic  Pay          :  69000.00
Allowances          :  16000.00
Deductions          :  8000.00
Netpay              :  77000.00
========================================

Employee  Number    :  5008
Employee  Name      :  Nitin  Otagiri
Department          :  PERSONAL
Basic  Pay          :  67000.00
Allowances          :  15800.00
Deductions          :  7000.00
Netpay              :  75800.00
========================================

Employee  Number    :  5009
Employee  Name      :  Kumar
Department          :  STATIONARY
Basic  Pay          :  65000.00
Allowances          :  15700.00
Deductions          :  7000.00
Netpay              :  73700.00
========================================

Employee  Number    :  5010
Employee  Name      :  Ravi  Chandran
Department          :  INVENTORY
Basic  Pay          :  55800.00
```

```
Allowances          :  15100.00
Deductions          :  7000.00
Netpay              :  63900.00
========================================
```

The list () method will return empty List (not null reference) while the HQL retrieves no rows.

5.2.2 Selecting Individual Columns from Database Table

The following example selects only few fields of an entity.

```
// File Name: EmployeeManipulation.java
// Illustrates HQL: from clause

package com.hdemo;

import java.util.List;

import org.hibernate.Session;
import org.hibernate.SessionFactory;
import org.hibernate.Transaction;

public class EmployeeManipulation {

  @SuppressWarnings("unchecked")
  public static void main(String[] args) throws Exception {
  SessionFactory sessionFactory = HibernateUtil.getSessionFactory();
        Session session = sessionFactory.openSession();
        Transaction txn = session.beginTransaction();

        List list = session.createQuery("select empNumber, empName,
                                 netpay from Employee").list();
        for (int i = 0; i < list.size(); i++) {
              Object[] row = (Object[]) list.get(i);
              System.out.println("Employee Number : " + row[0]);
              System.out.println("Employee Name   : " + row[1]);
              System.out.println("Netpay          : " + row[2]);

  System.out.println("========================================\n\n");
```

```
            }

            txn.commit();
            session.close();
            sessionFactory.close();
        }
    }
```

```
Hibernate: select employee0_.EMP_NUMBER as col_0_0_, employee0_.
EMP_NAME as col_1_0_, employee0_.NETPAY as col_2_0_ from EMPLOYEE
employee0_
    Employee Number    : 5001
    Employee Name      : Ibrahim
    Netpay             : 113000.00
    ========================================

    Employee Number    : 5002
    Employee Name      : Ananad Desai
    Netpay             : 107000.00
    ========================================

    Employee Number    : 5003
    Employee Name      : Karan Singh
    Netpay             : 100500.00
    ========================================

    Employee Number    : 5004
    Employee Name      : Sudhir
    Netpay             : 93900.00
    ========================================

    Employee Number    : 5005
    Employee Name      : Ajay
    Netpay             : 87000.00
    ========================================

    Employee Number    : 5006
    Employee Name      : Achfa
    Netpay             : 84000.00
    ========================================
```

```
Employee  Number    : 5007
Employee  Name      : Indiran
Netpay              : 77000.00
========================================

Employee  Number    : 5008
Employee  Name      : Nitin  Otagiri
Netpay              : 75800.00
========================================

Employee  Number    : 5009
Employee  Name      : Kumar
Netpay              : 73700.00
========================================

Employee  Number    : 5010
Employee  Name      : Ravi  Chandran
Netpay              : 63900.00
========================================
```

5.2.3 Applying Conditions on Query

The following example illustrates how to apply conditions (where clause) on query.

You can use directly field name of an entity or alias name with field name of an entity to refer a field in condition.

Example

```
from Employee where empNumber = 5001

from Employee e where e.empNumber = 5001
```

If the `Employee` entity contains a field named `salary` as of type `Salary` entity, which contains a field named `incometax`. Then, this `incometax` field can be accessed as shown below.

```
from Employee e where e.salary.incometax < 10000
```

The following are some of the operators and functions that can be used in this `select` query.

Relational Operators : `=, !=, <>, <, <=, >, >=, like`

Logical Operators: `not, and, or`

Arithmetic Operators: `+, -, *, /`

Set Operators: `in, not in, is null, is not null, is empty, is not empty, between,member of, not member of`

The operators 'member of, not member of' are used to check whether an entity is part of collection or not.

CASE Statements: **CASE Multi-branch Statement (Entry Condition):**

```
CASE expression
  WHEN value1 THEN result1
  WHEN value2 THEN result2
  ...
  WHEN valueN THEN resultN
  [
        ELSE elseResult
  ]
  END
```

CASE Multi-branch Statement (Multiple Conditions):

```
CASE
      WHEN booleanExpression1 THEN result1
      WHEN booleanExpression2 THEN result2
      ...
      WHEN booleanExpressionN THEN resultN
      [
      ELSE elseResult
      ]
END
```

Built-in Functions: **Date functions:**

`current_date()` -Returns current date

`current_time()` -Returns current time

`current_timestamp()` -Returns current date and time

`day(date/timestamp field)`

-Returns day of date/timestamp field passed as argument

`month(date/timestamp field)`

-Returns month of date/timestamp field passed as argument

`year(date/timestamp field)`

-Returns year of date/timestamp field passed as argument

`hour(date/timestamp field)`

-Returns hour of date/timestamp field passed as argument

`minute(date/timestamp field)`

-Returns minute of date/timestamp field passed as argument

`second(date/timestamp field)`

-Returns second of date/timestamp field passed as argument

String Functions:

`concat(string1, string2)`

-Appends string2 to string1. We can also use `||` operator also for concatenation as `string1 || string2`

`lower(string)-`

Converts the specified string to lower case

`upper(string)`

-Converts the specified string to upper case

`length(string)`

-Returns the length (total number of characters) of the specified string

`str(numeric/date value)`

-Returns String representation of specified parameter value.

`trim(string)`

-Returns the string with leading and trailing spaces are removed

`substring(string, starting_offset, length)`

-Returns `length` number of characters from the specified `string` starting at `starting_offset`. Index starts from 1.

`locate(string1, string2)`

-Returns the first starting position of `string1` in `string2`. If not found, then returns 0. An optional third parameter can be specified to start search from that position. The index starts from 1.

Mathematical/Trigonometric Functions:

`abs(value)` -Returns absolute value (unsigned value) of specified parameter. `abs(-10) = 10, abs(10) = 10`

`sort(value)` -Returns square root value of the specified parameter

`bit_length(String)` -Returns the number of bits in a given string.

`mod(value1, value2)` -Returns modulus (Remainder of division) of the division `value1` by `value2.`

`mod(8,3) = 2` (Two times 3 is 6, remaining value is 2; Quotient = 2, Remainder = 2 (mod value)). `Mod(7,2) = 1`

Hibernate also supports functions specific to underlying Database. Some of them are,

`sin(value),`

`cos(value),`

`trunc(value), ...`

Checking `null` and empty values:

`IS NULL, IS NOT NULL` -Check for NULL fields.

`IS EMPTY, IS NOT EMPTY` -Check for empty value, usually used to test collection fields.

`coalesce(argument1, argument2, ...)` -Returns first non-null value of its arguments.

For example,
`coalesce(empName, empNumber, id)`

If empName is null and `empNumber` is also `null`, then it returns the value of `id`. If the `empName` is `null` and `empNumber` is not `null`, then it returns the value of `empNumber`. If the `empName` is not `null`, then it returns the value of `empName`.

The Boolean fields can be used for arithmetic operations (sum of true/false fields ...) by setting the `hibernate.query.substitutions` property as follows in hibernate configuration (in our case, `hibernate.cfg.xml` file).

```
<property name="hibernate.query.substitutions">true 1, false 0</
property>
```

The following example selects only record belongs to Employee Number 5005.

```
// File Name: EmployeeManipulation.java
```

```
// Illustrates HQL: from clause

package com.hdemo;

import java.util.List;

import org.hibernate.Session;
import org.hibernate.SessionFactory;
import org.hibernate.Transaction;

public class EmployeeManipulation {
   @SuppressWarnings("unchecked")
   public static void main(String[] args) throws Exception {
         SessionFactory sessionFactory =
                                 HibernateUtil.getSessionFactory();
         Session session = sessionFactory.openSession();
         Transaction txn = session.beginTransaction();

         List<Employee> employeeList = session.createQuery("from
                 Employee e where e.empNumber = 5005").list();
         for (int i = 0; i < employeeList.size(); i++) {
               Employee employee = employeeList.get(i);
               System.out.println("Employee Number  : " +
                                      employee.getEmpNumber());
               System.out.println("Employee Name    : " +
                                        employee.getEmpName());
               System.out.println("Department       : " +
                                     employee.getDepartment());
               System.out.println("Basic Pay        : " +
                                       employee.getBasicpay());
               System.out.println("Allowances       : " +
                                     employee.getAllowances());
               System.out.println("Deductions       : " +
                                     employee.getDeductions());
               System.out.println("Netpay             : " +
                                         employee.getNetpay());

   System.out.println("========================================\n\n");
```

```
        }

        txn.commit();
        session.close();
        sessionFactory.close();
    }
}
```

Hibernate: select employee0_.ID as ID0_, employee0_.ALLOWANCES as ALLOWANCES0_, employee0_.BASIC_PAY as BASIC3_0_, employee0_.DEDUCTIONS as DEDUCTIONS0_, employee0_.DEPT as DEPT0_, employee0_.EMP_NAME as EMP6_0_, employee0_.EMP_NUMBER as EMP7_0_, employee0_.NETPAY as NETPAY0_ from EMPLOYEE employee0_ where employee0_.EMP_NUMBER=5005

```
Employee Number   : 5005
Employee Name     : Ajay
Department        : SALES
Basic Pay         : 78000.00
Allowances        : 23000.00
Deductions        : 14000.00
Netpay            : 87000.00
========================================
```

Positional Parameters: You can also use positional parameters while specifying data to queries. Hibernate supports JDBC style (?) positional parameters and its own named string (`:string`) parameters. Note that JDBC style ? positional parameters start with 0, not from 1 (In JDBC, positional parameters start with 1).

The following program illustrates how to JDBC style positional parameters.

```
// File Name: EmployeeManipulation.java
// Illustrates HQL: from clause

package com.hdemo;

import java.util.List;

import org.hibernate.Session;
import org.hibernate.SessionFactory;
import org.hibernate.Transaction;

public class EmployeeManipulation {
```

```
    @SuppressWarnings("unchecked")
    public static void main(String[] args) throws Exception {
          SessionFactory sessionFactory =
                          HibernateUtil.getSessionFactory();
          Session session = sessionFactory.openSession();
          Transaction txn = session.beginTransaction();

          List<Employee> employeeList = session.createQuery("from
          Employee e where e.empNumber = ?").setInteger(0, 5005).list();
          for (int i = 0; i < employeeList.size(); i++) {
                Employee employee = employeeList.get(i);
                System.out.println("Employee Number : " +
                                    employee.getEmpNumber());
                System.out.println("Employee Name    : " +
                                    employee.getEmpName());
                System.out.println("Department        : " +
                                    employee.getDepartment());
                System.out.println("Basic Pay         : " +
                                    employee.getBasicpay());
                System.out.println("Allowances        : " +
                                    employee.getAllowances());
                System.out.println("Deductions        : " +
                                    employee.getDeductions());
                System.out.println("Netpay             : " +
                                    employee.getNetpay());

    System.out.println("====================================\n\n");
          }

          txn.commit();
          session.close();
          sessionFactory.close();
    }
}
```

```
Hibernate: select employee0_.ID as ID0_, employee0_.ALLOWANCES as ALLOWANCES0_, employee0_.BASIC_PAY as BASIC3_0_, employee0_.DEDUCTIONS as DEDUCTIONS0_, employee0_.DEPT as DEPT0_, employee0_.EMP_NAME as EMP6_0_, employee0_.EMP_NUMBER as EMP7_0_, employee0_.NETPAY as NETPAY0_ from EMPLOYEE employee0_ where employee0_.EMP_NUMBER=?
```

```
Employee Number   : 5005
Employee Name     : Ajay
Department        : SALES
Basic Pay         : 78000.00
Allowances        : 23000.00
Deductions        : 14000.00
Netpay            : 87000.00
========================================
```

The following program illustrates how to use Hibernate style named parameters.

```
// File Name: EmployeeManipulation.java
// Illustrates HQL: from clause

package com.hdemo;

import java.util.List;

import org.hibernate.Session;
import org.hibernate.SessionFactory;
import org.hibernate.Transaction;

public class EmployeeManipulation {

  @SuppressWarnings("unchecked")
  public static void main(String[] args) throws Exception {
        SessionFactory sessionFactory =
                          HibernateUtil.getSessionFactory();
        Session session = sessionFactory.openSession();
        Transaction txn = session.beginTransaction();

        List<Employee> employeeList = session.createQuery("from
Employee e where e.empNumber = :employeeNumber").setInteger
("employeeNumber", 5005).list();
        for (int i = 0; i < employeeList.size(); i++) {
              Employee employee = employeeList.get(i);
              System.out.println("Employee Number : " +
                                   employee.getEmpNumber());
              System.out.println("Employee Name   : " +
                                     employee.getEmpName());
```

```
            System.out.println("Department          : " +
                                    employee.getDepartment());
            System.out.println("Basic Pay           : " +
                                      employee.getBasicpay());
            System.out.println("Allowances          : " +
                                    employee.getAllowances());
            System.out.println("Deductions          : " +
                                    employee.getDeductions());
            System.out.println("Netpay                : " +
                                        employee.getNetpay());

     System.out.println("========================================\n\n");
        }

        txn.commit();
        session.close();
        sessionFactory.close();
    }
}
```

```
Hibernate: select employee0_.ID as ID0_, employee0_.ALLOWANCES as ALLOWANCES0_, employee0_.BASIC_PAY as BASIC3_0_, employee0_.DEDUCTIONS as DEDUCTIONS0_, employee0_.DEPT as DEPT0_, employee0_.EMP_NAME as EMP6_0_, employee0_.EMP_NUMBER as EMP7_0_, employee0_.NETPAY as NETPAY0_ from EMPLOYEE employee0_ where employee0_.EMP_NUMBER=?
Employee Number  : 5005
Employee Name    : Ajay
Department       : SALES
Basic Pay        : 78000.00
Allowances       : 23000.00
Deductions       : 14000.00
Netpay           : 87000.00
========================================
```

A named string parameters may occur multiple times in the same query as shown in the following example.

```
// File Name: EmployeeManipulation.java
// Illustrates Named String Parameter
```

```
package com.hdemo;

import org.hibernate.Session;
import org.hibernate.SessionFactory;
import org.hibernate.Transaction;

public class EmployeeManipulation {

   public static void main(String[] args) throws Exception {
         SessionFactory sessionFactory =
                              HibernateUtil.getSessionFactory();
         Session session = sessionFactory.openSession();
         Transaction txn = session.beginTransaction();

         Double result = ((Double) (session.createQuery("select (:b
- (:a + :a + :a)) from Employee").setDouble("a", 2.4).setDouble("b",
8.6).list().iterator().next())).doubleValue();

         System.out.println("\nResult: " + result);

         txn.commit();
         session.close();
         sessionFactory.close();
   }
}
```

Hibernate: select ?-(?+?+?) as col_0_0_ from EMPLOYEE employee0_

Result: 1.4

The following program illustrates how to use `like` operator. Note that the like operation is dependent on underlying database for case sensitiveness while matching pattern. In general like, 'A%' will not match any string value starting with 'a' (case sensitive). But, it is dependent on underlying database, for example if you use the above like operation in MySQL database, it ignores case sensitive so that 'A%' will match all strings starting with 'A' or 'a'.

```
// File Name: EmployeeManipulation.java
// Illustrates 'like' operator

package com.hdemo;

import java.util.List;
```

```
import org.hibernate.Session;
import org.hibernate.SessionFactory;
import org.hibernate.Transaction;

public class EmployeeManipulation {

  @SuppressWarnings("unchecked")
  public static void main(String[] args) throws Exception {
       SessionFactory sessionFactory =
                             HibernateUtil.getSessionFactory();
       Session session = sessionFactory.openSession();
       Transaction txn = session.beginTransaction();

       List<Employee> employeeList = session.createQuery("from
Employee e where e.empName like :employeeName").setString("employeeName",
"A%").list();
       for (int i = 0; i < employeeList.size(); i++) {
            Employee employee = employeeList.get(i);
            System.out.println("Employee Number : " +
                                   employee.getEmpNumber());
            System.out.println("Employee Name     : " +
                                   employee.getEmpName());
            System.out.println("Department         : " +
                                   employee.getDepartment());
            System.out.println("Basic Pay          : " +
                                   employee.getBasicpay());
            System.out.println("Allowances         : " +
                                   employee.getAllowances());
            System.out.println("Deductions         : " +
                                   employee.getDeductions());
            System.out.println("Netpay              : " +
                                   employee.getNetpay());

   System.out.println("====================================\n\n");
       }

       txn.commit();
       session.close();
```

```
            sessionFactory.close();
        }
    }
```

Hibernate: select employee0_.ID as ID0_, employee0_.ALLOWANCES as ALLOWANCES0_, employee0_.BASIC_PAY as BASIC3_0_, employee0_.DEDUCTIONS as DEDUCTIONS0_, employee0_.DEPT as DEPT0_, employee0_.EMP_NAME as EMP6_0_, employee0_.EMP_NUMBER as EMP7_0_, employee0_.NETPAY as NETPAY0_ from EMPLOYEE employee0_ where employee0_.EMP_NAME like ?

```
Employee Number    : 5002
Employee Name      : Ananad Desai
Department         : IT
Basic Pay          : 93000.00
Allowances         : 29000.00
Deductions         : 15000.00
Netpay             : 107000.00
========================================
Employee Number    : 5005
Employee Name      : Ajay
Department         : SALES
Basic Pay          : 78000.00
Allowances         : 23000.00
Deductions         : 14000.00
Netpay             : 87000.00
========================================
Employee Number    : 5006
Employee Name      : Achfa
Department         : SALES
Basic Pay          : 74000.00
Allowances         : 22500.00
Deductions         : 12500.00
Netpay             : 84000.00
========================================
```

The following program illustrates how to use logical and relational operators.

```
// File Name: EmployeeManipulation.java
// Illustrates how to use logical and relational operators

package com.hdemo;

import java.util.List;

import org.hibernate.Session;
import org.hibernate.SessionFactory;
import org.hibernate.Transaction;

public class EmployeeManipulation {

  @SuppressWarnings("unchecked")
  public static void main(String[] args) throws Exception {
        SessionFactory sessionFactory =
                              HibernateUtil.getSessionFactory();
        Session session = sessionFactory.openSession();
        Transaction txn = session.beginTransaction();

        List<Employee> employeeList = session.createQuery("from
Employee e where e.empName like :employeeName and e.netpay >
100000").setString("employeeName", "A%").list();
        for (int i = 0; i < employeeList.size(); i++) {
              Employee employee = employeeList.get(i);
              System.out.println("Employee Number : " +
                                        employee.getEmpNumber());
              System.out.println("Employee Name   : " +
                                          employee.getEmpName());
              System.out.println("Department      : " +
                                       employee.getDepartment());
              System.out.println("Basic Pay       : " +
                                         employee.getBasicpay());
              System.out.println("Allowances      : " +
                                       employee.getAllowances());
              System.out.println("Deductions      : " +
                                       employee.getDeductions());
              System.out.println("Netpay          : " +
                                           employee.getNetpay());
```

```
System.out.println("===========================================\n\n");
            }

            txn.commit();
            session.close();
            sessionFactory.close();
      }
   }
```

```
Hibernate: select employee0_.ID as ID0_, employee0_.ALLOWANCES as ALLOWANCES0_, employee0_.BASIC_PAY as BASIC3_0_, employee0_.DEDUCTIONS as DEDUCTIONS0_, employee0_.DEPT as DEPT0_, employee0_.EMP_NAME as EMP6_0_, employee0_.EMP_NUMBER as EMP7_0_, employee0_.NETPAY as NETPAY0_ from EMPLOYEE employee0_ where (employee0_.EMP_NAME like ?) and employee0_.NETPAY>100000
Employee Number   : 5002
Employee Name     : Ananad Desai
Department        : IT
Basic Pay         : 93000.00
Allowances        : 29000.00
Deductions        : 15000.00
Netpay            : 107000.00
=======================================
```

The following program illustrates how to use set operators.

```
// File Name: EmployeeManipulation.java
// Illustrates how to use set operators

package com.hdemo;

import java.util.List;

import org.hibernate.Session;
import org.hibernate.SessionFactory;
import org.hibernate.Transaction;

public class EmployeeManipulation {
```

```
    @SuppressWarnings("unchecked")
    public static void main(String[] args) throws Exception {
          SessionFactory sessionFactory =
                                   HibernateUtil.getSessionFactory();
          Session session = sessionFactory.openSession();
          Transaction txn = session.beginTransaction();

          List<Employee> employeeList = session.createQuery("from
          Employee e where e.empNumber in (5003, 5007, 5009)").list();
          for (int i = 0; i < employeeList.size(); i++) {
                Employee employee = employeeList.get(i);
                System.out.println("Employee Number : " +
                                        employee.getEmpNumber());
                System.out.println("Employee Name    : " +
                                          employee.getEmpName());
                System.out.println("Department       : " +
                                       employee.getDepartment());
                System.out.println("Basic Pay         : " +
                                         employee.getBasicpay());
                System.out.println("Allowances       : " +
                                       employee.getAllowances());
                System.out.println("Deductions       : " +
                                       employee.getDeductions());
                System.out.println("Netpay             : " +
                                           employee.getNetpay());

    System.out.println("===================================\n\n");
          }

          txn.commit();
          session.close();
          sessionFactory.close();
    }
  }
```

Hibernate: select employee0_.ID as ID0_, employee0_.ALLOWANCES as ALLOWANCES0_, employee0_.BASIC_PAY as BASIC3_0_, employee0_.DEDUCTIONS as DEDUCTIONS0_, employee0_.DEPT as DEPT0_, employee0_.EMP_NAME as

```
EMP6_0_, employee0_.EMP_NUMBER as EMP7_0_, employee0_.NETPAY as NETPAY0_
from EMPLOYEE employee0_ where employee0_.EMP_NUMBER in (5003, 5007,
5009)
    Employee Number  : 5003
    Employee Name    : Karan Singh
    Department       : SALES
    Basic Pay        : 88000.00
    Allowances       : 27000.00
    Deductions       : 14500.00
    Netpay           : 100500.00
    ========================================
    Employee Number  : 5007
    Employee Name    : Indiran
    Department       : PERSONAL
    Basic Pay        : 69000.00
    Allowances       : 16000.00
    Deductions       : 8000.00
    Netpay           : 77000.00
    ========================================
    Employee Number  : 5009
    Employee Name    : Kumar
    Department       : STATIONARY
    Basic Pay        : 65000.00
    Allowances       : 15700.00
    Deductions       : 7000.00
    Netpay           : 73700.00
    ========================================
```

The above program can be written as below by using a positional parameter.

```
// File Name: EmployeeManipulation.java
// Illustrates Set Operation (using named parameter)

package com.hdemo;

import java.util.ArrayList;
```

```
import java.util.List;

import org.hibernate.Session;
import org.hibernate.SessionFactory;
import org.hibernate.Transaction;

public class EmployeeManipulation {

   @SuppressWarnings("unchecked")
   public static void main(String[] args) throws Exception {
         SessionFactory sessionFactory =
                              HibernateUtil.getSessionFactory();

         Session session = sessionFactory.openSession();

         Transaction txn = session.beginTransaction();

         List alEmployeeNumbers = new ArrayList();
         alEmployeeNumbers.add(5003);
         alEmployeeNumbers.add(5007);
         alEmployeeNumbers.add(5009);

         List<Employee> employeeList = session.createQuery("from
         Employee e where e.empNumber in (:employeeNumbers)")

         .setParameterList("employeeNumbers", alEmployeeNumbers)
                                                      .list();

         for (int i = 0; i < employeeList.size(); i++) {
               Employee employee = employeeList.get(i);
               System.out.println("Employee Number : " +
                                        employee.getEmpNumber());

               System.out.println("Employee Name     : " +
                                          employee.getEmpName());

               System.out.println("Department          : " +
                                       employee.getDepartment());

               System.out.println("Basic Pay            : " +
                                         employee.getBasicpay());

               System.out.println("Allowances          : " +
                                       employee.getAllowances());

               System.out.println("Deductions          : " +
```

```
                                employee.getDeductions());
            System.out.println("Netpay                   : " +
                                employee.getNetpay());

      System.out.println("===================================\n\n");
        }

        txn.commit();
        session.close();
        sessionFactory.close();
    }
  }
```

```
Hibernate: select employee0_.ID as ID0_, employee0_.ALLOWANCES as ALLOWANCES0_, employee0_.BASIC_PAY as BASIC3_0_, employee0_.DEDUCTIONS as DEDUCTIONS0_, employee0_.DEPT as DEPT0_, employee0_.EMP_NAME as EMP6_0_, employee0_.EMP_NUMBER as EMP7_0_, employee0_.NETPAY as NETPAY0_ from EMPLOYEE employee0_ where employee0_.EMP_NUMBER in (? , ? , ?)
Employee Number   : 5003
Employee Name     : Karan Singh
Department        : SALES
Basic Pay         : 88000.00
Allowances        : 27000.00
Deductions        : 14500.00
Netpay            : 100500.00
===================================

Employee Number   : 5007
Employee Name     : Indiran
Department        : PERSONAL
Basic Pay         : 69000.00
Allowances        : 16000.00
Deductions        : 8000.00
Netpay            : 77000.00
===================================

Employee Number   : 5009
Employee Name     : Kumar
```

```
Department          : STATIONARY
Basic  Pay          : 65000.00
Allowances          : 15700.00
Deductions          : 7000.00
Netpay              : 73700.00
========================================
```

The following program illustrates the use of `case` (entry condition) statement. If any of the specified (`when`) value matches the result of the (`case`) expression, then the result of that block will be returned; if none matches, then the value specified in `else` block will be returned. Note that if any match found, the `case` statement ends without checking other cases.

```
// File Name: EmployeeManipulation.java
// Illustrates the use of case .. when .. else statement

package com.hdemo;

import java.util.Iterator;
import java.util.List;

import org.hibernate.Session;
import org.hibernate.SessionFactory;
import org.hibernate.Transaction;

public class EmployeeManipulation {

  @SuppressWarnings("unchecked")
  public static void main(String[] args) throws Exception {
        SessionFactory sessionFactory =
                              HibernateUtil.getSessionFactory();
        Session session = sessionFactory.openSession();
        Transaction txn = session.beginTransaction();

        List<Employee> employeeList = session.createQuery("select
empNumber, empName, case department  when 'IT' then (netpay + 10000)
when 'SALES' then (netpay + 5000)  else netpay end from Employee").list();
      for (Iterator it = employeeList.iterator(); it.hasNext();) {
            Object[] employeeRecord = (Object[])it.next();
```

```
                System.out.println("Employee Number : " +
                                                        employeeRecord[0]);
                System.out.println("Employee Name   : " +
                                                        employeeRecord[1]);
                System.out.println("Netpay          : " +
                                                        employeeRecord[2]);

      System.out.println("=======================================\n\n");
            }
            txn.commit();
            session.close();
            sessionFactory.close();
      }
   }
```

```
Hibernate: select employee0_.EMP_NUMBER as col_0_0_, employee0_.EMP_NAME as col_1_0_, case employee0_.DEPT when 'IT' then employee0_.NETPAY+10000 when 'SALES' then employee0_.NETPAY+5000 else employee0_.NETPAY end as col_2_0_ from EMPLOYEE employee0_
Employee Number   : 5001
Employee Name     : Ibrahim
Netpay            : 123000.00
=======================================

Employee Number   : 5002
Employee Name     : Ananad Desai
Netpay            : 117000.00
=======================================
Employee Number   : 5003
Employee Name     : Karan Singh
Netpay            : 105500.00
=======================================
Employee Number   : 5004
Employee Name     : Sudhir
Netpay            : 98900.00
=======================================
```

```
Employee Number   : 5005
Employee Name     : Ajay
Netpay            : 92000.00
========================================

Employee Number   : 5006
Employee Name     : Achfa
Netpay            : 89000.00
========================================

Employee Number   : 5007
Employee Name     : Indiran
Netpay            : 77000.00
========================================

Employee Number   : 5008
Employee Name     : Nitin Otagiri
Netpay            : 75800.00
========================================

Employee Number   : 5009
Employee Name     : Kumar
Netpay            : 73700.00
========================================

Employee Number   : 5010
Employee Name     : Ravi Chandran
Netpay            : 63900.00
========================================
```

The following program illustrates the use of `case` (multiple conditions) statement. If any of the specified (`when`) expression becomes true, then the result of corresponding block will be returned; if none becomes true, then the value specified in `else` block will be returned. The `case` statement will end without examining other cases, if one case is successful.

```
// File Name: EmployeeManipulation.java
// Illustrates the use of case when .. else statement
```

```
package com.hdemo;

import java.util.Iterator;
import java.util.List;

import org.hibernate.Session;
import org.hibernate.SessionFactory;
import org.hibernate.Transaction;

public class EmployeeManipulation {

   @SuppressWarnings("unchecked")
   public static void main(String[] args) throws Exception {
         SessionFactory sessionFactory =
                              HibernateUtil.getSessionFactory();
         Session session = sessionFactory.openSession();
         Transaction txn = session.beginTransaction();

         List<Employee> employeeList = session.createQuery("select
empNumber, empName, netpay, case  when (netpay > 100000) then (netpay
* 0.18)  when (netpay > 85000) then (netpay * 0.14)  when (netpay
> 75000) then (netpay * 0.11)  when (netpay > 65000) then (netpay *
0.09)  when (netpay > 45000) then (netpay * 0.07) else netpay end from
Employee").list();
       for (Iterator it = employeeList.iterator(); it.hasNext();) {
                Object[] employeeRecord = (Object[])it.next();
                System.out.println("Employee Number : " +
                                                employeeRecord[0]);
                System.out.println("Employee Name     : " +
                                                employeeRecord[1]);
                System.out.println("Netpay                : " +
                                                employeeRecord[2]);
                System.out.println("Tax                   : " +
                                                employeeRecord[3]);

     System.out.println("====================================\n\n");
         }

         txn.commit();
```

```
        session.close();
        sessionFactory.close();
    }
}
```

Hibernate: select employee0_.EMP_NUMBER as col_0_0_,employee0_.EMP_NAME as col_1_0_, employee0_.NETPAY as col_2_0_, case when employee0_.NETPAY>100000 then employee0_.NETPAY*0.18 when employee0_.NETPAY>85000 then employee0_.NETPAY*0.14 when employee0_.NETPAY>75000 then employee0_.NETPAY*0.11 when employee0_.NETPAY>65000 then employee0_.NETPAY*0.09 when employee0_.NETPAY>45000 then employee0_.NETPAY*0.07 else employee0_.NETPAY end as col_3_0_ from EMPLOYEE employee0_

```
Employee Number  : 5001
Employee Name    : Ibrahim
Netpay           : 113000.00
Tax              : 20340.0
========================================

Employee Number  : 5002
Employee Name    : Ananad Desai
Netpay           : 107000.00
Tax              : 19260.0
========================================

Employee Number  : 5003
Employee Name    : Karan Singh
Netpay           : 100500.00
Tax              : 18090.0
========================================

Employee Number  : 5004
Employee Name    : Sudhir
Netpay           : 93900.00
Tax              : 13146.0
========================================
```

```
Employee  Number   :  5005
Employee  Name     :  Ajay
Netpay             :  87000.00
Tax                :  12180.0
========================================

Employee  Number   :  5006
Employee  Name     :  Achfa
Netpay             :  84000.00
Tax                :  9240.0
========================================

Employee  Number   :  5007
Employee  Name     :  Indiran
Netpay             :  77000.00
Tax                :  8470.0
========================================

Employee  Number   :  5008
Employee  Name     :  Nitin  Otagiri
Netpay             :  75800.00
Tax                :  8338.0
========================================

Employee  Number   :  5009
Employee  Name     :  Kumar
Netpay             :  73700.00
Tax                :  6633.0
========================================

Employee  Number   :  5010
Employee  Name     :  Ravi  Chandran
Netpay             :  63900.00
Tax                :  4473.0
========================================
```

To illustrate the use of "`member of`" operator, we change our database data as follows.

Add the following line in *hibernate.cfg.xml* file before executing the main program.

```
<mapping class="com.hdemo.EmployeeCategory" />
// File Name: Employee.java
// Entity Class

package com.hdemo;

import java.io.Serializable;
import java.math.BigDecimal;

import javax.persistence.Column;
import javax.persistence.Entity;
import javax.persistence.GeneratedValue;
import javax.persistence.Id;
import javax.persistence.Table;

import org.hibernate.annotations.GenericGenerator;

@Entity
@Table(name = "EMPLOYEE")
public class Employee implements Serializable {

  private static final long serialVersionUID = 1L;

  @Id
  @GeneratedValue(generator = "idGen")
  @GenericGenerator(name = "idGen", strategy = "uuid.hex")
  @Column(name = "ID", length = 32)
  private String id = "";

  @Column(name = "EMP_NUMBER", nullable = false)
  private int empNumber;

  @Column(name = "EMP_NAME", nullable = false, length = 64)
  private String empName;

  @Column(name = "DEPT", nullable = false, length = 64)
  private String department;
```

```
    @Column(name = "BASIC_PAY", nullable = false, precision = 10, 
scale = 2)
    private BigDecimal basicpay;

    @Column(name = "ALLOWANCES", precision = 10, scale = 2)
    private BigDecimal allowances;

    @Column(name = "DEDUCTIONS", precision = 10, scale = 2)
    private BigDecimal deductions;

    @Column(name = "NETPAY", precision = 10, scale = 2)
    private BigDecimal netpay;

    Employee() {
    }

    Employee(int empNumber, String empName, String department, 
BigDecimal basicpay, BigDecimal allowances, BigDecimal deductions) {
        this.empNumber = empNumber;
        this.empName = empName;
        this.department = department;
        this.basicpay = basicpay;
        this.allowances = allowances;
        this.deductions = deductions;
        this.netpay = basicpay.add(allowances).subtract(deductions);
    }

    public String getId() {
        return id;
    }

    public void setId(String id) {
        this.id = id;
    }

    public int getEmpNumber() {
        return empNumber;
```

```
}

public void setEmpNumber(int empNumber) {
     this.empNumber = empNumber;
}

public String getEmpName() {
     return empName;
}

public void setEmpName(String empName) {
     this.empName = empName;
}

public String getDepartment() {
     return department;
}

public void setDepartment(String department) {
     this.department = department;
}

public BigDecimal getBasicpay() {
     return basicpay;
}

public void setBasicpay(BigDecimal basicpay) {
     this.basicpay = basicpay;
}

public BigDecimal getAllowances() {
     return allowances;
}

public void setAllowances(BigDecimal allowances) {
     this.allowances = allowances;
}

public BigDecimal getDeductions() {
```

```
        return deductions;
    }

    public void setDeductions(BigDecimal deductions) {
        this.deductions = deductions;
    }

    public BigDecimal getNetpay() {
        return netpay;
    }

    public void setNetpay(BigDecimal netpay) {
        this.netpay = netpay;
    }

}

// File Name: EmployeeCategory.java
// Entity class

package com.hdemo;

import java.io.Serializable;
import java.util.HashSet;
import java.util.Set;

import javax.persistence.CascadeType;
import javax.persistence.Column;
import javax.persistence.Entity;
import javax.persistence.FetchType;
import javax.persistence.GeneratedValue;
import javax.persistence.Id;
import javax.persistence.JoinColumn;
import javax.persistence.OneToMany;
import javax.persistence.Table;

import org.hibernate.annotations.GenericGenerator;
```

```
@Entity
@Table(name = "EMPLOYEE_CATEGORY")
public class EmployeeCategory implements Serializable {
  private static final long serialVersionUID = 1L;

  @Id
  @GeneratedValue(generator = "idGen")
  @GenericGenerator(name = "idGen", strategy = "uuid.hex")
  @Column(name = "ID", length = 32)
  private String id = "";

  @OneToMany(cascade=CascadeType.ALL,  fetch=FetchType.EAGER)
  @JoinColumn(name="PERMANENT_EMPLOYEES")
  private Set<Employee> permanentEmployees = new HashSet<Employee>();

  @OneToMany(cascade=CascadeType.ALL,  fetch=FetchType.EAGER)
  @JoinColumn(name="CONTRACT_EMPLOYEES")
  private Set<Employee> contractEmployees = new HashSet<Employee>();

  public String getId() {
       return id;
  }

  public void setId(String id) {
       this.id = id;
  }

  public Set<Employee> getPermanentEmployees() {
       return permanentEmployees;
  }

  public void setPermanentEmployees(Set<Employee> permanentEmployees){
       this.permanentEmployees = permanentEmployees;
  }

  public Set<Employee> getContractEmployees() {
```

```
        return contractEmployees;
    }

    public void setContractEmployees(Set<Employee> contractEmployees)
{
        this.contractEmployees = contractEmployees;
    }

}

// File Name: EmployeeManipulation.java
// Main Program

package com.hdemo;

import java.math.BigDecimal;
import java.util.HashSet;
import java.util.Set;

import org.hibernate.Session;
import org.hibernate.SessionFactory;
import org.hibernate.Transaction;

public class EmployeeManipulation {

    public static void main(String[] args) throws Exception {
        SessionFactory sessionFactory =
                                HibernateUtil.getSessionFactory();
        Session session = sessionFactory.openSession();
        Transaction txn = session.beginTransaction();

    Employee employee1 = new Employee(5001, "Ibrahim", "IT", new
BigDecimal(98000.0), new BigDecimal(30000.0), new BigDecimal(15000.0));
    Employee employee2 = new Employee(5002, "Ananad Desai", "IT", new
BigDecimal(93000.0), new BigDecimal(29000.0), new BigDecimal(15000.0));
    Employee employee3 = new Employee(5003, "Karan Singh", "SALES",
new BigDecimal(88000.0), new BigDecimal(27000.0), new
BigDecimal(14500.0));
```

```
Employee employee4 = new Employee(5004, "Sudhir", "SALES", new BigDecimal(83000.0), new BigDecimal(25000.0), new BigDecimal(14100.0));
Employee employee5 = new Employee(5005, "Ajay", "SALES", new BigDecimal(78000.0), new BigDecimal(23000.0), new BigDecimal(14000.0));
Employee employee6 = new Employee(5006, "Achfa", "SALES", new BigDecimal(74000.0), new BigDecimal(22500.0), new BigDecimal(12500.0));
Employee employee7 = new Employee(5007, "Indiran", "PERSONAL", new BigDecimal(69000.0), new BigDecimal(16000.0), new BigDecimal(8000.0));
Employee employee8 = new Employee(5008, "Nitin Otagiri", "PERSONAL", new BigDecimal(67000.0), new BigDecimal(15800.0), new BigDecimal(7000.0));
Employee employee9 = new Employee(5009, "Kumar", "STATIONARY", new BigDecimal(65000.0), new BigDecimal(15700.0), new BigDecimal(7000.0));
Employee employee10 = new Employee(5010, "Ravi Chandran", "INVENTORY", new BigDecimal(55800.0), new BigDecimal(15100.0), new BigDecimal(7000.0));

        session.persist(employee1);
        session.persist(employee2);
        session.persist(employee3);
        session.persist(employee4);
        session.persist(employee5);
        session.persist(employee6);
        session.persist(employee7);
        session.persist(employee8);
        session.persist(employee9);
        session.persist(employee10);
        System.out.println("The employee objects are persisted with session");

        Set<Employee> permanentEmployees = new HashSet<Employee>();
        permanentEmployees.add(employee1);
        permanentEmployees.add(employee2);
        permanentEmployees.add(employee4);
        permanentEmployees.add(employee6);

        Set<Employee> contractEmployees = new HashSet<Employee>();
        contractEmployees.add(employee3);
```

```
    contractEmployees.add(employee5);
    contractEmployees.add(employee7);
    contractEmployees.add(employee8);
    contractEmployees.add(employee9);
    contractEmployees.add(employee10);

    EmployeeCategory employeeCategory = new EmployeeCategory();
    employeeCategory.setPermanentEmployees(permanentEmployees);
    employeeCategory.setContractEmployees(contractEmployees);
    session.persist(employeeCategory);
    System.out.println("Employee category is persisted with session");

    txn.commit();
    System.out.println("Transaction on this session is committed");
    session.close();
    sessionFactory.close();
    }
}
```

```
The employee objects are persisted with session
Employee category is persisted with session
Hibernate: insert into EMPLOYEE (ALLOWANCES, BASIC_PAY, DEDUCTIONS, DEPT, EMP_NAME, EMP_NUMBER, NETPAY, ID) values (?, ?, ?, ?, ?, ?, ?, ?)
Hibernate: insert into EMPLOYEE (ALLOWANCES, BASIC_PAY, DEDUCTIONS, DEPT, EMP_NAME, EMP_NUMBER, NETPAY, ID) values (?, ?, ?, ?, ?, ?, ?, ?)
Hibernate: insert into EMPLOYEE (ALLOWANCES, BASIC_PAY, DEDUCTIONS, DEPT, EMP_NAME, EMP_NUMBER, NETPAY, ID) values (?, ?, ?, ?, ?, ?, ?, ?)
Hibernate: insert into EMPLOYEE (ALLOWANCES, BASIC_PAY, DEDUCTIONS, DEPT, EMP_NAME, EMP_NUMBER, NETPAY, ID) values (?, ?, ?, ?, ?, ?, ?, ?)
Hibernate: insert into EMPLOYEE (ALLOWANCES, BASIC_PAY, DEDUCTIONS, DEPT, EMP_NAME, EMP_NUMBER, NETPAY, ID) values (?, ?, ?, ?, ?, ?, ?, ?)
Hibernate: insert into EMPLOYEE (ALLOWANCES, BASIC_PAY, DEDUCTIONS, DEPT, EMP_NAME, EMP_NUMBER, NETPAY, ID) values (?, ?, ?, ?, ?, ?, ?, ?)
Hibernate: insert into EMPLOYEE (ALLOWANCES, BASIC_PAY, DEDUCTIONS, DEPT, EMP_NAME, EMP_NUMBER, NETPAY, ID) values (?, ?, ?, ?, ?, ?, ?, ?)
Hibernate: insert into EMPLOYEE (ALLOWANCES, BASIC_PAY, DEDUCTIONS, DEPT, EMP_NAME, EMP_NUMBER, NETPAY, ID) values (?, ?, ?, ?, ?, ?, ?, ?)
```

```
Hibernate: insert into EMPLOYEE (ALLOWANCES, BASIC_PAY, DEDUCTIONS, DEPT, EMP_NAME, EMP_NUMBER, NETPAY, ID) values (?, ?, ?, ?, ?, ?, ?, ?)
Hibernate: insert into EMPLOYEE (ALLOWANCES, BASIC_PAY, DEDUCTIONS, DEPT, EMP_NAME, EMP_NUMBER, NETPAY, ID) values (?, ?, ?, ?, ?, ?, ?, ?)
Hibernate: insert into EMPLOYEE_CATEGORY (ID) values (?)
Hibernate: update EMPLOYEE set CONTRACT_EMPLOYEES=? where ID=?
Hibernate: update EMPLOYEE set CONTRACT_EMPLOYEES=? where ID=?
Hibernate: update EMPLOYEE set CONTRACT_EMPLOYEES=? where ID=?
Hibernate: update EMPLOYEE set CONTRACT_EMPLOYEES=? where ID=?
Hibernate: update EMPLOYEE set CONTRACT_EMPLOYEES=? where ID=?
Hibernate: update EMPLOYEE set CONTRACT_EMPLOYEES=? where ID=?
Hibernate: update EMPLOYEE set PERMANENT_EMPLOYEES=? where ID=?
Hibernate: update EMPLOYEE set PERMANENT_EMPLOYEES=? where ID=?
Hibernate: update EMPLOYEE set PERMANENT_EMPLOYEES=? where ID=?
Hibernate: update EMPLOYEE set PERMANENT_EMPLOYEES=? where ID=?
Transaction on this session is committed

mysql> desc employee;
```

Field	Type	Null	Key	Default	Extra
ID	varchar(32)	NO	PRI	NULL	
ALLOWANCES	decimal(10,2)	YES		NULL	
BASIC_PAY	decimal(10,2)	NO		NULL	
DEDUCTIONS	decimal(10,2)	YES		NULL	
DEPT	varchar(64)	NO		NULL	
EMP_NAME	varchar(64)	NO		NULL	
EMP_NUMBER	int(11)	NO		NULL	
NETPAY	decimal(10,2)	YES		NULL	
PERMANENT_EMPLOYEES	varchar(32)	YES	MUL	NULL	
CONTRACT_EMPLOYEES	varchar(32)	YES	MUL	NULL	

```
10 rows in set (0.00 sec)
```

```
mysql> desc employee_category;
```

Field	Type	Null	Key	Default	Extra
ID	varchar(32)	NO	PRI	NULL	

```
1 row in set (0.00 sec)

mysql> select * from employee_category;
```

ID
402881f81ede3c90011ede3c971d000b

```
1 row in set (0.00 sec)
```

Now, we have some sample data in database. Change the `hbm2ddl.auto` property as `update` in *hibernate.cfg.xml* to keep these data, before running the following program, which illustrate the use of '`member of`' operator.

```
// File Name: EmployeeManipulation.java
// Illustrates 'member of' operator

package com.hdemo;

import java.util.Iterator;
import java.util.List;

import org.hibernate.Session;
import org.hibernate.SessionFactory;
import org.hibernate.Transaction;

public class EmployeeManipulation {

  @SuppressWarnings("unchecked")
  public static void main(String[] args) throws Exception {
        SessionFactory sessionFactory =
                                   HibernateUtil.getSessionFactory();
```

```
        Session session = sessionFactory.openSession();
        Transaction txn = session.beginTransaction();

        List<Employee> employeeList = session.createQuery("select
e.empNumber, e.empName, e.netpay from Employee e, EmployeeCategory ec
where e member of ec.permanentEmployees").list();
        for (Iterator it = employeeList.iterator(); it.hasNext();){
            Object[] employeeRecord = (Object[])it.next();
            System.out.println("Employee Number : " +
                                        employeeRecord[0]);
            System.out.println("Employee Name   : " +
                                        employeeRecord[1]);
            System.out.println("Netpay          : " +
                                        employeeRecord[2]);

    System.out.println("========================================\n\n");
        }

        txn.commit();
        session.close();
        sessionFactory.close();
    }
}
```

```
Hibernate: select employee0_.EMP_NUMBER as col_0_0_,
employee0_.EMP_NAME as col_1_0_, employee0_.NETPAY as col_2_0_ from
EMPLOYEE employee0_, EMPLOYEE_CATEGORY employeeca1_ where employee0_.ID
in (select permanente2_.ID from EMPLOYEE permanente2_ where
employeeca1_.ID=permanente2_.PERMANENT_EMPLOYEES)
  Employee Number  : 5001
  Employee Name    : Ibrahim
  Netpay           : 113000.00
  ========================================

  Employee Number  : 5002
  Employee Name    : Ananad Desai
  Netpay           : 107000.00
  ========================================
```

```
Employee Number   : 5004
Employee Name     : Sudhir
Netpay            : 93900.00
========================================

Employee Number   : 5006
Employee Name     : Achfa
Netpay            : 84000.00
========================================
```

Now, we will create new Entity to test Date oriented functions. Remove `EmployeeCategory` entity mapping from configuration (it is included for previous example). And change `hbm2ddl.auto` property to `create` in *hibernate.cfg.xml* to re-create entity. Change the `Employee` entity as follows which contains employee's date-of-joining as Date field. Then execute the given main program.

```
// File Name: Employee.java
// Data for illustrating Date functions

package com.hdemo;

import java.io.Serializable;
import java.math.BigDecimal;
import java.util.Date;

import javax.persistence.Column;
import javax.persistence.Entity;
import javax.persistence.GeneratedValue;
import javax.persistence.Id;
import javax.persistence.Table;
import javax.persistence.Temporal;
import javax.persistence.TemporalType;

import org.hibernate.annotations.GenericGenerator;

@Entity
@Table(name = "EMPLOYEE")
public class Employee implements Serializable {

  private static final long serialVersionUID = 1L;
```

```
@Id
@GeneratedValue(generator = "idGen")
@GenericGenerator(name = "idGen", strategy = "uuid.hex")
@Column(name = "ID", length = 32)
private String id = "";

@Column(name = "EMP_NUMBER", nullable = false)
private int empNumber;

@Column(name = "EMP_NAME", nullable = false, length = 64)
private String empName;

@Temporal(value=TemporalType.DATE)
@Column (name="DATE_OF_JOINING")
private Date doj;

@Column(name = "DEPT", nullable = false, length = 64)
private String department;

@Column(name = "BASIC_PAY", nullable = false, precision = 10,
                                                   scale = 2)
private BigDecimal basicpay;

@Column(name = "ALLOWANCES", precision = 10, scale = 2)
private BigDecimal allowances;

@Column(name = "DEDUCTIONS", precision = 10, scale = 2)
private BigDecimal deductions;

@Column(name = "NETPAY", precision = 10, scale = 2)
private BigDecimal netpay;

Employee() {
}

Employee(int empNumber, String empName, Date doj, String department,
BigDecimal basicpay, BigDecimal allowances, BigDecimal deductions) {
      this.empNumber = empNumber;
      this.empName = empName;
```

```
        this.doj = doj;
        this.department = department;
        this.basicpay = basicpay;
        this.allowances = allowances;
        this.deductions = deductions;
        this.netpay = basicpay.add(allowances).subtract(deductions);
    }

    public String getId() {
        return id;
    }

    public void setId(String id) {
        this.id = id;
    }

    public int getEmpNumber() {
        return empNumber;
    }

    public void setEmpNumber(int empNumber) {
        this.empNumber = empNumber;
    }

    public String getEmpName() {
        return empName;
    }

    public void setEmpName(String empName) {
        this.empName = empName;
    }

    public Date getDoj() {
        return doj;
    }

    public void setDoj(Date doj) {
```

```
        this.doj = doj;
    }

    public String getDepartment() {
        return department;
    }

    public void setDepartment(String department) {
        this.department = department;
    }

    public BigDecimal getBasicpay() {
        return basicpay;
    }

    public void setBasicpay(BigDecimal basicpay) {
        this.basicpay = basicpay;
    }

    public BigDecimal getAllowances() {
        return allowances;
    }

    public void setAllowances(BigDecimal allowances) {
        this.allowances = allowances;
    }

    public BigDecimal getDeductions() {
        return deductions;
    }

    public void setDeductions(BigDecimal deductions) {
        this.deductions = deductions;
    }

    public BigDecimal getNetpay() {
        return netpay;
    }
```

```
    public void setNetpay(BigDecimal netpay) {
          this.netpay = netpay;
    }

}

// File Name: EmployeeManipulation.java
// Data for illustrating Date functions

package com.hdemo;

import java.math.BigDecimal;
import java.util.Calendar;

import org.hibernate.Session;
import org.hibernate.SessionFactory;
import org.hibernate.Transaction;

public class EmployeeManipulation {

    public static void main(String[] args) throws Exception {
          SessionFactory sessionFactory =
                              HibernateUtil.getSessionFactory();
          Session session = sessionFactory.openSession();
          Transaction txn = session.beginTransaction();

          Calendar c = Calendar.getInstance();
          c.set(2001, 7, 2);  // (year, month, date) format, month
          starts from 0
          Employee employee1 = new Employee(5001, "Ibrahim",
          c.getTime(), "IT", new BigDecimal(98000.0), new
          BigDecimal(30000.0), new BigDecimal(15000.0));
          c.set(2001, 9, 1);
          Employee employee2 = new Employee(5002, "Ananad Desai",
          c.getTime(), "IT", new BigDecimal(93000.0), new
          BigDecimal(29000.0), new BigDecimal(15000.0));
          c.set(2002, 1, 15);
          Employee employee3 = new Employee(5003, "Karan Singh",
```

```
c.getTime(), "SALES", new BigDecimal(88000.0), new
BigDecimal(27000.0), new BigDecimal(14500.0));

c.set(2003, 6, 5);

Employee employee4 = new Employee(5004, "Sudhir", c.getTime(),
"SALES", new BigDecimal(83000.0), new BigDecimal(25000.0),
new BigDecimal(14100.0));

c.set(2004, 11, 1);

Employee employee5 = new Employee(5005, "Ajay", c.getTime(),
"SALES", new BigDecimal(78000.0), new BigDecimal(23000.0),
new BigDecimal(14000.0));

c.set(2005, 0, 2);

Employee employee6 = new Employee(5006, "Achfa", c.getTime(),
"SALES", new BigDecimal(74000.0), new BigDecimal(22500.0),
new BigDecimal(12500.0));

c.set(2000, 2, 5);

Employee employee7 = new Employee(5007, "Indiran",
c.getTime(), "PERSONAL", new BigDecimal(69000.0), new
BigDecimal(16000.0), new BigDecimal(8000.0));

c.set(2000, 5, 1);

Employee employee8 = new Employee(5008, "Nitin Otagiri",
c.getTime(), "PERSONAL", new BigDecimal(67000.0), new
BigDecimal(15800.0), new BigDecimal(7000.0));

c.set(2001, 7, 1);

Employee employee9 = new Employee(5009, "Kumar", c.getTime(),
"STATIONARY", new BigDecimal(65000.0), new
BigDecimal(15700.0), new BigDecimal(7000.0));

c.set(2004, 9, 1);

Employee employee10 = new Employee(5010, "Ravi Chandran",
c.getTime(), "INVENTORY", new BigDecimal(55800.0), new
BigDecimal(15100.0), new BigDecimal(7000.0));

session.persist(employee1);

session.persist(employee2);

session.persist(employee3);

session.persist(employee4);

session.persist(employee5);

session.persist(employee6);

session.persist(employee7);
```

```
    session.persist(employee8);
    session.persist(employee9);
    session.persist(employee10);
    System.out.println("The employee objects are persisted with
session");

    txn.commit();
    System.out.println("Transaction on this session is committed");
    session.close();
    sessionFactory.close();
    }
  }
```

```
The employee objects are persisted with session
Hibernate: insert into EMPLOYEE (ALLOWANCES, BASIC_PAY, DEDUCTIONS,
DEPT, DATE_OF_JOINING, EMP_NAME, EMP_NUMBER, NETPAY, ID) values (?,
?, ?, ?, ?, ?, ?, ?, ?)
Hibernate: insert into EMPLOYEE (ALLOWANCES, BASIC_PAY, DEDUCTIONS,
DEPT, DATE_OF_JOINING, EMP_NAME, EMP_NUMBER, NETPAY, ID) values (?,
?, ?, ?, ?, ?, ?, ?, ?)
Hibernate: insert into EMPLOYEE (ALLOWANCES, BASIC_PAY, DEDUCTIONS,
DEPT, DATE_OF_JOINING, EMP_NAME, EMP_NUMBER, NETPAY, ID) values (?,
?, ?, ?, ?, ?, ?, ?, ?)
Hibernate: insert into EMPLOYEE (ALLOWANCES, BASIC_PAY, DEDUCTIONS,
DEPT, DATE_OF_JOINING, EMP_NAME, EMP_NUMBER, NETPAY, ID) values (?,
?, ?, ?, ?, ?, ?, ?, ?)
Hibernate: insert into EMPLOYEE (ALLOWANCES, BASIC_PAY, DEDUCTIONS,
DEPT, DATE_OF_JOINING, EMP_NAME, EMP_NUMBER, NETPAY, ID) values (?,
?, ?, ?, ?, ?, ?, ?, ?)
Hibernate: insert into EMPLOYEE (ALLOWANCES, BASIC_PAY, DEDUCTIONS,
DEPT, DATE_OF_JOINING, EMP_NAME, EMP_NUMBER, NETPAY, ID) values (?,
?, ?, ?, ?, ?, ?, ?, ?)
Hibernate: insert into EMPLOYEE (ALLOWANCES, BASIC_PAY, DEDUCTIONS,
DEPT, DATE_OF_JOINING, EMP_NAME, EMP_NUMBER, NETPAY, ID) values (?,
?, ?, ?, ?, ?, ?, ?, ?)
Hibernate: insert into EMPLOYEE (ALLOWANCES, BASIC_PAY, DEDUCTIONS,
DEPT, DATE_OF_JOINING, EMP_NAME, EMP_NUMBER, NETPAY, ID) values (?,
?, ?, ?, ?, ?, ?, ?, ?)
```

```
Hibernate: insert into EMPLOYEE (ALLOWANCES, BASIC_PAY, DEDUCTIONS,
DEPT, DATE_OF_JOINING, EMP_NAME, EMP_NUMBER, NETPAY, ID) values (?,
?, ?, ?, ?, ?, ?, ?, ?)
Hibernate: insert into EMPLOYEE (ALLOWANCES, BASIC_PAY, DEDUCTIONS,
DEPT, DATE_OF_JOINING, EMP_NAME, EMP_NUMBER, NETPAY, ID) values (?,
?, ?, ?, ?, ?, ?, ?, ?)
Transaction on this session is committed
```

Keep the generated sample data by setting `hbm2ddl.auto` property to `update` in *hibernate.cfg.xml* and execute the following main program.

```
// File Name: EmployeeManipulation.java
// Illustrates Date functions

package com.hdemo;

import java.text.SimpleDateFormat;
import java.util.Iterator;
import java.util.List;

import org.hibernate.Session;
import org.hibernate.SessionFactory;
import org.hibernate.Transaction;

public class EmployeeManipulation {

   @SuppressWarnings("unchecked")
   public static void main(String[] args) throws Exception {
         SessionFactory sessionFactory =
                              HibernateUtil.getSessionFactory();
         Session session = sessionFactory.openSession();
         Transaction txn = session.beginTransaction();

         SimpleDateFormat sdf = new SimpleDateFormat("dd/MM/yyyy");

         List employeeList = session.createQuery("select e.empNumber,
                        e.empName, e.doj from Employee e").list();
```

```
        for (Iterator it = employeeList.iterator(); it.hasNext();) {
              Object[] employeeRecord = (Object[])it.next();
              System.out.println("Employee Number : " +
                                            employeeRecord[0]);
              System.out.println("Employee Name   : " +
                                            employeeRecord[1]);
              System.out.println("Joined Date     : " +
                                sdf.format(employeeRecord[2]));

   System.out.println("======================================\n\n");
        }

        txn.commit();
        session.close();
        sessionFactory.close();
    }
}
```

```
Hibernate: select employee0_.EMP_NUMBER as col_0_0_, employee0_.EMP_NAME as col_1_0_, employee0_.DATE_OF_JOINING as col_2_0_ from EMPLOYEE employee0_
   Employee Number : 5001
   Employee Name   : Ibrahim
   Joined Date     : 02/08/2001
   ======================================

   Employee Number : 5002
   Employee Name   : Ananad Desai
   Joined Date     : 01/10/2001
   ======================================

   Employee Number : 5003
   Employee Name   : Karan Singh
   Joined Date     : 15/02/2002
   ======================================
```

```
Employee Number  : 5004
Employee Name    : Sudhir
Joined Date      : 05/07/2003
=========================================

Employee Number  : 5005
Employee Name    : Ajay
Joined Date      : 01/12/2004
=========================================

Employee Number  : 5006
Employee Name    : Achfa
Joined Date      : 02/01/2005
=========================================

Employee Number  : 5007
Employee Name    : Indiran
Joined Date      : 05/03/2000
=========================================

Employee Number  : 5008
Employee Name    : Nitin Otagiri
Joined Date      : 01/06/2000
=========================================

Employee Number  : 5009
Employee Name    : Kumar
Joined Date      : 01/08/2001
=========================================

Employee Number  : 5010
Employee Name    : Ravi Chandran
Joined Date      : 01/10/2004
=========================================
```

The following program demonstrates some Date oriented built-in functions.

```
// File Name: EmployeeManipulation.java
// Illustrates Date functions
```

```
package com.hdemo;

import java.util.List;

import org.hibernate.Session;
import org.hibernate.SessionFactory;
import org.hibernate.Transaction;

public class EmployeeManipulation {

  @SuppressWarnings("unchecked")
  public static void main(String[] args) throws Exception {
        SessionFactory sessionFactory =
                                HibernateUtil.getSessionFactory();
        Session session = sessionFactory.openSession();
        Transaction txn = session.beginTransaction();

        List list = session.createQuery("select current_date() from
        Employee").list();
        System.out.println("\nDate using current_date(): " +
        list.get(0));

        list = session.createQuery("select current_time() from
        Employee").list();
        System.out.println("\nDate using current_time(): " +
        list.get(0));

        list = session.createQuery("select current_timestamp() from
        Employee").list();
        System.out.println("\nDate using current_timestamp(): " +
        list.get(0));

        list = session.createQuery("select day(doj) || '/' ||
        month(doj) || '/' || year(doj) from Employee where empNumber
        = 5001").list();
        System.out.println("\nJoined Date of Employee 5001: " +
        list.get(0));

        txn.commit();
        session.close();
        sessionFactory.close();
```

```
    }
  }
```

```
Hibernate: select current_date as col_0_0_ from EMPLOYEE employee0_

Date using current_date(): 2009-01-19
Hibernate: select current_time as col_0_0_ from EMPLOYEE employee0_

Date using current_time(): 11:16:10
Hibernate: select current_timestamp as col_0_0_ from EMPLOYEE
employee0_

Date using current_timestamp(): 2009-01-19 11:16:10.0
Hibernate: select concat(day(employee0_.DATE_OF_JOINING), '/',
month(employee0_.DATE_OF_JOINING), '/', year(employee0_
.DATE_OF_JOINING)) as col_0_0_ from EMPLOYEE employee0_ where
employee0_.EMP_NUMBER=5001

Joined Date of Employee 5001: 2/8/2001
```

The following example illustrates some string oriented functions.

```
// File Name: EmployeeManipulation.java
// Illustrates String functions

package com.hdemo;

import java.util.Iterator;
import java.util.List;

import org.hibernate.Session;
import org.hibernate.SessionFactory;
import org.hibernate.Transaction;

public class EmployeeManipulation {

  @SuppressWarnings("unchecked")
  public static void main(String[] args) throws Exception {
       SessionFactory sessionFactory =
                             HibernateUtil.getSessionFactory();
       Session session = sessionFactory.openSession();
```

```
        Transaction txn = session.beginTransaction();

        List list = session.createQuery("select empName,
        bit_length(empName), locate('n', empName), locate('n',
        empName, 3), mod(7,2), coalesce(empName, empNumber, id)
        from Employee where empNumber = 5007").list();

        for (Iterator it = list.iterator(); it.hasNext();) {
            Object[] record = (Object[])it.next();
            System.out.println("\nEmployee Name: " + record[0]);
            System.out.println("\nBit Length of Employee Name: "
            + record[1]);
            System.out.println("\nLocation of 'n' in [" + record[0]
            + "]: " + record[2]);
            System.out.println("\nLocation of 'n' in [" + record[0]
            + "]. Search from 3rd position: " + record[3]);
            System.out.println("\nmod(7,2): " + record[4]);
            // coalesce function returns first non-null value of
            its arguments
            System.out.println("\ncoalesce(empName, empNumber, id):
            " + record[5]);
        }

        txn.commit();
        session.close();
        sessionFactory.close();
    }
}
```

```
Hibernate: select employee0_.EMP_NAME as col_0_0_,
bit_length(employee0_.EMP_NAME) as col_1_0_, locate('n',
employee0_.EMP_NAME) as col_2_0_, locate('n', employee0_.EMP_NAME, 3)
as col_3_0_, mod(7, 2) as col_4_0_, coalesce(employee0_.EMP_NAME,
employee0_.EMP_NUMBER, employee0_.ID) as col_5_0_ from EMPLOYEE employee0_
where employee0_.EMP_NUMBER=5007

Employee Name: Indiran

Bit Length of Employee Name: 56
```

```
Location of 'n' in [Indiran]: 2

Location of 'n' in [Indiran]. Search from 3rd position: 7

mod(7,2): 1

coalesce(empName, empNumber, id): Indiran
```

In the example below, an object of the entity Salary is a member of the entity Employee and vice versa (Redefine Entities and adjust settings in configuration file). While selecting Employee (from Employee), not only Employee objects, but also corresponding Salary objects are also retrieved. It is same while selecting Salary objects, that it also retrieves corresponding Employee objects.

```
// File Name: Employee.java
// Illustrates select: selecting member entity objects

package com.hdemo;

import javax.persistence.CascadeType;
import javax.persistence.Column;
import javax.persistence.Entity;
import javax.persistence.GeneratedValue;
import javax.persistence.Id;
import javax.persistence.JoinColumn;
import javax.persistence.OneToOne;
import javax.persistence.Table;

import org.hibernate.annotations.GenericGenerator;

@Entity
@Table(name = "EMPLOYEE")
public class Employee {

  private static final long serialVersionUID = 1L;

  @Id
  @GeneratedValue(generator = "idGen")
  @GenericGenerator(name = "idGen", strategy = "uuid.hex")
  @Column(name = "ID", length = 32)
```

```
    private String id = "";

    @Column(name = "EMP_NUMBER", unique = true, nullable = false)
    private Integer empNumber;

    @Column(name = "EMP_NAME", length = 64, nullable = false)
    private String empName;

    @OneToOne(cascade = {CascadeType.PERSIST, CascadeType.REMOVE})
    @JoinColumn(name = "EMP_SALARY", nullable=false, unique=true)
    private Salary salary;

    public String getId() {
          return id;
    }

    public void setId(String id) {
          this.id = id;
    }

    public Integer getEmpNumber() {
          return empNumber;
    }

    public void setEmpNumber(Integer empNumber) {
          this.empNumber = empNumber;
    }

    public String getEmpName() {
          return empName;
    }

    public void setEmpName(String empName) {
          this.empName = empName;
    }

    public Salary getSalary() {
          return salary;
```

```
   }

   public void setSalary(Salary salary) {
        this.salary = salary;
   }

}

// File Name: Salary.java
// Illustrates select: selecting member entity objects

package com.hdemo;

import java.io.Serializable;

import javax.persistence.Column;
import javax.persistence.Entity;
import javax.persistence.GeneratedValue;
import javax.persistence.Id;
import javax.persistence.OneToOne;
import javax.persistence.Table;

import org.hibernate.annotations.GenericGenerator;

@Entity
@Table(name = "SALARY")
public class Salary implements Serializable {

   private static final long serialVersionUID = 1L;

   @Id
   @GeneratedValue(generator = "idGen")
   @GenericGenerator(name = "idGen", strategy = "uuid.hex")
   @Column(name = "ID", length = 32)
   private String id = "";

   @Column(name = "BPAY")
   private Double basicPay;
```

```
@Column(name = "ALLOWANCES")
private Double allowances;

@Column(name = "DEDUCTIONS")
private Double deductions;

@Column(name = "NETPAY")
private Double netPay;

@OneToOne(mappedBy = "salary")
private Employee employee;

public String getId() {
      return id;
}

public void setId(String id) {
      this.id = id;
}

public Double getBasicPay() {
      return basicPay;
}

public void setBasicPay(Double basicPay) {
      this.basicPay = basicPay;
}

public Double getAllowances() {
      return allowances;
}

public void setAllowances(Double allowances) {
      this.allowances = allowances;
}

public Double getDeductions() {
      return deductions;
```

```
    }

    public void setDeductions(Double deductions) {
          this.deductions = deductions;
    }

    public Double getNetPay() {
          return netPay;
    }

    public void setNetPay(Double netPay) {
          this.netPay = netPay;
    }

    public Employee getEmployee() {
          return employee;
    }

    public void setEmployee(Employee employee) {
          this.employee = employee;
    }

}

// File Name: EmployeeManipulation.java
// Main Program

package com.hdemo;

import java.util.List;

import org.hibernate.Session;
import org.hibernate.SessionFactory;
import org.hibernate.Transaction;

public class EmployeeManipulation {

    @SuppressWarnings("unchecked")
    public static void main(String[] args) throws Exception {
```

```
SessionFactory sessionFactory =
                HibernateUtil.getSessionFactory();
Session session = sessionFactory.openSession();
Transaction txn = session.beginTransaction();

Employee employee1 = new Employee();
employee1.setEmpNumber(5001);
employee1.setEmpName("Ibrahim");
Salary salary1 = new Salary();
salary1.setBasicPay(10000.00);
salary1.setAllowances(3000.00);
salary1.setDeductions(2000.00);
salary1.setNetPay(salary1.getBasicPay() +
    salary1.getAllowances() - salary1.getDeductions());
employee1.setSalary(salary1);
session.persist(employee1);
System.out.println("The object employee1 is persisted with
session");

Employee employee2 = new Employee();
employee2.setEmpNumber(5002);
employee2.setEmpName("Kumar");
Salary salary2 = new Salary();
salary2.setBasicPay(5000.00);
salary2.setAllowances(1500.00);
salary2.setDeductions(1000.00);
salary2.setNetPay(salary2.getBasicPay() +
    salary2.getAllowances() - salary2.getDeductions());
employee2.setSalary(salary2);
session.persist(employee2);
System.out.println("The object employee2 is persisted with
session");

Employee employee3 = new Employee();
employee3.setEmpNumber(5003);
employee3.setEmpName("Ajay");
```

```
        Salary salary3 = new Salary();
        salary3.setBasicPay(15000.00);
        salary3.setAllowances(4000.00);
        salary3.setDeductions(2500.00);
        salary3.setNetPay(salary3.getBasicPay() +
                salary3.getAllowances() - salary3.getDeductions());
        employee3.setSalary(salary3);
        session.persist(employee3);
        System.out.println("The object employee3 is persisted with
        session");

        txn.commit();
        System.out.println("Transaction on this session is committed");

        session = sessionFactory.openSession();
        txn = session.beginTransaction();

        System.out.println("\n\nAccessing Employee Objects\n\n");
        List<Employee> employeeList = session.createQuery("from
        Employee").list();
        for (int i = 0; i < employeeList.size(); i++) {
            Employee employee = employeeList.get(i);
            System.out.println("Employee Number: " +
                                    employee.getEmpNumber());
            System.out.println("Employee Name   : " +
                                    employee.getEmpName());
            Salary salary = employee.getSalary();
            System.out.println("Basic Pay        : " +
                                    salary.getBasicPay());
            System.out.println("Allowances       : " +
                                    salary.getAllowances());
            System.out.println("Deductions       : " +
                                    salary.getDeductions());
            System.out.println("Netpay           : " +
                                    salary.getNetPay());

    System.out.println("======================================\n\n");
```

```
        }

        System.out.println("\n\nAccessing Salary Objects\n\n");
        List<Salary> salaryList = session.createQuery("from
        Salary").list();
        for (int i = 0; i < salaryList.size(); i++) {
              Salary salary = salaryList.get(i);
              Employee employee = salary.getEmployee();
              System.out.println("Employee Number : " +
                                  employee.getEmpNumber());
              System.out.println("Employee Name   : " +
                                    employee.getEmpName());
              System.out.println("Basic Pay       : " +
                                     salary.getBasicPay());
              System.out.println("Allowances      : " +
                                  salary.getAllowances());
              System.out.println("Deductions      : " +
                                  salary.getDeductions());
              System.out.println("Netpay          : " +
                                       salary.getNetPay());

  System.out.println("========================================\n\n");
        }

        txn.commit();
        sessionFactory.close();
  }
}
```

```
The object employee1 is persisted with session
The object employee2 is persisted with session
The object employee3 is persisted with session
Hibernate: insert into SALARY (ALLOWANCES, BPAY, DEDUCTIONS, NETPAY,
ID) values (?, ?, ?, ?, ?)
Hibernate: insert into EMPLOYEE (EMP_NAME, EMP_NUMBER, EMP_SALARY,
ID) values (?, ?, ?, ?)
Hibernate: insert into SALARY (ALLOWANCES, BPAY, DEDUCTIONS, NETPAY,
```

```
ID) values (?, ?, ?, ?, ?)
Hibernate: insert into EMPLOYEE (EMP_NAME, EMP_NUMBER, EMP_SALARY,
ID) values (?, ?, ?, ?)
Hibernate: insert into SALARY (ALLOWANCES, BPAY, DEDUCTIONS, NETPAY,
ID) values (?, ?, ?, ?, ?)
Hibernate: insert into EMPLOYEE (EMP_NAME, EMP_NUMBER, EMP_SALARY,
ID) values (?, ?, ?, ?)
Transaction on this session is committed

Accessing Employee Objects

Employee Number : 5001
Employee Name   : Ibrahim
Basic Pay       : 10000.0
Allowances      : 3000.0
Deductions      : 2000.0
Netpay          : 11000.0
========================================
Employee Number : 5002
Employee Name   : Kumar
Basic Pay       : 5000.0
Allowances      : 1500.0
Deductions      : 1000.0
Netpay          : 5500.0
========================================
Employee Number : 5003
Employee Name   : Ajay
Basic Pay       : 15000.0
Allowances      : 4000.0
Deductions      : 2500.0
Netpay          : 16500.0
========================================
```

```
Accessing Salary Objects

Hibernate: select salary0_.ID as ID1_, salary0_.ALLOWANCES as ALLOWANCES1_, salary0_.BPAY as BPAY1_, salary0_.DEDUCTIONS as DEDUCTIONS1_, salary0_.NETPAY as NETPAY1_ from SALARY salary0_

Employee Number  : 5001
Employee Name    : Ibrahim
Basic Pay        : 10000.0
Allowances       : 3000.0
Deductions       : 2000.0
Netpay           : 11000.0
========================================

Employee Number  : 5002
Employee Name    : Kumar
Basic Pay        : 5000.0
Allowances       : 1500.0
Deductions       : 1000.0
Netpay           : 5500.0
========================================

Employee Number  : 5003
Employee Name    : Ajay
Basic Pay        : 15000.0
Allowances       : 4000.0
Deductions       : 2500.0
Netpay           : 16500.0
========================================
```

The following example illustrates how to retrieve Collection of values (in our example, List).

```
// File Name: Employee.java
// Illustrates how to access Collection of values

package com.hdemo;
```

```
import java.util.List;

import javax.persistence.CascadeType;
import javax.persistence.Column;
import javax.persistence.Entity;
import javax.persistence.GeneratedValue;
import javax.persistence.Id;
import javax.persistence.JoinColumn;
import javax.persistence.OneToMany;
import javax.persistence.Table;

import org.hibernate.annotations.GenericGenerator;

@Entity
@Table(name = "EMPLOYEE")
public class Employee {

  private static final long serialVersionUID = 1L;

  @Id
  @GeneratedValue(generator = "idGen")
  @GenericGenerator(name = "idGen", strategy = "uuid.hex")
  @Column(name = "ID", length = 32)
  private String id = "";

  @Column(name = "EMP_NUMBER", unique = true, nullable = false)
  private Integer empNumber;

  @Column(name = "EMP_NAME", length = 64, nullable = false)
  private String empName;

  @OneToMany(cascade = CascadeType.ALL)
  @JoinColumn(name = "EMPLOYEE_ADDRESS")
  private List<Address> addresses;

  public String getId() {
       return id;
```

```
    }

    public void setId(String id) {
        this.id = id;
    }

    public Integer getEmpNumber() {
        return empNumber;
    }

    public void setEmpNumber(Integer empNumber) {
        this.empNumber = empNumber;
    }

    public String getEmpName() {
        return empName;
    }

    public void setEmpName(String empName) {
        this.empName = empName;
    }

    public List<Address> getAddresses() {
        return addresses;
    }

    public void setAddresses(List<Address> addresses) {
        this.addresses = addresses;
    }
}
```

```
The object employee1 is persisted with session
The object employee2 is persisted with session
The object employee3 is persisted with session
Hibernate: insert into EMPLOYEE (EMP_NAME, EMP_NUMBER, ID) values
(?, ?, ?)
Hibernate: insert into ADDRESS (CITY_NAME, COUNTRY_NAME, HOUSE_NUMBER,
POSTAL_CODE, STREET_NAME, ID) values (?, ?, ?, ?, ?, ?)
```

```
Hibernate: insert into ADDRESS (CITY_NAME, COUNTRY_NAME, HOUSE_NUMBER, POSTAL_CODE, STREET_NAME, ID) values (?, ?, ?, ?, ?, ?)
Hibernate: insert into ADDRESS (CITY_NAME, COUNTRY_NAME, HOUSE_NUMBER, POSTAL_CODE, STREET_NAME, ID) values (?, ?, ?, ?, ?, ?)
Hibernate: insert into EMPLOYEE (EMP_NAME, EMP_NUMBER, ID) values (?, ?, ?)
Hibernate: insert into ADDRESS (CITY_NAME, COUNTRY_NAME, HOUSE_NUMBER, POSTAL_CODE, STREET_NAME, ID) values (?, ?, ?, ?, ?, ?)
Hibernate: insert into EMPLOYEE (EMP_NAME, EMP_NUMBER, ID) values (?, ?, ?)
Hibernate: update ADDRESS set EMPLOYEE_ADDRESS=? where ID=?
Hibernate: update ADDRESS set EMPLOYEE_ADDRESS=? where ID=?
Hibernate: update ADDRESS set EMPLOYEE_ADDRESS=? where ID=?
Hibernate: update ADDRESS set EMPLOYEE_ADDRESS=? where ID=?
Transaction on this session is committed
Accessing Employee Objects

Hibernate: select employee0_.ID as ID0_, employee0_.EMP_NAME as EMP2_0_, employee0_.EMP_NUMBER as EMP3_0_ from EMPLOYEE employee0_
Employee Number : 5001
Employee Name : Ibrahim
Employee Address(1): [House Number: C-13-4
Street Name : Jalan Munsi Abdullah
City Name : Kuala Lumpur
Country Name : Malaysia
Postal Code : 50100]
Employee Address(2): [House Number: 3-121
Street Name : Middle Street
City Name : Tiruchirapalli
Country Name : India
Postal Code : 621302]
Employee Address(3): [House Number: D-14
Street Name : Jalan Bunus
City Name : Penang
Country Name : Malaysia
Postal Code : 11950]
========================================
```

```
Employee Number        : 5002
Employee Name          : Kumar
Employee Address(1) : [House Number: T-4
Street Name            : Nehru Street
City Name              : Chennai
Country Name           : India
Postal Code            : 600020]
========================================
Employee Number        : 5003
Employee Name          : Ajay
========================================

Getting Address details

Hibernate: select addresses1_.ID as ID1_, addresses1_.CITY_NAME as CITY2_1_, addresses1_.COUNTRY_NAME as COUNTRY3_1_, addresses1_.HOUSE_NUMBER as HOUSE4_1_, addresses1_.POSTAL_CODE as POSTAL5_1_, addresses1_.STREET_NAME as STREET6_1_ from EMPLOYEE employee0_ inner join ADDRESS addresses1_ on employee0_.ID=addresses1_.EMPLOYEE_ADDRESS
[House Number          : C-13-4
Street Name            : Jalan Munsi Abdullah
City Name              : Kuala Lumpur
Country Name           : Malaysia
Postal Code            : 50100]

[House Number          : 3-121
Street Name            : Middle Street
City Name              : Tiruchirapalli
Country Name           : India
Postal Code            : 621302]

[House Number          : D-14
Street Name            : Jalan Bunus
```

```
City Name           : Penang
Country Name        : Malaysia
Postal Code         : 11950]

[House Number       : T-4
Street Name         : Nehru Street
City Name           : Chennai
Country Name        : India
Postal Code         : 600020]
```

5.3 JOIN QUERIES

Join conditions are used to combine (join) two or more tables and select the required data. General format of Join

```
table1 type-of-join table2
```

Based on the conditions on join, we can distinguish Joins as below.

(i) `INNER JOIN` or simply `JOIN`

-Returns all matching rows from table1 and table2 (returns rows from both tables when the specified condition columns match).

(ii) `OUTER JOIN`

This can be further classified into two types.

(a) `LEFT OUTER JOIN` or simply `LEFT JOIN`

-Returns all matching rows from both tables and also returns all rows from the left table (table1), even if there are no matches in the right table (table2).

(b) `RIGHT OUTER JOIN` or simply `RIGHT JOIN`

-Returns all matching rows from both tables and also returns all rows from the right table (table2), even if there are no matches in the left table (table1).

The following program generates some sample data to manipulate join operations. Add the following settings in *hibernate.cfg.xml* file.

```
<mapping class="com.hdemo.Customer" />
<mapping class="com.hdemo.Invoice" />
```

```
// File Name: Customer.java
// Illustrates Join operation

package com.hdemo;
```

```
import javax.persistence.Column;
import javax.persistence.Entity;
import javax.persistence.GeneratedValue;
import javax.persistence.Id;
import javax.persistence.Table;

import org.hibernate.annotations.GenericGenerator;

@Entity
@Table(name = "CUSTOMER")
public class Customer {

  @Id
  @GeneratedValue(generator = "idGen")
  @GenericGenerator(name = "idGen", strategy = "assigned")
  @Column(name = "IC_NUMBER", nullable = false)
  private int icNumber;

  @Column(name = "CUST_NAME", nullable = false, length = 80)
  private String customerName;

  @Column(name = "EMAIL", length = 80)
  private String email;

  public int getIcNumber() {
        return icNumber;
  }

  public void setIcNumber(int icNumber) {
        this.icNumber = icNumber;
  }

  public String getCustomerName() {
        return customerName;
  }

  public void setCustomerName(String customerName) {
```

```
        this.customerName = customerName;
    }

    public String getEmail() {
        return email;
    }

    public void setEmail(String email) {
        this.email = email;
    }

}

// File Name: Invoice.java
// Illustrates Join operation

package com.hdemo;

import javax.persistence.Column;
import javax.persistence.Entity;
import javax.persistence.GeneratedValue;
import javax.persistence.Id;
import javax.persistence.Table;

import org.hibernate.annotations.GenericGenerator;

@Entity
@Table(name="INVOICE")
public class Invoice {

    @Id
    @GeneratedValue(generator = "idGen")
    @GenericGenerator(name = "idGen", strategy = "assigned")
    @Column(name = "INVOICE_NUMBER", nullable = false)
    private int invoiceNum;

    @Column(name = "CUST_IC_NUMBER", nullable = false)
    private int customerICNumber;
```

```
    @Column(name = "AMOUNT")
    private double amount;

    public int getInvoiceNum() {
        return invoiceNum;
    }

    public void setInvoiceNum(int invoiceNum) {
        this.invoiceNum = invoiceNum;
    }

    public int getCustomerICNumber() {
        return customerICNumber;
    }

    public void setCustomerICNumber(int customerICNumber) {
        this.customerICNumber = customerICNumber;
    }

    public double getAmount() {
        return amount;
    }

    public void setAmount(double amount) {
        this.amount = amount;
    }

}

// File Name: SalesManipulation.java
// Illustrates Join operation

package com.hdemo;

import org.hibernate.Session;
import org.hibernate.SessionFactory;
import org.hibernate.Transaction;
```

```
public class SalesManipulation {

    public static void main(String[] args) throws Exception {
        SessionFactory sessionFactory =
HibernateUtil.getSessionFactory();
        Session session = sessionFactory.openSession();
        Transaction txn = session.beginTransaction();

        Customer customer1 = new Customer();
        customer1.setIcNumber(2008001501);
        customer1.setCustomerName("Mohamed Ibrahim");
        customer1.setEmail("bmohamedibrahim@yahoo.co.in");

        Customer customer2 = new Customer();
        customer2.setIcNumber(2008001602);
        customer2.setCustomerName("Ajit Kumar");
        customer2.setEmail("ajitkumar@email.net");

        Customer customer3 = new Customer();
        customer3.setIcNumber(2008001703);
        customer3.setCustomerName("Karan Singh");
        customer3.setEmail("karansingh@email2you.com");

        Customer customer4 = new Customer();
        customer4.setIcNumber(2008001804);
        customer4.setCustomerName("Nitin");
        customer4.setEmail("nitin@email.com");

        Invoice invoice1 = new Invoice();
        invoice1.setInvoiceNum(1001);
        invoice1.setCustomerICNumber(2008001501);
        invoice1.setAmount(10000.0);

        Invoice invoice2 = new Invoice();
        invoice2.setInvoiceNum(1002);
        invoice2.setCustomerICNumber(2008001501);
        invoice2.setAmount(8500.0);
```

```
        Invoice invoice3 = new Invoice();
        invoice3.setInvoiceNum(1003);
        invoice3.setCustomerICNumber(2008001703);
        invoice3.setAmount(4500.0);

        Invoice invoice4 = new Invoice();
        invoice4.setInvoiceNum(1004);
        invoice4.setCustomerICNumber(1009001101);
        invoice4.setAmount(12345.0);

        Invoice invoice5 = new Invoice();
        invoice5.setInvoiceNum(1005);
        invoice5.setCustomerICNumber(2008001804);
        invoice5.setAmount(18230.0);

        session.save(customer1);
        session.save(customer2);
        session.save(customer3);
        session.save(customer4);

        session.save(invoice1);
        session.save(invoice2);
        session.save(invoice3);
        session.save(invoice4);
        session.save(invoice5);

        txn.commit();
        session.close();
        sessionFactory.close();
    }
}
```

The following are some SQL queries using Joins.

```
mysql> desc customer;
```

Field	Type	Null	Key	Default	Extra
IC_NUMBER	int(11)	NO	PRI	NULL	
CUST_NAME	varchar(80)	NO		NULL	
EMAIL	varchar(80)	YES		NULL	

```
3 rows in set (0.00 sec)
mysql> desc invoice;
```

Field	Type	Null	Key	Default	Extra
INVOICE_NUMBER	int(11)	NO	PRI	NULL	
AMOUNT	double	YES		NULL	
CUST_IC_NUMBER	int(11)	NO		NULL	

```
3 rows in set (0.00 sec)
mysql> select * from customer;
```

IC_NUMBER	CUST_NAME	EMAIL
2008001501	Mohamed Ibrahim	bmohamedibrahim@yahoo.co.in
2008001602	Ajit Kumar	ajitkumar@email.net
2008001703	Karan Singh	karansingh@email2you.com
2008001804	Nitin	nitin@email.com

```
4 rows in set (0.00 sec)
mysql> select * from invoice;
```

INVOICE_NUMBER	AMOUNT	CUST_IC_NUMBER
1001	10000	2008001501
1002	8500	2008001501
1003	4500	2008001703
1004	12345	1009001101
1005	18230	2008001804

```
5 rows in set (0.00 sec)
```

Error will be reported if you use the above style of JOIN HQL queries directly in Hibernate. Hibernate expects an entity (joining entity) should have a collection property (joined entity) of type joining entity for join operation.

The following example uses native (underlying database) SQL queries to illustrate join operations in Hibernate. Note that `createSQLQuery()` method is used to create native SQL query.

INNER JOIN:

```
// File Name: SalesManipulation.java
// Illustrates Join Operations (INNER JOIN) and Native Queries

package com.hdemo;

import java.util.Iterator;
import java.util.List;

import org.hibernate.Session;
import org.hibernate.SessionFactory;
import org.hibernate.Transaction;

public class SalesManipulation {

  @SuppressWarnings("unchecked")
  public static void main(String[] args) throws Exception {
        SessionFactory sessionFactory =
                              HibernateUtil.getSessionFactory();
        Session session = sessionFactory.openSession();
        Transaction txn = session.beginTransaction();

        List list = session.createSQLQuery("select * from customer
c INNER JOIN invoice i ON c.ic_number = i.cust_ic_number").list();

        System.out.printf("%-15s %-20s %-30s %-16s %10s  %-15s",
"IC_NUMBER", "CUST_NAME", "EMAIL", "INVOICE_NUMBER", "AMOUNT",
"CUST_IC_NUMBER");
        for (Iterator it = list.iterator(); it.hasNext();) {
              Object[] row = (Object[]) it.next();
              System.out.printf("\n%-15s %-20s %-30s %-16s %10s
%-15s", row[0], row[1], row[2], row[3], row[4], row[5]);
        }
```

```
            txn.commit();
            session.close();
            sessionFactory.close();
    }
}
```

Hibernate: select * from customer c INNER JOIN invoice i ON c.ic_number = i.cust_ic_number

IC_NUMBER	CUST_NAME	EMAIL	INVOICE _NUMBER	AMOUNT	CUST_IC_NUMBER
2008001501	Mohamed Ibrahim	bmohamedibrah im@yahoo.co.in	1001	10000.0	2008001501
2008001501	Mohamed Ibrahim	bmohamedibr ahim@yahoo.co.in	1002	8500.0	2008001501
2008001703	Karan Singh	karansingh @email2you.com	1003	4500.0	2008001703
2008001804	Nitin	nitin@email.com	1005	18230.0	2008001804

LEFT OUTER JOIN:

```
// File Name: EmployeeManipulation.java
// Illustrates Join Operations (LEFT OUTER JOIN) and Native Queries

package com.hdemo;

import java.util.Iterator;
import java.util.List;

import org.hibernate.Session;
import org.hibernate.SessionFactory;
import org.hibernate.Transaction;

public class SalesManipulation {

    @SuppressWarnings("unchecked")
    public static void main(String[] args) throws Exception {
```

```
        SessionFactory sessionFactory =
                            HibernateUtil.getSessionFactory();
        Session session = sessionFactory.openSession();
        Transaction txn = session.beginTransaction();

        List list = session.createSQLQuery("select * from customer
        c LEFT OUTER JOIN invoice i ON c.ic_number =
        i.cust_ic_number").list();

        System.out.printf("%-15s %-20s %-30s %-16s %10s  %-15s",
        "IC_NUMBER", "CUST_NAME", "EMAIL", "INVOICE_NUMBER", "AMOUNT",
        "CUST_IC_NUMBER");
        for (Iterator it = list.iterator(); it.hasNext();) {
            Object[] row = (Object[]) it.next();
            System.out.printf("\n%-15s %-20s %-30s %-16s %10s
            %-15s", row[0], row[1], row[2], row[3], row[4],
            row[5]);
        }

        txn.commit();
        session.close();
        sessionFactory.close();
    }
}
```

RIGHT OUTER JOIN:

```
// File Name: EmployeeManipulation.java
// Illustrates Join Operations (RIGHT OUTER JOIN) and Native
Queries

package com.hdemo;

import java.util.Iterator;
import java.util.List;

import org.hibernate.Session;
import org.hibernate.SessionFactory;
import org.hibernate.Transaction;
```

```
public class SalesManipulation {

  @SuppressWarnings("unchecked")
  public static void main(String[] args) throws Exception {
        SessionFactory sessionFactory =
                            HibernateUtil.getSessionFactory();
        Session session = sessionFactory.openSession();
        Transaction txn = session.beginTransaction();

        List list = session.createSQLQuery("select * from customer
        c RIGHT OUTER JOIN invoice i ON c.ic_number =
        i.cust_ic_number").list();

        System.out.printf("%-15s %-20s %-30s %-16s %10s  %-15s",
        "IC_NUMBER", "CUST_NAME", "EMAIL", "INVOICE_NUMBER", "AMOUNT",
        "CUST_IC_NUMBER");
        for (Iterator it = list.iterator(); it.hasNext();) {
              Object[] row = (Object[]) it.next();
              System.out.printf("\n%-15s %-20s %-30s %-16s %10s
              %-15s", row[0], row[1], row[2], row[3], row[4],row[5]);
        }

        txn.commit();
        session.close();
        sessionFactory.close();
  }
}
```

The following example illustrates how to use Join operations in HQL.

Execute the following program to generate sample data (Adjust configurations in *hibernate.cfg.xml* file, keep `hbm2ddl.auto` property as `create`).

```
// File Name: Customer.java
// Illustrates Join operations

package com.hdemo;

import java.util.HashSet;
import java.util.Set;

import javax.persistence.CascadeType;
```

```
import javax.persistence.Column;
import javax.persistence.Entity;
import javax.persistence.GeneratedValue;
import javax.persistence.Id;
import javax.persistence.JoinColumn;
import javax.persistence.OneToMany;
import javax.persistence.Table;

import org.hibernate.annotations.GenericGenerator;

@Entity
@Table(name = "CUSTOMER")
public class Customer {

  @Id
  @GeneratedValue(generator = "idGen")
  @GenericGenerator(name = "idGen", strategy = "uuid.hex")
  @Column(name = "ID", length = 32)
  private String id = "";

  @Column(name = "IC_NUMBER", nullable = false)
  private int icNumber;

  @Column(name = "CUST_NAME", nullable = false, length = 80)
  private String customerName;

  @Column(name = "EMAIL", length = 80)
  private String email;

  @OneToMany(cascade = CascadeType.ALL)
  @JoinColumn(name = "CUST_INVOICE")
  private Set<Invoice> invoices = new HashSet<Invoice>();

  public String getId() {
       return id;
  }

  public void setId(String id) {
       this.id = id;
  }
```

```
    public int getIcNumber() {
        return icNumber;
    }

    public void setIcNumber(int icNumber) {
        this.icNumber = icNumber;
    }

    public String getCustomerName() {
        return customerName;
    }

    public void setCustomerName(String customerName) {
        this.customerName = customerName;
    }

    public String getEmail() {
        return email;
    }

    public void setEmail(String email) {
        this.email = email;
    }

    public Set<Invoice> getInvoices() {
        return invoices;
    }

    public void setInvoices(Set<Invoice> invoices) {
        this.invoices = invoices;
    }
}

// File Name: Invoice.java
// Illustrates Join operations

package com.hdemo;
```

```
import javax.persistence.Column;
import javax.persistence.Entity;
import javax.persistence.GeneratedValue;
import javax.persistence.Id;
import javax.persistence.Table;

import org.hibernate.annotations.GenericGenerator;

@Entity
@Table(name = "INVOICE")
public class Invoice {

  @Id
  @GeneratedValue(generator = "idGen")
  @GenericGenerator(name = "idGen", strategy = "uuid.hex")
  @Column(name = "ID", length = 32)
  private String id = "";

  @Column(name = "INVOICE_NUMBER", nullable = false)
  private int invoiceNum;

  @Column(name = "AMOUNT")
  private double amount;

  public String getId() {
        return id;
  }

  public void setId(String id) {
        this.id = id;
  }

  public int getInvoiceNum() {
        return invoiceNum;
  }

  public void setInvoiceNum(int invoiceNum) {
        this.invoiceNum = invoiceNum;
  }
```

```
    public double getAmount() {
          return amount;
    }

    public void setAmount(double amount) {
          this.amount = amount;
    }

}


// File Name: SalesManipulation.java
// Illustrates Join operations

package com.hdemo;

import java.util.HashSet;
import java.util.Set;

import org.hibernate.Session;
import org.hibernate.SessionFactory;
import org.hibernate.Transaction;

public class SalesManipulation {

    public static void main(String[] args) throws Exception {
          SessionFactory sessionFactory =
HibernateUtil.getSessionFactory();
          Session session = sessionFactory.openSession();
          Transaction txn = session.beginTransaction();

          Customer customer1 = new Customer();
          customer1.setIcNumber(2008001501);
          customer1.setCustomerName("Mohamed Ibrahim");
          customer1.setEmail("bmohamedibrahim@yahoo.co.in");

          Customer customer2 = new Customer();
          customer2.setIcNumber(2008001602);
          customer2.setCustomerName("Ajit Kumar");
          customer2.setEmail("ajitkumar@email.net");

          Customer customer3 = new Customer();
          customer3.setIcNumber(2008001703);
```

```
customer3.setCustomerName("Karan Singh");
customer3.setEmail("karansingh@email2you.com");

Customer customer4 = new Customer();
customer4.setIcNumber(2008001804);
customer4.setCustomerName("Nitin");
customer4.setEmail("nitin@email.com");

Customer customer5 = new Customer();
customer5.setIcNumber(2008001950);
customer5.setCustomerName("Kiran");
customer5.setEmail("kiran@email.com");

Invoice invoice1 = new Invoice();
invoice1.setInvoiceNum(1001);
invoice1.setAmount(10000.0);

Invoice invoice2 = new Invoice();
invoice2.setInvoiceNum(1002);
invoice2.setAmount(8500.0);

Invoice invoice3 = new Invoice();
invoice3.setInvoiceNum(1003);
invoice3.setAmount(4500.0);

Invoice invoice4 = new Invoice();
invoice4.setInvoiceNum(1004);
invoice4.setAmount(12345.0);

Invoice invoice5 = new Invoice();
invoice5.setInvoiceNum(1005);
invoice5.setAmount(18230.0);

Invoice invoice6 = new Invoice();
invoice6.setInvoiceNum(1006);
invoice6.setAmount(4000.0);

Set<Invoice> customer1Invoices = new HashSet<Invoice>();
customer1Invoices.add(invoice1);
customer1Invoices.add(invoice2);
customer1.setInvoices(customer1Invoices);
```

```
        Set<Invoice> customer2Invoices = new HashSet<Invoice>();
        customer2Invoices.add(invoice3);
        customer2Invoices.add(invoice4);
        customer2.setInvoices(customer2Invoices);

        Set<Invoice> customer3Invoices = new HashSet<Invoice>();
        customer3Invoices.add(invoice5);
        customer3.setInvoices(customer3Invoices);

        customer4.setInvoices(null);

        customer5.setInvoices(null);

        session.save(customer1);
        session.save(customer2);
        session.save(customer3);
        session.save(customer4);
        session.save(customer5);

        session.save(invoice6);

        txn.commit();
        session.close();
        sessionFactory.close();
    }
}
```

```
mysql> desc customer;
```

Field	Type	Null	Key	Default	Extra
ID	varchar(32)	NO	PRI	NULL	
CUST_NAME	varchar(80)	NO		NULL	
EMAIL	varchar(80)	YES		NULL	
IC_NUMBER	int(11)	NO		NULL	

```
4 rows in set (0.06 sec)
```

```
mysql> desc invoice;
```

Field	Type	Null	Key	Default	Extra
ID	varchar(32)	NO	PRI	NULL	
AMOUNT	double	YES		NULL	
INVOICE_NUMBER	int(11)	NO		NULL	
CUST_INVOICE	varchar(32)	YES	MUL	NULL	

```
4 rows in set (0.00 sec)
```

The following are the sample programs, illustrates Join operations using HQL. Change the `hbm2ddl.auto` property as `update` to keep the generated sample data.

INNER JOIN:

```
// File Name: SalesManipulation.java
// Illustrates Join Operations (INNER JOIN) and HQL

package com.hdemo;

import java.util.Iterator;
import java.util.List;

import org.hibernate.Session;
import org.hibernate.SessionFactory;
import org.hibernate.Transaction;

public class SalesManipulation {

  @SuppressWarnings("unchecked")
  public static void main(String[] args) throws Exception {
        SessionFactory sessionFactory =
                        HibernateUtil.getSessionFactory();
        Session session = sessionFactory.openSession();
        Transaction txn = session.beginTransaction();

        List list = session.createQuery("from Customer c inner join
        c.invoices i").list();

        for (Iterator it = list.iterator(); it.hasNext();) {
```

```
            Object[] row = (Object[]) it.next();

            Customer customer = (Customer) row[0];
            if (customer != null)
            System.out.printf("%-35s \t %-15s \t %-20s \t %-35s
            \t", customer.getId(), customer.getIcNumber(),
            customer.getCustomerName(), customer.getEmail());
            else
            System.out.printf("%-35s \t %-15s \t %-20s \t %-35s
            \t", "NULL", "NULL", "NULL", "NULL");

            Invoice invoice = (Invoice) row[1];
            if (invoice != null)
            System.out.printf("%-35s \t %10s \t %10.2f \t",
            invoice.getId(), invoice.getInvoiceNum(), invoice
            .getAmount());
            else
            System.out.printf("%-35s \t %10s \t %10s \t",
            "NULL", "NULL", "NULL");

            System.out.println();
        }

        txn.commit();
        session.close();
        sessionFactory.close();
    }
}
```

LEFT OUTER JOIN:

```
// File Name: SalesManipulation.java
// Illustrates Join Operations (LEFT OUTER JOIN) and HQL

package com.hdemo;

import java.util.Iterator;
import java.util.List;

import org.hibernate.Session;
import org.hibernate.SessionFactory;
import org.hibernate.Transaction;
```

```
public class SalesManipulation {

   @SuppressWarnings("unchecked")
   public static void main(String[] args) throws Exception {
         SessionFactory sessionFactory =
                                   HibernateUtil.getSessionFactory();
         Session session = sessionFactory.openSession();
         Transaction txn = session.beginTransaction();

         List list = session.createQuery("from Customer c left outer
                                          join c.invoices i").list();

         for (Iterator it = list.iterator(); it.hasNext();) {
               Object[] row = (Object[]) it.next();

               Customer customer = (Customer) row[0];
               if (customer != null)
         System.out.printf("%-35s \t %-15s \t %-20s \t %-35s \t",
customer.getId(), customer.getIcNumber(), customer.getCustomerName(),
customer.getEmail());
               else
         System.out.printf("%-35s \t %-15s \t %-20s \t %-35s \t",
         "NULL", "NULL", "NULL", "NULL");

               Invoice invoice = (Invoice) row[1];
               if (invoice != null)
               System.out.printf("%-35s \t %10s \t %10.2f \t",
               invoice.getId(), invoice.getInvoiceNum(), invoice
               .getAmount());
               else
               System.out.printf("%-35s \t %10s \t %10s \t", "NULL",
               "NULL", "NULL");

               System.out.println();
         }

         txn.commit();
         session.close();
         sessionFactory.close();
   }
}
```

RIGHT OUTER JOIN:

```
// File Name: SalesManipulation.java
// Illustrates Join Operations (RIGHT OUTER JOIN) and HQL

package com.hdemo;

import java.util.Iterator;
import java.util.List;

import org.hibernate.Session;
import org.hibernate.SessionFactory;
import org.hibernate.Transaction;

public class SalesManipulation {

   @SuppressWarnings("unchecked")
   public static void main(String[] args) throws Exception {
         SessionFactory sessionFactory =
                             HibernateUtil.getSessionFactory();
         Session session = sessionFactory.openSession();
         Transaction txn = session.beginTransaction();

         List list = session.createQuery("from Customer c right
         outer join c.invoices i").list();

         for (Iterator it = list.iterator(); it.hasNext();) {
               Object[] row = (Object[]) it.next();

               Customer customer = (Customer) row[0];
               if (customer != null)
               System.out.printf("%-35s \t %-15s \t %-20s \t %-35s
               \t", customer.getId(), customer.getIcNumber(),
               customer.getCustomerName(), customer.getEmail());
               else
               System.out.printf("%-35s \t %-15s \t %-20s \t %-35s
               \t", "NULL", "NULL", "NULL", "NULL");

               Invoice invoice = (Invoice) row[1];
               if (invoice != null)
```

```
                System.out.printf("%-35s  \t  %10s  \t  %10.2f  \t",
                invoice.getId(), invoice.getInvoiceNum(), invoice
                .getAmount());
                else
                System.out.printf("%-35s \t %10s \t %10s \t", "NULL",
                "NULL", "NULL");

                System.out.println();
            }

            txn.commit();
            session.close();
            sessionFactory.close();
        }
    }
```

5.4 DYNAMIC ASSIGNMENT OF SELECTED VALUES ON VALUE OBJECTS

We can dynamically assign to any object while selecting values from entities. The following example selects `icNumber` and `amount` from entities `Customer` and `Invoice`, and then creates a `Sales` object by using its parameterized constructor. This `Sales` class is not needed to be included in hibernate configuration file and no need to be an entity.

Execute the following programs used to generate sample data (These programs are used in demonstrating Native SQL Join operations. The same programs are repeated here for easy reference.)

```
// File Name: Customer.java
// Illustrates Join operation

package com.hdemo;

import javax.persistence.Column;
import javax.persistence.Entity;
import javax.persistence.GeneratedValue;
import javax.persistence.Id;
import javax.persistence.Table;

import org.hibernate.annotations.GenericGenerator;

@Entity
@Table(name = "CUSTOMER")
public class Customer {
```

```
    @Id
    @GeneratedValue(generator = "idGen")
    @GenericGenerator(name = "idGen", strategy = "assigned")
    @Column(name = "IC_NUMBER", nullable = false)
    private int icNumber;

    @Column(name = "CUST_NAME", nullable = false, length = 80)
    private String customerName;

    @Column(name = "EMAIL", length = 80)
    private String email;

    public int getIcNumber() {
        return icNumber;
    }

    public void setIcNumber(int icNumber) {
        this.icNumber = icNumber;
    }

    public String getCustomerName() {
        return customerName;
    }

    public void setCustomerName(String customerName) {
        this.customerName = customerName;
    }

    public String getEmail() {
        return email;
    }

    public void setEmail(String email) {
        this.email = email;
    }
}
```

```
// File Name: Invoice.java
// Illustrates Join operation

package com.hdemo;

import javax.persistence.Column;
import javax.persistence.Entity;
import javax.persistence.GeneratedValue;
import javax.persistence.Id;
import javax.persistence.Table;

import org.hibernate.annotations.GenericGenerator;

@Entity
@Table(name="INVOICE")
public class Invoice {

  @Id
  @GeneratedValue(generator = "idGen")
  @GenericGenerator(name = "idGen", strategy = "assigned")
  @Column(name = "INVOICE_NUMBER", nullable = false)
  private int invoiceNum;

  @Column(name = "CUST_IC_NUMBER", nullable = false)
  private int customerICNumber;

  @Column(name = "AMOUNT")
  private double amount;

  public int getInvoiceNum() {
        return invoiceNum;
  }

  public void setInvoiceNum(int invoiceNum) {
        this.invoiceNum = invoiceNum;
  }

  public int getCustomerICNumber() {
        return customerICNumber;
```

```
    }

    public void setCustomerICNumber(int customerICNumber) {
        this.customerICNumber = customerICNumber;
    }

    public double getAmount() {
        return amount;
    }

    public void setAmount(double amount) {
        this.amount = amount;
    }

}

// File Name: SalesManipulation.java
// Illustrates Join operation

package com.hdemo;

import org.hibernate.Session;
import org.hibernate.SessionFactory;
import org.hibernate.Transaction;

public class SalesManipulation {

    public static void main(String[] args) throws Exception {
        SessionFactory sessionFactory =
                            HibernateUtil.getSessionFactory();
        Session session = sessionFactory.openSession();
        Transaction txn = session.beginTransaction();

        Customer customer1 = new Customer();
        customer1.setIcNumber(2008001501);
        customer1.setCustomerName("Mohamed Ibrahim");
        customer1.setEmail("bmohamedibrahim@yahoo.co.in");

        Customer customer2 = new Customer();
        customer2.setIcNumber(2008001602);
```

```
customer2.setCustomerName("Ajit  Kumar");
customer2.setEmail("ajitkumar@email.net");
Customer  customer3  =  new  Customer();
customer3.setIcNumber(2008001703);
customer3.setCustomerName("Karan  Singh");
customer3.setEmail("karansingh@email2you.com");

Customer  customer4  =  new  Customer();
customer4.setIcNumber(2008001804);
customer4.setCustomerName("Nitin");
customer4.setEmail("nitin@email.com");

Invoice  invoice1  =  new  Invoice();
invoice1.setInvoiceNum(1001);
invoice1.setCustomerICNumber(2008001501);
invoice1.setAmount(10000.0);

Invoice  invoice2  =  new  Invoice();
invoice2.setInvoiceNum(1002);
invoice2.setCustomerICNumber(2008001501);
invoice2.setAmount(8500.0);

Invoice  invoice3  =  new  Invoice();
invoice3.setInvoiceNum(1003);
invoice3.setCustomerICNumber(2008001703);
invoice3.setAmount(4500.0);

Invoice  invoice4  =  new  Invoice();
invoice4.setInvoiceNum(1004);
invoice4.setCustomerICNumber(1009001101);
invoice4.setAmount(12345.0);

Invoice  invoice5  =  new  Invoice();
invoice5.setInvoiceNum(1005);
invoice5.setCustomerICNumber(2008001804);
invoice5.setAmount(18230.0);
```

```
        session.save(customer1);
        session.save(customer2);
        session.save(customer3);
        session.save(customer4);

        session.save(invoice1);
        session.save(invoice2);
        session.save(invoice3);
        session.save(invoice4);
        session.save(invoice5);

        txn.commit();
        session.close();
        sessionFactory.close();
    }
}
```

Keep the same `Customer` and `Invoice` entities. And keep the generated sample data in database (Let the `hbm2ddl.auto` property be `update`).

```
// File Name: Sales.java
// Value Object

package com.hdemo;

public class Sales {

    private int icNumber;
    private double amount;

    public Sales(int icNumber, double amount) {
        this.icNumber = icNumber;
        this.amount = amount;
    }

    public int getIcNumber() {
        return icNumber;
    }

    public void setIcNumber(int icNumber) {
```

```
            this.icNumber = icNumber;
      }

      public double getAmount() {
            return amount;
      }

      public void setAmount(double amount) {
            this.amount = amount;
      }

}

// File Name: EmployeeManipulation.java
// Illustrates dynamic assignment of selected values to value objects

package com.hdemo;

import java.util.List;
import org.hibernate.Session;
import org.hibernate.SessionFactory;
import org.hibernate.Transaction;

public class SalesManipulation {

      @SuppressWarnings("unchecked")
      public static void main(String[] args) throws Exception {
            SessionFactory sessionFactory =
                                          HibernateUtil.getSessionFactory();
            Session session = sessionFactory.openSession();
            Transaction txn = session.beginTransaction();

            List salesList = session.createQuery("select new
            com.hdemo.Sales(c.icNumber, i.amount) from Customer c, Invoice
            i where c.icNumber = i.customerICNumber").list();

            System.out.printf("%-15s   %-10s", "IC_NUMBER", "AMOUNT");
            for (int i = 0; i < salesList.size(); i++) {
```

```
            Sales sales = (Sales) salesList.get(i);
            System.out.printf("\n%-15s %.2f", sales.getIcNumber(),
                                                  sales.getAmount());
        }

        txn.commit();
        session.close();
        sessionFactory.close();
    }
}
```

```
Hibernate: select customer0_.IC_NUMBER as col_0_0_, invoice1_.AMOUNT as col_1_0_ from CUSTOMER customer0_, INVOICE invoice1_ where customer0_.IC_NUMBER=invoice1_.CUST_IC_NUMBER

IC_NUMBER           AMOUNT
2008001501          10000.00
2008001501          8500.00
2008001703          4500.00
2008001804          18230.00
```

5.5 POLYMORPHIC QUERIES

The '`from`' clause not only retrieves the instances of the specified entity, but also its subclasses. This is called Polymorphic query.

We are defining three entity classes namely *Employee, EmployeeSalary*, and *EmployeeAddress*. The *Employee* acts as the super class, where the sub-classes *EmployeeSalary* and *EmployeeAddress* inherit it.

```
// File Name: Employee.java
// Illustrates Polymorphic Queries

package com.hdemo;

import javax.persistence.Column;
import javax.persistence.Entity;
import javax.persistence.GeneratedValue;
import javax.persistence.Id;
import javax.persistence.Table;
```

```
import org.hibernate.annotations.GenericGenerator;

@Entity
@Table(name = "EMPLOYEE")
public class Employee {

   @Id
   @GeneratedValue(generator = "idGen")
   @GenericGenerator(name = "idGen", strategy = "uuid.hex")
   @Column(name = "ID", length = 32)
   private String id;

   @Column(name = "EMP_NUMBER", unique = true, nullable = false)
   private Integer empNumber;

   @Column(name = "EMP_NAME", length = 64, nullable = false)
   private String empName;

   public String getId() {
         return id;
   }

   public void setId(String id) {
         this.id = id;
   }

   public Integer getEmpNumber() {
         return empNumber;
   }

   public void setEmpNumber(Integer empNumber) {
         this.empNumber = empNumber;
   }

   public String getEmpName() {
         return empName;
   }

   public void setEmpName(String empName) {
```

```
        this.empName = empName;
    }
}

// File Name: EmployeeSalary.java
// Illustrates Polymorphic Queries

package com.hdemo;

import javax.persistence.Column;
import javax.persistence.Entity;

@Entity
public class EmployeeSalary extends Employee {

    @Column(name = "BPAY")
    private Double basicPay;

    @Column(name = "ALLOWANCES")
    private Double allowances;

    @Column(name = "DEDUCTIONS")
    private Double deductions;

    @Column(name = "NETPAY")
    private Double netPay;

    public Double getBasicPay() {
        return basicPay;
    }

    public void setBasicPay(Double basicPay) {
        this.basicPay = basicPay;
    }

    public Double getAllowances() {
        return allowances;
    }

    public void setAllowances(Double allowances) {
```

```
        this.allowances = allowances;
    }

    public Double getDeductions() {
        return deductions;
    }

    public void setDeductions(Double deductions) {
        this.deductions = deductions;
    }

    public Double getNetPay() {
        return netPay;
    }

    public void setNetPay(Double netPay) {
        this.netPay = netPay;
    }
}
```

```
// File Name: EmployeeAddress.java
// Illustrates Polymorphic Queries

package com.hdemo;

import javax.persistence.Column;
import javax.persistence.Entity;

@Entity
public class EmployeeAddress extends Employee {

    @Column(name = "HOUSE_NUMBER", length=8)
    private String houseNumber;

    @Column(name = "STREET_NAME", length=64)
    private String streetName;

    @Column(name = "CITY_NAME", length=64)
    private String cityName;
```

```
@Column(name = "COUNTRY_NAME", length=64)
private String countryName;

@Column(name = "POSTAL_CODE", length=16)
private String postalCode;

public String getHouseNumber() {
      return houseNumber;
}

public void setHouseNumber(String houseNumber) {
      this.houseNumber = houseNumber;
}

public String getStreetName() {
      return streetName;
}

public void setStreetName(String streetName) {
      this.streetName = streetName;
}

public String getCityName() {
      return cityName;
}

public void setCityName(String cityName) {
      this.cityName = cityName;
}

public String getCountryName() {
      return countryName;
}

public void setCountryName(String countryName) {
      this.countryName = countryName;
}

public String getPostalCode() {
```

```
        return postalCode;
    }

    public void setPostalCode(String postalCode) {
        this.postalCode = postalCode;
    }

}
```

Don't forget to include the following mappings in *hibernate.cfg.xml* before running main class (`EmployeeManipulation.java`).

```
<mapping class="com.hdemo.Employee" />
<mapping class="com.hdemo.EmployeeSalary" />
<mapping class="com.hdemo.EmployeeAddress" />
```

```
// File Name: EmployeeManipulation.java
// Main Program for generating sample data for testing Polymorphic
Queries

package com.hdemo;

import org.hibernate.Session;
import org.hibernate.SessionFactory;
import org.hibernate.Transaction;

public class EmployeeManipulation {

    public static void main(String[] args) throws Exception {
        SessionFactory sessionFactory =
                        HibernateUtil.getSessionFactory();
        Session session = sessionFactory.getCurrentSession();
        Transaction txn = session.beginTransaction();

        Employee employee1 = new Employee();
        employee1.setEmpNumber(1001);
        employee1.setEmpName("David");
        session.save(employee1);

        Employee employee2 = new Employee();
        employee2.setEmpNumber(1002);
```

```
employee2.setEmpName("Mohamed Ismail");
session.save(employee2);

Employee employee3 = new Employee();
employee3.setEmpNumber(1003);
employee3.setEmpName("Dawood");
session.save(employee3);

EmployeeSalary employeeSalary1 = new EmployeeSalary();
employeeSalary1.setEmpNumber(2001);
employeeSalary1.setEmpName("Ibrahim");
employeeSalary1.setBasicPay(10000.00);
employeeSalary1.setAllowances(3000.00);
employeeSalary1.setDeductions(2000.00);
employeeSalary1.setNetPay(employeeSalary1.getBasicPay() +
employeeSalary1.getAllowances() - employeeSalary1.
getDeductions());
session.save(employeeSalary1);

EmployeeAddress employeeAddress1 = new EmployeeAddress();
employeeAddress1.setEmpNumber(3001);
employeeAddress1.setEmpName("Ajay");
employeeAddress1.setHouseNumber("D-46-5");
employeeAddress1.setStreetName("Jalan Bunus");
employeeAddress1.setCityName("Kuala Lumpur");
employeeAddress1.setCountryName("Malaysia");
employeeAddress1.setPostalCode("50100");
session.save(employeeAddress1);

EmployeeAddress employeeAddress2 = new EmployeeAddress();
employeeAddress2.setEmpNumber(3002);
employeeAddress2.setEmpName("Karan");
employeeAddress2.setHouseNumber("A-6");
employeeAddress2.setStreetName("Jalan TAR");
employeeAddress2.setCityName("Kuala Lumpur");
employeeAddress2.setCountryName("Malaysia");
employeeAddress2.setPostalCode("50132");
session.save(employeeAddress2);
```

```
        txn.commit();
        sessionFactory.close();
    }
}
```

The successful execution of the above main class results in the following changes in the database.

```
mysql> desc employee;
```

Field	Type	Null	Key	Default	Extra
DTYPE	varchar(31)	NO		NULL	
ID	varchar(32)	NO	PRI	NULL	
EMP_NAME	varchar(64)	NO		NULL	
EMP_NUMBER	int(11)	NO	UNI	NULL	
ALLOWANCES	double	YES		NULL	
BPAY	double	YES		NULL	
DEDUCTIONS	double	YES		NULL	
NETPAY	double	YES		NULL	
CITY_NAME	varchar(64)	YES		NULL	
COUNTRY_NAME	varchar(64)	YES		NULL	
HOUSE_NUMBER	varchar(8)	YES		NULL	
POSTAL_CODE	varchar(16)	YES		NULL	
STREET_NAME	varchar(64)	YES		NULL	

```
13 rows in set (0.00 sec)
```

Keep the generated sample data by setting `hbm2ddl.auto` property as `update` in *hibernate.cfg.xml* file.

```
// File Name: EmployeeManipulation.java
// Main Program to test Polymorphic Query

package com.hdemo;

import java.util.Iterator;
import java.util.List;

import org.hibernate.Session;
```

```
import org.hibernate.SessionFactory;
import org.hibernate.Transaction;

public class EmployeeManipulation {

  @SuppressWarnings("unchecked")
  public static void main(String[] args) throws Exception {
       SessionFactory sessionFactory =
                           HibernateUtil.getSessionFactory();
       Session session = sessionFactory.getCurrentSession();
       Transaction txn = session.beginTransaction();

       List list = session.createQuery("from Employee e").list();

       Iterator it = list.iterator();
       for (int record = 1; it.hasNext(); record++) {
            System.out.println("\nAccessing Record " + record);

            Object object = it.next();

            if (object instanceof EmployeeSalary) {
            System.out.println("Accessing EmployeeSalary Object");
            EmployeeSalary employeeSalary = (EmployeeSalary) object;
            System.out.println("Employee Number :" +
                              employeeSalary.getEmpNumber());
            System.out.println("Employee Name      :" +
                                employeeSalary.getEmpName());
            System.out.println("Basic Pay          :" +
                               employeeSalary.getBasicPay());
            System.out.println("Allowances         :" +
                             employeeSalary.getAllowances());
            System.out.println("Deductions         :" +
                             employeeSalary.getDeductions());
            System.out.println("Netpay              :" +
                                 employeeSalary.getNetPay());
            }

            else if (object instanceof EmployeeAddress) {
            System.out.println("Accessing EmployeeAddress Object");
```

```
                    EmployeeAddress employeeAddress =
                                    (EmployeeAddress) object;
                    System.out.println("Employee Number :" +
                                employeeAddress.getEmpNumber());
                    System.out.println("Employee Name   :" +
                                employeeAddress.getEmpName());
                    System.out.println("House Number    :" +
                                employeeAddress.getHouseNumber());
                    System.out.println("Street Name     :" +
                                employeeAddress.getStreetName());
                    System.out.println("City Name       :" +
                                employeeAddress.getCityName());
                    System.out.println("Country Name    :" +
                                employeeAddress.getCountryName());
                    System.out.println("Postal Code     :" +
                                employeeAddress.getPostalCode());

                }

                else if (object instanceof Employee) {
                    System.out.println("Accessing Employee Object");
                    Employee employee = (Employee) object;
                    System.out.println("Employee Number :" +
                                    employee.getEmpNumber());
                    System.out.println("Employee Name   :" +
                                    employee.getEmpName());

                }
            }

            txn.commit();
            sessionFactory.close();
        }
    }
```

Hibernate: select employee0_.ID as ID0_, employee0_.EMP_NAME as EMP3_0_, employee0_.EMP_NUMBER as EMP4_0_, employee0_.ALLOWANCES as ALLOWANCES0_, employee0_.BPAY as BPAY0_, employee0_.DEDUCTIONS as DEDUCTIONS0_, employee0_.NETPAY as NETPAY0_, employee0_.CITY_NAME as CITY9_0_, employee0_.COUNTRY_NAME as COUNTRY10_0_, employee0_.HOUSE_NUMBER as HOUSE11_0_, employee0_.POSTAL_CODE as POSTAL12_0_, employee0_.STREET_NAME as STREET13_0_, employee0_.DTYPE as DTYPE0_ from EMPLOYEE employee0_

```
Accessing Record 1
Accessing Employee Object
Employee Number    : 1001
Employee Name      : David

Accessing Record 2
Accessing Employee Object
Employee Number    : 1002
Employee Name      : Mohamed Ismail

Accessing Record 3
Accessing Employee Object
Employee Number    : 1003
Employee Name      : Dawood

Accessing Record 4
Accessing EmployeeSalary Object
Employee Number    : 2001
Employee Name      : Ibrahim
Basic Pay          : 10000.0
Allowances         : 3000.0
Deductions         : 2000.0
Netpay             : 11000.0
Accessing Record 5
Accessing EmployeeAddress Object
Employee Number    : 3001
Employee Name      : Ajay
House Number       : D-46-5
Street Name        : Jalan Bunus
City Name          : Kuala Lumpur
Country Name       : Malaysia
Postal Code        : 50100

Accessing Record 6
Accessing EmployeeAddress Object
Employee Number    : 3002
```

```
Employee Name      : Karan
House Number       : A-6
Street Name        : Jalan TAR
City Name          : Kuala Lumpur
Country Name       : Malaysia
Postal Code        : 50132
```

Observe from the above result that we are only selecting *Employee* objects, but it also selects objects of its sub-classes (*EmployeeSalary, EmployeeAddress*).

5.6 AGGREGATE FUNCTIONS, GROUP BY AND ORDER BY

The following are supported aggregate functions in HQL which can be used with `group by` clause.

`sum(field)` –Summation value of specified field,

`avg(field)` –Average value of specified field,

`min(field)` –Minimum value of specified field,

`max(field)` –Maximum value of specified field,

`count(*)` –Total number of records in the database table,

`count(field), count(all field)`

–Total number of not-null values of the specified field,

`count(distinct field)`

–Total number of distinct (different) and not-null values of the specified field

The following native SQL queries illustrates the different uses of `count()` function.

```
mysql> create table student (id int(10), rollnumber int(3), sname varchar(20), result varchar(4));
Query OK, 0 rows affected (0.13 sec)
mysql> desc student;
```

Field	Type	Null	Key	Default	Extra
id	int(10)	YES		NULL	
rollnumber	int(3)	YES		NULL	
sname	varchar(20)	YES		NULL	
result	varchar(4)	YES		NULL	

```
4 rows in set (0.01 sec)
```

```
mysql> insert into student (id, rollnumber, sname, result) values
(1000001, 101, 'Ibrahim', 'PASS');
Query OK, 1 row affected (0.03 sec)

mysql> insert into student (id, rollnumber, sname, result) values
(1000002, 102, 'Nitin', 'PASS');
Query OK, 1 row affected (0.05 sec)

mysql> insert into student (id, rollnumber, sname, result) values
(1000003, 103, 'Kiran', null);
Query OK, 1 row affected (0.03 sec)

mysql> insert into student (id, rollnumber, sname, result) values
(1000004, 104, 'Ameer', null);
Query OK, 1 row affected (0.03 sec)

mysql> insert into student (id, rollnumber, sname, result) values
(1000005, 105, 'Ajmal', 'FAIL');
Query OK, 1 row affected (0.06 sec)

mysql> insert into student (id, rollnumber, sname, result) values
(1000006, 106, 'Join', 'FAIL');
Query OK, 1 row affected (0.05 sec)

mysql> insert into student (id, rollnumber, sname, result) values
(1000007, 107, 'Salman', null);
Query OK, 1 row affected (0.05 sec)

mysql> select * from student;
```

id	rollnumber	sname	result
1000001	101	Ibrahim	PASS
1000002	102	Nitin	PASS
1000003	103	Kiran	NULL
1000004	104	Ameer	NULL
1000005	105	Ajmal	FAIL
1000006	106	Join	FAIL
1000007	107	Salman	NULL

```
7 rows in set (0.01 sec)
```

```
mysql> select count(*) from student;

  count(*)

  7

1 row in set (0.05 sec)

mysql> select count(id) from student;

  count(id)

  7

1 row in set (0.03 sec)

mysql> select count(result) from student;

  count(result)

  4

1 row in set (0.00 sec)

mysql> select count(distinct result) from student;

  count(distinct result)

  2

1 row in set (0.03 sec)

mysql> select count(all result) from student;

  count(all result)

  4

1 row in set (0.00 sec)

mysql>
```

General format of Order By clause

```
<HQL Select statement> order by field-name1 asc|desc,
                                field-name2 asc|desc, ...
```

It sorts the retrieved data based on specified order by fields. The keyword `asc` represents ascending order, the key word `desc` represents descending order, where `asc` is the default.

General format of `Group By` clause

```
<HQL Select statement> group by field-name1, field-name2, ...
                                         [having condition]
```

The optional part "`having condition`" specifies condition(s) to select the data.

Execute the following program to populate some sample data.

```
// File Name: Employee.java
// Generating sample data for demonstrate Aggregate Functions

package com.hdemo;

import java.io.Serializable;
import java.math.BigDecimal;

import javax.persistence.Column;
import javax.persistence.Entity;
import javax.persistence.GeneratedValue;
import javax.persistence.Id;
import javax.persistence.Table;

import org.hibernate.annotations.GenericGenerator;

@Entity
@Table(name = "EMPLOYEE")
public class Employee implements Serializable {

  private static final long serialVersionUID = 1L;

  @Id
  @GeneratedValue(generator = "idGen")
  @GenericGenerator(name = "idGen", strategy = "uuid.hex")
  @Column(name = "ID", length = 32)
  private String id = "";
```

```
    @Column(name = "EMP_NUMBER", nullable = false)
    private int empNumber;

    @Column(name = "EMP_NAME", nullable = false, length = 64)
    private String empName;

    @Column(name = "DEPT", nullable = false, length = 64)
    private String department;

    @Column(name = "BASIC_PAY", nullable = false, precision = 10,
    scale = 2)
    private BigDecimal basicpay;

    @Column(name = "ALLOWANCES", precision = 10, scale = 2)
    private BigDecimal allowances;

    @Column(name = "DEDUCTIONS", precision = 10, scale = 2)
    private BigDecimal deductions;

    @Column(name = "NETPAY", precision = 10, scale = 2)
    private BigDecimal netpay;

    Employee() {
    }

    Employee(int empNumber, String empName, String department,
BigDecimal basicpay, BigDecimal allowances, BigDecimal deductions) {
        this.empNumber = empNumber;
        this.empName = empName;
        this.department = department;
        this.basicpay = basicpay;
        this.allowances = allowances;
        this.deductions = deductions;
        this.netpay = basicpay.add(allowances).subtract(deductions);
    }

    public String getId() {
        return id;
    }

    public void setId(String id) {
```

```
        this.id = id;
    }

    public int getEmpNumber() {
        return empNumber;
    }

    public void setEmpNumber(int empNumber) {
        this.empNumber = empNumber;
    }

    public String getEmpName() {
        return empName;
    }

    public void setEmpName(String empName) {
        this.empName = empName;
    }

    public String getDepartment() {
        return department;
    }

    public void setDepartment(String department) {
        this.department = department;
    }

    public BigDecimal getBasicpay() {
        return basicpay;
    }

    public void setBasicpay(BigDecimal basicpay) {
        this.basicpay = basicpay;
    }

    public BigDecimal getAllowances() {
        return allowances;
    }
```

```
    public void setAllowances(BigDecimal allowances) {
        this.allowances = allowances;
    }

    public BigDecimal getDeductions() {
        return deductions;
    }

    public void setDeductions(BigDecimal deductions) {
        this.deductions = deductions;
    }

    public BigDecimal getNetpay() {
        return netpay;
    }

    public void setNetpay(BigDecimal netpay) {
        this.netpay = netpay;
    }

}

// File Name: EmployeeManipulation.java
// Main Program

package com.hdemo;

import java.math.BigDecimal;

import org.hibernate.Session;
import org.hibernate.SessionFactory;
import org.hibernate.Transaction;

public class EmployeeManipulation {

    public static void main(String[] args) throws Exception {
        SessionFactory sessionFactory =
                            HibernateUtil.getSessionFactory();
```

```
    Session session = sessionFactory.openSession();
    Transaction txn = session.beginTransaction();

    Employee employee1 = new Employee(5001, "Ibrahim", "IT", new BigDecimal(98000.0), new BigDecimal(30000.0), new BigDecimal(15000.0));
    Employee employee2 = new Employee(5002, "Ananad Desai", "IT", new BigDecimal(93000.0), new BigDecimal(29000.0), new BigDecimal(15000.0));
    Employee employee3 = new Employee(5003, "Karan Singh", "SALES", new BigDecimal(88000.0), new BigDecimal(27000.0), new BigDecimal(14500.0));
    Employee employee4 = new Employee(5004, "Sudhir", "SALES", new BigDecimal(83000.0), new BigDecimal(25000.0), new BigDecimal(14100.0));
    Employee employee5 = new Employee(5005, "Ajay", "SALES", new BigDecimal(78000.0), new BigDecimal(23000.0), new BigDecimal(14000.0));
    Employee employee6 = new Employee(5006, "Achfa", "SALES", new BigDecimal(74000.0), new BigDecimal(22500.0), new BigDecimal(12500.0));
    Employee employee7 = new Employee(5007, "Indiran", "PERSONAL", new BigDecimal(69000.0), new BigDecimal(16000.0), new BigDecimal(8000.0));
    Employee employee8 = new Employee(5008, "Nitin Otagiri", "PERSONAL", new BigDecimal(67000.0), new BigDecimal(15800.0), new BigDecimal(7000.0));
    Employee employee9 = new Employee(5009, "Kumar", "STATIONARY", new BigDecimal(65000.0), new BigDecimal(15700.0), new BigDecimal(7000.0));
    Employee employee10 = new Employee(5010, "Ravi Chandran", "INVENTORY", new BigDecimal(55800.0), new BigDecimal(15100.0), new BigDecimal(7000.0));

        session.persist(employee1);
        session.persist(employee2);
        session.persist(employee3);
        session.persist(employee4);
        session.persist(employee5);
        session.persist(employee6);
        session.persist(employee7);
        session.persist(employee8);
        session.persist(employee9);
        session.persist(employee10);
        System.out.println("The employee objects are persisted with session");
```

```
            txn.commit();
            System.out.println("Transaction on this session is
            committed");
            session.close();
            sessionFactory.close();
      }
   }
```

The following program uses `order by` clause, and selects records ordered by Employee Name. Default is ascending order.

```
   // File Name: EmployeeManipulation.java
   // Illustrates Order By clause

   package com.hdemo;

   import java.util.List;

   import org.hibernate.Session;
   import org.hibernate.SessionFactory;
   import org.hibernate.Transaction;

   public class EmployeeManipulation {

      @SuppressWarnings("unchecked")
      public static void main(String[] args) throws Exception {
            SessionFactory sessionFactory =
                                    HibernateUtil.getSessionFactory();
            Session session = sessionFactory.openSession();
            Transaction txn = session.beginTransaction();

            List<Employee> employeeList = session.createQuery("from
            Employee order by empName").list();
            for (int i = 0; i < employeeList.size(); i++) {
                  Employee employee = employeeList.get(i);
                  System.out.println("Employee Number : " +
                                          employee.getEmpNumber());
                  System.out.println("Employee Name   : " +
                                          employee.getEmpName());
```

```
            System.out.println("Department             : " +
                                    employee.getDepartment());
            System.out.println("Basic Pay               : " +
                                      employee.getBasicpay());
            System.out.println("Allowances             : " +
                                    employee.getAllowances());
            System.out.println("Deductions             : " +
                                    employee.getDeductions());
            System.out.println("Netpay                   : " +
                                        employee.getNetpay());

    System.out.println("======================================\n\n");
        }

        txn.commit();
        session.close();
        sessionFactory.close();
    }
}
```

```
Hibernate: select employee0_.ID as ID0_, employee0_.ALLOWANCES as ALLOWANCES0_, employee0_.BASIC_PAY as BASIC3_0_, employee0_.DEDUCTIONS as DEDUCTIONS0_, employee0_.DEPT as DEPT0_, employee0_.EMP_NAME as EMP6_0_, employee0_.EMP_NUMBER as EMP7_0_, employee0_.NETPAY as NETPAY0_ from EMPLOYEE employee0_ order by employee0_.EMP_NAME
Employee Number    : 5006
Employee Name      : Achfa
Department         : SALES
Basic Pay          : 74000.00
Allowances         : 22500.00
Deductions         : 12500.00
Netpay             : 84000.00
======================================

Employee Number    : 5005
Employee Name      : Ajay
Department         : SALES
```

```
Basic Pay           : 78000.00
Allowances          : 23000.00
Deductions          : 14000.00
Netpay              : 87000.00
========================================
Employee Number     : 5002
Employee Name       : Ananad Desai
Department          : IT
Basic Pay           : 93000.00
Allowances          : 29000.00
Deductions          : 15000.00
Netpay              : 107000.00
========================================

Employee Number     : 5001
Employee Name       : Ibrahim
Department          : IT
Basic Pay           : 98000.00
Allowances          : 30000.00
Deductions          : 15000.00
Netpay              : 113000.00
========================================

Employee Number     : 5007
Employee Name       : Indiran
Department          : PERSONAL
Basic Pay           : 69000.00
Allowances          : 16000.00
Deductions          : 8000.00
Netpay              : 77000.00
========================================

Employee Number     : 5003
Employee Name       : Karan Singh
Department          : SALES
Basic Pay           : 88000.00
```

```
Allowances          : 27000.00
Deductions          : 14500.00
Netpay              : 100500.00
=============================================
Employee Number     : 5009
Employee Name       : Kumar
Department          : STATIONARY
Basic Pay           : 65000.00
Allowances          : 15700.00
Deductions          : 7000.00
Netpay              : 73700.00
=============================================
Employee Number     : 5008
Employee Name       : Nitin Otagiri
Department          : PERSONAL
Basic Pay           : 67000.00
Allowances          : 15800.00
Deductions          : 7000.00
Netpay              : 75800.00
=============================================
Employee Number     : 5010
Employee Name       : Ravi Chandran
Department          : INVENTORY
Basic Pay           : 55800.00
Allowances          : 15100.00
Deductions          : 7000.00
Netpay              : 63900.00
=============================================
Employee Number     : 5004
Employee Name       : Sudhir
Department          : SALES
Basic Pay           : 83000.00
Allowances          : 25000.00
```

```
Deductions          : 14100.00
Netpay              : 93900.00
========================================
```

The following example selects records based on descending order of department, from each department group further ordered by employee name of ascending order.

```
// File Name: EmployeeManipulation.java
// Illustrates Order By clause

package com.hdemo;

import java.util.List;

import org.hibernate.Session;
import org.hibernate.SessionFactory;
import org.hibernate.Transaction;

public class EmployeeManipulation {

  @SuppressWarnings("unchecked")
  public static void main(String[] args) throws Exception {
        SessionFactory sessionFactory =
                               HibernateUtil.getSessionFactory();
        Session session = sessionFactory.openSession();
        Transaction txn = session.beginTransaction();

        List<Employee> employeeList = session.createQuery("from
        Employee order by department desc, empName").list();
        for (int i = 0; i < employeeList.size(); i++) {
              Employee employee = employeeList.get(i);
              System.out.println("Employee Number : " +
                                      employee.getEmpNumber());
              System.out.println("Employee Name     : " +
                                        employee.getEmpName());
              System.out.println("Department          : " +
                                     employee.getDepartment());
              System.out.println("Basic Pay            : " +
                                       employee.getBasicpay());
              System.out.println("Allowances          : " +
                                     employee.getAllowances());
```

```
                System.out.println("Deductions           : " +
                                            employee.getDeductions());
                System.out.println("Netpay                  : " +
                                                employee.getNetpay());

      System.out.println("========================================\n\n");
            }

            txn.commit();
            session.close();
            sessionFactory.close();
      }
   }
```

```
Hibernate: select employee0_.ID as ID0_, employee0_.ALLOWANCES as ALLOWANCES0_, employee0_.BASIC_PAY as BASIC3_0_, employee0_.DEDUCTIONS as DEDUCTIONS0_, employee0_.DEPT as DEPT0_, employee0_.EMP_NAME as EMP6_0_, employee0_.EMP_NUMBER as EMP7_0_, employee0_.NETPAY as NETPAY0_ from EMPLOYEE employee0_ order by employee0_.DEPT desc, employee0_.EMP_NAME
Employee  Number    : 5009
Employee  Name      : Kumar
Department          : STATIONARY
Basic  Pay          : 65000.00
Allowances          : 15700.00
Deductions          : 7000.00
Netpay              : 73700.00
========================================

Employee  Number    : 5006
Employee  Name      : Achfa
Department          : SALES
Basic  Pay          : 74000.00
Allowances          : 22500.00
Deductions          : 12500.00
Netpay              : 84000.00
========================================
Employee  Number    : 5005
Employee  Name      : Ajay
```

```
Department          : SALES
Basic Pay           : 78000.00
Allowances          : 23000.00
Deductions          : 14000.00
Netpay              : 87000.00
======================================

Employee Number     : 5003
Employee Name       : Karan Singh
Department          : SALES
Basic Pay           : 88000.00
Allowances          : 27000.00
Deductions          : 14500.00
Netpay              : 100500.00
======================================
Employee Number     : 5004
Employee Name       : Sudhir
Department          : SALES
Basic Pay           : 83000.00
Allowances          : 25000.00
Deductions          : 14100.00
Netpay              : 93900.00
======================================

Employee Number     : 5007
Employee Name       : Indiran
Department          : PERSONAL
Basic Pay           : 69000.00
Allowances          : 16000.00
Deductions          : 8000.00
Netpay              : 77000.00
======================================
Employee Number     : 5008
Employee Name       : Nitin Otagiri
Department          : PERSONAL
```

```
Basic Pay           : 67000.00
Allowances          : 15800.00
Deductions          : 7000.00
Netpay              : 75800.00
=========================================

Employee Number     : 5002
Employee Name       : Ananad Desai
Department          : IT
Basic Pay           : 93000.00
Allowances          : 29000.00
Deductions          : 15000.00
Netpay              : 107000.00
=========================================

Employee Number     : 5001
Employee Name       : Ibrahim
Department          : IT
Basic Pay           : 98000.00
Allowances          : 30000.00
Deductions          : 15000.00
Netpay              : 113000.00
=========================================

Employee Number     : 5010
Employee Name       : Ravi Chandran
Department          : INVENTORY
Basic Pay           : 55800.00
Allowances          : 15100.00
Deductions          : 7000.00
Netpay              : 63900.00
=========================================
```

The following example uses `Group By` clause.

```
// File Name: EmployeeManipulation.java
// Illustrates Group By clause
```

```
package com.hdemo;

import java.util.Iterator;
import java.util.List;

import org.hibernate.Session;
import org.hibernate.SessionFactory;
import org.hibernate.Transaction;

public class EmployeeManipulation {

  @SuppressWarnings("unchecked")
  public static void main(String[] args) throws Exception {
        SessionFactory sessionFactory =
                              HibernateUtil.getSessionFactory();
        Session session = sessionFactory.openSession();
        Transaction txn = session.beginTransaction();

// Finds Number of Employees in each department, Sum of Basic Pay
in each department, Average of Basic Pay in each department,
// Minimum Basic Pay in each department, Maximum Basic Pay in each
department
List list = session.createQuery("select department, count(*),
sum(basicpay), avg(basicpay), min(basicpay), max(basicpay) from
Employee group by department").list();
System.out.printf("%-15s %-30s %25s %25s %25s %25s", "Department",
"No. of Employees in Department", "SUM OF BASIC PAY", "AVERAGE OF
BASIC PAY", "MINIMUM BASIC PAY", "MAXIMUM BASIC PAY");
        for (Iterator it = list.iterator(); it.hasNext();) {
              Object[] row = (Object[])it.next();
              System.out.printf("\n%-15s %30s %25s %25s %25s %25s",
              row[0], row[1], row[2], row[3], row[4], row[5]);
        }
        txn.commit();
        session.close();
        sessionFactory.close();
  }
}
```

Hibernate: select employee0_.DEPT as col_0_0_, count(*) as col_1_0_, sum(employee0_.BASIC_PAY) as col_2_0_, avg(employee0_.BASIC_PAY) as col_3_0_, min(employee0_.BASIC_PAY) as col_4_0_, max(employee0_.BASIC_PAY) as col_5_0_ from EMPLOYEE employee0_ group by employee0_.DEPT

DEPARTMENT	NO. OF EMPLOYEES IN DEPARTMENT	SUM OF BASIC PAY	AVERAGE OF BASIC PAY	MINIMUM BASIC PAY	MAXIMUM BASIC PAY
INVENTORY	1	55800.00	55800.0	55800.00	55800.00
IT	2	191000.00	95500.0	93000.00	98000.00
PERSONAL	2	136000.00	68000.0	67000.00	69000.00
SALES	4	323000.00	80750.0	74000.00	88000.00
STATIONARY	1	65000.00	65000.0	65000.00	65000.00

```
mysql> select dept as Department, count(*) as "Number of Employees in Department",
    -> sum(basic_pay) as "SUM OF BASIC PAY", avg(basic_pay) as "AVERAGE OF BASIC PAY",
    -> min(basic_pay) as "MINIMUM BASIC PAY", max(basic_pay) as "MAXIMUM BASIC PAY"
    -> from EMPLOYEE group by dept;
```

DEPARTMENT	NO. OF EMPLOYEES IN DEPARTMENT	SUM OF BASIC PAY	AVERAGE OF BASIC PAY	MINIMUM BASIC PAY	MAXIMUM BASIC PAY
INVENTORY	1	55800.00	55800.00	55800.00	55800.00
IT	2	191000.00	95500.00	93000.00	98000.00
PERSONAL	2	136000.00	68000.00	67000.00	69000.00
SALES	4	323000.00	80750.00	74000.00	88000.00
STATIONARY	1	65000.00	65000.00	65000.00	65000.00

5 rows in set (0.00 sec)

The following example uses both `group by` and `having` clause to find total number of employees in 'IT' and 'SALES' department.

```
// File Name: EmployeeManipulation.java
// Illustrates Group By ... Having clause

package com.hdemo;

import java.util.Iterator;
import java.util.List;

import org.hibernate.Session;
import org.hibernate.SessionFactory;
import org.hibernate.Transaction;

public class EmployeeManipulation {

  @SuppressWarnings("unchecked")
  public static void main(String[] args) throws Exception {
        SessionFactory sessionFactory =
                              HibernateUtil.getSessionFactory();
        Session session = sessionFactory.openSession();
        Transaction txn = session.beginTransaction();

        // Finds howmany employees under departments 'IT' and 'SALES'
        List list = session.createQuery("select department,
        count(department) from Employee group by department having
        department in ('IT', 'SALES')").list();
        System.out.printf("%-15s %-30s", "Department", "No. of
        Employees in Department");
        for (Iterator it = list.iterator(); it.hasNext();) {
              Object[] row = (Object[])it.next();
              System.out.printf("\n%-15s %30s", row[0], row[1]);
        }
```

```
        txn.commit();
        session.close();
        sessionFactory.close();
    }
}
```

```
Hibernate: select employee0_.DEPT as col_0_0_, count(employee0_.DEPT) as col_1_0_ from EMPLOYEE employee0_ group by employee0_.DEPT having employee0_.DEPT in ('IT' , 'SALES')
Department           No. of Employees in Department
IT                   2
SALES                4
```

5.7 SUB-QUERIES

A query used in another query (usually in `select` and `where` clause) is called sub-query. The following example uses sub-query to retrieve the Employee who is having least basic pay.

```
// File Name: EmployeeManipulation.java
// Illustrates Sub-query

package com.hdemo;

import java.util.List;

import org.hibernate.Session;
import org.hibernate.SessionFactory;
import org.hibernate.Transaction;
public class EmployeeManipulation {
    @SuppressWarnings("unchecked")
    public static void main(String[] args) throws Exception {
        SessionFactory sessionFactory =
                                HibernateUtil.getSessionFactory();
        Session session = sessionFactory.openSession();
        Transaction txn = session.beginTransaction();

        List<Employee> employeeList = session.createQuery("from
        Employee where basicpay = (select min(basicpay) from
        Employee)").list();
```

```
            for (int i = 0; i < employeeList.size(); i++) {
                  Employee employee = employeeList.get(i);
                  System.out.println("Employee Number : " +
                                             employee.getEmpNumber());
                  System.out.println("Employee Name     : " +
                                               employee.getEmpName());
                  System.out.println("Department         : " +
                                            employee.getDepartment());
                  System.out.println("Basic Pay            : " +
                                              employee.getBasicpay());
                  System.out.println("Allowances          : " +
                                            employee.getAllowances());
                  System.out.println("Deductions          : " +
                                            employee.getDeductions());
                  System.out.println("Netpay                : " +
                                                employee.getNetpay());

      System.out.println("======================================\n\n");
            }

            txn.commit();
            session.close();
            sessionFactory.close();
      }
   }
```

```
Hibernate: select employee0_.ID as ID0_, employee0_.ALLOWANCES as ALLOWANCES0_, employee0_.BASIC_PAY as BASIC3_0_, employee0_.DEDUCTIONS as DEDUCTIONS0_, employee0_.DEPT as DEPT0_, employee0_.EMP_NAME as EMP6_0_, employee0_.EMP_NUMBER as EMP7_0_, employee0_.NETPAY as NETPAY0_ from EMPLOYEE employee0_ where employee0_.BASIC_PAY=(select min(employee1_.BASIC_PAY) from EMPLOYEE employee1_)
   Employee Number  : 5010
   Employee Name    : Ravi Chandran
   Department       : INVENTORY
   Basic Pay        : 55800.00
   Allowances       : 15100.00
   Deductions       : 7000.00
   Netpay           : 63900.00
   ========================================
```

5.8 RESTRICTING SIZE OF QUERY'S RESULT SET

The `Query` interface has the following methods to restrict the result set size. It is very much used for pagination while listing.

`setFirstResult(offset)`

-Sets the offset location for the first row to retrieve. Index starts from 0.

`setMaxResults(limit)`

-Sets the maximum number of rows to retrieve.

The following example retrieves 2 rows from 4th row of Employee table.

```
// File Name: EmployeeManipulation.java
// Illustrates Restricting Query Result Set Size

package com.hdemo;

import java.util.List;

import org.hibernate.Query;
import org.hibernate.Session;
import org.hibernate.SessionFactory;
import org.hibernate.Transaction;

public class EmployeeManipulation {

  @SuppressWarnings("unchecked")
  public static void main(String[] args) throws Exception {
        SessionFactory sessionFactory =
                                  HibernateUtil.getSessionFactory();
        Session session = sessionFactory.openSession();
        Transaction txn = session.beginTransaction();

        System.out.println("Selecting All Employee Records\n");
        Query query1 = session.createQuery("from Employee order by
        empName");
        List<Employee> employeeList1 = query1.list();
        for (int i = 0; i < employeeList1.size(); i++) {
              Employee employee = employeeList1.get(i);
              System.out.println("Employee Number : " +
                                          employee.getEmpNumber());
```

```
            System.out.println("Employee Name      : " +
                                              employee.getEmpName());
            System.out.println("Department         : " +
                                              employee.getDepartment());
            System.out.println("Basic Pay          : " +
                                              employee.getBasicpay());
            System.out.println("Allowances         : " +
                                              employee.getAllowances());
            System.out.println("Deductions         : " +
                                              employee.getDeductions());
            System.out.println("Netpay             : " +
                                              employee.getNetpay());

    System.out.println("=======================================\n");
        }

        System.out.println("\nSelecting 2 Employee Records from 4th
        row. [Index starts from 0]\n");
        Query query2 = session.createQuery("from Employee order by
        empName");
        query2.setFirstResult(3);
        query2.setMaxResults(2);
        List<Employee> employeeList2 = query2.list();
        for (int i = 0; i < employeeList2.size(); i++) {
            Employee employee = employeeList2.get(i);
            System.out.println("Employee Number : " +
                                              employee.getEmpNumber());
            System.out.println("Employee Name      : " +
                                              employee.getEmpName());
            System.out.println("Department         : " +
                                              employee.getDepartment());
            System.out.println("Basic Pay          : " +
                                              employee.getBasicpay());
            System.out.println("Allowances         : " +
                                              employee.getAllowances());
            System.out.println("Deductions         : " +
                                              employee.getDeductions());
            System.out.println("Netpay             : " +
                                              employee.getNetpay());
```

```
    System.out.println("========================================\n");
        }

        txn.commit();
        session.close();
        sessionFactory.close();
    }
}
```

```
Selecting All Employee Records

Hibernate: select employee0_.ID as ID0_, employee0_.ALLOWANCES as ALLOWANCES0_, employee0_.BASIC_PAY as BASIC3_0_, employee0_.DEDUCTIONS as DEDUCTIONS0_, employee0_.DEPT as DEPT0_, employee0_.EMP_NAME as EMP6_0_, employee0_.EMP_NUMBER as EMP7_0_, employee0_.NETPAY as NETPAY0_ from EMPLOYEE employee0_ order by employee0_.EMP_NAME
Employee Number    : 5006
Employee Name      : Achfa
Department         : SALES
Basic Pay          : 74000.00
Allowances         : 22500.00
Deductions         : 12500.00
Netpay             : 84000.00
========================================

Employee Number    : 5005
Employee Name      : Ajay
Department         : SALES
Basic Pay          : 78000.00
Allowances         : 23000.00
Deductions         : 14000.00
Netpay             : 87000.00
========================================

Employee Number    : 5002
Employee Name      : Ananad Desai
Department         : IT
Basic Pay          : 93000.00
```

```
Allowances          : 29000.00
Deductions          : 15000.00
Netpay              : 107000.00
========================================

Employee  Number    : 5001
Employee  Name      : Ibrahim
Department          : IT
Basic  Pay          : 98000.00
Allowances          : 30000.00
Deductions          : 15000.00
Netpay              : 113000.00
========================================

Employee  Number    : 5007
Employee  Name      : Indiran
Department          : PERSONAL
Basic  Pay          : 69000.00
Allowances          : 16000.00
Deductions          : 8000.00
Netpay              : 77000.00
========================================

Employee  Number    : 5003
Employee  Name      : Karan  Singh
Department          : SALES
Basic  Pay          : 88000.00
Allowances          : 27000.00
Deductions          : 14500.00
Netpay              : 100500.00
========================================

Employee  Number    : 5009
Employee  Name      : Kumar
Department          : STATIONARY
Basic  Pay          : 65000.00
```

```
Allowances          : 15700.00
Deductions          : 7000.00
Netpay              : 73700.00
========================================

Employee Number     : 5008
Employee Name       : Nitin Otagiri
Department          : PERSONAL
Basic Pay           : 67000.00
Allowances          : 15800.00
Deductions          : 7000.00
Netpay              : 75800.00
========================================
Employee Number     : 5010
Employee Name       : Ravi Chandran
Department          : INVENTORY
Basic Pay           : 55800.00
Allowances          : 15100.00
Deductions          : 7000.00
Netpay              : 63900.00
========================================

Employee Number     : 5004
Employee Name       : Sudhir
Department          : SALES
Basic Pay           : 83000.00
Allowances          : 25000.00
Deductions          : 14100.00
Netpay              : 93900.00
========================================

Selecting 2 Employee Records from 4th row. [Index starts from 0]

Hibernate: select employee0_.ID as ID0_, employee0_.ALLOWANCES as ALLOWANCES0_, employee0_.BASIC_PAY as BASIC3_0_, employee0_.DEDUCTIONS as DEDUCTIONS0_, employee0_.DEPT as DEPT0_, employee0_.EMP_NAME as EMP6_0_, employee0_.EMP_NUMBER as EMP7_0_, employee0_.NETPAY as NETPAY0_ from EMPLOYEE employee0_ order by employee0_.EMP_NAME limit ?, ?
```

```
Employee Number    : 5001
Employee Name      : Ibrahim
Department         : IT
Basic Pay          : 98000.00
Allowances         : 30000.00
Deductions         : 15000.00
Netpay             : 113000.00
========================================

Employee Number    : 5007
Employee Name      : Indiran
Department         : PERSONAL
Basic Pay          : 69000.00
Allowances         : 16000.00
Deductions         : 8000.00
Netpay             : 77000.00
========================================
```

5.9 SCROLLABLE RESULTS

We can obtain Scrollable Result Set (we can traverse both front and back in the result set) from `Query` interface, if the underlying database supports Scrollable Result Set.

The sample data on the database table are as selected below.

The following example demonstrates this feature.

```
// File Name: EmployeeManipulation.java
// Illustrates Scrollable Results

package com.hdemo;

import org.hibernate.Query;
import org.hibernate.ScrollableResults;
import org.hibernate.Session;
import org.hibernate.SessionFactory;
import org.hibernate.Transaction;

public class EmployeeManipulation {
```

```
public static void main(String[] args) throws Exception {
      SessionFactory sessionFactory =
                          HibernateUtil.getSessionFactory();
      Session session = sessionFactory.openSession();
      Transaction txn = session.beginTransaction();

      System.out.println("Selecting All Employee Records\n");
      Query query1 = session.createQuery("from Employee order by
      empName");
      ScrollableResults records = query1.scroll();

      while (records.next()) {
            Employee employee = (Employee) records.get(0);
            printRecord(employee);
      }

      System.out.println("\nRetrieving First Record");
      if (records.first()) {
            Employee employee = (Employee) records.get(0);
            printRecord(employee);
      }
      else
            System.out.println("\n [First] Record is not found");

      System.out.println("\nRetrieving Last Record");
      if (records.last()) {
            Employee employee = (Employee) records.get(0);
            printRecord(employee);
      }
      else
            System.out.println("\n [Last] Record is not found");

      System.out.println("\nRetrieving Previous of Last Record");
      if (records.last()) {
            if (records.previous()) {
                  Employee employee = (Employee) records.get(0);
```

```
                printRecord(employee);
            }
            else
            System.out.println("\n [Previous of Last] Record is
            not found");
        }
        else
            System.out.println("\nRetrieving Previous of Last
            Record: No record found");

        System.out.println("\nRetrieving Third Record");
        records.beforeFirst();
        // scroll() -Scrolls an arbitrary number of locations
        if (records.scroll(3)) {
            Employee employee = (Employee) records.get(0);
            printRecord(employee);
        }
        else
        System.out.println("\nRetrieving Third Record: No sufficient
        records to scroll\n");

        System.out.println("\nAgain Scroll 2 more records");
        if (records.scroll(2)) {
            Employee employee = (Employee) records.get(0);
            printRecord(employee);
        }
        else
        System.out.println("\nAgain Scroll 2 more records: No
        sufficient records to scroll");

System.out.println("\nRow Number [" + records.getRowNumber() + "]");
        System.out.println("\nScroll 20 more records");
        if (records.scroll(20)) {
            Employee employee = (Employee) records.get(0);
            printRecord(employee);
```

```
        }
        else
        System.out.println("\nScroll 20 more records: No sufficient
        records to scroll");

    System.out.println("\nRow Number [" + records.getRowNumber() + "]");

        // setRowNumber() -Sets the current location in the result
        set. For this, Index starts from 0.
        // Use negative value to set current location from last
        record.
        System.out.println("\nSetting Index to 3rd Location");
        if (records.setRowNumber(2)) {
            Employee employee = (Employee) records.get(0);
            printRecord(employee);
        }
        else
        System.out.println("\nSetting Offset to 3rd Location: No
        sufficient records");

        System.out.println("\nSetting Index to 3rd Location from
        Last Record");
        if (records.setRowNumber(-3)) {
            Employee employee = (Employee) records.get(0);
            printRecord(employee);
        }
        else
        System.out.println("\nSetting Offset to 3rd Location from
        Last Record: No sufficient records");

        txn.commit();
        session.close();
        sessionFactory.close();
    }

    static void printRecord(Employee employee) {
        System.out.println("Employee Number : " +
```

```
                                        employee.getEmpNumber());
            System.out.println("Employee Name     : " +
                                        employee.getEmpName());
            System.out.println("Department        : " +
                                        employee.getDepartment());
            System.out.println("Basic Pay         : " +
                                        employee.getBasicpay());
            System.out.println("Allowances        : " +
                                        employee.getAllowances());
            System.out.println("Deductions        : " +
                                        employee.getDeductions());
            System.out.println("Netpay            : " +
                                        employee.getNetpay());

        System.out.println("========================================\n");
    }
}
```

```
Selecting All Employee Records

Hibernate: select employee0_.ID as ID0_, employee0_.ALLOWANCES as ALLOWANCES0_, employee0_.BASIC_PAY as BASIC3_0_, employee0_.DEDUCTIONS as DEDUCTIONS0_, employee0_.DEPT as DEPT0_, employee0_.EMP_NAME as EMP6_0_, employee0_.EMP_NUMBER as EMP7_0_, employee0_.NETPAY as NETPAY0_ from EMPLOYEE employee0_ order by employee0_.EMP_NAME

Employee Number : 5006
Employee Name   : Achfa
Department      : SALES
Basic Pay       : 74000.00
Allowances      : 22500.00
Deductions      : 12500.00
Netpay          : 84000.00
========================================

Employee Number : 5005
Employee Name   : Ajay
Department      : SALES
Basic Pay       : 78000.00
```

```
Allowances        :  23000.00
Deductions        :  14000.00
Netpay            :  87000.00
=========================================

Employee Number   :  5002
Employee Name     :  Ananad Desai
Department        :  IT
Basic Pay         :  93000.00
Allowances        :  29000.00
Deductions        :  15000.00
Netpay            :  107000.00
=========================================

Employee Number   :  5001
Employee Name     :  Ibrahim
Department        :  IT
Basic Pay         :  98000.00
Allowances        :  30000.00
Deductions        :  15000.00
Netpay            :  113000.00
=========================================

Employee Number   :  5007
Employee Name     :  Indiran
Department        :  PERSONAL
Basic Pay         :  69000.00
Allowances        :  16000.00
Deductions        :  8000.00
Netpay            :  77000.00
=========================================

Employee Number   :  5003
Employee Name     :  Karan Singh
Department        :  SALES
Basic Pay         :  88000.00
```

```
Allowances       :  27000.00
Deductions       :  14500.00
Netpay           :  100500.00
========================================

Employee Number  :  5009
Employee Name    :  Kumar
Department       :  STATIONARY
Basic Pay        :  65000.00
Allowances       :  15700.00
Deductions       :  7000.00
Netpay           :  73700.00
========================================

Employee Number  :  5008
Employee Name    :  Nitin Otagiri
Department       :  PERSONAL
Basic Pay        :  67000.00
Allowances       :  15800.00
Deductions       :  7000.00
Netpay           :  75800.00
========================================

Employee Number  :  5010
Employee Name    :  Ravi Chandran
Department       :  INVENTORY
Basic Pay        :  55800.00
Allowances       :  15100.00
Deductions       :  7000.00
Netpay           :  63900.00
========================================

Employee Number  :  5004
Employee Name    :  Sudhir
Department       :  SALES
Basic Pay        :  83000.00
```

```
Allowances       :  25000.00
Deductions       :  14100.00
Netpay           :  93900.00
========================================

Retrieving First Record
Employee Number  :  5006
Employee Name    :  Achfa
Department       :  SALES
Basic Pay        :  74000.00
Allowances       :  22500.00
Deductions       :  12500.00
Netpay           :  84000.00
========================================

Retrieving Last Record
Employee Number  :  5004
Employee Name    :  Sudhir
Department       :  SALES
Basic Pay        :  83000.00
Allowances       :  25000.00
Deductions       :  14100.00
Netpay           :  93900.00
========================================

Retrieving Previous of Last Record
Employee Number  :  5010
Employee Name    :  Ravi Chandran
Department       :  INVENTORY
Basic Pay        :  55800.00
Allowances       :  15100.00
Deductions       :  7000.00
Netpay           :  63900.00
========================================
```

```
Retrieving Third Record
Employee Number : 5002
Employee Name   : Ananad Desai
Department      : IT
Basic Pay       : 93000.00
Allowances      : 29000.00
Deductions      : 15000.00
Netpay          : 107000.00
========================================

Again Scroll 2 more records
Employee Number : 5007
Employee Name   : Indiran
Department      : PERSONAL
Basic Pay       : 69000.00
Allowances      : 16000.00
Deductions      : 8000.00
Netpay          : 77000.00
========================================

Row Number [4]

Scroll 20 more records

Scroll 20 more records: No sufficient records to scroll

Row Number [-1]

Setting Index to 3rd Location
Employee Number : 5002
Employee Name   : Ananad Desai
Department      : IT
Basic Pay       : 93000.00
Allowances      : 29000.00
Deductions      : 15000.00
Netpay          : 107000.00
========================================
```

```
Setting Index to 3rd Location from Last Record
Employee Number  :  5008
Employee Name    :  Nitin Otagiri
Department       :  PERSONAL
Basic Pay        :  67000.00
Allowances       :  15800.00
Deductions       :  7000.00
Netpay           :  75800.00
========================================
```

5.10 NATIVE SQL QUERIES

Hibernate supports native SQL queries (underlying database queries; JDBC queries) including call to Stored Procedures. However, since Hibernate is based on object world, native queries are not recommended and also native queries are dependent on the underlying database. If the query is written in HQL, then the same query will work at all databases (if those databases support used features); just configuring database settings are enough.

As `Query` interface is used for HQL, the `SQLQuery` interface is used for native SQL operations, which can be instantiated using `createSQLQuery()` method of `Session`.

5.10.1 Selecting Data from Database Tables

Just like HQL, pass native (underlying database) SQL query as the argument to `createSQLQuery()` method. The result of the query will be in the form of list of Object arrays (`List<Object[]>`) and their data-types are based on its JDBC `ResultSetMetadata` (it is one interface in JDBC, used to get data about data (meta-data) such as column names, data types of the columns from the associated result set).

```
// File Name: EmployeeManipulation.java
// Illustrates Native SQL Queries

package com.hdemo;

import java.util.List;

import org.hibernate.SQLQuery;
import org.hibernate.Session;
import org.hibernate.SessionFactory;
import org.hibernate.Transaction;

public class EmployeeManipulation {
```

```
public static void main(String[] args) throws Exception {
        SessionFactory sessionFactory =
        HibernateUtil.getSessionFactory();
        Session session = sessionFactory.openSession();
        Transaction txn = session.beginTransaction();

        System.out.println("Selecting All Employee Records\n");
        SQLQuery query = session.createSQLQuery("select * from
        employee");
        List list = query.list();

        for (int i = 0; i < list.size(); i++) {
                System.out.println("RECORD [" + (i+1) + "]");
                Object[] row = (Object[]) list.get(i);
                if (row != null) {
                        for (int j = 0; j < row.length; j++) {
                                System.out.println("Value " + j + "
                                                     [" + row[j] + "]");
                        }
                }
        System.out.println("=================================\n");
        }
        txn.commit();
        session.close();
        sessionFactory.close();
    }
}
```

```
Selecting All Employee Records

Hibernate: select * from Employee
RECORD [1]
Value 0 [402881f81ef2c60d011ef2c60e9d0001]
Value 1 [30000.00]
Value 2 [98000.00]
```

```
Value 3 [15000.00]
Value 4 [IT]
Value 5 [Ibrahim]
Value 6 [5001]
Value 7 [113000.00]
=========================================

RECORD [2]
Value 0 [402881f81ef2c60d011ef2c60ea60002]
Value 1 [29000.00]
Value 2 [93000.00]
Value 3 [15000.00]
Value 4 [IT]
Value 5 [Ananad Desai]
Value 6 [5002]
Value 7 [107000.00]
=========================================

RECORD [3]
Value 0 [402881f81ef2c60d011ef2c60ea60003]
Value 1 [27000.00]
Value 2 [88000.00]
Value 3 [14500.00]
Value 4 [SALES]
Value 5 [Karan Singh]
Value 6 [5003]
Value 7 [100500.00]
=========================================

RECORD [4]
Value 0 [402881f81ef2c60d011ef2c60ea60004]
Value 1 [25000.00]
Value 2 [83000.00]
Value 3 [14100.00]
Value 4 [SALES]
Value 5 [Sudhir]
```

```
Value 6 [5004]
Value 7 [93900.00]
=====================================

RECORD [5]
Value 0 [402881f81ef2c60d011ef2c60ea60005]
Value 1 [23000.00]
Value 2 [78000.00]
Value 3 [14000.00]
Value 4 [SALES]
Value 5 [Ajay]
Value 6 [5005]
Value 7 [87000.00]
=====================================

RECORD [6]
Value 0 [402881f81ef2c60d011ef2c60ea60006]
Value 1 [22500.00]
Value 2 [74000.00]
Value 3 [12500.00]
Value 4 [SALES]
Value 5 [Achfa]
Value 6 [5006]
Value 7 [84000.00]
=====================================

RECORD [7]
Value 0 [402881f81ef2c60d011ef2c60ea60007]
Value 1 [16000.00]
Value 2 [69000.00]
Value 3 [8000.00]
Value 4 [PERSONAL]
Value 5 [Indiran]
Value 6 [5007]
Value 7 [77000.00]
=====================================
```

```
RECORD [8]
Value 0 [402881f81ef2c60d011ef2c60ea60008]
Value 1 [15800.00]
Value 2 [67000.00]
Value 3 [7000.00]
Value 4 [PERSONAL]
Value 5 [Nitin Otagiri]
Value 6 [5008]
Value 7 [75800.00]
======================================
RECORD [9]
Value 0 [402881f81ef2c60d011ef2c60ea60009]
Value 1 [15700.00]
Value 2 [65000.00]
Value 3 [7000.00]
Value 4 [STATIONARY]
Value 5 [Kumar]
Value 6 [5009]
Value 7 [73700.00]
======================================
RECORD [10]
Value 0 [402881f81ef2c60d011ef2c60ea6000a]
Value 1 [15100.00]
Value 2 [55800.00]
Value 3 [7000.00]
Value 4 [INVENTORY]
Value 5 [Ravi Chandran]
Value 6 [5010]
Value 7 [63900.00]
======================================
```

We can override this default data-type mapping by specifying column-names and their corresponding data-types in `addScalar()` methods.

```
// File Name: EmployeeManipulation.java
// Illustrates Native SQL Queries

package com.hdemo;

import java.util.List;

import org.hibernate.Hibernate;
import org.hibernate.SQLQuery;
import org.hibernate.Session;
import org.hibernate.SessionFactory;
import org.hibernate.Transaction;

public class EmployeeManipulation {

  @SuppressWarnings("unchecked")
  public static void main(String[] args) throws Exception {
        SessionFactory sessionFactory =
                          HibernateUtil.getSessionFactory();
        Session session = sessionFactory.openSession();
        Transaction txn = session.beginTransaction();

        System.out.println("Selecting All Employee Records\n");
        SQLQuery query = session.createSQLQuery("select * from
        employee")
                    .addScalar("EMP_NUMBER", Hibernate.INTEGER)
                    .addScalar("EMP_NAME", Hibernate.STRING)
                    .addScalar("NETPAY", Hibernate.DOUBLE);

        List list = query.list();

        for (int i = 0; i < list.size(); i++) {
              System.out.println("RECORD [" + (i+1) + "]");
              Object[] row = (Object[]) list.get(i);
              if (row != null) {
                    for (int j = 0; j < row.length; j++) {
                          System.out.println("Value " + j + " [" +
                          row[j] + "]");
                    }
```

```
            }

        System.out.println("===================================\n");
         }

         txn.commit();
         session.close();
         sessionFactory.close();
    }
}
```

```
Selecting All Employee Records

Hibernate: select * from employee
RECORD [1]
Value 0 [5001]
Value 1 [Ibrahim]
Value 2 [113000.0]
===================================

RECORD [2]
Value 0 [5002]
Value 1 [Ananad Desai]
Value 2 [107000.0]
===================================

RECORD [3]
Value 0 [5003]
Value 1 [Karan Singh]
Value 2 [100500.0]
===================================

RECORD [4]
Value 0 [5004]
Value 1 [Sudhir]
Value 2 [93900.0]
===================================
```

```
RECORD [5]
Value 0 [5005]
Value 1 [Ajay]
Value 2 [87000.0]
=====================================
RECORD [6]
Value 0 [5006]
Value 1 [Achfa]
Value 2 [84000.0]
=====================================
RECORD [7]
Value 0 [5007]
Value 1 [Indiran]
Value 2 [77000.0]
=====================================
RECORD [8]
Value 0 [5008]
Value 1 [Nitin Otagiri]
Value 2 [75800.0]
=====================================
RECORD [9]
Value 0 [5009]
Value 1 [Kumar]
Value 2 [73700.0]
=====================================
RECORD [10]
Value 0 [5010]
Value 1 [Ravi Chandran]
Value 2 [63900.0]
=====================================
```

Note that even though we selected all columns (`select * from Employee`), only those columns defined their data types using `setScalar()` are returned, that is if you use `setScalar()` method(s), then those Scalar set columns only be returned.

Some of the allowed data types found in `org.hibernate.Hibernate` class, which can be used to specify column data type in `setScalar()` method, are as follows.

Constant	Data Type
Hibernate.BYTE	Hibernate byte type
Hibernate.SHORT	Hibernate short type
Hibernate.INTEGER	Hibernate integer type
Hibernate.LONG	Hibernate long type
Hibernate.FLOAT	Hibernate float type
Hibernate.DOUBLE	Hibernate double type
Hibernate.BOOLEAN	Hibernate boolean type
Hibernate.CHARACTER	Hibernate character type
Hibernate.BIG_INTEGER	Hibernate big_integer type
Hibernate.BIG_DECIMAL	Hibernate big_decimal type
Hibernate.BINARY	Hibernate binary type
Hibernate.STRING	Hibernate string type
Hibernate.TEXT	Hibernate text type
Hibernate.DATE	Hibernate date type
Hibernate.CALENDAR	Hibernate calendar type
Hibernate.TIMESTAMP	Hibernate timestamp type
Hibernate.CLASS	Hibernate class type
Type.OBJECT	Hibernate object type
Type.CLOB	Hibernate clob type
Type.BLOB	Hibernate blob type

It is also possible to specify data types for some columns and keep JDBC ResultSetMetadata based data type for other columns. Just do not specify any data type in `setScalar()` method to keep `ResultSetMetadata` based data type for a column. The following example illustrates how to do it.

```
// File Name: EmployeeManipulation.java
// Illustrates Native SQL Queries -addScalar() method

package com.hdemo;
```

```
import java.util.List;

import org.hibernate.Hibernate;
import org.hibernate.SQLQuery;
import org.hibernate.Session;
import org.hibernate.SessionFactory;
import org.hibernate.Transaction;

public class EmployeeManipulation {

  public static void main(String[] args) throws Exception {
       SessionFactory sessionFactory =
                              HibernateUtil.getSessionFactory();
       Session session = sessionFactory.openSession();
       Transaction txn = session.beginTransaction();

       System.out.println("Selecting All Employee Records\n");
       SQLQuery query = session.createSQLQuery("select * from
       employee")
                        .addScalar("ID")
                        .addScalar("EMP_NUMBER", Hibernate.INTEGER)
                        .addScalar("EMP_NAME", Hibernate.STRING)
                        .addScalar("DEPT")
                        .addScalar("BASIC_PAY", Hibernate.DOUBLE)
                        .addScalar("ALLOWANCES")
                        .addScalar("DEDUCTIONS")
                        .addScalar("NETPAY", Hibernate.DOUBLE);
       List list = query.list();

       for (int i = 0; i < list.size(); i++) {
            System.out.println("RECORD [" + (i + 1) + "]");
            Object[] row = (Object[]) list.get(i);
             System.out.println("ID              : " + row[0]);
             System.out.println("Employee Number : " + row[1]);
             System.out.println("Employee Name   : " + row[2]);
```

```
            System.out.println("Department        : " + row[3]);
            System.out.println("Basic Pay         : " + row[4]);
            System.out.println("Allowances        : " + row[5]);
            System.out.println("Deductions        : " + row[6]);
            System.out.println("Netpay            : " + row[7]);

    System.out.println("======================================\n");
        }

        txn.commit();
        session.close();
        sessionFactory.close();
    }
}
```

```
Selecting All Employee Records

Hibernate: select * from Employee
RECORD [1]
ID                : 402881f81ef2c60d011ef2c60e9d0001
Employee Number   : 5001
Employee Name     : Ibrahim
Department        : IT
Basic Pay         : 98000.0
Allowances        : 30000.00
Deductions        : 15000.00
Netpay            : 113000.0
======================================

RECORD [2]
ID                : 402881f81ef2c60d011ef2c60ea60002
Employee Number   : 5002
Employee Name     : Ananad Desai
Department        : IT
Basic Pay         : 93000.0
Allowances        : 29000.00
```

```
Deductions        : 15000.00
Netpay            : 107000.0
========================================

RECORD [3]
ID                : 402881f81ef2c60d011ef2c60ea60003
Employee Number   : 5003
Employee Name     : Karan Singh
Department        : SALES
Basic Pay         : 88000.0
Allowances        : 27000.00
Deductions        : 14500.00
Netpay            : 100500.0
========================================

RECORD [4]
ID                : 402881f81ef2c60d011ef2c60ea60004
Employee Number   : 5004
Employee Name     : Sudhir
Department        : SALES
Basic Pay         : 83000.0
Allowances        : 25000.00
Deductions        : 14100.00
Netpay            : 93900.0
========================================

RECORD [5]
ID                : 402881f81ef2c60d011ef2c60ea60005
Employee Number   : 5005
Employee Name     : Ajay
Department        : SALES
Basic Pay         : 78000.0
Allowances        : 23000.00
Deductions        : 14000.00
Netpay            : 87000.0
========================================
```

```
RECORD [6]
ID                : 402881f81ef2c60d011ef2c60ea60006
Employee Number   : 5006
Employee Name     : Achfa
Department        : SALES
Basic Pay         : 74000.0
Allowances        : 22500.00
Deductions        : 12500.00
Netpay            : 84000.0
========================================

RECORD [7]
ID                : 402881f81ef2c60d011ef2c60ea60007
Employee Number   : 5007
Employee Name     : Indiran
Department        : PERSONAL
Basic Pay         : 69000.0
Allowances        : 16000.00
Deductions        : 8000.00
Netpay            : 77000.0
========================================

RECORD [8]
ID                : 402881f81ef2c60d011ef2c60ea60008
Employee Number   : 5008
Employee Name     : Nitin Otagiri
Department        : PERSONAL
Basic Pay         : 67000.0
Allowances        : 15800.00
Deductions        : 7000.00
Netpay            : 75800.0
========================================

RECORD [9]
ID                : 402881f81ef2c60d011ef2c60ea60009
Employee Number   : 5009
```

```
Employee Name     : Kumar
Department        : STATIONARY
Basic Pay         : 65000.0
Allowances        : 15700.00
Deductions        : 7000.00
Netpay            : 73700.0
========================================

RECORD [10]
ID                : 402881f81ef2c60d011ef2c60ea6000a
Employee Number   : 5010
Employee Name     : Ravi Chandran
Department        : INVENTORY
Basic Pay         : 55800.0
Allowances        : 15100.00
Deductions        : 7000.00
Netpay            : 63900.0
========================================
```

We can simply use `addEntity()` method to map the retrieved database table rows to an Entity class.

```
// File Name: EmployeeManipulation.java
// Illustrates Native SQL Queries -addEntity() method

package com.hdemo;

import java.util.List;

import org.hibernate.SQLQuery;
import org.hibernate.Session;
import org.hibernate.SessionFactory;
import org.hibernate.Transaction;

public class EmployeeManipulation {

   @SuppressWarnings("unchecked")
   public static void main(String[] args) throws Exception {
```

```
        SessionFactory sessionFactory =
                            HibernateUtil.getSessionFactory();
        Session session = sessionFactory.openSession();
        Transaction txn = session.beginTransaction();

        System.out.println("Selecting All Employee Records\n");
        SQLQuery query = session.createSQLQuery("select * from
        employee").addEntity(Employee.class);
        List<Employee> list = query.list();
        for (int i = 0; i < list.size(); i++) {
              System.out.println("RECORD [" + (i + 1) + "]");
              Employee employee = list.get(i);
              printRecord(employee);
        }

        txn.commit();
        session.close();
        sessionFactory.close();
}

static void printRecord(Employee employee) {
        System.out.println("Employee Number   : " +
                                     employee.getEmpNumber());
        System.out.println("Employee Name    : " +
                                       employee.getEmpName());
        System.out.println("Department       : " +
                                    employee.getDepartment());
        System.out.println("Basic Pay          : " +
                                      employee.getBasicpay());
        System.out.println("Allowances       : " +
                                    employee.getAllowances());
        System.out.println("Deductions       : " +
                                    employee.getDeductions());
        System.out.println("Netpay                : " +
                                        employee.getNetpay());
System.out.println("==========================================\n");
}
```

```
}

Selecting All Employee Records

Hibernate: select * from Employee
RECORD [1]
Employee Number  : 5001
Employee Name    : Ibrahim
Department       : IT
Basic Pay        : 98000.00
Allowances       : 30000.00
Deductions       : 15000.00
Netpay           : 113000.00
========================================

RECORD [2]
Employee Number  : 5002
Employee Name    : Ananad Desai
Department       : IT
Basic Pay        : 93000.00
Allowances       : 29000.00
Deductions       : 15000.00
Netpay           : 107000.00
========================================
RECORD [3]
Employee Number  : 5003
Employee Name    : Karan Singh
Department       : SALES
Basic Pay        : 88000.00
Allowances       : 27000.00
Deductions       : 14500.00
Netpay           : 100500.00
========================================

RECORD [4]
Employee Number  : 5004
Employee Name    : Sudhir
```

```
Department       : SALES
Basic  Pay       : 83000.00
Allowances       : 25000.00
Deductions       : 14100.00
Netpay           : 93900.00
========================================

RECORD  [5]
Employee  Number : 5005
Employee  Name   : Ajay
Department       : SALES
Basic  Pay       : 78000.00
Allowances       : 23000.00
Deductions       : 14000.00
Netpay           : 87000.00
========================================

RECORD  [6]
Employee  Number : 5006
Employee  Name   : Achfa
Department       : SALES
Basic  Pay       : 74000.00
Allowances       : 22500.00
Deductions       : 12500.00
Netpay           : 84000.00
========================================

RECORD  [7]
Employee  Number : 5007
Employee  Name   : Indiran
Department       : PERSONAL
Basic  Pay       : 69000.00
Allowances       : 16000.00
Deductions       : 8000.00
Netpay           : 77000.00
========================================
```

```
RECORD [8]
Employee Number  : 5008
Employee Name    : Nitin Otagiri
Department       : PERSONAL
Basic Pay        : 67000.00
Allowances       : 15800.00
Deductions       : 7000.00
Netpay           : 75800.00
========================================

RECORD [9]
Employee Number  : 5009
Employee Name    : Kumar
Department       : STATIONARY
Basic Pay        : 65000.00
Allowances       : 15700.00
Deductions       : 7000.00
Netpay           : 73700.00
========================================

RECORD [10]
Employee Number  : 5010
Employee Name    : Ravi Chandran
Department       : INVENTORY
Basic Pay        : 55800.00
Allowances       : 15100.00
Deductions       : 7000.00
Netpay           : 63900.00
========================================
```

However, we have to select all the required columns for the entity in order to map using `addEntity()` method. The following statement will result in error.

```
SQLQuery query =
     session.createSQLQuery("SELECT ID, EMP_NUMBER, EMP_NAME, NETPAY
FROM EMPLOYEE")
```

```
                .addEntity(Employee.class);
List list = query.list();
```

If you execute the above code (not selecting all the columns of EMPLOYEE table), then you will get error message like shown below.

```
ERROR org.hibernate.util.JDBCExceptionReporter
                             - Column 'ALLOWANCES' not found.
```

We can overcome this issue by using `setResultTransformer()` method, which is used to map selected values to an unmanaged entity (ordinary Java class) as shown below.

```
// File Name: EmployeeManipulation.java
// Illustrates Native SQL Queries -setResultTransformer() method

package com.hdemo;

import java.util.List;

import org.hibernate.Session;
import org.hibernate.SessionFactory;
import org.hibernate.Transaction;
import org.hibernate.transform.Transformers;

public class EmployeeManipulation {

   @SuppressWarnings("unchecked")
   public static void main(String[] args) throws Exception {
         SessionFactory sessionFactory =
                              HibernateUtil.getSessionFactory();
         Session session = sessionFactory.openSession();
         Transaction txn = session.beginTransaction();

         System.out.println("Selecting All Employee Records\n");
         List list = session.createSQLQuery("SELECT EMP_NUMBER,
         EMP_NAME, NETPAY FROM EMPLOYEE")

.setResultTransformer(Transformers.aliasToBean(EmployeeDisplay.class)).list();

         for (int i = 0; i < list.size(); i++) {
```

```
                System.out.println("RECORD [" + (i + 1) + "]");
                EmployeeDisplay employeeDisplay = (EmployeeDisplay)
                list.get(i);
                printRecord(employeeDisplay);
            }

            txn.commit();
            session.close();
            sessionFactory.close();
        }

        static void printRecord(EmployeeDisplay employeeDisplay) {
            System.out.println("Employee Number : " +
                                          employeeDisplay.getEMP_NUMBER());
            System.out.println("Employee Name     : " +
                                            employeeDisplay.getEMP_NAME());
            System.out.println("Netpay                : " +
                                              employeeDisplay.getNETPAY());

         System.out.println("=====================================\n");
        }
    }

    // File Name: Employee.java
    // Helper class for storing Employee data

    package com.hdemo;

    import java.math.BigDecimal;

    public class EmployeeDisplay {

        private int EMP_NUMBER;

        private String EMP_NAME;

        private BigDecimal NETPAY;

        public int getEMP_NUMBER() {
```

```
        return EMP_NUMBER;
    }

    public void setEMP_NUMBER(int emp_number) {
        EMP_NUMBER = emp_number;
    }

    public String getEMP_NAME() {
        return EMP_NAME;
    }

    public void setEMP_NAME(String emp_name) {
        EMP_NAME = emp_name;
    }

    public BigDecimal getNETPAY() {
        return NETPAY;
    }

    public void setNETPAY(BigDecimal netpay) {
        NETPAY = netpay;
    }

}
```

```
Selecting All Employee Records

Hibernate: SELECT EMP_NUMBER, EMP_NAME, NETPAY FROM EMPLOYEE
RECORD [1]
Employee Number : 5001
Employee Name   : Ibrahim
Netpay          : 113000.00
========================================

RECORD [2]
Employee Number : 5002
Employee Name   : Ananad Desai
Netpay          : 107000.00
========================================
```

```
RECORD [3]
Employee Number : 5003
Employee Name   : Karan Singh
Netpay          : 100500.00
========================================

RECORD [4]
Employee Number : 5004
Employee Name   : Sudhir
Netpay          : 93900.00
========================================

RECORD [5]
Employee Number : 5005
Employee Name   : Ajay
Netpay          : 87000.00
========================================

RECORD [6]
Employee Number : 5006
Employee Name   : Achfa
Netpay          : 84000.00
========================================

RECORD [7]
Employee Number : 5007
Employee Name   : Indiran
Netpay          : 77000.00
========================================

RECORD [8]
Employee Number : 5008
Employee Name   : Nitin Otagiri
Netpay          : 75800.00
========================================
```

```
RECORD [9]
Employee Number : 5009
Employee Name   : Kumar
Netpay          : 73700.00
========================================

RECORD [10]
Employee Number : 5010
Employee Name   : Ravi Chandran
Netpay          : 63900.00
========================================
```

Native SQL queries in Hibernate support positional as well as Hibernate style named parameters, like HQL. Note that Hibernate ? Positional parameters start with 0, not from 1 (JDBC positional parameters start with 1).

```
// File Name: EmployeeManipulation.java
// Illustrates Native SQL Queries -Positional Parameters

package com.hdemo;

import java.util.List;

import org.hibernate.Session;
import org.hibernate.SessionFactory;
import org.hibernate.Transaction;

public class EmployeeManipulation {

  @SuppressWarnings("unchecked")
  public static void main(String[] args) throws Exception {
        SessionFactory sessionFactory =
                                   HibernateUtil.getSessionFactory();
        Session session = sessionFactory.openSession();
        Transaction txn = session.beginTransaction();

        List list =  session.createSQLQuery("SELECT * FROM EMPLOYEE
        WHERE EMP_NAME LIKE ? AND NETPAY > :EmpNetpay")
                          .addEntity(Employee.class)
                          .setString(0, "a%")
```

```
                        .setDouble("EmpNetpay", 85000.0)
                        .list();

        for (int i = 0; i < list.size(); i++) {
            System.out.println("RECORD [" + (i + 1) + "]");
            Employee employee = (Employee) list.get(i);
            printRecord(employee);
        }

        txn.commit();
        session.close();
        sessionFactory.close();
    }
    static void printRecord(Employee employee) {
        System.out.println("Employee Number  : " +
                                        employee.getEmpNumber());
        System.out.println("Employee Name    : " +
                                        employee.getEmpName());
        System.out.println("Department       : " +
                                        employee.getDepartment());
        System.out.println("Basic Pay        : " +
                                        employee.getBasicpay());
        System.out.println("Allowances       : " +
                                        employee.getAllowances());
        System.out.println("Deductions       : " +
                                        employee.getDeductions());
        System.out.println("Netpay                          : " +
                                        employee.getNetpay());

      System.out.println("========================================\n");
    }
}
```

```
Hibernate: SELECT * FROM EMPLOYEE WHERE EMP_NAME LIKE ? AND NETPAY
> ?
RECORD [1]
Employee Number : 5002
Employee Name   : Ananad Desai
Department      : IT
```

```
Basic  Pay          :  93000.00
Allowances          :  29000.00
Deductions          :  15000.00
Netpay              :  107000.00
========================================

RECORD  [2]
Employee  Number  :  5005
Employee  Name    :  Ajay
Department        :  SALES
Basic  Pay        :  78000.00
Allowances        :  23000.00
Deductions        :  14000.00
Netpay            :  87000.00
========================================
```

5.11 SQL ALIASES

We can use alias names, enclosed in braces ({}) for table-names to simply queries and assign values to Entity objects defined in Hibernate. That is, the alias-name enclosed in braces refers an Entity object of type specified in `addScalar()` method. Different scripts of alias notations enclosed in braces give specific meanings to Hibernate. Some of alias possibilities are given below.

Accessing a member → `{alias_name.property_name}`

Accessing All the members → `{alias_name.*}`

Accessing an element of an collection → `{alias_name.element}`

Accessing a property of an element of an collection →

`{alias_name.element.property_name}`

Accessing all properties of an element of an collection → `{alias_name.element.*}`

Use the following program to generate sample data to test aliases. Take care of appropriate settings in *hiberante.cfg.xml* to keep the generated data.

```
// File Name: Employee.java
// Generates sample data for testing aliases

package com.hdemo;
```

```
import javax.persistence.CascadeType;
import javax.persistence.Column;
import javax.persistence.Entity;
import javax.persistence.GeneratedValue;
import javax.persistence.Id;
import javax.persistence.JoinColumn;
import javax.persistence.OneToOne;
import javax.persistence.Table;

import org.hibernate.annotations.GenericGenerator;

@Entity
@Table(name = "EMPLOYEE")
public class Employee {

   private static final long serialVersionUID = 1L;

   @Id
   @GeneratedValue(generator = "idGen")
   @GenericGenerator(name = "idGen", strategy = "uuid.hex")
   @Column(name = "ID", length = 32)
   private String id = "";

   @Column(name = "EMP_NUMBER", unique = true, nullable = false)
   private Integer empNumber;


   @Column(name = "EMP_NAME", length = 64, nullable = false)
   private String empName;

   @OneToOne(cascade = {CascadeType.PERSIST, CascadeType.REMOVE})
   @JoinColumn(name = "EMP_SALARY", unique=true)
   private Salary salary;

   public String getId() {
         return id;
   }

   public void setId(String id) {
```

```
        this.id = id;
    }

    public Integer getEmpNumber() {
        return empNumber;
    }

    public void setEmpNumber(Integer empNumber) {
        this.empNumber = empNumber;
    }

    public String getEmpName() {
        return empName;
    }

    public void setEmpName(String empName) {
        this.empName = empName;
    }

    public Salary getSalary() {
        return salary;
    }

    public void setSalary(Salary salary) {
        this.salary = salary;
    }

}

// File Name: Salary.java
// Generates sample data for testing aliases

package com.hdemo;

import java.io.Serializable;

import javax.persistence.Column;
import javax.persistence.Entity;
import javax.persistence.GeneratedValue;
```

```
import javax.persistence.Id;
import javax.persistence.Table;

import org.hibernate.annotations.GenericGenerator;

@Entity
@Table(name = "SALARY")
public class Salary implements Serializable {

  private static final long serialVersionUID = 1L;

  @Id
  @GeneratedValue(generator = "idGen")
  @GenericGenerator(name = "idGen", strategy = "uuid.hex")
  @Column(name = "ID", length = 32)
  private String id = "";

  @Column(name = "BPAY")
  private Double basicPay;

  @Column(name = "ALLOWANCES")
  private Double allowances;

  @Column(name = "DEDUCTIONS")
  private Double deductions;

  @Column(name = "NETPAY")
  private Double netPay;

  public String getId() {
        return id;
  }

  public void setId(String id) {
        this.id = id;
  }

  public Double getBasicPay() {
        return basicPay;
```

```
	}

	public void setBasicPay(Double basicPay) {
		this.basicPay = basicPay;
	}

	public Double getAllowances() {
		return allowances;
	}

	public void setAllowances(Double allowances) {
		this.allowances = allowances;
	}

	public Double getDeductions() {
		return deductions;
	}

	public void setDeductions(Double deductions) {
		this.deductions = deductions;
	}

	public Double getNetPay() {
		return netPay;
	}

	public void setNetPay(Double netPay) {
		this.netPay = netPay;
	}
}

// File Name: EmployeeManipulation.java
// Main Program

package com.hdemo;

import org.hibernate.Session;
import org.hibernate.SessionFactory;
import org.hibernate.Transaction;
```

```
public class EmployeeManipulation {

    public static void main(String[] args) throws Exception {
        SessionFactory sessionFactory =
            HibernateUtil.getSessionFactory();
        Session session = sessionFactory.getCurrentSession();
        Transaction txn = session.beginTransaction();

        Employee employee1 = new Employee();
        employee1.setEmpNumber(5001);
        employee1.setEmpName("Ibrahim");
        Salary salary1 = new Salary();
        salary1.setBasicPay(10000.00);
        salary1.setAllowances(3000.00);
        salary1.setDeductions(2000.00);
        salary1.setNetPay(salary1.getBasicPay() +
            salary1.getAllowances() - salary1.getDeductions());
        employee1.setSalary(salary1);
        session.persist(employee1);

        Employee employee2 = new Employee();
        employee2.setEmpNumber(5002);
        employee2.setEmpName("Kumar");
        Salary salary2 = new Salary();
        salary2.setBasicPay(5000.00);
        salary2.setAllowances(1500.00);
        salary2.setDeductions(1000.00);
        salary2.setNetPay(salary2.getBasicPay() +
            salary2.getAllowances() - salary2.getDeductions());
        employee2.setSalary(salary2);
        session.persist(employee2);

        Employee employee3 = new Employee();
        employee3.setEmpNumber(5003);
        employee3.setEmpName("Ajay");
        Salary salary3 = new Salary();
```

```
        salary3.setBasicPay(15000.00);
        salary3.setAllowances(4000.00);
        salary3.setDeductions(2500.00);
        salary3.setNetPay(salary3.getBasicPay() +
salary3.getAllowances() - salary3.getDeductions());
        employee3.setSalary(salary3);
        session.persist(employee3);

        txn.commit();
        sessionFactory.close();
    }
}
```

The following program illustrates the use of aliases.

```
// File Name: EmployeeManipulation.java
// Illustrates Native SQL Queries -Aliases
package com.hdemo;

import java.util.List;

import org.hibernate.Session;
import org.hibernate.SessionFactory;
import org.hibernate.Transaction;

public class EmployeeManipulation {

    @SuppressWarnings("unchecked")
    public static void main(String[] args) throws Exception {
        SessionFactory sessionFactory =
                                HibernateUtil.getSessionFactory();

        Session session = sessionFactory.openSession();
        Transaction txn = session.beginTransaction();

        List<Employee> list = session.createSQLQuery("SELECT {emp.*}
        FROM EMPLOYEE {emp}")
                        .addEntity("emp", Employee.class)
                        .list();
```

```
        for (int i = 0; i < list.size(); i++) {
              System.out.println("RECORD [" + (i + 1) + "]");
              Employee employee = (Employee) list.get(i);
              printRecord(employee);
        }

        txn.commit();
        session.close();
        sessionFactory.close();
    }

    static void printRecord(Employee employee) {
        System.out.println("Employee Number : " +
                                        employee.getEmpNumber());
        System.out.println("Employee Name   : " +
                                        employee.getEmpName());
        System.out.println("Basic Pay      : " +
                              employee.getSalary().getBasicPay());
        System.out.println("Allowances      : " +
                           employee.getSalary().getAllowances());
        System.out.println("Deductions      : " +
                           employee.getSalary().getDeductions());
        System.out.println("Netpay         : " +
                                employee.getSalary().getNetPay());

     System.out.println("=========================================\n");
    }
}
```

```
Hibernate: SELECT emp.ID as ID0_0_, emp.EMP_NAME as EMP2_0_0_,
emp.EMP_NUMBER as EMP3_0_0_, emp.EMP_SALARY as EMP4_0_0_ FROM EMPLOYEE
emp
Hibernate: select salary0_.ID as ID1_0_, salary0_.ALLOWANCES as
ALLOWANCES1_0_, salary0_.BPAY as BPAY1_0_, salary0_.DEDUCTIONS as
DEDUCTIONS1_0_, salary0_.NETPAY as NETPAY1_0_ from SALARY salary0_
where salary0_.ID=?
Hibernate: select salary0_.ID as ID1_0_, salary0_.ALLOWANCES as
ALLOWANCES1_0_, salary0_.BPAY as BPAY1_0_, salary0_.DEDUCTIONS as
DEDUCTIONS1_0_, salary0_.NETPAY as NETPAY1_0_ from SALARY salary0_
where salary0_.ID=?
```

```
Hibernate: select salary0_.ID as ID1_0_, salary0_.ALLOWANCES as ALLOWANCES1_0_, salary0_.BPAY as BPAY1_0_, salary0_.DEDUCTIONS as DEDUCTIONS1_0_, salary0_.NETPAY as NETPAY1_0_ from SALARY salary0_ where salary0_.ID=?
RECORD [1]
Employee Number  : 5001
Employee Name    : Ibrahim
Basic Pay        : 10000.0
Allowances       : 3000.0
Deductions       : 2000.0
Netpay           : 11000.0
========================================

RECORD [2]
Employee Number  : 5002
Employee Name    : Kumar
Basic Pay        : 5000.0
Allowances       : 1500.0
Deductions       : 1000.0
Netpay           : 5500.0
========================================

RECORD [3]
Employee Number  : 5003
Employee Name    : Ajay
Basic Pay        : 15000.0
Allowances       : 4000.0
Deductions       : 2500.0
Netpay           : 16500.0
========================================
```

We can select individual fields from database table and can assign to Hibernate alias as follows.

```
// File Name: EmployeeManipulation.java
// Illustrates Native SQL Queries -Aliases

package com.hdemo;
```

```
import java.util.List;

import org.hibernate.Session;
import org.hibernate.SessionFactory;
import org.hibernate.Transaction;

public class EmployeeManipulation {

    @SuppressWarnings("unchecked")
    public static void main(String[] args) throws Exception {
        SessionFactory sessionFactory =
            HibernateUtil.getSessionFactory();
        Session session = sessionFactory.openSession();
        Transaction txn = session.beginTransaction();

        List<Employee> list = session.createSQLQuery("SELECT {emp}.ID
AS {emp.id}, {emp}.EMP_NUMBER AS {emp.empNumber}, {emp}.EMP_NAME AS
{emp.empName}, {emp}.EMP_SALARY AS {emp.salary} FROM EMPLOYEE {emp}")
                                .addEntity("emp", Employee.class)
                                .list();

        for (int i = 0; i < list.size(); i++) {
            System.out.println("RECORD [" + (i + 1) + "]");
            Employee employee = (Employee) list.get(i);
            printRecord(employee);
        }

        txn.commit();
        session.close();
        sessionFactory.close();
    }

    static void printRecord(Employee employee) {
        System.out.println("Employee Number : " +
                                            employee.getEmpNumber());
        System.out.println("Employee Name   : " +
                                              employee.getEmpName());
        System.out.println("Basic Pay       : " +
                                 employee.getSalary().getBasicPay());
```

```
            System.out.println("Allowances       : " +
                               employee.getSalary().getAllowances());
            System.out.println("Deductions       : " +
                               employee.getSalary().getDeductions());
            System.out.println("Netpay            :   " +
employee.getSalary().getNetPay());
System.out.println("=====================================\n");
        }
    }
```

```
Hibernate: SELECT emp.ID AS ID0_0_, emp.EMP_NUMBER AS EMP3_0_0_, emp.EMP_NAME AS EMP2_0_0_, emp.EMP_SALARY AS EMP4_0_0_ FROM EMPLOYEE emp
Hibernate: select salary0_.ID as ID1_0_, salary0_.ALLOWANCES as ALLOWANCES1_0_, salary0_.BPAY as BPAY1_0_, salary0_.DEDUCTIONS as DEDUCTIONS1_0_, salary0_.NETPAY as NETPAY1_0_ from SALARY salary0_ where salary0_.ID=?
Hibernate: select salary0_.ID as ID1_0_, salary0_.ALLOWANCES as ALLOWANCES1_0_, salary0_.BPAY as BPAY1_0_, salary0_.DEDUCTIONS as DEDUCTIONS1_0_, salary0_.NETPAY as NETPAY1_0_ from SALARY salary0_ where salary0_.ID=?
Hibernate: select salary0_.ID as ID1_0_, salary0_.ALLOWANCES as ALLOWANCES1_0_, salary0_.BPAY as BPAY1_0_, salary0_.DEDUCTIONS as DEDUCTIONS1_0_, salary0_.NETPAY as NETPAY1_0_ from SALARY salary0_ where salary0_.ID=?
RECORD [1]
Employee Number : 5001
Employee Name   : Ibrahim
Basic Pay       : 10000.0
Allowances      : 3000.0
Deductions      : 2000.0
Netpay          : 11000.0
=====================================

RECORD [2]
Employee Number : 5002
Employee Name   : Kumar
Basic Pay       : 5000.0
Allowances      : 1500.0
```

```
Deductions        :  1000.0
Netpay            :  5500.0
========================================
RECORD  [3]
Employee  Number  :  5003
Employee  Name    :  Ajay
Basic  Pay        :  15000.0
Allowances        :  4000.0
Deductions        :  2500.0
Netpay            :  16500.0
========================================
```

5.12 CALLING STORED PROCEDURES

The following example illustrates how to call stored procedures. The same approach can be used for executing native SQL queries also.

Create a stored procedure named GET_EMPLOYEE_SP in MySQL (Note that the syntax may vary for other databases).

Be sure that you are having rights to create stored procedures. Otherwise, login as root and give rights to you (Usually the super-user will do it for you).

Giving all rights on everything to the user 'huser':

Login as root, and issue the following command.

```
grant all privileges on *.* to huser@localhost
            identified by 'hpword' with grant option;
```

Now, login as 'huser' (normal user, this is the user-login we are using for our demonstrations) and create the stored procedure as follows.

```
mysql> DELIMITER //
mysql> CREATE PROCEDURE GET_EMPLOYEE_SP()
    -> BEGIN
    -> SELECT * FROM EMPLOYEE;
    -> END //
Query OK, 0 rows affected (0.00 sec)
```

```
mysql> DELIMITER ;
mysql>
mysql> CALL GET_EMPLOYEE_SP();
```

ID	EMP_NAME	EMP_NUMBER	EMP_SALARY
402881f81f 016ab7011f016 abc470001 402881f81f 016ab7011f016 abc490002	Ibrahim	5001	—
402881f81f 016ab7011f016 abc510003 402881f81f 016ab7011f016 abc510004	Kumar	5002	—
402881f81f 016ab7011f016 abc510005 402881f81f 016ab7011f016 abc510006	Ajay	5003	—

```
3 rows in set (0.00 sec)

Query OK, 0 rows affected (0.03 sec)
```

Just include one `NamedSQLQuery` in the Entity and keep the already existing data (Keep hbm2ddl.auto property as update).

```
// File Name: Employee.java
// Illustrates @NamedNativeQuery and how to call Stored Procedures

package com.hdemo;

import javax.persistence.CascadeType;
import javax.persistence.Column;
import javax.persistence.Entity;
import javax.persistence.GeneratedValue;
import javax.persistence.Id;
import javax.persistence.JoinColumn;
import javax.persistence.NamedNativeQuery;
import javax.persistence.OneToOne;
```

```
import javax.persistence.QueryHint;
import javax.persistence.Table;

import org.hibernate.annotations.GenericGenerator;

@Entity
@Table(name = "EMPLOYEE")

//At Entity Level
@NamedNativeQuery(name = "QUERY_GET_EMPLOYEE_SP",
            resultClass = Employee.class,
            query = "{call GET_EMPLOYEE_SP()}",
            hints = { @QueryHint(name = "org.hibernate.callable",
            value = "true"),
              @QueryHint(name = "org.hibernate.readOnly", value =
              "true") })
   public class Employee {

   private static final long serialVersionUID = 1L;

   @Id
   @GeneratedValue(generator = "idGen")
   @GenericGenerator(name = "idGen", strategy = "uuid.hex")
   @Column(name = "ID", length = 32)
   private String id = "";

   @Column(name = "EMP_NUMBER", unique = true, nullable = false)
   private Integer empNumber;

   @Column(name = "EMP_NAME", length = 64, nullable = false)
   private String empName;

   @OneToOne(cascade = { CascadeType.PERSIST, CascadeType.REMOVE })
   @JoinColumn(name = "EMP_SALARY", unique = true)
   private Salary salary;

   public String getId() {
         return id;
   }

   public void setId(String id) {
         this.id = id;
   }
```

```
    public Integer getEmpNumber() {
          return empNumber;
    }

    public void setEmpNumber(Integer empNumber) {
          this.empNumber = empNumber;
    }

    public String getEmpName() {
          return empName;
    }

    public void setEmpName(String empName) {
          this.empName = empName;
    }

    public Salary getSalary() {
          return salary;
    }

    public void setSalary(Salary salary) {
          this.salary = salary;
    }

}
```

Execute the following main program and observe that the Stored Procedure is called and it returns all the rows of Employee table.

```
// File Name: EmployeeManipulation.java
// Illustrates @NamedNativeQuery and how to call Stored Procedures

package com.hdemo;

import java.util.List;

import org.hibernate.Query;
import org.hibernate.Session;
import org.hibernate.SessionFactory;
import org.hibernate.Transaction;

public class EmployeeManipulation {
```

```
    @SuppressWarnings("unchecked")
    public static void main(String[] args) throws Exception {
          SessionFactory sessionFactory =
                                 HibernateUtil.getSessionFactory();
          Session session = sessionFactory.openSession();
          Transaction txn = session.beginTransaction();

          Query query = session.getNamedQuery("QUERY_GET_EMPLOYEE_SP");
          List list = query.list();

          for (int i = 0; i < list.size(); i++) {
                System.out.println("RECORD [" + (i + 1) + "]");
                Employee employee = (Employee) list.get(i);
                printRecord(employee);
          }

          txn.commit();
          session.close();
          sessionFactory.close();
    }

    static void printRecord(Employee employee) {
          System.out.println("Employee Number : " +
                                        employee.getEmpNumber());
          System.out.println("Employee Name   : " +
                                          employee.getEmpName());
          System.out.println("Basic Pay       : " +
                            employee.getSalary().getBasicPay());
          System.out.println("Allowances      : " +
                          employee.getSalary().getAllowances());
          System.out.println("Deductions      : " +
                          employee.getSalary().getDeductions());
          System.out.println("Netpay          : " +
                              employee.getSalary().getNetPay());

      System.out.println("====================================\n");
    }
}
```

```
Hibernate: {call GET_EMPLOYEE_SP()}
```

```
Hibernate: select salary0_.ID as ID1_0_, salary0_.ALLOWANCES as
ALLOWANCES1_0_, salary0_.BPAY as BPAY1_0_, salary0_.DEDUCTIONS as
DEDUCTIONS1_0_, salary0_.NETPAY as NETPAY1_0_ from SALARY salary0_
where salary0_.ID=?
Hibernate: select salary0_.ID as ID1_0_, salary0_.ALLOWANCES as
ALLOWANCES1_0_, salary0_.BPAY as BPAY1_0_, salary0_.DEDUCTIONS as
DEDUCTIONS1_0_, salary0_.NETPAY as NETPAY1_0_ from SALARY salary0_
where salary0_.ID=?
Hibernate: select salary0_.ID as ID1_0_, salary0_.ALLOWANCES as
ALLOWANCES1_0_, salary0_.BPAY as BPAY1_0_, salary0_.DEDUCTIONS as
DEDUCTIONS1_0_, salary0_.NETPAY as NETPAY1_0_ from SALARY salary0_
where salary0_.ID=?
RECORD [1]
Employee Number  : 5001
Employee Name    : Ibrahim
Basic Pay        : 10000.0
Allowances       : 3000.0
Deductions       : 2000.0
Netpay           : 11000.0
========================================

RECORD [2]
Employee Number  : 5002
Employee Name    : Kumar
Basic Pay        : 5000.0
Allowances       : 1500.0
Deductions       : 1000.0
Netpay           : 5500.0
========================================

RECORD [3]
Employee Number  : 5003
Employee Name    : Ajay
Basic Pay        : 15000.0
Allowances       : 4000.0
Deductions       : 2500.0
Netpay           : 16500.0
========================================
```

Now we will change the stored procedure to accept one IN argument.

```
mysql> DROP PROCEDURE IF EXISTS GET_EMPLOYEE_SP;
Query OK, 0 rows affected (0.00 sec)

mysql> DELIMITER //
mysql> CREATE PROCEDURE GET_EMPLOYEE_SP(IN ENAME CHAR(64))
      -> BEGIN
       -> SELECT * FROM EMPLOYEE WHERE EMP_NAME LIKE CONCAT('%',
        ENAME, '%');
      -> END //
Query OK, 0 rows affected (0.00 sec)

mysql> DELIMITER ;

// File Name: Employee.java
// Illustrates @NamedNativeQuery and how to call Stored Procedures
with arguments

package com.hdemo;

import javax.persistence.CascadeType;
import javax.persistence.Column;
import javax.persistence.Entity;
import javax.persistence.GeneratedValue;
import javax.persistence.Id;
import javax.persistence.JoinColumn;
import javax.persistence.NamedNativeQuery;
import javax.persistence.OneToOne;
import javax.persistence.QueryHint;
import javax.persistence.Table;

import org.hibernate.annotations.GenericGenerator;

@Entity
@Table(name = "EMPLOYEE")

//At Entity Level
```

```
@NamedNativeQuery(name = "QUERY_GET_EMPLOYEE_SP",
          resultClass = Employee.class,
          query = "{call GET_EMPLOYEE_SP(:EmpName)}",
          hints = { @QueryHint(name = "org.hibernate.callable",
          value = "true"),
          @QueryHint(name = "org.hibernate.readOnly", value = "true")
          })
  public class Employee {

  private static final long serialVersionUID = 1L;

  @Id
  @GeneratedValue(generator = "idGen")
  @GenericGenerator(name = "idGen", strategy = "uuid.hex")
  @Column(name = "ID", length = 32)
  private String id = "";

  @Column(name = "EMP_NUMBER", unique = true, nullable = false)
  private Integer empNumber;

  @Column(name = "EMP_NAME", length = 64, nullable = false)
  private String empName;

  @OneToOne(cascade = { CascadeType.PERSIST, CascadeType.REMOVE })
  @JoinColumn(name = "EMP_SALARY", unique = true)
  private Salary salary;

  public String getId() {
        return id;
  }

  public void setId(String id) {
        this.id = id;
  }

  public Integer getEmpNumber() {
        return empNumber;
  }
```

```
    public void setEmpNumber(Integer empNumber) {
        this.empNumber = empNumber;
    }

    public String getEmpName() {
        return empName;
    }

    public void setEmpName(String empName) {
        this.empName = empName;
    }

    public Salary getSalary() {
        return salary;
    }

    public void setSalary(Salary salary) {
        this.salary = salary;
    }

}

// File Name: EmployeeManipulation.java
// Illustrates @NamedNativeQuery and how to call Stored Procedures
with arguments

package com.hdemo;

import java.util.List;

import org.hibernate.Query;
import org.hibernate.Session;
import org.hibernate.SessionFactory;
import org.hibernate.Transaction;

public class EmployeeManipulation {

    @SuppressWarnings("unchecked")
```

```
    public static void main(String[] args) throws Exception {
        SessionFactory sessionFactory =
                              HibernateUtil.getSessionFactory();
        Session session = sessionFactory.openSession();
        Transaction txn = session.beginTransaction();

        Query query = session.getNamedQuery("QUERY_GET_EMPLOYEE_SP");
        query.setParameter("EmpName", "ja");
        List list = query.list();

        for (int i = 0; i < list.size(); i++) {
            System.out.println("RECORD [" + (i + 1) + "]");
            Employee employee = (Employee) list.get(i);
            printRecord(employee);
        }

        txn.commit();
        session.close();
        sessionFactory.close();
    }

    static void printRecord(Employee employee) {
        System.out.println("Employee Number : " +
                                    employee.getEmpNumber());
        System.out.println("Employee Name   : " +
                                      employee.getEmpName());
        System.out.println("Basic Pay       : " +
                         employee.getSalary().getBasicPay());
        System.out.println("Allowances      : " +
                       employee.getSalary().getAllowances());
        System.out.println("Deductions      : " +
                       employee.getSalary().getDeductions());
        System.out.println("Netpay           : " +
                           employee.getSalary().getNetPay());

     System.out.println("=======================================\n");
    }
}
```

```
Hibernate: {call GET_EMPLOYEE_SP(?)}
Hibernate: select salary0_.ID as ID1_0_, salary0_.ALLOWANCES as ALLOWANCES1_0_, salary0_.BPAY as BPAY1_0_, salary0_.DEDUCTIONS as DEDUCTIONS1_0_, salary0_.NETPAY as NETPAY1_0_ from SALARY salary0_ where salary0_.ID=?
RECORD [1]
Employee Number : 5003
Employee Name   : Ajay
Basic Pay       : 15000.0
Allowances      : 4000.0
Deductions      : 2500.0
Netpay          : 16500.0
=========================================
```

5.13 BULK DATABASE OPERATIONS: INSERT, UPDATE AND DELETE STATEMENTS

HQL also supports insert, update and delete statements. Their syntaxes are almost similar to SQL, but uses object references.

General format of `INSERT` statement

```
INSERT INTO EntityName properties_list SELECT_STATEMENT
```

HQL supports only the above '`INSERT INTO .. SELECT`' format of `INSERT` statement, it currently does not support '`INSERT INTO .. VALUES`' format, that is direct insertion of values are not supported.

To illustrate this `INSERT` statement, we will create a new *Employee* entity and we try to insert some sample data. Adjust hbm2ddl.auto property in *hiberate.cfg.xml* file.

```
// File Name: Employee.java
// Generating sample data to illustrate Bulk Database operations

package com.hdemo;

import java.util.Date;

import javax.persistence.Column;
import javax.persistence.Entity;
import javax.persistence.GeneratedValue;
import javax.persistence.Id;
import javax.persistence.Table;
import javax.persistence.Temporal;
```

```
import javax.persistence.TemporalType;

import org.hibernate.annotations.GenericGenerator;

@Entity
@Table(name = "EMPLOYEE")
public class Employee {

  private static final long serialVersionUID = 1L;

  @Id
  @GeneratedValue(generator = "idGen")
  @GenericGenerator(name = "idGen", strategy = "uuid.hex")
  @Column(name = "ID", length = 32)
  private String id = "";

  @Column(name = "EMP_NUMBER", unique = true, nullable = false)
  private Integer empNumber;

  @Column(name = "EMP_NAME", length = 64, nullable = false)
  private String empName;

  @Temporal(value = TemporalType.DATE)
  @Column(name = "DOJ")
  private Date doj;       //Date Of Joining

  public String getId() {
       return id;
  }

  public void setId(String id) {
       this.id = id;
  }

  public Integer getEmpNumber() {
       return empNumber;
  }
```

```
    public void setEmpNumber(Integer empNumber) {
        this.empNumber = empNumber;
    }

    public String getEmpName() {
        return empName;
    }

    public void setEmpName(String empName) {
        this.empName = empName;
    }

    public Date getDoj() {
        return doj;
    }

    public void setDoj(Date doj) {
        this.doj = doj;
    }

}
```

```
// File Name: EmployeeManipulation.java
// Illustrates HQL INSERT Statement

package com.hdemo;

import java.text.SimpleDateFormat;
import java.util.Calendar;
import java.util.List;

import org.hibernate.Query;
import org.hibernate.Session;
import org.hibernate.SessionFactory;
import org.hibernate.Transaction;

public class EmployeeManipulation {
```

```
@SuppressWarnings("unchecked")
public static void main(String[] args) throws Exception {
     SessionFactory sessionFactory =
                          HibernateUtil.getSessionFactory();
     Session session = sessionFactory.openSession();
     Transaction txn = session.beginTransaction();
     Calendar doj = Calendar.getInstance();

     Employee employee1 = new Employee();
     employee1.setEmpNumber(5001);
     employee1.setEmpName("Ibrahim");
     doj.set(2001, 6, 2);
     employee1.setDoj(doj.getTime());
     session.persist(employee1);

     Employee employee2 = new Employee();
     employee2.setEmpNumber(5002);
     employee2.setEmpName("Kumar");
     doj.set(2002, 7, 3);
     employee2.setDoj(doj.getTime());
     session.persist(employee2);

     Employee employee3 = new Employee();
     employee3.setEmpNumber(5003);
     employee3.setEmpName("Ajay");
     doj.set(2003, 5, 1);
     employee3.setDoj(doj.getTime());
     session.persist(employee3);

     Query queryEmployeeInsert = session.createQuery("insert into
     Employee (id, empNumber, empName, doj) select '1', e.empNumber
     + 100, concat('Mr.', e.empName), e.doj from Employee e
     where e.empNumber = 5002");
     int affectedRows = queryEmployeeInsert.executeUpdate();
     if (affectedRows > 0)
     System.out.println("Employee Row is inserted successfully");
     else
```

```
                System.out.println("Failed to insert the Employee row");

            System.out.println("\n");

            Query query = session.createQuery("from Employee");
            List list = query.list();
            for (int i = 0; i < list.size(); i++) {
                Employee employee = (Employee) list.get(i);
                printRecord(employee);
            }

            txn.commit();
            session.close();
            sessionFactory.close();
        }

        static void printRecord(Employee employee) {
            System.out.println("Employee Number : " +
                                          employee.getEmpNumber());
            System.out.println("Employee Name   : " +
                                            employee.getEmpName());
            System.out.println("DOJ             : " +
          new SimpleDateFormat("dd/MM/yyyy").format(employee.getDoj()));

         System.out.println("=======================================\n");
        }
    }
```

```
Hibernate: insert into EMPLOYEE (DOJ, EMP_NAME, EMP_NUMBER, ID)
values (?, ?, ?, ?)
Hibernate: insert into EMPLOYEE (DOJ, EMP_NAME, EMP_NUMBER, ID)
values (?, ?, ?, ?)
Hibernate: insert into EMPLOYEE (DOJ, EMP_NAME, EMP_NUMBER, ID)
values (?, ?, ?, ?)
Hibernate: insert into EMPLOYEE ( ID, EMP_NUMBER, EMP_NAME, DOJ )
select '1' as col_0_0_, employee0_.EMP_NUMBER+100 as col_1_0_,
concat('Mr.', employee0_.EMP_NAME) as col_2_0_, employee0_.DOJ as
col_3_0_ from EMPLOYEE employee0_ where employee0_.EMP_NUMBER=5002
Employee Row is inserted successfully
```

```
Hibernate: select employee0_.ID as ID0_, employee0_.DOJ as DOJ0_,
employee0_.EMP_NAME as EMP3_0_, employee0_.EMP_NUMBER as EMP4_0_ from
EMPLOYEE employee0_
    Employee Number : 5102
    Employee Name   : Mr.Kumar
    DOJ             : 03/08/2002
    ========================================

    Employee Number : 5001
    Employee Name   : Ibrahim
    DOJ             : 02/07/2001
    ========================================

    Employee Number : 5002
    Employee Name   : Kumar
    DOJ             : 03/08/2002
    ========================================

    Employee Number : 5003
    Employee Name   : Ajay
    DOJ             : 01/06/2003
    ========================================
```

General format of `UPDATE` statement

```
  UPDATE EntityName set property = value, ... [where condition]
// File Name: EmployeeManipulation.java
// Illustrates HQL UPDATE Statement

package com.hdemo;

import java.text.SimpleDateFormat;
import java.util.List;

import org.hibernate.Query;
import org.hibernate.Session;
import org.hibernate.SessionFactory;
import org.hibernate.Transaction;
```

```
public class EmployeeManipulation {

   @SuppressWarnings("unchecked")
   public static void main(String[] args) throws Exception {
         SessionFactory sessionFactory =
                                 HibernateUtil.getSessionFactory();
         Session session = sessionFactory.openSession();
         Transaction txn = session.beginTransaction();

         Query queryEmployeeUpdate = session.createQuery("UPDATE
         Employee e SET e.empName = concat(e.empName, ' Ji') where
         e.empNumber in (5001,5002)");
         int affectedRows = queryEmployeeUpdate.executeUpdate();
         if (affectedRows > 0)
               System.out.println("Employee Row(s) are updated
               successfully");
         else
               System.out.println("Failed to update the Employee
               row(s)");

         System.out.println("\n");

         Query query = session.createQuery("from Employee");
         List list = query.list();
         for (int i = 0; i < list.size(); i++) {
               Employee employee = (Employee) list.get(i);
               printRecord(employee);
         }

         txn.commit();
         session.close();
         sessionFactory.close();
   }

   static void printRecord(Employee employee) {
         System.out.println("Employee Number : " +
                                       employee.getEmpNumber());
         System.out.println("Employee Name   : " +
                                         employee.getEmpName());
```

```
        System.out.println("DOJ            : " +
      new  SimpleDateFormat("dd/MM/yyyy").format(employee.getDoj()));

     System.out.println("=====================================\n");
   }
}
```

```
Hibernate: update EMPLOYEE set EMP_NAME=concat(EMP_NAME, ' Ji') where EMP_NUMBER in (5001 , 5002)
Employee Row(s) are updated successfully

Hibernate: select employee0_.ID as ID0_, employee0_.DOJ as DOJ0_, employee0_.EMP_NAME as EMP3_0_, employee0_.EMP_NUMBER as EMP4_0_ from EMPLOYEE employee0_
Employee Number : 5102
Employee Name   : Mr.Kumar
DOJ             : 03/08/2002
=====================================
Employee Number : 5001
Employee Name   : Ibrahim Ji
DOJ             : 02/07/2001
=====================================
Employee Number : 5002
Employee Name   : Kumar Ji
DOJ             : 03/08/2002
=====================================
Employee Number : 5003
Employee Name   : Ajay
DOJ             : 01/06/2003
=====================================
```

The following program updates 'doj' (Date data-type) column.

```
// File Name: EmployeeManipulation.java
// Illustrates HQL UPDATE Statement
```

```
package com.hdemo;

import java.text.SimpleDateFormat;
import java.util.Date;
import java.util.List;

import org.hibernate.Query;
import org.hibernate.Session;
import org.hibernate.SessionFactory;
import org.hibernate.Transaction;

public class EmployeeManipulation {

  @SuppressWarnings("unchecked")
  public static void main(String[] args) throws Exception {
        SessionFactory sessionFactory =
                              HibernateUtil.getSessionFactory();
        Session session = sessionFactory.openSession();
        Transaction txn = session.beginTransaction();

        Query queryEmployeeUpdate = session.createQuery("UPDATE
        Employee e SET e.doj = :doj where e.empNumber = 5001");
        queryEmployeeUpdate.setTimestamp("doj", new Date());
        int affectedRows = queryEmployeeUpdate.executeUpdate();
        if (affectedRows > 0)
        System.out.println("Employee Row is updated successfully");
        else
              System.out.println("Failed to update the Employee row");

        System.out.println("\n");

        Query query = session.createQuery("from Employee");
        List list = query.list();
        for (int i = 0; i < list.size(); i++) {
              Employee employee = (Employee) list.get(i);
              printRecord(employee);
        }

        txn.commit();
        session.close();
```

```
        sessionFactory.close();
    }

    static void printRecord(Employee employee) {
        System.out.println("Employee Number : " +
                                        employee.getEmpNumber());
        System.out.println("Employee Name   : " +
                                        employee.getEmpName());
        System.out.println("DOJ             : " +
      new SimpleDateFormat("dd/MM/yyyy").format(employee.getDoj()));

     System.out.println("=====================================\n");
    }
}
```

```
Hibernate: update EMPLOYEE set DOJ=? where EMP_NUMBER=5001
Employee Row is updated successfully

Hibernate: select employee0_.ID as ID0_, employee0_.DOJ as DOJ0_,
employee0_.EMP_NAME as EMP3_0_, employee0_.EMP_NUMBER as EMP4_0_ from
EMPLOYEE employee0_
Employee Number : 5102
Employee Name   : Mr.Kumar
DOJ             : 03/08/2002
=====================================

Employee Number : 5001
Employee Name   : Ibrahim Ji
DOJ             : 28/01/2009
=====================================

Employee Number : 5002
Employee Name   : Kumar Ji
DOJ             : 03/08/2002
=====================================

Employee Number : 5003
Employee Name   : Ajay
DOJ             : 01/06/2003
=====================================
```

General format of DELETE statement

```
DELETE EntityName [where condition]
```

```
// File Name: EmployeeManipulation.java
// Illustrates HQL DELETE Statement

package com.hdemo;

import java.text.SimpleDateFormat;
import java.util.List;

import org.hibernate.Query;
import org.hibernate.Session;
import org.hibernate.SessionFactory;
import org.hibernate.Transaction;

public class EmployeeManipulation {

  @SuppressWarnings("unchecked")
  public static void main(String[] args) throws Exception {
        SessionFactory sessionFactory =
                              HibernateUtil.getSessionFactory();
        Session session = sessionFactory.openSession();
        Transaction txn = session.beginTransaction();

        Query queryEmployeeUpdate = session.createQuery("DELETE
        Employee e WHERE e.empNumber = :empNumber");
        queryEmployeeUpdate.setInteger("empNumber", 5001);
        int affectedRows = queryEmployeeUpdate.executeUpdate();
        if (affectedRows > 0)
        System.out.println("Employee Row is deleted successfully");
        else
             System.out.println("Failed to delete the Employee row");

        System.out.println("\n");

        Query query = session.createQuery("from Employee");
        List list = query.list();
```

```
        for (int i = 0; i < list.size(); i++) {
             Employee employee = (Employee) list.get(i);
             printRecord(employee);
        }

        txn.commit();
        session.close();
        sessionFactory.close();
    }

    static void printRecord(Employee employee) {
        System.out.println("Employee Number : " +
                                          employee.getEmpNumber());
        System.out.println("Employee Name : " +
                                            employee.getEmpName());
        System.out.println("DOJ            : " +
      new SimpleDateFormat("dd/MM/yyyy").format(employee.getDoj()));

      System.out.println("=======================================\n");
    }
}
```

```
Hibernate: delete from EMPLOYEE where EMP_NUMBER=?
Employee Row is deleted successfully
Hibernate: select employee0_.ID as ID0_, employee0_.DOJ as DOJ0_, employee0_.EMP_NAME as EMP3_0_, employee0_.EMP_NUMBER as EMP4_0 from EMPLOYEE employee0_
Employee Number : 5102
Employee Name   : Mr.Kumar
DOJ             : 03/08/2002
=======================================
Employee Number : 5002
Employee Name   : Kumar Ji
DOJ             : 03/08/2002
=======================================
```

```
Employee Number  : 5003
Employee Name    : Ajay
DOJ              : 01/06/2003
============================================
```

5.14 GETTING JDBC CONNECTION

It is also possible to get JDBC `Connection` object from Hibernate Session. Once you get JDBC `Connection` object, you can do what ever allowed with JDBC Connection such as executing native SQL statements, calling stored procedures, etc.

The `connection()` method of `Session` interface returns the underlying JDBC Connection. The programmer must take care about closing connections. This method is currently deprecated (old API, will be removed from next version of the Software) and will be removed from Hibernate Version 4. In the new version, there will be an alternate to access and use JDBC API. However, the following program uses this deprecated method to get JDBC `Connection`.

```
// File Name: Employee.java
// Illustrates how to access JDBC Connection

package com.hdemo;

import java.util.Date;

import javax.persistence.Column;
import javax.persistence.Entity;
import javax.persistence.GeneratedValue;
import javax.persistence.Id;
import javax.persistence.Table;
import javax.persistence.Temporal;
import javax.persistence.TemporalType;

import org.hibernate.annotations.GenericGenerator;

@Entity
@Table(name = "EMPLOYEE")
public class Employee {

  private static final long serialVersionUID = 1L;

  @Id
  @GeneratedValue(generator = "idGen")
```

```
@GenericGenerator(name = "idGen", strategy = "uuid.hex")
@Column(name = "ID", length = 32)
private String id = "";

@Column(name = "EMP_NUMBER", unique = true, nullable = false)
private Integer empNumber;

@Column(name = "EMP_NAME", length = 64, nullable = false)
private String empName;

@Temporal(value = TemporalType.DATE)
@Column(name = "DOJ")
private Date doj;        //Date Of Joining

public String getId() {
      return id;
}

public void setId(String id) {
      this.id = id;
}

public Integer getEmpNumber() {
      return empNumber;
}

public void setEmpNumber(Integer empNumber) {
      this.empNumber = empNumber;
}

public String getEmpName() {
      return empName;
}

public void setEmpName(String empName) {
      this.empName = empName;
}

public Date getDoj() {
```

```
        return doj;
    }

    public void setDoj(Date doj) {
        this.doj = doj;
    }

}

// File Name: EmployeeManipulation.java
// Illustrates how to get JDBC Connection

package com.hdemo;

import java.sql.Connection;
import java.sql.PreparedStatement;
import java.sql.ResultSet;
import java.sql.Statement;
import java.sql.Timestamp;
import java.util.Calendar;
import java.util.Date;

import org.hibernate.Session;
import org.hibernate.SessionFactory;
import org.hibernate.Transaction;

public class EmployeeManipulation {

    public static void main(String[] args) throws Exception {
        SessionFactory sessionFactory =
HibernateUtil.getSessionFactory();
        Session session = sessionFactory.openSession();
        Transaction txn = session.beginTransaction();

        Connection con = null;
        Statement st = null;
        PreparedStatement ps = null;
        ResultSet rs = null;
```

```
try {
        con = session.connection();

        st = con.createStatement();
        st.executeUpdate("INSERT INTO EMPLOYEE (ID, EMP_NUMBER,
        EMP_NAME, DOJ) VALUES ('1', 1001, 'Ibrahim',
        str_to_date('02/07/2001', '%d/%m/%Y'))");
        st.executeUpdate("INSERT INTO EMPLOYEE (ID, EMP_NUMBER,
        EMP_NAME, DOJ) VALUES ('2', 1002, 'Ajay',
        str_to_date('01/02/2001', '%d/%m/%Y'))");
        st.executeUpdate("INSERT INTO EMPLOYEE (ID, EMP_NUMBER,
        EMP_NAME, DOJ) VALUES ('3', 1003, 'Akfha',
        str_to_date('16/08/2002', '%d/%m/%Y'))");
        st.executeUpdate("INSERT INTO EMPLOYEE (ID, EMP_NUMBER,
        EMP_NAME, DOJ) VALUES ('4', 1004, 'Kumar',
        str_to_date('16/02/2004', '%d/%m/%Y'))");
        st.executeUpdate("INSERT INTO EMPLOYEE (ID, EMP_NUMBER,
        EMP_NAME, DOJ) VALUES ('5', 1005, 'Karan',
        str_to_date('01/05/2005', '%d/%m/%Y'))");
        System.out.println("Five Employee records are inserted
        using Statement interface");

        ps = con.prepareStatement("INSERT INTO EMPLOYEE (ID,
        EMP_NUMBER, EMP_NAME, DOJ) VALUES (?, ?, ?, ?)");
        ps.setString(1, "6");
        ps.setInt(2, 1006);
        ps.setString(3, "Ameer");
        Calendar c = Calendar.getInstance();
        c.set(2007, 11, 16);
        ps.setTimestamp(4, new Timestamp(c.getTimeInMillis()));
        ps.executeUpdate();

        ps.setString(1, "7");
        ps.setInt(2, 1007);
        ps.setString(3, "Salman");
        c.set(2000, 0, 5);
        ps.setTimestamp(4, new Timestamp(c.getTimeInMillis()));
        ps.executeUpdate();
```

```
            System.out.println("Two Employee records are inserted
            using PreparedStatement interface");

            displayEmployees(st);

            System.out.println("\nUpdating EMPLOYEE table");
            int rowsAffected = st.executeUpdate("UPDATE EMPLOYEE
            SET EMP_NAME = concat('Mr.' , EMP_NAME)");
    System.out.println(rowsAffected + " records are updated \n");

            displayEmployees(st);

    System.out.println("\nDeleting some rows from EMPLOYEE table");
            ps = con.prepareStatement("DELETE FROM EMPLOYEE WHERE
            UPPER(EMP_NAME) like UPPER(?)");
            ps.setString(1, "%K%");
            rowsAffected = ps.executeUpdate();
    System.out.println(rowsAffected + " records are deleted \n");

            displayEmployees(st);
        }
        catch (Exception e) {
            System.out.println("ERROR OCCURRED. ERROR [" +
            e.getMessage() + "]");
            e.printStackTrace();
        }
        finally {
            if (st != null)
                st.close();
            if (ps != null)
                ps.close();
            if (rs != null)
                rs.close();
            if (session.isConnected()) // Is Underlying JDBC
            Connection is connected
```

```
                session.disconnect();    // Disconnect the
                underlying JDBC Connection
        }

        txn.commit();
        session.close();
        sessionFactory.close();
    }

    static void displayEmployees(Statement st) throws Exception {
        System.out.println("Selecting all records of EMPLOYEE table");
        ResultSet rs = st.executeQuery("SELECT EMP_NUMBER, EMP_NAME,
        DOJ FROM EMPLOYEE");
        while (rs.next()) {
            int empNumber = rs.getInt("EMP_NUMBER");
            String empName = rs.getString("EMP_NAME");
            Timestamp tsDOJ = rs.getTimestamp("DOJ");
            Date doj = null;
            if (tsDOJ != null)
                doj = new Date(rs.getTimestamp("DOJ").getTime());

            System.out.printf("%10s %-30s %td/%tm/%tY \n",
            empNumber, empName, doj, doj, doj);
        }
    }
}
```

```
Five Employee records are inserted using Statement interface
Two Employee records are inserted using PreparedStatement interface
Selecting all records of EMPLOYEE table
      1001 Ibrahim                        02/07/2001
      1002 Ajay                           01/02/2001
      1003 Akfha                          16/08/2002
      1004 Kumar                          16/02/2004
      1005 Karan                          01/05/2005
```

```
        1006 Ameer                                  16/12/2007
        1007 Salman                                 05/01/2000

Updating EMPLOYEE table
7 records are updated

Selecting all records of EMPLOYEE table
        1001 Mr.Ibrahim                            02/07/2001
        1002 Mr.Ajay                               01/02/2001
        1003 Mr.Akfha                              16/08/2002
        1004 Mr.Kumar                              16/02/2004
        1005 Mr.Karan                              01/05/2005
        1006 Mr.Ameer                              16/12/2007
        1007 Mr.Salman                             05/01/2000

Deleting some rows from EMPLOYEE table
3 records are deleted

Selecting all records of EMPLOYEE table
        1001 Mr.Ibrahim                           02/07/2001
        1002 Mr.Ajay                              01/02/2001
        1006 Mr.Ameer                             16/12/2007
        1007 Mr.Salman                            05/01/2000

Data at Database:

mysql> select * from Employee;
```

ID	DOJ	EMP_NAME	EMP_NUMBER
1	2001-07-02	Mr.Ibrahim	1001
2	2001-02-01	Mr.Ajay	1002
6	2007-12-16	Mr.Ameer	1006
7	2000-01-05	Mr.Salman	1007

```
4 rows in set (0.00 sec)
```

Calling Stored Procedure via JDBC:

Using this JDBC `Connection`, we can invoke Stored Procedures directly using `CallableStatement` as shown below.

We will take the already created stored procedure `GET_EMPLOYEE_SP`, which accept a string as parameter and returns all employee records where the employee names contain the parameter string.

```
mysql> DROP PROCEDURE IF EXISTS GET_EMPLOYEE_SP;
Query OK, 0 rows affected (0.00 sec)

mysql> DELIMITER //
mysql> CREATE PROCEDURE GET_EMPLOYEE_SP(IN ENAME CHAR(64))
      -> BEGIN
     ->   SELECT * FROM EMPLOYEE WHERE EMP_NAME LIKE CONCAT('%',
        ENAME, '%');
      -> END //
Query OK, 0 rows affected (0.00 sec)

mysql> DELIMITER ;
```

To invoke the created stored procedure, just use the `CallableStatement` which is available in JDBC. It is not required to declare any `@NamedNativeQuery` in *Employee* entity as we already shown, which is used to invoke Stored Procedure using Hibernate API.

```
// File Name: EmployeeManipulation.java
// Illustrates how to invoke Stored Procedure using JDBC Connection

package com.hdemo;

import java.sql.CallableStatement;
import java.sql.Connection;
import java.sql.ResultSet;
import java.sql.Timestamp;
import java.util.Date;

import org.hibernate.Session;
import org.hibernate.SessionFactory;
import org.hibernate.Transaction;

public class EmployeeManipulation {
```

```
public static void main(String[] args) throws Exception {
    SessionFactory sessionFactory =
                        HibernateUtil.getSessionFactory();

    Session session = sessionFactory.openSession();
    Transaction txn = session.beginTransaction();

    Connection con = null;
    ResultSet rs = null;

    try {
        con = session.connection();

        CallableStatement cs = con.prepareCall("{ call
        GET_EMPLOYEE_SP(?) }");
        cs.setString(1, "ja");
        rs = cs.executeQuery();

        System.out.println("Stored Procedure is invoked.
        Iterating the Resultset...");
        displayEmployees(rs);
    }
    catch (Exception e) {
        System.out.println("ERROR OCCURRED. ERROR [" +
        e.getMessage() + "]");
        e.printStackTrace();
    }
    finally {
        if (rs != null)
            rs.close();
        if (session.isConnected()) // Is Underlying JDBC
        Connection is connected
            session.disconnect();  // Disconnect the
            underlying JDBC Connection
    }

    txn.commit();
    session.close();
    sessionFactory.close();
```

```
        }

        static void displayEmployees(ResultSet rs) throws Exception {
                while (rs.next()) {
                        int empNumber = rs.getInt("EMP_NUMBER");
                        String empName = rs.getString("EMP_NAME");
                        Timestamp tsDOJ = rs.getTimestamp("DOJ");
                        Date doj = null;
                        if (tsDOJ != null)
                                doj = new Date(rs.getTimestamp("DOJ").getTime());

                        System.out.printf("%10s %-30s %td/%tm/%tY \n",
                        empNumber, empName, doj, doj, doj);
                }
        }
}
```

```
Stored Procedure is invoked. Iterating the Resultset...
      1002 Mr.Ajay                        01/02/2001
```

SUMMARY

This chapter uses HQL for demonstration; JPA QL syntaxes are almost same like HQL. The user can easily understand JPQ QL, if he know HQL and vice versa. The syntaxes of HQL / JPA QL are similar to SQL, but they are based on object references. HQL supports all possible way to select data and supports all types of Join operations while retrieving data. It contains rich set of built-in functions and it also allows us to use functions those are supported by the underlying database. It provides ways to use underlying database specific features such as invoking scrollable result set, calling stored procedures, etc. It also provides direct `UPDATE`, `DELETE`, and `INSERT_FROM_SELECT` statements for bulk database operations. It provides Polymorphic Queries feature, not available in normal SQL, which selects all sub-class objects while selecting parent class object. Hibernate provides API to invoke native SQL statements directly. With HQL, we can achieve almost all the operations that those we are doing using JDBC. However, if you feel that it is good to do some operations with JDBC, then it is possible to get JDBC `Connection` object from Hibernate Session.

CHAPTER

6

CRITERIA QUERIES

6.0 INTRODUCTION

Even though the HQL is based on object references, its query syntaxes are similar to SQL, so the programmer still needs to know SQL syntaxes and relational mappings to write HQL queries. The Hibernate provides *Criteria API* which is purely based object-oriented approach; using this Criteria API, the programmer can use Java code for manipulating data with database, and no need to know SQL and relational mappings for building queries.

6.1 GENERATING SAMPLE DATA FOR DEMONSTRATIONS

Before we begin demonstrate the features of Criteria API, we will have a database table "EMPLOYEE" with some initial data. The required files for generating these sample data are given below. Follow the already explained instructions to run these programs.

Configuration File (hibernate.cfg.xml):

```
<?xml version='1.0' encoding='utf-8'?>
<!DOCTYPE hibernate-configuration PUBLIC
        "-//Hibernate/Hibernate Configuration DTD 3.0//EN"
        "http://hibernate.sourceforge.net/hibernate-configuration-
        3.0.dtd">
<hibernate-configuration>
   <session-factory>
        <property name="connection.driver_class">com.mysql.jdbc.
        Driver</property>
        <property name="connection.url">jdbc:mysql://localhost:3306/
        hdemodb</property>
        <property name="connection.username">huser</property>
        <property name="connection.password">hpword</property>
```

```
        <property  name="dialect">org.hibernate.dialect.MySQLDialect</
        property>

        <property  name="hibernate.c3p0.minPoolSize">1</property>
        <property  name="hibernate.c3p0.maxPoolSize">1</property>
        <property  name="hibernate.c3p0.timeout">10</property>
        <property  name="hibernate.c3p0.max_statement">50</property>
        <property name="hibernate.c3p0.testConnectionOnCheckout">
        false</property>

        <property name="current_session_context_class">thread</
        property>
        <property  name="cache.provider_class">org.hibernate.cache.
        NoCacheProvider</property>
        <property  name="show_sql">true</property>
        <property  name="hbm2ddl.auto">create</property>

        <mapping  class="com.hdemo.Employee"  />

    </session-factory>
</hibernate-configuration>
```

Entity File:

```
// File Name: Employee.java
// Entity class

package com.hdemo;

import java.io.Serializable;
import java.math.BigDecimal;

import javax.persistence.Column;
import javax.persistence.Entity;
import javax.persistence.GeneratedValue;
import javax.persistence.Id;
import javax.persistence.Table;

import org.hibernate.annotations.GenericGenerator;
```

```
@Entity
@Table(name = "EMPLOYEE")
public class Employee implements Serializable {

    private static final long serialVersionUID = 1L;

    @Id
    @GeneratedValue(generator = "idGen")
    @GenericGenerator(name = "idGen", strategy = "uuid.hex")
    @Column(name = "ID", length = 32)
    private String id = "";

    @Column(name = "EMP_NUMBER", nullable = false)
    private int empNumber;

    @Column(name = "EMP_NAME", nullable = false, length = 64)
    private String empName;

    @Column(name = "DEPT", nullable = false, length = 64)
    private String department;

    @Column(name = "BASIC_PAY", nullable = false, precision = 10,
                                                          scale = 2)
    private BigDecimal basicpay;

    @Column(name = "ALLOWANCES", precision = 10, scale = 2)
    private BigDecimal allowances;

    @Column(name = "DEDUCTIONS", precision = 10, scale = 2)
    private BigDecimal deductions;

    @Column(name = "NETPAY", precision = 10, scale = 2)
    private BigDecimal netpay;

    Employee() {
    }

    Employee(int empNumber, String empName, String department,
BigDecimal basicpay, BigDecimal allowances, BigDecimal deductions) {
```

```
        this.empNumber = empNumber;
        this.empName = empName;
        this.department = department;
        this.basicpay = basicpay;
        this.allowances = allowances;
        this.deductions = deductions;
        this.netpay = basicpay.add(allowances).subtract(deductions);
    }

    public String getId() {
        return id;
    }

    public void setId(String id) {
        this.id = id;
    }

    public int getEmpNumber() {
        return empNumber;
    }

    public void setEmpNumber(int empNumber) {
        this.empNumber = empNumber;
    }

    public String getEmpName() {
        return empName;
    }

    public void setEmpName(String empName) {
        this.empName = empName;
    }

    public String getDepartment() {
        return department;
    }

    public void setDepartment(String department) {
```

```
        this.department = department;
    }

    public BigDecimal getBasicpay() {
        return basicpay;
    }

    public void setBasicpay(BigDecimal basicpay) {
        this.basicpay = basicpay;
    }

    public BigDecimal getAllowances() {
        return allowances;
    }

    public void setAllowances(BigDecimal allowances) {
        this.allowances = allowances;
    }

    public BigDecimal getDeductions() {
        return deductions;
    }

    public void setDeductions(BigDecimal deductions) {
        this.deductions = deductions;
    }

    public BigDecimal getNetpay() {
        return netpay;
    }

    public void setNetpay(BigDecimal netpay) {
        this.netpay = netpay;
    }
}
```

`SessionFactory` **Helper File:**

```
// File Name: HibernateUtil.java
```

```
// Helper class to ger SessionFactory object

package com.hdemo;

import org.hibernate.SessionFactory;
import org.hibernate.cfg.AnnotationConfiguration;

public class HibernateUtil {

  private static final SessionFactory sessionFactory;
  static {
       try {
              sessionFactory = new AnnotationConfiguration().
                                     configure().buildSessionFactory();
       }
       catch (Throwable e) {
              System.err.println("Error in crerating SessionFactory.
                                                              " + e);
              throw new ExceptionInInitializerError(e);
       }
  }

  public static SessionFactory getSessionFactory() {
       return sessionFactory;
  }
}
```

Main Program:

```
// File Name: EmployeeManipulation.java
// Main Program

package com.hdemo;

import java.math.BigDecimal;

import org.hibernate.Session;
import org.hibernate.SessionFactory;
import org.hibernate.Transaction;
```

```
public class EmployeeManipulation {

    public static void main(String[] args) throws Exception {
        SessionFactory sessionFactory = HibernateUtil.getSession
                                                    Factory();
        Session session = sessionFactory.openSession();
        Transaction txn = session.beginTransaction();

        Employee employee1 = new Employee(5001, "Ibrahim", "IT",
new BigDecimal(98000.0), new BigDecimal(30000.0), new
BigDecimal(15000.0));
        Employee employee2 = new Employee(5002, "Ananad Desai",
"IT", new BigDecimal(93000.0), new BigDecimal(29000.0), new
BigDecimal(15000.0));
        Employee employee3 = new Employee(5003, "Karan Singh",
"SALES", new BigDecimal(88000.0), new BigDecimal(27000.0), new
BigDecimal(14500.0));
        Employee employee4 = new Employee(5004, "Sudhir", "SALES",
new BigDecimal(83000.0), new BigDecimal(25000.0), new
BigDecimal(14100.0));
        Employee employee5 = new Employee(5005, "Ajay", "SALES",
new BigDecimal(78000.0), new BigDecimal(23000.0), new
BigDecimal(14000.0));
        Employee employee6 = new Employee(5006, "Achfa", "SALES",
new BigDecimal(74000.0), new BigDecimal(22500.0), new
BigDecimal(12500.0));
        Employee employee7 = new Employee(5007, "Indiran", "PERSONAL",
new BigDecimal(69000.0), new BigDecimal(16000.0), new BigDecimal(8000.0));
        Employee employee8 = new Employee(5008, "Nitin Otagiri",
"PERSONAL", new BigDecimal(67000.0), new BigDecimal(15800.0), new
BigDecimal(7000.0));
        Employee employee9 = new Employee(5009, "Kumar", "STATIONARY",
new BigDecimal(65000.0), new BigDecimal(15700.0), new BigDecimal(7000.0));
        Employee employee10 = new Employee(5010, "Ravi Chandran",
"INVENTORY", new BigDecimal(55800.0), new BigDecimal(15100.0), new
BigDecimal(7000.0));

        session.persist(employee1);
        session.persist(employee2);
        session.persist(employee3);
```

```
        session.persist(employee4);
        session.persist(employee5);
        session.persist(employee6);
        session.persist(employee7);
        session.persist(employee8);
        session.persist(employee9);
        session.persist(employee10);
        System.out.println("The employee objects are persisted with
                                                        session");

        txn.commit();
        System.out.println("Transaction on this session is
                                                      committed");
        session.close();
        sessionFactory.close();
    }
}
```

Program Result:

```
The employee objects are persisted with session

Transaction on this session is committed
```

Database Result:

```
mysql> select * from employee;
```

ID	ALLOWA-NCES	BASIC_PAY	DEDUC-TIONS	DEPT	EMP_NAME	EMP_NUMBER	NETPAY
402881f81f206e6d011f206e6ffb0001	30000.00	98000.00	15000.00	IT	Ibrahim	5001	113000.00
402881f81f206e6d011f206e70070002	29000.00	93000.00	15000.00	IT	Ananad Desai	5002	107000.00
402881f81f206e6d011f206e70070003	27000.00	88000.00	14500.00	SALES	Karan Singh	5003	100500.00
402881f81f206e6d011f206e70070004	25000.00	83000.00	14100.00	SALES	Sudhir	5004	93900.00

```
402881f81f206  23000.00  78000.00  14000.00  SALES      Ajay      5005   87000.00
e6d011f206
e70080005
402881f81f206  22500.00  74000.00  12500.00  SALES      Achfa     5006   84000.00
e6d011f206
e70080006
402881f81f206  16000.00  69000.00  8000.00   PERSONAL   Indiran   5007   77000.00
e6d011f206
e70080007
402881f81f206  15800.00  67000.00  7000.00   PERSONAL   Nitin     5008   75800.00
e6d011f206                                              Otagiri
e70080008
402881f81f206  15700.00  65000.00  7000.00   STATIONARY  Kumar    5009   73700.00
e6d011f206
e70080009
402881f81f206  15100.00  55800.00  7000.00   INVENTORY  Ravi      5010   63900.00
e6d011f206                                              Chandran
e7008000a
10 rows in set (0.00 sec)
```

6.2 THE CRITERIA INTERFACE (org.hibernate.Criteria)

Create an instance of Criteria using createCriteria() method of Session by passing the required Entity class as its argument.

Use list() method of Criteria to get all the rows associated with the specified entity.

```
// File Name: EmployeeManipulation.java
// Criteria Queries: Selecting records from a table

package com.hdemo;

import java.util.List;

import org.hibernate.Criteria;
import org.hibernate.Session;
import org.hibernate.SessionFactory;
import org.hibernate.Transaction;

public class EmployeeManipulation {
```

```
@SuppressWarnings("unchecked")
public static void main(String[] args) throws Exception {
      SessionFactory sessionFactory = HibernateUtil.getSession
                                                        Factory();
      Session session = sessionFactory.openSession();
      Transaction txn = session.beginTransaction();

      Criteria criteria = session.createCriteria(Employee.class);
      List<Employee> employeeList = criteria.list();
      for (int i = 0; i < employeeList.size(); i++) {
            Employee employee = employeeList.get(i);
            System.out.println("Employee Number : " +
                                        employee.getEmpNumber());
            System.out.println("Employee Name   : " +
                                          employee.getEmpName());
            System.out.println("Department      : " +
                                       employee.getDepartment());
            System.out.println("Basic Pay       : " +
                                         employee.getBasicpay());
            System.out.println("Allowances      : " +
                                       employee.getAllowances());
            System.out.println("Deductions      : " +
                                       employee.getDeductions());
            System.out.println("Netpay           : " +
                                           employee.getNetpay());

  System.out.println("======================================\n\n");
      }

      txn.commit();
      session.close();
      sessionFactory.close();
  }
}
```

Hibernate: select this_.ID as ID0_0_, this_.ALLOWANCES as

```
ALLOWANCES0_0_, this_.BASIC_PAY as BASIC3_0_0_, this_.DEDUCTIONS as
DEDUCTIONS0_0_, this_.DEPT as DEPT0_0_, this_.EMP_NAME as EMP6_0_0_,
this_.EMP_NUMBER as EMP7_0_0_, this_.NETPAY as NETPAY0_0_ from EMPLOYEE
this_
    Employee Number   : 5001
    Employee Name     : Ibrahim
    Department        : IT
    Basic Pay         : 98000.00
    Allowances        : 30000.00
    Deductions        : 15000.00
    Netpay            : 113000.00
    ========================================

    Employee Number   : 5002
    Employee Name     : Ananad Desai
    Department        : IT
    Basic Pay         : 93000.00
    Allowances        : 29000.00
    Deductions        : 15000.00
    Netpay            : 107000.00
    ========================================

    Employee Number   : 5003
    Employee Name     : Karan Singh
    Department        : SALES
    Basic Pay         : 88000.00
    Allowances        : 27000.00
    Deductions        : 14500.00
    Netpay            : 100500.00
    ========================================

    Employee Number   : 5004
    Employee Name     : Sudhir
    Department        : SALES
    Basic Pay         : 83000.00
    Allowances        : 25000.00
    Deductions        : 14100.00
    Netpay            : 93900.00
```

```
==========================================

Employee  Number   :  5005
Employee  Name     :  Ajay
Department         :  SALES
Basic  Pay         :  78000.00
Allowances         :  23000.00
Deductions         :  14000.00
Netpay             :  87000.00
==========================================

Employee  Number   :  5006
Employee  Name     :  Achfa
Department         :  SALES
Basic  Pay         :  74000.00
Allowances         :  22500.00
Deductions         :  12500.00
Netpay             :  84000.00
==========================================

Employee  Number   :  5007
Employee  Name     :  Indiran
Department         :  PERSONAL
Basic  Pay         :  69000.00
Allowances         :  16000.00
Deductions         :  8000.00
Netpay             :  77000.00
==========================================

Employee  Number   :  5008
Employee  Name     :  Nitin  Otagiri
Department         :  PERSONAL
Basic  Pay         :  67000.00
Allowances         :  15800.00
Deductions         :  7000.00
Netpay             :  75800.00
```

```
========================================

Employee Number    : 5009
Employee Name      : Kumar
Department         : STATIONARY
Basic Pay          : 65000.00
Allowances         : 15700.00
Deductions         : 7000.00
Netpay             : 73700.00
========================================

Employee Number    : 5010
Employee Name      : Ravi Chandran
Department         : INVENTORY
Basic Pay          : 55800.00
Allowances         : 15100.00
Deductions         : 7000.00
Netpay             : 63900.00
========================================
```

Some important methods in `Criteria` interface are given below.

`Criteria add(Criterion criterion)`

→ Adds a `Restrictions` condition to retrieve data

`Criteria addOrder(Order order)`

→ Defines the sort order (ascending / descending) of the result set

Order class constructor:

`Order(String property_name, boolean sort_order)`

Order class methods:

`static Order asc(string property_name)`

-ascending order of the specified property_name

`static Order desc(String property_name)`

-descending order of the specified property_name

`Order ignoreCase()` -Ignores case sensitiveness while sorting

A Note on ignore Case: Some databases consider cases (upper case and lower case) while sorting, some other databases do not consider this case sensitiveness. So, case sensitive sorting is depended on underlying database. For example, Oracle database will do case sensitive sorting by default, but MySQL database ignores case sensitive while sorting (by default). However, this `ignoreCase()` method forces the database to ignore case sensitiveness while sorting.

```
Criteria criteria = session.createCriteria(Employee.class);
criteria.addOrder(Order.asc("empName").ignoreCase());
```

The above code will sort *Employee* records in ascending order of Employee_Name and ignores cases for sorting operation. In case sensitive sorting, the capital case letters occur first and then small case letters follow them (as in ASCII chart). So, the capital case letter 'Z' comes first than the small case letter 'a'.

```
Criteria createAlias(String association_path, String alias)
```

While joining an association (`employee.salary`, where Employee and Salary are the entities and `salary` is a property in `employee`), it is used to create alias name to the joined association.

For example,

```
CreateAlias("employee.salary", "sal")
```

We can use the alias name "`sal`" wherever you want to refer `salary` object present in the `employee` object

```
Criteria createCriteria(String association_path)
```

Creates a new Criteria, rooted at (starting from) the associated entity

```
List list()
```

Returns the records of the Criteria query. If no records matches, it returns empty list (not null value).

```
ScrollableResults scroll()
```

Get the Criteria query result as `ScrollableResults` object.

(If the underling database supports Scrollable Result Set, which allows to navigate result set rows in both directions, scroll to a specified position, ...)

```
Criteria setFetchMode(String association_path, FetchMode mode)
```

Sets the records fetch (retrieve) mode for the specified association_path (entity object(s) in entity object)

The second argument should be a value (object) of type

`org.hibernate.FetchMode class.`

Do not use `org.hibernate.annotations.FetchMode` class, which is used when `FetchMode` is specified for a filed while declaring an Entity like shown below.

```
@JoinColumn(name = "EMP_SALARY", unique = true)
@Fetch(org.hibernate.annotations.FetchMode.JOIN)
private Salary salary;
```

Allowed Fetch Modes (static constants in **`org.hibernate.FetchMode`**) are,

`FetchMode.DEFAULT` -Default fetch mode specified in Entity using Annotations / Configuration file (mapping files if you are not using Annotations)

`FetchMode.JOIN` -Fetches associated entity object(s) using an outer join (Use this as alternative to deprecated `FetchMode.EAGAR` (Eagar fetch -fetch always all data))

`FetchMode.SELECT` -Fetches associated entity object(s) using a separate select statements (Use this as alternate to deprecated `FetchMode.LAZY` (Lazy fetch -fetch only when referred in the program))

`Criteria setFirstResult(int offset)`

Sets the first result row is to be retrieved. Offset stats from 0. It is very much used for Pagination purpose

`Criteria setMaxResults(int limit)`

Sets the maximum limit to retrieve rows

`Criteria setProjection(Projection projection)`

Sets the specified projection which uses aggregate functions and group by specification, ...

`Criteria setResultTransformer(ResultTransformer resultTransformer)`

Sets the specified `ResultTransformer`, which transforms the result of Criteria query into application-visible query result list such as distinct rows.

The `CriteriaSpecification` interface provides the following constants of type `ResultTransformer`.

`CriteriaSpecification.DISTINCT_ROOT_ENTITY` -Transforms the result of Criteria query result as each row of the result is a distinct instance of the root entity (specified while creating root `Criteria` object). Only distinct rows will be the result. Note that this transformer uses (Java's) `hashCode()` method for comparison; the comparison is not done at database level (as `SELECT DISTINCT` statement)

`CriteriaSpecification.ROOT_ENTITY` -Transforms the result of Criteria query as each row of the result is an instance of the root entity (specified while creating root `Criteria` object).

`CriteriaSpecification.ALIAS_TO_ENTITY_MAP`-Each row of the result is a Map, which contains data of alias, which is specified reference to parent entity instance (from alias to entity instance)

The above three result transformers do not require using Projection in order to use them.

`CriteriaSpecification.PROJECTION` -Default. This result transformer is selected implicitly by calling `setProjection() method.`

`Object uniqueResult()`

Returns a single instance (result row) of the invoked Query or returns `null` if the Query returns no rows.

Here, Unique Result does not mean distinct rows from the result set. This method can be used along with Queries that those will return only one or no value (row) as a result. Instead of invoking `list()` method and getting the first row (single value result), we can use this method which return the retrieved value directly.

6.3 THE RESTRICTION CLASS (org.hibernate.criterion.Restrictions)

The `Restrictions` class provides several static methods, which are used to create relational and logical conditions (criterions). These methods return an object of type `Criterion` interface / object of a class which implemented the `Criterion` interface. These criterions can be added to a Criteria query using `add(Criterion criterion)` method. Some of the methods in this `Restrictions` class are as follows.

```
SimpleExpression eq(String propertyName, Object value)
```

Checks the value of specified `propertyName` of the underlying Entity is equals to the specified value

```
Criterion allEq(Map propertyNameValues)
```

Checks an "equals" constraint to each property in the key set with its corresponding value of the Map

```
PropertyExpression eqProperty(String propertyName1,
String propertyName2)
```

Checks the value of `propertyName1` is equals to the value of `propertyName2`

```
SimpleExpression ne(String propertyName, Object value)
```

Checks the value of the `propertyName` is not equal to the specified value

```
PropertyExpression ne Property(String propertyName1,
                                String propertyName2)
```

Checks the value of `propertyName1` is not equal to the value of `propertyName2`

```
SimpleExpression lt(String propertyName, Object value)
```

Checks the value of the `propertyName` is less than the specified value

```
PropertyExpression ltProperty(String propertyName1,
String propertyName2)
```

Checks the value of `propertyName1` is not equals to the value of `propertyName2`

```
SimpleExpression le(String propertyName, Object value)
```

Checks the value of `propertyName` is less than or equals to the specified value

`PropertyExpression leProperty(String propertyName1, String propertyName2)`

Checks the value of `propertyName1` is less than or equals to the value of `propertyName2`

`SimpleExpression gt(String propertyName, Object value)`

Checks the value of `propertyName` is greater than the specified value

`PropertyExpression gtProperty(String propertyName1, String propertyName2)`

Checks the value of `propertyName1` is greater than the value of `propertyName2`

`SimpleExpression ge(String propertyName, Object value)`

Checks the value of `propertyName` is greater than or equals to the specified value

`PropertyExpression geProperty(String propertyName1, String propertyName2)`

Checks the value of `propertyName1` is greater than or equals to the value of `propertyName2`

`Criterion between(String propertyName, Object lowValue, Object highValue)`

Checks the value of `propertyName` lies between specified `lowValue` and `highValue`

`Criterion isNull(String propertyName)`

Checks the `propertyName` is null

`Criterion isNotNull(String propertyName)`

Checks `propertyName` is not null

`Criterion isEmpty(String propertyName)`

Checks the specified `propertyName` (collection valued property) is empty (zero size)

`Criterion isNotEmpty(String propertyName)`

Checks the specified `propertyName` (collection valued property) is not empty (zero size)

`SimpleExpression like(String propertyName, Object value)`

Applies like operator (checks for matching strings, the search string may contain wild-card characters % (all) and _ (one character)) on the value of `propertyName` by the search string value specified in second argument.

Note that the pattern matching is case sensitive. However, it is dependent on underlying database. For example, in MySQL, SQL patterns are case-insensitive by default. In Oracle, SQL patterns are case-sensitive.

`SimpleExpression like(String propertyName,`

```
String value,
MatchMode matchMode)
```

It applies like operator on the value of `propertyName` by the search string passed as second parameter. Instead of using wild-card character to search at beginning or ending or all, we can use the third parameter which defined the search string matching mode. The acceptable values for this match mode are as below.

`MatchMode.START` -Matches the start of the string to the search pattern

`MatchMode.END` -Matches the end of the string to the search pattern

`MatchMode.ANYWHERE` -Matches the search pattern anywhere in the string

`MatchMode.EXACT` -Matches the entire string to the search pattern (equals to)

Note that the pattern matching is case sensitive. However, it is dependent on underlying database. For example, in MySQL, SQL patterns are case-insensitive by default. In Oracle, SQL patterns are case-sensitive.

```
Criterion ilike(String propertyName, Object value)
```

Applies *like* operation on the value of `propertyName` by the search pattern specified in second argument. It ignores case-sensitive.

```
Criterion ilike(String propertyName,
                String value,
                MatchMode matchMode)
```

Applies *like* operation on the value of `propertyName` by the search pattern specified in second argument and match mode specified in third argument. It ignores case-sensitive.

```
Criterion in(String propertyName, Collection values)
```

Applies an "`in`" constraint to the value of `propertyName` in the values of Java Collection (List, Set, ...). Checks whether the value of `propertyName` matches any value found in the Java Collection object specified in the second argument.

Note: Hibernate does not expect empty array / Collection for this in operation. Otherwise, it throws an exception.

```
Criterion in(String propertyName, Object[] values)
```

Applies an "`in`" constraint to the value of `propertyName` in the array of values. Checks whether the value of `propertyName` presents in the array of values specified in the second argument.

```
LogicalExpression and(Criterion criterion1,
                      Criterion criterion2)
```

Performs an "`and`" operation (conjunction) on specified two Criterions (Expressions)

```
LogicalExpression or(Criterion criterion1,
                     Criterion criterion2)
```

Performs an "or" operation (disjunction) on specified two Criterions (Expressions)

`Criterion not(Criterion criterion)`

Returns the negation (`not` value) of the specified Criterion (Expression)

`Conjunction conjunction()`

Performs `"and"` operation on group of expressions

(`Exp1 and Exp2 and Exp3` ...)

`Restrictions.conjunction().add(Exp1).add(Exp2).add(Exp3)`

where `Exp` is a `Restrictions` Criterion.

Example

```
Criteria criteria =
        session.createCriteria(Employee.class)
    .add( Restrictions.conjunction()
         .add( Restrictions.isNotNull("empNumber") )
         .add( Restrictions.eq("empNumber", 1002 ) )
         .add( Restrictions.like("empName","Ib", MatchMode.START ))
    );
```

`Disjunction disjunction()`

Performs `"or"` operation on group of expressions

(`Exp1 or Exp2 or Exp3` ...)

`Restrictions.disjunction().add(Exp1).add(Exp2).add(Exp3)`

where `Exp` is a `Restrictions` Criterion.

Example

```
Criteria criteria =
         session.createCriteria(Employee.class)
        .add( Restrictions.disjunction()
                  .add( Restrictions.eq("empNumber", 1002 ) )
       .add( Restrictions.like("empName", "Ib", MatchMode.START) )
       );
```

`Criterion idEq(Object value)`

Restricts the selection to select the corresponding entity record whose `id` value (defined through `@Id`) is equal to the specified value.

`Criterion sizeEq(String propertyName, int size)`

Checks the size of the Collection (List, Set, ...) `propertyName` is equal to the specified size (in second argument)

`Criterion sizeNe(String propertyName, int size)`

Checks the size of the Collection `propertyName` is not equal to the specified size

`Criterion sizeLt(String propertyName, int size)`

Checks the size of the Collection `propertyName` is less than the specified size

`Criterion sizeLe(String propertyName, int size)`

Checks the size of the Collection `propertyName` is less than or equals to the specified size

`Criterion sizeGt(String propertyName, int size)`

Checks the size of the Collection `propertyName` is greater than to the specified size

`Criterion sizeGe(String propertyName, int size)`

Checks the size of the Collection `propertyName` is greater than or equals to the specified size

`Criterion sqlRestriction(String sql)`

Applies the specified constraint expressed in SQL (use native SQL query condition, do not express in HQL manner)

Example

```
Criteria criteria = session.createCriteria(Employee.class);
criteria.add(Restrictions.sqlRestriction("EMP_NAME like 'I%'"));
```

The above Criteria selects, if selected, all employee records those Employee Name starts with letter 'I'.

where `EMP_NAME` is a column in the `EMPLOYEE` database table.

Any occurrences of {`alias`} will be replaced by the table alias.

```
Criteria criteria = session.createCriteria(Employee.class);
criteria.add(Restrictions.sqlRestriction("{alias}.EMP_NAME like
'I%'"));
```

`Criterion sqlRestriction(String sql, Object value, Type type)`

Applies the specified constraint expressed in SQL (contains positional parameter, will be filled by second parameter), with the given JDBC parameter (second parameter) and its data type (third parameter)

```
Criteria criteria = session.createCriteria(Employee.class);
criteria.add(Restrictions
.sqlRestriction("EMP_NAME like ?", "I%", Hibernate.STRING));
```

The third parameter Type is an interface, specifies the data type of positional parameter.

`Criterion sqlRestriction(String sql, Object[] values, Type[] types)`

Applies the specified constraint expressed in SQL (contains positional parameters, will be filled by array-type second parameter), with the given JDBC parameters (array type second parameter) and its data types (array type third parameter)

```
Criteria criteria = session.createCriteria(Employee.class);
criteria.add(Restrictions
```

```
                .sqlRestriction("EMP_NAME like ? AND EMP_NUMBER = ?",
                        new Object[] {"I%", new Integer(5001)},
                            new Type[] {Hibernate.STRING,
                                        Hibernate.INTEGER})).
```

6.4 THE PROJECTIONS CLASS (org.hibernate.criterion.Projections)

The following method in Criteria is used to set Projection (group by, count specification ...). The Projection is a fundamental relational database operation that produces the result set from selected columns, not all columns of one or more existing tables.

```
Criteria setProjection(Projection projection)
```

We can pass any object of a class which implements Projection interface.

The Projections class in Hibernate provides several useful methods for projection operations. All these methods are static and returns an object of Projection (org.hibernate.criterion.Projection) interface/object of a class which implemented Projection. This returned object can be passed as argument to the setProjection() method of Criteria.

Some of the methods under Projections class are given below.

`CountProjection count(String propertyName)`

Counts the total number of (not-null) values of propertyName

`CountProjection countDistinct(String propertyName)`

Counts the total number of distinct (non-repeated and not-null) values of propertyName

`Projection rowCount()`

Counts the total number of resultant rows of the Query

`AggregateProjection sum(String propertyName)`

Finds the summation value of propertyName (columns)

`AggregateProjection avg(String propertyName)`

Finds the average value of propertyName

`AggregateProjection max(String propertyName)`

Finds the maximum value of propertyName

`AggregateProjection min(String propertyName)`

Finds the minimum value of propertyName

`PropertyProjection property(String propertyName)`

A projected property value (This property will be selected for resultant row)

`PropertyProjection groupProperty(String propertyName)`

A grouping property value (This property is applied to group values in database table, i.e., `group by propertyName`)

```
Projection distinct(Projection projection)
```

Creates a distinct projection from a projection

```
Projection sqlProjection(String sql,
                         String[] columnAliases,
                         Type[] types)
```

A SQL projection, we can specify native SQL select columns as first parameter. The column alias names used in the first parameter are specified as String array in second parameter, and their data types are specified in third parameter.

```
criteria.setProjection(
   Projections.sqlProjection(
   "CONCAT('Mr.', EMP_NAME) as EmployeeName, (NETPAY - 500.0) as
Netpay",
   new String[] { "EmployeeName", "Netpay" },
   new Type[] { Hibernate.STRING, Hibernate.DOUBLE }));
```

The above query returns Employee Name prefixed with "Mr." and Net pay deducted by 500.

```
Projection sqlGroupProjection(String sql,
                              String groupBy,
                              String[] columnAliases,
                              Type[] types)
```

A grouping SQL projection, the first parameter contains database select columns (may use group functions), the second parameter specifies group by column name (database column name), and third and fourth parameters specify the column alias names and their data types.

```
criteria.setProjection(
   Projections.sqlGroupProjection(
  "EMP_NAME AS EmployeeName, DEPT as Department, MAX(NETPAY) as
Netpay",
   "DEPT",
   new String[] { "EmployeeName", "Department", "Netpay" },
  new Type[] { Hibernate.STRING, Hibernate.STRING, Hibernate.DOUBLE
}))
```

The generated native SQL by Hibernate is shown below.

```
select EMP_NAME AS EmployeeName, DEPT as Department, MAX(NETPAY) as
Netpay from EMPLOYEE this_ group by DEPT
```

```
ProjectionList projectionList()
```

Create a new projection list. A set of Projections can be added to this list and set to the `Criteria` using a single call to `setProjection()` method.

```
Criteria criteria = session.createCriteria(Employee.class);
ProjectionList projectionList = Projections.projectionList();
projectionList.add (Projections.property("empName"));
projectionList.add(Projections.max ("netpay"));
projectionList.add (Projections.groupProperty("department"));
criteria.setProjection(projectionList);
```

The generated SQL by Hibernate is as follows.

```
select this_.EMP_NAME as y0_, max(this_.NETPAY) as y1_,
this_.DEPT as y2_ from EMPLOYEE this_ group by this_.DEPT
```

Note that the group_by property is automatically selected. And the selection of columns (returned columns' order; which column is first, which is next) is based on the order you are adding Projections to ProjectionList. For example, if the Projection for "*department*" is added next to Projection for "*empName*", then department column will become as second column in selection, as shown in the generated SQL below.

```
Criteria criteria = session.createCriteria(Employee.class);
ProjectionList projectionList = Projections.projectionList();
projectionList.add( Projections.property("empName"));
projectionList.add(Projections.groupProperty ("department"));
projectionList.add(Projections.max("netpay"));
criteria.setProjection(projectionList);
```

Generated SQL:

```
select this_.EMP_NAME as y0_, this_.DEPT as y1_,
max(this_.NETPAY) as y2_ from EMPLOYEE this_ group by this_.DEPT
```

The `add(Projection projection)` is very important method in `ProjectionList`, which is used to add one Projection into it.

6.5 THE PROPERTY CLASS (org.hibernate.criterion.Property)

We can also use `Property` for restricting conditions in retrieving data, as an alternate to `Restrictions` class.

For example,

```
criteria.add(Restrictions.eq("empNumber", 5001))
```

The above code can be written using `Property` as follows.

```
criteria.add(Property.forName("empNumber").eq(5001))
```

The static method `forName()` returns an object of type `Property` for the specified field name in the corresponding Criteria entity.

The methods in this `Property` class and their functions are similar to the methods available in `Restrictions` class. However, these methods are not static (except `forName()`).

Some of the methods under `Property` class are as below.

`SimpleExpression eq(Object value)`

Checks the value of the property is equal to the passed parameter value.

`PropertyExpression eqProperty(Property|String property)`

Checks the value of the property is equal to the value of the passed parameter property. The argument passed to this method is a field of the Entity in the format of String or in the format of `Property`.

```
criteria.add(Property.forName("allowances").eq("deductions"))
```

The above code can also be written as below.

```
criteria.add(Property.forName("allowances").eq(Property.forName("deductions")))
```

`SimpleExpression ne(Object value)`

Checks the value of the property is not equal to the passed parameter value.

`PropertyExpression neProperty(Property|String property)`

Checks the value of the property is not equal to the value of the passed parameter property.

`SimpleExpression lt(Object value)`

Checks the value of the property is less than the passed parameter value.

`PropertyExpression ltProperty(Property|String property)`

Checks the value of the property is less than the value of the passed parameter property.

`SimpleExpression le(Object value)`

Checks the value of the property is less than or equals to the passed parameter value.

`PropertyExpression leProperty(Property|String property)`

Checks the value of the property is less than or equal to the value of the passed parameter property.

`SimpleExpression gt(Object value)`

Checks the value of the property is greater than the passed parameter value.

`PropertyExpression gtProperty(Property|String property)`

Checks the value of the property is greater than the value of the passed parameter property.

`SimpleExpression ge(Object value)`

Checks the value of the property is greater than or equals to the passed parameter value.

`PropertyExpression gePropertyProperty(Property|String property)`

Checks the value of the property is greater than or equals to the passed parameter property.

`Criterion between(Object min, Object max)`

Checks the value of the property lies between specified minimum and maximum values.

`Criterion in(Collection values)`

Check the property value matches any value in the specified Collection (List, Set ...).

`Criterion in(Object[] values)`

Check the property value matches any value in the specified Array.

`SimpleExpression like(Object value)`

like operation (can use wild card characters)

`SimpleExpression like(String value, MatchMode matchMode)`

like operation, we can also use `MatchMode` instead of wild card characters.

The acceptable values for this match mode are as below.

`MatchMode.START`-Matches the start of the string to the search pattern

`MatchMode.END`-Matches the end of the string to the search pattern

`MatchMode.ANYWHERE`-Matches the search pattern anywhere in the string

`MatchMode.EXACT`-Matches the entire string to the search pattern (equals to)

`Criterion isNull()`

Checks for `null` value (checks the associated property is `null`)

`Criterion isNotNull()`

Checks for not `null` value (checks the associated property is not `null`)

`Criterion isEmpty()`

Checks for empty value

`Criterion isNotEmpty()`

Checks for non-empty value

`CountProjection count()`

Returns Total number of not `null` values of the associated property column.

`AggregateProjection max()`

Returns Maximum value of the associated property column.

`AggregateProjection min()`

Returns Minimum value of the associated property column.

`AggregateProjection avg()`

Returns Average value of the associated property column.

`PropertyProjection group()`

Treats the associated property columns as "`group by`" column.

`Order asc()`

Sort the records by the associated property column in ascending order

`Order desc()`

Sort the records by the associated property column in descending order

6.6 EXAMPLES USING `org.hibernate.Criteria` API

This section lists some example programs illustrating the uses of `org.hibernate.Criteria` API and required Classes / Interfaces for its methods as arguments.

6.6.1 Examples using `Criteria add()`

The following examples use several restriction conditions that can be added to Criteria.

6.6.1.1 Example using `Restrictions.eq()`

```
// File Name: EmployeeManipulation.java
// Criteria Queries: Restrictions.eq()

package com.hdemo;

import java.util.List;

import org.hibernate.Criteria;
import org.hibernate.Session;
import org.hibernate.SessionFactory;
import org.hibernate.Transaction;
import org.hibernate.criterion.Restrictions;

public class EmployeeManipulation {

  @SuppressWarnings("unchecked")
  public static void main(String[] args) throws Exception {
  SessionFactory sessionFactory = HibernateUtil.getSession Factory();
        Session session = sessionFactory.openSession();
        Transaction txn = session.beginTransaction();

        Criteria criteria = session.createCriteria(Employee.class);
```

```
        criteria.add( Restrictions.eq("empNumber", 5001) );
        List<Employee> employeeList = criteria.list();
        for (int i = 0; i < employeeList.size(); i++) {
    Employee employee = employeeList.get(i);
        System.out.println("Employee Number : " +
                                        employee.getEmpNumber());
        System.out.println("Employee Name     : " +
                                        employee.getEmpName());
        System.out.println("Department          : " +
                                        employee.getDepartment());
        System.out.println("Basic Pay            : " +
                                        employee.getBasicpay());
        System.out.println("Allowances          : " +
                                        employee.getAllowances());
        System.out.println("Deductions          : " +
                                        employee.getDeductions());
        System.out.println("Netpay                : " +
                                        employee.getNetpay());

    System.out.println("==========================================\n\n");
        }

        txn.commit();
        session.close();
        sessionFactory.close();
    }
}
```

```
Hibernate: select this_.ID as ID0_0_, this_.ALLOWANCES as ALLOWANCES0_0_, this_.BASIC_PAY as BASIC3_0_0_, this_.DEDUCTIONS as DEDUCTIONS0_0_, this_.DEPT as DEPT0_0_, this_.EMP_NAME as EMP6_0_0_, this_.EMP_NUMBER as EMP7_0_0_, this_.NETPAY as NETPAY0_0_ from EMPLOYEE this_ where this_.EMP_NUMBER=?
Employee Number : 5001
Employee Name   : Ibrahim
Department      : IT
Basic Pay       : 98000.00
```

```
Allowances          : 30000.00
Deductions          : 15000.00
Netpay              : 113000.00
=======================================
```

6.6.1.2 Example using `Restrictions.allEq()`

```
// File Name: EmployeeManipulation.java
// Criteria Queries: Restrictions.allEq()
package com.hdemo;

import java.math.BigDecimal;
import java.util.HashMap;
import java.util.List;
import java.util.Map;

import org.hibernate.Criteria;
import org.hibernate.Session;
import org.hibernate.SessionFactory;
import org.hibernate.Transaction;
import org.hibernate.criterion.Restrictions;

public class EmployeeManipulation {

  @SuppressWarnings("unchecked")
  public static void main(String[] args) throws Exception {
        SessionFactory sessionFactory = HibernateUtil.getSession
                                                        Factory();
        Session session = sessionFactory.openSession();
        Transaction txn = session.beginTransaction();

        Map criterionMap = new HashMap();
        criterionMap.put("department", "PERSONAL");
        criterionMap.put("deductions", new BigDecimal(7000.0));

        Criteria criteria = session.createCriteria(Employee.class);

        criteria.add( Restrictions.allEq(criterionMap) );
```

```
        List<Employee> employeeList = criteria.list();
        for (int i = 0; i < employeeList.size(); i++) {
        Employee employee = employeeList.get(i);
        System.out.println("Employee Number : " +
                                        employee.getEmpNumber());
        System.out.println("Employee Name    : " +
                                          employee.getEmpName());
        System.out.println("Department       : " +
                                       employee.getDepartment());
        System.out.println("Basic Pay        : " +
                                         employee.getBasicpay());
        System.out.println("Allowances       : " +
                                       employee.getAllowances());
        System.out.println("Deductions       : " +
                                       employee.getDeductions());
        System.out.println("Netpay              : " +
                                           employee.getNetpay());

  System.out.println("===================================\n\n");
        }

        txn.commit();
        session.close();
        sessionFactory.close();
    }
  }
```

```
Hibernate: select this_.ID as ID0_0_, this_.ALLOWANCES as ALLOWANCES0_0_, this_.BASIC_PAY as BASIC3_0_0_, this_.DEDUCTIONS as DEDUCTIONS0_0_, this_.DEPT as DEPT0_0_, this_.EMP_NAME as EMP6_0_0_, this_.EMP_NUMBER as EMP7_0_0_, this_.NETPAY as NETPAY0_0_ from EMPLOYEE this_ where (this_.DEDUCTIONS=? and this_.DEPT=?)
   Employee Number  : 5008
   Employee Name    : Nitin Otagiri
   Department       : PERSONAL
   Basic Pay        : 67000.00
   Allowances       : 15800.00
```

```
Deductions          : 7000.00
Netpay              : 75800.00
========================================
```

6.6.1.3 Example using `Restrictions.between()`

```
// File Name: EmployeeManipulation.java
// Criteria Queries: Restrictions.between()

package com.hdemo;

import java.util.List;

import org.hibernate.Criteria;
import org.hibernate.Session;
import org.hibernate.SessionFactory;
import org.hibernate.Transaction;
import org.hibernate.criterion.Restrictions;

public class EmployeeManipulation {

  @SuppressWarnings("unchecked")
   public static void main(String[] args) throws Exception {
        SessionFactory sessionFactory = HibernateUtil.getSession
Factory();
        Session session = sessionFactory.openSession();
        Transaction txn = session.beginTransaction();

        Criteria criteria = session.createCriteria(Employee.class);
        criteria.add( Restrictions.between("empNumber", 5002, 5004));

        List<Employee> employeeList = criteria.list();
        for (int i = 0; i < employeeList.size(); i++) {
              Employee employee = employeeList.get(i);
              System.out.println("Employee Number : " +
                                      employee.getEmpNumber());
              System.out.println("Employee Name   : " +
                                        employee.getEmpName());
              System.out.println("Department        : " +
```

```
                                        employee.getDepartment());
                  System.out.println("Basic Pay          : " +
                                        employee.getBasicpay());
                  System.out.println("Allowances         : " +
                                        employee.getAllowances());
                  System.out.println("Deductions         : " +
                                        employee.getDeductions());
                  System.out.println("Netpay                : " +
                                        employee.getNetpay());

System.out.println("========================================\n\n");
            }

            txn.commit();
            session.close();
            sessionFactory.close();
        }
    }
```

Hibernate: select this_.ID as ID0_0_, this_.ALLOWANCES as ALLOWANCES0_0_, this_.BASIC_PAY as BASIC3_0_0_, this_.DEDUCTIONS as DEDUCTIONS0_0_, this_.DEPT as DEPT0_0_, this_.EMP_NAME as EMP6_0_0_, this_.EMP_NUMBER as EMP7_0_0_, this_.NETPAY as NETPAY0_0_ from EMPLOYEE this_ where this_.EMP_NUMBER between ? and ?

```
Employee Number   : 5002
Employee Name     : Ananad Desai
Department        : IT
Basic Pay         : 93000.00
Allowances        : 29000.00
Deductions        : 15000.00
Netpay            : 107000.00
========================================

Employee Number   : 5003
Employee Name     : Karan Singh
Department        : SALES
Basic Pay         : 88000.00
```

```
Allowances          :  27000.00
Deductions          :  14500.00
Netpay              :  100500.00
========================================

Employee  Number    :  5004
Employee  Name      :  Sudhir
Department          :  SALES
Basic  Pay          :  83000.00
Allowances          :  25000.00
Deductions          :  14100.00
Netpay              :  93900.00
========================================
```

6.6.1.4 Example using `Restrictions.eqProperty()`

```
// File Name: EmployeeManipulation.java
// Criteria Queries: Restrictions.eqProperty()

package com.hdemo;

import java.util.List;

import org.hibernate.Criteria;
import org.hibernate.Session;
import org.hibernate.SessionFactory;
import org.hibernate.Transaction;
import org.hibernate.criterion.Restrictions;

public class EmployeeManipulation {

  @SuppressWarnings("unchecked")
  public static void main(String[] args) throws Exception {
        SessionFactory sessionFactory = HibernateUtil.getSession
                                                          Factory();
        Session session = sessionFactory.openSession();
        Transaction txn = session.beginTransaction();

        Criteria criteria = session.createCriteria(Employee.class);
        // deductions > allowances
```

```
        criteria.add( Restrictions.gtProperty("deductions",
"allowances") );

        List<Employee> employeeList = criteria.list();
        for (int i = 0; i < employeeList.size(); i++) {
            Employee employee = employeeList.get(i);
        System.out.println("Employee Number : " +
                                        employee.getEmpNumber());
        System.out.println("Employee Name : " +
                                        employee.getEmpName());
        System.out.println("Department : " +
                                        employee.getDepartment());
        System.out.println("Basic Pay : " +
                                        employee.getBasicpay());
        System.out.println("Allowances : " +
                                        employee.getAllowances());
        System.out.println("Deductions : " +
                                        employee.getDeductions());
        System.out.println("Netpay : " +
                                        employee.getNetpay());

System.out.println("====================================\n\n");
        }

        txn.commit();
        session.close();
        sessionFactory.close();
    }
}
```

```
Hibernate: select this_.ID as ID0_0_, this_.ALLOWANCES as
ALLOWANCES0_0_, this_.BASIC_PAY as BASIC3_0_0_, this_.DEDUCTIONS as
DEDUCTIONS0_0_, this_.DEPT as DEPT0_0_, this_.EMP_NAME as EMP6_0_0_,
this_.EMP_NUMBER as EMP7_0_0_, this_.NETPAY as NETPAY0_0_ from EMPLOYEE
this_ where this_.DEDUCTIONS>this_.ALLOWANCES
```

6.6.1.5 Example using `Restrictions.ilike()`

```
// File Name: EmployeeManipulation.java
```

```
// Criteria Queries: Restrictions.ilike()

package com.hdemo;

import java.util.List;

import org.hibernate.Criteria;
import org.hibernate.Session;
import org.hibernate.SessionFactory;
import org.hibernate.Transaction;
import org.hibernate.criterion.Restrictions;

public class EmployeeManipulation {
    @SuppressWarnings("unchecked")
    public static void main(String[] args) throws Exception {
        SessionFactory sessionFactory = HibernateUtil.getSession
Factory();
        Session session = sessionFactory.openSession();
        Transaction txn = session.beginTransaction();

        Criteria criteria = session.createCriteria(Employee.class);
        criteria.add(Restrictions.ilike("empName", "a_h%"));

        List<Employee> employeeList = criteria.list();
        for (int i = 0; i < employeeList.size(); i++) {
            Employee employee = employeeList.get(i);
            System.out.println("Employee Number : " +
                                        employee.getEmpNumber());
            System.out.println("Employee Name : " +
                                        employee.getEmpName());
            System.out.println("Department       : " +
                                        employee.getDepartment());
            System.out.println("Basic Pay        : " +
                                        employee.getBasicpay());
            System.out.println("Allowances       : " +
                                        employee.getAllowances());
            System.out.println("Deductions       : " +
                                        employee.getDeductions());
```

```
                System.out.println("Netpay          : " +
                                        employee.getNetpay());

    System.out.println("======================================\n\n");
        }

        txn.commit();
        session.close();
        sessionFactory.close();
    }
}
```

```
Hibernate: select this_.ID as ID0_0_, this_.ALLOWANCES as ALLOWANCES0_0_, this_.BASIC_PAY as BASIC3_0_0_, this_.DEDUCTIONS as DEDUCTIONS0_0_, this_.DEPT as DEPT0_0_, this_.EMP_NAME as EMP6_0_0_, this_.EMP_NUMBER as EMP7_0_0_, this_.NETPAY as NETPAY0_0_ from EMPLOYEE this_ where lower(this_.EMP_NAME) like ?
Employee Number   : 5006
Employee Name     : Achfa
Department        : SALES
Basic Pay         : 74000.00
Allowances        : 22500.00
Deductions        : 12500.00
Netpay            : 84000.00
======================================
```

6.6.1.6 Example using `Restrictions.ilike()` and `MatchMode.START`

```
// File Name: EmployeeManipulation.java
// Criteria Queries: Restrictions.ilike() and MatchMode.START

package com.hdemo;

import java.util.List;

import org.hibernate.Criteria;
import org.hibernate.Session;
```

```
import org.hibernate.SessionFactory;
import org.hibernate.Transaction;
import org.hibernate.criterion.MatchMode;
import org.hibernate.criterion.Restrictions;

public class EmployeeManipulation {

  @SuppressWarnings("unchecked")
  public static void main(String[] args) throws Exception {
        SessionFactory sessionFactory = HibernateUtil.getSession
Factory();
        Session session = sessionFactory.openSession();
        Transaction txn = session.beginTransaction();

        Criteria criteria = session.createCriteria(Employee.class);
        criteria.add(Restrictions.ilike("empName", "a",
MatchMode.START));

        List<Employee> employeeList = criteria.list();
        for (int i = 0; i < employeeList.size(); i++) {
  Employee employee = employeeList.get(i);
System.out.println("Employee Number : " + employee.getEmpNumber());
System.out.println("Employee Name   : " + employee.getEmpName());
System.out.println("Department      : " + employee.getDepartment());
System.out.println("Basic Pay       : " + employee.getBasicpay());
System.out.println("Allowances      : " + employee.getAllowances());
System.out.println("Deductions      : " + employee.getDeductions());
System.out.println("Netpay          : " + employee.getNetpay());

  System.out.println("======================================\n\n");
        }

        txn.commit();
        session.close();
        sessionFactory.close();
  }
}
```

```
Hibernate: select this_.ID as ID0_0_, this_.ALLOWANCES as ALLOWANCES0_0_, this_.BASIC_PAY as BASIC3_0_0_, this_.DEDUCTIONS as DEDUCTIONS0_0_, this_.DEPT as DEPT0_0_, this_.EMP_NAME as EMP6_0_0_, this_.EMP_NUMBER as EMP7_0_0_, this_.NETPAY as NETPAY0_0_ from EMPLOYEE this_ where lower(this_.EMP_NAME) like ?
Employee Number   : 5002
Employee Name     : Ananad Desai
Department        : IT
Basic Pay         : 93000.00
Allowances        : 29000.00
Deductions        : 15000.00
Netpay            : 107000.00
========================================

Employee Number   : 5005
Employee Name     : Ajay
Department        : SALES
Basic Pay         : 78000.00
Allowances        : 23000.00
Deductions        : 14000.00
Netpay            : 87000.00
========================================

Employee Number   : 5006
Employee Name     : Achfa
Department        : SALES
Basic Pay         : 74000.00
Allowances        : 22500.00
Deductions        : 12500.00
Netpay            : 84000.00
========================================
```

6.6.1.7 Example using Restrictions.like() and MatchMode.EXACT

```
// File Name: EmployeeManipulation.java
// Criteria Queries: Restrictions.like() and MatchMode.EXACT

package com.hdemo;
```

```
import java.util.List;

import org.hibernate.Criteria;
import org.hibernate.Session;
import org.hibernate.SessionFactory;
import org.hibernate.Transaction;
import org.hibernate.criterion.MatchMode;
import org.hibernate.criterion.Restrictions;

public class EmployeeManipulation {

  @SuppressWarnings("unchecked")
  public static void main(String[] args) throws Exception {
        SessionFactory sessionFactory = HibernateUtil.getSession
                                                          Factory();
        Session session = sessionFactory.openSession();
        Transaction txn = session.beginTransaction();

        Criteria criteria = session.createCriteria(Employee.class);
        criteria.add(Restrictions.like("empName", "Ravi Chandran",
                                                  MatchMode.EXACT));

        List<Employee> employeeList = criteria.list();
        for (int i = 0; i < employeeList.size(); i++) {
        Employee employee = employeeList.get(i);
   System.out.println("Employee Number: " + employee.getEmpNumber());
   System.out.println("Employee Name   : " + employee.getEmpName());
   System.out.println("Department      : " + employee.getDepartment());
   System.out.println("Basic Pay       : " + employee.getBasicpay());
   System.out.println("Allowances      : " + employee.getAllowances());
   System.out.println("Deductions      : " + employee.getDeductions());
   System.out.println("Netpay          : " + employee.getNetpay());

   System.out.println("======================================\n\n");
        }

        txn.commit();
```

```
        session.close();
        sessionFactory.close();
    }
}
```

```
Hibernate: select this_.ID as ID0_0_, this_.ALLOWANCES as ALLOWANCES0_0_, this_.BASIC_PAY as BASIC3_0_0_, this_.DEDUCTIONS as DEDUCTIONS0_0_, this_.DEPT as DEPT0_0_, this_.EMP_NAME as EMP6_0_0_, this_.EMP_NUMBER as EMP7_0_0_, this_.NETPAY as NETPAY0_0_ from EMPLOYEE this_ where this_.EMP_NAME like ?
Employee Number   : 5010
Employee Name     : Ravi Chandran
Department        : INVENTORY
Basic Pay         : 55800.00
Allowances        : 15100.00
Deductions        : 7000.00
Netpay            : 63900.00
========================================
```

6.6.1.8 Example using `Restrictions.ilike()` and `MatchMode.ANYWHERE`

```
// File Name: EmployeeManipulation.java
// Criteria Queries: Restrictions.ilike() and MatchMode.ANYWHERE

package com.hdemo;

import java.util.List;

import org.hibernate.Criteria;
import org.hibernate.Session;
import org.hibernate.SessionFactory;
import org.hibernate.Transaction;
import org.hibernate.criterion.MatchMode;
import org.hibernate.criterion.Restrictions;

public class EmployeeManipulation {

  @SuppressWarnings("unchecked")
```

```
    public static void main(String[] args) throws Exception {
        SessionFactory sessionFactory = HibernateUtil.getSession
                                                          Factory();
        Session session = sessionFactory.openSession();
        Transaction txn = session.beginTransaction();

        Criteria criteria = session.createCriteria(Employee.class);
        criteria.add(Restrictions.ilike("empName", "D",
                                         MatchMode.ANYWHERE));

        List<Employee> employeeList = criteria.list();
        for (int i = 0; i < employeeList.size(); i++) {
            Employee employee = employeeList.get(i);
            System.out.println("Employee Number : " +
                                        employee.getEmpNumber());
            System.out.println("Employee Name     : " +
                                          employee.getEmpName());
            System.out.println("Department          : " +
                                       employee.getDepartment());
            System.out.println("Basic Pay            : " +
                                         employee.getBasicpay());
            System.out.println("Allowances          : " +
                                       employee.getAllowances());
            System.out.println("Deductions          : " +
                                       employee.getDeductions());
            System.out.println("Netpay                : " +
                                           employee.getNetpay());

   System.out.println("========================================\n\n");
        }

        txn.commit();
        session.close();
        sessionFactory.close();
    }
}
```

Hibernate: select this_.ID as ID0_0_, this_.ALLOWANCES as ALLOWANCES0_0_, this_.BASIC_PAY as BASIC3_0_0_, this_.DEDUCTIONS as

```
DEDUCTIONS0_0_, this_.DEPT as DEPT0_0_, this_.EMP_NAME as EMP6_0_0_,
this_.EMP_NUMBER as EMP7_0_0_, this_.NETPAY as NETPAY0_0_ from EMPLOYEE
this_ where lower(this_.EMP_NAME) like ?
    Employee Number   : 5002
    Employee Name     : Ananad Desai
    Department        : IT
    Basic Pay         : 93000.00
    Allowances        : 29000.00
    Deductions        : 15000.00
    Netpay            : 107000.00
    ====================================

    Employee Number   : 5004
    Employee Name     : Sudhir
    Department        : SALES
    Basic Pay         : 83000.00
    Allowances        : 25000.00
    Deductions        : 14100.00
    Netpay            : 93900.00
    ====================================
    Employee Number   : 5007
    Employee Name     : Indiran
    Department        : PERSONAL
    Basic Pay         : 69000.00
    Allowances        : 16000.00
    Deductions        : 8000.00
    Netpay            : 77000.00
    ====================================

    Employee Number   : 5010
    Employee Name     : Ravi Chandran
    Department        : INVENTORY
    Basic Pay         : 55800.00
    Allowances        : 15100.00
    Deductions        : 7000.00
    Netpay            : 63900.00
    ====================================
```

6.6.1.9 Example using `Restrictions.in(Array)`

```
// File Name: EmployeeManipulation.java
// Criteria Queries: Restrictions.in(Array)

package com.hdemo;

import java.util.List;

import org.hibernate.Criteria;
import org.hibernate.Session;
import org.hibernate.SessionFactory;
import org.hibernate.Transaction;
import org.hibernate.criterion.Restrictions;

public class EmployeeManipulation {

    @SuppressWarnings("unchecked")
    public static void main(String[] args) throws Exception {
        SessionFactory sessionFactory = HibernateUtil.getSession
                                                        Factory();

        Session session = sessionFactory.openSession();
        Transaction txn = session.beginTransaction();

        Integer empNum[] = {5002, 5004, 5006}; //Auto-boxing will
                conver scaler int values in to Integer Objects

        Criteria criteria = session.createCriteria(Employee.class);
        criteria.add(Restrictions.in("empNumber", empNum));

        List<Employee> employeeList = criteria.list();
        for (int i = 0; i < employeeList.size(); i++) {
            Employee employee = employeeList.get(i);
            System.out.println("Employee Number : " +
                                        employee.getEmpNumber());
            System.out.println("Employee Name    : " +
                                        employee.getEmpName());
```

```
                System.out.println("Department            : " +
                                        employee.getDepartment());
                System.out.println("Basic Pay              : " +
                                          employee.getBasicpay());
                System.out.println("Allowances             : " +
                                        employee.getAllowances());
                System.out.println("Deductions             : " +
                                        employee.getDeductions());
                System.out.println("Netpay                 : " +
                                            employee.getNetpay());

      System.out.println("=======================================\n\n");
        }

        txn.commit();
        session.close();
        sessionFactory.close();
    }
  }
```

Hibernate: select this_.ID as ID0_0_, this_.ALLOWANCES as ALLOWANCES0_0_, this_.BASIC_PAY as BASIC3_0_0_, this_.DEDUCTIONS as DEDUCTIONS0_0_, this_.DEPT as DEPT0_0_, this_.EMP_NAME as EMP6_0_0_, this_.EMP_NUMBER as EMP7_0_0_, this_.NETPAY as NETPAY0_0_ from EMPLOYEE this_ where this_.EMP_NUMBER in (?, ?, ?)

```
Employee Number    : 5002
Employee Name      : Ananad Desai
Department         : IT
Basic Pay          : 93000.00
Allowances         : 29000.00
Deductions         : 15000.00
Netpay             : 107000.00
=======================================

Employee Number    : 5004
Employee Name      : Sudhir
Department         : SALES
Basic Pay          : 83000.00
```

```
Allowances          :  25000.00
Deductions          :  14100.00
Netpay              :  93900.00
========================================

Employee  Number    :  5006
Employee  Name      :  Achfa
Department          :  SALES
Basic  Pay          :  74000.00
Allowances          :  22500.00
Deductions          :  12500.00
Netpay              :  84000.00
========================================
```

6.6.1.10 Example using `Restrictions.in(Collection)`

```
// File Name: EmployeeManipulation.java
// Criteria Queries: Restrictions.in(Collection)

package com.hdemo;

import java.util.ArrayList;
import java.util.List;

import org.hibernate.Criteria;
import org.hibernate.Session;
import org.hibernate.SessionFactory;
import org.hibernate.Transaction;
import org.hibernate.criterion.Restrictions;

public class EmployeeManipulation {

  @SuppressWarnings("unchecked")
  public static void main(String[] args) throws Exception {
  SessionFactory sessionFactory = HibernateUtil.getSessionFactory();
       Session session = sessionFactory.openSession();
       Transaction txn = session.beginTransaction();
```

```
        ArrayList<Integer> alEmpNum = new ArrayList<Integer>();
        alEmpNum.add(5002);
        alEmpNum.add(5004);
        alEmpNum.add(5006);

        Criteria criteria = session.createCriteria(Employee.class);
        criteria.add(Restrictions.in("empNumber", alEmpNum));

        List<Employee> employeeList = criteria.list();
        for (int i = 0; i < employeeList.size(); i++) {
        Employee employee = employeeList.get(i);
              System.out.println("Employee Number : " +
                                              employee.getEmpNumber());
              System.out.println("Employee Name  : " +
                                                employee.getEmpName());
              System.out.println("Department :        " +
                                             employee.getDepartment());
              System.out.println("Basic Pay:          " +
                                               employee.getBasicpay());
              System.out.println("Allowances:         " +
                                             employee.getAllowances());
              System.out.println("Deductions:         " +
                                             employee.getDeductions());
              System.out.println("Netpay     :        " +
                                                 employee.getNetpay());

   System.out.println("======================================\n\n");
        }

        txn.commit();
        session.close();
        sessionFactory.close();
    }
  }
```

```
Hibernate: select this_.ID as ID0_0_, this_.ALLOWANCES as
ALLOWANCES0_0_, this_.BASIC_PAY as BASIC3_0_0_, this_.DEDUCTIONS as
```

```
DEDUCTIONS0_0_, this_.DEPT as DEPT0_0_, this_.EMP_NAME as EMP6_0_0_,
this_.EMP_NUMBER as EMP7_0_0_, this_.NETPAY as NETPAY0_0_ from EMPLOYEE
this_ where this_.EMP_NUMBER in (?, ?, ?)
    Employee Number  : 5002
    Employee Name    : Ananad Desai
    Department       : IT
    Basic Pay        : 93000.00
    Allowances       : 29000.00
    Deductions       : 15000.00
    Netpay           : 107000.00
    ========================================
    Employee Number  : 5004
    Employee Name    : Sudhir
    Department       : SALES
    Basic Pay        : 83000.00
    Allowances       : 25000.00
    Deductions       : 14100.00
    Netpay           : 93900.00
    ========================================
    Employee Number  : 5006
    Employee Name    : Achfa
    Department       : SALES
    Basic Pay        : 74000.00
    Allowances       : 22500.00
    Deductions       : 12500.00
    Netpay           : 84000.00
    ========================================
```

6.6.1.11 Example using `Restrictions.idEq()`

```
// File Name: EmployeeManipulation.java
// Criteria Queries: Restrictions.idEq()

package com.hdemo;

import java.util.List;

import org.hibernate.Criteria;
import org.hibernate.Session;
```

```
import  org.hibernate.SessionFactory;
import  org.hibernate.Transaction;
import  org.hibernate.criterion.Restrictions;

public  class  EmployeeManipulation  {

    @SuppressWarnings("unchecked")
    public  static  void  main(String[]  args)  throws  Exception  {
    SessionFactory sessionFactory = HibernateUtil.getSession Factory();
          Session  session  =  sessionFactory.openSession();
          Transaction  txn  =  session.beginTransaction();

          Criteria  criteria  =  session.createCriteria(Employee.class);

criteria.add(Restrictions.idEq("402881f81f206e6d011f206e70080008"));  //
Pass  Id  value  of  the  required  Entity  as  parameter

          List<Employee>  employeeList  =  criteria.list();
          if  (employeeList.size()  >  0)  {
                Employee  employee  =  employeeList.get(0);
                System.out.println("Id  :  "  +  employee.getId());
                System.out.println("Employee  Number  :  "  +
                                                employee.getEmpNumber());
                System.out.println("Employee  Name  :  "  +
                                                  employee.getEmpName());
                System.out.println("Department      :  "  +
                                               employee.getDepartment());
                System.out.println("Basic  Pay     :  "  +
                                                 employee.getBasicpay());
                System.out.println("Allowances     :  "  +
                                               employee.getAllowances());
                System.out.println("Deductions     :  "  +
                                               employee.getDeductions());
                System.out.println("Netpay          :  "  +
                                                   employee.getNetpay());
```

```
  System.out.println("========================================\n\n");
        }
        else
              System.out.println("No Employee record found with the
                                                    specified Id");

        txn.commit();
        session.close();
        sessionFactory.close();
  }
}
```

Hibernate: select this_.ID as ID0_0_, this_.ALLOWANCES as ALLOWANCES0_0_, this_.BASIC_PAY as BASIC3_0_0_, this_.DEDUCTIONS as DEDUCTIONS0_0_, this_.DEPT as DEPT0_0_, this_.EMP_NAME as EMP6_0_0_, this_.EMP_NUMBER as EMP7_0_0_, this_.NETPAY as NETPAY0_0_ from EMPLOYEE this_ where this_.ID = ?

```
Id                  :  402881f81f206e6d011f206e70080008
Employee Number     : 5008
Employee Name       : Nitin Otagiri
Department          : PERSONAL
Basic Pay           : 67000.00
Allowances          : 15800.00
Deductions          : 7000.00
Netpay              : 75800.00
========================================
```

6.6.1.12 Example using `Restrictions.not()`

```
// File Name: EmployeeManipulation.java
// Criteria Queries: Restrictions.not()
package com.hdemo;

import java.util.ArrayList;
import java.util.List;

import org.hibernate.Criteria;
```

```
import org.hibernate.Session;
import org.hibernate.SessionFactory;
import org.hibernate.Transaction;
import org.hibernate.criterion.Restrictions;

public class EmployeeManipulation {

  @SuppressWarnings("unchecked")
  public static void main(String[] args) throws Exception {
        SessionFactory sessionFactory = HibernateUtil.getSession
                                                        Factory();
        Session session = sessionFactory.openSession();
        Transaction txn = session.beginTransaction();

        ArrayList<Integer> alEmpNum = new ArrayList<Integer>();
        alEmpNum.add(5002);
        alEmpNum.add(5004);
        alEmpNum.add(5006);

        Criteria criteria = session.createCriteria(Employee.class);
        criteria.add(Restrictions.not(Restrictions.in("empNumber",
                                                       alEmpNum)));

        List<Employee> employeeList = criteria.list();
        for (int i = 0; i < employeeList.size(); i++) {
              Employee employee = employeeList.get(i);
              System.out.println("Employee Number : " +
                                          employee.getEmpNumber());
              System.out.println("Employee Name     : " +
                                            employee.getEmpName());
              System.out.println("Department        : " +
                                         employee.getDepartment());
              System.out.println("Basic Pay         : " +
                                           employee.getBasicpay());
              System.out.println("Allowances        : " +
                                         employee.getAllowances());
              System.out.println("Deductions        : " +
                                         employee.getDeductions());
```

```
            System.out.println("Netpay                  : " +
                                            employee.getNetpay());

    System.out.println("======================================\n\n");
        }

        txn.commit();
        session.close();
        sessionFactory.close();
    }
}
```

```
Hibernate: select this_.ID as ID0_0_, this_.ALLOWANCES as ALLOWANCES0_0_, this_.BASIC_PAY as BASIC3_0_0_, this_.DEDUCTIONS as DEDUCTIONS0_0_, this_.DEPT as DEPT0_0_, this_.EMP_NAME as EMP6_0_0_, this_.EMP_NUMBER as EMP7_0_0_, this_.NETPAY as NETPAY0_0_ from EMPLOYEE this_ where not (this_.EMP_NUMBER in (?, ?, ?))
Employee Number   : 5001
Employee Name     : Ibrahim
Department        : IT
Basic Pay         : 98000.00
Allowances        : 30000.00
Deductions        : 15000.00
Netpay            : 113000.00
======================================

Employee Number   : 5003
Employee Name     : Karan Singh
Department        : SALES
Basic Pay         : 88000.00
Allowances        : 27000.00
Deductions        : 14500.00
Netpay            : 100500.00
======================================

Employee Number   : 5005
Employee Name     : Ajay
```

```
Department          :  SALES
Basic  Pay          :  78000.00
Allowances          :  23000.00
Deductions          :  14000.00
Netpay              :  87000.00
========================================

Employee  Number    :  5007
Employee  Name      :  Indiran
Department          :  PERSONAL
Basic  Pay          :  69000.00
Allowances          :  16000.00
Deductions          :  8000.00
Netpay              :  77000.00
========================================

Employee  Number    :  5008
Employee  Name      :  Nitin  Otagiri
Department          :  PERSONAL
Basic  Pay          :  67000.00
Allowances          :  15800.00
Deductions          :  7000.00
Netpay              :  75800.00
========================================

Employee  Number    :  5009
Employee  Name      :  Kumar
Department          :  STATIONARY
Basic  Pay          :  65000.00
Allowances          :  15700.00
Deductions          :  7000.00
Netpay              :  73700.00
========================================

Employee  Number    :  5010
Employee  Name      :  Ravi  Chandran
```

```
Department          :  INVENTORY
Basic  Pay          :  55800.00
Allowances          :  15100.00
Deductions          :  7000.00
Netpay              :  63900.00
=======================================
```

6.6.1.13 Example using `Restrictions.and()` and `Restrictions.conjunction()`

We can specify multiple restrictions to a Criteria query by adding all the restriction to the Criteria as shown in the following example.

```
// File Name: EmployeeManipulation.java
// Criteria Queries: Multiple Restrictions

package com.hdemo;

import java.math.BigDecimal;
import java.util.ArrayList;
import java.util.List;

import org.hibernate.Criteria;
import org.hibernate.Session;
import org.hibernate.SessionFactory;
import org.hibernate.Transaction;
import org.hibernate.criterion.Restrictions;

public class EmployeeManipulation {

  @SuppressWarnings("unchecked")
  public static void main(String[] args) throws Exception {
        SessionFactory sessionFactory = HibernateUtil.getSession
                                                      Factory();

        Session session = sessionFactory.openSession();
        Transaction txn = session.beginTransaction();

        ArrayList<Integer> alEmpNum = new ArrayList<Integer>();
        alEmpNum.add(5002);
        alEmpNum.add(5004);
```

```
        alEmpNum.add(5006);

        Criteria criteria = session.createCriteria(Employee.class);
        criteria.add(Restrictions.ilike("empName", "a%"));
        criteria.add(Restrictions.ge("netpay", new BigDecimal
(100000.0)));

        List<Employee> employeeList = criteria.list();
        for (int i = 0; i < employeeList.size(); i++) {
            Employee employee = employeeList.get(i);
            System.out.println("Employee Number : " +
                                    employee.getEmpNumber());
            System.out.println("Employee Name     : " +
                                    employee.getEmpName());
            System.out.println("Department        : " +
                                    employee.getDepartment());
            System.out.println("Basic Pay         : " +
                                    employee.getBasicpay());
            System.out.println("Allowances        : " +
                                    employee.getAllowances());
            System.out.println("Deductions        : " +
                                    employee.getDeductions());
            System.out.println("Netpay            : " +
                                    employee.getNetpay());

    System.out.println("======================================\n\n");
        }

        txn.commit();
        session.close();
        sessionFactory.close();
    }
}
```

```
Hibernate: select this_.ID as ID0_0_, this_.ALLOWANCES as ALLOWANCES0_0_, this_.BASIC_PAY as BASIC3_0_0_, this_.DEDUCTIONS as DEDUCTIONS0_0_, this_.DEPT as DEPT0_0_, this_.EMP_NAME as EMP6_0_0_, this_.EMP_NUMBER as EMP7_0_0_, this_.NETPAY as NETPAY0_0_ from EMPLOYEE this_ where lower(this_.EMP_NAME) like ? and this_.NETPAY>=?
```

```
Employee Number   : 5002
Employee Name     : Ananad Desai
Department        : IT
Basic Pay         : 93000.00
Allowances        : 29000.00
Deductions        : 15000.00
Netpay            : 107000.00
=========================================
```

The following example uses `Restrictions.and()` to specify multiple conjunction conditions.

```
// File Name: EmployeeManipulation.java
// Criteria Queries: Restrictions.and()

package com.hdemo;

import java.math.BigDecimal;
import java.util.List;

import org.hibernate.Criteria;
import org.hibernate.Session;
import org.hibernate.SessionFactory;
import org.hibernate.Transaction;
import org.hibernate.criterion.Restrictions;

public class EmployeeManipulation {

  @SuppressWarnings("unchecked")
  public static void main(String[] args) throws Exception {
        SessionFactory sessionFactory = HibernateUtil.getSession
                                                        Factory();
        Session session = sessionFactory.openSession();
        Transaction txn = session.beginTransaction();

        Criteria criteria = session.createCriteria(Employee.class);
        criteria.add(Restrictions.and(Restrictions.ilike("empName",
"a%"), Restrictions.ge("netpay", new BigDecimal(100000.0))));
```

```
        List<Employee> employeeList = criteria.list();
        for (int i = 0; i < employeeList.size(); i++) {
              Employee employee = employeeList.get(i);
              System.out.println("Employee Number : " +
                                        employee.getEmpNumber());
              System.out.println("Employee Name    : " +
                                          employee.getEmpName());
              System.out.println("Department        : " +
                                       employee.getDepartment());
              System.out.println("Basic Pay          : " +
                                         employee.getBasicpay());
              System.out.println("Allowances        : " +
                                       employee.getAllowances());
              System.out.println("Deductions        : " +
                                       employee.getDeductions());
              System.out.println("Netpay              : " +
                                           employee.getNetpay());

  System.out.println("=====================================\n\n");
        }

        txn.commit();
        session.close();
        sessionFactory.close();
  }
}
```

```
Hibernate: select this_.ID as ID0_0_, this_.ALLOWANCES as
ALLOWANCES0_0_, this_.BASIC_PAY as BASIC3_0_0_, this_.DEDUCTIONS as
DEDUCTIONS0_0_, this_.DEPT as DEPT0_0_, this_.EMP_NAME as EMP6_0_0_,
this_.EMP_NUMBER as EMP7_0_0_, this_.NETPAY as NETPAY0_0_ from EMPLOYEE
this_ where (lower(this_.EMP_NAME) like ? and this_.NETPAY>=?)
Employee Number  : 5002
Employee Name    : Ananad Desai
Department       : IT
Basic Pay        : 93000.00
Allowances       : 29000.00
```

```
Deductions           : 15000.00
Netpay               : 107000.00
========================================
```

You can not specify more than two Criterions in one `and()` method. If you want, then you can use `conjunction()` method as shown below.

```
// File Name: EmployeeManipulation.java
// Criteria Queries: Restrictions.conjunction()

package com.hdemo;

import java.math.BigDecimal;
import java.util.List;

import org.hibernate.Criteria;
import org.hibernate.Session;
import org.hibernate.SessionFactory;
import org.hibernate.Transaction;
import org.hibernate.criterion.Restrictions;

public class EmployeeManipulation {

  @SuppressWarnings("unchecked")
  public static void main(String[] args) throws Exception {
        SessionFactory sessionFactory = HibernateUtil.getSession
                                                          Factory();
        Session session = sessionFactory.openSession();
        Transaction txn = session.beginTransaction();

        Criteria criteria = session.createCriteria(Employee.class);
        criteria.add(Restrictions.conjunction()
                      .add(Restrictions.ilike("empName", "a%"))
                      .add(Restrictions.ge("netpay", new
                                        BigDecimal(85000.0)))
                      .add(Restrictions.eq("department",
                                                  "SALES")));

        List<Employee> employeeList = criteria.list();
```

```
            for (int i = 0; i < employeeList.size(); i++) {
                Employee employee = employeeList.get(i);
                System.out.println("Employee Number  :  " +
                                        employee.getEmpNumber());
                System.out.println("Employee Name    :  " +
                                        employee.getEmpName());
                System.out.println("Department       :  " +
                                        employee.getDepartment());
                System.out.println("Basic Pay        :  " +
                                        employee.getBasicpay());
                System.out.println("Allowances       :  " +
                                        employee.getAllowances());
                System.out.println("Deductions       :  " +
                                        employee.getDeductions());
                System.out.println("Netpay           :  " +
                                        employee.getNetpay());

        System.out.println("=========================================\n\n");
            }

            txn.commit();
            session.close();
            sessionFactory.close();
        }
    }
```

```
Hibernate: select this_.ID as ID0_0_, this_.ALLOWANCES as ALLOWANCES0_0_, this_.BASIC_PAY as BASIC3_0_0_, this_.DEDUCTIONS as DEDUCTIONS0_0_, this_.DEPT as DEPT0_0_, this_.EMP_NAME as EMP6_0_0_, this_.EMP_NUMBER as EMP7_0_0_, this_.NETPAY as NETPAY0_0_ from EMPLOYEE this_ where (lower(this_.EMP_NAME) like ? and this_.NETPAY>=? and this_.DEPT=?)
  Employee Number  : 5005
  Employee Name    : Ajay
  Department       : SALES
  Basic Pay        : 78000.00
  Allowances       : 23000.00
```

```
Deductions          : 14000.00
Netpay              : 87000.00
==========================================
```

6.6.1.14 Example using `Restrictions.or()` and `Restrictions.disjunction()`

The following example uses `Restrictions.or()` to specify multiple disjunction conditions.

```
// File Name: EmployeeManipulation.java
// Criteria Queries: Restrictions.or()

package com.hdemo;

import java.math.BigDecimal;
import java.util.List;

import org.hibernate.Criteria;
import org.hibernate.Session;
import org.hibernate.SessionFactory;
import org.hibernate.Transaction;
import org.hibernate.criterion.Restrictions;

public class EmployeeManipulation {

  @SuppressWarnings("unchecked")
  public static void main(String[] args) throws Exception {
        SessionFactory sessionFactory = HibernateUtil.getSession
                                                    Factory();
        Session session = sessionFactory.openSession();
        Transaction txn = session.beginTransaction();

        Criteria criteria = session.createCriteria(Employee.class);
        criteria.add(Restrictions.or(Restrictions.ilike("empName",
    "a%"), Restrictions.ge("netpay", new BigDecimal(100000.0))));

        List<Employee> employeeList = criteria.list();
        for (int i = 0; i < employeeList.size(); i++) {
              Employee employee = employeeList.get(i);
  System.out.println("Employee Number : " + employee.getEmpNumber());
```

```
                System.out.println("Employee Name      : " +
                                            employee.getEmpName());
                System.out.println("Department          : " +
                                        employee.getDepartment());
                System.out.println("Basic  Pay          : " +
                                          employee.getBasicpay());
                System.out.println("Allowances          : " +
                                        employee.getAllowances());
                System.out.println("Deductions          : " +
                                        employee.getDeductions());
                System.out.println("Netpay               : " +
                                             employee.getNetpay());

      System.out.println("========================================\n\n");
            }

            txn.commit();
            session.close();
            sessionFactory.close();
      }
    }
```

```
Hibernate: select this_.ID as ID0_0_, this_.ALLOWANCES as ALLOWANCES0_0_, this_.BASIC_PAY as BASIC3_0_0_, this_.DEDUCTIONS as DEDUCTIONS0_0_, this_.DEPT as DEPT0_0_, this_.EMP_NAME as EMP6_0_0_, this_.EMP_NUMBER as EMP7_0_0_, this_.NETPAY as NETPAY0_0_ from EMPLOYEE this_ where (lower(this_.EMP_NAME) like ? or this_.NETPAY>=?)
   Employee Number  : 5001
   Employee Name    : Ibrahim
   Department       : IT
   Basic  Pay       : 98000.00
   Allowances       : 30000.00
   Deductions       : 15000.00
   Netpay           : 113000.00
   ========================================
```

```
Employee Number    : 5002
Employee Name      : Ananad Desai
Department         : IT
Basic Pay          : 93000.00
Allowances         : 29000.00
Deductions         : 15000.00
Netpay             : 107000.00
========================================

Employee Number    : 5003
Employee Name      : Karan Singh
Department         : SALES
Basic Pay          : 88000.00
Allowances         : 27000.00
Deductions         : 14500.00
Netpay             : 100500.00
========================================

Employee Number    : 5005
Employee Name      : Ajay
Department         : SALES
Basic Pay          : 78000.00
Allowances         : 23000.00
Deductions         : 14000.00
Netpay             : 87000.00
========================================

Employee Number    : 5006
Employee Name      : Achfa
Department         : SALES
Basic Pay          : 74000.00
Allowances         : 22500.00
Deductions         : 12500.00
Netpay             : 84000.00
========================================
```

You can not specify more than two Criterions in one `or()` method. If you want, then you can use `disjunction()` method as shown below.

```
// File Name: EmployeeManipulation.java
// Criteria Queries: Restrictions.disjunction()

package com.hdemo;

import java.math.BigDecimal;
import java.util.List;

import org.hibernate.Criteria;
import org.hibernate.Session;
import org.hibernate.SessionFactory;
import org.hibernate.Transaction;
import org.hibernate.criterion.Restrictions;

public class EmployeeManipulation {

  @SuppressWarnings("unchecked")
  public static void main(String[] args) throws Exception {
        SessionFactory sessionFactory = HibernateUtil.getSession
                                                      Factory();
        Session session = sessionFactory.openSession();
        Transaction txn = session.beginTransaction();

        Criteria criteria = session.createCriteria(Employee.class);
        criteria.add(Restrictions.disjunction()

          .add(Restrictions.ilike("empName", "a%"))

          .add(Restrictions.ge("netpay", new BigDecimal(100000.0)))

          .add(Restrictions.eq("department", "PERSONAL")));

        List<Employee> employeeList = criteria.list();
        for (int i = 0; i < employeeList.size(); i++) {
              Employee employee = employeeList.get(i);
              System.out.println("Employee Number : " +
                                        employee.getEmpNumber());
```

```
            System.out.println("Employee Name     : " +
                                    employee.getEmpName());
            System.out.println("Department         : " +
                                 employee.getDepartment());
            System.out.println("Basic Pay          : " +
                                   employee.getBasicpay());
            System.out.println("Allowances         : " +
                                 employee.getAllowances());
            System.out.println("Deductions         : " +
                                 employee.getDeductions());
            System.out.println("Netpay              : " +
                                     employee.getNetpay());
    System.out.println("====================================\n\n");
        }

        txn.commit();
        session.close();
        sessionFactory.close();
    }
}
```

```
Hibernate: select this_.ID as ID0_0_, this_.ALLOWANCES as ALLOWANCES0_0_, this_.BASIC_PAY as BASIC3_0_0_, this_.DEDUCTIONS as DEDUCTIONS0_0_, this_.DEPT as DEPT0_0_, this_.EMP_NAME as EMP6_0_0_, this_.EMP_NUMBER as EMP7_0_0_, this_.NETPAY as NETPAY0_0_ from EMPLOYEE this_ where (lower(this_.EMP_NAME) like ? or this_.NETPAY>=? or this_.DEPT=?)
    Employee Number  : 5001
    Employee Name    : Ibrahim
    Department       : IT
    Basic Pay        : 98000.00
    Allowances       : 30000.00
    Deductions       : 15000.00
    Netpay           : 113000.00
    ====================================
```

```
Employee Number   : 5002
Employee Name     : Ananad Desai
Department        : IT
Basic Pay         : 93000.00
Allowances        : 29000.00
Deductions        : 15000.00
Netpay            : 107000.00
========================================

Employee Number   : 5003
Employee Name     : Karan Singh
Department        : SALES
Basic Pay         : 88000.00
Allowances        : 27000.00
Deductions        : 14500.00
Netpay            : 100500.00
========================================

Employee Number   : 5005
Employee Name     : Ajay
Department        : SALES
Basic Pay         : 78000.00
Allowances        : 23000.00
Deductions        : 14000.00
Netpay            : 87000.00
========================================

Employee Number   : 5006
Employee Name     : Achfa
Department        : SALES
Basic Pay         : 74000.00
Allowances        : 22500.00
Deductions        : 12500.00
Netpay            : 84000.00
========================================
```

```
Employee  Number    :  5007
Employee  Name      :  Indiran
Department          :  PERSONAL
Basic  Pay          :  69000.00
Allowances          :  16000.00
Deductions          :  8000.00
Netpay              :  77000.00
========================================
Employee  Number    :  5008
Employee  Name      :  Nitin  Otagiri
Department          :  PERSONAL
Basic  Pay          :  67000.00
Allowances          :  15800.00
Deductions          :  7000.00
Netpay              :  75800.00
========================================
```

6.6.1.15 Example using `Restrictions.sqlRestriction()`

```
// File Name: EmployeeManipulation.java
// Criteria Queries: Restrictions.sqlRestriction()
package com.hdemo;
import java.util.List;
import org.hibernate.Criteria;
import org.hibernate.Session;
import org.hibernate.SessionFactory;
import org.hibernate.Transaction;
import org.hibernate.criterion.Restrictions;

public class EmployeeManipulation {

  @SuppressWarnings("unchecked")
  public static void main(String[] args) throws Exception {
```

```
        SessionFactory sessionFactory = HibernateUtil.getSession
                                                         Factory();
        Session session = sessionFactory.openSession();
        Transaction txn = session.beginTransaction();

        Criteria criteria = session.createCriteria(Employee.class);
        criteria.add(Restrictions.sqlRestriction("EMP_NAME like
                                                           'I%'"));

        List<Employee> employeeList = criteria.list();
        for (int i = 0; i < employeeList.size(); i++) {
              Employee employee = employeeList.get(i);
              System.out.println("Employee Number : " +
                                          employee.getEmpNumber());
              System.out.println("Employee Name     : " +
                                            employee.getEmpName());
              System.out.println("Department          : " +
                                         employee.getDepartment());
              System.out.println("Basic Pay            : " +
                                           employee.getBasicpay());
              System.out.println("Allowances           : " +
                                         employee.getAllowances());
              System.out.println("Deductions           : " +
                                         employee.getDeductions());
              System.out.println("Netpay                : " +
                                             employee.getNetpay());

    System.out.println("====================================\n\n");
        }

        txn.commit();
        session.close();
        sessionFactory.close();
    }
}
```

Hibernate: select this_.ID as ID0_0_, this_.ALLOWANCES as ALLOWANCES0_0_, this_.BASIC_PAY as BASIC3_0_0_, this_.DEDUCTIONS as

```
DEDUCTIONS0_0_, this_.DEPT as DEPT0_0_, this_.EMP_NAME as EMP6_0_0_,
this_.EMP_NUMBER as EMP7_0_0_, this_.NETPAY as NETPAY0_0_ from EMPLOYEE
this_ where EMP_NAME like 'I%'
    Employee Number   : 5001
    Employee Name     : Ibrahim
    Department        : IT
    Basic Pay         : 98000.00
    Allowances        : 30000.00
    Deductions        : 15000.00
    Netpay            : 113000.00
    ==================================
    Employee Number   : 5007
    Employee Name     : Indiran
    Department        : PERSONAL
    Basic Pay         : 69000.00
    Allowances        : 16000.00
    Deductions        : 8000.00
    Netpay            : 77000.00
    ==================================
```

The following example illustrates how to use Positional Parameter in `Restrictions.sqlRestriction()`

```
// File Name: EmployeeManipulation.java
// Criteria Queries: Restrictions.sqlRestriction() with Positional
Parameter

package com.hdemo;

import java.util.List;

import org.hibernate.Criteria;
import org.hibernate.Hibernate;
import org.hibernate.Session;
import org.hibernate.SessionFactory;
import org.hibernate.Transaction;
import org.hibernate.criterion.Restrictions;
```

```
public class EmployeeManipulation {

    @SuppressWarnings("unchecked")
    public static void main(String[] args) throws Exception {
          SessionFactory sessionFactory = HibernateUtil.getSession
                                                          Factory();

          Session session = sessionFactory.openSession();
          Transaction txn = session.beginTransaction();

          Criteria criteria = session.createCriteria(Employee.class);
          criteria.add(Restrictions.sqlRestriction("EMP_NAME like ?",
                                             "A%", Hibernate.STRING));

          List<Employee> employeeList = criteria.list();
          for (int i = 0; i < employeeList.size(); i++) {
                Employee employee = employeeList.get(i);
                System.out.println("Employee Number : " +
                                            employee.getEmpNumber());
                System.out.println("Employee Name    : " +
                                              employee.getEmpName());
                System.out.println("Department       : " +
                                           employee.getDepartment());
                System.out.println("Basic Pay        : " +
                                             employee.getBasicpay());
                System.out.println("Allowances       : " +
                                           employee.getAllowances());
                System.out.println("Deductions       : " +
                                           employee.getDeductions());
                System.out.println("Netpay           : " +
                                               employee.getNetpay());

    System.out.println("======================================\n\n");
          }

          txn.commit();
          session.close();
          sessionFactory.close();
```

```
    }
}
```

```
Hibernate: select this_.ID as ID0_0_, this_.ALLOWANCES as ALLOWANCES0_0_, this_.BASIC_PAY as BASIC3_0_0_, this_.DEDUCTIONS as DEDUCTIONS0_0_, this_.DEPT as DEPT0_0_, this_.EMP_NAME as EMP6_0_0_, this_.EMP_NUMBER as EMP7_0_0_, this_.NETPAY as NETPAY0_0_ from EMPLOYEE this_ where EMP_NAME like ?
Employee Number  : 5002
Employee Name    : Ananad Desai
Department       : IT
Basic Pay        : 93000.00
Allowances       : 29000.00
Deductions       : 15000.00
Netpay           : 107000.00
==========================================

Employee Number  : 5005
Employee Name    : Ajay
Department       : SALES
Basic Pay        : 78000.00
Allowances       : 23000.00
Deductions       : 14000.00
Netpay           : 87000.00
==========================================

Employee Number  : 5006
Employee Name    : Achfa
Department       : SALES
Basic Pay        : 74000.00
Allowances       : 22500.00
Deductions       : 12500.00
Netpay           : 84000.00
==========================================
```

The following example illustrates how to use multiple Positional Parameters in `Restrictions.sqlRestriction()`

```
// File Name: EmployeeManipulation.java
// Criteria Queries: Restrictions.sqlRestriction() with Positional Parameter

package com.hdemo;

import java.util.List;

import org.hibernate.Criteria;
import org.hibernate.Hibernate;
import org.hibernate.Session;
import org.hibernate.SessionFactory;
import org.hibernate.Transaction;
import org.hibernate.criterion.Restrictions;
import org.hibernate.type.Type;

public class EmployeeManipulation {

  @SuppressWarnings("unchecked")
  public static void main(String[] args) throws Exception {
        SessionFactory sessionFactory = HibernateUtil.getSession
                                                            Factory();
        Session session = sessionFactory.openSession();
        Transaction txn = session.beginTransaction();

        Criteria criteria = session.createCriteria(Employee.class);
        criteria.add(Restrictions.sqlRestriction("EMP_NAME like ? AND NETPAY > ?", new Object[] {"A%", new Double(100000.0)}, new Type[] {Hibernate.STRING, Hibernate.DOUBLE}));

        List<Employee> employeeList = criteria.list();
        for (int i = 0; i < employeeList.size(); i++) {
              Employee employee = employeeList.get(i);
              System.out.println("Employee Number : " +
                                          employee.getEmpNumber());
              System.out.println("Employee Name   : " +
                                            employee.getEmpName());
```

```
            System.out.println("Department            : " +
                                    employee.getDepartment());
            System.out.println("Basic  Pay            : " +
                                      employee.getBasicpay());
            System.out.println("Allowances            : " +
                                    employee.getAllowances());
            System.out.println("Deductions            : " +
                                    employee.getDeductions());
            System.out.println("Netpay                 : " +
                                        employee.getNetpay());

     System.out.println("=================================\n\n");
        }

        txn.commit();
        session.close();
        sessionFactory.close();
    }
}
```

Hibernate: select this_.ID as ID0_0_, this_.ALLOWANCES as ALLOWANCES0_0_, this_.BASIC_PAY as BASIC3_0_0_, this_.DEDUCTIONS as DEDUCTIONS0_0_, this_.DEPT as DEPT0_0_, this_.EMP_NAME as EMP6_0_0_, this_.EMP_NUMBER as EMP7_0_0_, this_.NETPAY as NETPAY0_0_ from EMPLOYEE this_ where EMP_NAME like ? AND NETPAY > ?

```
Employee Number   : 5002
Employee Name     : Ananad Desai
Department        : IT
Basic  Pay        : 93000.00
Allowances        : 29000.00
Deductions        : 15000.00
Netpay            : 107000.00
=================================
```

6.6.2 Example Using `Criteria addOrder()`

```
// File Name: EmployeeManipulation.java
```

```
// Criteria Queries: Criteria ==> addOrder()

package com.hdemo;

import java.util.List;

import org.hibernate.Criteria;
import org.hibernate.Session;
import org.hibernate.SessionFactory;
import org.hibernate.Transaction;
import org.hibernate.criterion.Order;

public class EmployeeManipulation {

  @SuppressWarnings("unchecked")
  public static void main(String[] args) throws Exception {
        SessionFactory sessionFactory = HibernateUtil.getSession
                                                          Factory();
        Session session = sessionFactory.openSession();
        Transaction txn = session.beginTransaction();

        //First sorted by department, then each group is sorted by
                                                            empName
        Criteria criteria = session.createCriteria(Employee.class);
        criteria.addOrder(Order.asc("department"));
        criteria.addOrder(Order.asc("empName"));

        List<Employee> employeeList = criteria.list();
        System.out.printf("%-15s   %-20s   %-15s   %10s   %10s
                                               %10s   %10s \n",
        "EMP. NUMBER", "EMP. NAME", "DEPT.", "BASIC PAY",
                           "ALLOWANCES", "DEDUCTIONS", "NETPAY");
        for (int i = 0; i < employeeList.size(); i++) {
              Employee employee = employeeList.get(i);
              System.out.printf("%-15d   %-20s   %-15s   %10.2f
                                   %10.2f  %10.2f   %10.2f \n",
```

```
                                        employee.getEmpNumber(),
employee.getEmpName(), employee.getDepartment(), employee.getBasicpay(),
                                        employee.getAllowances(),
employee.getDeductions(),  employee.getNetpay());
            }

            txn.commit();
            session.close();
            sessionFactory.close();
      }
  }
```

```
Hibernate: select this_.ID as ID0_0_, this_.ALLOWANCES as ALLOWANCES0_0_, this_.BASIC_PAY as BASIC3_0_0_, this_.DEDUCTIONS as DEDUCTIONS0_0_, this_.DEPT as DEPT0_0_, this_.EMP_NAME as EMP6_0_0_, this_.EMP_NUMBER as EMP7_0_0_, this_.NETPAY as NETPAY0_0_ from EMPLOYEE this_ order by this_.DEPT asc, this_.EMP_NAME asc
```

EMP. NUMBER	EMP. NAME	DEPT.	BASIC PAY	ALLOWA-NCES	DEDUCT-IONS	NETPAY
5010	Ravi Chandran	INVENTORY	55800.00	15100.00	7000.00	63900.00
5002	Ananad Desai	IT	93000.00	29000.00	15000.00	107000.00
5001	Ibrahim	IT	98000.00	30000.00	15000.00	113000.00
5007	Indiran	PERSONAL	69000.00	16000.00	8000.00	77000.00
5008	Nitin Otagiri	PERSONAL	67000.00	15800.00	7000.00	75800.00
5006	Achfa	SALES	74000.00	22500.00	12500.00	84000.00
5005	Ajay	SALES	78000.00	23000.00	14000.00	87000.00
5003	Karan Singh	SALES	88000.00	27000.00	14500.00	100500.00
5004	Sudhir	SALES	83000.00	25000.00	14100.00	93900.00
5009	Kumar	STATIONARY	65000.00	15700.00	7000.00	73700.00

6.6.3 Example Using `Criteria scroll()`

We can obtain Scrollable Result Set (we can traverse both front and back in the result set) from `Query` interface, if the underlying database supports Scrollable Result Set.

The sample data on the database table are as selected below.

mysql> select * from employee order by emp_name;

ID	ALLO-WANCES	BASIC_PAY	DEDU-CTIONS	DEPT	EMP_NAME	EMP_NUMBER	NETPAY
402881f81f206e6d011f206e70080006	22500.00	74000.00	12500.00	SALES	Achfa	5006	84000.00
402881f81f206e6d011f206e70080005	23000.00	78000.00	14000.00	SALES	Ajay	5005	87000.00
402881f81f206e6d011f206e70070002	29000.00	93000.00	15000.00	IT	Ananad Desai	5002	107000.00
402881f81f206e6d011f206e6ffb0001	30000.00	98000.00	15000.00	IT	Ibrahim	5001	113000.00
402881f81f206e6d011f206e70080007	16000.00	69000.00	8000.00	PERSONAL	Indiran	5007	77000.00
402881f81f206e6d011f206e70070003	27000.00	88000.00	14500.00	SALES	Karan Singh	5003	100500.00
402881f81f206e6d011f206e70080009	15700.00	65000.00	7000.00	STATIONARY	Kumar	5009	73700.00
402881f81f206e6d011f206e70080008	15800.00	67000.00	7000.00	PERSONAL	Nitin Otagiri	5008	75800.00
402881f81f206e6d011f206e7008000a	15100.00	55800.00	7000.00	INVENTORY	Ravi Chandran	5010	63900.00
402881f81f206e6d011f206e70070004	25000.00	83000.00	14100.00	SALES	Sudhir	5004	93900.00

10 rows in set (0.01 sec)

The following example demonstrates this feature.

```
// File Name: EmployeeManipulation.java
// Illustrates how to use Scrollable Resultset

package com.hdemo;

import org.hibernate.Criteria;
import org.hibernate.ScrollableResults;
import org.hibernate.Session;
import org.hibernate.SessionFactory;
import org.hibernate.Transaction;
import org.hibernate.criterion.Order;

public class EmployeeManipulation {

  public static void main(String[] args) throws Exception {
        SessionFactory sessionFactory = HibernateUtil.getSession
                                                        Factory();
        Session session = sessionFactory.openSession();
        Transaction txn = session.beginTransaction();

        Criteria criteria = session.createCriteria(Employee.class);
        criteria.addOrder(Order.asc("empName"));
        ScrollableResults records = criteria.scroll();

        System.out.printf("%-15s   %-20s   %-15s   %10s   %10s
                                           %10s   %10s \n",
        "EMP. NUMBER", "EMP. NAME", "DEPT.", "BASIC PAY",
                        "ALLOWANCES", "DEDUCTIONS", "NETPAY");

        while (records.next()) {
              Employee employee = (Employee) records.get(0);
              printRecord(employee);
        }

        System.out.println("\nRetrieving First Record");
        if (records.first()) {
              Employee employee = (Employee) records.get(0);
              printRecord(employee);
```

```
        }
        else
              System.out.println("\n [First] Record is not found");

        System.out.println("\nRetrieving Last Record");
        if (records.last()) {
              Employee employee = (Employee) records.get(0);
              printRecord(employee);
        }
        else
              System.out.println("\n [Last] Record is not found");

        System.out.println("\nRetrieving Previous of Last Record");
        if (records.last()) {
              if (records.previous()) {
                    Employee employee = (Employee) records.get(0);
                    printRecord(employee);
              }
              else
              System.out.println("\n [Previous of Last] Record is
                                                       not found");
        }
        else
              System.out.println("\nRetrieving Previous of Last
                                           Record: No record found");

        System.out.println("\nRetrieving Third Record");
        records.beforeFirst();
        // scroll() -Scrolls an arbitrary number of locations
        if (records.scroll(3)) {
              Employee employee = (Employee) records.get(0);
              printRecord(employee);
        }
        else
              System.out.println("\nRetrieving Third Record: No
                                    sufficient records to scroll\n");
```

```
System.out.println("\nAgain Scroll 2 more records");
if (records.scroll(2)) {
     Employee employee = (Employee) records.get(0);
     printRecord(employee);
}
else
     System.out.println("\nAgain Scroll 2 more records: No
                              sufficient records to scroll");

System.out.println("\nRow Number [" + records.getRowNumber()
                                                    + "]");
System.out.println("\nScroll 20 more records");
if (records.scroll(20)) {
     Employee employee = (Employee) records.get(0);
     printRecord(employee);
}
else
System.out.println("\nScroll 20 more records: No sufficient
                                     records to scroll");

System.out.println("\nRow Number [" + records.getRowNumber()
                                                    + "]");

// setRowNumber() -Sets the current location in the result
                        set. For this, Index starts from 0.
// Use negative value to set current location from last
                                                   record.
System.out.println("\nSetting Index to 3rd Location");
if (records.setRowNumber(2)) {
     Employee employee = (Employee) records.get(0);
     printRecord(employee);
}
else
     System.out.println("\nSetting Offset to 3rd Location:
                                No sufficient records");

System.out.println("\nSetting Index to 3rd Location from
                                             Last Record");
if (records.setRowNumber(-3)) {
```

```
                Employee employee = (Employee) records.get(0);
                printRecord(employee);
            }
            else
                System.out.println("\nSetting Offset to 3rd Location
                        from Last Record: No sufficient records");

            txn.commit();
            session.close();
            sessionFactory.close();
        }

        static void printRecord(Employee employee) {
            System.out.printf("%-15d %-20s %-15s %10.2f %10.2f
%10.2f %10.2f \n", employee.getEmpNumber(), employee.getEmpName(),
employee.getDepartment(), employee.getBasicpay(), employee.getAllowances(),
employee.getDeductions(), employee.getNetpay());
        }
    }
```

6.6.4 Restricting Size of Query's Result Set

```
Criteria setFirstResult(int offset)
Criteria setMaxResults(int limit)
```

The following example retrieves 2 rows from 4th row of Employee table.

```
// File Name: EmployeeManipulation.java
// Illustrates Criteria Query: setFirstResult(), setMaxResults()

package com.hdemo;

import java.util.List;

import org.hibernate.Criteria;
import org.hibernate.Query;
import org.hibernate.Session;
import org.hibernate.SessionFactory;
import org.hibernate.Transaction;
import org.hibernate.criterion.Order;
```

```
public class EmployeeManipulation {
    @SuppressWarnings("unchecked")
    public static void main(String[] args) throws Exception {
          SessionFactory sessionFactory = HibernateUtil.getSession
                                                          Factory();
          Session session = sessionFactory.openSession();
          Transaction txn = session.beginTransaction();

          System.out.println("Selecting All Employee Records\n");
          Criteria criteria1 = session.createCriteria(Employee.class);
          criteria1.addOrder(Order.asc("empName"));
          List<Employee> employeeList1 = criteria1.list();
          System.out.printf("%-15s %-20s %-15s %10s %10s
                                                   %10s %10s \n",
             "EMP. NUMBER", "EMP. NAME", "DEPT.", "BASIC PAY",
                          "ALLOWANCES", "DEDUCTIONS", "NETPAY");
          for (int i = 0; i < employeeList1.size(); i++) {
               Employee employee = employeeList1.get(i);
               System.out.printf("%-15d %-20s %-15s %10.2f
%10.2f %10.2f %10.2f \n", employee.getEmpNumber(),
employee.getEmpName(), employee.getDepartment(), employee.getBasicpay(),
employee.getAllowances(), employee.getDeductions(), employee.getNetpay());
          }

          System.out.println("\nSelecting 2 Employee Records from 4th
                                   row. [Index starts from 0]\n");
          Criteria criteria2 = session.createCriteria(Employee.class);
          criteria2.addOrder(Order.asc("empName"));
          criteria2.setFirstResult(3);
          criteria2.setMaxResults(2);
          List<Employee> employeeList2 = criteria2.list();
          for (int i = 0; i < employeeList2.size(); i++) {
               Employee employee = employeeList2.get(i);
               System.out.printf("%-15d %-20s %-15s %10.2f
%10.2f %10.2f %10.2f \n", employee.getEmpNumber(),
```

```
employee.getEmpName(), employee.getDepartment(), employee.getBasicpay(),
employee.getAllowances(), employee.getDeductions(), employee.getNetpay());
            }

            txn.commit();
            session.close();
            sessionFactory.close();
        }
    }
```

Selecting All Employee Records

Hibernate: select this_.ID as ID0_0_, this_.ALLOWANCES as ALLOWANCES0_0_, this_.BASIC_PAY as BASIC3_0_0_, this_.DEDUCTIONS as DEDUCTIONS0_0_, this_.DEPT as DEPT0_0_, this_.EMP_NAME as EMP6_0_0_, this_.EMP_NUMBER as EMP7_0_0_, this_.NETPAY as NETPAY0_0_ from EMPLOYEE this_ order by this_.EMP_NAME asc

EMP. NUMBER	EMP. NAME	DEPT.	BASIC PAY	ALLOWA-NCES	DEDUCT-IONS	NETPAY
5006	Achfa	SALES	74000.00	22500.00	12500.00	84000.00
5005	Ajay	SALES	78000.00	23000.00	14000.00	87000.00
5002	Ananad Desai	IT	93000.00	29000.00	15000.00	107000.00
5001	Ibrahim	IT	98000.00	30000.00	15000.00	113000.00
5007	Indiran	PERSONAL	69000.00	16000.00	8000.00	77000.00
5003	Karan Singh	SALES	88000.00	27000.00	14500.00	100500.00
5009	Kumar	STATIONARY	65000.00	15700.00	7000.00	73700.00
5008	Nitin Otagiri	PERSONAL	67000.00	15800.00	7000.00	75800.00
5010	Ravi Chandran	INVENTORY	55800.00	15100.00	7000.00	63900.00
5004	Sudhir	SALES	83000.00	25000.00	14100.00	93900.00

Selecting 2 Employee Records from 4th row. [Index starts from 0]

Hibernate: select this_.ID as ID0_0_, this_.ALLOWANCES as ALLOWANCES0_0_, this_.BASIC_PAY as BASIC3_0_0_, this_.DEDUCTIONS as DEDUCTIONS0_0_, this_.DEPT as DEPT0_0_, this_.EMP_NAME as EMP6_0_0_, this_.EMP_NUMBER as EMP7_0_0_, this_.NETPAY as NETPAY0_0_ from EMPLOYEE this_ order by this_.EMP_NAME asc limit ?, ?

EMP. NUMBER	EMP. NAME	DEPT.	BASIC PAY	ALLOWA-NCES	DEDUCT-IONS	NETPAY
5001	Ibrahim	IT	98000.00	30000.00	15000.00	113000.00
5007	Indiran	PERSONAL	69000.00	16000.00	8000.00	77000.00

6.6.5 Example Using `Criteria uniqueResult()`

Note that the Query should return only one value or no value as the result, then only you can use this `uniqueResult()` method to retrieve that value. You may use `setMaxResults()` method to restrict the Query result to 1 row, before invoking this `uniqueResult()` method. If you try to use this method with a Query which returns more than one row, then an exception will be thrown.

```
// File Name: EmployeeManipulation.java
// Illustrates Criteria Query: uniqueResult()

package com.hdemo;

import org.hibernate.Criteria;
import org.hibernate.Session;
import org.hibernate.SessionFactory;
import org.hibernate.Transaction;
import org.hibernate.criterion.Restrictions;

public class EmployeeManipulation {

   public static void main(String[] args) throws Exception {
        SessionFactory sessionFactory = HibernateUtil.getSession
                                                          Factory();
        Session session = sessionFactory.openSession();
        Transaction txn = session.beginTransaction();

        System.out.println("Selecting All Employee Records\n");
        Criteria criteria = session.createCriteria(Employee.class);

criteria.add(Restrictions.idEq("402881f81f206e6d011f206e6ffb0001"));
        Employee employee = (Employee) criteria.uniqueResult();
        if (employee != null) {
```

```
                System.out.printf("%-15s       %-20s       %-15s       %10s
%10s   %10s    %10s \n", "EMP. NUMBER", "EMP. NAME", "DEPT.", "BASIC
PAY", "ALLOWANCES", "DEDUCTIONS", "NETPAY");
                System.out.printf("%-15d    %-20s     %-15s    %10.2f
%10.2f    %10.2f     %10.2f  \n",  employee.getEmpNumber(),
employee.getEmpName(), employee.getDepartment(), employee.getBasicpay(),
employee.getAllowances(), employee.getDeductions(), employee.getNetpay());
            }
            else
                System.out.println("No matching record found");

            txn.commit();
            session.close();
            sessionFactory.close();
        }
    }
```

Selecting All Employee Records

Hibernate: select this_.ID as ID0_0_, this_.ALLOWANCES as ALLOWANCES0_0_, this_.BASIC_PAY as BASIC3_0_0_, this_.DEDUCTIONS as DEDUCTIONS0_0_, this_.DEPT as DEPT0_0_, this_.EMP_NAME as EMP6_0_0_, this_.EMP_NUMBER as EMP7_0_0_, this_.NETPAY as NETPAY0_0_ from EMPLOYEE this_ where this_.ID = ?

EMP. NUMBER	EMP. NAME	DEPT.	BASIC PAY	ALLOWA-NCES	DEDUCT-IONS	NETPAY
5001	Ibrahim	IT	98000.00	30000.00	15000.00	113000.00

6.6.6 Example Using `Criteria setProjection()`

```
// File Name: EmployeeManipulation.java
// Illustrates Criteria Query: Projections

package com.hdemo;

import java.math.BigDecimal;

import org.hibernate.Criteria;
import org.hibernate.Session;
import org.hibernate.SessionFactory;
```

```
import org.hibernate.Transaction;
import org.hibernate.criterion.Projections;

public class EmployeeManipulation {

  public static void main(String[] args) throws Exception {
        SessionFactory sessionFactory = HibernateUtil.getSession
                                                      Factory();
        Session session = sessionFactory.openSession();
        Transaction txn = session.beginTransaction();

        Criteria criteria = session.createCriteria(Employee.class);
        criteria.setProjection(Projections.sum("netpay"));
        Object sumOfNetpay = criteria.uniqueResult();
        System.out.printf("Sum of Netpay: " + (BigDecimal)
                                                    sumOfNetpay);

        txn.commit();
        session.close();
        sessionFactory.close();
  }
}
```

```
Hibernate: select sum(this_.NETPAY) as y0_ from EMPLOYEE this_
Sum of Netpay: 875800.00
```

If you want to specify more projections, then add them into a `ProjectionList` and set with `Criteria`. Of course, the `ProjectionList` can be used to specify only one Projection also. We should not set multiple Projections as follows, which makes the last set Projection only take effect.

```
Criteria criteria = session.createCriteria(Employee.class);
criteria.setProjection(Projections.rowCount());
criteria.setProjection(Projections.sum("basicpay"));
criteria.setProjection(Projections.avg("basicpay"));
criteria.setProjection(Projections.min("basicpay"));
criteria.setProjection(Projections.max("basicpay"));
List list = criteria.list();
```

The above list will contain only one value of the last set projection (maximum of *basicpay* of Employee).

The following example uses ProjectionList to specify more projections.

```
// File Name: EmployeeManipulation.java
// Illustrates Criteria Query: Projections

package com.hdemo;

import java.util.List;

import org.hibernate.Criteria;
import org.hibernate.Session;
import org.hibernate.SessionFactory;
import org.hibernate.Transaction;
import org.hibernate.criterion.ProjectionList;
import org.hibernate.criterion.Projections;

public class EmployeeManipulation {

  @SuppressWarnings("unchecked")
  public static void main(String[] args) throws Exception {
      SessionFactory sessionFactory = HibernateUtil.getSession
                                                      Factory();
      Session session = sessionFactory.openSession();
      Transaction txn = session.beginTransaction();

      Criteria criteria = session.createCriteria(Employee.class);
      ProjectionList projectionList = Projections.projectionList();
      projectionList.add(Projections.rowCount());
      projectionList.add(Projections.sum("basicpay"));
      projectionList.add(Projections.avg("basicpay"));
      projectionList.add(Projections.min("basicpay"));
      projectionList.add(Projections.max("basicpay"));
      criteria.setProjection(projectionList);
      List list = criteria.list();

      Object[] values = (Object[])list.get(0);
      System.out.println("Total records         : " + values[0]);
```

```
        System.out.println("Sum of Basicpay      : " + values[1]);
        System.out.println("Average of Basicpay  : " + values[2]);
        System.out.println("Minimum Basicpay     : " + values[3]);
        System.out.println("Maximum Basicpay     : " + values[4]);

        txn.commit();
        session.close();
        sessionFactory.close();
    }
}
```

```
Hibernate: select count(*) as y0_, sum(this_.BASIC_PAY) as y1_, avg(this_.BASIC_PAY) as y2_, min(this_.BASIC_PAY) as y3_, max(this_.BASIC_PAY) as y4_ from EMPLOYEE this_
Total records         : 10
Sum of Basicpay       : 770800.00
Average of Basicpay   : 77080.0
Minimum Basicpay      : 55800.00
Maximum Basicpay      : 98000.00
```

The following example uses group property ("group by" feature of SQL).

```
// File Name: EmployeeManipulation.java
// Illustrates Criteria Query: Projections

package com.hdemo;

import java.util.Iterator;
import java.util.List;

import org.hibernate.Criteria;
import org.hibernate.Session;
import org.hibernate.SessionFactory;
import org.hibernate.Transaction;
import org.hibernate.criterion.ProjectionList;
import org.hibernate.criterion.Projections;

public class EmployeeManipulation {

  @SuppressWarnings("unchecked")
```

```
    public static void main(String[] args) throws Exception {
        SessionFactory sessionFactory = HibernateUtil.getSession
                                                        Factory();
        Session session = sessionFactory.openSession();
        Transaction txn = session.beginTransaction();

        // Finds Number of Employees in each department, Sum of
Basic Pay in each department, Average of Basic Pay in each department,
        // Minimum Basic Pay in each department, Maximum Basic Pay
                                                 in each department
        Criteria criteria = session.createCriteria(Employee.class);
        ProjectionList projectionList = Projections.projectionList();

        projectionList.add(Projections.groupProperty("department"));
        projectionList.add(Projections.rowCount());
        projectionList.add(Projections.sum("basicpay"));
        projectionList.add(Projections.avg("basicpay"));
        projectionList.add(Projections.min("basicpay"));
        projectionList.add(Projections.max("basicpay"));
        criteria.setProjection(projectionList);

        List list = criteria.list();
        System.out.printf("%-15s %-30s %25s %25s %25s %25s",
"Department", "No. of Employees in Department", "SUM OF BASIC PAY",
"AVERAGE OF BASIC PAY", "MINIMUM BASIC PAY", "MAXIMUM BASIC PAY");
        for (Iterator it = list.iterator(); it.hasNext();) {
            Object[] row = (Object[])it.next();
            System.out.printf("\n%-15s %30s %25s %25s %25s %25s",
              row[0], row[1], row[2], row[3], row[4], row[5]);
        }

        txn.commit();
        session.close();
        sessionFactory.close();
    }
}
```

```
Hibernate: select this_.DEPT as y0_, count(*) as y1_,
```

sum(this_.BASIC_PAY) as y2_, avg(this_.BASIC_PAY) as y3_, min(this_.BASIC_PAY) as y4_, max(this_.BASIC_PAY) as y5_ from EMPLOYEE this_ group by this_.DEPT

DEPARTMENT	NO. OF EMPLOYEES IN DEPARTMENT	SUM OF BASIC PAY	AVERAGE OF BASIC PAY	MINIMUM BASIC PAY	MAXIMUM BASIC PAY
INVENTORY	1	55800.00	55800.0	55800.00	55800.00
IT	2	191000.00	95500.0	93000.00	98000.00
PERSONAL	2	136000.00	68000.0	67000.00	69000.00
SALES	4	323000.00	80750.0	74000.00	88000.00
STATIONARY	1	65000.00	65000.0	65000.00	65000.00

The following example illustrates how to use alias names for group/aggregate properties.

```
// File Name: EmployeeManipulation.java
// Illustrates Criteria Query: Projections

package com.hdemo;

import java.util.Iterator;
import java.util.List;

import org.hibernate.Criteria;
import org.hibernate.Session;
import org.hibernate.SessionFactory;
import org.hibernate.Transaction;
import org.hibernate.criterion.Order;
import org.hibernate.criterion.ProjectionList;
import org.hibernate.criterion.Projections;

public class EmployeeManipulation {

  @SuppressWarnings("unchecked")
  public static void main(String[] args) throws Exception {
        SessionFactory sessionFactory = HibernateUtil.getSession
                                                          Factory();

        Session session = sessionFactory.openSession();
        Transaction txn = session.beginTransaction();
```

```
        // Finds Number of Employees in each department, Sum of
Basic Pay in each department, Average of Basic Pay in each department,
        // Minimum Basic Pay in each department, Maximum Basic Pay
                                                in each department
        // Order By Number of Employees in each department in
                                                 decending order
        Criteria criteria = session.createCriteria(Employee.class);
        ProjectionList projectionList = Projections.projectionList();

        projectionList.add(Projections.groupProperty("department"));
        projectionList.add(Projections.rowCount(), "RowCount");
        projectionList.add(Projections.sum("basicpay"));
        projectionList.add(Projections.avg("basicpay"));
        projectionList.add(Projections.min("basicpay"));
        projectionList.add(Projections.max("basicpay"));
        criteria.addOrder(Order.desc("RowCount"));
        criteria.setProjection(projectionList);

        List list = criteria.list();
        System.out.printf("%-15s %-30s %25s %25s %25s %25s",
"Department", "No. of Employees in Department", "SUM OF BASIC PAY",
"AVERAGE OF BASIC PAY", "MINIMUM BASIC PAY", "MAXIMUM BASIC PAY");
        for (Iterator it = list.iterator(); it.hasNext();) {
            Object[] row = (Object[])it.next();
            System.out.printf("\n%-15s %30s %25s %25s %25s %25s",
              row[0], row[1], row[2], row[3], row[4], row[5]);
        }

        txn.commit();
        session.close();
        sessionFactory.close();
    }
}
```

```
Hibernate: select this_.DEPT as y0_, count(*) as y1_, sum(this_.BASIC_PAY) as y2_, avg(this_.BASIC_PAY) as y3_, min(this_.BASIC_PAY) as y4_, max(this_.BASIC_PAY) as y5_ from EMPLOYEE this_ group by this_.DEPT order by y1_ desc
```

DEPARTMENT	NO. OF EMPLOYEES IN DEPARTMENT	SUM OF BASIC PAY	AVERAGE OF BASIC PAY	MINIMUM BASIC PAY	MAXIMUM BASIC PAY
SALES	4	323000.00	80750.0	74000.00	88000.00
IT	2	191000.00	95500.0	93000.00	98000.00
PERSONAL	2	136000.00	68000.0	67000.00	69000.00
STATIONARY	1	65000.00	65000.0	65000.00	65000.00
INVENTORY	1	55800.00	55800.0	55800.00	55800.00

The following example illustrates other ways to use alias names for properties.

```
// File Name: EmployeeManipulation.java
// Illustrates Criteria Query: Projections

package com.hdemo;

import java.util.Iterator;
import java.util.List;

import org.hibernate.Criteria;
import org.hibernate.Session;
import org.hibernate.SessionFactory;
import org.hibernate.Transaction;
import org.hibernate.criterion.Order;
import org.hibernate.criterion.ProjectionList;
import org.hibernate.criterion.Projections;

public class EmployeeManipulation {

  @SuppressWarnings("unchecked")
  public static void main(String[] args) throws Exception {
     SessionFactory sessionFactory = HibernateUtil.getSession
                                                    Factory();
```

```
        Session session = sessionFactory.openSession();
        Transaction txn = session.beginTransaction();

        // Finds Number of Employees in each department
        // Order By department decending
        System.out.println("Using direct field name");
        Criteria criteria1 = session.createCriteria(Employee.class);
        ProjectionList projectionList1 = Projections.projectionList();
      projectionList1.add(Projections.groupProperty("department"));
        projectionList1.add(Projections.rowCount());
        criteria1.addOrder(Order.desc("department"));
        criteria1.setProjection(projectionList1);

        List list1 = criteria1.list();
        System.out.printf("%-15s %-30s", "Department", "No. of
Employees in Department");
        for (Iterator it = list1.iterator(); it.hasNext();) {
              Object[] row = (Object[])it.next();
              System.out.printf("\n%-15s %30s", row[0], row[1]);
        }

        System.out.println("\n\nUsing alias-name (created from add
                                        method's second argument)");
        Criteria criteria2 = session.createCriteria(Employee.class);
        ProjectionList projectionList2 = Projections.projectionList();

       projectionList2.add(Projections.groupProperty("department"),
                                                     "DEPARTMENT");
        projectionList2.add(Projections.rowCount());
        criteria2.addOrder(Order.desc("DEPARTMENT"));
        criteria2.setProjection(projectionList2);

        List list2 = criteria2.list();
        System.out.printf("%-15s %-30s", "Department", "No. of
                                          Employees in Department");
```

```
        for (Iterator it = list2.iterator(); it.hasNext();) {
              Object[] row = (Object[])it.next();
              System.out.printf("\n%-15s %30s", row[0], row[1]);
        }

        System.out.println("\n\nUsing alias-name (created using 'as()'
                                                              method)");
        Criteria criteria3 = session.createCriteria(Employee.class);
        ProjectionList projectionList3 = Projections.projectionList();
        projectionList3.add(Projections.groupProperty("department")
                                                    .as("DEPARTMENT"));
        projectionList3.add(Projections.rowCount());
        criteria3.addOrder(Order.desc("DEPARTMENT"));
        criteria3.setProjection(projectionList3);

        List list3 = criteria3.list();
        System.out.printf("%-15s %-30s", "Department", "No. of
                                          Employees in Department");
        for (Iterator it = list3.iterator(); it.hasNext();) {
              Object[] row = (Object[])it.next();
              System.out.printf("\n%-15s %30s", row[0], row[1]);
        }

        txn.commit();
        session.close();
        sessionFactory.close();
    }
}
```

```
Using direct field name
Hibernate: select this_.DEPT as y0_, count(*) as y1_ from EMPLOYEE
this_ group by this_.DEPT order by this_.DEPT desc
Department             No. of Employees in Department
STATIONARY                               1
SALES                                    4
PERSONAL                                 2
```

```
IT                          2
INVENTORY                   1

Using alias-name (created from add method's second argument)
Hibernate: select this_.DEPT as y0_, count(*) as y1_ from EMPLOYEE
this_ group by this_.DEPT order by y0_ desc
Department            No. of Employees in Department
STATIONARY                  1
SALES                       4
PERSONAL                    2
IT                          2
INVENTORY                   1

Using alias-name (created using 'as()' method)
Hibernate: select this_.DEPT as y0_, count(*) as y1_ from EMPLOYEE
this_ group by this_.DEPT order by y0_ desc
Department            No. of Employees in Department
STATIONARY                  1
SALES                       4
PERSONAL                    2
IT                          2
INVENTORY                   1
```

The following example is given for demonstrating how to include additional required fields in the result set of group expression (suing `Projections.property()`method).

```
// File Name: EmployeeManipulation.java
// Illustrates Criteria Query: Projections

package com.hdemo;

import java.util.Iterator;
import java.util.List;

import org.hibernate.Criteria;
import org.hibernate.Session;
```

```
import  org.hibernate.SessionFactory;
import  org.hibernate.Transaction;
import  org.hibernate.criterion.ProjectionList;
import  org.hibernate.criterion.Projections;

public  class  EmployeeManipulation  {

  @SuppressWarnings("unchecked")
  public  static  void  main(String[]  args)  throws  Exception  {
       SessionFactory  sessionFactory  =  HibernateUtil.getSession
                                                        Factory();
       Session  session  =  sessionFactory.openSession();
       Transaction  txn  =  session.beginTransaction();

       //Projections.property()  selects  the  specified  field  also
                                                   for  the  result
       Criteria  criteria  =  session.createCriteria(Employee.class);
       ProjectionList projectionList = Projections.projectionList();
       projectionList.add(Projections.property("department"));
       projectionList.add(Projections.count("department"));
       projectionList.add(Projections.groupProperty("department"));
       criteria.setProjection(projectionList);

       List  list  =  criteria.list();
       System.out.printf("%-15s %-30s %25s \n", "Department", "No.
                   of  Employees  in  Department",  "Department");
       for  (Iterator  it  =  list.iterator();  it.hasNext();)  {
            Object[]  row  =  (Object[])  it.next();
            System.out.printf("%-15s %-30s %25s \n", row[0], row[1],
                                                          row[2]);
       }

       txn.commit();
       session.close();
```

```
            sessionFactory.close();
      }
   }
```

```
   Hibernate: select this_.DEPT as y0_, count(this_.DEPT) as y1_,
this_.DEPT as y2_ from EMPLOYEE this_ group by this_.DEPT
   Department        No. of Employees in Department    Department
   INVENTORY                        1                   INVENTORY
   IT                               2                      IT
   PERSONAL                         2                   PERSONAL
   SALES                            4                     SALES
   STATIONARY                       1                  STATIONARY
```

The following example uses `ProjectionList` to limit the fields to retrieve for result set.

```
// File Name: EmployeeManipulation.java
// Illustrates Criteria Query: Projections

package com.hdemo;

import java.util.Iterator;
import java.util.List;

import org.hibernate.Criteria;
import org.hibernate.Session;
import org.hibernate.SessionFactory;
import org.hibernate.Transaction;
import org.hibernate.criterion.ProjectionList;
import org.hibernate.criterion.Projections;

public class EmployeeManipulation {

   @SuppressWarnings("unchecked")
   public static void main(String[] args) throws Exception {
```

```
        SessionFactory sessionFactory = HibernateUtil.getSession
                                                        Factory();
        Session session = sessionFactory.openSession();
        Transaction txn = session.beginTransaction();

        //Projections.property() selects the specified field also
                                                   for the result
        Criteria criteria = session.createCriteria(Employee.class);
        ProjectionList projectionList = Projections.projectionList();
        projectionList.add(Projections.property("empNumber"));
        projectionList.add(Projections.property("empName"));
        projectionList.add(Projections.property("department"));
        projectionList.add(Projections.property("netpay"));
        criteria.setProjection(projectionList);

        List list = criteria.list();
        System.out.printf("%-15s %-25s %-15s %10s \n", "EMP. NUMBER",
                         "EMP. NAME", "DEPARTMENT", "NETPAY");
        for (Iterator it = list.iterator(); it.hasNext();) {
            Object[] row = (Object[]) it.next();
            System.out.printf("%-15s %-25s %-15s %10.2f \n",
                             row[0], row[1], row[2], row[3]);
        }

        txn.commit();
        session.close();
        sessionFactory.close();
    }
}
```

Hibernate: select this_.EMP_NUMBER as y0_, this_.EMP_NAME as y1_, this_.DEPT as y2_, this_.NETPAY as y3_ from EMPLOYEE this_

EMP. NUMBER	EMP. NAME	DEPARTMENT	NETPAY
5001	Ibrahim	IT	113000.00
5002	Ananad Desai	IT	107000.00
5003	Karan Singh	SALES	100500.00
5004	Sudhir	SALES	93900.00
5005	Ajay	SALES	87000.00
5006	Achfa	SALES	84000.00
5007	Indiran	PERSONAL	77000.00
5008	Nitin Otagiri	PERSONAL	75800.00
5009	Kumar	STATIONARY	73700.00
5010	Ravi Chandran	INVENTORY	63900.00

The following example uses `Projections.sqlProjection()` method, which allows us to use native SQL columns of database table to retrieve data.

```
// File Name: EmployeeManipulation.java
// Illustrates Criteria Query: Projections

package com.hdemo;

import java.util.Iterator;
import java.util.List;

import org.hibernate.Criteria;
import org.hibernate.Hibernate;
import org.hibernate.Session;
import org.hibernate.SessionFactory;
import org.hibernate.Transaction;
import org.hibernate.criterion.Projections;
import org.hibernate.type.Type;

public class EmployeeManipulation {

  @SuppressWarnings("unchecked")
  public static void main(String[] args) throws Exception {
```

```
        SessionFactory sessionFactory = HibernateUtil.getSession
                                                        Factory();
        Session session = sessionFactory.openSession();
        Transaction txn = session.beginTransaction();

        Criteria criteria = session.createCriteria(Employee.class);

    criteria.setProjection(Projections.sqlProjection("CONCAT('Mr.  ',
       EMP_NAME) as EmployeeName, (NETPAY - 500.0) as Netpay",
        new String[] { "EmployeeName", "Netpay" },
        new Type[] { Hibernate.STRING, Hibernate.DOUBLE }));

        List list = criteria.list();
        System.out.printf("%-25s %10s \n", "EMP. NAME", "NETPAY");
        for (Iterator it = list.iterator(); it.hasNext();) {
              Object[] row = (Object[]) it.next();
              System.out.printf("%-25s %10.2f \n", row[0], row[1]);
        }

        txn.commit();
        session.close();
        sessionFactory.close();
    }
}
```

```
Hibernate: select CONCAT('Mr. ', EMP_NAME) as EmployeeName, (NETPAY
- 500.0) as Netpay from EMPLOYEE this_
```

EMP. NAME	NETPAY
Mr. Ibrahim	112500.00
Mr. Ananad Desai	106500.00
Mr. Karan Singh	100000.00
Mr. Sudhir	93400.00
Mr. Ajay	86500.00
Mr. Achfa	83500.00
Mr. Indiran	76500.00
Mr. Nitin Otagiri	75300.00
Mr. Kumar	73200.00
Mr. Ravi Chandran	63400.00

The following example uses `Projections.sqlGroupProjection()` method, which allows us to use native SQL column names of database table to retrieve "*group by*" data.

```
// File Name: EmployeeManipulation.java
// Illustrates Criteria Query: Projections

package com.hdemo;

import java.util.Iterator;
import java.util.List;

import org.hibernate.Criteria;
import org.hibernate.Hibernate;
import org.hibernate.Session;
import org.hibernate.SessionFactory;
import org.hibernate.Transaction;
import org.hibernate.criterion.Projections;
import org.hibernate.type.Type;

public class EmployeeManipulation {

   @SuppressWarnings("unchecked")
   public static void main(String[] args) throws Exception {
         SessionFactory sessionFactory = HibernateUtil.getSession
                                                      Factory();
         Session session = sessionFactory.openSession();
         Transaction txn = session.beginTransaction();

         //Finds which employee is having highest netpay in each
                                                      department
         Criteria criteria = session.createCriteria(Employee.class);

criteria.setProjection(Projections.sqlGroupProjection("EMP_NAME AS
EmployeeName, DEPT as Department, MAX(NETPAY) as Netpay",

   "DEPT",
```

```
        new String[] { "EmployeeName", "Department", "Netpay" },
    new Type[] { Hibernate.STRING, Hibernate.STRING,
                                        Hibernate.DOUBLE}));

        List list = criteria.list();
        System.out.printf("%-25s %-20s %10s \n", "EMP. NAME",
                                    "DEPARTMENT", "NETPAY");
        for (Iterator it = list.iterator(); it.hasNext();) {
            Object[] row = (Object[]) it.next();
            System.out.printf("%-25s %-20s %10.2f \n", row[0],
                                        row[1], row[2]);
        }

        txn.commit();
        session.close();
        sessionFactory.close();
    }
}
```

Hibernate: select EMP_NAME AS EmployeeName, DEPT as Department, MAX(NETPAY) as Netpay from EMPLOYEE this_ group by DEPT

EMP. NAME	DEPARTMENT	NETPAY
Ravi Chandran	INVENTORY	63900.00
Ibrahim	IT	113000.00
Indiran	PERSONAL	77000.00
Karan Singh	SALES	100500.00
Kumar	STATIONARY	73700.00

The following example uses `Projections.countDistinct()` method.

```
// File Name: EmployeeManipulation.java
// Illustrates Criteria Query: Projections

package com.hdemo;

import org.hibernate.Criteria;
```

```
import org.hibernate.Session;
import org.hibernate.SessionFactory;
import org.hibernate.Transaction;
import org.hibernate.criterion.Projections;

public class EmployeeManipulation {

  public static void main(String[] args) throws Exception {
      SessionFactory sessionFactory = HibernateUtil.getSession
                                                     Factory();
      Session session = sessionFactory.openSession();
      Transaction txn = session.beginTransaction();

      Criteria criteria = session.createCriteria(Employee.class);

    criteria.setProjection(Projections.countDistinct("deductions"));

      Integer totalNetpays = (Integer) criteria.uniqueResult();
      System.out.printf("Total different Netpays : " +
                                                 totalNetpays);

      txn.commit();
      session.close();
      sessionFactory.close();
  }
}
```

```
Hibernate: select count(distinct this_.DEDUCTIONS) as y0_ from
EMPLOYEE this_
Total different Netpays :7
```

The following example uses `Projections.distinct()` method.

```
// File Name: EmployeeManipulation.java
// Illustrates Criteria Query: Projections

package com.hdemo;

import org.hibernate.Criteria;
```

```
import org.hibernate.Session;
import org.hibernate.SessionFactory;
import org.hibernate.Transaction;
import org.hibernate.criterion.Projections;

public class EmployeeManipulation {

  public static void main(String[] args) throws Exception {
      SessionFactory sessionFactory = HibernateUtil.getSession
                                                        Factory();
      Session session = sessionFactory.openSession();
      Transaction txn = session.beginTransaction();

      Criteria criteria = session.createCriteria(Employee.class);
         criteria.setProjection(Projections.distinct(Projections.
                                  property("deductions")));

      int totalDistinctDeductions = criteria.list().size();
      System.out.printf("Total distinct deductions : " +
                                  totalDistinctDeductions);

      txn.commit();
      session.close();
      sessionFactory.close();
  }
}
```

```
Hibernate: select distinct this_.DEDUCTIONS as y0_ from EMPLOYEE
this_
Total distinct deductions : 7
```

6.7 EXAMPLES USING `org.hibernate.criterion.Property` API

This `Property` class may be used as an alternate to `Restrictions` class to specify conditions in `Criteria` query.

6.7.1 Example Using `eq()`

```
// File Name: EmployeeManipulation.java
// Criteria Queries: eq()
```

```
package com.hdemo;

import java.util.List;

import org.hibernate.Criteria;
import org.hibernate.Session;
import org.hibernate.SessionFactory;
import org.hibernate.Transaction;
import org.hibernate.criterion.Property;

public class EmployeeManipulation {

    @SuppressWarnings("unchecked")
    public static void main(String[] args) throws Exception {
        SessionFactory sessionFactory = HibernateUtil.getSession
                                                        Factory();
        Session session = sessionFactory.openSession();
        Transaction txn = session.beginTransaction();

        Criteria criteria = session.createCriteria(Employee.class);
        criteria.add(Property.forName("empNumber").eq(5001));

        List<Employee> employeeList = criteria.list();
        for (int i = 0; i < employeeList.size(); i++) {
            Employee employee = employeeList.get(i);
            System.out.println("Employee Number : " +
                                        employee.getEmpNumber());
            System.out.println("Employee Name    : " +
                                          employee.getEmpName());

            System.out.println("Department       : " +
                                       employee.getDepartment());
            System.out.println("Basic Pay         : " +
                                         employee.getBasicpay());
            System.out.println("Allowances       : " +
                                       employee.getAllowances());
            System.out.println("Deductions       : " +
                                       employee.getDeductions());
```

```
                System.out.println("Netpay                 : " +
                                                employee.getNetpay());

      System.out.println("========================================\n\n");
            }

            txn.commit();
            session.close();
            sessionFactory.close();
      }
   }
```

```
Hibernate: select this_.ID as ID0_0_, this_.ALLOWANCES as ALLOWANCES0_0_, this_.BASIC_PAY as BASIC3_0_0_, this_.DEDUCTIONS as DEDUCTIONS0_0_, this_.DEPT as DEPT0_0_, this_.EMP_NAME as EMP6_0_0_, this_.EMP_NUMBER as EMP7_0_0_, this_.NETPAY as NETPAY0_0_ from EMPLOYEE this_ where this_.EMP_NUMBER=?
   Employee Number   : 5001
   Employee Name     : Ibrahim
   Department        : IT
   Basic Pay         : 98000.00
   Allowances        : 30000.00
   Deductions        : 15000.00
   Netpay            : 113000.00
   ========================================
```

6.7.2 Example Using between()

```
   // File Name: EmployeeManipulation.java
   // Criteria Queries: between()

   package com.hdemo;

   import java.util.List;

   import org.hibernate.Criteria;
   import org.hibernate.Session;
   import org.hibernate.SessionFactory;
```

```
import org.hibernate.Transaction;
import org.hibernate.criterion.Property;

public class EmployeeManipulation {

   @SuppressWarnings("unchecked")
   public static void main(String[] args) throws Exception {
         SessionFactory sessionFactory = HibernateUtil.getSession
                                                        Factory();
         Session session = sessionFactory.openSession();
         Transaction txn = session.beginTransaction();

         Criteria criteria = session.createCriteria(Employee.class);
         criteria.add(Property.forName("empNumber").between
                                                   (5002, 5004));

         List<Employee> employeeList = criteria.list();
         for (int i = 0; i < employeeList.size(); i++) {
               Employee employee = employeeList.get(i);
               System.out.println("Employee Number : " +
                                          employee.getEmpNumber());
               System.out.println("Employee Name     : " +
                                            employee.getEmpName());
               System.out.println("Department          : " +
                                         employee.getDepartment());
               System.out.println("Basic Pay            : " +
                                           employee.getBasicpay());
               System.out.println("Allowances          : " +
                                         employee.getAllowances());
               System.out.println("Deductions          : " +
                                         employee.getDeductions());
               System.out.println("Netpay                  : " +
                                             employee.getNetpay());

  System.out.println("=====================================\n\n");
         }

         txn.commit();
```

```
        session.close();
        sessionFactory.close();
    }
}
```

```
Hibernate: select this_.ID as ID0_0_, this_.ALLOWANCES as ALLOWANCES0_0_, this_.BASIC_PAY as BASIC3_0_0_, this_.DEDUCTIONS as DEDUCTIONS0_0_, this_.DEPT as DEPT0_0_, this_.EMP_NAME as EMP6_0_0_, this_.EMP_NUMBER as EMP7_0_0_, this_.NETPAY as NETPAY0_0_ from EMPLOYEE this_ where this_.EMP_NUMBER between ? and ?
Employee Number   : 5002
Employee Name     : Ananad Desai
Department        : IT
Basic Pay         : 93000.00
Allowances        : 29000.00
Deductions        : 15000.00
Netpay            : 107000.00
========================================
Employee Number   : 5003
Employee Name     : Karan Singh
Department        : SALES
Basic Pay         : 88000.00
Allowances        : 27000.00
Deductions        : 14500.00
Netpay            : 100500.00
========================================
Employee Number   : 5004
Employee Name     : Sudhir
Department        : SALES
Basic Pay         : 83000.00
Allowances        : 25000.00
Deductions        : 14100.00
Netpay            : 93900.00
========================================
```

6.7.3 Example Using eqProperty()

```
// File Name: EmployeeManipulation.java
// Criteria Queries: eqProperty()

package com.hdemo;

import java.util.List;

import org.hibernate.Criteria;
import org.hibernate.Session;
import org.hibernate.SessionFactory;
import org.hibernate.Transaction;
import org.hibernate.criterion.Property;


public class EmployeeManipulation {

  @SuppressWarnings("unchecked")
  public static void main(String[] args) throws Exception {
        SessionFactory sessionFactory = HibernateUtil.getSession
                                                      Factory();
        Session session = sessionFactory.openSession();
        Transaction txn = session.beginTransaction();

        Criteria criteria = session.createCriteria(Employee.class);
        // deductions > allowances
             criteria.add(Property.forName("deductions").eqProperty
                                                 ("allowances"));

        List<Employee> employeeList = criteria.list();
        for (int i = 0; i < employeeList.size(); i++) {
             Employee employee = employeeList.get(i);
             System.out.println("Employee Number : " +
                                          employee.getEmpNumber());
             System.out.println("Employee Name   : " +
                                            employee.getEmpName());
             System.out.println("Department      : " +
                                         employee.getDepartment());
```

```
                System.out.println("Basic Pay              : " +
                                              employee.getBasicpay());
                System.out.println("Allowances            : " +
                                            employee.getAllowances());
                System.out.println("Deductions            : " +
                                            employee.getDeductions());
                System.out.println("Netpay                  : " +
                                                employee.getNetpay());

      System.out.println("======================================\n\n");
         }

         txn.commit();
         session.close();
         sessionFactory.close();
    }
  }
```

```
Hibernate: select this_.ID as ID0_0_, this_.ALLOWANCES as
ALLOWANCES0_0_, this_.BASIC_PAY as BASIC3_0_0_, this_.DEDUCTIONS as
DEDUCTIONS0_0_, this_.DEPT as DEPT0_0_, this_.EMP_NAME as EMP6_0_0_,
this_.EMP_NUMBER as EMP7_0_0_, this_.NETPAY as NETPAY0_0_ from EMPLOYEE
this_ where this_.DEDUCTIONS=this_.ALLOWANCES
```

6.7.4 Example Using `like()`

```
// File Name: EmployeeManipulation.java
// Criteria Queries: like()

package com.hdemo;

import java.util.List;

import org.hibernate.Criteria;
import org.hibernate.Session;
import org.hibernate.SessionFactory;
import org.hibernate.Transaction;
import org.hibernate.criterion.Property;

public class EmployeeManipulation {
```

```
@SuppressWarnings("unchecked")
public static void main(String[] args) throws Exception {
      SessionFactory sessionFactory = HibernateUtil.getSession
                                                       Factory();
      Session session = sessionFactory.openSession();
      Transaction txn = session.beginTransaction();

      Criteria criteria = session.createCriteria(Employee.class);
      criteria.add(Property.forName("empName").like("A_h%"));

      List<Employee> employeeList = criteria.list();
      for (int i = 0; i < employeeList.size(); i++) {
            Employee employee = employeeList.get(i);
            System.out.println("Employee Number : " +
                                         employee.getEmpNumber());
            System.out.println("Employee Name    : " +
                                           employee.getEmpName());
            System.out.println("Department        : " +
                                        employee.getDepartment());
            System.out.println("Basic Pay          : " +
                                          employee.getBasicpay());
            System.out.println("Allowances        : " +
                                        employee.getAllowances());
            System.out.println("Deductions        : " +
                                        employee.getDeductions());
            System.out.println("Netpay              : " +
                                            employee.getNetpay());

  System.out.println("========================================\n\n");
      }

      txn.commit();
      session.close();
      sessionFactory.close();
   }
}
```

Hibernate: select this_.ID as ID0_0_, this_.ALLOWANCES as

```
ALLOWANCES0_0_, this_.BASIC_PAY as BASIC3_0_0_, this_.DEDUCTIONS as
DEDUCTIONS0_0_, this_.DEPT as DEPT0_0_, this_.EMP_NAME as EMP6_0_0_,
this_.EMP_NUMBER as EMP7_0_0_, this_.NETPAY as NETPAY0_0_ from EMPLOYEE
this_ where this_.EMP_NAME like ?
   Employee Number   : 5006
   Employee Name     : Achfa
   Department        : SALES
   Basic Pay         : 74000.00
   Allowances        : 22500.00
   Deductions        : 12500.00
   Netpay            : 84000.00
   ========================================
```

6.7.5 Example Using `like()` and `MatchMode.START`

```
// File Name: EmployeeManipulation.java
// Criteria Queries: like() and MatchMode.START

package com.hdemo;

import java.util.List;

import org.hibernate.Criteria;
import org.hibernate.Session;
import org.hibernate.SessionFactory;
import org.hibernate.Transaction;
import org.hibernate.criterion.MatchMode;
import org.hibernate.criterion.Property;

public class EmployeeManipulation {
  @SuppressWarnings("unchecked")
  public static void main(String[] args) throws Exception {
      SessionFactory sessionFactory = HibernateUtil.getSession
                                                     Factory();
      Session session = sessionFactory.openSession();
      Transaction txn = session.beginTransaction();

      Criteria criteria = session.createCriteria(Employee.class);
```

```
        criteria.add(Property.forName("empName").like("A",
                                              MatchMode.START));
        List<Employee> employeeList = criteria.list();
        for (int i = 0; i < employeeList.size(); i++) {
            Employee employee = employeeList.get(i);
            System.out.println("Employee Number : " +
                                        employee.getEmpNumber());
            System.out.println("Employee Name    : " +
                                          employee.getEmpName());
            System.out.println("Department       : " +
                                       employee.getDepartment());
            System.out.println("Basic Pay        : " +
                                         employee.getBasicpay());
            System.out.println("Allowances       : " +
                                       employee.getAllowances());
            System.out.println("Deductions       : " +
                                       employee.getDeductions());
            System.out.println("Netpay           : " +
                                           employee.getNetpay());

    System.out.println("====================================\n\n");
        }

        txn.commit();
        session.close();
        sessionFactory.close();
    }
}
```

```
Hibernate: select this_.ID as ID0_0_, this_.ALLOWANCES as ALLOWANCES0_0_, this_.BASIC_PAY as BASIC3_0_0_, this_.DEDUCTIONS as DEDUCTIONS0_0_, this_.DEPT as DEPT0_0_, this_.EMP_NAME as EMP6_0_0_, this_.EMP_NUMBER as EMP7_0_0_, this_.NETPAY as NETPAY0_0_ from EMPLOYEE this_ where this_.EMP_NAME like ?
Employee Number   : 5002
Employee Name     : Ananad Desai
Department        : IT
Basic Pay         : 93000.00
```

```
Allowances          : 29000.00
Deductions          : 15000.00
Netpay              : 107000.00
=========================================

Employee  Number    : 5005
Employee  Name      : Ajay
Department          : SALES
Basic  Pay          : 78000.00
Allowances          : 23000.00
Deductions          : 14000.00
Netpay              : 87000.00
=========================================
Employee  Number    : 5006
Employee  Name      : Achfa
Department          : SALES
Basic  Pay          : 74000.00
Allowances          : 22500.00
Deductions          : 12500.00
Netpay              : 84000.00
=========================================
```

6.7.6 Example Using `like()` and `MatchMode.EXACT`

```
// File Name: EmployeeManipulation.java
// Criteria Queries: like() and MatchMode.EXACT

package com.hdemo;

import java.util.List;

import org.hibernate.Criteria;
import org.hibernate.Session;
import org.hibernate.SessionFactory;
import org.hibernate.Transaction;
import org.hibernate.criterion.MatchMode;
import org.hibernate.criterion.Property;
```

```
public class EmployeeManipulation {

   @SuppressWarnings("unchecked")
   public static void main(String[] args) throws Exception {
         SessionFactory sessionFactory = HibernateUtil.getSession
                                                        Factory();
         Session session = sessionFactory.openSession();
         Transaction txn = session.beginTransaction();

         Criteria criteria = session.createCriteria(Employee.class);
         criteria.add(Property.forName("empName").like("Ravi Chandran",
                                                 MatchMode.EXACT));

         List<Employee> employeeList = criteria.list();
         for (int i = 0; i < employeeList.size(); i++) {
               Employee employee = employeeList.get(i);
               System.out.println("Employee Number : " +
                                          employee.getEmpNumber());
               System.out.println("Employee Name    : " +
                                            employee.getEmpName());
               System.out.println("Department         : " +
                                         employee.getDepartment());
               System.out.println("Basic Pay          : " +
                                           employee.getBasicpay());
               System.out.println("Allowances         : " +
                                         employee.getAllowances());
               System.out.println("Deductions         : " +
                                         employee.getDeductions());
               System.out.println("Netpay               : " +
                                             employee.getNetpay());

  System.out.println("====================================\n\n");
         }

         txn.commit();
         session.close();
         sessionFactory.close();
```

```
    }
  }
```

```
Hibernate: select this_.ID as ID0_0_, this_.ALLOWANCES as ALLOWANCES0_0_, this_.BASIC_PAY as BASIC3_0_0_, this_.DEDUCTIONS as DEDUCTIONS0_0_, this_.DEPT as DEPT0_0_, this_.EMP_NAME as EMP6_0_0_, this_.EMP_NUMBER as EMP7_0_0_, this_.NETPAY as NETPAY0_0_ from EMPLOYEE this_ where this_.EMP_NAME like ?
Employee Number   : 5010
Employee Name     : Ravi Chandran
Department        : INVENTORY
Basic Pay         : 55800.00
Allowances        : 15100.00
Deductions        : 7000.00
Netpay            : 63900.00
========================================
```

6.7.7 Example Using `in(Collection)`

```
// File Name: EmployeeManipulation.java
// Criteria Queries: in(Collection)

package com.hdemo;

import java.util.ArrayList;
import java.util.List;

import org.hibernate.Criteria;
import org.hibernate.Session;
import org.hibernate.SessionFactory;
import org.hibernate.Transaction;
import org.hibernate.criterion.Property;

public class EmployeeManipulation {

  @SuppressWarnings("unchecked")
  public static void main(String[] args) throws Exception {
      SessionFactory sessionFactory = HibernateUtil.getSession
                                                   Factory();
```

```
        Session session = sessionFactory.openSession();
        Transaction txn = session.beginTransaction();

        ArrayList<Integer> alEmpNum = new ArrayList<Integer>();
        alEmpNum.add(5002);
        alEmpNum.add(5004);
        alEmpNum.add(5006);

        Criteria criteria = session.createCriteria(Employee.class);
        criteria.add(Property.forName("empNumber").in(alEmpNum));

        List<Employee> employeeList = criteria.list();
        for (int i = 0; i < employeeList.size(); i++) {
              Employee employee = employeeList.get(i);
              System.out.println("Employee Number : " +
                                        employee.getEmpNumber());
              System.out.println("Employee Name     : " +
                                          employee.getEmpName());
              System.out.println("Department         : " +
                                       employee.getDepartment());
              System.out.println("Basic Pay          : " +
                                         employee.getBasicpay());
              System.out.println("Allowances         : " +
                                       employee.getAllowances());
              System.out.println("Deductions         : " +
                                       employee.getDeductions());
              System.out.println("Netpay               : " +
                                           employee.getNetpay());

  System.out.println("=====================================\n\n");
        }

        txn.commit();
        session.close();
        sessionFactory.close();
  }
}
```

```
Hibernate: select this_.ID as ID0_0_, this_.ALLOWANCES as ALLOWANCES0_0_, this_.BASIC_PAY as BASIC3_0_0_, this_.DEDUCTIONS as DEDUCTIONS0_0_, this_.DEPT as DEPT0_0_, this_.EMP_NAME as EMP6_0_0_, this_.EMP_NUMBER as EMP7_0_0_, this_.NETPAY as NETPAY0_0_ from EMPLOYEE this_ where this_.EMP_NUMBER in (?, ?, ?)
Employee Number   : 5002
Employee Name     : Ananad Desai
Department        : IT
Basic Pay         : 93000.00
Allowances        : 29000.00
Deductions        : 15000.00
Netpay            : 107000.00
=========================================
Employee Number   : 5004
Employee Name     : Sudhir
Department        : SALES
Basic Pay         : 83000.00
Allowances        : 25000.00
Deductions        : 14100.00
Netpay            : 93900.00
=========================================

Employee Number   : 5006
Employee Name     : Achfa
Department        : SALES
Basic Pay         : 74000.00
Allowances        : 22500.00
Deductions        : 12500.00
Netpay            : 84000.00
=========================================
```

6.7.8 Example Using avg()

```
// File Name: EmployeeManipulation.java
// Illustrates Criteria Query: Property avg()
```

```
package com.hdemo;

import org.hibernate.Criteria;
import org.hibernate.Session;
import org.hibernate.SessionFactory;
import org.hibernate.Transaction;
import org.hibernate.criterion.Property;

public class EmployeeManipulation {

  public static void main(String[] args) throws Exception {
        SessionFactory sessionFactory = HibernateUtil.getSession
                                                        Factory();
        Session session = sessionFactory.openSession();
        Transaction txn = session.beginTransaction();

        Criteria criteria = session.createCriteria(Employee.class);
        criteria.setProjection(Property.forName("netpay").avg());
        Object avgOfNetpay = criteria.uniqueResult();
        System.out.printf("Average of Netpay: " + avgOfNetpay);

        txn.commit();
        session.close();
        sessionFactory.close();
  }
}
```

```
Hibernate: select avg(this_.NETPAY) as y0_ from EMPLOYEE this_
Average of Netpay: 87580.0
```

6.7.9 Aggregate Functions: `count()`, `min()`, `max()`

```
// File Name: EmployeeManipulation.java
// Illustrates Property's Aggregate Functions

package com.hdemo;

import java.util.Iterator;
import java.util.List;
```

```
import org.hibernate.Criteria;
import org.hibernate.Session;
import org.hibernate.SessionFactory;
import org.hibernate.Transaction;
import org.hibernate.criterion.ProjectionList;
import org.hibernate.criterion.Projections;
import org.hibernate.criterion.Property;

public class EmployeeManipulation {

  @SuppressWarnings("unchecked")
  public static void main(String[] args) throws Exception {
       SessionFactory sessionFactory = HibernateUtil.getSession
                                                  Factory();

       Session session = sessionFactory.openSession();
       Transaction txn = session.beginTransaction();

       // Finds Number of Employees in each department, Sum of
Basic Pay in each department, Average of Basic Pay in each department,
       // Minimum Basic Pay in each department, Maximum Basic Pay
in each department
       Criteria criteria = session.createCriteria(Employee.class);
       ProjectionList projectionList = Projections.projectionList();
       projectionList.add(Property.forName("department").group());
       projectionList.add(Property.forName("id").count());
       projectionList.add(Projections.sum("basicpay"));
       projectionList.add(Property.forName("basicpay").avg());
       projectionList.add(Property.forName("basicpay").min());
       projectionList.add(Property.forName("basicpay").max());
       criteria.setProjection(projectionList);

       List list = criteria.list();
       System.out.printf("%-15s %-30s %25s %25s %25s %25s",
"Department", "No. of Employees in Department", "SUM OF BASIC PAY",
"AVERAGE OF BASIC PAY", "MINIMUM BASIC PAY", "MAXIMUM BASIC PAY");
       for (Iterator it = list.iterator(); it.hasNext();) {
```

```
                Object[] row = (Object[])it.next();
                System.out.printf("\n%-15s %30s %25s %25s %25s %25s",
row[0], row[1], row[2], row[3], row[4], row[5]);
            }

            txn.commit();
            session.close();
            sessionFactory.close();
        }
    }
```

```
Hibernate: select this_.DEPT as y0_, count(this_.ID) as y1_, sum(this_.BASIC_PAY) as y2_, avg(this_.BASIC_PAY) as y3_, min(this_.BASIC_PAY) as y4_, max(this_.BASIC_PAY) as y5_ from EMPLOYEE this_ group by this_.DEPT
```

DEPARTMENT	NO. OF EMPLOYEES IN DEPARTMENT	SUM OF BASIC PAY	AVERAGE OF BASIC PAY	MINIMUM BASIC PAY	MAXIMUM BASIC PAY
INVENTORY	1	55800.00	55800.00	55800.00	55800.00
IT	2	191000.00	95500.00	93000.00	98000.00
PERSONAL	2	136000.00	68000.00	67000.00	69000.00
SALES	4	323000.00	80750.00	74000.00	88000.00
STATIONARY	1	65000.00	65000.00	65000.00	65000.00

6.7.10 Example using `asc()`, `desc()`

```
// File Name: EmployeeManipulation.java
// Criteria Queries: Property

package com.hdemo;

import java.util.List;

import org.hibernate.Criteria;
import org.hibernate.Session;
import org.hibernate.SessionFactory;
import org.hibernate.Transaction;
import org.hibernate.criterion.Property;
```

```
public class EmployeeManipulation {

  @SuppressWarnings("unchecked")
    public static void main(String[] args) throws Exception {
         SessionFactory sessionFactory = HibernateUtil.getSession
                                                          Factory();
         Session session = sessionFactory.openSession();
         Transaction txn = session.beginTransaction();

         //First sorted by department, then each group is sorted by
                                                              empName
         Criteria criteria = session.createCriteria(Employee.class);
         criteria.addOrder(Property.forName("department").desc());
         criteria.addOrder(Property.forName("empName").asc());

         List<Employee> employeeList = criteria.list();
         System.out.printf("%-15s %-20s %-15s %10s %10s
                                                  %10s %10s \n",
                                         "EMP. NUMBER", "EMP. NAME",
"DEPT.", "BASIC PAY", "ALLOWANCES", "DEDUCTIONS", "NETPAY");
         for (int i = 0; i < employeeList.size(); i++) {
              Employee employee = employeeList.get(i);
              System.out.printf("%-15d %-20s %-15s %10.2f
                                       %10.2f %10.2f %10.2f \n",
              employee.getEmpNumber(), employee.getEmpName(),
                 employee.getDepartment(), employee.getBasicpay(),
              employee.getAllowances(), employee.getDeductions(),
                                              employee.getNetpay());
         }

         txn.commit();
         session.close();
         sessionFactory.close();

    }
}
```

6.8 DetachedCriteria AND SUB-QUERIES

Query used within another query is called sub-query. These sub-queries are very much used to simplify complex conditions/constraints while selecting data.

The following example lists the details about the employee who is having minimum net pay.

```
// File Name: EmployeeManipulation.java
// Criteria Queries: Sub-query

package com.hdemo;

import java.util.List;

import org.hibernate.Criteria;
import org.hibernate.Session;
import org.hibernate.SessionFactory;
import org.hibernate.Transaction;
import org.hibernate.criterion.DetachedCriteria;
import org.hibernate.criterion.Property;

public class EmployeeManipulation {

  @SuppressWarnings("unchecked")
  public static void main(String[] args) throws Exception {
        SessionFactory sessionFactory = HibernateUtil.getSession
                                                          Factory();
        Session session = sessionFactory.openSession();
        Transaction txn = session.beginTransaction();

        // Find employee who is having minimum netpay

        DetachedCriteria dCriteriaMaxNetpay = Detached
                                   Criteria.forClass(Employee.class);

  CriteriaMaxNetpay.setProjection(Property.forName("netpay").min());

        Criteria criteria = session.createCriteria(Employee.class);

    criteria.add(Property.forName("netpay").eq(dCriteriaMaxNetpay));

        List<Employee> employeeList = criteria.list();
```

```
            System.out.printf("%-15s    %-20s    %-15s    %10s    %10s
%10s    %10s \n", "EMP. NUMBER", "EMP. NAME", "DEPT.", "BASIC PAY",
"ALLOWANCES", "DEDUCTIONS", "NETPAY");
            for (int i = 0; i < employeeList.size(); i++) {
                  Employee employee = employeeList.get(i);
                  System.out.printf("%-15d    %-20s    %-15s    %10.2f
%10.2f    %10.2f    %10.2f \n", employee.getEmpNumber(),
employee.getEmpName(), employee.getDepartment(), employee.getBasicpay(),
employee.getAllowances(), employee.getDeductions(), employee.getNetpay());
            }

            txn.commit();
            session.close();
            sessionFactory.close();
      }
  }
```

```
Hibernate: select this_.ID as ID0_0_, this_.ALLOWANCES as
ALLOWANCES0_0_, this_.BASIC_PAY as BASIC3_0_0_, this_.DEDUCTIONS as
DEDUCTIONS0_0_, this_.DEPT as DEPT0_0_, this_.EMP_NAME as EMP6_0_0_,
this_.EMP_NUMBER as EMP7_0_0_, this_.NETPAY as NETPAY0_0_ from EMPLOYEE
this_ where this_.NETPAY = (select min(this_.NETPAY) as y0_ from
EMPLOYEE this_)
```

EMP. NUMBER	EMP. NAME	DEPT.	BASIC PAY	ALLOWA-NCES	DEDUCT-IONS	NETPAY
5010	Ravi Chandran	INVENTORY	55800.00	15100.00	7000.00	63900.00

The `org.hibernate.criterion.DetachedCriteria` class is used to create "*detached*" Criteria, which is detached (not attached) from Hibernate Session.

Normally, `Criteria` is created using `createCriteria()` method of `Session` object.

Example:

```
Session session = sessionFactory.openSession();
Criteria criteria = session.createCriteria(Employee.class);
```

The **`DetachedCriteria`** is created with out using `Session` object as follows.

```
DetachedCriteria dCriteriaMaxNetpay = DetachedCriteria.forClass
(Employee.class);
```

The DetachedCriteria is similar like Criteria and the defined methods in DetachedCriteria are functionally same to the corresponding method in Criteria. But, DetachedCriteria is detached (separated) from Session so that we can not run this **DetachedCriteria** query directly.

The following method attaches specified Hibernate Session with the invoking DetachedCriteria query and returns Criteria object, which can be run to get the result.

```
Criteria  getExecutableCriteria(Session  session)
```

Some other methods in this DetachedCriteria class are as follows.

```
DetachedCriteria  add(Criterion  criterion)

DetachedCriteria  addOrder(Order  order)

DetachedCriteria  createAlias(String  associationPath,  String  alias)

DetachedCriteria  createCriteria(String  associationPath)

DetachedCriteria createCriteria(String associationPath, String alias)

static  DetachedCriteria  forClass(Class  clazz)

static  DetachedCriteria   forClass(Class  clazz,  String  alias)

static  DetachedCriteria  forEntityName(String  entityName)

static DetachedCriteria forEntityName(String entityName, String alias)

DetachedCriteria setFetchMode(String associationPath, FetchMode mode)

DetachedCriteria  setProjection(Projection  projection)

DetachedCriteria  setResultTransformer(ResultTransformer
                                                    resultTransformer)
```

The following example shows how to make run DetachedCriteria query.

```
//  File  Name:  EmployeeManipulation.java
//  Criteria  Queries:  DetachedCriteria

package  com.hdemo;

import  java.util.List;
```

```
import org.hibernate.Criteria;
import org.hibernate.Session;
import org.hibernate.SessionFactory;
import org.hibernate.Transaction;
import org.hibernate.criterion.DetachedCriteria;
public class EmployeeManipulation {

   @SuppressWarnings("unchecked")
   public static void main(String[] args) throws Exception {

          DetachedCriteria detachedCriteria = Detached
                                        Criteria.forClass(Employee.class);

          SessionFactory sessionFactory = HibernateUtil.getSession
                                                            Factory();
          Session session = sessionFactory.openSession();
          Transaction txn = session.beginTransaction();

          Criteria criteria = detachedCriteria.getExecutable
                                                     Criteria(session);

          List<Employee> employeeList = criteria.list();
          System.out.printf("%-15s    %-20s    %-15s    %10s    %10s
%10s    %10s \n", "EMP. NUMBER", "EMP. NAME", "DEPT.", "BASIC PAY",
"ALLOWANCES", "DEDUCTIONS", "NETPAY");
          for (int i = 0; i < employeeList.size(); i++) {
                Employee employee = employeeList.get(i);
                System.out.printf("%-15d    %-20s    %-15s    %10.2f
%10.2f    %10.2f     %10.2f \n", employee.getEmpNumber(),
employee.getEmpName(), employee.getDepartment(), employee.getBasicpay(),
employee.getAllowances(), employee.getDeductions(), employee.getNetpay());
          }

          txn.commit();
          session.close();
          sessionFactory.close();
   }
}
```

6.8.1 Sub-Queries with `org.hibernate.criterion.Property` Methods

This `DetachedCriteria` can be used to express a sub-query (Query with in another query). To simplify sub-query operations with `DetachedCriteria`, the `org.hibernate.criterion.Property` class provides the following methods; each method accepts `DetachedCriteria` as its argument and returns `Criterion` object, which can be passed as argument to the `add()` method of `Criteria/DetachedCriteria` to define one criterion condition.

```
Criterion  eq(DetachedCriteria  subselect)
Criterion  eqAll(DetachedCriteria  subselect)
Criterion  ge(DetachedCriteria  subselect)
Criterion  geAll(DetachedCriteria  subselect)
Criterion  geSome(DetachedCriteria  subselect)
Criterion  gt(DetachedCriteria  subselect)
Criterion  gtAll(DetachedCriteria  subselect)
Criterion  gtSome(DetachedCriteria  subselect)
Criterion  in(DetachedCriteria  subselect)
Criterion  le(DetachedCriteria  subselect)
Criterion  leAll(DetachedCriteria  subselect)
Criterion  leSome(DetachedCriteria  subselect)
Criterion  lt(DetachedCriteria  subselect)
Criterion  ltAll(DetachedCriteria  subselect)
Criterion  ltSome(DetachedCriteria  subselect)
Criterion  ne(DetachedCriteria  subselect)
Criterion  notIn(DetachedCriteria  subselect)
```

The following example demonstrates how to use some of the above methods.

```
//  File  Name:  EmployeeManipulation.java
//  Criteria  Queries:  DetachedCriteria


package  com.hdemo;

import  java.math.BigDecimal;
import  java.util.List;
```

```
import org.hibernate.Criteria;
import org.hibernate.Session;
import org.hibernate.SessionFactory;
import org.hibernate.Transaction;
import org.hibernate.criterion.DetachedCriteria;
import org.hibernate.criterion.Projections;
import org.hibernate.criterion.Property;
import org.hibernate.criterion.Restrictions;

public class EmployeeManipulation {

  public static void main(String[] args) throws Exception {

        SessionFactory sessionFactory = HibernateUtil.getSession
                                                        Factory();
        Session session = sessionFactory.openSession();
        Transaction txn = session.beginTransaction();

        DetachedCriteria detachedCriteria = DetachedCriteria.forClass
                                                  (Employee.class);

  detachedCriteria.setProjection(Projections.property("empNumber"));
        detachedCriteria.add(Restrictions.between("netpay", new
        BigDecimal(85000.00), new BigDecimal(100000.0)));

        System.out.println(" in() method");
        Criteria criteria = session.createCriteria(Employee.class);

   criteria.add(Property.forName("empNumber").in(detachedCriteria));
        displayList(criteria);

        System.out.println("\n notIn() method");
        criteria = session.createCriteria(Employee.class);

criteria.add(Property.forName("empNumber").notIn(detachedCriteria));
        displayList(criteria);
```

```
        System.out.println("\n  ltAll()  method  (ALL)");
        criteria  =  session.createCriteria(Employee.class);

    criteria.add(Property.forName("empNumber").ltAll(detachedCriteria));
        displayList(criteria);

        System.out.println("\n  ltSome()  method  (ANY)");
        criteria  =  session.createCriteria(Employee.class);

   criteria.add(Property.forName("empNumber").ltSome(detachedCriteria));
        displayList(criteria);

        txn.commit();
        session.close();
        sessionFactory.close();
    }

    @SuppressWarnings("unchecked")
    static  void  displayList(Criteria  criteria)  {
        List<Employee>  employeeList  =  criteria.list();
        System.out.printf("%-15s     %-20s     %-15s     %10s     %10s
%10s     %10s \n",  "EMP.  NUMBER",  "EMP.  NAME",  "DEPT.",  "BASIC  PAY",
"ALLOWANCES",  "DEDUCTIONS",  "NETPAY");
        for  (int  i  =  0;  i  <  employeeList.size();  i++)  {
            Employee  employee  =  employeeList.get(i);
            System.out.printf("%-15d     %-20s     %-15s     %10.2f
%10.2f     %10.2f      %10.2f  \n",   employee.getEmpNumber(),
employee.getEmpName(),  employee.getDepartment(),  employee.getBasicpay(),
employee.getAllowances(), employee.getDeductions(), employee.getNetpay());
        }

    }
}
```

The ALL keyword requires that all values from the sub-select comply with the comparison operator. The SOME and ANY keywords require that at least one pair complies.

The expression = ANY (equal any) is equivalent to the keyword IN. The expression <> ALL (not equal all) is equivalent to using the NOT IN keyword. The keywords ANY and SOME are equivalent. The following SQL operations illustrate the difference between ALL and SOME (ANY).

6.8.2 Sub-Queries with `org.hibernate.criterion.Subqueries` Methods

The `org.hibernate.criterion.Subqueries` class provides several sophisticated methods (all are static), which are used to deal with sub-queries (may be used as an alternative to the listed methods of `org.hibernate.criterion.Property` class in the previous section).

```
Criterion eq(Object value, DetachedCriteria dc)
Criterion eqAll(Object value, DetachedCriteria dc)
Criterion exists(DetachedCriteria dc)
Criterion ge(Object value, DetachedCriteria dc)
Criterion geAll(Object value, DetachedCriteria dc)
Criterion geSome(Object value, DetachedCriteria dc)
Criterion gt(Object value, DetachedCriteria dc)
Criterion gtAll(Object value, DetachedCriteria dc)
Criterion gtSome(Object value, DetachedCriteria dc)
Criterion in(Object value, DetachedCriteria dc)
Criterion le(Object value, DetachedCriteria dc)
Criterion leAll(Object value, DetachedCriteria dc)
Criterion leSome(Object value, DetachedCriteria dc)
Criterion lt(Object value, DetachedCriteria dc)
Criterion ltAll(Object value, DetachedCriteria dc)
Criterion ltSome(Object value, DetachedCriteria dc)
Criterion ne(Object value, DetachedCriteria dc)
Criterion notExists(DetachedCriteria dc)
Criterion notIn(Object value, DetachedCriteria dc)
Criterion propertyEq(String propertyName, DetachedCriteria dc)
Criterion propertyEqAll(String propertyName, DetachedCriteria dc)
Criterion propertyGe(String propertyName, DetachedCriteria dc)
Criterion propertyGeAll(String propertyName, DetachedCriteria dc)
Criterion propertyGeSome(String propertyName, DetachedCriteria dc)
Criterion propertyGt(String propertyName, DetachedCriteria dc)
```

```
Criterion propertyGtAll(String propertyName, DetachedCriteria dc)
Criterion propertyGtSome(String propertyName, DetachedCriteria dc)
Criterion propertyIn(String propertyName, DetachedCriteria dc)
Criterion propertyLe(String propertyName, DetachedCriteria dc)
Criterion propertyLeAll(String propertyName, DetachedCriteria dc)
Criterion propertyLeSome(String propertyName, DetachedCriteria dc)
Criterion propertyLt(String propertyName, DetachedCriteria dc)
Criterion propertyLtAll(String propertyName, DetachedCriteria dc)
Criterion propertyLtSome(String propertyName, DetachedCriteria dc)
Criterion propertyNe(String propertyName, DetachedCriteria dc)
Criterion propertyNotIn(String propertyName, DetachedCriteria dc)
```

The following example lists the details about the employee who is having minimum net pay.

```
// File Name: EmployeeManipulation.java
// Criteria Queries: Sub-query

package com.hdemo;

import java.util.List;

import org.hibernate.Criteria;
import org.hibernate.Session;
import org.hibernate.SessionFactory;
import org.hibernate.Transaction;
import org.hibernate.criterion.DetachedCriteria;
import org.hibernate.criterion.Property;
import org.hibernate.criterion.Subqueries;

public class EmployeeManipulation {

  @SuppressWarnings("unchecked")
  public static void main(String[] args) throws Exception {
        SessionFactory sessionFactory = HibernateUtil.getSession
                                                            Factory();
        Session session = sessionFactory.openSession();
        Transaction txn = session.beginTransaction();
```

```
        // Find employee who is having minimum netpay

        DetachedCriteria dCriteriaMaxNetpay = Detached
Criteria.forClass(Employee.class);

dCriteriaMaxNetpay.setProjection(Property.forName("netpay").min());

        Criteria criteria = session.createCriteria(Employee.class);
        criteria.add(Subqueries.propertyEq("netpay", dCriteria
MaxNetpay));

        List<Employee> employeeList = criteria.list();
        System.out.printf("%-15s    %-20s    %-15s    %10s    %10s
%10s    %10s \n", "EMP. NUMBER", "EMP. NAME", "DEPT.", "BASIC PAY",
"ALLOWANCES", "DEDUCTIONS", "NETPAY");
        for (int i = 0; i < employeeList.size(); i++) {
            Employee employee = employeeList.get(i);
            System.out.printf("%-15d    %-20s    %-15s    %10.2f
%10.2f    %10.2f    %10.2f \n", employee.getEmpNumber(),
employee.getEmpName(), employee.getDepartment(), employee.getBasicpay(),
employee.getAllowances(), employee.getDeductions(), employee.getNetpay());
        }

        txn.commit();
        session.close();
        sessionFactory.close();
    }
  }
```

Hibernate: select this_.ID as ID0_0_, this_.ALLOWANCES as ALLOWANCES0_0_, this_.BASIC_PAY as BASIC3_0_0_, this_.DEDUCTIONS as DEDUCTIONS0_0_, this_.DEPT as DEPT0_0_, this_.EMP_NAME as EMP6_0_0_, this_.EMP_NUMBER as EMP7_0_0_, this_.NETPAY as NETPAY0_0_ from EMPLOYEE this_ where this_.NETPAY = (select min(this_.NETPAY) as y0_ from EMPLOYEE this_)

EMP. NUMBER	EMP. NAME	DEPT.	BASIC PAY	ALLOWA-NCES	DEDUCT-IONS	NETPAY
5010	Ravi Chandran	INVENTORY	55800.00	15100.00	7000.00	63900.00

The following example illustrates some of the Subqueries methods to deal with "set" data.

```
// File Name: EmployeeManipulation.java
// Criteria Queries: Subqueries

package com.hdemo;

import java.math.BigDecimal;
import java.util.List;

import org.hibernate.Criteria;
import org.hibernate.Session;
import org.hibernate.SessionFactory;
import org.hibernate.Transaction;
import org.hibernate.criterion.DetachedCriteria;
import org.hibernate.criterion.Projections;
import org.hibernate.criterion.Restrictions;
import org.hibernate.criterion.Subqueries;

public class EmployeeManipulation {

   public static void main(String[] args) throws Exception {

         SessionFactory sessionFactory = HibernateUtil.getSession
                                                    Factory();
         Session session = sessionFactory.openSession();
         Transaction txn = session.beginTransaction();

         DetachedCriteria detachedCriteria = Detached
                              Criteria.forClass(Employee.class);

    detachedCriteria.setProjection(Projections.property("empNumber"));
         detachedCriteria.add(Restrictions.between("netpay", new
                BigDecimal(85000.00), new BigDecimal(100000.0)));

         System.out.println(" propertyIn() method");
         Criteria criteria = session.createCriteria(Employee.class);
         criteria.add(Subqueries.propertyIn("empNumber",
                                              detachedCriteria));
```

```
        displayList(criteria);

        System.out.println("\n  propertyNotIn()  method");
        criteria  =  session.createCriteria(Employee.class);
        criteria.add(Subqueries.propertyNotIn("empNumber",
                                              detachedCriteria));
        displayList(criteria);

        System.out.println("\n  propertyLtAll()  method  (ALL)");
        criteria  =  session.createCriteria(Employee.class);
        criteria.add(Subqueries.propertyLtAll("empNumber",
                                              detachedCriteria));
        displayList(criteria);

        System.out.println("\n  propertyLtSome()  method  (ANY)");
        criteria  =  session.createCriteria(Employee.class);
        criteria.add(Subqueries.propertyLtSome("empNumber",
                                              detachedCriteria));
        displayList(criteria);

        txn.commit();
        session.close();
        sessionFactory.close();
    }

    @SuppressWarnings("unchecked")
    static  void  displayList(Criteria  criteria)  {
        List<Employee>  employeeList  =  criteria.list();
        System.out.printf("%-15s    %-20s    %-15s    %10s    %10s
%10s    %10s  \n",  "EMP.  NUMBER",  "EMP.  NAME",  "DEPT.",  "BASIC  PAY",
"ALLOWANCES",  "DEDUCTIONS",  "NETPAY");
        for  (int  i  =  0;  i  <  employeeList.size();  i++)  {
        Employee  employee  =  employeeList.get(i);
        System.out.printf("%-15d   %-20s   %-15s    %10.2f    %10.2f
%10.2f    %10.2f  \n",  employee.getEmpNumber(),  employee.getEmpName(),
employee.getDepartment(), employee.getBasicpay(), employee.getAllowances(),
employee.getDeductions(),  employee.getNetpay());
        }
```

```
    }
  }
```

propertyIn() method

Hibernate: select this_.ID as ID0_0_, this_.ALLOWANCES as ALLOWANCES0_0_, this_.BASIC_PAY as BASIC3_0_0_, this_.DEDUCTIONS as DEDUCTIONS0_0_, this_.DEPT as DEPT0_0_, this_.EMP_NAME as EMP6_0_0_, this_.EMP_NUMBER as EMP7_0_0_, this_.NETPAY as NETPAY0_0_ from EMPLOYEE this_ where this_.EMP_NUMBER in (select this_.EMP_NUMBER as y0_ from EMPLOYEE this_ where this_.NETPAY between ? and ?)

EMP. NUMBER	EMP. NAME	DEPT.	BASIC PAY	ALLOWA-NCES	DEDUCT-IONS	NETPAY
5004	Sudhir	SALES	83000.00	25000.00	14100.00	93900.00
5005	Ajay	SALES	78000.00	23000.00	14000.00	87000.00

propertyNotIn() method

Hibernate: select this_.ID as ID0_0_, this_.ALLOWANCES as ALLOWANCES0_0_, this_.BASIC_PAY as BASIC3_0_0_, this_.DEDUCTIONS as DEDUCTIONS0_0_, this_.DEPT as DEPT0_0_, this_.EMP_NAME as EMP6_0_0_, this_.EMP_NUMBER as EMP7_0_0_, this_.NETPAY as NETPAY0_0_ from EMPLOYEE this_ where this_.EMP_NUMBER not in (select this_.EMP_NUMBER as y0_ from EMPLOYEE this_ where this_.NETPAY between ? and ?)

EMP. NUMBER	EMP. NAME	DEPT.	BASIC PAY	ALLOWA-NCES	DEDUCT-IONS	NETPAY
5001	Ibrahim	IT	98000.00	30000.00	15000.00	113000.00
5002	Ananad Desai	IT	93000.00	29000.00	15000.00	107000.00
5003	Karan Singh	SALES	88000.00	27000.00	14500.00	100500.00
5006	Achfa	SALES	74000.00	22500.00	12500.00	84000.00
5007	Indiran	PERSONAL	69000.00	16000.00	8000.00	77000.00
5008	Nitin Otagiri	PERSONAL	67000.00	15800.00	7000.00	75800.00
5009	Kumar	STATIONARY	65000.00	15700.00	7000.00	73700.00
5010	Ravi Chandran	INVENTORY	55800.00	15100.00	7000.00	63900.00

propertyLtAll() method (ALL)

Hibernate: select this_.ID as ID0_0_, this_.ALLOWANCES as ALLOWANCES0_0_, this_.BASIC_PAY as BASIC3_0_0_, this_.DEDUCTIONS as

DEDUCTIONS0_0_, this_.DEPT as DEPT0_0_, this_.EMP_NAME as EMP6_0_0_, this_.EMP_NUMBER as EMP7_0_0_, this_.NETPAY as NETPAY0_0_ from EMPLOYEE this_ where this_.EMP_NUMBER < all (select this_.EMP_NUMBER as y0_ from EMPLOYEE this_ where this_.NETPAY between ? and ?)

EMP. NUMBER	EMP. NAME	DEPT.	BASIC PAY	ALLOWA-NCES	DEDUCT-IONS	NETPAY
5001	Ibrahim	IT	98000.00	30000.00	15000.00	113000.00
5002	Ananad Desai	IT	93000.00	29000.00	15000.00	107000.00
5003	Karan Singh	SALES	88000.00	27000.00	14500.00	100500.00

propertyLtSome() method (ANY)

Hibernate: select this_.ID as ID0_0_, this_.ALLOWANCES as ALLOWANCES0_0_, this_.BASIC_PAY as BASIC3_0_0_, this_.DEDUCTIONS as DEDUCTIONS0_0_, this_.DEPT as DEPT0_0_, this_.EMP_NAME as EMP6_0_0_, this_.EMP_NUMBER as EMP7_0_0_, this_.NETPAY as NETPAY0_0_ from EMPLOYEE this_ where this_.EMP_NUMBER < some (select this_.EMP_NUMBER as y0_ from EMPLOYEE this_ where this_.NETPAY between ? and ?)

EMP. NUMBER	EMP. NAME	DEPT.	BASIC PAY	ALLOWA-NCES	DEDUCT-IONS	NETPAY
5001	Ibrahim	IT	98000.00	30000.00	15000.00	113000.00
5002	Ananad Desai	IT	93000.00	29000.00	15000.00	107000.00
5003	Karan Singh	SALES	88000.00	27000.00	14500.00	100500.00
5004	Sudhir	SALES	83000.00	25000.00	14100.00	93900.00

The following example illustrates how to use org.hibernate.criterion.Subqueries methods; those are accepting Object values as their first parameter.

```
// File Name: EmployeeManipulation.java
// Criteria Queries: Subqueries eq() method
package com.hdemo;

import org.hibernate.Criteria;
import org.hibernate.Session;
import org.hibernate.SessionFactory;
import org.hibernate.Transaction;
```

```
import org.hibernate.criterion.DetachedCriteria;
import org.hibernate.criterion.Property;
import org.hibernate.criterion.Subqueries;

public class EmployeeManipulation {

    public static void main(String[] args) throws Exception {
        SessionFactory sessionFactory = HibernateUtil.getSession
                                                        Factory();
        Session session = sessionFactory.openSession();
        Transaction txn = session.beginTransaction();

        // Find the minimum netpay
        DetachedCriteria dCriteriaMaxNetpay = Detached
                                   Criteria.forClass(Employee.class);

    dCriteriaMaxNetpay.setProjection(Property.forName("netpay").min());

        // Find Employee Number who is having minimum netpay (from
                 the dCriteriaMaxNetpay DetachedCriteria query)
        DetachedCriteria dCriteriaMaxNetpayEmpNumber =
                            DetachedCriteria.forClass(Employee.class);

        dCriteriaMaxNetpayEmpNumber.setProjection(Property.
                                            forName("empNumber"));
        dCriteriaMaxNetpayEmpNumber.add(Property.forName("netpay")
                                         .eq(dCriteriaMaxNetpay));

        // Check the Emp_Number of the Employee who is having
                                      minimum netpay is 5010 ?
        Criteria criteria = session.createCriteria(Employee.class);
      criteria.add(Subqueries.eq(5010, dCriteriaMaxNetpayEmpNumber));

        if (criteria.list().size() > 0)
            System.out.println("Yes, The Minimum netpay earning
              employee is the one whose Emp_Number is 5010.");
        else
            System.out.println("The Minimum netpay earning employee
                  is not the one whose Emp_Number is 5010.");
```

```
            txn.commit();
            session.close();
            sessionFactory.close();
        }
    }
```

Hibernate: select this_.ID as ID0_0_, this_.ALLOWANCES as ALLOWANCES0_0_, this_.BASIC_PAY as BASIC3_0_0_, this_.DEDUCTIONS as DEDUCTIONS0_0_, this_.DEPT as DEPT0_0_, this_.EMP_NAME as EMP6_0_0_, this_.EMP_NUMBER as EMP7_0_0_, this_.NETPAY as NETPAY0_0_ from EMPLOYEE this_ where ? = (select this_.EMP_NUMBER as y0_ from EMPLOYEE this_ where this_.NETPAY = (select min(this_.NETPAY) as y0_ from EMPLOYEE this_))

Yes, The Minimum netpay earning employee is the one whose Emp_Number is 5010.

6.9 FETCHING DATA FOR ENTITY WITH ASSOCIATION

To illustrate methods used for Association, we will generate some sample data using the following programs. Here, the Employee entity contains one field of type another entity named Salary along with normal fields. Change `hbm2ddl.auto` property in *hibernate.cfg.xml* file to `create`, for clean database tables. And do not forget to add mappings for Employee and Salary entities.

```
            <mapping class="com.hdemo.Employee" />
            <mapping class="com.hdemo.Salary" />
    // File Name: Employee.java
    // Criteria Queries: Associations

    package com.hdemo;

    import javax.persistence.CascadeType;
    import javax.persistence.Column;
    import javax.persistence.Entity;
    import javax.persistence.GeneratedValue;
    import javax.persistence.Id;
    import javax.persistence.JoinColumn;
    import javax.persistence.OneToOne;
    import javax.persistence.Table;

    import org.hibernate.annotations.GenericGenerator;
```

```
@Entity
@Table(name = "EMPLOYEE")
public class Employee {

  @Id
  @GeneratedValue(generator = "idGen")
  @GenericGenerator(name = "idGen", strategy = "uuid.hex")
  @Column(name = "ID", length = 32)
  private String id = "";

  @Column(name = "EMP_NUMBER", unique = true, nullable = false)
  private Integer empNumber;

  @Column(name = "EMP_NAME", length = 64, nullable = false)
  private String empName;

  @OneToOne(cascade = { CascadeType.PERSIST, CascadeType.REMOVE })
  @JoinColumn(name = "EMP_SALARY", unique = true)
  private Salary salary;

  public String getId() {
        return id;
  }

  public void setId(String id) {
        this.id = id;
  }

  public Integer getEmpNumber() {
        return empNumber;
  }

  public void setEmpNumber(Integer empNumber) {
        this.empNumber = empNumber;
  }

  public String getEmpName() {
```

```
        return empName;
    }

    public void setEmpName(String empName) {
        this.empName = empName;
    }

    public Salary getSalary() {
        return salary;
    }

    public void setSalary(Salary salary) {
        this.salary = salary;
    }

}

// File Name: Salary.java
// Criteria Queries: Associations

package com.hdemo;

import javax.persistence.Column;
import javax.persistence.Entity;
import javax.persistence.GeneratedValue;
import javax.persistence.Id;
import javax.persistence.Table;

import org.hibernate.annotations.GenericGenerator;

@Entity
@Table(name = "SALARY")
public class Salary {

    @Id
    @GeneratedValue(generator = "idGen")
    @GenericGenerator(name = "idGen", strategy = "uuid.hex")
    @Column(name = "ID", length = 32)
    private String id = "";
```

```
@Column(name = "BPAY")
private Double basicpay;

@Column(name = "ALLOWANCES")
private Double allowances;

@Column(name = "DEDUCTIONS")
private Double deductions;

@Column(name = "NETPAY")
private Double netpay;

public String getId() {
      return id;
}

public void setId(String id) {
      this.id = id;
}

public Double getBasicpay() {
      return basicpay;
}

public void setBasicpay(Double basicpay) {
      this.basicpay = basicpay;
}

public Double getAllowances() {
      return allowances;
}

public void setAllowances(Double allowances) {
      this.allowances = allowances;
}

public Double getDeductions() {
      return deductions;
```

```
    }

    public void setDeductions(Double deductions) {
          this.deductions = deductions;
    }

    public Double getNetpay() {
          return netpay;
    }

    public void setNetpay(Double netpay) {
          this.netpay = netpay;
    }

}

// File Name: EmployeeManipulation.java
// Main Program

package com.hdemo;

import java.util.List;

import org.hibernate.Criteria;
import org.hibernate.Session;
import org.hibernate.SessionFactory;
import org.hibernate.Transaction;

public class EmployeeManipulation {
    @SuppressWarnings("unchecked")
    public static void main(String[] args) throws Exception {
          SessionFactory sessionFactory = HibernateUtil.getSession
                                                            Factory();
          Session session = sessionFactory.openSession();
          Transaction txn = session.beginTransaction();

          Employee employee1 = new Employee();
          employee1.setEmpNumber(5001);
```

```
        employee1.setEmpName("Ibrahim");
        Salary salary1 = new Salary();
        salary1.setBasicpay(10000.00);
        salary1.setAllowances(3000.00);
        salary1.setDeductions(2000.00);
        salary1.setNetpay(salary1.getBasicpay() + salary1.get
                          Allowances() - salary1.getDeductions());
        employee1.setSalary(salary1);
        session.persist(employee1);

        Employee employee2 = new Employee();
        employee2.setEmpNumber(5002);
        employee2.setEmpName("Kumar");
        Salary salary2 = new Salary();
        salary2.setBasicpay(5000.00);
        salary2.setAllowances(1500.00);
        salary2.setDeductions(1000.00);
        salary2.setNetpay(salary2.getBasicpay() + salary2.get
                          Allowances() - salary2.getDeductions());
        employee2.setSalary(salary2);
        session.persist(employee2);

        Employee employee3 = new Employee();
        employee3.setEmpNumber(5003);
        employee3.setEmpName("Ajay");
        Salary salary3 = new Salary();
        salary3.setBasicpay(15000.00);
        salary3.setAllowances(4000.00);
        salary3.setDeductions(2500.00);
        salary3.setNetpay(salary3.getBasicpay() + salary3.get
                          Allowances() - salary3.getDeductions());
        employee3.setSalary(salary3);
        session.persist(employee3);

        txn.commit();
        session.close();
        session = sessionFactory.openSession();
        txn = session.beginTransaction();

        Criteria criteria = session.createCriteria(Employee.class);
```

```
        List<Employee> list = criteria.list();
        for (int i = 0; i < list.size(); i++) {
              Employee employee = list.get(i);
              System.out.println("\nEmployee Number : " +
employee.getEmpNumber());
              System.out.println("Employee Name : " +
employee.getEmpName());
              System.out.println("Employee Basicpay : " +
employee.getSalary().getBasicpay());
              System.out.println("Employee Allowances : " +
employee.getSalary().getAllowances());
              System.out.println("Employee Deductions : " +
employee.getSalary().getDeductions());
              System.out.println("Employee Netpay : " +
employee.getSalary().getNetpay());
        }

        txn.commit();
        session.close();

        sessionFactory.close();
    }
}
```

```
Hibernate: insert into SALARY (ALLOWANCES, BPAY, DEDUCTIONS, NETPAY, ID) values (?, ?, ?, ?, ?)
Hibernate: insert into EMPLOYEE (EMP_NAME, EMP_NUMBER, EMP_SALARY, ID) values (?, ?, ?, ?)
Hibernate: insert into SALARY (ALLOWANCES, BPAY, DEDUCTIONS, NETPAY, ID) values (?, ?, ?, ?, ?)
Hibernate: insert into EMPLOYEE (EMP_NAME, EMP_NUMBER, EMP_SALARY, ID) values (?, ?, ?, ?)
Hibernate: insert into SALARY (ALLOWANCES, BPAY, DEDUCTIONS, NETPAY, ID) values (?, ?, ?, ?, ?)
Hibernate: insert into EMPLOYEE (EMP_NAME, EMP_NUMBER, EMP_SALARY, ID) values (?, ?, ?, ?)
Hibernate: select this_.ID as ID0_1_, this_.EMP_NAME as EMP2_0_1_, this_.EMP_NUMBER as EMP3_0_1_, this_.EMP_SALARY as EMP4_0_1_, salary2_.ID as ID1_0_, salary2_.ALLOWANCES as ALLOWANCES1_0_, salary2_.BPAY as BPAY1_0_, salary2_.DEDUCTIONS as DEDUCTIONS1_0_, salary2_.NETPAY as NETPAY1_0_ from EMPLOYEE this_ left outer join SALARY salary2_ on
```

```
this_.EMP_SALARY=salary2_.ID

    Employee Number      : 5001
    Employee Name        : Ibrahim
    Employee Basicpay    : 10000.0
    Employee Allowances  : 3000.0
    Employee Deductions  : 2000.0
    Employee Netpay      : 11000.0

    Employee Number      : 5002
    Employee Name        : Kumar
    Employee Basicpay    : 5000.0
    Employee Allowances  : 1500.0
    Employee Deductions  : 1000.0
    Employee Netpay      : 5500.0

    Employee Number      : 5003
    Employee Name        : Ajay
    Employee Basicpay    : 15000.0
    Employee Allowances  : 4000.0
    Employee Deductions  : 2500.0
    Employee Netpay      : 16500.0

    mysql> desc employee;
     Field          Type           Null     Key    Default  Extra
     ID              varchar(32)    NO      PRI     NULL
     EMP_NAME       varchar(64)     NO              NULL
     EMP_NUMBER     int(11)         NO      UNI     NULL
     EMP_SALARY     varchar(32)    YES      UNI     NULL
    4 rows in set (0.00 sec)

    mysql> desc salary;
     Field          Type           Null     Key    Default  Extra
     ID             varchar(32)     NO      PRI     NULL
     ALLOWANCES     double         YES              NULL
     BPAY           double         YES              NULL
     DEDUCTIONS     double         YES              NULL
     NETPAY         double         YES              NULL
    5 rows in set (0.00 sec)

    mysql> select * from employee;
```

ID	EMP_NAME	EMP_NUMBER	EMP_SALARY
402881f81f6e5a1a011f6e5a1f5b0001 402881f81f6e5a1a011f6e5a1f600002	Ibrahim	5001	
402881f81f6e5a1a011f6e5a1f680003 402881f81f6e5a1a011f6e5a1f680004	Kumar	5002	
402881f81f6e5a1a011f6e5a1f690005 402881f81f6e5a1a011f6e5a1f690006	Ajay	5003	

```
3 rows in set (0.00 sec)

mysql> select * from salary;
```

ID	ALLOWANCES	BPAY	DEDUCTIONS	NETPAY
402881f81f6e5a1a011f6e5a1f600002	3000	10000	2000	11000
402881f81f6e5a1a011f6e5a1f680004	1500	5000	1000	5500
402881f81f6e5a1a011f6e5a1f690006	4000	15000	2500	16500

Now, change the hbm2ddl.auto property in *hibernate.cfg.xml* file to update to keep the generated sample data.

The following example uses createCriteria() method to get Criteria object for "salary" field (object of Salary Entity) from Employee's Criteria object to make conditions on the association Entity object "salary".

```
// File Name: EmployeeManipulation.java
// Criteria Queries: Association

package com.hdemo;

import java.util.List;

import org.hibernate.Criteria;
import org.hibernate.Session;
import org.hibernate.SessionFactory;
import org.hibernate.Transaction;
import org.hibernate.criterion.Restrictions;

public class EmployeeManipulation {

  @SuppressWarnings("unchecked")
  public static void main(String[] args) throws Exception {
        SessionFactory sessionFactory = HibernateUtil.getSession
                                                        Factory();
        Session session = sessionFactory.openSession();
        Transaction txn = session.beginTransaction();

        //Find Employees, those having netpay more than 10000
        Criteria employeeCriteria = session.create
                                        Criteria(Employee.class);
        Criteria salaryInEmployeeCriteria = employee
                                 Criteria.createCriteria("salary");
        salaryInEmployeeCriteria.add(Restrictions.gt("netpay",
                                                         10000.0));

        List<Employee> list = employeeCriteria.list();
        for (int i = 0; i < list.size(); i++) {
              Employee employee = list.get(i);
```

```
            System.out.println("\nEmployee Number : " +
                                    employee.getEmpNumber());

            System.out.println("Employee Name    : " +
                                      employee.getEmpName());
            System.out.println("Employee Basicpay : " +
                        employee.getSalary().getBasicpay());
            System.out.println("Employee Allowances : " +
                      employee.getSalary().getAllowances());

            System.out.println("Employee Deductions : " +
                      employee.getSalary().getDeductions());

            System.out.println("Employee Netpay : " +
                          employee.getSalary().getNetpay());

        }

        txn.commit();

        session.close();

        sessionFactory.close();

    }

}
```

Hibernate: select this_.ID as ID0_1_, this_.EMP_NAME as EMP2_0_1_, this_.EMP_NUMBER as EMP3_0_1_, this_.EMP_SALARY as EMP4_0_1_, salary1_.ID as ID1_0_, salary1_.ALLOWANCES as ALLOWANCES1_0_, salary1_.BPAY as BPAY1_0_, salary1_.DEDUCTIONS as DEDUCTIONS1_0_, salary1_.NETPAY as NETPAY1_0_ from EMPLOYEE this_ inner join SALARY salary1_ on this_.EMP_SALARY=salary1_.ID where salary1_.NETPAY>?

```
Employee Number      : 5001
Employee Name        : Ibrahim
Employee Basicpay    : 10000.0
Employee Allowances  : 3000.0
Employee Deductions  : 2000.0
Employee Netpay      : 11000.0

Employee Number      : 5003
Employee Name        : Ajay
Employee Basicpay    : 15000.0
Employee Allowances  : 4000.0
```

```
Employee Deductions  : 2500.0
Employee Netpay      : 16500.0
```

The `createCriteria()` method used in the above program creates a new instance (object) of `Criteria` for referring "salary" field. We can re-write the above program using `createAlias()` as below, which does not create new instance of `Criteria` for accessing "salary" field.

```
// File Name: EmployeeManipulation.java
// Criteria Queries: Association

package com.hdemo;

import java.util.List;

import org.hibernate.Criteria;
import org.hibernate.Session;
import org.hibernate.SessionFactory;
import org.hibernate.Transaction;
import org.hibernate.criterion.Restrictions;

public class EmployeeManipulation {

   @SuppressWarnings("unchecked")
   public static void main(String[] args) throws Exception {
          SessionFactory sessionFactory = HibernateUtil.getSession
                                                              Factory();
          Session session = sessionFactory.openSession();
          Transaction txn = session.beginTransaction();

          //Find Employees, those having netpay more than 10000
          Criteria employeeCriteria = session.create
                                            Criteria(Employee.class);
          employeeCriteria.createAlias("salary", "sal");       //
                                             (field_name, alias_name)
          employeeCriteria.add(Restrictions.gt("sal.netpay", 10000.0));

          List<Employee> list = employeeCriteria.list();
          for (int i = 0; i < list.size(); i++) {
                Employee employee = list.get(i);
                System.out.println("\nEmployee Number : " +
                                            employee.getEmpNumber());
```

```
                System.out.println("Employee Name       : " +
                                        employee.getEmpName());
                System.out.println("Employee Basicpay  :  " +
                               employee.getSalary().getBasicpay());
                System.out.println("Employee Allowances  :  " +
                             employee.getSalary().getAllowances());
                System.out.println("Employee Deductions  :  " +
                             employee.getSalary().getDeductions());
                System.out.println("Employee Netpay  :  " +
                                 employee.getSalary().getNetpay());
            }

            txn.commit();
            session.close();

            sessionFactory.close();
        }
    }
```

Hibernate: select this_.ID as ID0_1_, this_.EMP_NAME as EMP2_0_1_, this_.EMP_NUMBER as EMP3_0_1_, this_.EMP_SALARY as EMP4_0_1_, sal1_.ID as ID1_0_, sal1_.ALLOWANCES as ALLOWANCES1_0_, sal1_.BPAY as BPAY1_0_, sal1_.DEDUCTIONS as DEDUCTIONS1_0_, sal1_.NETPAY as NETPAY1_0_ from EMPLOYEE this_ inner join SALARY sal1_ on this_.EMP_SALARY=sal1_.ID where sal1_.NETPAY>?

```
Employee Number       : 5001
Employee Name         : Ibrahim
Employee Basicpay     : 10000.0
Employee Allowances   : 3000.0
Employee Deductions   : 2000.0
Employee Netpay       : 11000.0

Employee Number       : 5003
Employee Name         : Ajay
Employee Basicpay     : 15000.0
Employee Allowances   : 4000.0
```

```
Employee Deductions   : 2500.0
Employee Netpay       : 16500.0
```

The following example uses `FetchMode.JOIN` mode to access "salary" field of "Employee" entity.

```
// File Name: EmployeeManipulation.java
// Criteria Queries: Association

package com.hdemo;

import java.util.List;

import org.hibernate.Criteria;
import org.hibernate.FetchMode;
import org.hibernate.Session;
import org.hibernate.SessionFactory;
import org.hibernate.Transaction;

public class EmployeeManipulation {

  @SuppressWarnings("unchecked")
  public static void main(String[] args) throws Exception {
       SessionFactory sessionFactory = HibernateUtil.getSession
                                                       Factory();
       Session session = sessionFactory.openSession();
       Transaction txn = session.beginTransaction();

       Criteria employeeCriteria = session.create
                                  Criteria(Employee.class);
       employeeCriteria.setFetchMode("salary", FetchMode.JOIN);

       List<Employee> list = employeeCriteria.list();
       for (int i = 0; i < list.size(); i++) {
            Employee employee = list.get(i);
            System.out.println("\nEmployee Number : " +
                                  employee.getEmpNumber());
            System.out.println("Employee Name   : " +
                                    employee.getEmpName());
```

```
            System.out.println("Employee Basicpay : " +
                          employee.getSalary().getBasicpay());
            System.out.println("Employee Allowances : " +
                          employee.getSalary().getAllowances());
            System.out.println("Employee Deductions : " +
                          employee.getSalary().getDeductions());
            System.out.println("Employee Netpay : " +
                          employee.getSalary().getNetpay());
        }

        txn.commit();
        session.close();

        sessionFactory.close();
    }
}
```

```
Hibernate: select this_.ID as ID0_1_, this_.EMP_NAME as EMP2_0_1_, this_.EMP_NUMBER as EMP3_0_1_, this_.EMP_SALARY as EMP4_0_1_, salary2_.ID as ID1_0_, salary2_.ALLOWANCES as ALLOWANCES1_0_, salary2_.BPAY as BPAY1_0_, salary2_.DEDUCTIONS as DEDUCTIONS1_0_, salary2_.NETPAY as NETPAY1_0_ from EMPLOYEE this_ left outer join SALARY salary2_ on this_.EMP_SALARY=salary2_.ID

Employee Number      : 5001
Employee Name        : Ibrahim
Employee Basicpay    : 10000.0
Employee Allowances  : 3000.0
Employee Deductions  : 2000.0
Employee Netpay      : 11000.0

Employee Number      : 5002
Employee Name        : Kumar
Employee Basicpay    : 5000.0
Employee Allowances  : 1500.0
Employee Deductions  : 1000.0
Employee Netpay      : 5500.0
```

```
Employee Number      : 5003
Employee Name        : Ajay
Employee Basicpay    : 15000.0
Employee Allowances  : 4000.0
Employee Deductions  : 2500.0
Employee Netpay      : 16500.0
```

The following example uses `FetchMode.SELECT` mode to access "salary" field of "Employee" entity.

```
// File Name: EmployeeManipulation.java
// Criteria Queries: Association

package com.hdemo;

import java.util.List;

import org.hibernate.Criteria;
import org.hibernate.FetchMode;
import org.hibernate.Session;
import org.hibernate.SessionFactory;
import org.hibernate.Transaction;

public class EmployeeManipulation {

  @SuppressWarnings("unchecked")
  public static void main(String[] args) throws Exception {
        SessionFactory sessionFactory = HibernateUtil.getSession
                                                          Factory();
        Session session = sessionFactory.openSession();
        Transaction txn = session.beginTransaction();

        Criteria employeeCriteria = session.create
                                         Criteria(Employee.class);
        employeeCriteria.setFetchMode("salary", FetchMode.SELECT);

        List<Employee> list = employeeCriteria.list();
        for (int i = 0; i < list.size(); i++) {
              Employee employee = list.get(i);
```

```
                System.out.println("\nEmployee Number : " +
                                          employee.getEmpNumber());
                System.out.println("Employee Name     : " +
                                            employee.getEmpName());
                System.out.println("Employee Basicpay : " +
                                 employee.getSalary().getBasicpay());
                System.out.println("Employee Allowances : " +
                               employee.getSalary().getAllowances());
                System.out.println("Employee Deductions : " +
                               employee.getSalary().getDeductions());
                System.out.println("Employee Netpay : " +
                                   employee.getSalary().getNetpay());

            }

            txn.commit();
            session.close();

            sessionFactory.close();
        }
    }
```

Hibernate: select this_.ID as ID0_0_, this_.EMP_NAME as EMP2_0_0_, this_.EMP_NUMBER as EMP3_0_0_, this_.EMP_SALARY as EMP4_0_0_ from EMPLOYEE this_

Hibernate: select salary0_.ID as ID1_0_, salary0_.ALLOWANCES as ALLOWANCES1_0_, salary0_.BPAY as BPAY1_0_, salary0_.DEDUCTIONS as DEDUCTIONS1_0_, salary0_.NETPAY as NETPAY1_0_ from SALARY salary0_ where salary0_.ID=?

Hibernate: select salary0_.ID as ID1_0_, salary0_.ALLOWANCES as ALLOWANCES1_0_, salary0_.BPAY as BPAY1_0_, salary0_.DEDUCTIONS as DEDUCTIONS1_0_, salary0_.NETPAY as NETPAY1_0_ from SALARY salary0_ where salary0_.ID=?

Hibernate: select salary0_.ID as ID1_0_, salary0_.ALLOWANCES as ALLOWANCES1_0_, salary0_.BPAY as BPAY1_0_, salary0_.DEDUCTIONS as DEDUCTIONS1_0_, salary0_.NETPAY as NETPAY1_0_ from SALARY salary0_ where salary0_.ID=?

```
Employee Number     : 5001
Employee Name       : Ibrahim
```

```
Employee Basicpay      : 10000.0
Employee Allowances    : 3000.0
Employee Deductions    : 2000.0
Employee Netpay        : 11000.0

Employee Number        : 5002
Employee Name          : Kumar
Employee Basicpay      : 5000.0
Employee Allowances    : 1500.0
Employee Deductions    : 1000.0
Employee Netpay        : 5500.0

Employee Number        : 5003
Employee Name          : Ajay
Employee Basicpay      : 15000.0
Employee Allowances    : 4000.0
Employee Deductions    : 2500.0
Employee Netpay        : 16500.0
```

6.10 FETCHING `Collection` DATA FOR ENTITY

Execute the following programs to generate some sample data for testing Collection fields. Adjust the required configurations in *hibernate.cfg.xml* file.

```
// File Name: Employee.java
// Criteria Queries: Associations

package com.hdemo;

import java.util.List;

import javax.persistence.CascadeType;
import javax.persistence.Column;
import javax.persistence.Entity;
import javax.persistence.GeneratedValue;
import javax.persistence.Id;
import javax.persistence.JoinColumn;
import javax.persistence.OneToMany;
```

```
import javax.persistence.Table;

import org.hibernate.annotations.GenericGenerator;

@Entity
@Table(name = "EMPLOYEE")
public class Employee {

  private static final long serialVersionUID = 1L;

  @Id
  @GeneratedValue(generator = "idGen")
  @GenericGenerator(name = "idGen", strategy = "uuid.hex")
  @Column(name = "ID", length = 32)
  private String id = "";

  @Column(name = "EMP_NUMBER", unique = true, nullable = false)
  private Integer empNumber;

  @Column(name = "EMP_NAME", length = 64, nullable = false)
  private String empName;

  @OneToMany(cascade = CascadeType.ALL)
  @JoinColumn(name = "EMPLOYEE_ADDRESS")
  private List<Address> addresses;

  public String getId() {
       return id;
  }

  public void setId(String id) {
       this.id = id;
  }

  public Integer getEmpNumber() {
       return empNumber;
  }

  public void setEmpNumber(Integer empNumber) {
```

```
            this.empNumber = empNumber;
      }

      public String getEmpName() {
            return empName;
      }

      public void setEmpName(String empName) {
            this.empName = empName;
      }

      public List<Address> getAddresses() {
            return addresses;
      }

      public void setAddresses(List<Address> addresses) {
            this.addresses = addresses;
      }

}

// File Name: Address.java
// Criteria Queries: Associations

package com.hdemo;

import java.io.Serializable;

import javax.persistence.Column;
import javax.persistence.Entity;
import javax.persistence.GeneratedValue;
import javax.persistence.Id;
import javax.persistence.Table;

import org.hibernate.annotations.GenericGenerator;

@Entity
@Table(name = "ADDRESS")
public class Address implements Serializable {
```

```
private static final long serialVersionUID = 1L;

@Id
@GeneratedValue(generator = "idGen")
@GenericGenerator(name = "idGen", strategy = "uuid.hex")
@Column(name = "ID", length = 32)
private String id = "";

@Column(name = "HOUSE_NUMBER", length = 8)
private String houseNumber;

@Column(name = "STREET_NAME", length = 64)
private String streetName;

@Column(name = "CITY_NAME", length = 64)
private String cityName;

@Column(name = "COUNTRY_NAME", length = 64)
private String countryName;

@Column(name = "POSTAL_CODE", length = 16)
private String postalCode;

public String getId() {
      return id;
}

public void setId(String id) {
      this.id = id;
}

public String getHouseNumber() {
      return houseNumber;
}

public void setHouseNumber(String houseNumber) {
      this.houseNumber = houseNumber;
}
```

```
public String getStreetName() {
     return streetName;
}

public void setStreetName(String streetName) {
     this.streetName = streetName;
}

public String getCityName() {
     return cityName;
}

public void setCityName(String cityName) {
     this.cityName = cityName;
}

public String getCountryName() {
     return countryName;
}

public void setCountryName(String countryName) {
     this.countryName = countryName;
}

public String getPostalCode() {
     return postalCode;
}

public void setPostalCode(String postalCode) {
     this.postalCode = postalCode;
}

public String toString() {
  return "[House Number: " + houseNumber +
  "\nStreet Name   : " + streetName +
  "\nCity Name     : " + cityName +
  "\nCountry Name  : " + countryName +
```

```
        "\nPostal Code   : " + postalCode +
                  "]";
    }
}

// File Name: EmployeeManipulation.java
// Criteria Queries: Associations

package com.hdemo;

import java.util.ArrayList;
import java.util.List;

import org.hibernate.Session;
import org.hibernate.SessionFactory;
import org.hibernate.Transaction;

public class EmployeeManipulation {

  @SuppressWarnings("unchecked")
  public static void main(String[] args) throws Exception {
        SessionFactory sessionFactory = HibernateUtil.getSession
                                                    Factory();
        Session session = sessionFactory.openSession();
        Transaction txn = session.beginTransaction();

        Employee employee1 = new Employee();
        employee1.setEmpNumber(5001);

        employee1.setEmpName("Ibrahim");
        Address employee1Address1 = new Address();
        employee1Address1.setHouseNumber("C-13-4");
        employee1Address1.setStreetName("Jalan Munsi Abdullah");
        employee1Address1.setCityName("Kuala Lumpur");
        employee1Address1.setCountryName("Malaysia");
        employee1Address1.setPostalCode("50100");
        Address employee1Address2 = new Address();
        employee1Address2.setHouseNumber("3-121");
```

```
employee1Address2.setStreetName("Middle  Street");
employee1Address2.setCityName("Tiruchirapalli");
employee1Address2.setCountryName("India");
employee1Address2.setPostalCode("621302");
List<Address> employee1Addresses = new ArrayList<Address>();
employee1Addresses.add(employee1Address1);
employee1Addresses.add(employee1Address2);
employee1.setAddresses(employee1Addresses);
session.save(employee1);
System.out.println("The  object  employee1  is  persisted  with
                                                        session");
Employee  employee2  =  new  Employee();
employee2.setEmpNumber(5002);
employee2.setEmpName("Kumar");
Address  employee2Address1  =  new  Address();
employee2Address1.setHouseNumber("T-4");
employee2Address1.setStreetName("Nehru  Street");
employee2Address1.setCityName("Chennai");
employee2Address1.setCountryName("India");
employee2Address1.setPostalCode("600020");
List<Address> employee2Addresses = new ArrayList<Address>();
employee2Addresses.add(employee2Address1);
employee2.setAddresses(employee2Addresses);
session.save(employee2);
System.out.println("The  object  employee2  is  persisted  with
                                                        session");
Employee  employee3  =  new  Employee();
employee3.setEmpNumber(5003);
employee3.setEmpName("Ajay");
employee3.setAddresses(null);
session.save(employee3);
System.out.println("The  object  employee3  is  persisted  with
                                                        session");
txn.commit();
```

```
        System.out.println("Transaction on this session is
                                                    committed");
        txn = session.beginTransaction();
        System.out.println("Accessing Employee Objects\n\n");
        List<Employee> employeeList = session.create
                                Criteria(Employee.class).list();
        for (int i = 0; i < employeeList.size(); i++) {
              Employee employee = employeeList.get(i);
              System.out.println("Employee Number : " +
                                          employee.getEmpNumber());
   System.out.println("Employee Name   : " + employee.getEmpName());
   List<Address> addresses = employee.getAddresses();
              for (int j=0; addresses != null && j <
                                          addresses.size(); j++) {
        System.out.println("Employee Address (" + (j+1) + ") : "
                                              + addresses.get(j));
              }
  System.out.println("=======================================\n\n");
        }

        txn.commit();
        sessionFactory.close();
  }
}
```

```
The object employee1 is persisted with session
The object employee2 is persisted with session
The object employee3 is persisted with session
Hibernate: insert into EMPLOYEE (EMP_NAME, EMP_NUMBER, ID) values
(?, ?, ?)
Hibernate: insert into ADDRESS (CITY_NAME, COUNTRY_NAME, HOUSE_NUMBER,
POSTAL_CODE, STREET_NAME, ID) values (?, ?, ?, ?, ?, ?)
Hibernate: insert into ADDRESS (CITY_NAME, COUNTRY_NAME, HOUSE_NUMBER,
POSTAL_CODE, STREET_NAME, ID) values (?, ?, ?, ?, ?, ?)
Hibernate: insert into EMPLOYEE (EMP_NAME, EMP_NUMBER, ID) values
(?, ?, ?)
```

```
Hibernate: insert into ADDRESS (CITY_NAME, COUNTRY_NAME, HOUSE_NUMBER,
        POSTAL_CODE, STREET_NAME, ID) values (?, ?, ?, ?, ?, ?)
Hibernate: insert into EMPLOYEE (EMP_NAME, EMP_NUMBER, ID) values
                                                          (?, ?, ?)
Hibernate: update ADDRESS set EMPLOYEE_ADDRESS=? where ID=?
Hibernate: update ADDRESS set EMPLOYEE_ADDRESS=? where ID=?
Hibernate: update ADDRESS set EMPLOYEE_ADDRESS=? where ID=?
Transaction on this session is committed
Accessing Employee Objects

Hibernate: select this_.ID as ID0_0_, this_.EMP_NAME as EMP2_0_0_,
               this_.EMP_NUMBER as EMP3_0_0_ from EMPLOYEE this_
Employee Number     : 5001
Employee Name       : Ibrahim
Employee Address (1) : [House Number: C-13-4
Street Name         : Jalan Munsi Abdullah
City Name           : Kuala Lumpur
Country Name        : Malaysia
Postal Code         : 50100]
Employee Address(2): [House Number: 3-121
Street Name         : Middle Street
City Name           : Tiruchirapalli
Country Name        : India
Postal Code         : 621302]
========================================

Employee Number     : 5002
Employee Name       : Kumar
Employee Address (1) : [House Number: T-4
Street Name         : Nehru Street
City Name           : Chennai
Country Name        : India
Postal Code         : 600020]
========================================

Employee Number     : 5003
Employee Name       : Ajay
========================================
```

```
mysql> desc employee;
```

Field	Type	Null	Key	Default	Extra
ID	varchar(32)	NO	PRI	NULL	
EMP_NAME	varchar(64)	NO		NULL	
EMP_NUMBER	int(11)	NO	UNI	NULL	

```
3 rows in set (0.00 sec)

mysql> desc address;
```

Field	Type	Null	Key	Default	Extra
ID	varchar(32)	NO	PRI	NULL	
CITY_NAME	varchar(64)	YES		NULL	
COUNTRY_NAME	varchar(64)	YES		NULL	
HOUSE_NUMBER	varchar(8)	YES		NULL	
POSTAL_CODE	varchar(16)	YES		NULL	
STREET_NAME	varchar(64)	YES		NULL	
EMPLOYEE_ADDRESS	varchar(32)	YES	MUL	NULL	

```
7 rows in set (0.00 sec)

mysql> select * from employee;
```

ID	EMP_NAME	EMP_NUMBER
402881f81f6ecdce011f6ecdd2840001	Ibrahim	5001
402881f81f6ecdce011f6ecdd29c0004	Kumar	5002
402881f81f6ecdce011f6ecdd29c0006	Ajay	5003

```
3 rows in set (0.00 sec)

mysql> select * from address;
```

ID	CITY_ NAME	COUNTRY_ NAME	HOUSE_ NUMBER	POSTAL_ CODE	STREET_ NAME	EMPLOYEE_ ADDRESS
402881f81f6ecdce011f6ecdd29b0002	Kuala Lumpur	Malaysia	C-13-4	50100	Jalan Munsi Abdullah	402881f81f6ecdce011f6ecdd2840001

```
402881f81f6ecdce   Tiruchi-  India    3-121   621302  Middle
011f6ecdd29c0003   rapalli                            Street
402881f81f6ecdce
011f6ecdd2840001

402881f81f6ecdce
011f6ecdd29c0005   Chennai   India    T-4     600020  Nehru
402881f81f6ecdce                                      Street
011f6ecdd29c0004

3 rows in set (0.00 sec)
```

The following example lists employees, those are having more than one addresses.

(using `Restrictions's static Criterion sizeEq(String propertyName, int size)` method)

```
// File Name: EmployeeManipulation.java
// Criteria Queries: Associations

package com.hdemo;

import java.util.List;

import org.hibernate.Session;
import org.hibernate.SessionFactory;
import org.hibernate.Transaction;
import org.hibernate.criterion.Restrictions;

public class EmployeeManipulation {

  @SuppressWarnings("unchecked")
  public static void main(String[] args) throws Exception {
        SessionFactory sessionFactory = HibernateUtil.getSession
                                                        Factory();
        Session session = sessionFactory.openSession();
        Transaction txn = session.beginTransaction();

        System.out.println("Select all Employees, those are having
                                  more than one address \n\n");
        List<Employee> employeeList = session.create
Criteria(Employee.class).add(Restrictions.sizeGe("addresses", 2)).list();
```

```
        for (int i = 0; i < employeeList.size(); i++) {
              Employee employee = employeeList.get(i);
              System.out.println("Employee Number : " + employee.
                                                          getEmpNumber());
              System.out.println("Employee Name     : " +
                                                   employee.getEmpName());
              List<Address> addresses = employee.getAddresses();
              for (int j=0; addresses != null && j <
                                             addresses.size(); j++) {
                    System.out.println("Employee Address (" + (j+1)
                                         + ") : " + addresses.get(j));
              }

    System.out.println("========================================\n\n");
        }

        txn.commit();
        sessionFactory.close();
    }
  }
```

Select all Employees, those are having more than one address

Hibernate: select this_.ID as ID0_0_, this_.EMP_NAME as EMP2_0_0_, this_.EMP_NUMBER as EMP3_0_0_ from EMPLOYEE this_ where ? <= (select count(*) from ADDRESS where this_.ID=EMPLOYEE_ADDRESS)

Employee Number : 5001

Employee Name : Ibrahim

Hibernate: select addresses0_.EMPLOYEE_ADDRESS as EMPLOYEE7_1_, addresses0_.ID as ID1_, addresses0_.ID as ID1_0_, addresses0_.CITY_NAME as CITY2_1_0_, addresses0_.COUNTRY_NAME as COUNTRY3_1_0_, addresses0_.HOUSE_NUMBER as HOUSE4_1_0_, addresses0_.POSTAL_CODE as POSTAL5_1_0_, addresses0_.STREET_NAME as STREET6_1_0_ from ADDRESS addresses0_ where addresses0_.EMPLOYEE_ADDRESS=?

```
Employee Address (1) : [House Number: C-13-4
Street Name          : Jalan Munsi Abdullah
City Name            : Kuala Lumpur
Country Name         : Malaysia
Postal Code          : 50100]
```

```
Employee Address(2)  : [House Number: 3-121
Street Name          : Middle Street
City Name            : Tiruchirapalli
Country Name         : India
Postal Code          : 621302]
========================================
```

Observe in the result of the above program that Hibernate uses `SELECT` statement when the (selected) `Collection` field is referred (object used for display Address information), *i.e.,* Hibernate used Lazy fetching for Collection data. Rewrite the above main program with out referring `Collection` field (do not display Address Information) as below and run it.

```
// File Name: EmployeeManipulation.java
// Criteria Queries: Associations

package com.hdemo;

import java.util.List;

import org.hibernate.Session;
import org.hibernate.SessionFactory;
import org.hibernate.Transaction;
import org.hibernate.criterion.Restrictions;

public class EmployeeManipulation {

  @SuppressWarnings("unchecked")
  public static void main(String[] args) throws Exception {
        SessionFactory sessionFactory = HibernateUtil.getSession
                                                          Factory();
        Session session = sessionFactory.openSession();
        Transaction txn = session.beginTransaction();

        System.out.println("Select all Employees, those are having
                                  more than one address \n\n");
        List<Employee>  employeeList  =  session.create
Criteria(Employee.class).add(Restrictions.sizeGe("addresses", 2)).list();
        for (int i = 0; i < employeeList.size(); i++) {
              Employee employee = employeeList.get(i);
              System.out.println("Employee Number : " +
                                        employee.getEmpNumber());
```

```
                System.out.println("Employee Name      :  " +
                                                employee.getEmpName());

      System.out.println("========================================\n\n");
        }

        txn.commit();
        sessionFactory.close();
    }
}
```

```
Select all Employees, those are having more than one address

Hibernate: select this_.ID as ID0_0_, this_.EMP_NAME as EMP2_0_0_, this_.EMP_NUMBER as EMP3_0_0_ from EMPLOYEE this_ where ? <= (select count(*) from ADDRESS where this_.ID=EMPLOYEE_ADDRESS)
Employee Number    : 5001
Employee Name      : Ibrahim
========================================
```

Observe that Hibernate did not generate the query for retrieving Address details (`Collection` field) as it follows `SELECT` (Lazy Fetch) fetch while retrieving values for the "addresses" Collection.

The above code is same as below (explicitly specified `SELECT` fetch mode).

```
// File Name: EmployeeManipulation.java
// Criteria Queries: Associations

package com.hdemo;

import java.util.List;

import org.hibernate.FetchMode;
import org.hibernate.Session;
import org.hibernate.SessionFactory;
import org.hibernate.Transaction;
import org.hibernate.criterion.Restrictions;

public class EmployeeManipulation {

    @SuppressWarnings("unchecked")
    public static void main(String[] args) throws Exception {
```

```
        SessionFactory sessionFactory = HibernateUtil.getSession
                                                        Factory();

        Session session = sessionFactory.openSession();
        Transaction txn = session.beginTransaction();

        System.out.println("Select all Employees, those are having
                                        more than one address \n\n");
    List<Employee> employeeList = session.create Criteria(Employee.class)

                    .add(Restrictions.sizeGe("addresses", 2))
                    .setFetchMode("addresses", FetchMode.SELECT)

                                                    .list();
        for (int i = 0; i < employeeList.size(); i++) {
            Employee employee = employeeList.get(i);
            System.out.println("Employee Number : " +
                                        employee.getEmpNumber());
            System.out.println("Employee Name    : " +
                                        employee.getEmpName());
    System.out.println("=======================================\n\n");
        }

        txn.commit();
        sessionFactory.close();
    }
}
```

```
Select all Employees, those are having more than one address

Hibernate: select this_.ID as ID0_0_, this_.EMP_NAME as EMP2_0_0_,
this_.EMP_NUMBER as EMP3_0_0_ from EMPLOYEE this_ where ? <= (select
count(*) from ADDRESS where this_.ID=EMPLOYEE_ADDRESS)
Employee Number : 5001
Employee Name   : Ibrahim
========================================
```

We will change the fetch type to `FetchMode.JOIN` in the above code; then all addresses are also fetched even though they are not referred in the program (Observe the generated SQL).

```
// File Name: EmployeeManipulation.java
// Criteria Queries: Associations

package com.hdemo;

import java.util.List;

import org.hibernate.FetchMode;
import org.hibernate.Session;
import org.hibernate.SessionFactory;
import org.hibernate.Transaction;
import org.hibernate.criterion.Restrictions;

public class EmployeeManipulation {

  @SuppressWarnings("unchecked")
  public static void main(String[] args) throws Exception {
        SessionFactory sessionFactory =
                          HibernateUtil.getSessionFactory();

        Session session = sessionFactory.openSession();
        Transaction txn = session.beginTransaction();

        System.out.println("Select all Employees, those are having
                          more than one address \n\n");
        List<Employee> employeeList = session.create
                                  Criteria(Employee.class)

                       .add(Restrictions.sizeGe("addresses", 2))
                .setFetchMode("addresses", FetchMode.JOIN)

                                       .list();

        for (int i = 0; i < employeeList.size(); i++) {
              Employee employee = employeeList.get(i);
              System.out.println("Employee Number : " +
                                  employee.getEmpNumber());
              System.out.println("Employee Name   : " +
                                    employee.getEmpName());

  System.out.println("======================================\n\n");
```

```
        }

        txn.commit();
        sessionFactory.close();
    }
}
```

```
Select all Employees, those are having more than one address

Hibernate: select this_.ID as ID0_1_, this_.EMP_NAME as EMP2_0_1_, this_.EMP_NUMBER as EMP3_0_1_, addresses2_.EMPLOYEE_ADDRESS as EMPLOYEE7_3_, addresses2_.ID as ID3_, addresses2_.ID as ID1_0_, addresses2_.CITY_NAME as CITY2_1_0_, addresses2_.COUNTRY_NAME as COUNTRY3_1_0_, addresses2_.HOUSE_NUMBER as HOUSE4_1_0_, addresses2_.POSTAL_CODE as POSTAL5_1_0_, addresses2_.STREET_NAME as STREET6_1_0_ from EMPLOYEE this_ left outer join ADDRESS addresses2_ on this_.ID=addresses2_.EMPLOYEE_ADDRESS where ? <= (select count(*) from ADDRESS where this_.ID=EMPLOYEE_ADDRESS)

Employee Number   : 5001
Employee Name     : Ibrahim
========================================
```

Observe from the generated SQL that all data from addresses collection are also selected even though they are not referred in the program. Hibernate uses outer join to fetch the data in our case, so that we are having two rows of same data. We can eliminate this duplication easily using `CriteriaSpecification.DISTINCT_ROOT_ENTITY` result transformer as shown below.

```
// File Name: EmployeeManipulation.java
// Criteria Queries: Associations

package com.hdemo;

import java.util.List;

import org.hibernate.FetchMode;
import org.hibernate.Session;
import org.hibernate.SessionFactory;
import org.hibernate.Transaction;
import org.hibernate.criterion.CriteriaSpecification;
```

```
import org.hibernate.criterion.Restrictions;

public class EmployeeManipulation {

  @SuppressWarnings("unchecked")
  public static void main(String[] args) throws Exception {
        SessionFactory sessionFactory =
                          HibernateUtil.getSessionFactory();
        Session session = sessionFactory.openSession();
        Transaction txn = session.beginTransaction();

        System.out.println("Select all Employees, those are having
                            more than one address \n\n");
        List<Employee> employeeList = session.create
                                    Criteria(Employee.class)
                          .add(Restrictions.sizeGe("addresses", 2))
                .setFetchMode("addresses", FetchMode.JOIN)
   .setResultTransformer(CriteriaSpecification.DISTINCT_ROOT_ENTITY)
                                              .list();
        for (int i = 0; i < employeeList.size(); i++) {
              Employee employee = employeeList.get(i);
              System.out.println("Employee Number : " +
                                   employee.getEmpNumber());
              System.out.println("Employee Name   : " +
                                     employee.getEmpName());
  System.out.println("====================================\n\n");
        }

        txn.commit();
        sessionFactory.close();
  }
}
```

```
Select all Employees, those are having more than one address
```

```
Hibernate: select this_.ID as ID0_1_, this_.EMP_NAME as EMP2_0_1_, this_.EMP_NUMBER as EMP3_0_1_, addresses2_.EMPLOYEE_ADDRESS as EMPLOYEE7_3_, addresses2_.ID as ID3_, addresses2_.ID as ID1_0_, addresses2_.CITY_NAME as CITY2_1_0_, addresses2_.COUNTRY_NAME as COUNTRY3_1_0_, addresses2_.HOUSE_NUMBER as HOUSE4_1_0_, addresses2_.POSTAL_CODE as POSTAL5_1_0_, addresses2_.STREET_NAME as STREET6_1_0_ from EMPLOYEE this_ left outer join ADDRESS addresses2_ on this_.ID=addresses2_.EMPLOYEE_ADDRESS where ? <= (select count(*) from ADDRESS where this_.ID=EMPLOYEE_ADDRESS)

Employee Number   : 5001
Employee Name     : Ibrahim
=========================================
```

The following example uses `CriteriaSpecification.ALIAS_TO_ENTITY_MAP` result transformer to retrieve *addresses* (only) which met the specified criteria (Country Name is India).

```
// File Name: EmployeeManipulation.java
// Criteria Queries: Associations, CriteriaSpecification.
ALIAS_TO_ENTITY_MAP

package com.hdemo;

import java.util.List;
import java.util.Map;

import org.hibernate.Session;
import org.hibernate.SessionFactory;
import org.hibernate.Transaction;
import org.hibernate.criterion.CriteriaSpecification;
import org.hibernate.criterion.Restrictions;

public class EmployeeManipulation {

   @SuppressWarnings("unchecked")
   public static void main(String[] args) throws Exception {
          SessionFactory sessionFactory = HibernateUtil.getSession
                                                          Factory();

          Session session = sessionFactory.openSession();
          Transaction txn = session.beginTransaction();

          System.out.println("Select all Employees\n\n");
```

```
        List  list  =  session.createCriteria(Employee.class)
                            .createCriteria("addresses",  "addr")

    .add(Restrictions.eq("countryName",  "India"))

    .setResultTransformer(CriteriaSpecification.ALIAS_TO_ENTITY_MAP)
                                            .list();

        for  (int  i  =  0;  i  <  list.size();  i++)  {
              Map  map  =  (Map)  list.get(i);
          Employee  employee  =  (Employee)  map.get(Criteria
                                                Specification.ROOT_ALIAS);
              System.out.println("Employee  Number  :  "  +
                                                employee.getEmpNumber());
              System.out.println("Employee  Name     :  "  +
                                                  employee.getEmpName());

              Address  address  =  (Address)  map.get("addr");
              System.out.println("Employee  Address  "  +  address);

    System.out.println("==========================================\n\n");
        }

        txn.commit();
        sessionFactory.close();
    }
}
```

Select all Employees

Hibernate: select this_.ID as ID0_1_, this_.EMP_NAME as EMP2_0_1_, this_.EMP_NUMBER as EMP3_0_1_, addr1_.ID as ID1_0_, addr1_.CITY_NAME as CITY2_1_0_, addr1_.COUNTRY_NAME as COUNTRY3_1_0_, addr1_.HOUSE_NUMBER as HOUSE4_1_0_, addr1_.POSTAL_CODE as POSTAL5_1_0_, addr1_.STREET_NAME as STREET6_1_0_ from EMPLOYEE this_ inner join ADDRESS addr1_ on this_.ID=addr1_.EMPLOYEE_ADDRESS where addr1_.COUNTRY_NAME=?

Employee Number : 5001

Employee Name : Ibrahim

Employee Address [House Number: 3-121

```
Street Name        : Middle Street
City Name          : Tiruchirapalli
Country Name       : India
Postal Code        : 621302]
=========================================

Employee Number    : 5002
Employee Name      : Kumar
Employee Address [House Number: T-4
Street Name        : Nehru Street
City Name          : Chennai
Country Name       : India
Postal Code        : 600020]
=========================================
```

If you did not use `CriteriaSpecification.ALIAS_TO_ENTITY_MAP` result transformer, then the Criteria will not be applied (not pre-filtered) to "*addresses*" List (Note that it is List, not a simple entity field) of each associated Employee. So, you will get unwanted result (all addresses, including those Country Name is not India, will be selected) as shown below.

```
// File Name: EmployeeManipulation.java
// Criteria Queries: Associations

package com.hdemo;

import java.util.List;

import org.hibernate.Session;
import org.hibernate.SessionFactory;
import org.hibernate.Transaction;
import org.hibernate.criterion.Restrictions;

public class EmployeeManipulation {

  @SuppressWarnings("unchecked")
  public static void main(String[] args) throws Exception {
        SessionFactory sessionFactory = HibernateUtil.getSession
                                                            Factory();
        Session session = sessionFactory.openSession();
        Transaction txn = session.beginTransaction();
```

```
        System.out.println("Select all Employees\n\n");
        List list = session.createCriteria(Employee.class)
                    .createCriteria("addresses", "addr")
                    .add(Restrictions.eq("countryName", "India"))
                                .list()

        for (int i = 0; i < list.size(); i++) {
              Employee employee = (Employee) list.get(i);
              System.out.println("Employee Number : " +
                                      employee.getEmpNumber());
              System.out.println("Employee Name    : " +
                                      employee.getEmpName());

              System.out.println("Employee Address " +
                                      employee.getAddresses());

    System.out.println("======================================\n\n");
        }

        txn.commit();
        sessionFactory.close();

    }

}
```

```
Select all Employees

Hibernate: select this_.ID as ID0_1_, this_.EMP_NAME as EMP2_0_1_, this_.EMP_NUMBER as EMP3_0_1_, addr1_.ID as ID1_0_, addr1_.CITY_NAME as CITY2_1_0_, addr1_.COUNTRY_NAME as COUNTRY3_1_0_, addr1_.HOUSE_NUMBER as HOUSE4_1_0_, addr1_.POSTAL_CODE as POSTAL5_1_0_, addr1_.STREET_NAME as STREET6_1_0_ from EMPLOYEE this_ inner join ADDRESS addr1_ on this_.ID=addr1_.EMPLOYEE_ADDRESS where addr1_.COUNTRY_NAME=?
Employee Number  : 5001
Employee Name      : Ibrahim
Hibernate: select addresses0_.EMPLOYEE_ADDRESS as EMPLOYEE7_1_, addresses0_.ID as ID1_, addresses0_.ID as ID1_0_, addresses0_.CITY_NAME as CITY2_1_0_, addresses0_.COUNTRY_NAME as COUNTRY3_1_0_, addresses0_.HOUSE_NUMBER as HOUSE4_1_0_, addresses0_.POSTAL_CODE as POSTAL5_1_0_, addresses0_.STREET_NAME as STREET6_1_0_ from ADDRESS addresses0_ where addresses0_.EMPLOYEE_ADDRESS=?
```

```
Employee Address [[House Number: C-13-4
Street Name  : Jalan Munsi Abdullah
City Name    : Kuala Lumpur
Country Name : Malaysia
Postal Code  : 50100], [House Number: 3-121
Street Name  : Middle Street
City Name    : Tiruchirapalli
Country Name : India
Postal Code  : 621302]]
========================================
Employee Number  : 5002
Employee Name    : Kumar
Hibernate: select addresses0_.EMPLOYEE_ADDRESS as EMPLOYEE7_1_, addresses0_.ID as ID1_, addresses0_.ID as ID1_0_, addresses0_.CITY_NAME as CITY2_1_0_, addresses0_.COUNTRY_NAME as COUNTRY3_1_0_, addresses0_.HOUSE_NUMBER as HOUSE4_1_0_, addresses0_.POSTAL_CODE as POSTAL5_1_0_, addresses0_.STREET_NAME as STREET6_1_0_ from ADDRESS addresses0_ where addresses0_.EMPLOYEE_ADDRESS=?
Employee Address [[House Number: T-4
Street Name  : Nehru Street
City Name    : Chennai
Country Name : India
Postal Code  : 600020]]
========================================
```

6.11 QUERY BY EXAMPLE (QBE)

We can utilize the feature of Hibernate to construct Criteria queries automatically through an "example" object. The object should be an instance of the persistent class you want to query. Create an object (instance) of the entity (Criteria Entity) and partially populate the object (act as conditions), set this object as example (template) so that the Hibernate creates the required Criteria for you. You are not needed to build Criteria by specifying restrictions/constraints as we did in earlier sections. That is, by simply submitting an example object, Hibernate automatically generates the required query (Criteria object) based on the values set in the example object. This approach of creating Criteria query is called "Query By Example".

Keep the same sample data (Employee – Addresses) generated for above section (Data generated for demonstration on Fetching Collection Data for Entity).

The following main program selects and displays details of the Employee whose Emp_Number is 5002. The identifier property (@Id), null-valued properties, and associations are ignored in comparison by default.

```
// File Name: EmployeeManipulation.java
// Criteria Queries: Query By Example

package com.hdemo;

import java.util.List;

import org.hibernate.Criteria;
import org.hibernate.Session;
import org.hibernate.SessionFactory;
import org.hibernate.Transaction;
import org.hibernate.criterion.Example;

public class EmployeeManipulation {

  @SuppressWarnings("unchecked")
  public static void main(String[] args) throws Exception {
      SessionFactory sessionFactory = HibernateUtil.getSession
                                                        Factory();
      Session session = sessionFactory.openSession();
      Transaction txn = session.beginTransaction();

      Employee exampleEmployee = new Employee();
      exampleEmployee.setEmpNumber(5002);

      Example example = Example.create(exampleEmployee);

      Criteria criteria = session.createCriteria(Employee.class);
      criteria.add(example);

      List list = criteria.list();

      for (int i = 0; i < list.size(); i++) {
          Employee employee = (Employee) list.get(i);
          System.out.println("Employee Number : " +
                                      employee.getEmpNumber());
          System.out.println("Employee Name   : " +
                                        employee.getEmpName());
```

```
                        System.out.println("Employee Address " +
                                                   employee.getAddresses());

      System.out.println("=======================================\n\n");
            }

            txn.commit();
            sessionFactory.close();
      }
  }
```

```
Hibernate: select this_.ID as ID0_0_, this_.EMP_NAME as EMP2_0_0_, this_.EMP_NUMBER as EMP3_0_0_ from EMPLOYEE this_ where (this_.EMP_NUMBER=?)

Employee Number    : 5002

Employee Name      : Kumar

Hibernate: select addresses0_.EMPLOYEE_ADDRESS as EMPLOYEE7_1_, addresses0_.ID as ID1_, addresses0_.ID as ID1_0_, addresses0_.CITY_NAME as CITY2_1_0_, addresses0_.COUNTRY_NAME as COUNTRY3_1_0_, addresses0_.HOUSE_NUMBER as HOUSE4_1_0_, addresses0_.POSTAL_CODE as POSTAL5_1_0_, addresses0_.STREET_NAME as STREET6_1_0_ from ADDRESS addresses0_ where addresses0_.EMPLOYEE_ADDRESS=?

Employee Address [[House Number: T-4

Street Name        : Nehru Street

City Name          : Chennai

Country Name       : India

Postal Code        : 600020]]

=======================================
```

In the above program, an Employee object is created and the value `5002` is set as Emp_Number on that object.

```
Employee exampleEmployee = new Employee();

exampleEmployee.setEmpNumber(5002);
```

This object will act as "Example" object in "Query By Example" approach, when its `org.hibernate.criterion.Example` instance is added to the `Criteria` object of the Entity.

The following code creates an instance of `org.hibernate.criterion.Example` class by invoking `create()` method of `Example class`.

```
Example example = Example.create(exampleEmployee);
```

The `create()` method is a static method in `Example` class, which accepts one object (of the required Entity) as its argument.

This "*Example*" object can be added to the Criteria using add() method as follows, then Hibernate build that Criteria query based on the values specified in the *Example* object.

```
Criteria criteria = session.createCriteria(Employee.class);
criteria.add(example);
```

Some of the methods in `org.hibernate.criterion.Example` class are given below.

`static Example create(Object entity)`

Creates a new `Example` instance of the augmented Entity object, which includes all non-null properties by default

`Example enableLike()`

Applies the "like" operations (includes wild-card characters) for all string type properties

`Example enableLike(MatchMode matchMode)`

Applies the "like" operations with `MatchMode`

`(MatchMode.START, MatchMode.END, MatchMode.ANYWHERE, MatchMode.EXACT)`

for all string type properties

`Example excludeProperty(String name)`

Excludes the specified property (Excludes for comparison while creating Criteria query)

`Example excludeZeroes()`

Excludes zero-valued properties

`Example excludeNone()`

Includes all properties including null or zero-valued properties. (Does not exclude null or zero-valued properties)

`Example ignoreCase()`

Ignores case sensitiveness for all string type properties

The following example uses `enableLike()` method.

```
// File Name: EmployeeManipulation.java
// Criteria Queries: Query By Example

package com.hdemo;

import java.util.List;

import org.hibernate.Criteria;
import org.hibernate.Session;
import org.hibernate.SessionFactory;
```

```
import org.hibernate.Transaction;
import org.hibernate.criterion.Example;

public class EmployeeManipulation {
  @SuppressWarnings("unchecked")
  public static void main(String[] args) throws Exception {
        SessionFactory sessionFactory = HibernateUtil.getSession
                                                        Factory();
        Session session = sessionFactory.openSession();
        Transaction txn = session.beginTransaction();

        Employee exampleEmployee = new Employee();
        exampleEmployee.setEmpName("%r%");

        Example example = Example.create(exampleEmployee);
        example.enableLike();

        Criteria criteria = session.createCriteria(Employee.class);
        criteria.add(example);
        List list = criteria.list();

        for (int i = 0; i < list.size(); i++) {
              Employee employee = (Employee) list.get(i);
              System.out.println("Employee Number : " +
                                         employee.getEmpNumber());
              System.out.println("Employee Name : " +
                                           employee.getEmpName());
              System.out.println("Employee Address " +
                                         employee.getAddresses());
   System.out.println("======================================\n\n");
        }

        txn.commit();
        sessionFactory.close();
  }
}
```

```
Hibernate: select this_.ID as ID0_0_, this_.EMP_NAME as EMP2_0_0_, this_.EMP_NUMBER as EMP3_0_0_ from EMPLOYEE this_ where (this_.EMP_NAME like ?)

Employee Number   : 5001
Employee Name     : Ibrahim

Hibernate: select addresses0_.EMPLOYEE_ADDRESS as EMPLOYEE7_1_, addresses0_.ID as ID1_, addresses0_.ID as ID1_0_, addresses0_.CITY_NAME as CITY2_1_0_, addresses0_.COUNTRY_NAME as COUNTRY3_1_0_, addresses0_.HOUSE_NUMBER as HOUSE4_1_0_, addresses0_.POSTAL_CODE as POSTAL5_1_0_, addresses0_.STREET_NAME as STREET6_1_0_ from ADDRESS addresses0_ where addresses0_.EMPLOYEE_ADDRESS=?

Employee Address [[House Number: C-13-4
Street Name       : Jalan Munsi Abdullah
City Name         : Kuala Lumpur
Country Name      : Malaysia
Postal Code       : 50100], [House Number: 3-121
Street Name       : Middle Street
City Name         : Tiruchirapalli
Country Name      : India
Postal Code       : 621302]]
========================================

Employee Number   : 5002
Employee Name     : Kumar

Hibernate: select addresses0_.EMPLOYEE_ADDRESS as EMPLOYEE7_1_, addresses0_.ID as ID1_, addresses0_.ID as ID1_0_, addresses0_.CITY_NAME as CITY2_1_0_, addresses0_.COUNTRY_NAME as COUNTRY3_1_0_, addresses0_.HOUSE_NUMBER as HOUSE4_1_0_, addresses0_.POSTAL_CODE as POSTAL5_1_0_, addresses0_.STREET_NAME as STREET6_1_0_ from ADDRESS addresses0_ where addresses0_.EMPLOYEE_ADDRESS=?

Employee Address [[House Number: T-4
Street Name       : Nehru Street
City Name         : Chennai
Country Name      : India
Postal Code       : 600020]]
========================================
```

The following example uses `enableLike(MatchMode matchMode)` method.

```
// File Name: EmployeeManipulation.java
// Criteria Queries: Query By Example

package com.hdemo;

import java.util.List;

import org.hibernate.Criteria;
import org.hibernate.Session;
import org.hibernate.SessionFactory;
import org.hibernate.Transaction;
import org.hibernate.criterion.Example;
import org.hibernate.criterion.MatchMode;

public class EmployeeManipulation {

   @SuppressWarnings("unchecked")
   public static void main(String[] args) throws Exception {
         SessionFactory sessionFactory = HibernateUtil.getSession
                                                          Factory();
         Session session = sessionFactory.openSession();
         Transaction txn = session.beginTransaction();

         Employee exampleEmployee = new Employee();
         exampleEmployee.setEmpName("r");

         Example example = Example.create(exampleEmployee);
         example.enableLike(MatchMode.ANYWHERE);

         Criteria criteria = session.createCriteria(Employee.class);
         criteria.add(example);

         List list = criteria.list();

         for (int i = 0; i < list.size(); i++) {
              Employee employee = (Employee) list.get(i);
              System.out.println("Employee Number : " +
                                          employee.getEmpNumber());
              System.out.println("Employee Name    : " +
                                            employee.getEmpName());
```

```
                System.out.println("Employee Address " +
                                            employee.getAddresses());

      System.out.println("=====================================\n\n");
          }

          txn.commit();
          sessionFactory.close();
      }
  }
```

Hibernate: select this_.ID as ID0_0_, this_.EMP_NAME as EMP2_0_0_, this_.EMP_NUMBER as EMP3_0_0_ from EMPLOYEE this_ where (this_.EMP_NAME like ?)

```
Employee Number   : 5001
Employee Name     : Ibrahim
```

Hibernate: select addresses0_.EMPLOYEE_ADDRESS as EMPLOYEE7_1_, addresses0_.ID as ID1_, addresses0_.ID as ID1_0_, addresses0_.CITY_NAME as CITY2_1_0_, addresses0_.COUNTRY_NAME as COUNTRY3_1_0_, addresses0_.HOUSE_NUMBER as HOUSE4_1_0_, addresses0_.POSTAL_CODE as POSTAL5_1_0_, addresses0_.STREET_NAME as STREET6_1_0_ from ADDRESS addresses0_ where addresses0_.EMPLOYEE_ADDRESS=?

```
Employee Address [[House Number: C-13-4
Street Name       : Jalan Munsi Abdullah
City Name         : Kuala Lumpur
Country Name      : Malaysia
Postal Code       : 50100], [House Number: 3-121
Street Name       : Middle Street
City Name         : Tiruchirapalli
Country Name      : India
Postal Code       : 621302]]
=====================================

Employee Number   : 5002
Employee Name     : Kumar
```

Hibernate: select addresses0_.EMPLOYEE_ADDRESS as EMPLOYEE7_1_, addresses0_.ID as ID1_, addresses0_.ID as ID1_0_, addresses0_.CITY_NAME as CITY2_1_0_, addresses0_.COUNTRY_NAME as COUNTRY3_1_0_,

```
addresses0_.HOUSE_NUMBER as HOUSE4_1_0_, addresses0_.POSTAL_CODE as
POSTAL5_1_0_, addresses0_.STREET_NAME as STREET6_1_0_ from ADDRESS
addresses0_ where addresses0_.EMPLOYEE_ADDRESS=?
    Employee Address [[House Number: T-4
    Street Name         : Nehru Street
    City Name           : Chennai
    Country Name        : India
    Postal Code         : 600020]]
    ========================================
```

The following example uses `excludeProperty(String name)` method. In our example, Emp_Number is included with the condition "empNumber = 5002" in `Example` object and then excluded. So, this condition will not be included while creating Criteria query.

```
// File Name: EmployeeManipulation.java
// Criteria Queries: Query By Example

package com.hdemo;

import java.util.List;

import org.hibernate.Criteria;
import org.hibernate.Session;
import org.hibernate.SessionFactory;
import org.hibernate.Transaction;
import org.hibernate.criterion.Example;

public class EmployeeManipulation {

  @SuppressWarnings("unchecked")
  public static void main(String[] args) throws Exception {
        SessionFactory sessionFactory = HibernateUtil.getSession
                                                        Factory();
        Session session = sessionFactory.openSession();
        Transaction txn = session.beginTransaction();

        Employee exampleEmployee = new Employee();
        exampleEmployee.setEmpNumber(5002);

        Example example = Example.create(exampleEmployee);
        example.excludeProperty("empNumber");
```

```
        Criteria criteria = session.createCriteria(Employee.class);
        criteria.add(example);

        List list = criteria.list();

        for (int i = 0; i < list.size(); i++) {
              Employee employee = (Employee) list.get(i);
              System.out.println("Employee Number : " +
                                   employee.getEmpNumber());
              System.out.println("Employee Name   : " +
                                     employee.getEmpName());

              System.out.println("Employee Address " +
                                   employee.getAddresses());

    System.out.println("=======================================\n\n");
        }

        txn.commit();
        sessionFactory.close();

    }

}
```

```
Hibernate: select this_.ID as ID0_0_, this_.EMP_NAME as EMP2_0_0_, this_.EMP_NUMBER as EMP3_0_0_ from EMPLOYEE this_ where (1=1)
Employee Number : 5001
Employee Name   : Ibrahim
Hibernate: select addresses0_.EMPLOYEE_ADDRESS as EMPLOYEE7_1_, addresses0_.ID as ID1_, addresses0_.ID as ID1_0_, addresses0_.CITY_NAME as CITY2_1_0_, addresses0_.COUNTRY_NAME as COUNTRY3_1_0_, addresses0_.HOUSE_NUMBER as HOUSE4_1_0_, addresses0_.POSTAL_CODE as POSTAL5_1_0_, addresses0_.STREET_NAME as STREET6_1_0_ from ADDRESS addresses0_ where addresses0_.EMPLOYEE_ADDRESS=?
Employee Address [[House Number: C-13-4
Street Name      : Jalan Munsi Abdullah
City Name        : Kuala Lumpur
Country Name     : Malaysia
Postal Code      : 50100], [House Number: 3-121
```

```
Street Name       : Middle Street
City Name         : Tiruchirapalli
Country Name      : India
Postal Code       : 621302]]
========================================

Employee Number   : 5002
Employee Name     : Kumar
Hibernate: select addresses0_.EMPLOYEE_ADDRESS as EMPLOYEE7_1_, addresses0_.ID as ID1_, addresses0_.ID as ID1_0_, addresses0_.CITY_NAME as CITY2_1_0_, addresses0_.COUNTRY_NAME as COUNTRY3_1_0_, addresses0_.HOUSE_NUMBER as HOUSE4_1_0_, addresses0_.POSTAL_CODE as POSTAL5_1_0_, addresses0_.STREET_NAME as STREET6_1_0_ from ADDRESS addresses0_ where addresses0_.EMPLOYEE_ADDRESS=?
Employee Address [[House Number: T-4
Street Name       : Nehru Street
City Name         : Chennai
Country Name      : India
Postal Code       : 600020]]
========================================

Employee Number   : 5003
Employee Name     : Ajay
Hibernate: select addresses0_.EMPLOYEE_ADDRESS as EMPLOYEE7_1_, addresses0_.ID as ID1_, addresses0_.ID as ID1_0_, addresses0_.CITY_NAME as CITY2_1_0_, addresses0_.COUNTRY_NAME as COUNTRY3_1_0_, addresses0_.HOUSE_NUMBER as HOUSE4_1_0_, addresses0_.POSTAL_CODE as POSTAL5_1_0_, addresses0_.STREET_NAME as STREET6_1_0_ from ADDRESS addresses0_ where addresses0_.EMPLOYEE_ADDRESS=?
Employee Address []
========================================
```

The following example uses `excludeZeroes()method`. In our example, if you do not use `excludeZeroes()`, then the zero set `Emp_Number` will be included for condition and as the result, no rows will be returned. We can also add additional criterions to Criteria (in addition to those generated by Hibernate as the result of QBE) as usual.

```
// File Name: EmployeeManipulation.java
// Criteria Queries: Query By Example

package com.hdemo;
```

```
import java.util.List;

import org.hibernate.Criteria;
import org.hibernate.Session;
import org.hibernate.SessionFactory;
import org.hibernate.Transaction;
import org.hibernate.criterion.Example;
import org.hibernate.criterion.Restrictions;

public class EmployeeManipulation {

   @SuppressWarnings("unchecked")
   public static void main(String[] args) throws Exception {
        SessionFactory sessionFactory = HibernateUtil.getSession
                                                          Factory();
        Session session = sessionFactory.openSession();
        Transaction txn = session.beginTransaction();

        Employee exampleEmployee = new Employee();
        exampleEmployee.setEmpNumber(0);

        Example example = Example.create(exampleEmployee);
        example.excludeZeroes();

        Criteria criteria = session.createCriteria(Employee.class);
        criteria.add(example);
        criteria.add(Restrictions.like("empName", "%ja%"));

        List list = criteria.list();

        for (int i = 0; i < list.size(); i++) {
             Employee employee = (Employee) list.get(i);
             System.out.println("Employee Number : " +
                                          employee.getEmpNumber());
             System.out.println("Employee Name   : " +
                                            employee.getEmpName());

             System.out.println("Employee Address " +
                                          employee.getAddresses());
```

```
  System.out.println("=======================================\n\n");
        }

        txn.commit();
        sessionFactory.close();
  }
}
```

Hibernate: select this_.ID as ID0_0_, this_.EMP_NAME as EMP2_0_0_, this_.EMP_NUMBER as EMP3_0_0_ from EMPLOYEE this_ where (1=1) and this_.EMP_NAME like ?

Employee Number : 5003

Employee Name : Ajay

Hibernate: select addresses0_.EMPLOYEE_ADDRESS as EMPLOYEE7_1_, addresses0_.ID as ID1_, addresses0_.ID as ID1_0_, addresses0_.CITY_NAME as CITY2_1_0_, addresses0_.COUNTRY_NAME as COUNTRY3_1_0_, addresses0_.HOUSE_NUMBER as HOUSE4_1_0_, addresses0_.POSTAL_CODE as POSTAL5_1_0_, addresses0_.STREET_NAME as STREET6_1_0_ from ADDRESS addresses0_ where addresses0_.EMPLOYEE_ADDRESS=?

Employee Address []

=======================================

The following example uses Association condition in QBE (Selects Employee(s)), whose name contains the letter 'm' and Country is Malaysia.

```
// File Name: EmployeeManipulation.java
// Criteria Queries: Query By Example

package com.hdemo;

import java.util.List;

import org.hibernate.Criteria;
import org.hibernate.Session;
import org.hibernate.SessionFactory;
import org.hibernate.Transaction;
import org.hibernate.criterion.Example;
import org.hibernate.criterion.MatchMode;

public class EmployeeManipulation {
```

```
@SuppressWarnings("unchecked")
public static void main(String[] args) throws Exception {
      SessionFactory sessionFactory = HibernateUtil.getSession
                                                    Factory();
      Session session = sessionFactory.openSession();
      Transaction txn = session.beginTransaction();

      Employee employee = new Employee();
      employee.setEmpName("%m%");
      Example exampleEmployee = Example.create(employee);
      exampleEmployee.enableLike();
      exampleEmployee.ignoreCase();

      Address address = new Address();
      address.setCountryName("MALAYSIA");
      Example exampleAddress = Example.create(address);
      exampleAddress.enableLike(MatchMode.EXACT);
      exampleAddress.ignoreCase();

      Criteria criteria = session.createCriteria(Employee.class);
      criteria.createCriteria("addresses").add(exampleAddress);
      criteria.add(exampleEmployee);

      List list = criteria.list();

      for (int i = 0; i < list.size(); i++) {
            Employee emp = (Employee) list.get(i);
            System.out.println("Employee Number : " +
                                          emp.getEmpNumber());
            System.out.println("Employee Name : " +
                                            emp.getEmpName());

            System.out.println("Employee Address " +
                                          emp.getAddresses());

   System.out.println("=====================================\n\n");
      }
      txn.commit();
      sessionFactory.close();
}
```

```
}
Hibernate: select this_.ID as ID0_1_, this_.EMP_NAME as EMP2_0_1_, this_.EMP_NUMBER as EMP3_0_1_, address1_.ID as ID1_0_, address1_.CITY_NAME as CITY2_1_0_, address1_.COUNTRY_NAME as COUNTRY3_1_0_, address1_.HOUSE_NUMBER as HOUSE4_1_0_, address1_.POSTAL_CODE as POSTAL5_1_0_, address1_.STREET_NAME as STREET6_1_0_ from EMPLOYEE this_ inner join ADDRESS address1_ on this_.ID=address1_.EMPLOYEE_ADDRESS where (lower(address1_.COUNTRY_NAME) like ?) and (lower(this_.EMP_NAME) like ?)
Employee Number   : 5001
Employee Name     : Ibrahim
Hibernate: select addresses0_.EMPLOYEE_ADDRESS as EMPLOYEE7_1_, addresses0_.ID as ID1_, addresses0_.ID as ID1_0_, addresses0_.CITY_NAME as CITY2_1_0_, addresses0_.COUNTRY_NAME as COUNTRY3_1_0_, addresses0_.HOUSE_NUMBER as HOUSE4_1_0_, addresses0_.POSTAL_CODE as POSTAL5_1_0_, addresses0_.STREET_NAME as STREET6_1_0_ from ADDRESS addresses0_ where addresses0_.EMPLOYEE_ADDRESS=?
Employee Address [[House Number: C-13-4
Street Name       : Jalan Munsi Abdullah
City Name         : Kuala Lumpur
Country Name      : Malaysia
Postal Code       : 50100], [House Number: 3-121
Street Name       : Middle Street
City Name         : Tiruchirapalli
Country Name      : India
Postal Code       : 621302]]
========================================
```

SUMMARY

Even though the HQL works on Java objects instead on database tables as in the case of Native SQL, its syntaxes are based on SQL. So, the developer still has to know the SQL syntaxes to write HQL queries. Hibernate provides Criteria API (also called as Criteria Queries) as an alternate to HQL, and this Criteria queries are completely based on object oriented approach without falling back on a relational technology. These Criteria queries are generated at runtime and executed on the fly. These Criteria queries are well suited for implementing Multiple-Criteria Search (Screen with Multiple Filters) functionalities, where HQL is not very effective. However, Criteria query has its own limitations.

INDEX

A

B

C

D

E

F

G

H

I

J

L

M

N

O

P

Q

R

S

T

U

V